Quebec

Montreal

Sault Ste. Marie

N. H.

MASS.

NEW
YORK

Portsmouth

Boston
Plymouth

Albany

MASS.

MASSACHUSETTS AND VIRGINIA

MASS.
AND N.Y.

CT.

R. I.

Detroit

PENN.

Princeton

N. Y.

CONNECTICUT AND VIRGINIA

Germantown
Philadelphia

N. J.

Pittsburgh

MD.

Baltimore

DEL.

Kaskaskia

VIRGINIA

Jamestown

Vincennes

Cahokia

Williamsburg

Norfolk

NORTH   CAROLINA

New Bern

Wilmington

SOUTH
CAROLINA

GEORGIA

Charleston

Natchitoches

Savannah

cogdoches

S P A N I S H   F L O R I D A

Mobile

Pensacola

St. Augustine

New Orleans

M
i
s
s
i
s
s
i
p
p
i

R.

CLIFTON E. OLMSTEAD
Professor of Religion, The George Washington University

History of Religion
in the
United States

PRENTICE-HALL, INC., ENGLEWOOD CLIFFS, N.J.

Current printing (last digit):
15   14   13   12   11   10

PRINTED IN THE UNITED STATES OF AMERICA

39194-C

To Glenda

$\mathscr{P}$reface

DURING THE PAST SEVERAL DECADES, STUDENTS OF AMERICAN CIVILIZATION have demonstrated an increasing predilection for the exploration of intellectual and cultural themes. Particularly noteworthy has been the enthusiasm on the part of both secular and church historians for the study of American religious history. The result has been a steady production of scholarly monographs and treatises on numerous phases of national religious life and thought. It has seemed imperative that the results of mature scholarship be brought together and made available in a relatively comprehensive yet concise one-volume survey which traces the history of American religion from colonial times to the present. That is the *raison d'être* of this book.

Recognizing that no movement exists in a vacuum, I have endeavored to set the story of American religion within the broad sweep of political, economic, social, and intellectual history. In keeping with the growing propensity among church historians to emphasize the role of theology, the present work has been written from a somewhat fuller theological perspective than previous volumes in the same general field. Some professional readers will prefer even more emphasis in that direction; others may prefer a more sociological orientation. My primary aim has been to achieve a fairly balanced treatment of American religion, taking into account the vast interplay of forces which have acted upon and through ecclesiastical institutions.

One of the perennial problems in scholarly publication is documentation. In a comprehensive volume, in which the author has drawn upon the works of literally hundreds of scholars, a rather liberal use of footnotes may seem desirable. Publication costs, however, render this impractical. The decision in this case was to document only quotations of a paragraph or more taken from primary sources.

It is my pleasant duty to thank publicly the many kind friends and fellow students of American religion who have contributed much to the authorship and production of this work. For their helpful criticisms and suggestions at various stages of the writing process I wish to express appreciation to my esteemed colleague, Wood Gray, The George Washington University; Leland Jamison, Syracuse University; Howard Kee, Drew University; and especially to my greatly admired friend and former mentor in graduate study, Lefferts A. Loetscher, Princeton Theological Seminary. Thanks are also due to the Office of Publication and Distribution of the National Council of the Churches of Christ in the United States of America for permission to quote statistical data found in the 1959 edition of the *Yearbook of American Churches*. Finally, I am grateful to my wife for her valued assistance during the years of manuscript preparation, especially for typing the entire final draft, and to Dick Hansen, Maurine Lewis, Don Martinetti, and George Karydes of the Prentice-Hall staff, who have given unstintingly of their time and talent in preparing the volume for publication.

CLIFTON E. OLMSTEAD

Contents

The European Heritage

THAT COMPLEX AND DIVERSIFIED PHENOMENON KNOWN AS "AMERICAN RE-ligion" is a product of the cultural heritage of Old Europe adapted and molded in the crucible of the American physical environment. The heritage is not only British but European, even Asian; not only of the six-teenth and seventeenth and eighteenth centuries but of twenty-five hundred years. Granted that the institutions of American religion are the immediate offspring of Reformation and Counter-Reformation movements, their roots, nevertheless, lie deeply embedded in the matrix of ancient Palestine, Greece, and Rome. We should, therefore, first turn to the broad cultural setting in which the Judaeo-Christian tradition found nourish-ment, so that we may more adequately assay the interplay of forces which contributed to the making of the American religious mind.

PRE-REFORMATION CHRISTENDOM

As a religious movement, the Protestant Reformation of the sixteenth century proposed to return the church to the pristine purity of Apostolic Christianity. It was, however, not unmixed in either its motivation or its goals, being aided and sometimes controlled by multifarious forces antagonistic toward the medieval world view. Thus, while the movement was most certainly religious in its inception and inspired by leaders of

deep spiritual conviction, it was so solidly grounded in the great awakening of the times that it affected every domain of human life.

To a unique degree, medieval Europe had achieved a synthesis of
Palestinian religion, Greek philosophy, and Roman law. In the first
century, primitive Christianity had ventured out into the Graeco-Roman
world, a pure and undefiled offspring from Judaism. Encountering the
challenging forces of the Greek philosophies and oriental mystery religions, it had found it necessary to systematize and regulate its faith,
presenting it in terms familiar to the Hellenistic mind.

After three centuries of sporadic and ultimately futile persecution, it
had been adopted as a child of the Roman Empire and accorded all the
benefits and impunities of a church establishment. From that time it had
ever more drawn to its bosom the orderly principles of Roman law and
had appropriated for itself the Latin genius for administration. The
result was that even before the collapse of the empire in the West, the
Church had singularly equipped itself to assume political responsibilities.

At the dawning of the Middle Ages, the Christian Church had faced
the challenge of bringing unity to a Europe torn by repeated invasions,
by internal strife and dissension, and culturally weakened by the relative
ignorance and social immaturity resulting from these forces. Being conscious of its sacred commission to make the world one in Christ, and following in the Platonic tradition, it had envisioned the universe as one
well-articulated whole, pervaded by a divinely instituted harmony. Every
separate aim or object of any individual or group would require regulation and control by the aim or object of the universe. Only in this way
could unity be preserved. From this it had followed that every earthly
organization should appear as an organic member of that *Civitas Dei*
which included both the heavens and the earth.

Mankind was a mystical body typified in two aspects, the spiritual
and the temporal; and represented by two persons, the world-priest and
the world-monarch. Obviously, the dualism of these two persons could
not have been final but called for reconciliation in some higher unity.
The central problem of the Middle Ages, therefore, had been to determine how this unity could be achieved. In attempting to work out a
solution, the agents of church and state had been thrown into almost
constant competition, the papacy gradually extending its power and
influence through the help of an awe-inspiring sacramentarian system,
until, in the thirteenth century, under Innocent III, it had reached its
zenith.

Antecedent to the political decline of the papacy in the fourteenth and
fifteenth centuries, there had arisen certain forces which would contribute to the breakdown of medieval unity and the rise of the modern
spirit of individualism. First, there had been the emergence of national-

ism, especially in France and England. It had been aided indirectly and unwittingly by the papacy, which had hoped to weaken the imperial power through its support of popular causes. Other obvious points of transition which favored the free enterprise system of modern capitalism had been the decline of the trade associations or guilds and the waning of prejudice against usury. Connected with this had been the rise of the new moneyed class known as *bourgeoisie,* with its predilection for commerce and industry.

Intellectual and spiritual forces had also played their part in the creation of a new order. Their origins could be found in a growing dissatisfaction over the ineptitudes and unprincipled practices of the hierarchy. Granted that their immorality had not reached the depths described by biased opponents, it was still true that the Church had grown more worldly and decadent, that the scholastic theologians had spent more time in vain disputations, that the monastic orders had grown more opulent, that unworthy priests had become more numerous. After the unfortunate Babylonian Captivity of the papacy and the deplorable papal schism of the fourteenth and fifteenth centuries, several attempts to reform the Church had been made at the ecumenical councils of Pisa, Constance, and Basel early in the fifteenth century. All had ended in failure.

Popular movements antagonistic to the papacy had arisen as early as the twelfth century in the Cathari and the Waldenses. Rejecting the medieval sacraments, which had been held essential for salvation, they had taken the Scripture as their sole authority and had stressed the importance of the laity. Similar movements had sprung up later under John Wycliffe in England and John Huss in Bohemia.

In the intellectual realm, humanism had rebelled against the dogmatism and scholasticism of the medieval Church, thus reviving the classical past and contributing to the rediscovery of the world and man. Though Renaissance humanism had proved itself to be basically a revival of Hellenism, it had directed attention to Christian origins chiefly through critical Scriptural study. It had further sought to lift the level of common piety.

Finally, there had been the influence of fourteenth and fifteenth century Flemish and German mysticism, which had reacted to the orthodox rationalism of the Scholastics on the ground that such dogmatism had crushed the spontaneous movements of the soul toward God. Its emphasis had rested upon the free and personal communion between the soul and God and a pietistic interpretation of the Christian life. Such forces, when acting in concert, contributed directly to the religious upheaval of the sixteenth and seventeenth centuries and so indirectly influenced the development of religion in America.

THE RIGHT WING OF THE REFORMATION

As a religious movement, the Protestant Reformation took as its common characteristic the rejection of the authority of the Roman Church, whether speaking through pope or ecumenical council. In the minds of its leaders, this action, deemed necessary after repeated failures to win reform, constituted no schism from the church. It was rather a schism in the church. The Reformers claimed to be scions and heirs of the church's biblical and patristic heritage. They appealed to Jesus Christ himself for their authority and taught that God's redemptive activity was final in Him. Basically, they conceived of Christianity as an individual relation between the soul and God, grounded in the act of redemption and sustained by the inner presence of the Holy Spirit. It was obvious that so individualistic a doctrine would necessarily lead ultimately to a variety of formal religious expressions, thus accounting for a diversity of denominations and sects in the Protestant tradition.

For the most part, the earliest products of the Reformation were the great churchly systems which retained a Catholic sense of the church even though they broke with Rome. Closely allied with strong nationalistic forces in their countries, they were invariably accorded the privileges pertaining to an establishment. These systems, which belonged to the right wing of the Reformation, were the Lutheran, the Reformed, the Anglican, and with some justification, the Puritan.

Lutheranism

While the Reformation was precipitated by Martin Luther's historic theses of 1517 on the misuse of indulgences, its mature development depended upon the treatment of more vital issues. This need was met by Luther himself in his three treatises of 1520, which defined the essence of Protestant faith.

In his *Address to the Christian Nobility of the German Nation,* he asserted the right of the civil power to reform the church. Attacking the exalted state of the clergy, he argued that every baptized Christian is a priest, despite the priests' claims to be on a higher level of divinity. Since all persons had immediate access to God through faith, the spiritual position and privileges of the clergy could not exceed those of the laity. Next to the idea of justification by faith, this was probably the most distinctive concept in Luther's thinking.

In his *Babylonish Captivity of the Church,* Luther struck a vigorous blow at the sacramental system of the Roman Church, maintaining that only the sacraments of baptism, the Lord's Supper, and possibly penance could be justified on the basis of the New Testament.

Luther's third treatise, entitled *The Freedom of a Christian Man*, emphasized the doctrine of justification by faith. This was the cornerstone of Reformation theology. To Luther, justification was not a change in the nature or character of man, nor was it an overcoming in him of sin; it was a change in his relation to divine justice. Through justification, the righteousness of Christ was imputed to man as his own righteousness.

This concept was inseparably linked to his idea of faith, which he defined as the unquestioning acceptance and appropriation of the Gospel. It was a trust of the heart and commitment of the will, born of a sense of man's utter helplessness and evoked by God's grace. Its result was a joyous reconciliation with God, bearing fruit in works of righteousness. The effect of such doctrines could be only to stir up discontent with the sacerdotal, hierarchical system of the day and set the stage for the formation of new ecclesiastical institutions in which the stress would be upon the fellowship of justified believers.

Luther was reluctant to break with the church and refrained from taking this step until he realized that the fundamental disparities between the Roman system and his own interpretation of religion were too great to permit reconciliation. In 1521, Charles V, Emperor of the Holy Roman Empire and champion of the church, summoned a legislative diet to meet at Worms on the Rhine. At this session, Luther was directed to state whether he still held the positions taken in his writings, which had already been proscribed by Rome. He asserted his independence and declared that he took his stand on the Bible as his authority, refusing to recant unless he could be proved false by Scripture. The emperor forced an edict of condemnation through the diet, and Luther was brought under the ban of the empire. It was then that Luther's Saxon friends, recognizing his importance to the cause of German nationalism, carried him off by night to the castle of the Wartburg. There he remained in safety for a year, commencing his famous translation of the Bible into German.

The Lutheran movement opened the way for certain radical tendencies, both social and religious. The country peasants had revolted several times in the hope that the church might release them from their feudal obligations to ecclesiastical and secular lords. Their unrest had nothing to do with the Reformation, nor did Luther's teaching in any way occasion it. Since he taught truth and justice, however, and turned to the New Testament for authority, it seems scarcely remarkable that the peasants should have seen in the new religious order the coming remedy for their ills.

A further uprising resulted, in 1525, in the Peasants' War. Luther, though he was sympathetic to the needs of the peasantry, was opposed to any form of radicalism and condemned them in the most vehement manner. Thenceforth he favored ever more the direction of religion by the state, the result being that German Lutheranism followed an Erastian pattern of domination by the state and was deprived of any effective religious criticism of society.

For a considerable period, Lutheran organization was in a transitional state. Luther, himself, had no fixed opinion on organization, and it was uncertain whether the revolt from the Roman Church was to be a permanent one. Few Catholic bishops became Protestant; but in certain communities, individual congregations renounced their allegiance to their old priests and chose pastors of their own. Though Luther at first favored popular direction of religion, it was not long before he became convinced that the ruler should be the ultimate ecclesiastical authority. Saxony led in reorganization, and other states followed. By the mid-1520's, Germany was divided into Lutheran and Catholic camps. So great was the tension, that in 1526 the Diet of Speyer adopted the policy of leaving each state to direct its own religious affairs. This policy was essentially reaffirmed in 1555 by the Peace of Augsburg.

In the realm of worship, evangelical practices gradually took the place of Catholic forms. Luther retained the mass as the focal point of worship but eliminated its sacrificial character. The sermon was elevated to first-rank importance; for if personal faith was to be evoked, the inspiration of the spoken word was necessary. This new emphasis on the sermon was to become a cardinal feature of the Protestant movement.

In the Scandinavian countries, a similarly Erastian form of Lutheranism was introduced as early as 1520. King Christian of Denmark, like the German princes, was anxious to curb the power of the chief clerical officials, and to this end he attempted certain disciplinary reforms. His successor, Frederick I, who reigned from 1523 to 1533, came out openly for Lutheranism. Finally, in 1536, a Danish diet at Copenhagen pronounced Lutheranism to be the state religion. The Lutheran tendencies were much less developed in Norway; but since Norway was a vassal of Denmark, the same law applied there. In Sweden, Gustavus Vasa, elected king after leading a successful revolt against the Danes in 1523, brought the church under the power of the realm and adopted a distinctly Swedish model of Lutheranism. Within a century, Sweden would become the leader of the Protestant forces of northern Europe, assuming a dominant role in the devastating Thirty Years' War.

Of the Lutheran nations, only Sweden took an early interest in American colonization. Because of its involvement in the Thirty Years' War, it was unable to divert much of its attention to America; and its little colony on the Delaware, founded in 1638, never flourished. It finally fell to the Dutch in 1655. As for the German Lutherans, they did not arrive in significant numbers in the colonies until the eighteenth century; the great Scandinavian migration would not begin until a century later.

In any case, the religious contribution of Martin Luther did not have to depend upon the German and Scandinavian immigrant for its transmission to America. It was too important a legacy to become the sole property of any one religious tradition. The result was that the Protestant principles of justification by faith, the authority of the Bible, and the priesthood of all believers found their way into the broad stream of Reformation thought and were carried by each of the Protestant immigrant groups to the American scene. In this indirect way, Lutheranism made its greatest impact upon American religious thought and life and bequeathed a priceless heritage to generations yet unborn.

The Reformed Churches

Almost simultaneously with the Lutheran movement in Germany, a similar movement sprang up in Switzerland under the leadership of Ulrich Zwingli (1484–1531). But largely because of dissimilar political and social conditions in Switzerland, it took a widely divergent course. Besides, Luther's background and training had been scholastic; Zwingli's was humanistic. He had studied the New Learning at Berne, Basel, and Vienna, maintaining a close personal friendship with Erasmus, whom he regarded as the ideal scholar.

During his service as people's priest in Zurich, Zwingli began to react against certain principles of the Roman Catholic system, especially the ascetic life, veneration of the saints, and the belief in purgatory. He came to accept the Scriptures as the supreme authority in religion and Christ as sufficient Saviour without the mediation of the church. The movement soon spread to other cantons, beginning with the important city of Berne. It also reached as far as Strassburg, in southern Germany, where reforms were accomplished in a similar way by the City Council, and where humanistic preparation inclined the Reformers to Zwinglian rather than Lutheran ways of thinking.

By the 1520's, Zwingli was calling for the removal of images from the churches and insisting that the Lord's Supper was only a memorial. As a result of his efforts, the City Council abolished images, the mass, and the monasteries. A visitation of the churches was prescribed and biblical instruction was appointed for clergy and laity alike. Zwingli gave the central place in his system to a theoretical doctrine of the absolute will of God, rather than to a personal religious experience of divine forgiveness. He saw the Christian life not as a spontaneous expression of gratitude to God, but as obedience to the divine will. In these respects, the Reformed Churches followed him instead of Luther.

About the same time, a well-known humanist named Jacques Lefèvre d'Étaples was furthering the Reformation in France through his studies of the New Testament. In a commentary on the Pauline epistles, published in 1512, he argued eloquently for the final authority of Scripture and justification by faith alone. Lefèvre, like Erasmus and numerous other humanists, never broke with the Roman Church, believing that the necessary reforms could be achieved without schism.

Many of Lefèvre's disciples, however, went further. If they had enjoyed the support of the crown, their movement would undoubtedly have made great progress. But since the French were already an independent nation and had experienced unusual success in curbing the claims of the papacy, they had little reason to identify Protestantism with Frenchness, as their eastern neighbor had identified it with German nationalism. It was hardly surprising, then, that the French crown opposed the new religious movement, persecuted its supporters, and forced many of them to seek refuge in Germany and Switzerland.

One of the French exiles, William Farel, introduced the Reformation into Geneva. Realizing his limited capacities for organization, he enlisted the services of John Calvin, a French refugee who was visiting the city. Calvin's social background was middle class, his intellectual preparation humanistic, including five years of theological study at the University of Paris. Owing to the influence of Lefèvre, he became sympathetic with the Protestant cause and, as a result, was forced to flee to Basel. There he published, in 1536, the first edition of his *Institutes of the Christian Religion,* which was destined to become one of the foremost Protestant treatments of systematic theology. Calvin received so much publicity after the release of this work that he soon became the recognized Protestant leader in France, as he was also to become at Geneva.

As Calvin viewed the Genevan situation, it seemed necessary to sort the people by their religious preferences, thus enabling him to determine how far he might carry his reforms. He would then be able to purify the church by discipline and begin an adequate program of religious education. The religious census resulted in a majority decision for Calvin; but when he attempted to enforce discipline, a reaction set in and he was banished from the city. Affairs in Geneva suffered from the loss of Calvin's dynamic leadership, and by 1541 the people were eager to invite him back. He accepted and served Geneva until his demise in 1564.

Calvin's interpretation of Christianity differed significantly from that of Luther. First, he conducted a much more thorough reform of church worship and organization. The pulpit with the open Bible became the focal point of worship, and the service centered in preaching, prayer, and the singing of hymns. Like Luther, Calvin accepted two sacraments: baptism and the Lord's Supper; but he went much further than Luther in changing their theological meaning. Far from becoming the substance of Christ's body and blood, as in the Roman Catholic doctrine of transubstantiation, Calvin held that the elements contained the spiritual presence of Christ and performed a work of grace for those alone who received them in faith.

At the pinnacle of Calvin's theological system stood his doctrine of God as absolute sovereign will. God not only brought the world and all things in it into being, but maintains them through every moment of their existence. Although the Deity disclosed His will to man in nature and human reason, man is no longer able to perform it because of his total depravity. In this sinful state he is unable to choose God and work out his own salvation. Taking cognizance of man's predicament, God has taken special means to save those whom He will. Following the view of Augustine, Calvin developed the doctrines of election and predestination. Since all men are sinners, their just reward is eternal perdition. But the Gospel reveals that beyond God's justice lies mercy, and that in His own providence He elects some men to salvation. Men cannot know of a certainty that they are numbered among the elect; yet, if they respond to the witness of the Holy Spirit and lead righteous lives, this may be an indication of their election.

The Calvinistic interpretation of election contributed directly to the building of a vigorous morality. God's way of accomplishing His will on earth was through the elect, who were appointed to carry out His plan. Their commission was to make all human life conform to the will of a holy and majestic God. Thus, while Calvin was pessimistic in his view of natural man, he was optimistic in his view of history. Here, in a religious form, was the doctrine of progress. And how was progress to be won? Calvin believed it could be accomplished through the application of the doctrines and commandments to every detail of life. Drawing their ethics as much from Moses as from Jesus, and seeking to impose them on the whole of society, his followers were apt to insist upon every jot and tittle of the law. Nevertheless, evaluations which portray Calvinists as somber, morose people devoid of humor, have oversimplified historical fact. The Calvinist experienced much joy and peace in the reflection that he was one of God's agents on earth.

In the realm of social ethics, Calvinism allied itself economically with the rising middle class. Calvin stood in sharp antagonism to medieval Catholic teaching when he permitted his followers to accept payments of interest, a practice which is basic in a capitalistic economy. Max Weber, the nineteenth century German sociologist, in his *Protestant Ethic and the Spirit of Capitalism,* has practically claimed that Calvin was the ethical source of modern capitalism. Certainly there is a modicum of truth in his thesis, but it must also be pointed out that the system flourished in Roman Catholic nations such as Italy, France and Belgium, where Calvinism had relatively little influence. Indirectly, Calvin gave aid and comfort to the current economic forces through his emphasis on the virtues of thrift, hard work and industry. Sloth and laziness he considered to be the worst of vices, a sign of depravity and sin.

Politically, Calvin stood for a mixture of aristocracy and democracy, though his own practices were frequently far from democratic. Still, in his representative church government, derived from the New Testament and the Genevan Republic, authority comes from the people. Calvin was a great respecter of states, yet he taught that when earthly rulers rise up against God they lose their divine right and must be put down. His deep sense of original sin led further to an abiding suspicion of pressure groups in government and to the idea of safeguarding checks and balances in a democratic society. In this way, he and his followers stood in the vanguard of resistance to political absolutism and indirectly prospered the growth of democracy.

The importance of Calvinism to American history stems from its expansion in France, the Lowlands, Scotland and England, from whence it was carried to the colonies. In France, the Calvinists had gained sufficient strength by 1559 to hold a synod in Paris, where they adopted the Gallican Confession as their symbol of faith, together with a Calvinistic model of church organization and discipline. These French Protestants came to be known as Huguenots, a term of uncertain origin. That same year Henry II died, and the nobles in sympathy with Protestantism came out openly in its behalf. Soon the nation was plunged into a bitter civil war over religious differences. Whether Protestantism should be permitted to survive became a leading political question.

The long struggle was characterized by massacres and assassinations which debilitated the nation and robbed it of many of its most useful citizens. Many Huguenots fled the country, one group coming to Florida in 1562. The climax of the war came with the Massacre of St. Bartholomew in 1572, in which a multitude of Huguenots were liquidated at the order of the Regent, Catherine de Medici. Although the Protestants never wholly recovered their strength, the war went on until 1594, when Henry of Navarre, the collateral heir to the throne and a Protestant, in order to establish peace, accepted Roman Catholicism upon becoming king.

Four years later, Henry announced a policy of toleration in the Edict of Nantes, which brought protection to French Huguenots for almost a century. When the edict was finally revoked by Louis XIV in 1685, another period of persecution and forced conversion of the Protestants came with it. Many escaped the country, though emigration was banned, and within a few years there was not a colony in America without a representation of Huguenots.

At the outbreak of the Reformation, the Low Countries had achieved unity in neither race nor government, being a curious amalgam of Dutch, Flemish, and Celtic elements under the suzerainty of the Holy Roman Emperor, Charles V. The Catholicism of the area had been influenced by movements of pietism, mysticism, and humanism, thus accounting for their eager response to the writings of Luther and the preaching of the Anabaptists. Charles V dealt with these movements promptly and severely, and without success.

Gradually Calvinism supplanted Lutheranism, particularly among the Dutch, many of whom organized themselves into churches on the model of the French Huguenots. In 1561, Guy de Bray, a Walloon who had studied at Geneva, drafted the Belgic Confession, a decidedly Calvinistic document, which became the standard of the Dutch Reformed Church. At the Synod of Emden in 1571, the Dutch Calvinists perfected their machinery of local consistories, the governing body of ministers and elders in every church, district presbyteries which were known as classes, and the general synod.

In the meantime, the country stood upon the verge of war. Charles V had abdicated in 1555, and his son, Philip II, a devout Catholic and political autocrat, had succeeded him. Philip, who had no intention of permitting either civil or religious freedom, continued the process of consolidating the region under Spanish rule and ferreting out heretics. His determined policy, which included the introduction of the Inquisition, provoked William, Prince of Orange, to lead an armed revolt against the Hispanic oppressor. Retaliation by the hated Duke of Alva came swiftly, with eighteen thousand patriots being put to the sword and many times that number taking refuge in Germany and England. The seven northern provinces, however, finally won their independence and declared themselves an independent republic in 1581.

William of Orange, though now a communicant of the Reformed Church, was religiously tolerant of Lutherans and Anabaptists. Roman Catholics, however, were forbidden public worship and the holding of public office. It was not long before The Netherlands became a religious haven for the persecuted of other lands. Anabaptists, Huguenots, Scotch Covenanters, and English Puritans and Separatists found comfort on its shores, spinning dreams of a future which would become history in the New World.

As for the Reformed Church, which enjoyed the status of an establishment by 1619, the center of interest was more theological than geographical. It was focused upon the Arminian controversy and the question of free will versus predestination. Of only secondary interest was the infant colony in New Netherland, spiritually undernourished for want of a settled ministry. For the moment, the struggle to preserve Calvinistic orthodoxy held the stage.

At the opening of the sixteenth century, the church in Scotland was in desperate need of reform. Many high ecclesiastical posts had fallen into the hands of sons of the nobility, who used them solely for their own aggrandizement. The lower clergy were more often than not ignorant and ineffectual men who were more interested in stipends than in standards. Here and there Protestant influences from the Continent were felt, especially those of the Lutheran movement. In 1528, Patrick Hamilton, a nobleman, was burned at the stake because of his Lutheran views.

Another early reformer was George Wishart, who had studied on the Continent and had accepted Calvinism. After returning home to preach his new convictions, he was arrested and sent to the stake in 1546.

The man who more than anyone else shaped the course of Scottish Protestantism was John Knox. Following in the steps of Wishart, he preached Protestant views at St. Andrews castle, was captured, and spent nineteen months as a prisoner on a French war galley. After his release, Knox went to England, where the Reformation was making notable progress under Edward VI. When Mary Tudor became Queen of England, he escaped to the Continent where he studied for a time under Calvin in Geneva.

In the meantime, the forces of Scottish nationalism and Protestantism were becoming more closely allied, lending prestige to the party hostile to Catholic France and friendly to England. Still, French influence saw to it that Princess Mary, later Queen of Scots, married the heir to the French throne. Her French mother, Mary of Lorraine, served as regent of Scotland in her place, and was intensely unpopular. Hoping to bring about her downfall, a large number of the nobles who were antagonistic toward both Roman Catholicism and French rule urged Knox to return home and head a reformation movement. These men gathered at Edinburgh and joined in a covenant to maintain their principles, thus becoming known as Covenanters.

At the risk of his life, Knox returned to Scotland and went about the country preaching with such vigor and force that rioting broke out, followed by civil war in 1559. English troops were sent by Queen Elizabeth to aid the Protestants, forcing the French to retire by the summer of 1560. The Scottish Parliament promptly adopted a confession of faith modeled upon Calvinism. Knox and his associates then drew up the *First Book of Discipline* for the organization and administration of the church. Its government was representative and presbyterian, having four ascending courts or judicatories to conduct the affairs of the church, a kirk session, a district presbytery, a regional synod, and a national general assembly. In the courts of the church all men were to be treated without discrimination, since "before God there is no respect of persons," a principle which contributed much to an independent and democratic spirit.

Scottish Presbyterianism followed a rocky road of hazards and pitfalls. With the return of the widowed Mary in 1560, Knox and his friends faced strong opposition. It might have proved overwhelming had not the Queen injudiciously become involved in court intrigues and matrimonial ventures which ruined her reputation and drove her out of the country. As it was, the church had to contend with James VI, later James I of England, who attempted to impose episcopacy upon it; and with his son, Charles I, who was determined to bring its services into conformity with the English Book of Common Prayer. The raising of Scottish ire over these attempts was directly contributory to the civil war which cost the Stuart king his life.

In one respect, the Stuart campaign against Presbyterianism scored a success. James I, hoping to gain control of all Ireland, lured large numbers of Scottish Presbyterians to the four northeastern counties of Ulster, with the promise of economic advantage. After they settled there, the government began to apply severe economic and political pressures which ultimately led them to seek security in the colonies. It was thus through the Scotch-Irish that Calvinism in its Presbyterian form made its greatest impact on American culture.

Anglicanism

Unlike the Reformation on the Continent which was essentially popular and theological, the English Reformation began as chiefly political and liturgical. The two movements were grounded in different principles and reached different goals. The English set out to reject the universal authority of the Roman Church. Doctrinal and ethical problems which so troubled Luther and Calvin were at first given only secondary importance. A recasting of Catholic doctrine was certainly not intended by Henry VIII, nor did he reject any part of Roman teaching, except the papal claim to universal jurisdiction. While Luther began with the recognition of practical abuses and the discovery of justification by faith, turning only later to renounce the papacy and to construct his own church, the English moved in the opposite direction. They began by renouncing the pope's authority, and only gradually turned to a reconstruction of doctrine.

A host of influences acted to bring about the English revolt. The Lollard movement of Wycliffe, with its anticlericalism and its emphasis on the authority of the Bible, was still a force among the common people. The Humanistic movement was encouraging practical reforms and stressing the study of the Scriptures. John Colet introduced new methods into the study of the New Testament at Oxford as early as 1496. Luther's writings also were having their effect on the universities to such an extent that Henry VIII prohibited them and wrote a defense of the seven sacraments in 1521, which won for him the title "Defensor Fidei" from the pope.

Within a dozen years the "Defender of the Faith" broke with the papacy and declared the church in England independent of Rome. This action could hardly be attributed to sympathy with the principles of the reformers. Henry, like most nationally minded Englishmen, had felt a sense of dissatisfaction with the papacy over political, social, and economic matters for some time. The unfortunate episode over the termination of Henry's marriage to Catherine of Aragon and his subsequent marriage to Anne Boleyn has little meaning when lifted from the broad general context. It was a convenient occasion for the king to declare himself supreme head of the Church of England in 1534, thus placing the church under the control of the state in Erastian fashion.

Political motives at one point prompted Henry to enter into friendly relations with the Protestant princes of Germany. This is reflected in the Ten Articles of 1536, which emphasized the free grace of God in justification and affirmed only three sacraments, baptism, the holy communion, and penance. But a reaction soon set in, largely because of public indignation over the government's suppression of the monasteries, and in 1539, the Six Articles, decidedly conservative and Catholic in character, were issued.

With the accession of the boy king Edward VI in 1547, the government came under the aegis of the Protestant party. The Six Articles were repealed and significant reforms were put into effect. Images were removed from the churches, prayers to the saints were forbidden, communion in both kinds was commanded, and clerical marriage was permitted. But the two monumental contributions made under the guidance of Thomas Cranmer, Archbishop of Canterbury, were the Book of Common Prayer, possibly the greatest liturgical work of the English-speaking world, and the Forty-two Articles. The latter, issued in 1553, show Cranmer's Lutheran influence in their stress upon justification by faith alone and the supreme authority of Scripture.

From 1553 to 1558, Roman Catholicism was restored under Mary Tudor. It was a time of violent persecution and scores of Protestant leaders, among them Cranmer, were put to death. Many who had turned against Protestantism because of the suppression of the monasteries, turned back out of disgust over this wholesale persecution, which won for the queen the ineradicable title of "Bloody Mary." In 1558, Mary died, and was succeeded by her half-sister, Elizabeth.

Elizabeth I was her father's daughter in every sense. She sought to rule England with all the Tudor despotism characteristic of Henry VIII. Although she permitted the reestablishment of practically every reform achieved under Edward VI, she was suspicious of popular religious exercises for fear that they might lead to a demand for fuller political liberty. She was not a pious woman, but she was devoted to the welfare of her people and spent much of her time trying to increase England's power.

In 1571, the Forty-two Articles were pruned to Thirty-nine, their present form. In doctrinal matters they followed the Continental reformers by emphasizing the things in which all agreed. But they reveal a slight leaning toward Calvinism, especially in the articles covering predestination and the Lord's Supper. The only serious objection to them came from the Puritan party in the church, which favored more sweeping reforms. This group would prove to be a most disturbing influence during Elizabeth's later life and during the reign of the Stuarts.

Puritanism

The Puritan movement began as an agitation within the Church of England in the latter half of the sixteenth century. It stood for the conviction that the church should be restored to the simplicity and purity of the first century fellowship and that reforms in England were thus far inadequate. Its adherents often disagreed among themselves concerning the length of sermons, spontaneous prayer, and plainer vestments; but in one matter they stood in perfect harmony: there should be an established church.

Ultimately, Puritans and Anglicans divided because of dissimilar interpretations of the Scriptures and their role in ecclesiastical government. Both sides believed in the authority of the Bible. The difference was that the Anglican did not believe everything in the Scriptures to be literally binding on all men. On the other hand, the Puritans, rooted and grounded in Calvinism, found the Bible to be a complete body of laws, inerrant in every respect. They found it so plain and explicit that any man of reasonable learning could establish its meaning and intention for any situation. In their opinion, the church had gone especially far afield in matters of worship and ceremony. They saw the observance of Christmas and the use of the cross and priestly vestments as innovations of Romanism which were to be abhorred. In 1603, they drew up a formal list of abuses in the Millenary Petition. James I granted only one request: the production of the celebrated Authorized Version of the Bible.

At the heart of the Puritan system was the Federal theology, which stressed the covenant relationship between God and man. Grounded in Calvinism, it regarded the Bible as essentially a history of redemption falling into three dispensations: the ante-legal, before man's fall; the legal, in which the covenant was the law; and the post-legal, in which God sent Jesus Christ to establish a covenant of grace.

Instead of centering attention on the eternal decree of God, the Federal theology stressed God's historical activity in dealing with men, first one way and then another. The effect was to place more emphasis on the role of man in salvation, since a covenant has no value unless two parties accept it. Another effect could be seen in the Westminster Confession of Faith of 1646, which was somewhat vague on the doctrine of predestination. Perhaps the Scottish-English group which prepared it saw some inconsistency in the doctrine with that of the covenant relationship. In any case, Federalism contributed to more liberal tendencies within the church; especially would this be true among the Puritans who came to New England.

The most significant contribution of the Puritans lay in the area of society and government. In Puritan thought, society was not an aggregation of individuals, but rather an organism functioning for a definite purpose. All persons residing in the community had as their duty the furtherance of society's chief purpose, which was to do the will of God. Since natural man was sinful, it followed that God's will could be done only if government were in the hands of the holy and regenerate (those who held Puritan views).

When it appeared that such a condition could not be achieved in England, a large number of Puritans migrated to New England in the 1620's, and especially in the 1630's, where they established governments controlled by the "holy and regenerate." There they put into effect certain principles which they had developed in England, among them freedom of conscience based on the clear and explicit teaching of Scripture, rule by fundamental law as contained in the Bible, and government by the consent of the governed. When broadened and liberalized, these ideas would exercise a profound influence on the shaping of American democratic thought.

THE LEFT WING OF THE REFORMATION

Almost simultaneously with the rise of the great churchly systems of Protestantism, there sprang up a number of religious groups or schools of thought which gave full expression to the divisive and individualistic tendencies latent within the Reformation. They were generally built around some particular emphasis which the members of the fellowship believed to be expressive of the essence of Christianity. Coming as they did out of the mass of the common people, they invariably began as "sect" phenomena, rejected by society and uncomfortable in "the world."

Protestants of the left wing conceived of the church as a fellowship rather than an organization and deemed a soul-searching personal decision as prerequisite to communicant membership. Their forms of polity were simple, generally of the congregational type. Although they gradually took on a more churchly character, they neither became nor aspired to become church establishments. Their strength lay in the piety of their adherents and the strictness of their discipline. Symbolic of the common man as they were, they seldom produced leaders of more than secondary importance. Yet their influence was deeply felt in Europe, and in America their religious character and type became normative.

The Anabaptists

In the first stage of the Reformation, the most numerous and influential followers of left-wing Protestantism in Germany and Switzerland were called Anabaptists or Rebaptizers. The appellation covered the widest range of religious opinion, since each Anabaptist exercised complete control in interpreting Scripture and in defining his own concept of the essentials of the Christian faith. Most Anabaptists concerned themselves primarily with the restoration of the beliefs and practices of primitive Christianity as described in the New Testament.

While the Anabaptists held to the major religious principles of the reformers, they differed from them in certain notable respects. They held that the church, since it is the community of saints composed of true believers alone, could not be coextensive with the state. The only way to make the Christian community a truly visible embodiment of the Kingdom of God would be to withdraw from the state churches. Into the true church they would receive only those persons who gave evidence in character and conduct of having been regenerated, accepting Christ publicly and receiving believers' baptism. The practice of infant baptism was repudiated, since baptism was only a symbol of regeneration which had already taken place in the believer and not a sacrament conferring special grace. Some Anabaptists practiced immersion in baptism, but affusion and sprinkling were the preferred modes during the early years of the movement.

One of the cardinal tenets of the Anabaptists was the complete separation of church and state. They postulated a dualism, with each institution being supreme in its own sphere and totally irrelevant to the other. Civil government might be of divine appointment, but Christians should not take part in affairs of state or hold official positions. Experience had taught the Anabaptists that where there was a union between church and state, persecution of dissenting groups invariably followed. It was their conviction that physical compulsion could not properly be exercised in matters of faith.

To be sure, the Anabaptists claimed the right to excommunicate the heretical and ungodly, but their authority was spiritual only. Beyond that, they believed in freedom of conscience and condemned religious persecution of any kind. In thus championing intellectual liberty, they followed in the path of Renaissance individualism and anticipated modern views of the dignity of human personality.

In 1525, the Anabaptists, encouraged by initial successes, felt that they were sponsoring the most important phase of the Reformation. Yet, within a decade, the movement had almost been destroyed by extremist tendencies, such as those exhibited by fanatical agitators in Münster in 1534. By the end of the Reformation period, Anabaptism had crystallized into a number of denominations such as the Mennonites, Baptists, Dunkers, Schwenkfelders, and Moravians. In the meantime, it had been carried to England where it contributed greatly to the rise of the Separatist movement.

The Separatists

In addition to the Puritans who believed in the union of church and state, there was a smaller group in England whose theology was essentially Puritan, but whose polity was quite different. Their principles were set forth chiefly by Robert Browne (1550–1633), an Englishman who had developed a close association with the Dutch Anabaptists. Like them, he taught that the church is a company of saints instituted by a voluntary covenant with God. The purpose of the church is not to build the Kingdom of God in the world, but rather to provide for the mutual spiritual growth and edification of its members. It can become a really spiritual institution only when it is independent of the state.

Browne believed that the church is nothing more than a local company of Christians who freely enter into a covenant with God and with one another and who carry on their Christian life and work as a united fellowship. Wherever redeemed persons enter into such a covenant, there is a true church. This idea became one of the fundamental principles of the Congregational churches. Consistent with this position was Browne's teaching that church officers should be chosen by and be responsible to the congregation. Even the power of ordination was a congregational right.

The principal difference between Browne and the Anabaptists was in regard to his concept of the covenant. Although he did not consider infant baptism a sacrament, he accepted it on the ground that children ought to be dedicated to God and the church. This led Browne to stress the idea of the voluntary covenant as the characteristic mark of the church. Those who could not agree with his teaching on infant baptism withdrew and founded what was to become the English Baptist Church. This group, already Separatist in sympathy, had settled in Amsterdam about 1607, under the leadership of John Smyth. Due to the influence of the Mennonites, Smyth rebaptized himself and his congregation. When they returned to London in 1612, they founded the first Baptist church in England. By 1638, a Baptist congregation under the spiritual leadership of Roger Williams was worshipping in Rhode Island.

Robert Browne was persecuted for his views and sought asylum in The Netherlands. Another Separatist group, under the leadership of John Robinson, William Brewster, and William Bradford, fled from England in 1609 and settled for a time in Leyden. It was part of this congregation that sailed across the Atlantic in 1620 to found Plymouth Colony.

The Friends

While the main stream of the Reformation was moving toward a careful systematization of doctrine and polity, another movement was stressing the importance of the mystical experience or inner light. On the Continent, it found its leadership in such men as Caspar Schwenkfeld, Sebastian Franck, and Jacob Boehme. George Fox (1624–1691), the founder of the movement in its English phase, had been reared in a strict Puritan atmosphere. Feeling that religion should be an inner experience, he rebelled and left home at the age of nineteen. Three years later, he had a mystical experience in which he believed he heard God speaking to him. From that time, he carried on a peripatetic ministry, preaching the possibility of direct enlightenment through the influence of the Holy Spirit. Boehme must have had a tremendous influence on him, for in Fox's journal one notes phraseology almost identical with that in Boehme's writings.

The Friends, or Quakers, as they were derisively called by a judge whom Fox had commanded to tremble at the Word of God, took as their central theological position the doctrine of the inner light. They believed that the illuminating power of the Holy Spirit is conferred on all men and is not limited to truth already received through Scripture. Yet, nothing contrary to Scripture could be accepted as coming from God. Since all men were equally dependent on the Spirit and the individual was the final norm of spiritual experience, all persons should be equal in the church. No clergy would be necessary, for the Spirit would inspire persons in the congregation to speak concerning their experience.

In spite of persecution, the common people welcomed this unconventional type of religion. Few men of rank and station joined the movement; but William Penn, an admiral's son, planted a Quaker colony in Pennsylvania in 1681, and this group became a respected and prosperous element in society. The Friends came to be known for their rejection of oaths, their use of Christian names in conversation with others, and their adherence to simple modes of dress. Especially outstanding were their dominant spirit of Christian kindness and their absolute condemnation of war. Wherever they went they stood as pillars in defense of liberty for all men.

THE ROMAN CATHOLIC COUNTER-REFORMATION

Despite the significant losses which the Roman Church suffered as a result of the Protestant Reformation, it still had enough vitality to stage a remarkable recovery. To accomplish this, however, the church had to meet two needs. The first was to take the great mass of medieval doctrine and tradition and weld it together into a carefully defined doctrinal system. While the immediate stimulus for this work was to be found in the Protestant revolt, the task was dealt with in a most positive manner.

The calling of a general council was distasteful to the papacy, which had not forgotten the unfortunate experiences connected with the conciliar movement a century before. But so much pressure was applied by

Charles V and the Spanish Church for the calling of a council that this
action could scarcely be avoided. Finally, Pope Paul III called a council
which met intermittently from 1545 to 1563 at Trent, in the Austrian
Tyrol. This long, drawn-out council was torn between the insistence of
the Italian prelates upon a thorough definition of Catholic doctrines and
the demand of the Spanish prelates for a reform of abuses. In the end,
both matters were treated.

In the realm of doctrine, there was much need for discussion, for
medieval theology had been quite fluid. But the discussions at Trent
were limited to questions which had been raised by the Protestants. The
Council declared that the body of revealed truth for Christians was to
be found not only in the Bible but also in the unwritten tradition of
Christ's teaching, preserved by the church from the beginning under the
guidance of the Holy Spirit. No statement was made concerning who
might declare the tradition; but gradually the principle was accepted that
popes have equal authority with the Scriptures when they speak *ex
cathedra*. As for Scripture, the Council pronounced to be canonical all
the books of the Septuagint, which included the Old Testament Apocrypha. Jerome's Vulgate Version of the fourth century, in Latin, was
declared to be the authoritative text.

Concerning the doctrine of salvation, it was discovered that a number
of the members of the Council embraced the Protestant view that the
sinner becomes reconciled to God by faith in the merits of Christ, and
that good works are the natural expression of one's faith. Indeed, some
of these men, such as Cardinal Contarini, had even tried to effect a reconciliation with the Protestants at Regensburg in 1541. A few of them
withdrew from the Council and returned home. The official decision was
that the sinner is justified by the merits of Christ, if they produce merits
in him, so that he obeys the commandments of God and the church. It
was further held that the seven sacraments are necessary to salvation.
Through them one's salvation begins, develops, and is recovered when
lost. Thus it followed that outside the church there can be no truly
religious life.

Some noteworthy practical reforms were also accomplished at Trent.
Provision was made for the more adequate supervision of clerical morals
and for the improved education of the clergy. Priests were directed to
reside in their parishes, and bishops in their dioceses, that they might
properly discharge the duties of their respective offices. The clergy were
ordered to expound the Scriptures in the larger towns and to see that
everywhere the people were taught in a lucid way the things essential to
salvation.

The second need of the Roman Church at the outset of the Counter-
Reformation was a strong aggressive movement within the church to promote its ideas and practices and to impede the progress of Protestantism.

If such a movement were to succeed, it would have to be characterized by intellectual acumen, moral persuasiveness, and a passionate zeal to defend the church in the face of vigorous opposition. Such a movement was found in the order known as the Society of Jesus. More than any other single agency it furthered the work of the Counter-Reformation and shaped the course of Roman Catholic development in the modern period.

The Jesuit order originated in the mind of a young Spanish noble, Ignatius Loyola. Born in 1491, his religious experience had been shaped by the burning devotion and mystical tendencies of Spanish Catholics and by the practical reforms of the Hispanic Reformation under Cardinal Ximenes. After a brief career in the army, he was wounded in a battle with the French and rendered lame for life. During his illness, he experienced an intensive spiritual struggle. In a moment of crisis, the sufferer threw himself upon the mercy of God and received salvation. Instead of following the theological implications of his discovery, he gave himself over to mystical practices. In periods of ecstasy and vision, he saw into the Catholic mysteries, such as transubstantiation, the Trinity, and the Incarnation. Many of his experiences he incorporated in his *Spiritual Exercises,* a manual of devotion and discipline for the subjection of the will.

At the University of Paris, in 1528–1529, Loyola gathered a small band of disciples who were to constitute a new order pledged to the special service of the pope. In 1537, these men were ordained to the priesthood. Three years later, Pope Paul III recognized them officially as the Society of Jesus. The mind and character of Loyola was indelibly stamped upon the new order. It was an officers' corps, designed to lead everywhere in the work of the Roman Church, notably in missions, education, diplomacy, and in places of unusual danger. Its members were trained to work in any country and might be sent anywhere at a moment's notice. The general of the order was supreme dictator, subject only to the pope. He exercised absolute authority over the members.

With such zeal and unity, Loyola and his order could not help but have a tremendous effect on the Roman Church. They contributed greatly to the strengthening of the papacy, which culminated in the infallibility decree of 1870. They fostered education, both secondary and higher, founding universities wherever they went. They won new lands for the church, soon becoming the greatest missionary order. By 1556, they had penetrated every colony of Spain and Portugal. Their influence in America was powerful, whether in the Spanish missions to the South and Southwest or in the French missions in the Northeast and Mississippi Valley. They easily represented the most aggressive movement in the effort to stem the tide of Protestantism.

There are perhaps a number of reasons for the success of the Roman Catholic Counter-Reformation. Certainly the purification of administrative abuses won back many who had been disgusted with the church's corruption. The advantage of a closely knit and well-disciplined organization was also a factor. Then, too, the Protestant movement had not been able to express itself in a unified way; divisions were taking place almost with the advent of the Reformation. This contributed to a serious weakening of Protestant strength which proved ultimately beneficial to the papacy.

JUDAISM

With the fall of Jerusalem and the destruction of the second temple in 70 A.D., Palestine fell completely into foreign hands, and the Jews became homeless wanderers among the nations. Wherever they went, they carried with them the Torah, which became for them a kind of spiritual fatherland. The main function of the rabbis was to interpret the Torah and apply it to ever-changing situations. They embodied the results of their labors in the Mishnah and in the Palestinian and Babylonian Gemaras, which formed the Talmud, Judaism's encyclopaedia of tradition. In the eyes of Christians, who could not tolerate the existence of the Jews, it came to be regarded as a wicked, blasphemous book and was put on trial by the Inquisition and publicly burned.

In North Africa, Spain, and Portugal, after the Moslem invasions, Judaism developed a more inclusive spirit and fostered a quickening of intellectual life. A diversity of movements appeared, such as that of the eighth century Karaites who revived interest in the study of the biblical text. Rationalistic movements, based on Platonic and Aristotelian philosophy, also appeared, served by such men as Saadia in the tenth century and Maimonides in the twelfth. Their principal concern was to harmonize philosophy with revealed religion.

With the final expulsion of Moslem rule from the Hispanic world in the fifteenth century, persecution of the Jews began anew. The result was a revival of the older exclusive spirit, coupled with a penchant for mystical, esoteric doctrines, as in the case of the sixteenth century Spanish Cabbala. In such critical times, it was only normal for Jews to seek refuge in foreign lands. Thus, by the seventeenth century, there were Spanish and Portuguese Jews in northern Brazil where they had found asylum during Dutch possession. In 1654, when Brazil reverted to Portugal, they fled to New York to find another haven among the Dutch, thus representing the first Jewish penetration of America. As for the Jews of central Europe, more than a century passed before they could free themselves from the insulation of the ghettos and accommodate themselves to modern trends. Only when that had been accomplished would many of them turn their eyes toward free America.

THE AGE OF EXPLORATION AND SETTLEMENT

At the very moment Europe was going through a period of religious upheaval, it was also moving through a period of geographical expansion in which the leading powers would seek to gain wealth and influence in the Western Hemisphere. If political, economic, and social interests were sometimes, even frequently, fused with religious causes, it was therefore not by accident.

The motivation for the great western expansion, which began in the mid-fifteenth century, was manifold. Out of the Renaissance had sprung an era of adventure, made possible on the sea by the discovery of the mariner's compass and implemented by the possession of firearms. The Venetian trade monopoly had turned Western European minds to the search for an all-water route to India and China. Such a route would eliminate much of the heavy expense of shipping and result in greater profits. But the motivation was not merely greed and love of adventure. Some dreamed of a better, freer life in a new homeland, while others regarded themselves as part of the great plan of God to advance His Kingdom in the uttermost parts of the earth. Thus, conviction as well as daring characterized the period of European expansion, a factor of considerable significance in the building of the New World.

The Portuguese, in the late fifteenth century, were the first to open an all-water route to the Orient via the southern tip of Africa. Columbus, in the employ of Spain, attempted to find a better route by sailing west, Magellan by sailing southwest. Within a few years, evidence revealed that what Columbus had discovered in 1492 was not the East Indies, but a land barrier between Europe and Asia, a new land.

Spain followed up Columbus' voyages with alacrity. Here was a possible opportunity to gain untold wealth and prestige and to make use of the unemployed conquistadors. Expeditions were promptly dispatched to the West Indies and the American mainland; Cortez overran Mexico, Pizarro Peru. In both regions, the Spanish found gold and silver and docile populations which could at once be exploited and won to the Catholic faith. It was not long before Spain's American empire extended from Florida and California to Argentina.

Naturally, the Spanish success provoked envy. Portuguese rivalry was settled by a papal demarcation line in 1493–1494, which gave Brazil to Portugal, the rest of America to Spain. Other monarchies, quite logically, refused to accept this arrangement. As early as 1497, John Cabot established an English claim to Newfoundland; and forty years later, Jacques Cartier raised the standard of France in the valley of the St. Lawrence. Though late, the French were vigorous and thorough, and a host of *coureurs des bois* and priests pushed into the western unknown establishing trading posts and missions.

The English did not immediately take advantage of the efforts of John Cabot. They were still lagging behind Spain in trade, culture, and armed might. But with the concentration of power in the Crown and the encouragement of the middle classes accomplished by the Tudor dynasty, English influence spread abroad. Merchants began to open commercial routes, found trading posts, and send colonists to remote shores. In this way, the merchants were able to secure much-needed raw materials as well as to build markets for English products.

It was inevitable that the English should come into conflict with the Spaniards, especially when they started breaking into the Spanish trading monopoly. In 1562, Captain John Hawkins shipped a cargo of slaves to Spanish West Indian planters, returning home with sugar and other goods. His nephew, Francis Drake, brought profits through the seizure of treasure ships and the looting of Spanish colonial seaports. These activities were popular in England. Politically, they were harmful to England's natural enemy; religiously, they symbolized the Protestant struggle with Roman Catholicism. The resultant war with Spain ended in 1588 with an overwhelming English victory. England was now ready for colonial expansion, a fact which was realized in 1607 when she planted her first permanent settlement at Jamestown.

2

The Spanish and French

Missions

THE SAGA OF AMERICA OPENS UPON A DRAMATIC EFFORT BY THREE POWERFUL European nations to order the advance of empire. Each looked out upon the New World and saw that it was good, that the benefits of possession were part of its manifest destiny. In the furtherance of its goals, each nation came into conflict with the others, and the clash of arms reverberated across a vast continent. When the dove of peace once more flew over the land, England, the last of these nations to enter the lists, had emerged the victor. But the cultural imprint left by the Spanish and French who had come before could not be totally expunged from the American environment, and there were vestiges of influence which remained long after the political supremacy of England in America had perished.

THE MISSIONS OF NEW SPAIN

Almost a century before the English colonization of Virginia, Roman Catholic Spain was planting permanent settlements within the borders of

25

what is now the United States. Perhaps no nation entered the American forest primeval with more vigor and enthusiasm and sense of mission. Certainly none was able to blend more effectively its economic, political, and religious goals in a comprehensive and unified program for colonization.

There were several factors which account for the uncommon character of Spanish colonialism. Foremost is the remarkable way in which Spanish political vitality and religious fervor were fused in the national consciousness by the opening of the sixteenth century. Out of a background of subjugation by the Islamic Moors, Spanish nationalism and Catholic faith came to find a natural affinity and together they fanned the sparks of Hispanic patriotism into full flame. In 1492, just nine months before Columbus' epoch-making discovery, the last Moslem stronghold fell to Ferdinand and Isabella. Spain now moved into a period of national unity and was soon to become the most powerful Catholic state in Europe. Spanish political and religious cohesiveness was further strengthened by the outbreak of the Protestant Reformation and made militant by hostility toward the rising Protestant states to the North. Thus it was no sudden caprice which prompted his Catholic majesty, Charles V, in June, 1523, to instruct Lucas Vásquez de Ayllón to regard the conversion of the Floridian Indians as "the chief motive you are to bear and hold in this affair . . ." Every Spanish enterprise, in fact, came to be linked with the cause of Catholic missions; and every settlement in the New World became an agency for the dissemination of the faith.

Another factor of considerable import was the unusual extent to which the church in Spain was dominated by the state. As early as 1508, Pope Julius II issued a bull which provided that the Spanish government's approval was necessary before any church, monastery, or religious house might be opened. He also granted the state the perpetual right to make nominations to every ecclesiastical benefice in the colonies. The effect of these and other concessions was to create friction between the political and ecclesiastical leaders, a situation which contributed to many contests for power in America and seriously weakened the Spanish influence.

The most cursory reading of Spanish colonial records for the three centuries following Juan Ponce de León's explorations in Florida in 1521 will reveal how acrimonious could be the relationships between the authorities of church and state. There was an almost constant dispute over the control of the natives. The clergy wished to attach them to the missions where they might learn industry as well as religion, and so increase the economic resources of the church; the lay authorities wished to press them into their own service. Paradoxically, there still remained a semblance of unity, for both sides knew full well the importance of the other. The Roman Catholic mission system proved to be a most effective instrument for dealing with primitive aboriginal peoples; at the same time, it was dependent upon the civil and military authority for its physical maintenance. Neither side, therefore, was in any position to press its claims to the limit, and so the uneasy alliance persisted throughout the colonial period.

Early Missions on the Atlantic Coast

While the Spanish exploration of the North American mainland begins with Ponce de León, there is no record of clerical participation in the venture. In June, 1526, however, two Dominican priests and a lay-brother sailed with Lucas Vásquez de Ayllón for America. They began a settlement on the Chesapeake, near the future site of Jamestown, and it was probably there that the first mass within the present borders of the United States was celebrated. Within a year, only a minority of the settlers still survived, and these returned home in dejection.

More disastrous was the mission of Pánfilo de Narváez, who landed at Tampa Bay in 1527. Ignoring the advice of the secular and Franciscan priests who accompanied him, he waged an unsuccessful war with the Indians and was finally pushed back to the sea, only to discover that his ships had returned to Cuba. In desperation his men fashioned a crude ship, hoping to reach Mexico by sailing along the shores of the Gulf. But the ship was wrecked and all but five of the men perished. These survivors, after a period of enslavement by the Indians, escaped and traveled westward, reaching the Gulf of California in 1535 and Mexico the following year.

The first permanent Spanish settlement in Florida was inspired by antipathy for a French Huguenot colony which was established in that territory in 1562. The French, under Captain Jean Ribault, had erected a fort on the St. John's River. Because of internal difficulties, the colony presented no real threat to the Spaniards. Nevertheless, in 1565, Philip II sent Pedro Menéndez de Avilés to terminate its existence. This was accomplished by a surprise attack and the merciless slaughter of the French garrison, which was especially despised because of its Protestant persuasion. On this occasion Menéndez fortified the peninsula and called it San Augustín (St. Augustine), in honor of the saint, the day of whose commemoration, August 28, coincided with the date of his landing. In 1568, the French retaliated by taking similar action against the Spanish troops, but they made no further effort to colonize Florida.

The Spaniards now felt free to continue their missionary efforts, this time by the Jesuits. A number of them took up residence in St. Augustine, while a still larger group labored as far north as the Chesapeake. This mission met with failure, due to famine and Indian attacks. Finally, the entire Jesuit contingent in Florida and parts north was withdrawn and sent to Mexico City. No further significant efforts for the conversion of the natives would be made in that area until 1577, with the coming of the Franciscans.

The eight priests and three lay-brothers of the Franciscan Order who came to St. Augustine encountered almost insuperable difficulties. Sir Frances Drake sacked the city in 1586, and eleven years later six of the missionaries were massacred by the Indians. Still, the work grew and developed with persistence, so that by 1634 there were forty-four missions conducted by thirty-five Franciscans, serving twenty-five thousand native converts. But with success there came also a spirit of complacency; this resulted in laxity of effort and perfunctory service on the part of the missionaries. By 1674, the situation had become so distressing that the Bishop of Santiago found it necessary to order strict reform in preaching and the teaching of catechism. The reform was neither penetrating nor permanent. It was symbolic of the general decay of Spanish vitality and influence, a sign of futility in an age which anxiously beheld the nascent might of England.

The Rise of Missions in the West

In the meantime, considerable interest in the exploration of interior America had developed, and soldiers and missionaries by the hundreds were following the trails which led to the vast unknown West. The year 1541 found Hernando de Soto at the Mississippi and Francisco Vásquez de Coronado in southern Nebraska, each promoting the missionary cause as far as possible, but with modest, impermanent results. Several of the religious on the Coronado expedition elected to remain in New Mexico after the withdrawal of the army. Two were never heard of again; a third, Juan de Padilla, was finally martyred in southwestern Kansas. From that time there was no further attempt, until 1581, to evangelize New Mexico. In that year Augustino Rodriguez, a Franciscan lay-brother, persuaded two priests, Francisco Lopez and Juan de Santa Maria, to go with him there to found a mission. They labored in the vicinity of the present city of Albuquerque until their martyrdom at the hands of the Indians.

In 1588, a contract was made with Juan de Oñate, a wealthy Mexican, for the colonization of New Mexico. The expedition, which included several Franciscans, finally assembled in the vicinity of Santa Barbara in August, 1597, and proceeded up the Rio Grande. The first settlement was made at San Juan de los Caballeros in July, 1598. Two months later, mass was celebrated in the first church edifice to be completed in New Mexico. Santa Fé, which would later become the center of administration, was established by 1609.

As in Florida, the missionaries were superficially successful in winning converts to the faith. Because of numerical gains, the missions had to be organized into a custodia in 1621, under a friar whose territorial jurisdiction was equal to that of the governor, and whose influence was probably greater. Twenty-five missions were reported by the Franciscan superior in New Mexico in 1630, and the number of Christian Indians 35,000. Yet there soon sprang up a spirit of complacency among the ecclesiastical leaders, who were often more concerned with exploiting the free labor of the Indian than with improving his immediate spiritual welfare. There was also some frustration due to the intervention of state officials who, lacking a fundamental understanding of Indian psychology, permitted the continuance of pagan religious practices among those who were nominally Christian, supposing in vain that time would improve the quality of their faith. Actually these rites were illustrative of the fact that while the Pueblo Indians were willing to accept the Christian God as an additional protective power, they could not relinquish their own beliefs concerning the spirits of the universe without completely annihilating their organized tribal life. Every aspect of their communal life was affected by their concept of the relation of the tribe to the world.

The self-satisfied, arrogant demeanor of the civil and military authorities, especially in their dealings with the clergy, contributed to Spanish division on the frontier and rendered their efforts among the Indians ineffectual. Some of the secular officials were even hauled before the Inquisition and penalized for crimes against the church. In such circumstances, discipline faltered and immorality increased. At the same time, the Indians were granted no independence, and though their masters were at times tolerant, still they longed for freedom from the Spanish yoke. Unbeknown to the Spaniards, they met in secret conclaves and plotted the downfall of the invader. One of their medicine men, Popé, saw that a revolt would be successful only if it could be inspired by a revival of paganism, accompanied by burning hatred for the white man's institutions. This he was able to accomplish with such effectiveness that in 1680 the insurrection broke out in full force. In the violence which immediately followed, half the clergy and four hundred white settlers were massacred. The rest withdrew to El Paso.

It was not long before the Pueblos realized that the new regime left much to be desired. Popé proved to be a tyrant and their former allies, the Apaches, were becoming troublesome. Thus, when Diego de Vargas attempted a reconquest in 1692, the way was somewhat prepared for his coming. The Indians admitted the Spaniards without battle, and upon confession of their sins were received again into the church. Though there was a new rebellion in 1696, it was soon stamped out; and by 1700, the province was enjoying relative peace. Henceforth, the Spanish authorities were quick to check the slightest move toward paganism or political autonomy.

The first Spaniard to enter the neighboring territory of Arizona was Marcos de Niza, a Franciscan friar, who came on a mission of reconnaissance in 1539. The following year the Coronado expedition explored the area and some efforts were made to Christianize the Pimas, Papagoes, and Moquis. From time to time, there was apparent progress, but with the great Indian uprising of 1680, the Moquis were permanently lost to Spanish Catholicism. The first really successful mission work was begun in 1687 by Father Eusebio Francisco Kino, a Jesuit from the Mexican province of Sonora. He introduced the Indians to improved methods of agriculture and through his friendship and understanding brought thousands to a profession of Christianity.

Critical Years in Florida and the Southwest

With the advent of the eighteenth century, Spanish power and influence in the East entered a period of eclipse. In 1702, an English force from South Carolina captured St. Augustine and burned the town. The next forty years witnessed a series of retaliations and further attacks. In such a time of tension, the Catholic missionaries found progress difficult, especially from 1763 to 1783, when Florida was under English domination. Though Florida reverted to Spain in 1783, the political tensions continued until 1819, when the Spanish government ceded it to the United States. With that act the long-lived alliance of church and state came to an end. The rule of Roman Catholic Spain in Florida belonged to history.

In the West the situation was strikingly varied and dissimilar. The eighteenth century brought decline and decay to Spanish Christianity in New Mexico. Only reports of the exciting adventures of Father Francisco Escalante, who journeyed from Santa Fé to Utah and Colorado in 1776, and the customary contentions between the clergy and the secular authorities could create a ripple in the otherwise placid waters of platitudinous existence. Religion was popularly an object either of indifference or hatred. Significant changes in the population were also evident; the number of whites was increasing, the Indian population dwindling. When the Bishop of Durango visited the province in 1845, he found only twenty thousand Indians among the eighty thousand inhabitants. A mere seventeen priests constituted the clergy. Three years later New Mexico became a part of the United States and the Spanish-Mexican rule was ended.

Circumstances in Arizona also grew increasingly somber. There was considerable competition between the Franciscans and Jesuits, with the latter establishing missions at Bac and Guevavi in 1732. Further tensions sprang up when the Spaniards legalized compulsory labor at the missions by the Indians. Then, in 1767, Jesuit activities were curtailed as the result of Charles III's edict expelling them from all the Spanish dominions. Their properties in Arizona were turned over to the Franciscans, who doubtless rejoiced in the turn of events since they feared the rising prestige and influence of the Society of Jesus. From 1808 to 1821, during the Mexican struggle for independence, many loyal Spanish friars were expelled from Arizona, seriously weakening the work. About the same time, the Apaches took up the tomahawk, necessitating the abandonment of all settlements except Tubac and Tucson. Almost no sign of mission activity remained when the territory became a part of the United States through the Mexican cession of 1848 and the Gadsden Purchase of 1853.

Though the Spanish mission movement in Texas dates predominantly from the eighteenth century, there was prior religious activity. The leading pioneer efforts had been made in the 1670's, by the Franciscan Father Juan Larios. In 1685, the French explorer René Robert Cavelier, Sieur de la Salle, established a colony near Matagorda Bay. While it constituted no threat to the Spaniards, the latter commissioned Captain Alonzo de León in 1689 to hunt out the French and to found a settlement. The French had retired by the time of his arrival, and so he proceeded, in conjunction with Father Damian Massanet, to establish the mission of San Francisco de los Tejas. During the next few years no other settlements were founded, but the journey of the Frenchman Louis Juchereau de Saint Denis across Texas in 1714 hastened the founding of such permanent settlements as San Antonio, Nacogdoches, and Goliad, and the missions of San Antonio de Valero, Concepcion, and San Jose. Of these the most famous was the Mission San Antonio de Valero, founded by Franciscans in 1718, and popularly known as The Alamo. Had the Spanish government regarded Texas as more than a field on which to deter French aggression, the work of settlement might have prospered. Such was not the case; and by the close of the eighteenth century, there were scarcely seven thousand whites in the entire area.

During the 1820's large numbers of Americans began to settle in Texas. In a superficial sense they accepted Mexican jurisdiction and made an outward profession of Roman Catholicism, but they made little effort to assimilate the older culture. During these unsettled times, when Mexico was winning independence from Spain and territorial lines were almost constantly shifting, friction between Americans and Mexicans increased, finally leading to revolt, the creation of a new republic, and its annexation in 1845 to the United States. Ecclesiastical conditions were far from satisfactory. In fact, during the years of the Texas republic, there were only two priests in the territory, and they were disesteemed. The first signs of improvement came in 1841, when John Odin was appointed Vicar-Apostolic, but little could be accomplished until Texas' political affiliation was determined.

The Missions of California

Among the more colorful of the Spanish missions were those of California. As in the case of Texas, the Spanish occupation was prompted by fear of a rival settlement, English or Russian, a circumstance which later proved beneficial to the American Union. The California coast was known to Spanish explorers as early as 1542, and Jesuit missionaries were at work in Lower California by 1697; yet seventy years would pass before the development of interest in Upper California.

In 1769, a settlement was established at San Diego and on July 16, the Franciscan missionary, Father Junípero Serra, founded the mission of San Diego de Alcala, the first in a chain of Franciscan missions. He established eight other missions before his death in 1784, among them San Gabriel, San Antonio, San Luís Obispo, and San Juan Capistrano. Another important missionary was Father Fermín Francisco de Lasuén, founder of nine other mission stations.

During the period from 1769 to 1823, the mission, because of its economic and political as well as religious significance, proved to be the most effective institution of Hispanic control. It did much more than spread the faith; it served as dispenser of Spanish culture and civilization. Its task was unusually difficult because of the radical cultural inferiority of the Indians. It was not uncommon at first for a missionary to labor many months before winning a single convert. Unflagging patience and firm discipline were prerequisites for success in this arduous endeavor. The Indian neophytes had to be taught advanced methods in agriculture, building, craftsmanship, and the domestic arts, and encouraged to work at various trades. Some efforts toward the intellectual enrichment of the natives were made through frequent religious exercises and instruction in sacred music, but with notably poor results. It seemed impossible to impart more than the basic doctrines considered essential to the salvation of their souls. To accomplish even this the natives had to be stamped into the mold of complete dependency. This in itself proved ultimately disastrous, for when the pressure was removed they promptly relapsed into barbarism.

The relationships between the missionaries and their pupils were like those of fathers and their children. There was a lovable intimacy both at work and play, a circumstance which is revealed in the report of Fray Francisco Palóu to the Viceroy of Mexico, in December, 1773, concerning the Mission of San Antonio de Padua:

Since the founding of the mission, a hundred and fifty-eight have been baptized between old and young, of whom eight have died; fifteen of the young converts have been married and live quite contentedly on the mission premises.

The new site is now supplied with plenty of water from the neighboring stream. An irrigation ditch brings the water to a large field in the immediate vicinity of the mission, where a good sized piece of ground has already been prepared and where they are intending to sow two bushels of wheat, which is the only seed grain that they now have. In due season they hope to produce a sufficiently large crop of corn and beans to provide for the maintenance of the native Christians, and to attract the rest of the natives, who do not feel the least hesitation in accepting the faith of our Lord Jesus Christ nor in living beside the missionaries themselves, for whom they have manifested the most marked affection, providing them with wild grains, rabbits and squirrels which are not so bad for eating after all.[1]

The collapse of Spanish authority in Mexico in 1821 prompted the shift of California's loyalty to the new Mexican government the following year. For the missions this marked the beginning of ruin. Mexican politicians in the South were casting covetous eyes toward the wealthy missions, whose property had been held communally during Spanish rule. During the years 1834 to 1840, they confiscated the mission lands, removed the friars, and introduced secular priests who had relatively little interest in the progress of the Indians. Thus collapsed the work of sixty-five years, a work which had led to the baptism of one hundred thousand aborigines. There followed a time of hardship and exploitation for the Indians, who now reverted to their primitive ways. With few priests and widespread indifference, the churches fell into ruins. When Francisco Garcia-Diego, Mexican bishop of the two Californias, died in 1846, an epoch had come to its close. Two years later California would be ceded to the United States. This event was anticipated by the church when it assigned the administration of the Californian churches to Joseph Alemany, Provincial of the American Dominicans.

In assaying the ultimate worth of the Spanish missions it is easy to be critical. The clerics, like the soldiery, were agents of the Spanish crown and thoroughly imbued with the love of empire. On occasions that passion could and did subvert the noblest Christian ideals so that the Indian was more manipulated than marshalled. Undoubtedly, this tendency contributed much to the decline of Spanish influence. At the same time, the Spanish treatment of the Indian compares favorably with that of the English. To the Englishman the native was an obstacle which had to be removed; to the Spaniard he was a backward neighbor who needed to be prepared for a richer life in community. Thus the Spanish policy was to assimilate the aboriginal stock in race, religion, and culture. The result was a new civilization, in which both Spanish and Indian elements fused. To this day the great Southwest bears the cultural imprint of that historic encounter.

THE MISSIONS OF NEW FRANCE

If France was somewhat tardier than Spain in the planting of permanent settlements in America, the delay could not be charged to her want

[1] P. G. Mode, *Sourcebook and Bibliographical Guide for American Church History* (Banta, c. 1921), 313.

of vision. She was fully cognizant of the remarkable opportunities which the New World presented. The Breton fishermen who visited the Banks of Newfoundland and the bold Cartier who sailed up the St. Lawrence to "Mont Real" in the early years of the sixteenth century saw to that. It seems reasonable to suppose that, if France had enjoyed a fuller political and religious unity like that of the Spanish, her colonization efforts in the sixteenth century would have been more impressive. As it was, she was preoccupied with domestic troubles: the final struggles between the crown and the leading nobles, incessant dynastic conflicts with neighboring countries, and the bloody religious wars which culminated in the terrible slaughter of Protestants on St. Bartholomew's Day in 1572. Settlements there were, such as the fated Protestant colony of 1562 in Florida, whose Master Robert conducted services in the manner of the Reformed tradition. But it was not until the seventeenth century that significant progress was made in the colonization enterprise, and this was largely in Canada.

The daring exploits of soldiers and traders coupled with the heroic and inspiring ministrations of the Jesuit and Récollet fathers in New France contributed to the making of one of the most thrilling episodes in North American history. Their encounters with the Algonquins and Hurons in Canada during the first four decades of the seventeenth century were harbingers of more extensive activities among the Indians of the Ohio and Mississippi River valleys, as well as those of northern New York and New England.

Mission Work in Northeast America

The first missionary efforts by French Roman Catholics within the present borders of the United States came in direct answer to a felt challenge. By 1640, the Jesuits had erected five chapels among the Hurons west of Montreal and had baptized more than one hundred of the natives. Their work, however, was rendered extremely hazardous by the frequent raids of the Iroquois, the bitterest enemies of the Hurons, and conditions grew steadily worse as the decade progressed. It was quite evident that the conversion of the Iroquois was a prerequisite to further missionary advancement. An impassioned statement, expressing the urgency of this task, was that of Father Paul Le Jeune, Jesuit superior at Quebec, in his *Relation of 1640–1641:*

I see at the South and at the West a great number of Tribes that cultivate the land and that are entirely sedentary, but have never heard of Jesus Christ; the door to all these people has been shut against us by the Hiroquois. In all these vast tracts there are only the Hurons, and some other neighboring Tribes, to whom we have carried the good news of the Gospel; but then we are obliged to approach them by horrible roads and long detours, and in continual danger of being boiled or roasted and then eagerly devoured by the wretched Hiroquois. We do not lose courage on account of this; we believe that God will make a light in this darkness, and that some powerful Spirit will open the door to the Gospel of Jesus Christ in these vast regions, and that old France will save the life of the New, which is going to be lost, unless it be vigorously and speedily succored . . .[2]

The goal, however, was not to be reached without terrible sacrifice. In 1642, Father Isaac Jogues sought to bring Christianity to the Iroquois in what is now the State of New York. They captured him and subjected him to the tortures of burning and mutilation. Though he escaped in 1643, he returned three years later to win the martyr's crown.

In the year of Isaac Jogues' murder, the Jesuits sent Father Gabriel Druilletes as a missionary to the Abenakis, who dwelt along the Kennebec River within the present borders of Maine. They received him with kindness and welcomed his ministrations. In 1650, he traveled to Boston, where he caused something of a sensation, until the Puritan fathers forcibly ushered him out of the colony. From that time he labored among the Abenakis, finally abandoning his post in 1657 and returning to Quebec. Around 1680, the Jesuit fathers revived the work and established a mission at the falls of St. Francis de Sales, along the Chaudière River, not far from what is now the Maine border. So fruitful were their efforts that eight years later a secular priest was sent to found a second mission, this one at Nanransouock, in Maine. The Jesuits took it over in 1703, and remained in control until the mission was destroyed by the English and their Indian allies in 1724.

In the meantime, the wily Iroquois had encountered opposition from other tribes to the south and west and so found it beneficial, in 1653, to sign a treaty with the French and allow a mission to be set up among the Onondagas in central New York. For a time six priests worked with these duplicitous natives, but their efforts came to naught. Once more the Iroquois turned on the French, and by 1658 the missionaries had to flee for their lives. It was not until 1667 that the French soldiery was able to crush the Iroquois, making it possible for the Jesuits to renew their efforts. For twenty years they preached and taught their faith, receiving only the most meager response from the unappreciative savages. They were joined by the Sulpicians in 1668. By this time, however, the English had occupied New York and were stirring up the Iroquois against the French. The Roman Catholic governor of New York, Thomas Dongan, even brought in English Jesuits to impede the progress of their French confrères. So successful were the English in gaining their purposes that by 1687 the French felt obliged to abandon their permanent posts in

[2] *Ibid.*, 305–306.

Iroquois territory. With that action, local Jesuit missionary activity came to a virtual standstill.

Western Exploration and Evangelization

While the French missions were facing overwhelming difficulties in the East, new opportunities were opening in the West. For some years the majestic St. Lawrence had been luring French explorers such as Jean Nicolet and Pierre Esprit, Sieur de Radisson, into the vast, mysterious interior. Close behind had come the Jesuit missionaries, led by Father René Ménard in 1660. Within a decade their stations on the Upper Lakes had become dominant centers of Christian culture. About this time the French government, under Louis XIV, was adopting a more aggressive policy for colonial expansion. In keeping with this policy, Simon Francois Daumont, Sieur de Saint Lusson, took formal possession of the entire western territory in 1671; and, in the ceremony which took place in the presence of the chiefs of all the neighboring tribes of Sault Ste. Marie, he claimed it in the name of God and the King.

One of the most colorful of the Jesuit missionaries in the West was Father Jacques Marquette. He had come to Canada in 1666 and had been assigned to work with Father Claude Allouez. This priest had explored the Lake Superior region and had even ventured up the Illinois River, before establishing the mission of St. Ignace at the mouth of Lake Michigan in 1670 and reviving the mission at Sault Ste. Marie. As early as 1669, Marquette had been fascinated by reports of a great river to the south; but before he could accomplish his plan for exploration, he was driven out of his post in Wisconsin by the Sioux. From 1671 to 1673, he served at St. Ignace. In the latter year he joined forces with the adventurer, Louis Joliet, and together they set out across the north side of Lake Michigan, up Green Bay and the Fox River, through what is now Wisconsin. They then crossed to the Wisconsin River and followed it into the Mississippi River, which they explored down to its juncture with the Arkansas. Their return to Green Bay was by way of the Illinois River. According to the Jesuit *Relation of 1672–73*, his motive was "to seek toward the south sea nations new and unknown to us, in order to make them know our great God of whom they have been up to now ignorant." On a second journey in 1674, he undertook to found a mission at Kaskaskia, among the Indians of the Illinois River area; but on his way home in 1675, he died of natural causes.

The year which witnessed Father Marquette's death found Robert Cavalier de la Salle, the indomitable soldier of fortune, in France, winning a grant of land and commissions from Louis XIV to advance the cause of empire. By 1678, he was back in Canada. No friend of the Jesuits, he took as his chaplain a Récollet priest, Father Louis Hennepin, who had already spent two years among the Iroquois at Kenté. Sailing up the Great Lakes from Niagara, they reached the Illinois in 1679, and there founded the fort and mission of Crèvacoeur. The two men then parted and Hennepin is said to have explored the Mississippi as far north as the present site of Minneapolis and christened the Falls of St. Anthony. As for La Salle, after a series of disasters, he finally reached the mouth of the Mississippi in April, 1682, thus challenging the jurisdiction of Spain.

Had the French been able to maintain political and religious unity, they might have built one gigantic network of influence extending from the mouth of the St. Lawrence to the Gulf of Mexico. As it was, incessant quarrels took place between La Salle and the authorities in Canada; and there was open division between the Récollet and Jesuit orders. La Salle's murder in 1687 was symbolic of a dissension which would permanently separate Louisiana from Quebec. Not only that, but it signalized the withdrawal of the Récollets from the West and left the missionary cause in the hands of the Jesuits, whose missionaries in the South rarely communicated with their Canadian associates.

The Church in the Mississippi Valley

By the opening decade of the eighteenth century, it was becoming apparent that the French government was changing its policy in America. More and more it was regarding New France not so much as an enterprise for trade and evangelism as a base of operations against the English. Recognizing the extreme importance of the Mississippi, the French founded settlements near Mobile in 1702 and at New Orleans in 1718, and planted outposts on the Red and Arkansas Rivers. The lower Mississippi Basin and the Gulf Plains soon became the scene of a bitter contest between the Spanish, French, and English.

There was similar development farther to the north. In western Illinois, where missions had been established at Cahokia in 1699 and Kaskaskia in 1700, permanent settlements and forts were built by 1720. The French were at Detroit in 1701 and at Vincennes on the Wabash by 1732. At each of these places of population, the church continued to carry on its ministrations, sometimes maintaining separate chapels for the Indians. But there was a singular absence of the piety which had characterized the seventeenth century missionaries. Even the missions reflected the secular interests of the age. Especially difficult was the situation in the Illinois country, which was virtually cut off from Canada because of the hostility of the Fox Indians. Finally, in 1731, the Illinois settlements were formally incorporated with the southern province of Louisiana.

While tension was mounting east of the Mississippi, to the west new explorations were taking place. Starting from Montreal, in 1731, the adventurer, Pierre de la Vérendrye, traveled past the Great Lakes and, with the help of the Jesuit, Father Charles Mesaiger, founded a string of fortified settlements from the western end of Lake Superior to the region west of Lake of the Woods. In 1738, he penetrated Dakota territory in a mission which took him to the Mandan Indians. Four years later, two of his sons crossed the Missouri and explored the country to the southwest as far as the Big Horn mountains. Apparently, few if any efforts were made on this expedition to evangelize the Indians.

The Church in a Changing Political Order

At the outbreak of the French and Indian War, which was precipitated by the English and French contest for the Ohio Valley, there were only one Récollet, eleven Sulpician, and thirty-eight Jesuit priests in all of New France. Clearly, a minority of these dwelt within the present borders of the United States. When the struggle commenced, they did what they could to aid the French arms. They made bargains with the Christian Indians, gave directions to raiding parties, said mass in the forts, and cared for the wounded on the battlefields. But they could not save the French from defeat by overwhelming forces. With the fall of Quebec and Montreal, an English victory in Canada was assured. According to the terms of the Paris treaty of 1763, France ceded to Great Britain, Canada and all her territory east of the Mississippi, while New Orleans went with Louisiana to Spain. With this action the curtain fell upon one of the most colorful chapters in American history.

The English made no attempt to stamp out French Catholicism from the newly won territories, though the immigration of more priests from France was barred by English law. For the Jesuits, rule by the new conquerors proved to be something of a blessing in disguise. Had they remained under French domination, they would have been expelled in 1761 by an edict of Louis XV suppressing the Society of Jesus. Under the circumstances they kept their official recognition until they were banned by order of Pope Clement XIV in 1773. Even then they continued their operations until the old missionaries died at their posts and the work came naturally to a close. In Louisiana, however, thirteen Jesuit priests were expelled as soon as the Spanish took over the territory, their property being turned over to the Capuchin friars.

The French Catholic population in the West never overcame its enmity for the British; and when the Revolution broke out, it threw its support to the American side. When George Rogers Clark and his Virginia militiamen captured Kaskaskia in 1778, they received assistance from Father Pierre Gibault. This same priest helped them to take Cahokia and to win Vincennes. In this way he and others like him made their contribution to the building of a free America.

Perhaps the one trait which made the work of the French missionaries unique was their ability to blend their lives with those whom they sought to serve. If the Spanish played the role of mildly indulgent fathers in a family of wayward children, the French acted as brothers who won their status by deeds of kindness and courage. The Hispanic note of benevolent condescension was almost completely lacking among the French. Both came with the open and express purpose of converting the savage aborigines to Catholic Christianity, though their conduct often revealed as much zeal for the Crown as for the Cross. The difference was that the French developed their mission with an unrivalled degree of subtlety. They preferred to present their faith in terms of a heroism that smiles at torture and death. Only when complete confidence had been won did they present the doctrinal aspects of their religion. They were no more effective than the Spanish in impressing upon the Indian consciousness the fuller implications of their faith. At best, they were able to apply a thin and impermanent veneer of Christian idealism to a primitive culture, somewhat resentful of their intrusion. Thus the most that can be said for their efforts is that they exposed innumerable thousands to a limited knowledge of God and a more settled way of life.

Their sense of brotherhood proved to be both their strength and their undoing, for their close alliances with one tribe incurred for them the hatred of another. The friendship which they held for the Hurons certainly had a direct bearing on the hostility of the Iroquois and had much to do with their inability to thrive in the region south and east of Lake Erie. Yet, while they could be one in their social and political alliances and in their loyalty to the Crown, they were torn by habitual quarreling among themselves. This circumstance greatly reduced their effectiveness in presenting the unity of the faith.

Still, the French missionaries achieved some remarkable feats. The very fact that centuries after the collapse of French power in Northeast America Roman Catholicism has flourished in Quebec is indicative of a powerful and abiding clerical influence. Their record in converting the Indians to a nominal acceptance of Christianity is admittedly less impressive than that of the Spanish, but they were somewhat more successful when it came to planting permanent settlements on the frontier. From the Great Lakes to the Gulf of Mexico they left the imprint of their culture and civilization and so contributed significantly to the taming of the American Middle West.

3

The Rise and Progress of Colonial Anglicanism

TOWARD THE CLOSE OF THE SIXTEENTH CENTURY, ENGLAND FOUND HERSELF in a perilous economic condition. The rapid growth of population called for a commensurate development of industry in order to provide adequate employment and maintain a sound economy. Raw materials, especially wood, were vital to the preservation of industry, and they were becoming increasingly scarce. English businessmen recognized that if they could not find some satisfactory means of importing basic materials for the smelting, shipbuilding, and woolen industries, the country would experience a severe depression.

In the meantime, English navigators had returned home with glowing reports of extensive forest lands in America, of virgin territory rich in natural resources. And so, out of economic necessity, was born the English expansion into the New World. There were, of course, other important factors and motives in English colonization—the hope of discovering a new route to the East, the impulse to curb the power of Spain, the longing to find cheap land on which to settle, even the desire to convert the Indians. Still the basic purpose was economic, and it is highly doubtful that the Crown would ever have granted approval to dissenting religious groups such as the Pilgrims and Puritans to settle in America had they not offered promise of producing the raw materials essential to England. What was so disappointing to the English was that colonial economic life failed to follow the prearranged plan. In New England, the colonists turned to agriculture and shipbuilding; in the South, they devoted themselves to the cultivation of tobacco. As the years passed, the relation of the colonies to the mother country would be characterized less by cooperation than by competition.

Several decades before the founding of Jamestown in 1607, the English had attempted to found colonies in America. In each instance, they had provided for the ministrations of the Gospel. The ill-fated settlements of Sir Humphrey Gilbert in Newfoundland and Sir Walter Raleigh at Roanoke, during the 1580's, had each enjoyed religious rites of an informal nature. Formal services of the Church of England had been conducted at the short-lived colony founded by Raleigh Gilbert on the island of Monhegan, Maine, in the spring of 1607. These ephemeral settlements, however, contributed nothing of lasting historical significance.

THE CHURCH IN VIRGINIA AND MARYLAND

Dawning at Jamestown

The founding of the first permanent English colony in Virginia and the planting of the Church of England in America were synchronous events. In 1606, just two years before the French fortification of Quebec and three years prior to the Dutch exploration of the Hudson, King James I granted a charter to the London Company to found a colony in the New World. Its immediate purposes were to seek out mineral deposits, to investigate agricultural and industrial possibilities, and to discover the northwest passage to the Orient. Its jurisdiction was the area between 34° and 41° N. Latitude in the territory of Virginia. Governed by a Council of thirteen members in England, the company was to appoint a similar Council to administer affairs in the colony. The settlers were to be accorded all the rights and privileges belonging to Englishmen at home, among them the services of the Established Church.

One of the petitioners for the charter of the London Company was Robert Hunt, an Anglican clergyman. When the first group of about one hundred colonists disembarked on the north bank of the James River, in the spring of 1607, Hunt was among them. On the fourteenth of May, he celebrated the first Holy Communion upon Virginia soil. Captain John Smith had this to say about subsequent services:

When I went first to Virginia, I well remember wee did hang an awning (which is an old saile) to three or foure trees to shadow us from the Sunne, our walles were rales of wood, our seats unhewed trees till we cut plankes, our Pulpit a bar of wood nailed to two neighboring trees. In foule weather we shifted into an old rotten tent; for we had few better, and this came by the way of adventure for new. . . .

Yet wee had daily Common Prayer morning and evening, every Sunday two Sermons and every three moneths the holy Communion, till our Minister died: but our Prayers daily, with an Homily on Sundaies, we continued two or three years after till more Preachers came: and surely God did most mercifully heare us, till the continuall inundations of mistaking directions, factions, and numbers of unprovided Libertines neere consumed us all, as the Israelites in the wilderness.[1]

Nor was life in the new land without its perils. By the summer of 1610, only one hundred and fifty of the more than nine hundred settlers were still alive. Some had been massacred by Indians, but most had succumbed to starvation and fever. The remainder would undoubtedly have returned home had it not been for the arrival of fresh supplies and new leadership.

In 1610, Lord Delaware arrived at Jamestown and assumed the governorship. He was accompanied by a chaplain, who was probably the second clergyman in the colony. That same year a new charter was granted which provided for the formation of the Virginia Company, a corporation independent of the crown and empowered to appoint its own governors. Thomas Dale, who subsequently became governor, attempted to improve the discipline of the colony through the issuance of a set of severe laws in 1611. The first law dealing with religion is representative:

. . . I do strictly and commaund and charge all Captaines and Officers, of what qualitie or nature soeuer, whether commanders in the field, or in town, or townes, forts or fortresses, to haue a care that the Almighty God bee duly and daily serued, and that they call vpon their people to heare Sermons, as that also they diligently frequent Morning and Euening praier themselves by their owne exemplar and daily life, and dutie herein, encouraging others thereunto, and that such, who shall often and wilfully absent themselues, be duly punished according to the martiall law in that case prouided.[2]

Harsh penalties were also provided for blasphemy, unlawful oaths, and Sabbath breaking. Actually, the laws were seldom enforced; and in 1618, they were sharply modified.

The Union of Church and State

With the founding of the Jamestown settlement, there began a steady process pointing toward the creation of a church establishment. In 1618,

[1] Mode, *op. cit.,* 10.
[2] *Ibid.,* 11.

the Virginia Company instructed the governor to set aside one hundred acres of glebe land for the support of each member of the clergy. The following year, the Company was reorganized, and the new charter provided for a local legislature with an elective lower house or assembly of burgesses. This was the first popular legislative body in the American colonies. In 1619, the Assembly enacted a number of laws relative to the practice of religion. Among them were provisions which not only required all ministers to conduct services of worship in accordance with the usage of the Church of England, but also compelled all persons to attend divine service twice on Sundays, on pain of fine or bodily punishment.

The process of establishing Anglicanism in Virginia was completed shortly after the colony became a royal province in 1624. In June of that year, James I had procured the revocation of the charter of the Virginia Company, and from henceforth, until the American Revolution, Virginia was governed by officials appointed by the crown. Under the vigorous administration of Governor William Berkeley, who arrived in 1641, there was a noteworthy promotion of the church establishment. Ministers had to certify that they were episcopally ordained and pledge themselves to conformity. Tithes for the support of the clergy were made a legal requirement of the citizenry, and no person outside the Church of England was permitted suffrage. The Assembly also passed an act in 1641 creating vestries for the government of the parishes, in accordance with the practice of the church in England. It was decreed that in each parish there should be twelve vestrymen elected by the voters of the parish. After 1662, the vestries chose their own successors, thus enabling them to keep their own class in power.

Nonconformists were received with hostility. Most Virginians supposed that persons of the Roman Catholic faith were secretly in league with Spain. Thus they viewed their expanding colony in nearby Maryland with considerable concern. Virginia refused to permit Roman Catholic priests to enter the province, while laymen of that faith found themselves politically disqualified. As late as 1645, there were probably not more than two hundred nonconformists out of a population of almost fifteen thousand. A particular source of harassment was the Quaker missionaries. Their doctrines of the inner light, their pacifist beliefs, and their refusal to pay parish tithes rendered them odious to their Anglican neighbors. The law carried a death sentence for Quakers who returned three times after being expelled, but it was not enforced.

Strongly loyalist in sympathy, the Virginia Assembly enacted laws against the Puritans in 1642, at the outset of the English Civil War. During the period of the Commonwealth, the province had to submit to the authority of Parliament, but no attempt was made to interfere with colonial Anglican worship; distance alone would have made any Puritan legislation virtually impossible to enforce. Then came the Restoration in 1660 and the return to the episcopal establishment in England. The most immediate effect in Virginia was a quickening of the church's pulse, a most gratifying circumstance for a colony then in the throes of spiritual lethargy.

A new day for religious toleration dawned in 1687 when James II issued his "Declaration for Liberty of Conscience in Religious Matters." The edict was intended largely for the benefit of Roman Catholics, whose religion was practiced by the King, though it, of course, applied to other Christians as well. But there was little opportunity to apply the Declaration in the colonies, since it was automatically abolished the following year, with the accession to the throne of William and Mary. The famous Toleration Act of 1689 left in force all the existing restrictions against Roman Catholics, but it accorded new liberty to the Protestant dissenters. Ten years later, the Virginia Assembly officially adopted it as the law of the colony. Nevertheless, from time to time the activities of dissenting Christians were curtailed, usually on the ground that they were dangerous to the welfare of the state.

In the proprietary colony of Maryland, first settled in 1634, the relation of the Anglican Church to the state was highly unusual. Legally, the charter granted to Cecil Calvert, Lord Baltimore, provided for the organization of churches according to the ecclesiastical laws of England, which meant the Anglican Church. Lord Baltimore, however, was a Roman Catholic; and part of his motivation in founding the colony was to seek a refuge for his persecuted fellow-Catholics. Thus it came about that there were Jesuit priests but no Anglican clergy to minister to the needs of the citizenry, the larger percentage of whom were Protestants. A tactful and judicious man, Lord Baltimore urged his Roman Catholic confreres to be gracious and cooperative in dealings with their Protestant neighbors. There were, nevertheless, frequent and sometimes bitter quarrels between the various religious factions. By 1649, he found it necessary to push through the Assembly the famous Toleration Act in an ultimately futile effort to prevent the revocation of his charter. But during the Interregnum, Maryland came under Protestant control.

Despite the lack of an ordained ministry, the earliest Anglican settlers in Maryland erected a chapel at St. Mary's and conducted services with the help of a lay reader. The first clergyman of the Anglican Church known to have served in the colony was William Wilkinson, who arrived about 1650. Times were hard and his parishioners were unable to give him adequate support, and so he turned to trade in order to make a living. The cause of the church went forward slowly; by 1675, there were only three Anglican clergymen in the colony. One of them, John Yeo, reported to the Archbishop of Canterbury that "the province of Maryland is in a deplorable condition for want of an established ministry. . . .

The Lord's day is profaned; religion is despised; and all notorious vices are committed." He therefore asked that steps be taken to establish the Church of England in Maryland.

With the overthrow of King James II in 1688, a revolt was touched off in Maryland in which the Roman Catholic proprietor lost his power. The province was then made over into a royal colony under the immediate control of the Assembly, which was composed of Protestants. The policy of toleration was brought to an end and the Assembly took steps to bring about the establishment of the Church of England. The first two attempts, in 1692 and 1696, failed because of disapproval by the Board of Trade and Plantations in the mother country. In 1700, the Assembly passed another act of establishment; two years later it was approved and became law. The act decreed that each parish should elect a vestry of six members and that a poll tax of forty pounds of tobacco should be levied for the support of the churches and their ministers.

The provisions of the act were first enforced by Sir Francis Nicholson who became governor in 1694. Despite his high-handed and profane manners, he proved to be a true friend of the church and gave much attention to the building of new edifices and the enlistment of clergy for the parishes. Both Roman Catholics and Quakers were vigorous opponents of the establishment, but their efforts were fruitless. However, the large influx of Roman Catholic Irish about this time served to excite the fears of the Protestants that a revival of Roman Catholic power was in the offing; it contributed to a wave of intense activity in the Protestant camp. By 1715, the province was returned to the Calvert family, but only after the fourth Lord Baltimore had become a Protestant.

Parishes and Clergy

Virginia's government, on a local level, followed the pattern of the English parish. The parish was a local unit concerned with such matters as the conduct and support of the parish church, the supervision of morals, and the care of the poor. Its officers, who made up the vestry, were ordinarily influential and wealthy property holders chosen by a majority of the parishioners. They appointed the parish ministers, made local assessments, and investigated cases of moral offense for referral to the county court, the next higher judicatory. They also selected the church wardens, who audited the parish accounts and prosecuted morals cases. For several decades the system worked in a democratic fashion, but by the 1660's, the vestries had generally become self-perpetuating units made up of well-to-do landowners. This condition was sharply resented by the small farmers and servants.

The size of the parishes was dictated to a considerable extent by the placement of population. Jamestown, the chief center and capital of the colony for a century, could scarcely be thought of as a real town. The population was sparse, being settled on extensive plantations paralleling the river banks. This necessitated the creation of parishes many miles long—so long, in many cases, that a clergyman could not properly care for them. The Assembly was cognizant of the problem and attempted to find a solution in an act passed in 1631–1632.

Every mynister in this colony havings cure of soules shall preache one ser-mon every sunday in the yeare, having no lawful impediment, and yf the myn-isters shall neglect their charge by unnecessarie absence or otherwise the church wardens are to present it. But because in this colony the places of their cure are in many places ffar distant, It is thought fitt that the mynisters doe soe divide theire turnes as by joynt agreement of the parishoners they should be desired.[3]

As the population increased, the parishes, to some extent, changed in size and shape; but to the end of the colonial period many remained too large to be served adequately by one minister.

That attendance at divine worship was irregular was not surprising. Few had the perseverance to travel fifteen miles or more over ill-condi-tioned roads to participate in public worship, even in balmy weather. On stormy Sundays, the minister could expect to preach to vacant pews. The problem was lessened to a degree by the establishment of chapels in re-mote areas. These were invariably served by lay readers, the pastor mak-ing only a monthly visit. When such chapels were lacking, ministers were sometimes obliged to travel to the homes of their parishioners and con-duct what amounted to a private service. One clergyman reported with justifiable displeasure: "Sometimes after I have travell'd Fifty Miles to Preach at a Private House, the Weather happening to prove bad, on the day of our meeting, so that very few or none have met; or else being hindered by Rivers & Swamps rendered impassible with much rain, I have returned with doing of nothing to their benefit or mine own satis-faction."

Clergymen who valued strict conformity to the liturgy were often irritated by conditions which made such conformity impossible. They found particular dissatisfaction in the frequent use of lay readers in churches as well as in chapels. The practice, however, had developed out of sheer necessity and, with a shortage of clergy, there was no ideal solu-tion to the problem. Lay readers continued to officiate in place of the pastor. They were not permitted to prepare their own homilies, but they could and did read printed sermons. Under such circumstances, it was not surprising that both laity and clergy tended to become lax in the ob-servance of customs and ceremonies. Christmas and Good Friday alone

[3] *Ibid.,* 13.

among the church festivals were celebrated; the sacraments were often administered without the prescribed accouterments; the Holy Communion was received by persons who had never been confirmed.

Apparently many of the liturgical problems which so vexed the church in England were considered unimportant in America. In the mother country, the extreme Puritans in the church were protesting vigorously against the wearing of surplices and the use of liturgical forms in the Book of Common Prayer. Still, Alexander Whitaker, the minister at Henrico, could observe in 1614: "But I much more muse that so few of our English Ministers that were so hot against the Surplis and subscription, come hither where neither are spoken of." Technically, all clergy in the colony of Virginia were bound to conform to the practice of the church. But the somewhat casual attitude toward religious formalities in the colony, coupled with the desire of its authorities to attract any clergyman of good moral character, made it inadvisable to be overly sensitive about the application of ecclesiastical rules. There were even cases in which ministers without episcopal ordination were permitted to serve in Anglican parishes.

One of the perennial problems was the raising of sufficient salaries for the parish clergy. Many a parish numbered no more than one hundred families, most of whom could scarcely be called wealthy. Since the ministerial stipends came almost entirely through local tax levies, the only way of assuring a larger income would be to extend the geographical limits of the parish. Such action, however, created untenable situations for the local clergy, who could not possibly keep up with the work. During the first half of the seventeenth century there was wide variance in clerical salaries. The tax method was to assess each person in the colony an equal amount. But each pastor received only the funds collected in his own parish, which accounted for the disparity in income. One man might receive seventy pounds annually, another merely twenty-five.

In 1662, the Virginia Assembly passed an act making uniform all clerical salaries. The stipend was fixed at eighty pounds, the taxpayer being permitted to make his payment in tobacco. By this time, the market value of tobacco had declined sharply due to the navigation acts which forbade its shipment to foreign countries. When the clergy complained that their payments were inadequate to meet the rising costs of living, the assessments were increased. The stipends, however, were never adequate; and as late as 1724, the ministers insisted that a fixed income of forty or fifty pounds in England would be preferable to the arrangement which they tolerated in America.

Another step to improve the economic condition of the clergy was taken in 1661, when the Virginia Assembly required every parish to provide for its minister a glebe with suitable dwelling place, other buildings, and livestock. Most parishes complied with the law, so that many ecclesiastical leaders found themselves in command of small plantations. But the plan led only to greater difficulties. Few ministers had the funds, the time, or the knowledge to care for their holdings. By the end of the seventeenth century, many of the glebes were in a state of deterioration or completely deserted.

If the clergy were constantly harassed by poverty, they were outraged by the general treatment they received from the vestries. No clergyman had life tenure in his parish unless his vestry presented him to the governor for induction or installation. The vestries usually refused to present their pastors to the governor for fear that, once having been inducted, the clergy would no longer bow to their authority. On occasion, when a minister was regarded as exceptionally capable, the vestry would present him to the governor for life tenure, but probably not more than one-tenth of the pastors ever received such an honor. The fact that the vestries kept control over the clergy more often than not proved detrimental to the interests of the parish. Not only that, but it encouraged the abler ministers to remain in England, thus leaving the colonial pulpits staffed with mediocre divines. This circumstance seems not to have had the least instructive influence on the vestries, for they continued their policy with determination throughout the colonial period.

The Practice of Religion

The religion of the average Anglican in Virginia or Maryland might be characterized as pious but not prudish, formal but not fastidious. He believed in his religion and endeavored to practice it, without at the same time making it the foremost consideration in his life. His piety was evident in his choice of reading matter, in his public observances, in his laws. Most private libraries included one or more popular works on the practice of religion; thanksgiving days and "days of humiliation" belonged as much to Virginia as to New England; the regulations for the keeping of the Sabbath read like a page out of a Puritan law book. For all his outward professions of piety, however, the colonial Anglican often treated the ordinances of the church with reverent neglect. And in a land sparsely populated, with great distances between settlements, regular attendance at divine worship could hardly be enforced. If a phlegmatic settler happened to drift into the local tavern when he was supposed to be in church, few were eager to chastise him. The easy-going plantation life admitted a tolerance unknown to a more disciplined society.

Discipline there was, and of the most public character. A slanderous person might be sent to the ducking stool or made to apologize before the congregation. A conviction for drunkenness, profanity, or illicit sex relations might carry with it physical punishment. There were even trials for witchcraft. But in general, the Anglican clergy discouraged convictions on such charges. In the South, the fear of witchcraft seems to have stemmed more from folklore than from theology.

The attitude of the colonial Anglican toward the Indian provides a splendid insight into his practice of religion. From the outset of colonization, the sense of obligation to evangelize the Indian was apparent. According to a document issued by the Governor and Councillors of Virginia in 1609:

The Principal and *Maine Endes* (out of which are easily derived to any meane understanding infinitnesse, and yet great ones) were *first* to preach and baptize into *Christian Religion,* and by propagation of the *Gospell,* to recover out of the armes of the Divell, a number of poore and miserable soules, wrapt up unto death, in almost invincible *ignorance;* to endeavour the fulfilling, and accomplishment of the number of the elect, which shall be gathered from out all corners of the earth; and to add our myte to the Treasury of Heaven, that as we pray for the coming of the Kingdome of Glory, so to expresse in our actions, the same desire, if God, have pleased, to use so weak instruments, to the ripening and consummation thereof.[4]

Just how successful the first settlers were in communicating their faith to the Indians we do not know. Probably there was no organized missionary work during the earliest years because of the incessant warfare. By 1610, the situation had improved. The conversion of Pocahontas, the Indian princess, and her marriage to John Rolfe pointed to an era of good feeling between the whites and the Indians. During the period prior to the great massacre of 1622, some of the Indians, at least, became Christians. The visits of certain Indians in England, among them Pocahontas, aroused widespread interest and prompted church leaders to emphasize the need for Indian missions.

In 1617 and 1618, the Virginia settlers began to make plans for the founding of churches and schools for the Indians, eventually even a college. Definite action was taken by the Assembly in 1619:

Be it enacted by this present assembly, that for laying a surer foundation of the conversion of the Indians to Christian religion, eache towne, citty, Borough, & particular Plantation do obtaine unto themselves by just meanes a certaine number of the natives children to be educated by them in true Religion & civil course of life. Of wch children the most towardly boyes in witt & graces of nature to be brought up by them in the first Elements of litterature, so as to be fitted for the Colledge intended for them, that from thence they may be sent to that work of conversion.[5]

[4] *Ibid.,* 9.
[5] Quoted in G. M. Brydon, *Virginia's Mother Church* (Virginia Historical Society, 1947), I, 423.

King James I even made a special appeal to the church for funds, and the diocese of London alone raised a thousand pounds. Finally, it was decided to establish separate institutions for whites and Indians at Henrico. The work of clearing the land and erecting buildings was started. Then came the Indian massacre of 1622, the burning of the half-completed buildings, and the murder of the inhabitants. After that time, a strong feeling of distrust and resentment canceled out any humanitarian purposes on the part of the colonists, and henceforth they devoted themselves to the destruction of the Indian settlements.

Another challenge to the program of evangelism came with the introduction of the Negro into the colonies. As early as 1619, twenty indentured Negroes, from a Dutch cargo ship, were landed in Virginia. The Negro proved to be such an effective worker in the fields that gradually the system of indenture merged into slavery. But it was not until the Duke of York and the Royal African Company entered the slave trade, after 1660, that the importation of Negroes became significant. The number of Negroes in Virginia alone jumped from 300 in 1650 to 6,000 in 1700.

The presence of the Negro posed a religious problem for his white owner. If the slave should be converted and baptized, would he not have to be released on the ground that it was immoral to enslave a Christian? The matter was taken to the Virginia Assembly which, in 1667, ruled to the satisfaction of slave holders:

. . . the conferring of baptisme doth not alter the condition of the person as to his bondage or ffreedome; that diverse masters, ffreed from this doubt, may more carefully endeavour the propagation of christianity by permitting children, though slaves, or those of greater growth if capable to be admitted to that sacrament.[6]

The Anglican custom of baptizing infants was most likely followed in the case of slave infants, providing the owners would agree. There were probably few instances, however, in which instruction in Christian morals and doctrine was given. Occasionally, a voice would be raised in favor of evangelizing the Negro, as in the case of the Reverend Morgan Godwyn, in his *The Negro's and Indian's Advocate*, published in 1680. He called upon the Anglican Church to further the Christian instruction of Negro slaves and Indians in the colonies. The reaction to the pamphlet in Virginia could hardly be described as favorable. By this time, the trend was to regard the Negro as racially inferior and to discriminate against him on that ground. Christianity was primarily for the dominant white society and was to be administered to the Negro, if at all, in small and carefully prescribed doses.

[6] *Ibid.*, I, 470.

The Commissaries

As the seventeenth century drew to its close, the Anglican Church in Virginia was in a perilous condition. A majority of the parishes were vacant, while the minority were staffed by men of secondary ability and questionable character, who were poorly paid. Clergymen became frustrated and ultimately lethargic because parishes were too large to permit an effective ministry. It has been estimated that no more than one person in twenty was a member of the church. At least part of the difficulty rested with the weak and inefficient government of the church and the lack of close ties with the episcopal power in the mother country.

Throughout the entire colonial period, the only episcopal supervision which the Anglican Church in America knew was the jurisdiction exercised by the Bishop of London. As early as 1620, the Virginia Company had asked the bishop to appoint ministers for the colony and to render various other services. During the tenure of Bishop Laud (1628–1633), the Bishop of London's authority over the colonial church was greatly increased. In 1632 the Privy Council gave the bishop jurisdiction over English subjects outside the British Isles and charged him to maintain the proper observance of the liturgy and discipline.

After Henry Compton became bishop in 1675, instructions were issued to the colonial governors directing that no clergyman be received in the colonies without a certificate from the Bishop of London. Bishop Compton also became concerned over the employment of clergy by the vestries, the payment of clerical salaries in tobacco of poor quality, and the extensive use of the laity in services of public worship. He counseled the secular officials to take prompt measures to remedy the situation; they cooperated to an extent, but no significant reforms were made. Gradually it became apparent to the bishop that what he needed was a direct representative who could act with authority and dispatch. Such a person could not replace the bishop in all ecclesiastical functions. In the Anglican Church only a bishop could administer confirmation and ordination. But it was possible to delegate other functions such as supervision and administration. And so Bishop Compton began the practice of delegating certain of his functions to officials called commissaries.

The first commissary, James Blair, was appointed in 1689 to the colony of Virginia. An abler man could not have been chosen. He had already served as the rector of Henrico County for four years and was thoroughly conversant with conditions in the colony. Courageous and often astute in his dealings with others, he commanded the respect, if not always the support, of both secular and clerical officialdom and, until his death in 1743, performed a distinguished work for his church in Virginia.

Commissary Blair began his work by presenting a five-point plan for reform. First of all, it called for the raising of clerical salaries, which by this time were woefully inadequate. The crown gave full support to this proposal and even set aside a considerable sum for the purpose; but it was not until 1696 that legislation for better salaries, previously passed by the Virginia Assembly, was approved by the governor. Blair's second proposal, that the vestries should present their ministers to the governor for induction, encountered widespread opposition. When the governor threatened to collate ministers without the approval of the parish, the vestries protested and vowed that they would pay no salary to a clergyman so appointed. Since there was little the governor could do about such an impending situation, the matter was dropped. A third proposal, that the clergy should have a representative in the council of state to protect their interests in civil affairs, was favorably received. Dr. Blair was appointed to the council.

Much more frustrating was the commissary's attempt to reform the clergy. Discipline was at an all-time low and clerical morality left much to be desired. Drunkenness was fairly common among the ministers; laziness and indifference often marred their effectiveness and bred disrespect. Frequent admonitions from Blair seem not to have inspired any real inclination for reform. Indeed, the reform movement ended in total failure and with it came the steady weakening of the colonial church.

Perhaps the most important of James Blair's five proposals was the one which called for the founding of a college to train divinity students. Despite the traditional Anglican love for learning, education in Virginia had been sadly neglected except among the wealthy. After years of agitation for a charter and a trip to England to win the royal patronage, Blair succeeded in his plan. The College of William and Mary was chartered in 1693, the second college in the English colonies. In 1695, the erection of the main building was started at Williamsburg, a task which was not completed until 1700. When the institution finally opened, with Blair as its first president, it was little more than a grammar school. Advanced courses were added, but few students elected to take them. It was evident that not many young Virginians desired to enter the ministry, nor did they wish to take the long trip to England in order to receive ordination. The hazards of the journey and the fear of contracting smallpox after arrival were in themselves powerful deterrents. Disheartened by this turn of events, Blair realized that he would have to look almost entirely to the mother country for the recruitment of clergy. In this enlistment program he was notably successful; while, in 1700, more than half of the parishes were vacant, by the time of Blair's death only two parishes were without ministers.

The second commissary appointed by Bishop Compton was Dr. Thomas Bray. He was assigned to Maryland in 1696, and though he spent less than a year in the colony, his work is as important as that of

James Blair. In searching out ministers to send to the Maryland parishes, Bray discovered that the only interested persons were poor men who had no funds to buy books. This discovery started him on a course of activities which led to the founding of two societies, whose influence is still strongly felt. His first effort was to raise funds to buy libraries for the missionaries. The results were most favorable and this encouraged him to advance larger projects, such as the formation of the "Society for the Promotion of Christian Knowledge" in 1698.

As Commissary Bray labored to improve educational opportunities for the clergy, he endeavored to enlist their interest in colonial mission work. By the time he was ready to set sail for Maryland, the number of missionaries in that colony had risen to sixteen. Upon his arrival in America in March, 1700, Bray attended a meeting of the Maryland Assembly. It is likely that he had something to do with the passage of an act which required every person in the colony to attend Anglican worship. He also visited the parishes, giving assurance to the discouraged and censure to the indifferent members of the clergy.

After two and one-half months in the colony, Commissary Bray returned to England in order to win approval of the Assembly's church establishment act. It was finally approved in an amended form which harmonized with the provisions in the English Act of Toleration of 1689. Roman Catholics alone were denied freedom of worship.

In the meantime, Bray had published a report on the state of colonial religion, which emphasized the need for more ministers and recommended a drive to raise funds for the support of future missionaries. As a result of this effort, the Convocation of Canterbury appointed a committee, in 1701, to consider methods for improving the work in the colonies. In June of that year, the king granted a royal charter which brought into existence a society to provide for the "better support and Maintenance of an Orthodox Clergy in Forreigne Parts." It was known as the "Society for the Propagation of the Gospel in Foreign Parts." Its principal function was to further the ministrations of the Gospel among English colonials; at the same time, it was mindful of the need to evangelize the Indians and Negro slaves. The society's most important work, however, would be accomplished in colonies other than Maryland or Virginia.

In 1716, two commissaries were appointed to Maryland, to the Eastern and Western Shores respectively. They appear not to have been persuasive men, inasmuch as the ministers refused to recognize their authority. Discipline was conspicuously absent. With every passing decade of the eighteenth century, enthusiasm waned and the vigor of the established church declined. The future seemed to lie with the dissenting bodies, which were growing steadily in numbers and prestige.

THE CHURCH IN THE CAROLINAS AND GEORGIA

In 1663, Charles II granted a royal patent to the Earl of Clarendon and seven other proprietors for lands south of Virginia, which were called Carolina. The charter called for the toleration of dissenters despite "the unity and uniformity established in this nation." Nevertheless, the Fundamental Constitutions of 1669, prepared by the philosopher John Locke and his friend Lord Ashley Cooper, provided that only the Anglican Church was entitled to public support. Other religious persuasions were tolerated, however, for there was a provision that any seven persons of the same communion might organize a church, on the condition that they professed faith in God and a desire to worship Him. The following year a permanent settlement was founded at Albemarle Point near Charleston; two years later Charleston became the seat of government. Dissenters as well as Anglicans were immediately drawn to the new colony, and every year there was a considerable increase in the population.

The establishment clause in the Fundamental Constitutions was not taken seriously during the early years of the colony; there were too many dissenters to make it feasible. Not until 1698 did the Anglicans succeed in getting an act through the Assembly for the support of their minister in Charleston. In 1704, the Assembly passed a strict act of establishment. Certain provisions were disallowed by the English authorities, but finally an act was passed in 1706 which was acceptable. Unlike the situation in other colonies, ministers were to be selected by vote of the parishioners, though the vestries usually obtained the candidates through the help of the Bishop of London or the Society for the Propagation of the Gospel. Ministers did not have to be certified by the Bishop of London. The most unusual provision was the establishment of a commission of twenty laymen, whose task was to purchase land for churches and glebes and to administer all donations.

By 1708, there were five Anglican clergymen in South Carolina, men of high caliber who rendered able service. Their most difficult work was the evangelization of Indians and slaves. Only Francis Le Jau was able to make any real impact on the Negroes, and he was opposed by the planters. As the eighteenth century progressed, the Negroes came to outnumber the whites two to one, and slaveholders looked even more with disfavor upon missionary efforts on their behalf.

After South Carolina became a royal province in 1719, Anglicanism received added support from the government; and by 1723 the colony boasted thirteen prosperous parishes. Because of the influence of the Society for the Propagation of the Gospel a high standard was maintained in the church, which justified the praise of John Wesley during a visit in 1737. Later the society was relieved of responsibility and the church began to lose some of its effectiveness.

Theoretically, North and South Carolina were parts of the same province for half a century. Actually they were so far apart that it was necessary to maintain two separate governments. Each part had its own governor until 1691; then followed a period in which the governor at Charleston sent a deputy to rule in the north. After that the earlier pattern of rule by two governors was restored and was, of course, continued after 1729, when North Carolina became a legally separate royal colony.

At first, Anglicanism made very slow progress. Population was sparse and communities were few and far between. The colony seems to have attracted settlers who belonged predominantly to the dissenting bodies, especially Quakers, who from the beginning arrived in relatively large numbers. Only one Anglican clergyman served there during the seventeenth century. By the opening of the eighteenth century the Society for the Propagation of the Gospel found it possible to enlist a few men, but their stay was brief. As late as 1741, there were only two Anglican priests in the colony. One minister, Clement Hall, performed a prodigious amount of work during a period of eight years, baptizing some six thousand children and preaching almost seven hundred sermons to both whites and Negro slaves.

The North Carolina Assembly was somewhat dilatory in passing acts which would be beneficial to the Anglican Church. Strong opposition from Quakers and Presbyterians undoubtedly hindered the process, as in the case of the Vestry Act of 1701, which was disallowed by the proprietors after vigorous protest. In 1715, the Assembly passed an act of establishment. The act received the endorsement of the proprietors, but found little support in the colony because of the power of the dissenters. Another establishment act was passed in 1765, with the approval of the crown. The Anglican establishment, however, never became popular in North Carolina. Even the Anglicans resented the fact that, according to the law, the governor assumed virtually complete control over the selection of ministers to the parishes. In the long run establishment worked a decided hardship upon the church.

Georgia, founded in 1732 by Colonel James Oglethorpe, was a philanthropic venture on behalf of imprisoned debtors. It was administered by twenty-one trustees, among them five Church of England clergymen and such prominent lay Anglicans as Oglethorpe, the Earl of Egmont, and James Vernon. While it was expected that the Anglican Church would be established, the proprietors seem not to have been particularly concerned about the matter. Absorbed in their humanitarian enterprise they freely granted religious liberty to all Christians save Roman Catholics. On occasion they even helped to enlist ministers and acquire churches for the various dissenting bodies.

To the colony in its early days came the young John Wesley, then a missionary for the Society for the Propagation of the Gospel. Due to his unbending manner and his uncompromising discipline, his tenure was short and he returned home to find his destiny. Wesley was succeeded by George Whitefield, who would also win fame during the Great Awakening. In 1740, he became rector of Christ Church in Savannah. His principal contribution in Georgia was the founding of an orphanage which became Bethesda College.

In 1752 the proprietary charter expired and Georgia became a royal province, with a royal governor and a representative assembly. Almost immediately an attempt was made to gain the establishment of the Church of England. The first bill of establishment was passed in 1755, and was promptly rejected by the appointive Council on the ground that it would tend to discourage further immigrants from coming to Georgia. And yet, only three years later another act of establishment was passed and this time it was approved. Undoubtedly the influence of English officialdom was strong, for at the time of the act's passage there were only two members of the upper house who were Anglicans, and there was only one Anglican minister in the colony. In spite of this favorable legislation, the Anglican Church in Georgia failed to prosper, a circumstance which remained true throughout the rest of the colonial period. Indeed, it was unusual to have more than two clergymen of the established church in the colony at the same time.

THE CHURCH IN THE MIDDLE COLONIES

The only colony north of Maryland where there came to be anything resembling an Anglican establishment was New York. Prior to 1664, the colony had been known as New Netherland and had been under the control of the Dutch, who maintained an establishment of the Reformed Church. In that year, the English, under the Duke of York, took over the colony and put into effect a very generous policy, one that was exceptional for the seventeenth century. It provided for the toleration of all Protestant bodies and for the special recognition of the Reformed faith. The action was a diplomatic one, especially since the British were in no position to afford a quarrel with the large number of Protestant groups in New York, at least not at the beginning of their rule.

During the reign of James II, Thomas Dongan, a Roman Catholic, was Governor of New York, and toleration was broadened to include all religions. James himself was responsible for this broad toleration, which he favored largely because he desired to further the interests of the Roman Catholic Church, his own communion. But shortly after the overthrow of James, toleration in New York came to an end. William and Mary, the new sovereigns, sent over as their first governor, Henry Sloughter. He was instructed to push through an act establishing the Church of England.

In 1693, the Assembly passed a bill entitled "Act for Settling a Ministry, and raising a Maintenance for them in the City of New York, County of Richmond, Westchester and Queens' county." The act was later interpreted by the governors as establishing the Anglican Church in the counties named in the legislation. It is highly doubtful, however, if this was the intention of many who voted for the act. The document does not mention the Church of England. It provided only that the six named parishes were each to be served by a "good sufficient Protestant minister" and were to be supported by an annual tax. In English legal usage the phrase "good sufficient Protestant minister" meant a clergyman of the Church of England. This meaning was doubtless not understood by the Dutch members of the Assembly who voted for it, only to find themselves deceived.

It was not until 1697 that Trinity Church, the first Anglican parish in New York, was founded. William Vesey became the first rector. A few years later the Society for the Propagation of the Gospel began to send missionaries to the province. In 1702 a church was organized at Westchester; and shortly thereafter parishes were founded at Hempstead, Jamaica, Oyster Bay, Staten Island, and Albany. From 1702 to the opening of the Revolution the Society for the Propagation of the Gospel helped to maintain some fifty-eight missionaries in the colony.

The beginnings of Anglicanism in William Penn's Quaker colony of Pennsylvania were inauspicious. The very forces which attracted dissenters to the settlement prompted Anglicans to stay away. It was thus not until 1695 that the first parish, Christ Church in Philadelphia, was organized. The church's second rector, Evan Evans, was able to report six years later, however, that there were not less than five hundred Anglicans in his parish. Apparently Anglicanism had an appeal for wealthy Quakers, for in 1707 it was announced that many of them had been won over to the Anglican Church. It is interesting to note, in this connection, that the Quakers had been the most aggressive in opposing Anglican attempts to gain a footing.

Within a decade after the founding of Christ Church, Anglican missions sprang up at Chester, Oxford, and at New Castle and Dover, now in Delaware. All experienced real difficulties, especially in securing ministers. The Society for the Propagation of the Gospel did what it could, and before the outbreak of the Revolution supplied a total of forty-seven missionaries. But rarely, if ever, were there more than five or six men on active assignment at any one time.

In 1664, the Duke of York granted to Sir George Carteret and Lord John Berkeley a tract of land between the Hudson and Delaware Rivers named New Jersey. From 1676 to 1702 the province was divided into two parts, East and West Jersey. Immigrants from New England, in particular, came to populate the colony; but through purchases New

Jersey gradually came under the control of the Quakers. The Anglican Church carried on no organized activities there prior to the eighteenth century.

By 1703 George Keith and John Talbot, missionaries for the Society for the Propagation of the Gospel, were laboring at such towns as Amboy and Burlington. Keith, a converted Quaker, devoted special attention to the Quakers, often coming uninvited into their meetings and debating with them. He reported that invariably they received him with kindness and that he was able to persuade more than a hundred of them to unite with the Anglican Church. Talbot, who served at Burlington for twenty years, became noted for his efforts to have an episcopate established in the colonies. After 1751, his cause was championed, unsuccessfully, by Thomas Chandler, the rector at Elizabethtown. The chief support for the church came through the Society for the Propagation of the Gospel which, before the close of the colonial period, sent a total of forty-four missionaries to the province.

It is sometimes stated that the Anglican Church was established in New Jersey. This is because Lord Cornbury, the first royal governor, was instructed by Queen Anne in 1702 to see that worship in that province be conducted according to the usage of the Church of England. The New Jersey Assembly, however, never passed an act of establishment, which would have been necessary for the creation of a state church. If there was an establishment, it existed only in the minds of Lord Cornbury and Queen Anne.

THE CHURCH IN NEW ENGLAND

The introduction of Anglicanism into New England was marked by tension and discomfiture. In May, 1686, Robert Ratcliffe, an Anglican clergyman, arrived in Massachusetts Bay Colony with orders to found there a Church of England parish. This was quite a large assignment when one considers the pronounced views of the Puritans concerning the Anglican Church. Since 1660, the House of Stuart had been trying to force the New England Puritans to be obedient in ecclesiastical as well as political matters. Charles II advised the colonists that their charter gave evidence of the Crown's tolerance toward them and that they should reciprocate by extending freedom of worship to Anglicans in their midst. In 1664 Charles sent a royal commission to Massachusetts to bring about a softening of the colony's religious restrictions. The mission ended in virtual failure. After repeatedly being rebuffed in his efforts to win toleration for Anglicans, the king attacked the Massachusetts charter through the courts; and on October 3, 1684, he succeeded in having the charter revoked.

With the setting up of a royal government over Massachusetts and the coming of the king's representative, Sir Edmund Andros, in December 1686, a concerted effort was made to promote the cause of Anglicanism. Andros tried to persuade the Puritan ministers to permit Ratcliffe and his parishioners to use one of their meeting houses for worship. When the Puritans refused, the Anglicans were obliged to use the Town House. By the following spring a more conciliatory spirit prevailed, and the Anglicans moved into the South Meeting House.

When the Stuart dynasty met its nemesis in 1688, a revolution broke out in Massachusetts and a number of bitter attacks were made upon the Anglican Church. Increase Mather, an easily aroused Puritan leader, immediately put forth a pamphlet on the "Unlawfulness of the Common Prayer Worship." The Puritan authorities thought that with the coming of a new government their old charter might be restored, and they sent Increase Mather to make that request. In order to obtain a new charter he had to agree to the insertion of a provision that no religious tests should be permitted for the suffrage. This meant that Anglicans would have equal rights with Puritans in the government of Massachusetts, the only test for the suffrage being the ownership of property.

The most valuable support for Anglicanism came from the Society for the Propagation of the Gospel. Within a year after the Society's founding it sent George Keith and Patrick Gordon to the colonies in order to make a study of the church's needs and opportunities. Gordon died shortly after their arrival in Boston in July, 1702, and was succeeded by John Talbot. During the following two years Keith and Talbot went on a tour of inspection which took them from Maine to Carolina. Through these men and others like them, the Society for the Propagation of the Gospel was enabled to carry on an effective missionary program.

In Massachusetts an inestimable service was rendered by clergy of exceptionally high caliber. By 1722 there were so many Anglicans in Boston that it was necessary to organize a second church. A third was added in 1740. Some of these communicants were converts from Puritanism. Perhaps the best known convert was Timothy Cutler, formerly president of Yale College. He sailed to England in 1722 to receive episcopal ordination and upon his return assumed the rectorship of Christ Church, Boston.

The history of Anglicanism in Connecticut began in 1706, when George Muirson, the missionary at Rye, New York, began to conduct services at Stratford. Despite strong opposition from the magistrates, the congregation continued to grow, and by the 1720's was receiving the able ministrations of such missionaries as George Pigot and Samuel Johnson. A former Congregational pastor, Johnson adopted Anglicanism when he, along with his friend, Timothy Cutler, became convinced that episcopal ordination alone was valid. In 1727 a second Church of England congregation was founded at Fairfield; three years later a third was organized at New London. At the outset of the Revolution the Anglican Church had forty parishes and twenty clergymen in the colony.

The introduction of the church into Rhode Island was achieved by David Bethune, who became minister at Newport in 1700. The most important work, however, was performed by one of his successors, James Honeyman. Within a few years, churches were planted at Narragansett, Bristol, Providence, and Warwick, through the efforts of the Society for the Propagation of the Gospel.

The first permanent settlements in New Hampshire and Maine were established by Anglicans. As early as 1640 a parish was founded at Strawberry Bank, later known as Portsmouth. About the same time another congregation was being organized at Winter Harbor on the Saco River in Maine. However, as Puritan power began to develop in these areas, Anglican church life was virtually extinguished; and it was not until the eighteenth century that it could be revived. The first signs of regeneration came with the refounding of the parish at Portsmouth in 1734. Maine experienced a revival of Anglican activity in 1761 with the arrival of Jacob Bailey. But progress was slow, and only a few more parishes had been organized by the outbreak of the Revolution.

It is ironical that the Anglican Church in the colonies found its greatest disadvantage in the assistance that was offered by its ardent proponent, the English government. In the South, where the church was officially connected with the state and enjoyed the questionable benefits pertaining to an establishment, spiritual lethargy developed with unfailing regularity. Men of the highest ability and ideals could seldom be persuaded to accept a call to servility and uncertain tenure, subject to the whims of a vestry. Less committed and capable men were willing to accept an importunate situation and make the worst of it. There were notable exceptions, but not enough to place the clergy generally in a commanding position of respect.

In New England, where Anglicans were a despised minority, their support by the English crown rendered them even more suspect. The more vigorously the government prosecuted their claims, the more public resentment was aroused. The saving grace of the church was the Society for the Propagation of the Gospel, with its band of consecrated missionaries working against overwhelming odds to advance their faith.

A constant source of frustration was the absence of a colonial episcopate. Without the benefit of either confirmation or ordination on this side of the Atlantic, the church could not possibly assume a normal life. At best, it could become little more than a mission field. This thought failed to excite any real concern in the South, where clergy and laity alike were enjoying their freedom from episcopal interference. In the Middle

Colonies and New England, the situation was different. Determined efforts were made by the missionaries and their congregations to have a bishop appointed, but they were doomed to failure. The church would have no bishop in America until after the formation of a national government, independent of England.

4

The Puritan Adventure in New England

THE ENGLISH SETTING

The Puritans

BY THE MIDDLE OF THE SIXTEENTH CENTURY THE CHURCH OF ENGLAND HAD divided into two camps: the Anglican, which was in power; and the Puritan, which was agitating for supremacy. The latter, sparked by Calvinist missionaries, became entrenched in the eastern shires of Norfolk, Suffolk, and Essex and demanded a reformation similar to that of the Calvinists on the Continent. Puritanism stood for the repudiation of formalism. This was manifested in opposition to medieval ceremonies, clerical vestments, and the entire episcopal system of church government. It stood for the adoption by the established church of the Calvinist system of doctrine and the enforcement of that doctrine. The Puritans hoped to take the present society and transform it into the very model of perfection, thereby reflecting the will of God in history.

Queen Elizabeth had no love for Puritanism, preferring to follow the middle-of-the-road policy set forth in the Thirty-Nine Articles of 1571. Despite Puritan protests, she maintained the episcopal government, a creed which bore the imprint of Lutheranism, and a liturgy borrowed from medieval Roman Catholicism. Puritanism, however, made considerable progress during her reign, notably in Essex. There the Prayer Book was often laid aside in favor of services according to Calvinistic practice. Elizabeth made no effort to curtail their activities so long as they took place in the communion of the Church of England.

Most Puritans had no thought of withdrawing from the established church. They believed that it was in sorry condition, weakened by the neglect of Scripture's explicit teaching, but it was still the chosen vessel of God. None believed this more fervently than Thomas Cartwright (1535–1603), the acknowledged head of the movement. Nevertheless, disappointment over the church's persistent refusal to adopt the suggested reforms drove him to the acceptance of a polity which had congregational elements. He was certain that each local congregation should be able to call the minister of its choice, one who would be conformable to its ideas of worship. He also felt the congregation should handle disciplinary problems within its midst.

With the accession of James I to the throne in 1603, Puritan affairs took a turn for the worse. Their Millenary Petition for reform rejected and their leadership denounced by the king at the Hampton Court Conference the following year, the Puritans now realized that their hopes would not be fulfilled in England. It was inevitable that they should take still another step closer to congregationalism by affirming that their congregations existed by the authority not of the national church but of God.

Puritan thought was influenced predominantly by the writings of William Ames (1576–1633), a Cambridge divine who eventually had to take refuge in the Netherlands. His *Medulla Theologiae* became a standard textbook of Calvinist theology among the Puritans. In his *The First Book of Divinity*, Ames made the Church of England merely a collection of sovereign congregations loosely knit together as a federation. He maintained the right of the local congregation to call a pastor and insisted that the ordination of a minister should follow after his election to the church. But he was equally insistent that the state had the right and duty to suppress all ministers and religious persuasions which did not conform to the establishment. In this respect, if not in all others, Ames was in perfect agreement with Thomas Cartwright.

English Puritanism, in the congregational form which would take root in America, had thus crystallized during the reign of James I. It recognized the Church of England, but as a loose federation of congregations, each receiving its authority direct from God. It expected that these congregations, moreover, would be unified through the support of the state. The civil government would be responsible for the enforcement of church and civil law based upon the Scriptures, and the suppression of all heretical movements. Only one major obstacle blocked the realization of this cherished plan: the hostility of the government. When it became apparent that governmental opposition was increasing and that there was little prospect for the establishment of Puritanism in England, a saddened and despairing minority would seek an ultimate victory through emigration.

The Separatists

In the meantime, a division in the Puritan ranks had resulted in the formation of the Separatist movement under the leadership of Robert Browne (1550–1633). Though sympathetic to the Puritan cause in many respects, Browne could not tolerate the existence of an established church. At Norwich, he gathered a large congregation and preached revolutionary views which led to his imprisonment in 1581. The tenor of his criticism was that the Anglican Church was ungodly and corrupted by its connection with the civil government. He resolved to make the church a truly spiritual institution, independent of the state and patterned after the Scriptures.

Browne conceived the church to be nothing more than a company of Christians who make a covenant with God and with one another and who labor together for the advancement of their mutual Christian purposes. These purposes included neither the building of the Kingdom of God on earth nor the salvation of the world. The Separatist placed his emphasis upon the spiritual growth and edification of the local fellowship. Wherever redeemed persons effected a covenant, giving evidence of a satisfactory conversion experience and of their election to salvation, there was a true church. Browne did not suggest that persons outside his church could not be saved, for he never regarded church membership as essential to salvation. He did believe, however, that only those churches which followed principles similar to his own were true churches.

The democratic organization of the Separatist churches called for church officers to be chosen by and responsible to the entire congregation. Even the power of ordination resided with the people. Later, when the mantle of Separatist authority fell upon Henry Barrowe and John Greenwood, the principle was changed so that power in a local church rested not with the membership but with the pastor, elders, and teachers. Thus a modified Presbyterianism with rule by elders replaced Browne's congregational democracy.

For Browne, the essential mark of the church was undoubtedly the voluntary covenant. Since he rejected believers' baptism as the mark of the church, he was led to retain infant baptism as a sign of the dedication of children to God and the church. Children of the faithful thus became participants in the covenant relationship and were numbered among the people of God.

Many years later John Cotton in New England would deny any connection with either Browne or Barrowe. Nevertheless, Browne's idea of the congregational covenant and Barrowe's concept of the rule of the eldership became realized in the polity of the churches of the Massachusetts Bay Colony. The friction between Puritan and Separatist lay not so much in their concepts of the church as in their attitudes toward church establishments. In New England, the principle of establishment would prevail over Separatism.

The English government's persecution of the Separatists was vigorous and thorough and many of them were forced to flee the country. Those who remained were at all times under close scrutiny by the agents of the court, a circumstance which made it extremely perilous to hold meetings for worship. In 1608, a scattered congregation of Separatists, under the pastoral leadership of John Robinson of Scrooby, in Nottinghamshire, found asylum in Amsterdam. There they met many persons of like persuasion who had also fled England to seek religious toleration. Robinson and his congregation, however, continued to the city of Leyden, where they decided to settle. After a decade, the congregation had adjusted to Dutch economic life and had developed into a large and influential organization. Still the people did not feel at home in Holland; and when they heard reports of colonization in America, their interests turned in that direction. Thus began the movement which culminated in the establishment of Plymouth Colony.

THE FOUNDING OF PLYMOUTH

As early as 1617, representatives of the Leyden congregation were in England seeking a patent from the king which would grant them certain lands in northern Virginia. Two years later a patent was procured from the Virginia Company, probably through the good offices of Sir Edwin Sandys, a member of its Council. But the patent was never used. Finally, in 1620, their hopes were realized through the efforts of Thomas Weston, a London businessman. A joint-stock company was formed with all profits from fishing, trading, and other pursuits during the first seven years being equally divided between the settlers and the financiers. King James was suspicious of the Separatists, but since their settlement promised to provide much-needed raw materials, he grudgingly gave his consent to the enterprise.

In July, 1620, the Pilgrims departed for Southampton, from whence they would journey to America. The majority of the congregation, among them John Robinson, remained behind, hoping to join the vanguard at a later date. William Brewster (c.1566–1644), a ruling elder, became the spiritual leader of the adventurers. Other leading men were William Bradford, John Carver, Miles Standish, and Edward Winslow. Some of the one hundred and two prospective settlers were non-Separatist, a fact which accounts for some later friction, even open hostility, among the emigrants.

Of the two vessels provided by the Company, only the Mayflower proved seaworthy for the Atlantic voyage. After weeks of delay, the ship set sail; on the eleventh of November the crew cast anchor in Cape Cod Harbor. There the Separatist majority, fearing trouble from the non-Separatists and desiring some basis for a stable government, decided to draw up the document known as the Mayflower Compact before disembarkment:

In ye name of God, Amen. We whose names are underwriten, the loyall subjects of our dread soveraigne Lord, King James, by ye grace of God, of Great Britaine, Franc & Ireland king, defender of ye faith, &c., haveing undertaken, for ye glorie of God, and advancemente of ye Christian faith, and honour of our king & countrie, a voyage to plant ye first colonie in ye Northerne part of Virginia, doe by these presents solemnly & mutualy in ye presence of God, and one of another, covenant & combine our selves togeather into a civill body politick, for our better ordering & preservation & furtherance of ye ends aforesaid; and by vertue hearof to enacte, constitute, and frame such just & equall lawes, ordinances, acts, constitutions & offices, from time to time, as shall be thought most meete & convenient for ye generall good of ye Colonie, unto which we promise all due submission and obedience. In witnes wherof we have hereunder subscribed our names at Cap-Codd ye 11 of November, in ye year of ye raigne of our soveraigne lord, King James, of England, France & Ireland ye eighteenth, and of Scotland ye fiftie fourth An^o: Dom. 1620.

This was the first step by American colonists in the direction of framing a constitution or fundamental law. The Compact remained the legal basis of government until 1691, when Plymouth Colony was merged with Massachusetts.

The most immediate problem facing the colonists was their legal position in New England, since their patent provided for settlement in Virginia. After a period of uncertainty and vacillation, they decided to land at Plymouth, despite their lack of legal status. Fortunately for them they were able to obtain a patent from the New England Company the following year.

From the outset the Separatists were determined to hold the reins of power in the new colony. The suffrage was extended only to the original landowners and orthodox freemen. These qualified persons selected a governor to be elected annually and a Council of Assistants. Government by consent was therefore only partially realized, the defense being that it was the only possible way of preserving orthodoxy. Even so, the Separatists were more tolerant than their Puritan contemporaries and admitted Anglican settlers to the colony.

There was almost constant tension with the London financiers. Having no real interest in the religious inclinations of the Separatists, they sought to people the colony with young men, irrespective of denominational affiliation, who would be economically most productive. Certainly they did not encourage the coming of John Robinson who, they feared, would create more problems than solutions. Thus the Pilgrims had no minister for several years and had to content themselves with the services of their elder, William Brewster. A well-educated and devout man, he had no power to administer the sacraments, but preached frequently and with notable effectiveness in the simple "meeting house" which was furnished with bare wooden benches. To the satisfaction of his congregation, he avoided lengthy homiletical discourses and involved prayers, except on "solemne days of humiliation" and other special occasions.

The height of Separatist dissatisfaction with the London financiers was reached in 1624, when the latter had the temerity to send as the first minister, John Lyford, an Anglican priest. To make matters worse, it was soon discovered that Lyford was involved in a plan to create a rival colony and church. The result was that he was expelled from the colony.

Soon afterward steps were taken to terminate the partnership with the London merchants. According to the terms of settlement, the colony was to pay the merchants one thousand eight hundred pounds and meet the company's six hundred pound obligation to its creditors. As soon as the colonists gained complete possession, they made plans to bring over the remainder of their friends in Leyden. Within the next few years this was accomplished. But Pastor Robinson was not among the immigrants; he died in the Netherlands in 1626.

Economic conditions in Plymouth Colony improved after 1624, and though the colonists never became wealthy, exports of lumber, corn, and furs brought relative prosperity. Through trading contacts with the Indians, the colonists gained the opportunity to evangelize and instruct the friendlier and more docile natives. These attempts, unfortunately, seldom led the Indian to more than a flirtatious connection with Christianity. Intermittent hostilities with the natives further served to cast a pall over the well-meaning but ineffectual missionary enterprise.

The coming of Ralph Smith, a Separatist minister, in 1629, was heralded by those colonists who held to the Brownist persuasion. His presence offered encouragement to the Separatist element which was finding it ever more difficult to hold the colony to its religious foundation and, with Governor Bradford, was bemoaning the fact that "so many wicked persons and profane people should so quickly come over." The arrival of Roger Williams in the summer of 1631 brought further comfort to the beleaguered saints. Though he received neither formal appointment nor stipend, Williams assisted Ralph Smith for a period of two years. Bradford evaluated him as "a man godly and zealous, having many precious parts, but very unsettled in judgmente." His opinion might have been more favorable had Williams not alienated the colonists by insisting that the king had no right to grant them their lands without a previous settlement with the Indians. As it was, a sense of relief came over the colony when Williams decided to depart for Salem.

Despite the inroads made by non-Separatists, Plymouth Colony remained relatively free of theological controversy. Part of the reason lay in the fact that the Brownists, because of doctrinal and social inclinations, did not have the same admiration for education as did the Puritans. Men wih a university education, such as Brewster and Williams, were few though highly influential in shaping public opinion. Their libraries reveal an acquaintance with the Reformed theologians and even many Renaissance authors. William Bradford's highly creditable *History of Plimoth Plantation* reflects not only classical learning but a decidedly theological point of view. He portrays the Pilgrims as Christian saints afflicted by the stratagems of Satan, who were sent by God to establish a colony on the principles of Jesus Christ.

Worship was designedly simple and unadorned with pageantry. The principal parts of worship were prayer and the reading and exposition of Scripture. According to the experience of John Winthrop in 1632, it was customary for visitors and members of the congregation to join their minister in the discussion of some religious matter at a Sunday afternoon service. All "popish" observances, such as the celebration of Christmas, were soundly condemned. As early as Christmas, 1621, Governor Bradford rebuked a group of non-Separatists for merry-making and directed them to stop "gameing or revelling in ye streets." But the Pilgrims were not without diversion. Their observance of Thanksgiving Day, intended for the glorification of God, was marked by feasting and entertainment.

The Separatists were strenuously opposed to levity and never more so than on May Day with its Maypole festivities. In 1627 Thomas Morton, an aristocratic, pleasure-loving Anglican lawyer, celebrated the day at Merry Mount in a manner which proved shocking to the saints. Bradford, who had nothing but contempt for the man, called him a "lord of misrule" and accused him of promoting "Athisme" and "lasciviousness" and providing the Indians with firearms. "They allso set up a Maypole, drinking and dancing aboute it many days togeather, inviting the Indean women, for their consorts, dancing and frisking togither (like so many fairies, or furies rather,) and worse practices." The embarrassing episode came to and end with Morton's enforced deportation to England.

With the establishment of Massachusetts Bay Colony and the rapid influx of Puritan settlers during the 1630's, Plymouth looked to the newer

Puritan colony for most of its gains in population. In the end, Plymouth became absorbed into Massachusetts Bay. For some time the Plymouth colonists endeavored to obtain a separate royal charter but, failing in this, were obliged in 1691 to accept incorporation with Massachusetts.

THE PURITAN SETTLEMENT AT MASSACHUSETTS BAY

In the meantime, the Puritans in the mother country were undergoing the severest disabilities. James I, becoming ever more militant in his opposition to Puritanism, forced through Parliament in 1621 measures which required that baptized persons be confirmed by bishops, that they kneel at Holy Communion, and that they observe the festivals of Catholic Christianity. Such arbitrary treatment of Parliament served only to make the House of Commons more sympathetic with the Puritans.

If James I had proved difficult, Charles I, who succeeded him in 1625, was impossible. John Buchan has not unfairly described him as "part woman, part priest, and partly the bewildered delicate boy who had never quite grown up." From the outset, he had been associated with that strong-willed Anglican, William Laud (1573–1645), who hated Calvinism and was determined that there should be no church without bishops. Charles appointed Laud bishop of the diocese of London, a move calculated to raise the ire of that Puritan stronghold. By 1633, Laud was Archbishop of Canterbury. At his insistence, Charles harshly enforced religious uniformity and thus found himself in conflict with the House of Commons. The situation became so bad that Charles even dismissed the House in 1629 and for eleven years governed without it. During these critical years many Puritans made the decision to come to America; those who remained prepared the way for the inevitable—civil war.

As early as 1623, a group of Dorchester businessmen had founded a company for fishing purposes and had established a base of operations at Gloucester. When the company failed, the Puritan minister of Dorchester, John White, conceived a plan whereby the settlement might become a haven for the poor and a center of missionary activity. Later the idea would be broadened to include the creation of a Puritan State. The plan was taken up by a group of prominent Puritans who organized the New England Company and obtained a sizeable grant of land from the Council of New England. The history of Massachusetts Bay Colony begins with the arrival at Salem of their agent, John Endicott, and his followers in 1628. There were a few settlers already there when he arrived, and these did what they could to prevent his settlement by refusing to submit to his authority. But the odds were against them and they finally had to bow in submission. During the next twelve years some twenty thousand colonists would follow Endicott to New England. Only a minority would be Puritans, but the control of the colony would be in their hands.

A charter incorporating the Massachusetts Bay Company was granted in 1629 by Charles I. The king doubtless would not have taken such action had he been able to foresee the results of creating "The Governor and Company of Massachusetts Bay" and conferring upon them the powers of self-government. The charter, of course, had nothing to say about matters ecclesiastical. Nor did the Company make any suggestions concerning the type of church to be set up in the colony. It was simply a trading company founded for the purpose of creating in America a colony of its own. Nevertheless, the company did make provision for ministerial support and decreed that "convenient churches" should be built, half of the expenses being paid by the colonists and the other half by the company. The settlers were permitted to choose their mode of church government.

In the spring of 1629, two non-Separatist Puritan ministers, Samuel Skelton and Francis Higginson, arrived at Salem and within a few months had organized a church with a congregational polity. The people of the congregation adopted a Confession of Faith and a Covenant, pledging themselves to God and His service. Then they proceeded to ordain Skelton as pastor and Higginson as teacher, although both had received episcopal ordination. Thus was born the first non-Separatist church in America to be governed by congregational polity.

For many years it was held that the Puritan Church in Massachusetts was originally Presbyterian in its government, changing to a Congregational pattern only after establishing contact with the Plymouth Separatists. It was thought that Dr. Samuel Fuller, a deacon in the Plymouth Church, especially influenced Governor Endicott and his followers to found their church on the pattern of Plymouth, but this view has been repudiated by the investigations of Professor Perry Miller. He has shown that both the Puritans and Pilgrims were Congregationalists upon their arrival in America, the difference being that the former were non-Separatists.

Puritans and Pilgrims differed not only in their attitudes toward the church establishment but also in their views concerning the monarchy. The Puritans preferred to have a state without a monarch and worked persistently against the king. The Pilgrims totally rejected the Anglican Church but gave full allegiance to their sovereign. This dissimilarity was sharply delineated in a remark attributed to Francis Higginson as he beheld the shores of England disappear over the horizon:

We will not say as the Separatists were wont to say at their leaving of England, 'Farewel, Babylon! Farewel, Rome!' but we will say, Farewel, dear England! Farewel the Church of God in England, and all Christian friends there! We do not go to New England as Separatists from the Church of England;

though we cannot but separate from the corruptions in it, but we go to practise the positive part of church reformation and propagate the gospel in America.[1]

The "positive part of church reformation" did not include freedom of conscience or toleration. Religious liberty was no more a part of the seventeenth century Puritan vocabulary than it was of the Anglican or Roman Catholic. In their first confession of faith, the Massachusetts Bay Puritans included an article which banned all diversity and conferred certain powers upon magistrates in matters of religion. Endicott soon applied this provision in the case of John and Samuel Browne. These brothers, though Puritans, still favored the Anglican Church and its liturgy in many ways, and instituted a worship service of their own, using the Book of Common Prayer. Endicott summarily dispatched them to England.

The year 1630 witnessed the arrival in New England of seventeen ships carrying a thousand colonists. At once new settlements sprang up at Charlestown, Newtown, and Boston. There would be a significant increase in immigration as the decade progressed so that by 1640 the colony would number some twenty thousand settlers. Most important to the affairs of the colony was the arrival of the Charter in 1630. A group of emigrants had been able to gain its possession through the purchase of all the Massachusetts Bay Company's stock. Their removal of the Charter to America enabled them to establish a government of their own, without reference to a company in England or to the king. Most prominent in the group was John Winthrop, a man so widely respected for his fine mind and sterling character that he was asked to accept the governorship in America. During the nineteen years he spent in New England, he was chosen governor twelve times.

A definite step in the direction of a church establishment was made by the first General Court, which convened in May, 1631. At that session one hundred and ten people applied for admission as "Freemen." They took the oath of allegiance; but the court, fearing the outcome of so many people being given the franchise, passed the following rule: "It is ordered and agreed, that, for the time to come, noe man shall be admitted to the freedome of this body polliticke, but such as are members of some of the Churches within the lymitts of the same." This ruling, which ran counter to the terms of the Charter, was justified by the court on the ground that government must remain in the hands of "honest and good men." It has been estimated that by 1665, when the restriction was eased to a certain extent, the voteless residents outnumbered the freemen in the ratio of five to one. Apparently the desire to vote did not cause many to forsake

[1] Cotton Mather, *Magnalia Christi Americana* (Hartford, 1855), I, 362.

their religious convictions in order to obtain a certificate of good and regular standing in a Congregational church.

In 1636 an act of the General Court gave magistrates power over the churches. This was done to assure uniformity and to prevent all differences in ecclesiastical polity. Each congregation was free to use the ordinances of God according to the direction of Scripture, and could elect and ordain its officers on the condition that they were "able, pious, and orthodox." The act decreed: "This Court doeth not, nor will hereafter, approve of any such companyes of men as shall henceforthe ioyne in any pretended way of Church fellowship, without they shall first acquaint the magistrates and the elders of the greater part of the Churches in this jurisdiction with their intentions, and have their approbation herein."

The General Court took upon itself the function of investigating all persons who attempted to preach and forbade anyone to preach before an unauthorized society. In 1650, a Mr. Matthews was fined ten pounds for preaching in an unapproved church. This action was based on a court resolution of 1641, which held that "the civil authority . . . hath power and liberty to seek the peace, ordinances, and rules of Christ observed in every Church, according to His word. . . . It is the duty of the Christian magistrate to take care that his people be fed with wholesome and sound doctrine." The court further declared that no one should regularly preach or be ordained as a teaching elder if any two churches, the Council of State, or the General Court should declare him unworthy.

In 1668, the General Court decreed that "the Christian magistrate is bound by the word of God to preserve the peace, order, and liberty of the Churches of Christ, and by all due means to promote religion in doctrine and discipline." The choice of a minister was still in the hands of the people, but a law of 1692 provided that the county court should "take care that no town is destitute of a minister." In case there was a vacancy and the church neglected to call a minister, the court could appoint one and tax the town for his support.

Legislation was enacted to cover even matters of doctrine. The Act Against Heresy of 1646 decreed the banishment of anyone who denied the immortality of the soul, the resurrection, sin in the regenerate, redemption by Christ, justification through Christ, or the baptism of infants. Punishment was also prescribed for those who held either the Scriptures or the minister in contempt. The failure to attend services of worship was punishable by a fine of five shillings; to reject any of the books of the Bible could result in whipping, a fine, or even banishment. The violation of a law passed in 1697 against "Blasphemy and Atheism" might lead to imprisonment for six months, the pillory, whipping, boring the tongue with a hot iron, and sitting on the gallows with a rope about one's neck.

Dissenters of any kind were as welcome as a northeaster. The Reverend

Nathaniel Ward (1578–1652) summed up the mind of most Puritans when he wrote: "I dare take upon me, to be the Herauld of *New-England* so farre, as to proclaime to the world, in the name of our Colony, that all Familists, Antinomians, Anabaptists, and other Enthusiasts, shall have free Liberty to keep away from us, and such as will come to be gone as fast as they can, the sooner the better." The late difficulties with Roger Williams, Anne Hutchinson, Samuel Gorton, and others, the discussion of which belongs to a later chapter, doubtless inspired him to write in this vein. Nor were Roman Catholics permitted to settle in the colony. A special law was enacted in 1647 to keep out the Jesuits, who were considered very dangerous. It ordered that any who might come should be banished; and if they returned, they should be put to death. This law was applied as late as 1700.

In 1641, the General Court adopted a code drawn up by Nathaniel Ward entitled the "Body of Liberties." This legal document bears the influence not only of English law but of the Old Testament. Its chief interest for the historian of religion is its regulation concerning the forming of a church. "All the people of god within this Jurisdiction, who are not in a church way, and be orthodox in Judgement and not scandalous in life, shall have full libertie to gather themselves into a Church Estaite. Provided they doe it in a Christian way, with due observation of the rules of Christ revealed in his word." This was only a short step toward liberty, for it was perfectly possible for a magistrate to decide that a non-Congregational form of polity was in conflict with the rules of Christ. Still there was a growing disposition to permit freedom of worship to Presbyterians. Many thought that the "Body of Liberties" would settle many of the civil and ecclesiastical problems of Massachusetts. So convinced of this was the Reverend John Cotton, that learned teacher of the Boston church, that he wrote: "The order of the Churches and the Commonwealth is now so settled in New England by common consent, that it brings to mind the new heaven and the new earth wherein dwelleth righteousness."

While the Massachusetts Bay Colony purported to be a Christian state, its government was not by the clergy. To be sure, the ministers of the establishment could not help but attain a wide influence in community life. The magistrates would seek their advice on the most trivial matters, and by this means the clergy gained considerable power in civil affairs. They were well-educated, God-fearing men, and their advice was generally the best available in the colony; but they had no official role in government. The magistrates, on the other hand, did have official powers over the congregations, and they used them to the full limit of their office. Thus there is some justification for the judgment that the Massachusetts Bay Colony was not so much theocratic as Erastian.

THE PLANTING OF OTHER PURITAN COLONIES

The continuing pressure of immigration together with the strait-laced policies of the Puritan authorities persuaded many a newly arrived settler to seek his fortune in another colony. Not all who left Massachusetts Bay were discontented with the prevailing situation; clearly that was the case with the founders of New Haven. Most of the newer Puritan colonies, however, could trace their origins to some religious or political altercation in Massachusetts. The settlers fanned out along the coast and the inland waterways, establishing such colonies as Connecticut, New Hampshire, and New Haven, and migrating even to the northern coast of Long Island and northern New Jersey.

As early as 1633, the Dutch had established a trading post in Connecticut on the present site of Hartford. About the same time traders from Plymouth became interested in the area, and their glowing reports of the lands in the Connecticut River valley prompted a number of settlers in Massachusetts to migrate southward. In the winter of 1634–1635, colonists from Watertown founded Wethersfield. Within two years, settlers from Dorchester and Newton had established communities at Windsor and Hartford.

The principal leader of the movement was Thomas Hooker (1586–1647), the minister of the church at Newton. One of the most brilliant and eloquent of Puritan divines, he had been a prominent figure in England. When the pressure of persecution had become unbearable, he had fled to Holland and thence to New England. Apparently there was some unpleasantness with the Massachusetts authorities when Hooker proposed to lead his people to Hartford. Undaunted by the opposition, he pressed on to Connecticut and became the most powerful personage in the colony.

A plan of government was adopted in 1639 known as the "Fundamental Orders of Connecticut." It reveals no major departure from the system in Massachusetts, but manifests originality by omitting any religious test for citizenship. Hooker believed that the basis of authority should be the will of the people and that public officials should be chosen by the citizenry. It is sometimes supposed that, through the "Fundamental Orders," Hooker was enunciating a thoroughly democratic philosophy. In reality, his views were quite in harmony with those of other orthodox Puritans. Certainly he had no intention of allowing persons without social status to participate in government. Only those persons in the towns who held sufficient property, possessed a good character, and believed in religion, were permitted to vote for local officials and deputies to the General Court. The general affairs of the colony were in the hands of "freemen," who were elected to that status by the court. Probably not more than one-third of the colony's male adults were so classified.

Meanwhile, another migration to Connecticut had begun in 1638, when a band of Puritans who had landed in Massachusetts the previous year sailed from Boston to the coast of Connecticut and there founded the colony of New Haven. Their leaders were the Reverend John Davenport, who had been obliged to quit his London parish during the period of persecution initiated by Archbishop Laud, and Theophilus Eaton, a wealthy merchant who became the first governor. They had no charter or patent for the land; but through a treaty with the Quinnipiack Indians, they gained certain territories and within a few years had established several towns. Some seventy of these colonists met in June, 1639, for the purpose of organizing a government and founding a church. They drew up a "Plantation covenant" which recognized the Bible as the supreme rule in both civil and religious affairs. Their system of government followed the pattern of Massachusetts, including the requirement that church membership be prerequisite to the exercise of the suffrage. In 1644, the General Court ruled that the "judicial laws of God as they were declared by Moses" should be authoritative for all courts "till they be branched out into particulars hereafter." The effects of this decision can be seen in that series of harsh enactments known as the "Blue laws."

The New Haven colony flourished and soon other independent towns, such as Milford, Stamford, and Guilford, sprang up nearby. These four towns drew together under one government in 1643. Finally the colony was attached to Connecticut, according to the terms of the royal charter of 1662. A vigorous protest was raised by the New Haven settlers, but by 1665 they had assented to the union. In the united Colony of Connecticut no religious test was required for the suffrage.

The first serious efforts at colonization in New Hampshire and Maine were made by proprietors, notably Sir Ferdinando Gorges and John Mason, as early as the 1620's. Puritan Massachusetts was particularly inimical to Gorges and his associates because of their Anglicanism and promptly extended its influence to these areas. Both territories fell under the control of the Bay Colony, the union with Maine lasting until the nineteenth century. New Hampshire became a separate royal province in 1679; but during most of the years before 1741, it shared the same governor with Massachusetts. Religious exiles as well as Puritans settled these northern territories, adding to the disparity of religious views. Exeter, New Hampshire, for example, was founded by the Reverend John Wheelwright, who had been exiled from Massachusetts for his antinomian teaching that assurance of salvation was to be sought in the witness of the Holy Spirit and not in one's good works.

The bitterly fought Pequot War between settlers and Indians in 1637 clearly demonstrated the need for cooperation between the colonists in order to ward off common danger. After much discussion the colonies of Massachusetts, Plymouth, Connecticut, and New Haven founded the New England Confederation in 1643. This federal union was to be a "firm and perpetual league of friendship and amity, for offence and defence, mutual advice and succor upon all just occasions, both for preserving and propagating the truth and liberties of the gospel, and for their own mutual safety and welfare." Uniformity in religion was a requirement for membership in the confederation, the request of Rhode Island for admission being repeatedly denied because of its dissimilar religious beliefs and practices. The union, unfortunately, never proved to be very effectual and few mourned its dissolution in 1684. On the other hand, it did promote a tendency toward union and helped to prepare the colonial mind for further cooperative enterprises during the eighteenth century.

RELIGIOUS THOUGHT AND LIFE

The crowning glory of New England Puritanism was its vigorous intellectual activity. Other sects might eschew learning beyond the elementary level as unnecessary for the understanding of Scripture; but the Puritan ministers expected their people to comprehend the intricacies of an elaborate theological system. Their sermons are studded with gems of philosophical and theological speculation, skillfully drawn together and summarized with deftness and penetrating insight. How much they penetrated the minds of the listeners is conjectural. But Increase Mather, the most prominent minister in the second generation of New Englanders, thought it well to exhort his parishioners concerning the sin of "Sleeping at Sermons."

The theology of the New England Puritans was basically the modified Calvinism of the English dissenters. Its roots were laid in the Bible, especially as it was expounded by Augustine and John Calvin. Philosophically, it was grounded in the teachings of the Cambridge Platonists, who in turn were deeply indebted to Petrus Ramus (1515–1572), a French Calvinist trained in humanism. Through his denunciation of Aristotle and his development of a Platonic system, he had provided Puritanism with a rational, philosophical foundation and had enabled it to escape any reliance upon the individualistic "inner light" doctrines of certain other Protestant sects.

The Puritan God was a mysterious, incomprehensible Being, entirely beyond the realm of human understanding. Nevertheless, an imperfect description of God's nature might be obtained through reasoning out His attributes or representing the divine essence in finite conceptual terms. The Puritan deduced that the Deity was eternal, perfect, unchangeable, creative, holy, wise, just, and merciful, the sum of all His attributes. Most important of all, God was sovereign, the supreme ruler of the universe. The world exists because God created and sustains it. If He should terminate His creative activity, the world would lapse into nothingness. Everything depended upon the divine providence which guides all things to their appointed end.

At the center of Puritan theology stood a God who controlled all events according to His eternal arbitrary purpose. Every circumstance of life, however nonsensical from man's purview, was decreed by God. It was for man to accept and not to fathom the divine logic. All that man needed to know about the divine will was revealed by God in the Scriptures, the final rule in all matters of faith and life. For the Puritan, the Bible was a book of law, an infallible text which was authoritative not only for the religious life but for the social and political order. His duty, as a follower of the law, was to promote its observance in society through exhortation and, if necessary, by force.

While Puritan thought pronounced the world to be good since it was a creation of God, it found man to be tragically depraved. This unfortunate state came about through the curse of original sin transmitted through Adam, the federal representative of the human race, and through man's innate desire to sin. In true Augustinian fashion, the Puritan subscribed to the dictum, "In Adam's fall, we sinned all." Though weighed down with sinful propensities, man possessed faculties of reason and will which were free enough to render him responsible for his action. God, through His covenant with the human race, made the terms of salvation so reasonable and clear that no rational being could be excused for violating them. And yet God alone could perform the wonderful work of regeneration, restoring His image to the soul and its faculties. He alone could bestow grace upon whomsoever He chose for salvation. Such saving grace wrought a magical change in man's nature as well as his status; it empowered him to perform the works of righteousness.

The Puritan's meat was to be the willing servant of God. It was at once the sign of his election in the covenant of grace and the indication of his response to God's reasonable covenant. Since he had no way of knowing God's eternal plan for his life, he had to depend upon an analysis of his own thoughts and deeds in order to judge his spiritual standing. Through a slavish keeping of diaries, he recorded the testimony of his conscience from year to year as if it might be of help in charting his spiritual progress. Far from being antinomian, he stressed the place of good works and literally hurled himself into the task of building the Kingdom of God, which he saw to be society's chief purpose. At the same time, he saw that this purpose could be realized only if government were in the hands of the elect. To that end, he labored to create a society controlled by the regenerate and dedicated to keeping the divine law. The Puritan state would be founded upon a social compact with God.

The heart of Puritan ecclesiastical theory was the church covenant. The church was a company of regenerate persons who had met together and satisfied one another of their Christian experience and who had voluntarily covenanted together to do God's will. Authority was derived from the membership of saints, but was delegated to the pastors, teachers, elders, and deacons, who were the responsible officers of the church. Outside the church membership were the unregenerate inhabitants of the community. They could not participate in either church or civil affairs but were expected to attend services of worship, conduct themselves in an approved manner, and to contribute to the support of the church. Thus was preserved the rulership of the redeemed—a prerequisite to the establishment of the Kingdom.

Since this world was continually a place of temptation, the Puritan had to be constantly on his guard, lest he be found cavorting with the "Divel." His only security lay in following a rigid pattern of personal conduct. Moreover, his time was God's time; it was sinful to fritter it away on inanities. The Puritan colonies, therefore, passed laws from time to time against mixed dancing, playing cards, shuffleboard or bowling, making minced pies, and celebrating Christmas. Regulations for the observance of the Sabbath were particularly stringent. A Massachusetts law of 1653 made it illegal to travel, clean house, cook, or even to take a walk on Sunday. Such legislation must have proved a source of irritation to a great many of the settlers who had no particular religious inclinations. To the saints, it was a way of stamping out sin and redeeming the com· munity.

If the practice of the Puritan ethic did not approximate the ideal, it was not surprising. Pleasure has its enticements, even for the ascetic. Many a Puritan, the austere and sedate Cotton Mather included, imbibed freely; taverns offered flowing refreshment, smoking, and dancing, and almost any bookseller kept a stock of playing cards. Election day, a popular occasion in New England, became as noted for its "spirits" as its spirituality. Nor did the Ten Commandments remain inviolate. Every community had to reckon with the grosser sins of the flesh, a circumstance which brought keen embarrassment to the righteous.

At the center of Puritan community life stood the meetinghouse; the early Puritans would not call it church since it was used for town meetings and other secular purposes as well as public worship. At first it was usually a plain rectangular building without steeple or tower, placed at the center of town. But as the tendency to think of the meetinghouse as a church developed, so did appreciation of beauty in architecture. Later edifices were patterned after English styles, especially those of Sir Christopher Wren, with majestic square towers rising from the ground at the front of the edifices. The interior was customarily severe and uninviting. The sanctuary, which was uncommonly cold in winter, was filled with high square pews. These were assigned according to rank and purchased by the worshippers. Two pews in front faced the congregation, and were reserved for the elders and deacons. On the side, high above the pews, stood the pulpit.

Worship was simple, unadorned, edifying, and protracted. When the principal service began at nine o'clock in the morning, the people stood for a long prayer, during which the minister poured out a catalogue of his thoughts. Then followed the reading and exposition of Scripture. The emphasis fell upon the sermon, which generally lasted about one hour, though on occasion it might be stretched to two or three. Most congregations were fortunate in having outstanding preachers, distinguished men of learning who could expound on almost any subject—and usually did. A shorter prayer after the sermon closed the service. In addition to two Sunday services, there was a weekly afternoon meeting which featured an exposition of Scripture by the minister. The Lord's Supper was celebrated once a month, but as a memorial rather than a sacrament.

Congregational psalm-singing was a distinctive feature of Puritan worship. For many years the people sang *a cappella* because their leaders could find no warrant for musical instruments in the New Testament. It became necessary for an elder or deacon to pitch the tune and direct the singing. This arrangement left much to be desired, judging from the cacophonous sounds that sometimes were emitted by the worshippers. Metrical psalmody was, nevertheless, possessed of much beauty and capable of raising varied religious emotions when properly rendered. The Plymouth Separatists brought with them from the Netherlands a Psalm book prepared in 1612 by Henry Ainsworth. More famous was the Bay Psalm Book authored for Puritan use by Thomas Weld, John Eliot, and Richard Mather. It was published in 1640, the first book to be printed in the American colonies, and immediately replaced the older Sternhold and Hopkins version. The following rendition of the familiar Twenty-third Psalm reveals something of its literary merits and deficiencies:

> The Lord to mee a shepheard is, want therefore shall not I.
> 2   Hee in the folds of tender-grasse, doth cause mee downe to lie:
> To waters calme me gently leads   (3)   Restore my soule doth hee:
>   he doth in paths of righteousness: for his names sake leade mee.
> 4   Yea though in valley of deaths shade I walk, none ill I'le feare:
>   because thou art with mee, thy rod, and staffe my comfort are.
> 5   For mee a table thou hast spread, in presence of my foes:
>   thou dost annoynt my head with oyle, my cup it over-flowes.
> 6   Goodnes & mercy surely shall all my dayes follow mee:
>   and in the Lords house I shall dwell so long as dayes shall bee.[2]

The Puritan zeal for learning was reflected in the early and rapid rise of educational institutions, founded primarily for the training of clergy. This was a necessary course of action since the Puritans, unlike the Anglicans, could not look to England for a steady recruitment of ministers. There was also a desire to transmit to the next generation the stimulating

[2] Quoted in P. Miller and T. Johnson, *The Puritans* (American, c. 1938), 557.

spirit of the Renaissance, which many of the New England intelligentsia had received at Cambridge. These interests bore fruit in the establishment of Harvard College, the first college in English America. In 1636, the Massachusetts General Court voted four hundred pounds for the founding of a college. This grant was augmented two years later through a bequest by John Harvard, a minister at Charlestown, of his library and half his estate. That same year Harvard College opened at Cambridge. Nathaniel Eaton, the first teacher, proved to be something of a disappointment; in Cotton Mather's opinion he "was fitter to be master of a Bridewel than a Colledge." Henry Dunster, who became the school's master in 1640, sustained a more commendable record. A tract entitled *New Englands First Fruits*, published in London in 1643, described him as "a learned conscionable and industrious man, who hath so trained up, his Pupills in the tongues and Arts, and so seasoned them with the principles of Divinity and Christianity, that we have to our great comfort, (and in truth) beyond our hopes, beheld their progresse in Learning and godlinesse also . . ." In 1642, Dunster graduated his first class of nine scholars. He resigned his post in 1654 upon becoming a Baptist, but under his successors the school continued to prosper. By 1686, it had trained one hundred twenty-two men for the ministry and a lesser number for other pursuits.

Elementary education was also a pressing concern. A Massachusetts law of 1642 required parents to teach their children reading and writing so as to insure their ability to read the Scriptures. Five years later, the first steps were taken to require free elementary instruction in the towns. Education had a strongly theological bent as can be seen by the title of John Cotton's popular catechism of 1646: *Milk for Babes, Drawn Out of the Breasts of Both Testaments.*

The literary productiveness of the New England savants was phenomenal. Scores of sermons, pamphlets, and theological books streamed from the presses and found wide circulation. The Puritan philosophy of history, which saw the hand of God in every event, was ably presented in such representative works as William Bradford's *History of Plimouth Plantation*, Edward Johnson's *Wonder-Working Providence*, and Cotton Mather's *Magnalia Christi Americana*. Poetry, too, was nurtured in New England. Much of it was theology in verse, ponderous and morbid, as in Michael Wigglesworth's *Day of Doom* (1662). Conversely, the following stanza by Anne Bradstreet reveals a flash of inspiration:

> When I behold the heavens as in their prime,
> And then the earth (though old) stil clad in green,
> The stones and trees, insensible of time,
> Nor age nor wrinkle on their front are seen;
> If winter come, and greeness then do fade,

A Spring returns, and they more youthfull made;
But Man grows old, lies down, remains where once he's laid.[3]

Despite its preoccupation with learning, the New England mind was gripped by a superstitious fear of the supernatural. This was an inheritance from old Europe, where widespread popular belief in the occult led to a number of witchcraft trials in which hundreds of persons accused of conspiracy with the devil were put to death. In America, witchcraft hysteria could be found in most of the colonies, but only in New England were convicted witches executed. And there the epidemic was mild in comparison with the European mania. The unfortunate episode began in 1647, with the hanging of a witch at Windsor, Connecticut. Shortly thereafter executions took place at Charlestown, Massachusetts, and Hartford, Connecticut. Before the craze ceased for a time in 1663, eight victims had been hanged in Connecticut and six in Massachusetts.

The publication in 1684 of the Reverend Increase Mather's *An Essay for the Recording of Illustrious Providences* prepared the way for a witchhunt of more frightening proportions. The pestilence broke out again in 1688 and lasted until October, 1692. In Salem, two West Indian slaves stirred up latent fears through their tales of voodooism. When a group of young girls began to show signs of demon possession and accused their neighbors of being in league with Satan, the Inquisition began. The governor appointed a special court, one of its members being the revered Samuel Sewall, to hear the cases. The mantle of doom fell upon many a blameless and God-fearing person; even George Burroughs, a minister, became a victim of the terror. By the autumn of 1692 a score of persons and two dogs had been executed as witches and two hundred others stood under accusation. But when the finger of incrimination came to be pointed at certain influential citizens, Governor Phips brought the trials to an abrupt end. The Reverend Increase Mather, in a statement which came too late, advised extreme caution in judging alleged witches; but the clergy had already become publicly discredited for their part in the affair. Judge Samuel Sewall's belated confession of guilt, made openly in Old South Church five years later, was a fitting termination of one of the most shameful eras in New England history.

INDIANS AND NEGROES IN ZION

The New England Puritan was always something of an optimist. He believed that God had chosen him to build in the New World a redeemed society. Theoretically, this society extended to the Indians, who were considered ideal prospects for mass conversion. The charter of the Massachusetts Bay Colony rather fancifully depicted an Indian crying, "Come

[3] *Ibid.,* 567.

over and help us," as if the Puritans were his last white hope. In practice, the average Puritan regarded the aborigines as objects to be pitied, more frequently despised. He saw them as ignorant, shiftless, depraved savages; he saw them as things and only potentially as men. Some efforts were made to convert as well as to exploit the natives, but the missionary endeavors met with little success. Gradually the idea that the Indian belonged to an inferior and accursed race came to prevail, justifying his liquidation or enslavement by the colonists. When the Pequot War of 1637 came to an end, some of the Indian prisoners were enslaved by the settlers, while others were turned over to the Narragansett tribe or sent to the West Indies to be sold into bondage. These acts met with the overwhelming approval of the clergy, who were themselves not averse to keeping slaves.

If experience taught some English settlers to despise the Indian, it prompted others to seek his immediate conversion. In 1643, the Reverend Thomas Mayhew, Jr., began to labor among the Indians dwelling at Martha's Vineyard. By 1650, he had converted one hundred Indians to Christianity. The tragic news of his untimely death at sea seven years later, while on a voyage to England to solicit funds for his mission, brought the entire island into a state of mourning. His father, the governor of Martha's Vineyard, carried on the work effectively for more than twenty years. Shortly before the governor's demise, John Mayhew, one of his grandsons, became pastor and devoted much of his time to Indian missions. John Mayhew was succeeded by his son, Experience (1673–1758), who performed a prodigious work. Because of his close familiarity with the Indian language, he was able to produce highly accurate translations of the Psalms and the Gospel according to John. His book, *Indian Converts* (1727), is one of the most informative treatments of early Indian missions.

The most recognized among the Puritan missionaries of the first generation has been John Eliot (1604–1690), the "Apostle to the Indians." Educated at Cambridge, he assisted for a time at First Church after his arrival in Boston in 1631. The following year he became teacher at the Roxbury Church and remained there until his death. Feeling called to minister to the Indians, he became proficient in their language and then proceeded to translate the Ten Commandments and the Lord's Prayer, with the help of an Indian who understood English. In 1646, he began to preach to the Indians at nearby Nonantun in their own dialect. The Massachusetts government was so impressed by Eliot's success with the natives that certain lands were set aside for Christian Indian settlements. Several villages of "praying Indians" were established under the direction of Eliot and his fellow missionaries in the neighborhood of Boston. Most of the converts came from relatively weak tribes dwelling between the territories of the powerful and pugnacious Mohegans and Narragansetts.

Eliot's brilliant insight into Indian missionary problems becomes per-
spicuous in a report which he made in 1670:

In as much as now we have ordained *Indian Officers* unto the Ministry of the
Gospel, it is needful to add a word or two of Apology: I find it hopeless to expect *English* Officers in our *Indian* Churches; the work is full of hardship, hard
labour, and chargeable also, and the *Indians* not yet capable to give considerable support and maintenance; and Men have bodies, and must live of the Gospel: And what comes from England is liable to hazard and uncertainties. On
such grounds as these partly, but especially from the secret wise governance
of Jesus Christ, the Lord of the Harvest, there is no appearance of hope for
their souls feeding in that way: they must be trained up to be able to live of
themselves in the ways of the Gospel of Christ; and through the riches of God's
Grace and Love, sundry of themselves who are expert in the Scriptures, are able
to teach each other. . . .[4]

Eliot rendered a lasting service to the cause of Indian missions by trans-
lating the Bible and other religious works into the regional dialect of the
Algonquian tongue. In 1653, he published a *Catechism*, the first book to
be printed in the Indian language. The first edition of the New Testament
was issued in 1661; the Old Testament appeared two years later. There
can be little doubt that these literary achievements had a salutary effect
on the numerical growth of the missions. The fact that in 1675 there were
fourteen settlements of "praying Indians" and twenty-four congregations
in the area was due in large measure to the efforts of John Eliot and his
associates.

The work of missions went not without assistance from the mother
country. The circulation of several tracts, among them Eliot's *The Day-
Breaking if not the Sun-Rising of the Gospell with the Indians in New
England* (1647) and Thomas Shepard's *The Cleare Sunshine of the
Gospell Breaking Forth Upon the Indians in New England* (1648), ex-
cited the interest of the public. Through an act of the Long Parliament,
"The President and Society for the Propagation of the Gospell in New
England" was incorporated in 1649. The purpose of the society was to
raise funds to provide Christian literature and certain basic necessities
for the Indians and to pay the salaries of missionaries. Its efforts gave
added stimulus to Eliot's missions and to the Mayhew mission at Martha's
Vineyard. The society's charter was annulled with the Restoration of
1660, but a new one was granted the following year to a society which
bore a similar name and function.

King Philip's War (1675–1676), which originated in a mass Indian
uprising, took a heavy toll before the Indian power was broken. Most of
the Christian Indians remained at peace, but the resentment which was

[4] Mode, *op. cit.*, 525.

naturally evoked by the war caused a setback in the missionary enterprise. Christian work was still carried on, though in the face of greater obstacles. Many of the Indian congregations began to lose their identity as a result of interracial marriages which led to the absorption of the Indian into the Negro community. Not until the Great Awakening would there be another noteworthy advance in the cause of Indian missions.

Although the first cargoes of Negro slaves arrived in New England as early as 1676, it is certain that Negroes were in Connecticut before 1650. They were used primarily as domestic servants. By the end of the seventeenth century there were probably a thousand such slaves in the Puritan colonies. Slavery in New England did not flourish, however, largely because it was not profitable. The principal need was for skilled labor, a need which could not be met by the African savage. A slave who could perform the simple tasks involved in raising tobacco would be virtually useless as a blacksmith, carpenter, weaver, or seaman. There seems to have been no public sentiment against the institution of slavery on moral or religious grounds. Many of the clergy owned slaves and justified the practice as consistent with Scripture. That the institution waned and finally disappeared from New England was due more to economic than religious reasons.

THE WEAKENING OF THE FOUNDATIONS

It is an impressive albeit sobering fact that by 1643 only eleven per cent of the people of Massachusetts held citizenship. Since many of the non-citizens were wealthy and influential, it was only natural that they should have made many attempts to broaden the franchise. In 1646, a group of liberal thinkers headed by Dr. Robert Child petitioned the General Court to extend the franchise to all Englishmen who were "quiet, peaceable, and forward with heart, hand, and purse to promote the public good," and "allow divers sober, righteous, and godly men, members of the Church of England, to be taken into your congregation and to enjoy with you all the liberties and ordinances Christ hath purchased," or else be granted freedom to found churches of their own.

The court promptly ordered the petitioners to appear before it and accused them of making "contemtuous and seditious expressions." It rejected the petition and demanded an apology from its authors. They refused to do this, and so were fined. When some of them tried to carry their complaint to England through a statement signed by twenty-five men, their paper was seized and its signers were fined. Finally, in 1647, the complaint reached the mother country in the form of a pamphlet entitled "New England's Jonas Cast-Up at London." The English authorities took no action.

In the meantime, the General Court had thought it wise to call a synod of the churches in order to strengthen the defenses of the old system. Some of the ministers objected, stating that the court had no right to call a synod. In Boston, about thirty or forty persons asserted the right of the churches to meet in synod without the interference of the magistrates. The court, anxious for the meeting to be held, compromised by directing that "the call should be drawn up in the form of a motion and not of command," and addressed also to the churches of Plymouth, New Haven, and Connecticut. This satisfied everyone but the Bostonians, but they too were finally persuaded to send representatives. The synod met at Cambridge in September, 1646, and laid down plans for procedure. A second session was held in June, 1647, but after a few days it adjourned because of an epidemic and did not meet again until August, 1648. At its final session, the Cambridge Synod adopted the Westminster Confession, a Presbyterian symbol which was then the doctrinal standard of the Church of England, and a church polity based on the plan advocated by Henry Barrowe. These actions were set forth in the well-known "Cambridge Platform."

During the years 1640 to 1660, there was growing discontent among the populace with the repressive nature of the governmental system and disgust with the intolerance of the ministers and secular authorities. Dissent served only to make those in power more outspoken in their condemnation of nonconformity. Nathaniel Ward's *The Simple Cobler of Aggawam in America* (1647) offers an adequate presentation of conservative opinion: ". . . God doth no where in his word tolerate Christian States, to give Tolerations to such adversaries of his Truth, if they have power in their hands to prevent them. . . . My heart hath naturally detested . . . Tolerations of divers Religions, or of one Religion in segregant shapes . . ."

The success of the people and Parliament of England in their efforts to gain greater freedom and more representation had made an impression on the people of Massachusetts. They were troubled that there was now more freedom in England than in the Bay Colony. Malcontents who had been denied the vote were horrified at the thought of being more restricted in New England than they would have been at home. It was inevitable that the future should bring an ever-increasing disharmony.

For many years the Puritans had taught that the church consists of those who give proof of their regeneration, together with their children. The children were thought to be saints because they shared the covenant with their parents. But many of these children upon attaining maturity failed to have a conversion experience and so made no public profession of faith. In a sense, they were members of the church, yet it seemed questionable as to whether they could be admitted to the Lord's Supper. The problem became more acute when this unconverted second generation presented their children for baptism. If these children were permitted to receive it and be considered as church members upon reaching maturity, then the concept of the true church would have to be altered. If they were not considered members, then they could neither vote nor hold public office. In a colony where the voteless majority was becoming larger year by year, this was a matter of legitimate concern.

In 1657, the Ministerial Convention accepted a solution which provided that unregenerate members might transmit church membership and baptism to their children, but their progeny could neither partake of the Lord's Supper nor participate in church elections. This compromise, known as the Half-Way Covenant, was finally approved by a synod of the churches in 1662. The synod agreed that "the infant seed of confederate visible believers are members of the same Church with their parents and, when grown up, are personally under the watch, discipline, and government of the Church." Church members could request baptism for their children if they were "admitted in minority, understanding the doctrines of the faith, and publicly professing their assent thereto; not scandalous in life, and solemnly owning the covenant, wherein they give themselves to the government of Christ in the Church."

The Half-Way Covenant was accepted but not without opposition. When the synod reported its findings to the General Court, the opponents of the measure sprang into action. Most vigorous in their denunciation of the Half-Way Covenant were President Charles Chauncy of Harvard, John Davenport of New Haven, and Increase Mather of Boston. Their debate with the proponents of the measure continued for a number of years, though ultimately the declaration was accepted by a majority of the churches.

The passage of the Half-Way Covenant came to be regarded by many as an invitation to further laxity. In certain areas church membership was granted to any individual who would promise to lead an ethical life. The result was that during the 1660's a decline in religious zeal was evident throughout New England. Soon the advisability of admitting half-way church members to the Lord's Supper was being discussed. In 1677, Solomon Stoddard, pastor of the church at Northampton, began to allow unconverted church members to partake of the sacrament because it might serve as a means by which they would become converted. After that time the practice became known as Stoddardeanism. It came to be widely accepted throughout western Massachusetts. Spiritual vitality, nevertheless, continued to wane and the number of members in full communion with the church to decline. To many it seemed that the judgment of God was being poured out upon a sinful people.

The calling of the Synod in 1679 was a movement in the direction of reform. The delegates seem to have understood where the problems lay, judging from their report. They spoke feelingly of the curse of worldliness and the "great and visible decay of the power of Godliness." Their admonition to the people was to effect a solemn renewal of their covenant obligations and maintain a stricter discipline in the churches. The Synod also adopted the Savoy Confession, which had been issued by the English Congregationalists in 1658, as the standard of faith. It was essentially the same as the Westminster Confession, though there were some alterations in the doctrine of the church.

After 1660, the Puritan foundations were steadily weakened by pressures applied by the Crown. In 1662, Charles II ordered that liberty of worship be granted to Anglicans, that they be permitted to partake of the Lord's Supper in Congregational churches, and that baptism be extended to their children. The Puritans replied that they had come to "this Patmos" in order to worship as they saw fit and could not alter their practices without doing violence to their conscience. "The Congregational way is it, wherein we desire our orthodox brethren would bear with us."

Charles was dissatisfied with this answer and in 1664 he sent commissioners to Massachusetts to regulate the affair. They were instructed to give permission for Anglicans to use their prayer book, "it being very scandalous that any man should be debarred the exercise of his religion, according to ye laws and customs of England, by those who by ye indulgences granted have liberty left to be of what profession in religion they please. . . ." The commissioners gained nothing since the magistrates had no intention of satisfying the demands of the king. A second attempt, in 1665, also ended in failure.

In the matter of the franchise, the demands of the king were met. The General Court passed a new law in 1665 which provided that all Englishmen who were freeholders, members of some community church, orthodox and of good character, and twenty-four years of age might request the court "to be admitted to the freedom of the body politick, by the suffrage of the major part." The link between church and state was further weakened when, in 1676, the king threatened to revoke the charter. There was such consternation in the colony that the General Court called a synod of the churches to seek advice, since withdrawal of the charter would almost certainly alter the relation between church and state. But there was nothing which the Puritans could do to stop the inevitable; in 1684, the charter was revoked.

Charles II died in 1685 and was succeeded by James, the Duke of York. James II had the intention of uniting the American colonies under one royal governor, Sir Edmund Andros. When Andros arrived at Boston, in December, 1686, he was theoretically in control of the Dominion of New England, which included all New England, plus New York and New Jersey. Andros ruled with a heavy hand, abolishing representative assemblies, popular taxation, and freedom of the press. Although he commanded that everyone should be allowed freedom of worship, he did everything in his power to further the cause of the Anglican Church.

When word finally came that James had been removed from the throne, there was a popular uprising and Andros was deposed. With his overthrow, the Dominion of New England came to an end.

In the reorganization which followed the accession of William and Mary, Connecticut and Rhode Island resumed self-government under their old charters, while Massachusetts had to accept a royal governor with its new charter in 1691. Local government in Massachusetts remained undisturbed, though only the lower house of the legislature was to be elected by the people. All Christians, except Roman Catholics, were granted freedom of worship. Most distasteful to Puritans, however, was the provision which banned all religious tests for the suffrage. From that time, the church establishment was seriously weakened and rule by the saints was brought permanently to an end.

As the curtain dropped on the seventeenth century, it appeared to conservative leaders such as Increase Mather (1639–1723) and his son Cotton (1663–1728) that dangerous influences were abroad in the churches. At Harvard, the tutors William Brattle and John Leverett were encouraging changes in church polity and worship. They argued that persons seeking to be received into full communion with the church should not be required to make public testimony concerning their religious experience, that presentation by a professing Christian should be made the only prerequisite for infant baptism, and that all baptized persons who contributed to a church should have a voice in the selection of its pastor. Those who favored these views organized a fourth church in Boston, the Brattle Street Church, minus approval of the other congregations, and adopted them as standard practice. They introduced the Lord's Prayer and the reading of Scripture without comment into the worship service—a step toward Anglicanism in the opinion of the conservatives.

The Mathers and their associates saw that prompt action would have to be taken in order to stem the tide of liberalism. Their strategy was to protect orthodoxy through the strengthening of ministerial associations. In earlier decades ministerial meetings had been held, but gradually interest had declined and by 1676 the organizations had become defunct. The first of the revived organizations, composed of clergy from Boston and neighboring towns, had been founded in 1690. By the end of the decade at least five associations were meeting in Massachusetts.

In 1705, the conservatives came forward with a plan whereby the ministerial associations would be strengthened through gaining greater control over the local congregations; it was known as the *Massachusetts Proposals*. The document proposed, first, that all Congregational ministers organize themselves into ministerial associations, that these associations be empowered to examine and license candidates for the ministry, and that churches without pastor seek the advice of their association before calling a minister. This first proposal was adopted by the five associations, but not all the churches would agree to it. A second part proposed the creation of a standing council in each association composed of pastors and lay delegates. The council would serve as a continuing authority to supervise the churches and would have the power to make binding decisions. This proposal found little favor in the associations and was finally dropped.

There was widespread opposition to the *Massachusetts Proposals*. Many ministers and prominent laymen, among them the royal governor, felt that they threatened the freedom of the individual churches. A leading voice raised in protest was that of John Wise (1652–1725), the brilliant and outspoken minister at Ipswich. Deeply influenced by the writings of Locke, Pufendorf, and other political theorists, he had been captivated by the idea of a democratic social contract and the concept of the natural rights of man. In two tracts, *The Churches Quarrel Espoused* (1710) and *Vindication of the Government of the New England Churches* (1717), he defended church polity based on democratic principles and drew a connection between the natural rights of an individual under the social contract and the freedom of particular churches. He concluded that

. . . a democracy in church or state, is a very honorable and regular government according to the dictates of right reason, And, therefore . . . That these churches of New England, in their ancient constitution of church order, it being a democracy, are manifestly justified and defended by the law and light of nature.[5]

These works caused a stir among New England thinkers; they not only damaged the conservative argument but evoked a discussion of political and religious issues which would have bearing upon the coming American Revolution.

The failure of the conservative faction in Massachusetts prompted the Mathers to regroup their forces in Connecticut and prepare for a counter-attack. In order to neutralize the influence of Harvard, which was drifting steadily toward Arminianism, Deism, and Unitarianism, the development of a rival orthodox college was proposed. The struggling Collegiate School at Saybrook, founded in 1701, could serve as the nucleus. In 1718, a generous gift from Elihu Yale, a Boston-born capitalist who had become wealthy in the service of the East India Company, resulted in the renaming of the institution, which two years earlier had removed to New Haven, Yale College. The school, to the bitter disappointment of its founding fathers, soon proved to be as susceptible to liberalism as Harvard. Newtonian science, Berkeleian philosophy, and Anglican theology

---

[5] Quoted in V. L. Parrington, *Main Currents of American Thought* (Harcourt, Brace, c. 1927), I, 123.

undermined Yale's Congregational orthodoxy and some of its best teachers were lost to the Anglican Church.

In certain other respects the conservatives in Connecticut were more successful. In September, 1708, an assembly of Congregational ministers and lay delegates convened at Saybrook at the order of the Connecticut Legislature. This synod adopted the Savoy Confession as the doctrinal standard and fifteen articles dealing with church government and discipline. The articles provided for the establishment of consociations in each county, with powers of oversight over the local congregations; ministerial associations in each county, charged with the responsibility of advising and examining ministerial candidates; and a general association, with undefined functions, which was to meet annually. This semi-Presbyterian "Saybrook Platform" won the approval of the Connecticut government in October, 1708, but was not made binding on all the churches. Only those churches which adhered to the Platform, however, could enjoy the benefits of the establishment.

Gradually, the consociations took on more of the character of presbyteries; and the churches of Connecticut looked more to the Presbyterians of the Middle Colonies for Christian fellowship than to the Congregationalists of Massachusetts, whose polity retained greater independence for the local churches. The eighteenth century would witness a growing fraternization between Congregationalists and Presbyterians which would culminate in a union of wide significance.

Despite numerous appeals for reform on the part of the clergy, New England Puritanism manifested increasingly distinct signs of decay as the eighteenth century progressed. The vision of the fathers had faded; the stimulus of their times had given way before the easy peace of self-satisfaction. Nor had the relaxation of the church standards brought about a restoration of religious vitality; it had simply confirmed the phlegmatic proclivities of a spiritually lethargic people. Increase Mather was right: many of the rising generation were "profane Drunkards, Swearers, Licentious and scoffers at the power of Godliness." What was needed was a new crisis, a religious challenge which could capture the imagination and fire the soul. Such a challenge did not promise to issue from the unemotional and often pedantic utterances of the orthodox clergy. Only a religion which struck deep into the roots of a man and burned in his heart could suffice to change the spiritual and moral pattern of the times. Such a religion would blaze forth in the Great Awakening.

5

Religious Minorities in the English Colonies

AS THE SEVENTEENTH CENTURY PROGRESSED, THERE APPEARED IN THE ENG-
lish colonies the first signs of that religious diversification which was to
become normative in American life. No orderly pattern marked the emergence of the phenomenon. It was at once planned and spontaneous, immigrant and native born, concentrated and diffused. Its single element of
homogeneity lay in its vital principle—a passion for human rights. The
motivation behind this principle was complex, a curious blend of economic, social, political, and theological factors which could not readily
be isolated. It was perhaps inevitable that its application on the colonial
scene should have brought on conflict. Neither the Puritan saint nor the
Anglican divine was intellectually or socially geared to tolerate dissent.
Throughout the colonial period the erratic fires of authoritarianism alternately blazed and smoldered. But never could they consume the forces of
diversity. This chapter concerns the rise of religious heterogeneity in the
English colonies, the role played by three groups of nonconformists in
the early struggle for freedom.

THE ROMAN CATHOLICS

Since the reign of Henry VIII, Roman Catholics in England had been under restraint, even persecution. They had enjoyed a temporary restoration of power during the rule of Mary Tudor, but this was cut short in 1588 when once again they found themselves without favor. Under the weight of oppression, many Roman Catholic leaders, among them Sir Thomas More in his *Utopia,* advocated freedom of conscience. Even among the Anglican group, which was in power, there were certain leaders such as Lancelot Andrewes who spoke in favor of toleration. Neither church nor state was willing to grant carte blanche to dissenters, but there were times when the enforcement of religious uniformity was not rigorously applied. Many English nobles held to their Roman Catholic faith and suffered no serious disabilities. The attitude of the Stuart rulers becomes apparent in the case of George Calvert (c.1580–1632), who, after his conversion to Roman Catholicism, was elevated to the peerage by James I and granted the proprietary ownership of Maryland by Charles I.

The Calverts and the Founding of Maryland

Permanent Roman Catholic colonization in the English colonies was initiated in Maryland during the second quarter of the seventeenth century through the efforts of George Calvert. This nobleman, who was created Lord Baltimore in 1625, had for many years played an important role both in private business and in government. He had been a member of the London, or Virginia, Company and the New England Council, and had served as a member of Parliament and as one of the principal secretaries of state. From the latter office he felt compelled to resign in 1625, since as a newly converted Roman Catholic he could not take the required religious oath. James I, however, continued to favor him and raised him to the Irish peerage.

In 1621, Calvert had founded a small settlement in Newfoundland named Ferryland. Two years later he obtained a charter for the colony under the name of Avalon. At that time his interests were largely economic; after his conversion, the thought of providing a sanctuary for English Roman Catholics seems to have been uppermost in his mind. Within eight years, the forces of nature and the French caused him to abandon the settlement at a loss of between thirty and forty thousand pounds and turn his attention to Virginia. He made a short visit to Jamestown where he was received with mixed feelings of approbation and distrust. His refusal to take the oath acknowledging the ecclesiastical supremacy of the English monarch rendered him *persona non grata* in the colony. He returned to England and petitioned Charles I for a grant of land north of Virginia. The king acceded to his wishes, but before the charter of the Maryland palatinate could be issued, George Calvert was dead.

Cecil Calvert (1606–1675), Lord Baltimore's eldest son, inherited the title and the responsibilities of a new proprietaryship. A practical and judicious man with tenacity of purpose, he set out at once to raise a company of prospective settlers. He was able to secure the financial support of many prominent Roman Catholics, but not many of his co-religionists were interested in making their homes in the new colony. Undoubtedly a minority of the first band of pilgrims were of the Roman Catholic faith; most of the indentured servants were Protestants. In guiding the preparations for the colony's founding, the second Lord Baltimore revealed both tact and good will. His early advertisements of the project listed as one of its major purposes the conversion of the natives and then mentioned in a complimentary way the work already being undertaken by Anglicans and New England dissenters. In his private instructions to the Governor and Provincial Commissioners, he directed that they maintain peace among the passengers and not permit any cause for offense, especially in matters pertaining to religion. More specifically, he urged them to "cause all Acts" of their Roman Catholic faith to be done "as privately as may be" and to "treat the Protestants with as much mildness and favor as Justice will permit." At this juncture, Lord Baltimore could not chance the revocation of his charter because of any untoward act.

The first party of settlers set sail from England in November, 1633, pausing at the Isle of Wight to take on board two Jesuit priests and some lay Roman Catholics. Since Lord Baltimore chose to remain in England, the expedition was under the direction of Leonard Calvert, Cecil's younger brother and first governor of the palatinate. The following March, the settlers disembarked at St. Clement's Island, where mass was celebrated in honor of "the Annunciation of the Most Holy Virgin Mary." Through purchase from the Indians, the colonists acquired a large tract of land in what came to be known as St. Mary's and established their first settlement at St. Mary's City. Governor Calvert wisely ordered the cultivation of foodstuffs so as to avoid the blunders of the Virginians, who had faced famine because of their short-sighted preoccupation with the raising of tobacco. Under his leadership the colony flourished. In the first season, the settlers, having raised more corn than was needed, sent a cargo to New England and thus brought relief to the northern colonists in a desperate time of famine.

Although the government of Maryland was controlled by Roman Catholics and most of the large estates were owned by persons of that faith, all loyal English citizens who were Christians were, according to the terms of the charter, welcome in Maryland. The first Protestant settlers appear to have worshipped freely in the same chapel used by the

Roman Catholics. When a prominent Roman Catholic layman, in 1642, took away the keys to the chapel so that the Protestants could not gain admittance, he was brought before the Provincial Court and fined. Lord Baltimore, in 1636, even required his governors to take an oath that they would trouble no person who believed in Jesus Christ and would show no favoritism to any individual for religious reasons. It is sometimes asserted that the Proprietor, in taking such action, was motivated by political considerations. To a certain extent that is probably true. Nevertheless, his utterances show him to be a man of great understanding and tolerance, highly sensitive to the rights of his neighbors.

The spiritual well-being of the Roman Catholic population was in the competent hands of Jesuit fathers Andrew White, John Altham, John Brock, and Thomas Copley. These men devoted much time to the conversion of the Protestant settlers and the Indians, and with a large measure of success. In their report to the Superior General in Rome, in 1638, they stated:

Nevertheless, we have not ceased in an active manner to exert our endeavors for our neighbors; and although it is not yet permitted us by the rules of the province to live among the barbarians, both on account of the prevailing sickness and the hostile acts which the barbarians commit against the English . . . we hope in a short time that we will obtain one station of our own among the barbarians. In the interim we are more earnestly intent on the English, and since there are protestants as well as catholics in the colony, we have labored with both, and God has blessed our labors. For of the protestants who came from England this year, 1638, almost all have been converted to the faith, besides many others, with four servants that we bought for necessary use in Virginia, another colony of our empire. And of five workmen whom we hired for a month, we have in the meantime gained two.[1]

It was not long before friction developed between the Proprietor and the Jesuit fathers. In the opinion of Cecil Calvert, the government should not interfere with the churches in spiritual matters, but their temporal holdings should be under civil jurisdiction. This policy was ignored by the Jesuits, who proceeded to acquire real property directly from the Indians despite the terms of the charter which expressly stated that land grants in Maryland territory could be secured only from the Proprietor. The Jesuits not only held extensive tracts of land in the name of the Society of Jesus but demanded special privileges for themselves and their servants, among them being exemption from military service and from the payment of taxes. Their demands were not unusual; they were simply trying to gain the favors usually bestowed upon them in Roman Catholic countries.

[1] Mode, *op. cit.*, 27.

As Lord Baltimore viewed the situation, the Jesuits were challenging his claim to land already conveyed to him by royal charter. Neither he nor they proposed to capitulate without a struggle. The Jesuits had powerful lay support among the planters, notably Captain Thomas Cornwallis, the military commander of the palatinate. Lord Baltimore was represented by his forceful secretary, John Lewger, who managed to win for him an overwhelming victory. In 1642, the arrival of two secular priests to replace the Jesuit missionaries prompted the Jesuits to resolve their differences with Calvert and thereby win readmission. Father Henry More, the Jesuit Provincial in England, issued a statement canceling all Jesuit claims for legal exemptions; and the Society of Jesus released all lands which they had acquired from the natives. This was done on the basis of instructions from the General of the Order, who observed that it would be unfortunate "to see the first fruits, which are so beautifully developing in the Lord, nipped in their growth by the frost of cupidity." Although these concessions were clearly distressing to the Roman Catholic authorities, they did serve as an impediment to the establishment of religion in Maryland and helped to preserve equal civil advantages for all Christian denominations.

In the meantime, the people of Virginia, for economic and religious reasons, had demonstrated their hostility to the proprietary colony. Before the issuance of the charter to Lord Baltimore, they had endeavored to persuade the king not to grant it. Failing in this, they tried to arouse the Indians to attack the Maryland colonists. They even sent armed vessels to protect their trading interests within the boundaries of the palatinate. But not one of their hostile efforts ultimately succeeded.

Religion and the Decline of Proprietary Control

As time went on, Maryland became an asylum for dissenters from other colonies. Puritans who had been treated harshly in Virginia settled in Maryland, and nonconformists in Massachusetts were invited by Calvert to make their homes in the province. It was inevitable that differences between the Roman Catholic and Protestant elements in the population should have arisen. Further unrest was created by the outbreak of the English Civil War in 1642, a circumstance which caused the parliamentary faction in the colony to stage a revolt. The governor and his chief Roman Catholic supporters were obliged to flee for their lives; the insurrection was finally put down, however, and Calvert returned to his office. He died in 1647.

With the triumph of the parliamentary forces in England, Lord Baltimore feared that his charter would soon be revoked. In order to lessen that possibility, he took certain steps which were calculated to conciliate the ruling powers and refute the charge that Maryland was a haven for Roman Catholics. In 1649, he appointed William Stone, a Protestant, to the governorship and directed him not to molest for religious reasons any person who professed faith in Jesus Christ, especially if he was of the Roman Catholic persuasion. He then urged the General Assembly to enact legislation which would insure freedom of worship for all Christians.

The "Act Concerning Religion," passed by the Assembly in 1649, has frequently been heralded as one of the great advances in the history of religious freedom. Unquestionably it was liberal for its time, but it provided toleration for Christians alone. In its decree of death for persons who denied the deity of Jesus Christ, the Trinity, or the unity of the Godhead, it provided less toleration than had been the practice throughout the colony. It thus represented a concession to the strict Puritan element then in control of the home government. Persons who spoke disrespectfully of the Apostles or the Virgin Mary were to be fined or whipped and imprisoned. Any one in the province who called another person a "heritick, Scismatick, Idolator, puritan, Independant, Prespiterian, popish prest, Jesuite, Jesuited papist, Lutheran, Calvenist, Anabaptist, Brownist, Antinomian, Barrowist, Roundhead, Separatist, or any other name or terme in a reproachfull manner" was to receive a similar sentence. The principal philosophy of the act was made clear in the following declaration:

And whereas the inforceing of the conscience in matters of Religion hath frequently fallen out to be of dangerous Consequence in those commonwealthes where it hath been practised, And for the more quiett and peaceable governemt of this Province, and the better to pserve mutuall Love and amity amongst the Inhabitants thereof. Be it Therefore . . . Ordeyned & enacted . . . that noe person or psons whatsoever within this Province . . . professing to believe in Jesus Christ, shall from henceforth bee any waies troubled, Molested or discountenanced for or in respect of his or her religion nor in the free exercise thereof within this Province or the Islands thereunto belonging nor any way compelled to the beleife or exercise of any other Religion against his or her consent, soe as they be not unfaithfull to the Lord Proprietary, or molest or conspire against the civill Governemt established or to bee established in this Province vnder him or his heires.[2]

That the provisions of the act were not always enforced is evident in the case of Dr. Jacob Lumbrozo, a Jew who was charged with blasphemy against Jesus Christ. There was ample proof that he did not accept the Saviourhood of Jesus, but a conviction was never secured. Lumbrozo was even granted full rights of citizenship. Apparently the strict provisions of the act were more designed to impress the Puritans than to be taken seriously by the colonists.

[2] *Ibid.*, 31.

When word of the execution of Charles I reached Maryland, Thomas Greene, a Roman Catholic and acting governor in the absence of Governor Stone, unwisely declared Charles II, then in exile, to be the lawful sovereign. Although this action was repudiated by the Proprietor, the damage could not be undone. A commission of Parliament was dispatched to force the colony's allegiance to Parliament. When Governor Stone declined to recognize Parliament's authority over Maryland, he was replaced by a council. But being very popular and not opposed to compromise, he was soon restored to his office. Under the aegis of the Puritan party, the General Assembly met in 1654 and repealed the earlier act of toleration. Those who adhered to Roman Catholicism were no longer to enjoy the protection of the government and were to be denied the exercise of their faith. A new "Act Concerning Religion" was passed which provided heavy penalties for those convicted of "licentiousness." As interpreted by the Puritans, this could apply to any dissenter. The Assembly further discredited the authority of the Proprietor and invited the settlers to take lands without his knowledge or permission.

When Oliver Cromwell became Protector of England in 1653, Lord Baltimore sought his support. That Cromwell took his side in the dispute with the Maryland Puritans proved to be an important asset in the struggle to regain proprietary control. The opposition finally had to admit that Lord Baltimore's claims were just. No sooner did Calvert resume his authority than religious toleration was restored to the colony. This arrangement prevailed throughout the reigns of Charles II and James II, both of whom were committed to the Roman Catholic faith and aware that they could best serve its interests through the furtherance of toleration. Nor did the passing of Cecil Calvert in 1675 fundamentally alter the religious situation. His son, Charles, though politically more autocratic, maintained his ideal of freedom of conscience.

The forcible ejection of James II during the revolution of 1688 had powerful repercussions in Maryland. When word came of the succession of William and Mary, a group of malcontents, headed by the petty John Coode, revolted against the regime of Lord Baltimore; they forced its officials to surrender and set up an interim government. These "Associators" then petitioned William III, who was a Protestant, to end the proprietary rule. The petition was finally granted and in 1691 Sir Lionel Copley, an Anglican, was appointed the first royal governor of Maryland. The first act of Governor Copley upon his arrival in 1692 was to call a General Assembly, which was controlled by the revolutionary party. The Assembly abolished religious toleration for non-Trinitarians and Roman Catholics, an action which was in harmony with the English Toleration Act of 1689. It also passed the first legislation for the establishment of the Anglican Church, but the act was not approved in England until 1702.

The "Penal Age"

At no time in the seventeenth century had Roman Catholicism in Maryland presented a serious threat to the Protestant majority. There were conversions from Protestantism, and Indians were won to the faith through the kindness and understanding of the Jesuit priests. But the gains could scarcely be called phenomenal. At the opening of the eighteenth century, Roman Catholics constituted less than ten per cent of the colony's population. Nevertheless, Anglican establishment brought with it increasing pressure on the Roman Catholic community. In 1704, the General Assembly made it illegal for a priest to say mass or to baptize any child whose parents were not Roman Catholic. For a time, a statute prohibited Roman Catholic parents from sending their children abroad to be educated. Then, in 1718, Roman Catholics were denied the franchise.

The intolerable conditions in Maryland prompted many Roman Catholic families to move northward into the colony of Pennsylvania, newly founded in 1681. They were attracted by the tolerant spirit of William Penn and his Quaker co-religionists. The Jesuit Order acquired land in Cecil County as early as 1706 and founded the St. Xavier Mission. Joseph Greaton, a Jesuit priest, came to Philadelphia about 1734 and there conducted services in a little chapel. A few years later several Jesuits from Germany took up work among a large group of German Roman Catholic settlers who were emigrating from the Palatinate. Before the outbreak of the Revolution, Roman Catholics could be found in every one of the thirteen colonies, though in extremely small numbers outside of Maryland and Pennsylvania. Some came by mass deportation, as in the case of the six thousand Acadians who were uprooted from their homes in Nova Scotia by the English government and scattered through the colonies. In most of the settlements, Roman Catholics suffered from penal legislation until the establishment of American independence.

Internal problems also harassed the Roman Catholic Church. The absence of a bishop in America created important administrative problems. It also meant that the sacraments of confirmation and holy orders could not be conferred; both were necessary to the ongoing life of the church. The ordinances of religion were largely in the care of the Jesuit fathers, until the papacy suppressed the order in 1773. Never in the colonial period were there enough priests to minister to the growing Roman Catholic population. The result was that during the eighteenth century uncounted numbers of neglected Roman Catholic immigrants were permanently lost to the church. By the opening of the Revolution there were perhaps not more than 25,000 Roman Catholics in the colonies.

THE BAPTISTS

The maelstrom which swept wave upon wave of Puritans out of England was responsible also for the exodus of other diverse religious elements in the population. None felt more sharply the sting of the Laudian persecution than that exceedingly protean group generally known as the Separatists. There was little unanimity of religious opinion among these dissenters save for their abhorrence of established churches and government by bishops or presbyteries. Each congregation cherished its own doctrinal emphases—antinomianism, believers' baptism, biblical typology, and a host of others. Gradually these congregations having broadly similar tenets drew together on a loosely knit denominational basis. Even so, there was considerable fluidity in the arrangement and there were always some groups which defied easy classification. Nor was it uncommon for a Separatist sympathizer to oscillate between the various wings of the movement, as witness the case of Roger Williams. In early colonial America, the Separatist cause was most vigorously represented by the scores of Baptist congregations which sprang into being along the Eastern seaboard. No uniform pattern marked their establishment. It was as if a whirlwind had plucked the seeds of Baptist dissent from the soil of England and carried them safely across the great ocean to a land ready for their cultivation. The first flowering was in New England.

Roger Williams: New England Liberal

The arrival of Roger Williams in orthodox Boston on February 5, 1631, set the stage for one of the most important experiments in American history—the founding of a colony on the principle of religious liberty. He had received unique preparation for this task. Born in London, Roger Williams (c.1603–1683) was reared in a family of respectable middle-class Anglicans. It is probable but uncertain that he was baptized into the faith at St. Sepulchre's, the parish records having been lost in the London fire of 1666. While still a youth, his proficiency at shorthand attracted the attention of the eminent jurist, Sir Edward Coke, and won for him a position in the Star Chamber Court. Sir Edward's championship of common law against the divine right of kings theory asserted by James I undoubtedly proved influential in the shaping of Williams' liberal political philosophy.

Coke further proved his friendship by securing for the young man a scholarship to the Charterhouse School, where he matriculated in 1621. Later he won an appointment to Cambridge and received distinction in his studies at Pembroke College. During his years at Cambridge, Williams found himself turning against Anglicanism in favor of the Puritan system.

After being awarded his baccalaureate degree in 1627, he continued at Cambridge two years longer, his sympathies gradually becoming linked with the Separatist cause, though he accepted holy orders in the Anglican Church. A period of service as chaplain to Sir William Masham, in Essex, proved frustrating; and when the opportunity to migrate to New England appeared, Williams was enthusiastic. In the meantime, he married Mary Barnard in December, 1629. The following year they sailed for America.

Williams' Separatist inclinations were at once apparent. When the congregation of the Boston Church wanted him to assume the ministerial responsibilities during the absence of their pastor, John Wilson, he promptly refused. He could not serve a congregation which held fellowship with the Anglican Church and recognized the jurisdiction of magistrates in matters of conscience. Despite these unpopular views, Williams was called as teacher of the Salem Church, where the non-Separatist position was by no means as securely rooted. The authorities swiftly retaliated by sending a strong letter of protest to the Salem Church which led to his rejection by that congregation. He departed for Plymouth, where he stayed two years waiting for the storm to subside. In this colony, founded on Separatist principles, he was received with kindness and understanding. Governor Bradford pronounced him to be "a man godly and zealous, having many precious parts, but very unsettled in judgmente." He labored among the Narragansett Indians with some success and established friendships which would later prove invaluable. He served for a time as assistant to the Reverend Ralph Smith and, according to the report of Bradford, found favor among the people for his teaching. Eventually, however, friction developed between him and the congregation, probably over his advanced Separatist views. When the invitation came to return to Salem in 1633, Williams accepted it gladly.

Shortly after Williams began his duties as assistant to the Reverend Samuel Skelton at Salem, trouble broke out anew. In a treatise written that same year, the young theologian had been critical of King James' patents which conferred title to the lands of Massachusetts to the settlers. Since the land belonged to the Indians, how could James legally grant it to his subjects? The Puritans, through a rather ingenious method of allegory, had maintained that the Indians were an ungodly people and that it was just that they should be dispossessed of their territories by the new Israelites (the Puritans), whom God had providentially led into the Promised Land. Williams insisted that the significance of the Israelite conquest of Palestine was spiritual, that it had no direct bearing on the present situation. Indeed, the more he contemplated the issue, the more convinced he became that Israel was no model to be emulated at all, that to follow Israel was to repudiate Christianity.

What was so bothersome to the Massachusetts authorities was that Williams had attacked the charter, the very foundation of their Bible State. The critic was thus summarily ordered to appear before the General Court to give an accounting. This he did with great deference and, in apologetic humility, recanted and proffered his allegiance to the government. The matter was dropped, but only temporarily. Again Williams lashed out at the practices which seemed to him unjust, especially the interference of the civil power in religious matters and the reservation of the suffrage and public office for members of the established church. He further objected to compulsory attendance at religious services and to the civil tax for the support of the clergy.

This was too much for the members of the General Court. At a meeting in July, 1635, they charged him with "divers dangerous opinions" but decided not to pass sentence until Williams had been given the opportunity to humble himself. At the same time, they increased pressure on the Salem congregation by refusing to grant them title to certain lands to which they had made claim. Angered by their high-handed methods, Williams wrote to the other churches protesting the unjust action of the civil leaders. When the General Court met in October, the offensive Mr. Williams was summoned for questioning and ordered banished. At this session all the ministers of the colony were brought in for consultation, and the sentence of the court was approved by all but one of them. Because of Williams' poor health and the inclemency of the weather the court agreed to postpone his banishment until spring, provided he would refrain from airing his opinions. He continued to preach, however, and so officers were sent to take him and put him on a ship bound for England. A timely warning from friends enabled him to escape into the frozen wilderness, later to find refuge in the region of Narragansett Bay. A sense of relief came over the colony after his departure; the establishment had won, the rule of the saints had been vindicated. Henceforth, Roger Williams was anathema in Massachusetts Bay Colony. Two generations later, the pompous Cotton Mather, in his *Magnalia Christi Americana* (Book VII, Chapter II), likened him to a certain windmill in the Netherlands, which

. . . whirling round with such extraordinary violence, by reason of a violent storm, then blowing; the stone at length by its *rapid motion* became so intensely hot, as to fire the mill, from whence the flames, being dispersed by the high winds, did set a whole town *on fire*. But I can tell my reader that, about twenty years before this, there was a whole country in America like to be set on *fire* by the *rapid motion* of a windmill, in the head of one particular man. Know, then, that about the year 1630, arrived here one Mr. Roger Williams; who being a preacher that had less *light* than *fire* in him, hath by his own sad example, preached unto us the danger of that evil which the apostle mentions in Rom. x.2: "They have a zeal, but not according to knowledge."

Rhode Island: Citadel of Dissent

It was perhaps providential that after fourteen weeks of wandering in the wilderness, Roger Williams should have stumbled upon the camp of the Narragansett Indians, with whom he had been on the most friendly terms. They received him hospitably and he remained under their care throughout the winter. The following spring Williams and four other exiles founded a settlement at Seekonk. But when word came that they were trespassing on land which belonged to Plymouth, they moved on to the shore of Narragansett Bay where they founded Providence. This colony, named by Williams in remembrance of "God's merciful providence unto me in my distress," was to become "a shelter for those distressed in conscience." Within two years, so many accessions had been made to the settlement that its founder conveyed the lands granted to him by the Indians to twelve associates for thirty pounds. These persons incorporated themselves into a township and promised to render "an active or passive obedience to all such orders or agreements as shall be made for public good," by the will of the majority. But this obedience was to be only in civil matters.

In his insistence upon freedom of conscience, Roger Williams was championing a principle which was unique for his times. This principle was set forth clearly and forthrightly in his *The Bloudy Tenent of Persecution* (1644) and *The Bloody Tenent yet More Bloody* (1652). The argument which Williams used most frequently in defense of liberty was that religious persecution involved the violation of conscience. A man might very well be mistaken in his views, but if he was sincere he should not be molested. "I confess in this plea for freedom to all consciences (merely) of worship," wrote Williams, "I have impartially pleaded for the freedom of the consciences of the papists themselves, the greatest enemies and persecutors (in Europe) of the saints and truths of Jesus: yet I have pleaded for no more than is their due and right. . . ."

Williams' doctrine of the church called for a distinct separation between church and state. The church should not be identified with any nation since no nation is really Christian. Nor did a nation require Christianity as a prerequisite to just and effective government. "The commonwealth of Rome flourished five hundred years together, before ever the name of Christ was heard in it; which so great a glory of so great a continuance, mightily evinceth the distinction of the civil peace of a State from that which is Christian religion." From this Williams went on to aver that a man's religion had little effect upon his ability and worth as a magistrate. Religion should not be used as a test of the fitness of a candidate for office nor should an elected official interfere in any way in matters pertaining to conscience.

In Puritan theory, the ideal had been to found a national church after the pattern of ancient Israel. To Williams, the whole scheme was impossible. If the church wished to embrace the entire community then the standards for admission would have to be compromised in order to appeal to a large number. In the process, the church would lose its purity and distinctiveness and would no longer have the capacity to stand in judgment of society. If the standards were kept high, then it would be more difficult to gain conversions. Under those circumstances, if the church were to become coextensive with society, then it would prove necessary to apply constraint. Only in this way could a so-called Christian commonwealth be built.

John Cotton, the chief apologist for the national church, insisted that it was unnecessary to apply restraint in every regard. Some matters were of primary importance, justifying the use of coercion; others, being inconsequential, admitted an easy tolerance. To this Williams offered a sharp rebuttal. There was no such thing as a matter of lesser importance if God had commanded it. The standards of the church should be kept high so that only the regenerate might qualify for membership. But under no circumstances should coercion be applied to draw men into the church. For once force was permitted, it would be used not only to maintain the standards of the community but also to extend its influence. In either case, the sword would become the means of furthering the goals of the national church. Within the borders of the state, there would be religious persecution; beyond its borders uniformity in spiritual things would be advanced by wars of religion.

Force in matters pertaining to religion ought never to be permitted. There was too great a risk of making a mistake. To put oneself in the place of God or to act as His official interpreter was not the prerogative of man, especially since there were no infallible tests or infallible persons which might be used as a certain standard of judgment. For the state to use the sword in order to achieve religious uniformity would be demonic. Its right to wield the sword was valid only within the order of the flesh.

I hence observe, that there being in this Scripture held forth a twofold state, a civil state and a spiritual, civil officers and spiritual, civil weapons and spiritual weapons, civil vengeance and punishment and a spiritual vengeance and punishment: although the Spirit speaks not here expressly of civil magistrates and their civil weapons, yet, these states being of different natures and considerations, as far differing as spirit from flesh, I first observe, that civil weapons are most improper and unfitting in matters of the spiritual state and kingdom, though in the civil state most proper and suitable.[3]

Subsequent generations have honored Roger Williams chiefly for his

---

[3] Quoted in R. H. Bainton, *The Travail of Religious Liberty* (Westminster, c. 1951), 219.

contributions to political theory, notably his concept of government as a compact. Surely modern democracy owes him a debt of gratitude. But perhaps his most important legacy was his individualistic spirit, strong in personal conviction but avid in the defense of an opponent's rights. This was an important asset in an age which scarcely knew the meaning of tolerance.

It seems hardly surprising that from the outset the unchartered colony at Providence should have drawn dissenters of varied types to its vicinity. Among the first were Anne Hutchinson and her associates, who founded Portsmouth in 1638 and Newport in 1639. Anne Hutchinson had arrived in Boston in 1634 and had begun to hold religious meetings. Her distinctive teachings were that the covenant of grace had made obsolete the covenant of works, that no amount of sanctification or holiness could be considered as evidence of a justified state, and that the Holy Spirit personally dwells in a justified soul. One was a Christian not by works but by virtue of the divine spirit dwelling within him and illuminating his soul, kindling an awareness of personal salvation and union with God. She then made the alarming statement that most of the ministers were unconverted, being under the covenant of works. The clergy and most of the General Court members were outraged by her declarations. They had to move slowly, however, since she had several important officials on her side, among them Captain Underhill, the military leader, and Sir Harry Vane, the governor.

Matters went from bad to worse when the Reverend John Wheelwright, minister of the church at Wollaston and brother-in-law of Mrs. Hutchinson, preached a sermon defending the new views and criticizing some of the conditions which prevailed in Massachusetts Bay. The magistrate immediately arrested him on a charge of sedition. In 1637, a church synod was called at Newton to give an ecclesiastical judgment on the "heresy." Mrs. Hutchinson and her brother-in-law were examined and were pronounced guilty. The General Court met in May, 1637, and elected John Winthrop, who had sided with the clergy in the dispute, as governor to replace Vane. At this session a "Remonstrance" was presented, signed by sixty citizens, asking the court to refrain from interfering with Mrs. Hutchinson. But when the court called on the signers to admit their fault most of them were willing to remove their names and forget the whole matter. At its November session, the General Court banished Mrs. Hutchinson and Wheelwright from the colony.

Stranger perhaps was the case of Samuel Gorton, who came to Massachusetts "to enjoy liberty of conscience." In 1638, he was accused of "all manner of blasphemies" because he claimed an inner illumination by the Spirit and condemned the union of church and state. He was further attacked for his teaching that the ministry and sacraments have no rightful place among Christian disciples. After living for a time at Plymouth and Aquidneck, he moved to Providence. Later he founded a settlement at Shawomet which was renamed Warwick. But wherever he went he became involved in disputes over religion, politics, and property rights. Unquestionably, much of his difficulty sprang from the fact that the New England Puritans were experiencing a backwash of the English sectaries. Their subjective "Inner Light" emphasis was a deadly threat to the Calvinistic biblicism of the Puritans. Gorton's settlement in Rhode Island was symbolic of the restlessness of the times; it was a mecca for freethinkers and radicals and stood as the antithesis of the Puritan commonwealth.

The year 1643 found Roger Williams in England, seeking a charter for the Rhode Island settlements. The following March, a patent for "Providence Plantations" was granted to Providence, Portsmouth, and Newport. It gave the people full power "to govern and rule themselves and such others as shall inhabit within any part of the said tract of land, by such a form of civil government as by voluntary consent of all or the greatest part of them shall be found most serviceable in their estates and conditions." The first General Assembly met at Portsmouth in May, 1647, and adopted a code of laws based on democratic principles. It provided for absolute freedom of conscience so that the "saints of the Most High" might "walk in this Colony without molestation in the name of Jehovah, their God for ever and ever." Throughout the years, the colony remained faithful to this principle in both theory and practice, there being complete religious freedom for all. Until about 1680, religious influence in Rhode Island was predominantly Baptist; after that time the trend was toward the Society of Friends. That to the rest of New England the colony came to be known as "Rogues' Island" seems scarcely remarkable. The antagonism was so great that the little colony could not even be admitted into the New England Confederation, which was organized as a mutual protective agency against Indian aggression. The result was that Rhode Island suffered terribly during King Philip's War. Indeed, it was not until the nineteenth century that it was able to gain the full esteem of the rest of the nation.

The Birth and Expansion of the Baptist Movement

No sooner had Roger Williams established himself at Providence than he began to hold religious meetings in his home, preaching his doctrines of Separatism. Apparently he became impressed during this time by the teachings of certain Baptists who had arrived in the colony; their principles of adult conversion and believers' baptism seemed to him consistent with New Testament practice. In March, 1639, Williams received baptism from Ezekiel Holliman, and then proceeded to baptize Holliman plus ten other persons of like persuasion. The group, however, was not immersed, and there is no indication that this means was employed prior to 1649. Those who had been baptized organized themselves into a church, which some have claimed to be the first Baptist church in America. But after a few months, Williams withdrew from the fellowship, preferring to be known henceforth as a "Seeker." Later he confessed that he regarded the Baptist movement as more in harmony with early Christianity than any other, "and yet I have satisfaction neither in the authority by which it is done, nor in the manner; nor in the prophecies concerning the rising of Christ's kingdom after the desolation by Rome." One might only hope that God would yet reestablish a true church through some divine action.

The Providence Church soon became embroiled in theological controversy. Some of the members who, like Williams, were Calvinists were challenged by an Arminian faction which held to free will and the laying on of hands after baptism as a sign that the Holy Spirit had been received. Finally, in 1652, the congregation divided into two groups: an Arminian Six Principle group which developed steadily in strength, and a Calvinistic group which soon dissolved. Not until 1771 would a majority of the Providence congregation adopt again a Calvinistic confession, an action which would result in a further schism.

In the meantime, John Clarke, physician and minister, had organized a church at Newport, perhaps as early as 1638. But there are no extant records which clearly show it to be a Baptist church prior to 1648. As for Clarke, he had arrived in Massachusetts in the fall of 1637 just in time to raise his voice in behalf of Anne Hutchinson and to win the aversion of the saints. A lover of liberty, he was not a man who bowed easily to the rod of authority. Nor was he reluctant to face danger when duty summoned him. In 1651, at the request of an aged and lonely man, William Witter, Clarke, Obadiah Holmes, one-time minister at Seekonk, and John Crandall, a deputy from Newport in the Rhode Island General Court, had the temerity to journey to his home at Lynn, in Massachusetts. While conducting worship there, they were seized by constables and forced to attend the public services of the Puritan church. Their refusal to participate in those services together with Clarke's apologia for his Baptist principles, made before the congregation, led to their imprisonment the following day. Some days later they were taken before the court and sentenced to heavy fines or severe flogging. Anonymous friends paid the fines of Clarke and Crandall and offered to do the same for Holmes. The latter refused any help and bore stoically the thirty strokes of the lash. In 1652, Clarke published in England a work entitled *Ill Newes from New England,* which reported the persecution of the three Baptists and ended by preaching for a verdict. "Let him that readeth it consider which church is most like the Church of Christ (that Prince of Peace, that meek and gentle Lamb, that came into this World to save

Men's lives, not to destroy them), the Persecuted, or Persecuting." His argument for liberty of conscience was persuasive; a storm of protest arose in various quarters of England and Sir Richard Saltonstall was inspired to administer a public rebuke to the Massachusetts leaders for their "tyranny and persecution."

The confidence which John Clarke enjoyed in Rhode Island was directly responsible for his being sent to England in 1651 with Roger Williams to secure a charter for the colony. For more than a decade Clarke remained in the mother country watching over the interests of the settlement. Finally, in July, 1663, he obtained from Charles II a royal charter for Rhode Island and Providence Plantations. It confirmed all the rights granted in the earlier patent and provided that "no person within the said Colony, at any time hereafter, shall be anywise molested, punished, disquieted, or called in question, for any differences in opinion in matters of religion, that do not actually disturb the civil peace of our said Colony . . ." The value of Clarke's services was fully recognized when he returned to Rhode Island in 1664; his ministry at Newport was received with enthusiasm and further distinction came when he was called to the office of deputy governor. With the passage of time, Clarke's greatness tended to be obscured somewhat by the fame of Roger Williams; but though he ranked as a lesser luminary, his contributions to religious liberty were no less significant.

Until the latter part of the seventeenth century the Baptist movement made slow progress outside of Rhode Island. In 1663, a congregation of Welsh Baptists under the leadership of John Myles founded a church at Rehoboth in the colony of Plymouth. It was not long before Myles and his principal laymen were arrested and tried on the charge that they had conducted a public meeting for which permission had not been granted. After being fined, they decided to move to a place near the border of Rhode Island, which they named Swansea.

In Massachusetts, President Henry Dunster of Harvard, apparently troubled by the persecution of Clarke and his associates, began to study the claims made for believers' baptism with some thoroughness. For several years he had been inclined toward the Baptist position; by 1653, his conviction had become so strong that he refused to present his newly born child for infant baptism. Not only that, he felt compelled to speak out in public against the practice and on one occasion, in 1654, actually interrupted its administration in the church at Cambridge. During the twelve years he had served as president of Harvard, Dunster had won high respect and admiration for his brilliant achievements. If he had been willing to remain silent on the subject of baptism, doubtless he might have continued in his office. Under the circumstances, he brought too much embarrassment to the community to be permitted to remain. The resignation which Dunster had once offered was now demanded. He was summoned before the General Court in 1655, found guilty of disturbing public worship, and sentenced to receive a public rebuke. Shortly afterward he moved to Plymouth Colony where he became pastor of the church at Scituate. His successor at Harvard was Charles Chauncy, formerly minister of the church to which Dunster was called.

In 1665, the first Baptist church in Boston was organized in the home of Thomas Gould, who a decade before had refused to allow his child to receive baptism. Having been excommunicated from the Congregational Church, he and his followers were subjected to unusual trials in their new denominational connection. Those who were freemen were denied the franchise. Then, in 1666, Gould and certain of his associates were fined and imprisoned. Despite the persecution, the Baptists continued to gain converts and in 1678 they erected a meetinghouse. Gradually the opposition lessened, especially after the orthodox leaders were rebuffed by Charles II and various Congregational ministers in England for their intolerance. With the issuance of the new Charter in 1691, which stipulated that all Christians except Roman Catholics should enjoy freedom of conscience, persecution of Baptists virtually came to an end. Twenty-seven years later, Cotton Mather stood in the pulpit of the Baptist Church in Boston to preach the ordination sermon of Elisha Callender. It was entitled "Good Men United."

At Kittery in the province of Maine, a Baptist congregation was organized as early as 1682, with William Screven as minister. Two months later he was called before the Council, fined, and forbidden to hold further meetings. He paid no heed to these directions and continued his ministerial services in that area for a number of years. About 1696 he removed to South Carolina, taking some of his flock at Kittery with him.

The tardiness of Baptist growth in New England can be seen in the fact that by 1700 there were only ten churches with perhaps three hundred members. Connecticut's first Baptist church at Groton was not founded until 1705. By 1740, there were merely twenty-three Baptist churches in New England, of which eleven were in Rhode Island, eight in Massachusetts, and four in Connecticut. Not until the outbreak of the Great Awakening would there be a significant trend upward.

The most promising center of Baptist growth was the Middle Colonies. Many Baptists were drawn to the Philadelphia area inasmuch as religious toleration was practiced in Pennsylvania and New Jersey. In 1684, Thomas Dungan and a group of Baptists from Newport settled at Cold Spring, Pennsylvania and founded there a church. Four years later a church at Pennepack was organized by Elias Keach. Before the end of the century, congregations had been formed at Middletown, Piscataway, and Cohansey in New Jersey, and at Philadelphia, making advisable the formation of the Philadelphia Baptist Association, the first continuing Baptist association in America, in 1707. The Association had no power as a judicatory over its member churches; it was simply an advisory body. But if it lacked formal authority, it more than made up for it in prestige and influence. The churches and their members brought for its consideration almost every kind of ecclesiastical problem imaginable: requirements for church membership, the role of women in the congregation, the use of musical instruments in public worship, the question of slavery.

In 1742, the Association adopted as its doctrinal standard the London Confession of Particular Baptists of 1689. This denoted a decided trend among American Baptists toward Calvinism and away from the once predominant Arminian persuasion. In fact, it set the tone for the subsequent shaping of Baptist theology. A treatise on church discipline written by Benjamin Griffith and Jenkin Jones was also accepted. It was most urgently needed, for as the Association continued to grow the churches required direction as to their relation to it. By 1757, it had a membership of twenty-five churches scattered through Connecticut, the Middle Colonies, Maryland, and Virginia. The first membership report in 1762 listed 4,018 Baptist communicants.

In the South, Baptist penetration was unimpressive prior to the Great Awakening. Virginia made it clear from the beginning that dissenters were unwelcome, especially Baptists. This apparently did not dissuade a group of Arminian Baptists from settling in Isle of Wight County about 1700. Their first minister was Robert Nordin, who arrived from England in 1714 and organized a church at Burleigh. Another group moved into northern Virginia between the years 1743 and 1756 and founded three churches in Berkeley and Loudoun counties. While some of these Baptists continued to embrace Arminian principles, a majority accepted the more rigorous Calvinistic theology and were affiliated with the Philadelphia Association.

It is probable that the first Baptists in South Carolina arrived from Maine and England about 1683 and settled near Charleston. At the same time another group established themselves on Port Royal Island. They later became associated with William Screven's congregation. There is no record of Baptist activity in North Carolina prior to 1714, although it seems likely that some of the earlier settlers were of that persuasion. The first Baptist minister in the colony, Paul Palmer, arrived in 1720. Seven years later, he organized a church in Chowan Precinct. In 1729, another congregation was gathered at Shiloh in Camden County. Palmer, whose theology was Arminian, became known as a powerfully persuasive preacher who won hundreds of converts to the Baptist churches. For many years he carried on an effective itinerant ministry over a wide area, his influence extending into other colonies as well. In all likelihood, the first Baptist church in Maryland, organized at Chestnut Ridge in 1742, owed its existence largely to his efforts.

THE FRIENDS

The introduction of Quakerism into the American colonies was the result of a concerted effort by its missionaries to win converts and to replace Puritan orthodoxy. Only after several decades did the movement derive its strength largely through mass immigration. This explains the fact that small groups of Friends were meeting in various localities from New Hampshire to North Carolina a decade before the founding of the Quaker settlement of Pennsylvania in 1681. It also accounts for the extreme diffuseness of the society and its unique effectiveness over a wide area throughout the colonial period.

Beginnings in New England

Before the arrival of the first Quaker missionaries in New England, reports concerning their leader, George Fox, had filtered across the Atlantic to Massachusetts and had turned the colony into a state of alarm. Fox had preached a doctrine of the Inner Light of the Holy Spirit in man and had called for a return to the purity of primitive Christianity. His teachings, unfortunately, came to be confused with the wild rantings of the Fifth Monarchy Men, who plotted to overthrow Cromwell's government, and the Muggletonians, whose leaders, Lodowick Muggleton and John Reeve, contended that they were the two witnesses mentioned in the eleventh chapter of Revelation. The Puritan leaders, having no affinity for these or any other sectaries, planned a warm reception for any radicals who might plan to reform New England.

In 1656, two Friends, Ann Austin, mature mother of five, and Mary Fisher, young and unmarried, set sail from Barbados for Boston. Upon arrival, their books and papers were seized and burned and they were thrown into a jail the windows of which were boarded up in order to prevent anyone from conversing with them. The magistrates were stricken with the fear that somehow the community might become infected with the "pestilent heresy" of the "cursed sect of hereticks which are commonly called Quakers." After five weeks of indecision, they placed the undesirables aboard ship and sent them back to Barbados. Not many days later eight more Friends arrived from London. They were at once imprisoned and subjected to grueling interrogation. Eight weeks later, they were returned to England on the same ship that brought them to Boston. The problem, however, was not solved. No sooner had one group been deported before another arrived to take its place.

In October, 1656, the General Court enacted a law which provided that all Quakers entering Massachusetts be immediately thrown into prison, whipped with twenty stripes, and kept at hard labor until banished. Ship owners bringing Quakers into the colony were to be fined one hundred pounds, and a fine of forty shillings "for each hour of entertainment" was to be imposed upon those who opened their homes for the concealment of heretics. The Friends themselves could not only be imprisoned and whipped but mutilated and even executed. In 1658, Charles Chauncy, in a sermon preached at Boston, attempted to justify this persecution. He said, "Suppose you should catch six wolves in a trap, and ye cannot prove that they killed either sheep or lambs: and now you have them they will neither bark nor bite; yet they have the plain marks of wolves, and therefore ye knock them down."

In fairness to the Puritan authorities it should be pointed out that these early missionaries were at best rather annoying, being as different from their brethren of the present as day is from night. They conducted their activities in a spirit of frenzy and were wont to parade themselves in public in an eccentric fashion. There was no official dignity which they did not revile, nor any standard of social propriety which they did not deprecate. One woman wore sackcloth, her face smeared with grease; two others appeared at church and market place naked. Their attitude was polemical, especially in New England, and even the tolerant Roger Williams found them proud and contemptuous.

While Connecticut and New Haven, New Netherland and Virginia passed laws against the Friends, no other colony enacted laws as harsh as did Massachusetts. There four Quakers who refused to remain in exile were finally led to the gallows, namely, William Robinson and Marmaduke Stevenson in 1659, Mary Dyer in 1660, and William Leddra in 1661. The people in general did not approve of such extreme punishment even though they had no liking for the condemned persons. So strong was this sentiment that a reaction set in and imprisoned Quakers were released. In 1661, the General Court, probably at the insistence of Charles II, repealed the law permitting capital punishment for being a Friend. This does not mean that the sect was granted liberty. On the contrary, the law for the whipping of Quakers was back on the statutes by 1662, and in 1675 there was still a law which provided fines for any persons apprehended at a Quaker meeting. But by this time the movement had grown and few of its opponents were zealous in the application of the law. Most of the later Quakers were of irenic disposition and, except for refusing to join the militia or pay taxes for ministerial support, they obeyed the laws of the community. By 1677, the persecution of Friends in New England had all but disappeared.

Although the Friends suffered disabilities in the Puritan colonies, they enjoyed complete freedom in Rhode Island. This circumstance led to a vigorous protest from the United Colonies. The General Assembly of Rhode Island replied in March, 1657, that Rhode Island had been established on the basis of religious freedom, "which freedom we still prize as the greatest hapines that men can posess in this world," and that the

Friends might enter the colony as they pleased. But while the Quakers remained unmolested, they were vigorously opposed by Roger Williams, who became more vitriolic in his attacks as they grew in strength. In 1672, when George Fox visited Rhode Island, Williams sent a challenge to meet him in debate. Fox had left before it arrived, but a public meeting with three of his associates was arranged. Little was accomplished by the debate other than placing the major issues before the community. Williams retired to write a heated tract entitled *George Fox Digg'd out of his Burrowes*, a pun which victimized both Fox and his disciple Edward Burrough. Fox and John Burnyeat retaliated with *A New England Fire-Brand Quenched*. The contest was indecisive.

Progress through Expansion and Organization

During the last half of the seventeenth century the Quaker penetration of the colonies became ever more significant. In New Amsterdam, Friends appeared as early as 1657. Their presence threw the bewildered Dutch, who could not comprehend their frenzied cries and quakings, into a dither. One of the missionaries went to Long Island where he won many converts. The Dutch sentenced him to hard labor and when he refused to work they nearly beat him to death. Director Stuyvesant imprisoned the others for a time and then had them deported. The most celebrated case of persecution concerned John Bowne, who was jailed for holding a Quaker meeting in his home. After an involuntary journey to Amsterdam, he appealed to the Dutch West India Company; the officials rebuked Director Stuyvesant and ordered him to molest Bowne no more. Henceforth the Friends went about their work in peace.

In the Southern colonies, the Society of Friends made its most notable gains from among the unchurched. Josiah Coale and Thomas Thurston introduced the movement to Virginia in 1657. The success of their efforts prompted the authorities to pass legislation, in 1660, for the arrest, imprisonment, and banishment of all Quakers in the colony. Determined enforcement of the law apparently did not dampen the spirits of the missionaries, for they continued their labors with successful results. About the same time the movement made its first appearance in Maryland. There was some persecution there, but none of consequence. The situation was never as difficult in the South as it was in the New England colonies. In the Carolinas, where no efforts were made to suppress the religion, Quakerism was introduced not later than 1672.

The arrival of George Fox in the colonies in 1672 gave a considerable boost to the activities of the missionaries. Landing in Maryland in the spring of that year, he set out for Rhode Island where he remained two months, then started southward to Long Island and New Jersey, where he founded new meetings. His most important work, however, was accomplished in the South. In North Carolina, he gave support to the evangelistic labors of William Edmundson begun several months previously. From there he went to southern Virginia where his activities bore similar fruit. But the most encouraging experience was in Maryland, where a General Meeting was held on the Eastern Shore in October. It seems to have deeply gratified Fox and encouraged him as to the potential strength of the movement.

Fox's visit also led to some important advances in organization. Monthly Meetings for the conduct of business by a local congregation had already been founded in some areas, the first having been organized at Sandwich and Scituate in Massachusetts prior to 1660. There were also a few Quarterly Meetings, which brought a number of congregations together for the mutual consideration of spiritual and temporal matters; even a Yearly Meeting, which united the Monthly Meetings within its bounds and exercised general oversight of the congregations, had been established in 1661 in New England. But the process of organization was painfully slow until the coming of Fox breathed new life into the movement. Within the next quarter of a century five additional Yearly Meetings, from New York to North Carolina, would come into existence.

With the emergence of New Jersey and Pennsylvania as Quaker centers, the influence and prestige of the Society of Friends climbed with alacrity. In 1674, the ownership of New Jersey passed from the Duke of York to Sir George Carteret and John Lord Berkeley. Berkeley, who held control of West Jersey, soon sold his share to two Quakers and eventually the ownership and rule of West Jersey became vested in a land company dominated by Friends. For the first time in their as yet brief history, Friends were being charged with the responsibilities pertaining to government; they met the test with courage and self-assurance. When the province was opened to settlers, the proprietors announced that their purpose was to "lay a foundation for after ages to understand their liberty as men and Christians, that they may not be brought into bondage but by their own consent; for we put the power in the people." They were true to their word. The "Concessions and agreements of the Proprietors, Freeholders, and Inhabitants of West Jersey, in America," issued in March, 1677, provided that the settlers should elect annually their representatives to an assembly which should be a genuine legislature; judicial power should be exercised by judges and constables elected by popular vote; and trial by jury should be unrestricted and untrammeled. The right of every man to worship without interruption or molestation was made an established principle.

At once the population began to grow. In 1677, more than 200 Quakers founded a town at Burlington; the following year they established a Monthly Meeting. By 1681, New Jersey had received some 1400 settlers. That same year East Jersey, through purchase, came under Quaker control. The proprietors then appointed Robert Barclay, the eminent Quaker theologian, governor of the colony. This regime continued in power until 1688, when it was brought to an end by James II. In 1692, Quaker control of West Jersey was terminated when a group of Church of England men became the principal stockholders in the corporation. Ten years later, New Jersey became a royal province.

Perhaps the most prominent among Quaker proprietors of the Jerseys was William Penn. Born in 1644, the son of a British Admiral, he had been reared in the Anglican tradition, but from boyhood had exhibited certain tendencies toward Quakerism. His years at Oxford, followed by a period of study in France, only confirmed his "heretical" leanings. Later, in Ireland, he came under the influence of Thomas Loe, a well-known Quaker preacher, and was converted in 1667. As the son of Admiral Sir William Penn, the younger Penn enjoyed the favor of the court, even though his Quaker ideas rendered him somewhat suspect.

With the thought of establishing in America an asylum for the persecuted, William Penn, in 1680, petitioned the government for a grant of land. That his request was granted the following year was due to the fact that Charles II was trying to satisfy an old indebtedness to Penn's father. Thus Penn became sole proprietor of the territory which was to be named Pennsylvania. The following year he received from the Duke of York the lands which now comprise Delaware and governed them as part of Pennsylvania until 1703, when Delaware secured a separate legislature.

The enthusiasm Penn felt for his "Holy Experiment" was mirrored in the invitations which he extended to prospective colonists. He wanted them to know that while he had economic interests in the venture, a motive which was considered legitimate within Quaker circles, his main purpose was to build a free and self-governing society in which the will of one man might not hinder the good of the people. He saw that the role of government was "to support power in reverence with the people, and to secure the people from the abuse of power; for liberty without obedience is confusion, and obedience without liberty is slavery." With assurances of civil and religious freedom in conformity with these principles, he offered land at forty shillings for one hundred acres.

The response was all that Penn hoped it would be. The promise of freedom attracted the persecuted from the British Isles and from the Continent. At first the majority of the settlers were English and Welsh Quakers. Within a few years, however, immigrants would be coming in significant numbers from Germany, Holland, and France. It has been estimated that by the close of 1682, more than two thousand immigrants had arrived in Pennsylvania. Penn himself arrived in October of that year and spent ten months inspecting his lands, giving direction to the planning of Philadelphia, and preaching at Quaker meetings. During the first two years of the colony's existence, nine meetings for worship, one Monthly Meeting, and a Yearly Meeting were organized. And by the outbreak of the Revolution there were sixty-one Quaker congregations in Pennsylvania.

Penn's *Frame of Government of the Province of Pennsylvania*, issued in April, 1682, reflects some of the liberal views of such political philosophers as James Harrington, Algernon Sidney, and John Locke. He endorsed the social contract theory of government based upon the consent of the governed and the natural rights of men. This does not mean that he favored rule by the masses. Rather, his actions show that he believed in government by men of virtue and ability. This undoubtedly explains why voting and holding of public office were restricted to professing Christians. The first article of the *Frame of Government* clearly reveals Penn's belief that government is founded upon religion:

> In reverrence to God the Father of lights and Spirits the Author as well as object of all divine knowledge, faith and worship I do hereby declare for me and myn and establish it for the first fundamentall of the Government of my Country, that every Person that does or shall reside therein shall have and enjoy the Free Prossession of his or her faith and exersise of worsip towards God, in such way and manner As every Person shall in Conscience beleive is most acceptable to God and so long as every such Person useth not this Christian liberty to Licentiousness, that is to say to speak loosly and prophainly of God Christ or Religion, or to Committ any evill in their Conversation, he or she shall be protected in the enjoyment of the aforesaid Christian liberty by yᵉ civill Magistrate.[4]

Despite their avowed championship of freedom, Penn and his followers did not always relate this broad principle to every area of life. He and his Quaker neighbors saw no inconsistency in their holding of slaves, though it should be said that Penn freed them in his will. Some Friends, among them George Keith, opposed the institution publicly, but it was not until the eighteenth century that Quakers began to take a decided stand against slavery.

Nor did Penn always conform to the basic doctrines of the Friends. For example, he rejected the Quaker teaching of non-resistance and maintained that the use of force was legitimate when government was assaulted by revolutionaries or the rights of citizens were violated. On the other hand, he believed that Quakers and others who were conscientiously opposed to military service should not be conscripted. Most Quakers remained pacifists, interpreting literally the commandment "Thou shalt not kill." They were certain that peaceful persuasion was a powerful deterrent to aggression.

A study of Quaker religious life in Pennsylvania reveals an orientation which in some respects was not unlike the Puritan. Ascetic ideals and

[4] Mode, *op. cit.*, 160.

practices were as much a part of everyday life in Philadelphia as they were in Boston. In his *Conditions and Concessions to the Province of Pennsylvania,* Penn announced a policy of strict enforcement of laws pertaining to "slanders, drunkenness, swearing, cursing, pride in apparel, trespasses, distresses, replevins, weights and measures . . ." "Vain and evil sports and games" were also not to be tolerated. Simplicity was the ideal in matters of fashion and interior decoration; idle pursuits such as dancing and attendance at the theater were thought to be unworthy of Christians and definitely not in the spirit of the New Testament Church. Music and art were also attacked as sensuous and idolatrous pleasures, though this philosophy seems not to have influenced the celebrated Quaker painter of the eighteenth century, Benjamin West.

In other respects Quaker and Puritan ideals show a marked dissimilarity. While the Puritans esteemed an educated clergy and a theology which was intellectually appealing, the Friends preferred a ministry "called" but not trained and a plain pietistic faith which was emotionally satisfying. Many a Quaker regarded the university as a training ground of cold-hearted intellectuals destined for the service of a sterile church establishment. They wanted no part of it. William Penn could see the value of a basic education to the end that one might be able to read the Bible and the laws of the province. But he saw no need of learning ancient languages or of troubling oneself with the formalities of rhetoric and grammar in order to prepare for the Christian ministry; the spirit of God would fill the soul of his chosen messenger and send him forth to preach the truth regardless of his academic preparation.

From the standpoint of humanitarian principles, the Friends were far more advanced than their Puritan contemporaries. In Pennsylvania, the death penalty was provided only in cases of murder; punishment was much less brutal than in New England and prison conditions were superior to those in every other colony. Imprisonment of debtors was abolished by the personal action of William Penn, who had had practical experience with the institution and knew its folly. No other American settlement of the day could boast such an enlightened attitude toward its social problems.

One of the most outstanding of Penn's achievements was his harmonious relationship with the Indians. He consistently treated them with fairness and justice, even with fraternal affection. "I will consider you," he said to the Indians, "as the same flesh and blood with the Christians, and the same as if one man's body were to be divided into two parts." Upon receiving his charter, he wrote to the Indians to explain his intentions for the new land.

Now this great God hath been pleased to make me concerned in your parts of the world, and the King of the country where I live hath given unto me a great province therein, but I desire to enjoy it with your love and consent, that we may always live together as neighbors and friends, else what would the great God say to us Who hath made us not to devour and destroy one another but to live soberly and kindly together in the world?[5]

In 1683, Penn arranged a treaty with the Indians. It provided for the purchase of Indian lands, fair trade practices, and the same penal code for the Indians as for the whites. Penn sincerely hoped "to reduce the savage nations, by gentle and just means, to the love of civil society and the Christian religion." It is much to the credit of the Friends that the treaty was never broken and that Pennsylvania was not plagued by Indian wars so long as they were in control of the government.

Penn's second and last visit to his colony was in the years 1699–1701. During that time he carried on a rash of activities, preaching at meetings in Pennsylvania and New Jersey, arranging religious meetings for Negroes and Indians, and agitating for social reform. The rumor that all proprietary governments were to be transformed into royal colonies caused him to hasten to the mother country, never to return again. His remaining years, which were marked by disappointment and suffering, ended in 1718.

The eighteenth century opened auspiciously for the community of Friends in the Quaker colonies. Many an enterprising Quaker who believed in the dignity of honest toil became wealthy and influential, and, believing his wealth to be a trust from God, administered it with frugality. Economic security, however, was all too often accompanied by an apparent absence of the courage and spiritual fortitude which had typified the first settlers. Many who held positions of public trust maintained a formal allegiance to the Quaker movement, but it was evident that their affiliation was due more to upbringing than to personal commitment. The situation worsened after the London Yearly Meeting of 1737 declared that a man's family were to be considered members of the church if he held membership. And so the Friends followed in the steps of the Massachusetts Puritans and abandoned the necessary conversion experience in favor of membership by heredity. This road led downhill to an institutionalism that was both static and exclusive.

---

[5] Quoted in F. B. Tolles and E. G. Alderfer, *The Witness of William Penn* (Macmillan, 1957), 123.

The Transplanting of
Continental Protestantism

ENGLISH CONTROL OF THE EASTERN SEABOARD WAS NOT DESTINED TO REMAIN unchallenged. During the seventeenth century varied and complex forces in Continental Europe were setting the stage for a mass exodus which would divert the course of American colonial development. Early in that century the desire for political and economic advantage had committed the Dutch and the Swedes to the enterprise of carving out empires in the New World. The empires faded and expired, but from their residues emerged continuing societies which shone as beacons pointing the way to a land of opportunity. A later generation, seeking escape from religious persecution and the disasters of war and aspiring for freedom to propagate distinctive doctrines and to follow a particular way of life, would behold these lights from afar and respond to their invitation.

The wave of immigration from the European continent began in earnest towards the close of the seventeenth century. In 1690, the total colonial population of 250,000 represented largely English stock. English immigration, however, had by this time virtually come to a standstill. The fact that the population had multiplied ten times by 1775 was due in part to a non-English immigration which started almost imperceptibly in the 1680's with the coming of the Mennonites and Huguenots and was swept forward in the early decades of the eighteenth century by a surging tide of German immigrants who settled principally in Pennsylvania. Most of the Germans were refugees from the rich Palatinate region west of the Rhine River.

No part of Germany had suffered more from the ravages of the Thirty Years' War than the Palatinate. Its inhabitants had scarcely gained a measure of recovery before Louis XIV, in 1674, sent his armies into the area to burn and plunder. Again, in 1680 and 1688, the French monarch invaded the country, destroying crops, ruining vineyards, and driving thousands of citizens from their homes. The resultant conditions of famine and pestilence, together with the impossible tax burdens levied by the princes and the systematic persecution of Protestants, prompted many to migrate to Switzerland, the Netherlands, England, and eventually America. In England reports of the sufferings of these hapless victims elicited widespread sympathy. William Penn, deeply aroused after two visits to the Rhineland, invited the unfortunates to settle in Pennsylvania, where they might enjoy full religious and civil liberty. By the middle of the eighteenth century, some 150,000 to 200,000 Germans of various religious persuasions had made their homes in the colonies; of these, perhaps 70,000 were living in Pennsylvania.

EARLY DUTCH AND SWEDISH ESTABLISHMENTS

Religion in New Netherland

Torn by a long and bitter struggle with the Spanish which seriously depopulated their country, and preoccupied with trading concerns in the East, the Dutch had been slow to develop interest in American colonization. This situation began to change after Willem Usselinx, a pronounced Calvinist, published his first works on the economic possibilities of trade in America and Henry Hudson, in 1609, made his celebrated discovery of the river which bears his name. Mounting interest led to the organization of the Dutch West India Company in 1621, which was commissioned to establish trading posts and colonies. Three years later the company sent over Cornelis May, director of the projected settlement, and thirty Dutch and Walloon families; some of them went to Fort Orange (Albany), others to the Delaware, opposite the present site of Philadelphia. In 1626, Peter Minuit, an able leader soon to become the company's director, purchased Manhattan Island from the Indians and named it New Amsterdam. About 300 inhabitants were dwelling in the settlement by 1630.

The founders of New Netherland were men of bold and enterprising bent, whose principal end in colonization was unquestionably the acquisition of wealth. But reared in the established church of Holland, which was Calvinistic, they had developed a strong attachment to its faith and worship. They quite naturally, therefore, provided for the establishment of the Reformed religion in the new colony and took steps to institute services of worship. Yet it was not until 1626 that spiritual assistance was forthcoming in the arrival of two Comforters of the Sick. Persons appointed to this position, which was officially recognized by the Dutch Reformed Church, were authorized to assist in public worship, to conduct missionary activities when a minister was not available, and to serve as schoolmasters. Later they were permitted to baptize and officiate at weddings. With their coming, services were held in a large room over a horse mill which boasted a tower in which were placed church bells from Puerto Rico, probably captured from the Spanish in 1625.

At first, the West India Company assumed control of religion in the colony, together with responsibility for the appointment of church officers. The actual administration, however, was soon transformed to the Classis of Amsterdam, a church judicatory corresponding to a presbytery. In 1628, the first Reformed minister, Domine Jonas Michaelius, arrived at Manhattan. That very year he organized a church; Bastiaen Crol and Jan Huyck, Comforters of the Sick, and Director Minuit served as its first elders. Apparently the pastor was gratified by the first service of communion.

At the first administration of the Lord's Supper which was observed, not without great joy and comfort to many, we had fully fifty communicants—Walloons and Dutch; of whom, a portion made their first confession of faith before us, and others exhibited their church certificates. Others had forgotten to bring their certificates with them, not thinking that a church would be formed and established here; and some who brought them, had lost them unfortunately in a general conflagration, but they were admitted upon the satisfactory testimony of others to whom they were known, and also upon their daily good deportment, since one cannot observe strictly all the usual formalities in making a beginning under such circumstances.[1]

The Walloons, he went on to explain, understood so little Dutch that it was necessary for him to administer the sacrament and preach to them in French. He delivered the sermon from a manuscript, not trusting himself in the extemporaneous use of their language.

As for the Indians, Michaelius held little hope for their conversion. He found them to be a wicked and godless people, wholly uncivil and untrustworthy. "They have so much witchcraft, divination, sorcery and wicked arts, that they can hardly be held in by any bands or locks. They are as thievish and treacherous as they are tall; and in cruelty they are

[1] J. F. Jameson, *Narratives of New Netherland, 1609–1664* (Scribner, 1909), 124–125.

altogether inhuman, more than barbarous, far exceeding the Africans," whom he had come to know during a brief period of service on the west coast of Africa. He felt that the only workable scheme would be to remove the Indian children from their parents and place them under the care of Christian teachers who would train them in the faith. There is no indication that the proposal was carried out.

Michaelius was replaced in the spring of 1633 by Domine Everardus Bogardus; he arrived on the same ship which brought the new director, Wouter Van Twiller, successor to Bastiaen Crol. He served in New Amsterdam during the inefficient and corrupt administrations of Van Twiller (1633–1638) and William Kieft (1638–1647). From the outset, Bogardus proved to be a trial to his secular superiors. Incensed by Van Twiller's inept handling of government, he called the director "a child of the devil, a consummate villain" and attacked him publicly from the pulpit. Reports of the conflict drifted back to Amsterdam and, after investigation, Van Twiller was recalled. The next director, Van Kieft, took Bogardus to task for having entered his pulpit in a state of intoxication. The minister counterattacked with such forcefulness that Kieft refused to attend church and finally instituted civil proceedings against his foe. The feud ended indecisively without credit to either side.

During this era of friction, Van Twiller erected a little wooden church for the congregation which had hitherto worshipped in the room over the horse mill. Kieft, not to be outdone, pledged a thousand guilders from the company's funds for the erection of a stone church within the fort. In wily fashion, he contrived to raise substantial funds from the people on the occasion of a wedding feast held at the home of Domine Bogardus. After the wine had flowed freely, he passed around his subscription list. "Each then, with a light head, subscribed away at a handsome rate, one competing with the other; and although some heartily repented it when their senses came back, they were obliged nevertheless to pay; nothing could avail against it."

The pulpit of the new church was built high above the congregation as if to emphasize the authority of the minister. The voorleser or clerk stood in the baptistry below the pulpit and opened the service of worship by reading from the Scriptures and leading the congregation in psalm singing. The minister then entered the pulpit for the *exordium remotum*, an address which featured a chosen text and suggested its applicability to the sermon to follow. Then the deacons received the offering in a bag of velvet suspended from the end of a long pole, during which time the domine expatiated on the virtues of liberality. The sermon followed, usually an hour in length; at its close the voorleser handed to the domine the prayer requests of the communicants. When these had been read from the pulpit, the congregation sang another psalm and then filed out.

One of the most colorful of the early ministers was Domine Johannes

Megapolensis, who arrived in 1642. He was brought to the colony by Kiliaen Van Rensselaer, the wealthy patroon of Rensselaerwyck, near Albany. The West India Company had instituted the system of patroonships in 1629 as a means of attracting newcomers to the undersettled colony. Any member of the company who could bring over fifty colonists within four years would receive a large tract of land; within his domain he would be a semi-independent lord or patroon. One of the requirements for patroonship was to provide for the support of a minister and a schoolmaster. For a decade, Van Rensselaer evaded his responsibility in regard to the minister, but when Megapolensis became available, the patroon agreed to care for his temporal needs.

The scholarly domine labored for six years near Albany, conducting services in his home. It was agreed that a church should be built for him in 1643, but the promise never materialized. That same year he began preaching to the Indians, having learned the Mohawk language, and was apparently more successful with them than with his own people. He found the colonists indifferent to the ordinances of religion; they would sleep through his sermons and then spend the remainder of the Sabbath drinking and carousing. When his term of service had ended, he refused to remain. Arriving at New Amsterdam on his journey homeward, he was persuaded by the officials to assume the pastoral office there. Conditions in New Amsterdam left much to be desired; there was little enthusiasm for religion, and it has been estimated that approximately one-fourth of the town consisted of places for the sale of tobacco, beer, and brandy. Despite this unhappy situation, the domine continued to serve the congregation of about 170 until his death in 1670.

The principal threat to the security of the colony and its church lay in the irresponsible policies of its directors and the mercenary considerations of the company which they represented. Receiving neither protection nor encouragement from the homeland, the colony was forced to struggle along as best it could. The years brought increasing hardship. The apathetic Kieft, failing to conciliate the Indians, permitted the settlers on Staten Island to be massacred by the aborigines of New Jersey. Then, after a wanton attack on a tribe of friendly Algonquins, he placed the colony in jeopardy for two years (1643–1645), open to attack at every point and virtually unprepared to wage war. It was not until the coming of Peter Stuyvesant in 1647 that the colony's affairs took a turn for the better.

Despite its church establishment and its vigorous Calvinism, no country in seventeenth century Europe practiced more tolerance than Holland. This disposition was manifested in the regulations issued by the West India Company in 1638:

Religion shall be taught and practised there according to the Confession and formularies of union here publicly accepted, with which everyone shall be satisfied and content, without, however, it being inferred from this that any person shall hereby in any wise be constrained or aggrieved in his conscience, but every man shall be free to live up to his own in peace and decorum provided that he avoid frequenting any forbidden assemblies or conventicles, much less collect or get up any such. . . .

Each householder and inhabitant shall bear such tax and public charge as shall hereafter be considered proper for the maintenance of clergymen, comforters of the sick, schoolmasters, and such like necessary officers. . . .[2]

It is well known that the Dutch West India Company, for reasons of self-interest, urged toleration; however, there was much less toleration in New Netherland than was practiced in the Netherlands. Quakers were badly treated, and it was not until sometime after the English conquest of 1664 that Dutch Lutherans enjoyed real toleration.

Despite this minimal tolerance, in 1642, when the intrepid French Jesuit, Isaac Jogues, was captured by the Indians, some Dutch settlers, among them Domine Megapolensis, helped him to escape and brought him to New Amsterdam. While there were only two of his coreligionists dwelling there, he was received by the townspeople with cordiality. Deeply impressed by his experience, he wrote: "No religion is publicly exercised but the Calvinist, and orders are to admit none but Calvinists, but this is not observed; for besides the Calvinists there are in the colony Catholics, English Puritans, Lutherans, Anabaptists, here called Mnistes, etc."

With the arrival of Director Stuyvesant, the colony began to thrive and for a time a policy of toleration toward dissenters was maintained. Gradually, however, Stuyvesant imposed greater restrictions and it became evident that he stood for religious exclusiveness. His Puritanical bent was evidenced in his efforts to further Sabbath observance. He directed that Sunday drinking might be permitted only after two o'clock in the afternoon, except in the case of travelers and home consumers. The citizens were also expected to refrain from gainful employment or amusement during public worship.

That Stuyvesant's regime came to be characterized by religious tyranny must be credited in large measure to him, though his policies found considerable support among the clergy of the Dutch establishment. In 1654, he forbade the Lutherans on Manhattan Island to call a clergyman of their faith. Two years later the government made illegal all "conventicles and meetings whether public or private" which differed from the doctrine and practice of the establishment. Despite an enjoiner from the West India Company to treat the Lutherans mildly, Stuyvesant embarked on a campaign of persecution which led to the fining and imprisonment of nonconformists.

[2] Quoted in S. Van Rensselaer, *History of the City of New York in the Seventeenth Century* (Macmillan, 1909), I, 200.

None felt the weight of oppression more keenly than the Friends. Their first missionaries arrived in New Amsterdam in 1657; shortly thereafter two of them, women, were arrested and imprisoned for preaching unauthorized doctrines in the streets. Three others, going on to Long Island, were also apprehended and then deported to Rhode Island. To this action, the Dutch Reformed clergy gave their full approval. The most conspicuous case occurred in 1663, when Stuyvesant sent John Bowne, the leader of the Friends on Long Island, to stand trial in Holland. He was acquitted on the charge of illegal action and intent. The West India Company, realizing that a reputation for religious bigotry could seriously cripple their colonization program, prescribed toleration for New Netherland and directed Stuyvesant to follow a more liberal course. In this way, the persecution of dissenters was brought closer to an end.

In the meantime, a band of Jews, fleeing Portuguese persecution in Brazil, had landed on Manhattan Island in 1654. These Sephardic Jews, who originated in Spain and Portugal, had taken refuge from their European persecutors in northern Brazil, which for a time was owned by the more tolerant Dutch. When the territory reverted to Portugal in 1654, they fled to New Amsterdam, the first of their faith to settle on the North American mainland. Both Stuyvesant and Domine Megapolensis urged their immediate deportation, but the West India Company intervened and granted them the rights of settlers. At first, they encountered a certain prejudice against them, but this gradually died away; some Jews rose to positions of honor in the community. By 1700, there were about 100 Jews in the colony. During the eighteenth century they were joined by more of their Sephardic brethren, together with a few Ashkenazic Jews who had originated in Germany and Poland. Before the opening of the nineteenth century, other Jewish communities had been established at Newport, Rhode Island, Philadelphia, Charleston, Savannah, and Richmond. By the time of the Revolution, there were perhaps 2000 Jews in the colonies. The first rabbi with regular rabbinic ordination, however, would not be obtained until well into the nineteenth century.

The first Dutch Reformed church on Long Island was organized at Midwout in 1654 under the pastoral leadership of Domine Johannes Polhemus, who had been a missionary in Brazil. In 1660, Domine Henricus Selyns became minister at Breuckelen, a parish which numbered thirty-one families. Stuyvesant paid him 250 guilders a year to preach also at the Bowery village on Sunday afternoons. Two years later, a church was built at Bergen on the Hudson, the first within the present borders of New Jersey.

The Lutherans of New Sweden

When Peter Minuit was dismissed from the directorship of New Netherland in 1631, he turned to the task of developing a Swedish colony along the Delaware. As in the case of the Dutch, the motivation of the Swedes was economic and was inspired by Willem Usselinx, the Antwerp merchant who had convinced King Gustavus Adolphus of the value of trade in the New World. In 1638, two Swedish vessels under Minuit and Admiral Klas Fleming, a Finnish noble, sailed up the Delaware River to the present site of Wilmington and founded Fort Christina as a trading post. At least half of the new settlers sent under the auspices of the New Sweden Company were Finns.

The ordinances of the Lutheran Church, the established church of Sweden, were made available in New Sweden with the arrival of the first Lutheran minister, Reorus Torkillus, in 1639. He ministered there until 1643, when his life was cut short by a plague. His successor, Johan Campanius, arrived that same year with the new governor, Johan Printz. The latter had been instructed to

. . . take good measures that the divine service is performed according to the true confession of Augsburg, the Council of Upsala, and the ceremonies of the Swedish church, having care that all men, and especially the youth, be well instructed in all parts of Christianity, and that a good ecclesiastical discipline be observed and maintained.[3]

To Pastor Campanius went the honor of building the first Lutheran church on the island of Tinicum, near the present site of Essington, Pennsylvania. The new settlement was the seat of the governor's fort and mansion. Campanius served in the colony until 1648, ministering to both whites and Indians. So great was his concern for the aborigines that he mastered the Delaware language and made a translation of Luther's Small Catechism about 1646. It was used in manuscript form until its publication a half century later in Stockholm.

The constantly increasing number of Swedish colonists demanded a proportionate increase of clergy. Two additional ministers arrived in 1647, followed by two more in 1653. When New Sweden fell to the Dutch in 1655, there were three Lutheran ministers in the colony. One of them, Lars Lock, was permitted to remain and to conduct services of worship for his Lutheran parishioners. This arrangement continued when the colony was taken over by the English nine years later. The Swedish Lutheran churches, nevertheless, remained in virtually a static condition until 1697, when the Archbishop of Uppsala sent three clergymen to the Delaware. At that time there were probably between five and seven hundred Swedes dwelling in that area. For some years, the Swedish Lutheran churches thrived, especially during the ministry of Charles Magnus Wrangel which lasted from 1759 to 1768. Gradually, however, the Swedes became absorbed into their English environment and most of their congregations

---

[3] Quoted in W. W. Sweet, *Religion in Colonial America* (Scribner, 1949), 203–204.

eventually affiliated with the Anglican Church. Yet something of their character has been preserved in Holy Trinity Church (1699) in Wilmington and Gloria Dei Church (1700) in South Philadelphia, both of which still stand.

The Dutch Reformed Church under English Rule

In September, 1664, Stuyvesant, without a struggle, yielded New Amsterdam to English forces. The colony, which came under the control of James, Duke of York, was named New York and the establishment of the Dutch Reformed Church was ended. Any fears the Dutch might have had concerning the fate of their six ministers and thirteen churches were dispelled by the surrender agreement, which provided that they should enjoy freedom of conscience and worship and church discipline. The English had nothing to lose by the arrangement since they were scarcely in a position to create an Anglican establishment in a colony which was predominantly Dutch.

In February, 1665, the Duke of York issued laws very tolerant for the times but quite in harmony with the policy of Charles II to remove pressure from dissenting groups, knowing this would give relief to the Roman Catholics with whom he secretly sympathized. Article Ten states that "no congregations shall be disturbed in their private meetings, in the time of prayer, preaching, or other divine service; nor shall any person be molested, fined, or imprisoned, for differing in judgment in matters of religion, who professes Christianity." Shortly thereafter, the English governor directed the city authorities to raise tax moneys for the support of the Dutch ministers; and in 1670, the governor advised certain commissioners at Albany that the Reformed church there was to be considered the parochial church and that it should be maintained by taxation.

During 1673 and 1674 the Dutch, who were then at war with England, regained control of New York and reestablished the Reformed Church. But the colony was restored to the English in 1674 and henceforth the Dutch were shown fewer favors. Governor Andros permitted them to worship without fear of molestation; at the same time he insisted that they take an oath of allegiance to England. Not content with this accomplishment, Andros began to meddle in the affairs of the Dutch Church. He tried to foist an unwanted minister, Nicholas Van Rensselaer, on the church of Albany; the plan backfired and Andros had the embarrassing task of removing his own appointee.

During these critical years, the maintenance of sufficient clergy was at best difficult; in the decade which followed Stuyvesant's capitulation only one Dutch minister was received in the colony, while four were lost by death or departure. So acute was the need for ministers that in 1679 four of the Dutch clergy actually formed themselves into a classis and ordained Peter Tesschenmaeker, a theological graduate of the University of Utrecht, as minister for New Castle. Their action was approved by the Classis of Amsterdam. Three years later, Domine Henry Selyns, a man of remarkable talent and energy, arrived in New York. His vigorous leadership brought new life to the discouraged Dutch congregations and won for them added influence with the heads of state.

Another cause for hope was the appointment of Thomas Dongan in 1682 to the governorship. Liberally inclined, this Roman Catholic official quickly won his way into popular favor by his acts of tolerance. In 1683, he called a General Assembly composed of the people's representatives to frame laws for the welfare of the colony. The Assembly issued a Charter of Liberties which was approved by the governor. In matters of religion, it stipulated that Christians should enjoy the right to worship according to their conscience. When New York became a crown colony with the accession of James II in 1685, the Charter of Liberties was repealed and eventually the Assembly was dissolved. James instructed Dongan to persecute no one for religious reasons; state support, however, was to be given only to the Anglican communion. The governor, notwithstanding, preserved the most complete religious freedom throughout his administration. This is apparent in his report of 1687, in which he commented on religious conditions in New York.

Every town ought to have a minister. New York has, first, a Chaplain belonging to the Fort, of the Church of England; secondly, a Dutch Calvinist; thirdly, a French Calvinist; fourthly, a Dutch Lutheran. Here bee not many of the Church of England; few Roman Catholicks; abundance of Quaker preachers, men and Women especially; Singing Quakers; Ranting Quakers; Sabbatarians; Anti-Sabbatarians; some Anabaptists; some Jews: in short, of all sorts of opinions there are some, and the most part of none at all. The Great Church which serves both the English and the Dutch is within the Fort, which is found to be very inconvenient. Therefore, I desire that there may bee an order for their building another; ground being already layd out for that purpose, and they not wanting money in store wherewithall to build it. The most prevailing opinion is that of the Dutch Calvinists. It is the endeavor of all persons here to bring up their children and servants in that opinion which themselves profess; but this I observe, that they take no care of the conversion of their slaves . . .[4]

The overthrow of James II and the subsequent accession of William and Mary were well received in New York inasmuch as there was a growing fear that under James the Roman Catholic Church might someday come into power. In the period of turmoil which immediately followed, Lieu-

[4] Quoted in E. T. Corwin, *A History of the Reformed Church, Dutch* (Christian Literature Co., 1895), 87–88.

tenant-Governor Nicholson was forced to flee; and during the interim, Colonel Jacob Leisler and his anti-Catholic party were in power. Leisler was strenuously opposed by the Dutch Reformed clergy, a circumstance which placed the clergy in popular disrepute and led to their persecution by the new government. Finally, the king appointed Henry Sloughter to the governor's post. Leisler's enemies then brought him to trial on charges of treason and he was executed.

In accordance with instructions from his sovereign, Sloughter proclaimed toleration for all but Roman Catholics. But he was unsuccessful in getting the Assembly to pass an act for the proper maintenance of a minister in every town of forty or more families. His successor, Benjamin Fletcher, who arrived in 1692, achieved better results. Through persistent effort, he was able to obtain, in 1693, the passage of a Ministry Act, though it was not entirely to his satisfaction. He wanted an act of establishment for the Anglican Church; the Assembly, when it provided for the maintenance of a "good sufficient Protestant Minister," had no such intention. The crown's officials, however, chose to interpret the act as establishing the Church of England and undoubtedly the king so understood it when he granted royal confirmation in 1697. With the passage of time, many citizens came to believe that the Anglican Church was legally established in New York.

Meanwhile, the Dutch congregation at Manhattan was taking steps to insure the legal status of its church. Several times Domine Selyns and the Consistory petitioned for a charter; it was finally granted in 1696 after the church presented a handsome gift to the governor. During the eighteenth century, a number of Dutch churches won similar charters from the government. It was a period of prosperity for the Reformed churches, characterized by good will among the Dutch and English clergy. In 1700, there were twenty-nine Dutch Reformed churches as opposed to one Anglican church in the colony. The dominant position of the Dutch continued throughout the colonial period despite intermittent but ineffectual efforts on the part of the governors to advance the cause of Anglicanism or to take charge of the Dutch churches. In reality, the most serious obstacle to the Reformed churches was not the English government; it was an inflated sense of complacency. Not until the outset of the Great Awakening would the churches be startled out of their lethargy; even then rigid formalists would sally forth to do battle with the besieging forces of enthusiasm.

THE FRENCH HUGUENOTS

Twenty years before his revocation of the Edict of Nantes in 1685, Louis XIV initiated a policy of increasing pressure and persecution for French Protestants. He purposed to keep his victims within the homeland,

and to that end he placed a ban upon emigration; in this way he hoped to force their conversion to Roman Catholicism. But Louis was unsuccessful. Hundreds of these Huguenots surreptitiously fled the country to find refuge in other European sanctuaries or to make their way eventually to America.

Many of the colonies, having received word of the sincere piety of the Huguenots, gladly welcomed them into their midst. During Dutch rule, there were so many Huguenots in New York that the public documents had to be published in French as well as Dutch. They had no pastor, however, until the arrival of Pierre Daillé in 1683. He had been a professor at the well-known theological school at Saumur, which had been destroyed that very year by order of Louis XIV. Besides officiating in New York, Daillé ministered twice a year to the people at New Paltz. A few years later, the arrival of Pastors Peiret and De Bon Repos enabled him to broaden his field of endeavor and ultimately accept a call to Boston. One of the most interesting communities was New Rochelle, about twenty miles above the city of New York. Settled entirely by Huguenots from Rochelle, it retained its distinctiveness in language and custom until after the American Revolution.

As early as 1662, Huguenots were beginning to arrive in Massachusetts Bay colony. According to a record of that year, John Touton, a French physician from Rochelle, "made application to the General Court of Massachusetts, in behalf of himself and other Protestants, expelled from their habitations on account of their religion, that they might have liberty to live there, which was readily granted to them." In 1686, the French erected a church at Boston and ten years later called Pierre Daillé from New York to serve as their pastor.

Charles II of England, wishing to increase the export of raw materials from South Carolina, sent a company of Huguenots there in 1679 at his own expense to cultivate the soil. From that time there was extensive emigration of French Protestants to the English colonies. In 1690, William III dispatched a large number of them to Virginia; during the years immediately following, the immigration statistics climbed well beyond the thousand mark. And so it continued well into the eighteenth century, every year witnessing the arrival of more Huguenots, chiefly in the southern colonies.

In certain colonies where an established church was supported by taxation, special acts were passed to relieve Huguenots of such tax obligations and to grant them freedom of worship. Virginia enacted such a law in 1700:

Whereas a considerable number of French Protestant refugees have been lately imported into his majesty's colony and dominion, and several of which refugees have seated themselves above the fall of James's River, at or near the place commonly called and known by the name of the Monacan towns, etc., the said settlement be erected into a parish, not liable to other parochial assessments.[5]

Coming as they did into a predominantly English environment, the French could not hope to retain their separate identity for long. The second and third generations grew steadily less familiar with the French language and customs. In the end, most of them found their way into the Dutch Reformed, Presbyterian, or Anglican communions.

THE ARRIVAL OF THE GERMAN SECTARIES

Despite the tremendous spiritual energy which Martin Luther had infused into German Protestantism, the century following his death witnessed the steady ebb of the Protestant tide. The causes of the retrogression were threefold. The Lutheran establishment, being concerned largely with an intellectual formulation of scriptural truth, came to interpret saving faith in terms of intellectual assent. Strict orthodoxy became the *sine qua non* of religion, a condition which led to heresy trials, almost constant struggles with Roman Catholics, Reformed Protestants, and Anabaptists, and the consequent demoralization of the country's religious and moral life. The state control of the church inspired a legalistic and perfunctory attitude toward religion, thus contributing to the spiritual depression. No less important was the devastating Thirty Years' War, which left Germany exhausted and in a desolate state.

The first signs of religious revival appeared in the mid-seventeenth century with the nascence of German Pietism. Its message was that the inner spiritual life is more important than theological controversy. It stood for the mystical experience, practical and intense preaching, extensive pastoral work, the universal priesthood of believers, and piety and moderation in conduct. While the movement centered within the Lutheran Church, it affected all branches and phases of German Protestantism. None entered more completely into its spirit than the various sectaries which stemmed from the left wing of the Reformation. When the disastrous invasions of the Palatinate by Louis XIV forced them to flee their homes, many settled in the American colonies and in this way transmitted the pietistic strain to the New World environment.

The first German settlement was begun in 1683 at Germantown, near Philadelphia, with the arrival of a colony of religious refugees from the Palatinate. These immigrants were members of the Mennonite sect, which stood in the main stream of the Anabaptist movement. The sect took its name from the Dutch Anabaptist, Menno Simons (1492–1559), a leader noted for his wisdom and moderation. Its adherents were persecuted for their mystical and pietistic emphases by the orthodox churches, but with

[5] Quoted in R. Baird, *Religion in America* (Harper, 1856), 160.

undaunted zeal they continued to eschew outward ritualism and scholasticism in favor of a religion of the heart. Several visits of William Penn to the Continent convinced them of their oneness with the Society of Friends and bore fruit in a number of conversions to Quakerism. One of the converts was a young lawyer, Francis Daniel Pastorius, who would become agent of the Frankfort Company and, in its service, shepherd the first immigrants to Pennsylvania.

These first settlers were mostly weavers from Krefeld; some of them had already been won to the Society of Friends, while many others made the transition after their arrival in America. They soon established an enviable reputation for their integrity and for their application of the principle of human freedom. Somewhat more advanced than the Friends in their social views, they chided their neighbors for supporting slavery and the slave trade. "Have these poor negers not as much right to fight for their freedom," they demanded in 1688, "as you have to keep them slaves?" That same year they formed a Mennonite congregation at Germantown and constructed their first church edifice in 1708.

The second notable wave of German immigration to Pennsylvania was that of the German-speaking Swiss Mennonites, who arrived about 1710. They settled at Pequea Creek, in what is now Lancaster County. The rich, fertile farmlands attracted many others who followed in their footsteps, and soon Lancaster became the chief Mennonite center in America. Some of these settlers belonged to a conservative sect known as the Ammenites or Amish, which found its origins in a seventeenth century schism among the Mennonites. They became known for their doctrinal rigidity and their plain dress, especially their wearing of hooks and eyes in preference to buttons, which they thought was vain. But in matters such as the refusal to bear arms or take oaths and the insistence on believers' baptism, freedom of conscience, and the separation of church and state, they were in accord with the other Mennonite sects.

Another religious group having much in common with the Mennonites was the Dunkers or Tunkers. Their name is derived from the German word *eintunken,* to dip, thus suggesting their mode of baptism. Founded at Schwarzenau in 1708 by Alexander Mack, this sect adopted the New Testament as their only creed. They held to the principal doctrines and practices of the Mennonites, but stressed trine immersion, love feasts accompanied by feet-washing, and the anointment of the sick for healing. Like all the Baptist sectaries, their church government was congregational.

The first Dunker penetration of Pennsylvania was in 1719, when twenty families settled at Germantown, Conestoga, Skippack, and Oley. Their leader, Peter Becker, is best known for a revival which he conducted among them in 1723 and which led to many conversions. Before the revival, the Dunkers had met separately in private homes for their worship; now they were inspired to found a congregation, their first in America.

Becker was chosen as elder. In 1729, Alexander Mack arrived at the head of another band of colonists and immediately took command of the movement. Four years later, the coming of a third group under the leadership of John Naas brought further strength to the sect. There were about 700 Dunkers in Pennsylvania and New Jersey by the outbreak of the Revolution.

The most prominent Dunker in the colonial period was Christopher Saur, who published the first German newspaper in America. His publication, the first edition of which appeared in 1738, overshadowed Benjamin Franklin's efforts to publish for the German community. It gave publicity to the particular religious tenets of the German sectaries and consequently added to the influence of these groups. The contribution for which Saur is best known was his edition of the German Bible, first issued in 1743. It would be difficult to overstate its importance to the religious life of the early German settlers.

A unique secession from the Dunker fellowship eventually led to the formation of the Ephrata Society under the leadership of Johann Conrad Beissel. After his arrival in America in 1720, he was baptized into the Dunker faith and for some time served as elder of the Conestoga congregation. Constantly repudiated for his opposition to marriage and his insistence that the seventh day should be observed as the day of rest, Beissel and his followers withdrew and in 1732 founded the Ephrata Society in Lancaster County. It was developed along semi-monastic lines; the membership practiced a life of asceticism and devotion, and all property was owned by the order. Separate buildings were provided for the brothers and sisters who were clothed in monastic garb. The society owned a printing press from which issued a great number of religious books, among them the mystical writings of Beissel, and a constant supply of music for an order which excelled in singing. For a few decades the movement flourished and several Dunker congregations were brought within its fold. After Beissel's death in 1768, however, the society fell into a state of declension which it never overcame.

Another sect which came to Pennsylvania during the early part of the eighteenth century was the Schwenkfelders. Their founder, Kaspar Schwenkfeld von Ossig, was a contemporary of Luther. His insistence that the Bible does not contain everything necessary for salvation and that the sacraments were not means of grace led to his persecution by both Protestants and Roman Catholics. He continued, nevertheless, to preach the need of the living word communicated through the Holy Spirit. For well over a century his followers were oppressed because of their persistent faith. One group, forced into Saxony, took refuge on the estate of Count von Zinzendorf, then migrated to Pennsylvania in 1734. They established themselves in Montgomery, Bucks, and Berks counties. Though they selected George Weiss as their minister in 1741, they maintained no semblance of a congregational organization and held informal worship services in private homes. In 1762, the Schwenkfelders held a general conference which resulted in the issuance of a catechism and hymn book and the establishment of regular services of worship and formal religious instruction. This program, which continued twenty years, was administered wholly by laymen. The sect had neither a professional ministry nor a formal church structure. In 1782, however, the Schwenkfelders organized themselves into a church and eight years later erected their first church edifice.

THE MORAVIANS

Perhaps the most remarkable of the German sectaries was the Moravian Brethren or the Unitas Fratrum. The group's origin is traced to the evangelical movement in Bohemia inspired by John Huss in the fifteenth century. The original intention of the group, organized in 1457, was to form a Christian fellowship which would retain connections with the national church, even though they experienced no spiritual uplift in its rites. Persecution proved this hope to be unrealistic and prompted the group to meet a decade later as a synod and ordain three men to their priesthood. The rift was complete. Upon request, Bishop Stephen of the Austrian Waldenses granted episcopal consecration to Michael Bradacius who then reordained the three priests in order to validate their orders. The Unitas Fratrum were thoroughly evangelical in their emphases and were highly regarded by both German and Swiss leaders of the Reformation. But intensified persecutions in the sixteenth and seventeenth centuries seriously weakened the movement and led to the scattering of the church. That the Unitas Fratrum did not become extinct was due in large measure to the resourcefulness of Bishop John Amos Comenius (1592–1670).

Early in the eighteenth century, Christian David, a Moravian leader, made arrangements with a Saxon nobleman, Nicolaus Ludwig, Count von Zinzendorf (1700–1760), whereby he and his followers might sojourn on the Count's estates at Herrnhut. Zinzendorf, a Lutheran with pietistic inclinations, welcomed the opportunity to serve these oppressed evangelicals. In 1722, the little band of Moravians arrived at Herrnhut. As the months passed a steady stream of refugees poured into Zinzendorf's refuge until a sizeable population had been gathered. At first, the newcomers worshipped in the Lutheran parish church at Berthelsdorf, but finally they withdrew to form the Moravian Church. The Count soon found himself devoting more time to his neighbors and becoming increasingly involved in their activities until he emerged as their leader; he was consecrated bishop in 1737. Herrnhut now became the nucleus of a vast missionary enterprise which reached out far beyond the borders of Europe and, in a decade, touched America.

One of the groups which found shelter at Herrnhut was the Schwenk-felders. Because of their disputatiousness, Zinzendorf was eager to discover some irenic means of hastening them on their way. When he heard of Colonel James Oglethorpe and his new colony in Georgia, he began to explore the possibilities of securing a haven for them there. Oglethorpe and his trustees were amenable and in 1733 agreed to provide free passage and land for the Schwenkfelders. The latter then rather impulsively changed their plans and located in Pennsylvania. Since by this time opposition to the Moravians was developing in Saxony, it seemed wise for Zinzendorf's followers to occupy the Georgian tract. The site afforded a splendid base for missionary operations among the Cherokee and Creek Indians.

With the full approval of Oglethorpe, a group of nine Moravians under the leadership of Augustus Spangenberg arrived in April, 1735, to occupy some five hundred acres at Savannah. The following year twenty more colonists made the crossing on the same ship which bore John Wesley to America. Some missionary work was accomplished with the Indians, whose chief was on friendly terms with Spangenberg. A brief effort was even made to convert Negro slaves in South Carolina. But gradually the movement weakened because of mortality by fever, departure from the colony to Europe or Pennsylvania, and persecution due to refusal to participate in the struggle with Spain. When George Whitefield, in 1740, offered the remnant free passage to Philadelphia, they accepted with alacrity.

After their arrival in Pennsylvania, Whitefield employed them to assist in the building of a school for Negroes on a five thousand acre tract at the "Forks of the Delaware," which he named Nazareth. For a time the project went smoothly; then doctrinal differences began to divide Whitefield and Peter Böhler, the Moravian leader. The controversy finally became so intense that Whitefield discharged the Moravians and ordered them off the property. They spent the winter at Nazareth. The next April, Whitefield found himself in financial difficulty, being unable to make payment on a debt he had incurred in order to purchase the land. Since the Moravians showed willingness to buy the tract, Whitefield negotiated the sale and departed. That December Count Zinzendorf, who had devoted himself to missionary work since his banishment from Saxony in 1736, reached the Moravian settlement. At a celebration of the nativity on Christmas eve, he named the place Bethlehem.

It was Zinzendorf's hope that he might be able to unite all German Protestants in Pennsylvania into an evangelical alliance. To this end, he preached among the various denominations and during the next six months was successful in persuading them to hold seven synods to consider organic union. At the first four synods there were representatives from every German Protestant denomination in Pennsylvania, but after the fourth meeting all withdrew except the Moravians, the Lutherans, and the Reformed. After three additional synods, the remainder were convinced that the project was hopeless.

For a brief interval, Zinzendorf pastored the Lutheran congregation at Philadelphia, ministering also to the Reformed. When a certain faction opposed his preaching, he withdrew and built a stone church on Race Street at his own expense; it eventually became the first Moravian church in the city. During his remaining months in America, he took the lead in founding seven churches in Pennsylvania and two in New York, as well as organizing schools at Germantown, Fredericktown, Oley, and Heidelberg. Before he left New York in January, 1742, he appointed Peter Böhler to supervise the itinerant preachers and Bishop David Nitschmann to take charge of the Indian missions.

Zinzendorf also made several tours of Indian territory. On the first tour he covered the area which embraces the Blue Mountains and the Upper Schuylkill and, in an interview with the chiefs of the Six Nations, won permission for his coreligionists to travel freely through the Indian domains. A second tour brought him to the Mohican village of Shekomeko, where Christian Henry Rauch, the first Moravian missionary to the Indians, had been at work since 1740. Zinzendorf organized Rauch's converts into a congregation.

In the years immediately following Zinzendorf's departure, the Moravians at Bethlehem launched a wide-scale campaign to win converts to their Christocentric doctrine which emphasized the vicarious atonement. Again under Spangenberg's leadership they infiltrated every colony in the South, as well as New Jersey, New York, and most of the New England colonies. In order to support this extensive program, the Bethlehem and Nazareth communities had to accept a semi-communistic system which they called "Economy." Personal property might be held, but all profits from business had to be at the disposal of the church.

In the meantime, important developments were taking place in Europe, which would affect the church in America. The passage of a set of denominational regulations by the General Synod at Marienborn in 1745 brought to an end any thought of a German Protestant union in Pennsylvania. Also, the decision of the English Parliament in 1749 to recognize the Moravian Church as an ancient Protestant Episcopal church helped to clarify the situation. It meant that in the English colonies the Moravians might gain opportunities and concessions never before available. This inspired their leaders to negotiate for a tract of land in North Carolina where they might establish a missionary center. The transfer of land was made in 1753 and "Wachovia," as the tract was called, received recognition from the governor as the special diocese of the Moravians. Three years later, another settlement was begun at Lititz, Pennsylvania. During this decade increasing prosperity came to the church, making it possible to abolish the system of "Economy" which had demanded such sacrifice on the part of the membership. Unfortunately for the church in America, the General Synod, meeting at Marienborn in 1769, ruled that it was to be managed by boards called Provincial Helpers, which were responsible to the Elders' Conference rather than to the congregations in their jurisdiction. The loss of representation or self-government at the very time when the colonies were gaining independence would constitute a crippling blow to the Moravian Church in America.

During the period of tension which culminated in the French and Indian War, the Moravians were falsely reported to be in league with the French. Legislation denying them the right to give religious instruction to the Indians forced them to remove their missionaries from Shekomeko. They began another mission at Gnadenhütten, on the Mahoning, which soon attracted a congregation of about 500 Indians. Then, in November, 1755, hostile Indians raided the mission and massacred all but four of the occupants.

After peace had been restored, missionary efforts among the Indians were renewed. Under the leadership of David Zeisberger, a mission was established in 1765 on the north branch of the Susquehanna and named Friedenshütten, or Tents of Peace. During the next four years, additional missions were begun on the left bank of the Allegheny and on the Susquehanna. Under pressure of persecution by the unconverted Indians, Zeisberger and his fellow missionaries led their converts westward where in 1770 they settled on a tract along the Tuscarawas River in Ohio. There they founded the villages of Schönbrunn, Gnadenhütten, Lichtenau, and Salem. Judging from the reports of Colonel George Morgan, Indian agent for the Western District, they were blessed with phenomenal success. A remarkable degree of civilization was achieved and numerous bands of Indians were won to Christianity. Not until the outbreak of the Revolution would their activities be seriously hindered.

THE GERMAN LUTHERANS

The unfortunate circumstances which prompted the German sectaries to flee from the homeland to America were similarly evident in the decision of many Lutherans and Reformed to emigrate. But there the similarity ended. The Lutheran and Reformed groups, being accustomed to a close church-state relationship and a non-congregational polity, maintained full connections with European ecclesiastical bodies throughout the colonial period. Both looked to Halle, that center of pietism inspired by Philip Jacob Spener (1635–1705) and developed by August Hermann Francke (1663–1727), for advice and support. They were not disappointed.

From a numerical standpoint, the Lutherans were the most important of the German religious groups which settled in America. There were a few German Lutherans living near Philadelphia as early as 1682, but it was not until after the turn of the century that the colonies were deluged by German immigrants. Settling first in such places as Falckner's Swamp (New Hanover), Germantown, and Philadelphia, they gradually pushed farther into the interior, crossing the Susquehanna and moving southward to Maryland and Virginia. By 1750, there were 40,000 or more Lutherans in Pennsylvania alone.

The first regular pastor of a German Lutheran congregation in Pennsylvania was Daniel Falckner, who organized a church at New Hanover about 1703. Another early cleric was Anthony Jacob Henkel, who preached in Germantown and Philadelphia in 1717. The following year John Casper Stoever and his son, who had the same name, landed in Philadelphia. The elder Stoever ministered to the Lutherans in Virginia, while his son served for more than fifty years as a missionary in eastern Pennsylvania, Maryland, and Virginia.

Most of the early Lutheran settlers had been influenced by pietism and had come to regard the Christian life as one of devotion and love. They cherished not only their Bible and catechism but devotional classics such as Johann Arndt's *True Christianity*. Preaching and the sacraments were to them a great source of consolation. Unfortunately, ministerial service was seldom available in the colonies. The Swedish and Finnish Lutheran churches were always ready to help; yet, without a steady supply of clergy it was quite natural that some should go over to other religious bodies or simply allow their spiritual life to go unnurtured. Besides, in their destitute condition, few congregations were financially able to support a pastor. The vast majority worshipped in private homes at first; services were edifying but unadorned with liturgy. The first common liturgy was not adopted until 1748.

While Pennsylvania was the principal colony of entry for German Lutheran immigrants during the eighteenth century, a significant penetration of the South was also made. As the best farm lands in eastern Pennsylvania were occupied, some of the Lutheran settlers journeyed southwestward into Maryland and Virginia where they were offered land at a low price. By the 1730's there was a small Lutheran community at Monocacy Creek; it was organized into a congregation in 1738 through the missionary efforts of the younger Stoever. Other Lutheran communities sprang up near the present city of Hagerstown and at Baltimore. The first German Lutherans arrived in Virginia in 1717 and eight years later founded a church in Madison County. By the opening of the Revolution, congregations had been organized at Winchester, Strasburg, Rader's, Woodstock, and Pine Church.

In 1710, the first Lutheran settlers located in North Carolina. Their community at New Bern, however, was almost completely liquidated the following year by an Indian massacre. A score of years would pass before other Lutheran settlers would migrate to central and western North Carolina. The 1730's would also see the beginnings of Lutheranism in South Carolina, notably at Purysburg on the Savannah and at Charleston.

One of the most moving stories in American history concerns the planting of Lutheranism in Georgia. For almost two hundred years, stalwart Lutherans in the Austrian province of Salzburg had practiced their faith despite increasing persecution by the Roman Catholic majority. In 1731, the archbishop of Salzburg drove them from the province to wander in the dead of winter through the various nations of Europe. Finally the English people, touched by their suffering, arranged for the passage of 91 of these Salzburgers to the recently founded colony of Georgia. They arrived in 1734, and having been accorded all the rights of English citizens and freedom of conscience and worship, settled at Ebenezer on the Savannah River. Two instructors from the University of Halle, John Martin Boltzius and Israel Christian Gronau, accompanied them on their journey and served as their pastors. In 1735, 110 more refugees found their way to the colony. During the next five years the Salzburgers literally poured into Georgia so that by 1741 the population of Ebenezer had risen to 1200. Under wise and devoted leadership, the settlement flourished. When Pastor Gronau died in 1744, he was replaced by Hermann Henry Lemke, who served for nineteen years as Boltzius' faithful colleague.

The settlement was governed by its ministers, who were in turn subject to the Lutheran Church in Germany and the English Society for the Promotion of Christian Knowledge which had contributed handsomely to their cause. The two pastors constituted themselves a tribunal to rule on both spiritual and temporal matters, and it is said that they were preeminently just in their decisions. Their high moral sensitivities were apparent in the leadership which they gave to social and philanthropic causes. An orphanage was built, which served also as a church until an edifice could be erected. A considerable portion of the income from two grist-mills, a saw-mill, and a rice stamping-mill was devoted to charity. For some time, they took a strong position against the legalization of slavery in the colony and only upon extreme pressure withdrew their formal objections. Of tranquil disposition, they lived in peace with their Indian neighbors and even carried on some missionary work among them. Thomas Jones, in 1740, spoke of them thus:

. . . The people live in the greatest harmony with their ministers and with one another, as one family. They have no drunken, idle, or profligate people among them, but are industrious, and many have grown wealthy.[6]

[6] Quoted in A. B. Faust, *The German Element in the United States* (Houghton Mifflin, 1909), I, 241.

The principal problem which disturbed Lutheran congregations throughout the colonies was the scarcity of ministers. Closely related to it was the difficulty in raising adequate funds for a pastor's support, a challenge which they had not had to face in the homeland where the church was state-supported. In 1733, Pastor John Christian Schulz, who had united the three Lutheran congregations of Philadelphia, persuaded his people to send him and two laymen to Europe to enlist ministers and teachers and to raise funds. In London, where George II, a German, was on the English throne, they laid their problem before the king's chaplain, Pastor Frederick Michael Ziegenhagen. In Halle, they appealed to Professor August Hermann Francke. Both indicated their sympathetic concern but were reluctant to promise aid until the American congregations could commit themselves to the adequate support of a minister. This they could not do, and so the matter dragged on indecisively for a number of years. But when Count Zinzendorf arrived in Pennsylvania and undertook work among the Lutherans, the period of vacillation promptly ended. The Halle leaders breathlessly commissioned Henry Melchior Muhlenberg for the American post, and with that act a new era in colonial Lutheran history began.

Henry Melchior Muhlenberg (1711–1787), received his theological education at the University of Göttingen, served for fifteen months as a teacher at the Halle Orphanage, and later was pastor of a rural church in Saxony. Because of his strong leaning toward missionary work, the call from Francke to assume a pastorate in America was a veritable summons to Macedonia. He accepted without hesitation and in 1742 sailed to the colonies. Landing at Charleston, Muhlenberg spent some time with the Salzburgers before going on to Philadelphia. He found the Pennsylvania congregations in a state of distraction due largely to the influence of Zinzendorf. With indefatigable zeal he threw himself into the work of reformation and within a month emerged as master of the situation and as the installed pastor of the united congregations at Philadelphia, New Hanover, and The Trappe.

A man of broad vision, Muhlenberg saw unlimited opportunities for expansion in his new field. He assumed the pastoral oversight of the Germantown congregation and founded a school for each local church. Gradually he extended his influence into other areas and new congregations were organized. The demands upon his time finally became so great that he had to turn to the Halle authorities for assistance. Muhlenberg's *Halle Reports* were published in Germany, where they captured the imaginations of the people and as a result won both men and money for his cause. In 1745, Pastor Peter Brunnholz and two catechists, John Kurtz and John Schaum, arrived from Halle bringing funds to be used in building new churches.

Muhlenberg remained in command of Lutheran operations, but relinquished the pastoral oversight of the congregations at Philadelphia and Germantown to Brunnholz. This enabled Muhlenberg to devote more time to remote areas where the Lutherans were as yet unorganized. Congregations were soon organized at Upper Milford, Saucon, Easton, and Perkasie. Then, in 1747, the indomitable German went off on a pastoral tour which took him to Tulpehocken, Lancaster, York, and Hanover, Pennsylvania, and Frederick, Maryland. At each place he brought inspiration, renewed zeal, and organizational strength to the languishing congregations.

Undoubtedly, Muhlenberg's most important contribution to American Lutheranism was his forming of a synod in 1748. For some time he had recognized the need for increased cooperation among the pastors and churches and for unified standards to bind them together. To that end a synod was called to meet on August 26, 1748. Six pastors and twenty-four lay delegates representing ten congregations met at the newly dedicated St. Michael's Church in Philadelphia. The synod, then known as the "United Pastors," is now denominated the Ministerium of Pennsylvania. While at first it represented but one-seventh of the Lutheran congregations in the colonies, it grew rapidly in strength and set the standard for synodical organization in other areas. Its first act was to adopt a uniform liturgy suggested by Muhlenberg and two other pastors.

Through his leadership in the synod, Muhlenberg emerged as the foremost cleric in the church. As he saw it, the most formidable problem before him was the maintenance of an adequate supply of ministers. The Lutheran tide of immigration was swelling year by year, but few clergy arrived to care for the newcomers' spiritual needs. Because times demanded training a native ministry, Muhlenberg bought forty-nine acres of land in Philadelphia in 1749 for the purpose of erecting a school and seminary; his plan never came to fruition. But he did receive theological students into his home and trained them for the ministry. Among the students who went forth from this school were Muhlenberg's three sons.

From 1755 to 1759 there were no meetings of the synod. It was a time of discouragement, with opposition to the synod developing among the laymen and among those ministers who held no connection with Halle. To make matters worse, there was almost constant friction between the "United Pastors" and the European leaders who could not quite appreciate the needs of American Lutheranism. The arrival of Charles Magnus Wrangel in 1759 as provost of the Swedish churches was thus heralded, even among the Germans, as a sign of better things to come. Wrangel and Muhlenberg became fast friends, and the sound counsel which the latter received from the learned Swedish leader explains in large measure Muhlenberg's decision to revive the synod in 1760. Thenceforth the synod, with improved organization, exerted a powerful influence over the major proportion of American Lutherans and proved to be an important asset in the development of the church. By 1771 there were eighty-one congregations under Muhlenberg's pastoral oversight, and doubtless there were more independent congregations. With the outbreak of the Revolution, contacts with Halle were sharply curtailed; by 1779 they were non-existent. When the war finally came to an end, the American Lutheran Church had emerged as an independent spiritual entity.

THE GERMAN REFORMED

The same forces which prompted the German Lutherans to settle in the colonies were responsible for the arrival of their Reformed compatriots. Like the Lutherans, the Reformed received assistance from the Halle pietists. The first German Reformed ministers to settle in the colonies were Henry Hoeger, who founded a congregation at New Bern, North Carolina, in 1710, and Samuel Guldin, who arrived in Pennsylvania that same year and preached informally while making his living as a farmer. It was not until 1719 that a Reformed Church was built at Germantown. Apparently the congregation had no installed pastor at the time since the cornerstone was laid by a Swedish minister.

The guiding spirit of the Reformed Church in America was John Philip Boehm, a schoolteacher from Worms who settled in Montgomery County, Pennsylvania in 1720. Widely recognized for his piety, he was persuaded to conduct informal religious services among the pastorless people. In the meantime, congregations had been gathered at Falckner's Swamp, Skippack, and White Marsh. There being no likelihood that they would be able to attract a minister in the near future, they unanimously requested Boehm to accept the pastorate. He was reluctant to assume the office inasmuch as he was not ordained, but finally in 1725 he acceded to their wishes. For several years, he preached and administered baptism to hundreds of children in remote districts.

With the arrival of George Michael Weiss, an ordained minister, in 1727, Boehm's troubles began. Weiss declared him unfit for the work of a pastor due to his lack of ordination and took steps to deprive him of his position. Boehm's friends recognized the tenuous character of their case, but thought that it at least deserved a hearing. And so they applied to the Classis of Amsterdam for a decision. Their action not only brought about a favorable response from the Classis but inaugurated an era of close cooperation with the Dutch churches in America. The Classis ruled that under the circumstances Boehm's previous ministerial activities were legal but that "he must be ordained to the ministry according to ecclesiastical usage." Boehm was duly ordained in November, 1729, and the strife between him and Weiss came to an end. Weiss took charge of the congregations at Philadelphia and Germantown, having organized the former, while Boehm retained pastoral oversight of his three congregations.

During the next six or seven years there was a large influx of settlers from Switzerland, the immigrants making their homes in the area between the Delaware and Schuylkill Rivers. They and their German neighbors were served for a time by John Henry Goetschius and Conrad Wirtz, candidates for ordination who had been empowered to administer the sacraments. Both finally received ordination in the Presbyterian Church, though they continued to labor among Reformed congregations. That Reformed ministers should have applied to a Dutch classis or a Presbyterian presbytery is not as surprising as it at first might seem. These bodies were almost identical in their doctrinal tenets and church polity and their clergy could pass rather freely from one denomination to the other. The Heidelberg Catechism, doctrinal standard of the German Reformed Church, was thoroughly in harmony with the standards of Dutch Reformed and Presbyterian churches.

In 1729, George Weiss and Jacob Reiff, the latter a prominent layman in the Skippack Church, journeyed to the homeland in order to raise funds for their churches. Weiss returned two years later, bringing with him John Bartholomew Rieger, a physician who supplied the churches in the neighborhood of Lancaster. John Peter Miller arrived in 1730 with authority to administer the sacraments. A man of high scholarly attainment, he easily won Presbyterian ordination and soon afterward became pastor of the Reformed church at Tulpehocken, where he ministered for four years. At the end of that time, he came under the influence of Conrad Beissel, founder of the Ephrata Society, who had come to Tulpehocken with the thought of converting the young minister. Miller was so impressed with Beissel that he resigned his pastoral charge and led his elders and several members of the congregation into the monastic community. After Beissel's death, Miller became the head of the order, a position which he held until his death in 1796. He seems to have been too mystically inclined to have remained in the rather doctrinally centered Reformed Church; nevertheless, his loss was keenly felt by his former associates.

The unusual deprivations and divisions which plagued the German Protestant groups in the colonies challenged many leaders, among them Count Zinzendorf, to seek a solution through greater unity. The outstanding advocate of union in the Reformed camp was Henry Antes, a prosperous layman who proposed a federative union of the German churches. He played an important role in the interdenominational synods called by Zinzendorf. Another leading protagonist in this ecumenical adventure was John Bechtel, minister of the church at Germantown. For a time the friendliest relations existed between Lutherans, Reformed, and Moravians, but when it finally became apparent that only the Moravians were gaining much by the association, the unity movement began to fizzle. In 1744,

Bechtel was dismissed by his congregation and shortly thereafter united with the Moravian Church.

What Muhlenberg was to the Lutherans, Michael Schlatter was to the Reformed. A native of St. Gall, Switzerland, Schlatter (1716–1790) taught for some years in Holland, where he was ordained. In 1746, the Synods of Holland, having agreed to assume responsibility for the German Reformed congregations in America, appointed Schlatter to visit the scattered churches and to establish an ecclesiastical organization as soon as possible. He landed in Boston and three days later set out for New York and Philadelphia. At Philadelphia he discovered that there were only four Reformed ministers in Pennsylvania to care for a communicant membership estimated at 15,000. At once he began a tour of the settlements and endeavored to infuse new life into the congregations at Germantown, Goshenhoppen, Lancaster, and Tulpehocken.

On October 12, 1746, Pastors Boehm, Weiss, and Rieger met with Schlatter, at the latter's request, in Philadelphia for the purpose of laying the groundwork for the establishment of a synod or Coetus. The following September the Coetus, which was composed of thirty-one ministers and elders, met in Philadelphia. Four years later the Coetus sent Schlatter to Europe to raise funds for the destitute churches in America. His efforts resulted in a sum of 12,000 pounds being set aside for the benefit of the churches in Pennsylvania, but the sum could not be made available until the Coetus agreed to subordinate itself in all matters to the Classis of Amsterdam. It had to submit its minutes annually for approval and could not admit ministers who were not endorsed by the Classis. When Schlatter returned to America in 1752, he brought with him six young clergymen, as well as 700 Bibles which were distributed free of charge.

In England interest generated by Schlatter's appeals for help led to the formation of a Society for the Promotion of the Knowledge of God among the Germans. Some 20,000 pounds were raised to establish charity schools in Pennsylvania, especially among the Germans. But the manner in which the project was publicized was so imprudent and insulting that it seriously jeopardized its effectiveness in the German communities. When Schlatter accepted the superintendency of these charity schools, an avalanche of criticism was showered upon him. Popular opinion, aroused by the editorials of Christopher Saur, doomed the effort and brought about the reluctant resignation of Schlatter, who soon afterward went into retirement. His work, however, had not been in vain. The educational ideals which he had carefully nurtured were carried forward by his successors, and the ecclesiastical body which he founded continued to serve as a fitting reminder of his contributions to the American Reformed Church.

The Scotch-Irish

Presbyterians

AMERICAN PRESBYTERIANISM WAS THE NATURAL CHILD OF ENGLISH PURITAN-
ism and Scottish Presbyterianism, modified and reshaped in the colonial
environment. In England, Puritanism had only gradually split into Presbyterian and Congregational wings; and even in America, where the
Congregational form was dominant, there were always tendencies toward
Presbyterianism. Nowhere was the tendency more marked than in Connecticut. During the latter half of the seventeenth century, Puritans largely
from Connecticut planted churches on Long Island, in northern New Jersey, Pennsylvania, Maryland, Virginia, and South Carolina. Many invited
Scottish Presbyterian ministers to preach to them, while at the same time
they maintained their Congregational form of government. There were
instances in which Presbyterian congregations called Congregational ministers into their service. The denominational lines were not then sharply
drawn.

In theology, both Presbyterian and Congregational wings had been attracted to the Federal or Covenant system as it was enunciated in the
famous Westminster Confession, a document prepared by English Puri-

144

tans and Scottish Presbyterians in 1646. Following the line of reasoning of Scotsmen such as John Howie and Edward Fisher and Englishmen such as Thomas Cartwright and William Ames, it modified pure Calvinism by softening the decrees of God and placing more stress on man's responsibility. Presbyterians differed from Congregationalists chiefly in their doctrine of the church. In preference to a church which finds its reality in the local congregation, Presbyterians stressed the universal church, the congregation being merely a part of the body of Christ. Their ministry thus held its authority not from the local congregation, as in the case of Congregationalism, but from the church universal. Even their lay eldership derived its power from the same source. To Presbyterians, no individual church had the right to stand alone; it had to subject itself, as did its clergy, to the discipline of church courts which made its functioning complete. Despite these differences, Presbyterians and Congregationalists found that they could cooperate in numerous projects; during the latter half of the seventeenth century the Presbyterian and Congregational Union of London worked harmoniously with Connecticut and Massachusetts in sending ministers to Presbyterian pastorates in Pennsylvania and Delaware. With the coming of the Scotch-Irish in significant numbers during the eighteenth century, most of the Puritan churches in the middle and southern colonies eventually assumed a Presbyterian character.

THE SCOTCH-IRISH IMMIGRATION

The major strength of colonial Presbyterianism was derived from the great migration of Scots from North Ireland. Varied and complex forces contributed to their coming. Early in the seventeenth century, the English government tried to displace the Roman Catholic Irish population of northern Ireland by confiscating their property and inviting English and Scottish settlers to make their homes there. English officialdom supposed that this would bring an end to the almost ceaseless uprisings. Having seized some 3,800,000 acres, they divided the land into estates and granted it to wealthy and influential citizens who would agree to bring over colonists to work on the estates. These new settlers were to be kept as a closed social unit to avoid intermarriage with the Irish.

The response was all that the English had desired. A gigantic wave of emigrants poured forth, notably from southwestern Scotland. From 1610 to 1620 between 30,000 and 40,000 settlers arrived in northern Ireland. It has been estimated that by 1641, 100,000 Scots had settled in Ulster; most of them were Presbyterians. Within a period of forty years, the Presbyterian Church in Ireland numbered five presbyteries and nearly 100 congregations.

Unusual difficulties, however, were destined to plague the Scottish Presbyterians in this new land. Their leases, which originally had been granted at a modest rate in order to attract them, were soon doubled or even trebled. Then came governmental restrictions on the importation of foodstuffs into England, followed by the Woolens Act of 1699 which ruined the woolen industry in Ireland. To make matters worse, the Presbyterians were taxed for the support of the Anglican clergy, who represented the established church. Then, in 1704, the Irish Parliament, through the efforts of the bishops in the upper house, passed legislation which denied Presbyterians the right to hold public office unless they agreed to receive the sacraments of the Anglican Church. The right to officiate at weddings was also refused the Presbyterian clergy. Small wonder that in the early decades of the eighteenth century many of these harassed dissenters should have turned their attention to the New World.

Beginning as a mere trickle in the late sevententh century, the stream of immigration rose to full force after 1710. The first sizeable body of Presbyterians, numbering 600 to 800 laymen and two ministers, landed in Boston in 1718. Failing to receive an expected word of welcome, they moved on to the frontier, where they braved the attacks of savage Indians. Within a decade they had founded churches in Maine and New Hampshire as well as on the Massachusetts frontier. But so great was the opposition that most of the Presbyterian churches in that part of the country eventually became Congregational. At Milford, Connecticut, Presbyterians attempted to organize a congregation in 1741. They even extended a call to Samuel Finley, later to become president of the College of New Jersey. However, when he arrived to assume the pastorate he was clapped into jail, fined, and then unceremoniously ejected from the colony.

Disappointed but unperturbed by their reception in New England, the Presbyterian immigrants turned ever more to the Middle Colonies and to the South. Many of the later settlers from Ulster did not sail to New England, but disembarked at the Delaware River towns of Philadelphia, Lewes, and New Castle. Some sailed northward along the Delaware and founded settlements in Bucks County as early as 1720. Others about the same time reached the Susquehanna and from there moved across into Cumberland County. As James Logan observed in 1729: "It looks as if Ireland is to send all its inhabitants hither for last week not less than six ships arrived and every day two or three arrive also." Twenty years later one-fourth of the inhabitants of Pennsylvania were Scotch-Irish.

Another swarm of settlers poured into the Potomac Valley and traveled southwest into the Shenandoah as early as 1732. By 1740 there were Scotch-Irish settlements from Virginia to Georgia. Charleston, South Carolina, became a leading port of entry for these immigrants after 1750. From Charleston one group proceeded northward until it encountered the Scotch-Irish settlers sifting down from Pennsylvania and Virginia; another went southward into Georgia; while a third pressed on to the western frontier. By the mid-eighteenth century no colony was totally devoid of

Scotch-Irish, and in many colonies they were to be found in significant numbers.

THE BEGINNINGS OF PRESBYTERIAN ORGANIZATION

Any movement, if it is to flourish, must be endowed with able leadership. Such leadership for the Presbyterian movement in the colonies was found in the person of Francis Makemie (1658–1708). He was born in northern Ireland and educated at the University of Glasgow. After returning to Ireland, he was licensed by the Presbytery of Laggan in 1681 and the following year was ordained as a missionary to America. By 1683 he was at work in Maryland, but his early missionary labors took him over a much wider area, notably along the coasts of Virginia and North Carolina and even to Barbados. In 1692 he visited Philadelphia and inaugurated Presbyterian work there. On the eastern shore of Maryland and Virginia his missionary labors culminated in the establishment of five churches, the best known being at Rehoboth and Snow Hill. He made several trips to England to appeal for help in evangelizing America and was apparently successful. On a visit to London in 1704, he persuaded the United Brethren, an association of Presbyterian and Congregationalist ministers, to support two missionaries to the colonies, John Hampton and George McNish, both graduates of the University of Glasgow.

Returning to America with his two new associates, Makemie began to envision the possibility of creating unity among the widely scattered congregations through the creation of a presbytery. With such a judicatory it would be no longer necessary to look to Europe for clergy; the presbytery in America could license and ordain its own ministry. To this end, Makemie summoned Presbyterian leaders to meet with him in Philadelphia. At this meeting, which was probably held in the spring of 1706, the first presbytery was organized. Makemie was elected the first moderator. The other ministers who made up the charter membership were Samuel Davis, pastor at Lewes, Delaware; Jedediah Andrews of the church at Philadelphia; John Wilson of New Castle; Nathaniel Taylor of Patuxent, Maryland; and the two missionaries, Hampton and McNish. Three of the ministers were originally from New England. Most of the Puritan clergy in New York and New Jersey did not affiliate with the presbytery; probably they anticipated the imminent creation of a presbytery more conveniently located.

The first presbytery was unique in that it was the earliest American judicatory to bind its churches into an intercolonial system for assistance and control. It had the advantage of being able to ordain and install its own clergy and regulate the affairs of the congregations within its bounds without looking to some European ecclesiastical body for direction. It helped to foster a spirit of interdependence among its member organizations throughout the colonies and thus to prepare the way for a strong national body after the severance of ties with Britain.

Neither questions of doctrinal uniformity nor matters of organization occupied the minds of the presbyters at the first meetings. The result was that no constitution was drawn up and many details were left to be worked out later. If the presbytery was patterned after any model, it was after the Ulster form of presbytery. On the whole, however, the Presbyterian Church in America developed its own distinctive character and constituted an indigenous organization from its inception. That it received most of its early ministerial leadership and financial assistance from London and Boston rather than Ireland and Scotland is instructive. It betokened a growing rapport with the "Presbyterianized Congregationalists" of New England which would bear fruit in many cooperative ventures.

An unfortunate incident, which brought considerable discomfort to Moderator Makemie, proved to be the happy means whereby Presbyterianism was brought to the favorable attention of many American dissenters. Early in January, 1707, Makemie and John Hampton, having attended a meeting of presbytery at Freehold, New Jersey, made their way to New York on the first leg of a contemplated journey into New England. Makemie preached in a private home in New York; then the pair went on to Long Island, where once again Makemie preached at Newtown. Lord Cornbury, one of the most despotic governors ever to preside over the affairs of New York, ordered them arrested on the charge of preaching without a license. They were held in confinement until March. Shortly afterward the charges against Hampton were dropped; but Makemie had to stand trial in June. His defense was that his license to preach as a dissenting minister, which was issued in Barbados and recognized in Virginia, was equally valid in New York. Though the court ordered his acquittal, the vengeful Cornbury forced him to pay all costs of the trial. The following year, an irate Assembly passed a bill which rendered the action illegal; charges were preferred against the governor and he was recalled. The Presbyterians, now vindicated, emerged from the affair in a much stronger position.

Nevertheless, all was not sweetness and light. The Scotch-Irish congregations were poor, frequently unable to support a minister and sometimes unable to abide the minister they could support. There was much contention and strife within the congregations and the church courts were constantly involved in cases of discipline. In a letter written in 1723, the Reverend George Gillespie suggested some of the problems of his day.

As to the affairs of Christ in our parts of the world: There are a great many congregations erected, and now erecting; for wthin the space of five years by gone, near to two hundred Families have come into our parts from Ireland, and more are following: They are generally Presbyterians. So, it would appear, yt

Glorious Christ hath great designs in America; tho' I am afraid not to be effectuated in my days: for the mirs and congregations be multiplied with us; yet alas, there is little of the power and life of Religion with either: The Lord disappoint my fears. There are not above 30 ministers & probationer preachers in our Synod, and yet six of the said number have been grossly scandalous; Suspension for 4 Sabbaths hath been the greatest censure inflicted as yet.[1]

The misdemeanor which elicited the above penalty was committed by Robert Laing, who had the temerity to wash himself on "the Lord's Day."

Like their Puritan confreres, the Presbyterians placed a high value on education, especially for their clergy. When David Evans, a young Welsh layman, took it upon himself to preach to his countrymen in Pennsylvania, he was censured and advised to take instruction if he desired to preach. He did as the presbytery directed, and four years later, in 1710, received ordination. Candidates for the ministry were given rigorous training and were expected to show their proficiency in the original languages of Scripture, theology, and the homiletic arts. Once ordained and installed as pastors, they conducted simple services which featured long scholarly expositions of Scripture. Their congregations accustomed themselves to a protracted service of worship, at the conclusion of which they would repair to the local tavern for rest and refreshment, returning to the church in time for the afternoon service.

Not many years after the founding of the presbytery, a number of Puritan churches in New York and New Jersey decided to affiliate with this Presbyterian body. The New York congregations were composed almost entirely of New Englanders, while the Jersey churches were generally mixed because of the penetration of settlers from Britain, Holland, and France. Several new congregations were springing up in Pennsylvania, notably along the river valleys on the frontier, as wave upon wave of Scotch-Irish immigrants poured into the Middle Colonies. Only in Maryland and Virginia did the early gains prove abortive. In Maryland, many Presbyterian settlers departed for other colonies upon the establishment of Anglicanism there; the Virginia churches, which were largely dependent upon the Maryland congregations, were thus weakened and soon became defunct.

THE EXPANSION OF COLONIAL PRESBYTERIANISM

By 1716, 19 ministers, 40 churches, and 3000 communicant members were affiliated with the presbytery. No end to the sweeping tide of Scotch-Irish immigration was yet in sight. To Presbyterian leaders the time seemed right to divide the presbytery into four presbyteries and unite

[1] M. W. Armstrong, L. A. Loetscher and C. A. Anderson, *The Presbyterian Enterprise* (Westminster, c. 1956), 21–22.

them into a body which would then be known as the Synod. The original presbytery, consequently, decreed in 1716 that the presbyteries of Philadelphia, New Castle, Long Island, and Snow Hill should be constituted. But only the first three materialized. Most of Pennsylvania and New Jersey came within the bounds of Philadelphia Presbytery. New Castle Presbytery included Delaware, Maryland, and Virginia; while Long Island Presbytery embraced the province of New York.

The powers of the new synod, which met for the first time in September, 1717, were rather vague. Having been given no definite constitutional authority, it served as a kind of presbytery exercising general jurisdiction over three regional courts. In the future, difficulties would arise over the division of powers between the synod and its presbyteries. At this time, the Presbyterian churches in New England and South Carolina remained independent of the synod, though presbyteries had been organized in both areas. The Londonderry Presbytery, organized in 1730 for the churches in southern New Hampshire, was the first to be constituted in New England. A second was the Boston Presbytery, formed in 1745. The first judicatory in South Carolina was founded in 1722 and named the James Island Presbytery.

With the organization of the synod, the Presbyterian Church made some significant gains in leadership. Among the most prominent ministers to join its ranks were Jonathan Dickinson and John Pierson, pastors of the Puritan churches at Elizabethtown and Woodbridge, New Jersey. Dickinson (1688–1747), scion of a respected New England family, was educated in humanities at Yale, and ordained to the Congregational ministry in 1709. At that time he assumed the pastorate of the church at Elizabethtown, where he served for almost forty years. He was in favor of immediate affiliation with the new presbytery, but did not press the matter since a majority of the congregation preferred to remain independent. By 1717, he was successful in persuading his people to adopt Presbyterianism. Three years later he was appointed a member of the Standing Commission of the synod; in 1721 he became its moderator. His calm judgment and tact proved indispensible to the synod in its formative years. His fellow New Englander, Pierson, was also educated at Yale and was the son of its first president.

Another important though temporary accession to the church was a young man named Jonathan Edwards. After completing graduate studies at Yale in 1722, he accepted a call to the little Scottish Presbyterian church in New York. His decision was doubtless reflective of the then current movement to unite the presbyterianized Congregational churches of Connecticut with the synod. Nothing came of the movement; nevertheless, it had anticipated the coming union of 1801. As for Edwards, his pastorate terminated after eight months, and he did not serve the Presbyterian Church again until the last year of his life.

If New England gave its share of giants to colonial Presbyterianism, so did northern Ireland. One of its most eminent sons was William Tennent (1673–1746). He was educated at the University of Edinburgh and licensed by one of the Scottish presbyteries. But in 1704 he was ordained in the Anglican Church, perhaps because of pressure on the part of the state. In 1718, he arrived in Philadelphia and, upon application to the synod of Philadelphia, was enrolled as a minister after giving a satisfactory statement of his faith. That same year he became pastor of a church in East Chester, New York, which flourished under his leadership. In 1720, he was called to a larger parish at Bedford, New York. A brilliant scholar superbly trained in Latin, Greek, Hebrew, philosophy, and theology, he soon won a wide reputation for his learning. His major contribution to the church would be in the field of education.

During the period following the organization of the synod, the cause of Presbyterianism was advanced significantly in the South. After the death of Francis Makemie, the church in Virginia had gone out of existence. Then, in 1732, a new tide of Scotch-Irish immigrants began to sweep into the Shenandoah Valley, and Presbyterianism in Virginia was reborn. That very year sixteen families under the leadership of Joist Hite, a Dutchman, migrated from Philadelphia. Thereafter large numbers of Scotch-Irish settlers came southward from Pennsylvania and pushed through the valley into the Piedmont.

These pioneers entered the new land unaccompanied by ministers. But no sooner had they carved out settlements in the midst of the wilderness than they urged the presbyteries to send them pastors. The presbyteries were fully cognizant of the need and did what they could to supply the congregations. They encouraged pastors to leave their congregations for a time to go on missionary tours which might take several months. They required candidates for the ministry to serve on the frontier before admitting them to ordination. Still it was never possible to enlist enough men to meet the ever-expanding opportunities which the frontier afforded.

In Virginia, where early Presbyterian activities had been impeded by the government, John Caldwell and a group of prospective settlers petitioned Lieutenant Governor William Gooch, in 1738, to grant them freedom of worship. The Governor's answer was highly encouraging:

As I have always been inclined to favour the people who have lately removed from other provinces to settle on the western side of our great mountains so you may be assured that no interruption shall be given to any minister of your profession who shall come among them, so as they conform themselves to the rules prescribed by the act of toleration in England, by taking the oaths enjoined thereby, and registering the places of their meeting, and behave themselves peaceably towards the government.[2]

[2] Quoted in G. J. Slosser, ed., *They Seek a Country* (Macmillan, 1955), 69.

The Reverend Samuel Gelston entered the Valley of Virginia in 1737 as a missionary of Donegal Presbytery. James Anderson began to hold services in 1740; the following year John Thomson inaugurated an itinerant ministry. The first settled pastor in western Virginia was John Craig who, in 1740, came to the Augusta and Tinkling Spring congregations; he devoted the rest of his life to Presbyterian work in the valley.

After 1740, Scotch-Irish settlers appeared in greater numbers in central and western North Carolina; some traversed the mountains and made their homes in the Tennessee wilderness. In the 1750's, French and Indian attacks on the frontier caused many of the inhabitants to migrate southward into western South Carolina and Georgia. A decade later, Scotch-Irish immigrants landing at Charleston were encouraged by the colonial government to press on to the West. According to the report of a missionary sent out by the synod in 1768, there were then thirty-eight Presbyterian communities in South Carolina and five in Georgia; by the outbreak of the Revolution the combined figures would have risen to seventy. The history of evangelistic efforts among these Presbyterians of the South can best be seen in the discussion of the Great Awakening.

PROBLEMS OF FAITH AND ORDER

The opening decades of the eighteenth century witnessed a widening rift among Presbyterians in Britain and America over questions of theology and discipline. In Scotland and Ireland the courts of the church had combated the rising tides of heterodoxy by forcing subscription to the Westminster Confession of Faith as a prerequisite to ordination. Their decisions, however, instead of restoring peace to the church, served only to inspire widespread indignation. By the 1720's, tension in the Scottish and Irish judicatories had become explosive.

In America, the Scotch-Irish element found increasing dissatisfaction with the Puritan party, whose roots were embedded in New England Congregationalism. The latter were opposed to any compulsory subscription to creeds or confessions or articles of church polity. When the Reverend George Gillespie of New Castle Presbytery succeeded, in 1721, in getting an overture passed at synod to the effect that members might submit suggested legislation to the synod for adoption, the Puritan party objected strenuously; they feared that this was a move toward subscription. It was their conviction that should the Scotch-Irish wing be able to pass a subscription act they would be in a position to dominate the church.

In 1722, Jonathan Dickinson was invited to preach the opening sermon of synod; he saw this as his golden opportunity to further the cause of liberalism. He took a firm stand on the ground that the Scriptures are the only sufficient rule of faith and practice and that human interpretations of the Bible are too fallible to be made into official doctrinal

definitions of what is Scriptural truth. The fallibility of the human interpretations was evident in the fact that Roman Catholics, Anglicans, Presbyterians, and others held differing theological positions. He argued that
when credal statements are made officially binding then they, rather than
the Bible, become the final standard of faith. There is then no longer any
rule by which they can themselves be tested or reshaped. Eventually they
become ends in themselves. As a result of Dickinson's tactful but forceful
and persuasive leadership, tempers cooled and the synod was able to
reach a temporary compromise.

The controversy over subscription, however, soon broke out again and,
in 1727, the Reverend John Thomson introduced an overture in synod
which provided that all ministers and licentiates should subscribe strictly
to the Westminster Confession of Faith and Catechisms. The measure was
designed to protect American Presbyterianism from the corruption of its
doctrines by such "heresies" as Deism, Socinianism, and Arminianism,
which were flourishing in England at the time. The synod reached no decision during the current session, but when the measure was brought up
again in the synod in 1729, Dickinson led the liberal party in opposition
to it. His argument had not changed in the intervening years. Though he
himself personally accepted the Confession, he opposed the requirement
of subscription because of his love of liberty and his concern for the
church. The purity of the denomination would be preserved far better, he
felt, by examination of a candidate's religious experience as well as of his
beliefs. As Dickinson saw it, a creed was only a systematic statement of
the general beliefs of a given denomination and one of the many guides
available for the study of the Bible. When its purpose went beyond leading men to the Bible, there would be contention and strife within the
Christian fellowship; the function of religion would be reduced to the
formulation of rational truths about God.

The Adopting Act was finally passed in 1729, but thanks to the influence of Dickinson, it was a compromise measure and was adopted unanimously. The passage of a strict act would undoubtedly have split the
church asunder. The Adopting Act denied that synod had any right to
control the conscience. Nevertheless, in order to keep the church's doctrine pure and unadulterated,

. . . all the ministers of this Synod, or that shall hereafter be admitted into this
Synod, shall declare their agreement in, and approbation of, the Confession of
Faith, with the Larger and Shorter Catechisms of the Assembly of Divines at
Westminster, as being in all the essential and necessary articles, good forms of
sound words and systems of Christian doctrine, and do also adopt the said Confession and Catechisms as the confession of our faith . . . And in case any
minister of this Synod, or any candidate for the ministry, shall have any scruple
with respect to any article or articles of said Confession or Catechisms, he shall
at the time of his making said declaration declare his sentiments to the Presby-

tery or Synod, who shall, notwithstanding, admit him to the exercise of the ministry within our bounds, and to ministerial communion, if the Synod or Presbytery shall judge his scruple or mistake to be only about articles not essential and necessary in doctrine, worship, or government . . .[3]

Since the synod did not define what were the "necessary" articles, it meant that the matter could be left largely to the presbyteries. This arrangement appeared to offer more doctrinal latitude than strict subscription, and so won the support of the liberal party. But the conflict between the various warring elements in the church had not been fully resolved. It lingered as a smoldering fire which would again burst into full flame amid the tensions of the Great Awakening.

[3] Armstrong, Loetscher, and Anderson, *op. cit.*, 31–32.

8

The Great Awakening

TO MANY THOUGHTFUL OBSERVERS LIVING IN THE COLONIES DURING THE OPEN-
ing decades of the eighteenth century, it was all too apparent that the
well-springs of religious fervor in America were rapidly drying up. Where
once there was ardent devotion to things of the spirit now there were self-
satisfaction and lethargic indifference. The churches, once the supreme
arbiters of community faith and practice, were losing their hold on the
people. Drunkenness and debauchery were the order of the day; even
among the clergy there was ample evidence of egregious conduct. Samuel
Whitman's observation, in an election sermon preached in Connecticut in
1714, "that religion is on the wane among us," may well have been the
understatement of the year.

Multitudinous forces contributed to this unhappy condition. The development of commerce and increase of wealth in the colonies helped to
focus attention on materialistic interests. At the same time, the royal determination to abolish representative government and build up centralized
power through intercolonial union evoked such concern among the colonists that politics became a chief topic of discussion. Intermittent wars
plagued and harassed the settlers and added to the general tension of
the times. New Englanders especially felt the impact of the bitterly fought
King William's War (1689–1697) and Queen Anne's War (1701–1713).
Up and down the western frontier there were sporadic conflicts with the

Indians, such as the war which pitted North Carolinians against Tusca-roras in 1712. In such a situation, Americans had little time for the usual refinements of civilization; culture declined and with it interest in religion.

The problem, however, cannot be dismissed as purely extraecclesiasti-cal. Fervor and zeal were too often missing from the churches, since religion was confined to a vague discontent over sin in general and en-thusiasm in particular. In New England, the concessions made in the Half-Way Covenant and Stoddardeanism had proved to be self-defeating; unconsciously they had given comfort to the very liberal Arminian ideas which threatened the Puritan system. Among Anglicans the impossibility of attaining communicant membership on this side of the Atlantic had contributed to a careless attitude toward the formal ordinances of religion. More religious groups than not suffered from inability to secure ministers to man the parishes; in the absence of sound preaching and sacramental celebrations many an ordinarily religious settler lapsed into secularism. The times were thus ripe for some new emphasis which might shake the churches free from their extreme lethargy and present the people with some dynamic message which might inspire within them a burning faith. Such an emphasis was to be found in the revivalism of the Great Awak-ening.

THE ADVENT OF THE REVIVAL

The spark which kindled the flames of reawakened piety was ignited by a minister of the Dutch Reformed Church, Theodorus Jacobus Fre-linghuysen (1691–1747). A German educated under Dutch influence at the University of Lingen, he had accepted the Calvinism of the Heidel-berg Catechism and had followed in the footsteps of such eminent Dutch evangelicals as Brákel and Verschuir. He received ordination in the Dutch Church in 1717 and three years later began a powerful ministry to several Dutch congregations in New Jersey. Finding them in a lethargic state, comforted by routine orthodoxy, he launched a campaign of incisive re-form. It was supported by solid evangelistic preaching, regular pastoral visitation, and the maintenance of strict discipline. His labors in the Rari-tan River valley soon bore fruit in manifold conversions, while word of his success spread to other churches in the vicinity which in turn took up the revival.

Frelinghuysen soon found himself at the center of a raging storm of controversy. While many of his communicants supported his ministry with enthusiasm, there were numerous others who regarded his somewhat un-conventional methods of gaining converts as highly objectionable. Heated arguments often ended in congregational rifts, reports of which were car-ried to the sister churches and to the clerical leaders. The leading Dutch Reformed minister in New York, Domine Boel, attacked him publicly as a heretic and made a number of attempts to silence him. A visit by Boel to Frelinghuysen's people served only to stir up the existing disaffections and to prolong the controversy. Meanwhile, Frelinghuysen continued his direct and forceful preaching with astonishing results. Nor did the fact that his opponents published a volume in 1725, which was highly critical of his activities, have any effect in retarding the movement. By 1726, the revival had reached its height and was spreading like wildfire into other Dutch communities. From thence it would pass to the Presbyterian communities, which would carry it forward in its second phase. But to Frelinghuysen, as George Whitefield correctly adjudged, goes the credit for initiating "the great work" in that region.

The most noteworthy impetus to the Presbyterian revival was given by a family of Scotch-Irish ministers named Tennent. In 1727, William Tennent relinquished his pastorate at Bedford, New York, and moved to Neshaminy, Bucks County, Pennsylvania. There he established a school called the "Log College" for the training of a ministry. By 1733, Tennent's sons, Gilbert, John, and William, Jr., and Samuel Blair, all of whom had been trained by the elder Tennent, had been received as ministers into the synod.

The natural leader of the group was Gilbert Tennent who, having served for a brief period in the Presbytery of New Castle, was called in 1727 to the church at New Brunswick, New Jersey. He soon came to know and admire Domine Frelinghuysen and to look to him for guidance. But it was not until he was afflicted by a serious illness that he pledged himself, if spared, to a fervid evangelistic ministry. Thereafter he moved essentially in the main stream of English Puritanism and evangelical Dutch Reformed Protestantism, moving farther away from Scotch-Irish orthodoxy. He saw the root of the religious problem, as did Frelinghuysen, to be the "presumptuous Security" of his people and their false identification of sound doctrine with saving faith. He believed that his mission was to illumine their self-satisfied lives and inspire them to an inner conviction so dynamic that it must necessarily express itself in gracious works.

Gilbert Tennent went back to his pulpit and preached with flaming zeal. Many of his rough, untutored parishioners had been unaccustomed to forceful preaching which presented everlasting damnation or eternal joy and at once demanded a verdict; their violent reactions were thus to be expected. Sobs, shrieks, and groans emitted from the house of worship with members giving vent to their emotions. Other congregations soon caught the spirit of the revival and passed it on to hundreds of noncommunicants who, being moved by its persuasive appeal, identified themselves with the Christian fellowship. By 1738 so many new congregations had been organized that it was necessary to organize another judicatory, the Presbytery of New Brunswick.

By 1739 the revival was spreading over a much wider area. Many of the former Puritan churches, having been influenced by both the Middle Colony and New England revivals, began to respond to the new "enthusiasm." Jonathan Dickinson's congregation at Elizabeth, New Jersey, experienced a remarkable awakening of evangelical zeal. The young Aaron Burr, later to become president of the College of New Jersey, had even more sensational results at Newark. At Goshen, New York, another revival broke out under the forceful preaching of Silas Leonard, recently graduated from Yale. Farther to the south, within the jurisdiction of the Presbytery of Philadelphia, John Rowland was conducting an evangelistic campaign of unusual proportions among the congregations of Maidenhead, Hopewell, and Amwell. In 1740 an exceptionally successful revival was begun under the leadership of Samuel Blair at New Londonderry, or Fagg's Manor, Pennsylvania.

One of the most influential contributors to the revival was the prominent Anglican evangelist, George Whitefield (1714–1770). Educated at Oxford where he had been a member of the Holy Club and an associate of John and Charles Wesley, he was ordained in 1736. Two years later he spent a few months in Georgia, where he won popularity as a preacher and as a humanitarian whose chief passion was to found an orphan house. After returning to England, he preached effectively to thousands of persons at great outdoor services. By October, 1739, he was back in America, landing this time in Delaware. He proceeded to Philadelphia where there was such demand to hear him preach that he had to speak from the gallery of the Court House to nearly 6000 people standing in the streets. Benjamin Franklin was deeply impressed by his mild and reasonable preaching and complimented him in his writings.

A man of broad sympathies, Whitefield worked harmoniously with persons of all denominations. "I am of Catholic spirit," he said, "and if I see any man who loves the Lord Jesus in sincerity, I am not very solicitous to what communion he belongs." One of the men who influenced him most was Gilbert Tennent, in whose church he preached and with whom he traveled to New York. Tennent undoubtedly had much to do with Whitefield's change of theological position. The English evangelist, like John Wesley, owed much to the German pietists and Moravians, whom he had met in Georgia. Gradually, however, he shifted toward Calvinism, not because he knew or admired Calvin, but because he experienced its general truths. He was never an ivory-tower theologian and apparently never aspired to such a distinction. Though he remained within the Anglican Church, he paid no heed to laws and regulations which did not suit him and ignored all denominational barriers in his zeal to further the cause of the Kingdom in America. Possibly more than any other man he brought widespread attention and support to Middle Colonies revivalism. After visiting New York, Whitefield revisited the Philadelphia area, then pressed on to Georgia where he had the joy of laying the first brick for his orphan house.

THE PRESBYTERIAN RESPONSE

From the outset, Presbyterians had viewed the revival with mixed feelings. The Scotch-Irish party, essentially strong for subscription, had looked with jaundiced eyes upon the revivalists and had seen that their works were evil. The "Log College" graduates, though frequently better educated and more deeply grounded in religious conviction, constituted for the orthodox a threat which must be removed at all costs. It was all too apparent that the reason the revivalists were so eager for the establishment of the Presbytery of New Brunswick was that they wanted to possess the ecclesiastical machinery whereby they might ordain men of their own training and disposition. As a counter measure the opponents of the revival introduced an overture at the meeting of synod in 1738 which proposed that candidates for ordination who had not graduated from a New England or European college be required to take an examination before a committee of synod. The overture was passed.

The revivalist-controlled Presbytery of New Brunswick replied by licensing and later ordaining a graduate of the "Log College," John Rowland, in clear violation of synod's directive. This raised another question of primary importance. Did the right of ordination rest with synod or presbytery? The orthodox party insisted that it belonged to synod and, being in the majority, were able to declare Rowland's licensure illegal. It was a crushing defeat for the men of New Brunswick.

Tempers now rose to white heat. In March, 1740, Gilbert Tennent, never noted for his restraint, was invited to preach to the congregation at Nottingham on the border between Pennsylvania and Maryland. Aroused by what seemed to him to be the bigotry of the orthodox party, Tennent launched out with a sermon—more properly a polemical discourse—entitled "The Danger of an Unconverted Ministry." It was frank to the point of being defamatory. After referring to the orthodox as an "ungodly Ministry" and as "caterpillars" who "labour to devour every green Thing," he went on to bemoan the spiritual poverty of the congregations.

Poor Christians are stunted and starv'd, who are put to feed on such bare Pastures, and such dry Nurses; as the Rev. Mr. Hildersham justly calls them. It's only when the wise Virgins sleep, that they can bear with those dead Dogs, that can't bark; but when the LORD revives his People, they can't but abhor them! O! it is ready to break their very Hearts with Grief, to see, how lukewarm those Pharisee-Teachers are in their publick Discourses, while Sinners are sinking into Damnation, in Multitudes! . . .[1]

[1] Armstrong, Loetscher and Anderson, op. cit., 42.

The sermon was widely distributed, an unfortunate circumstance for the peace and purity of the church inasmuch as it produced much more heat than light. Nevertheless, it did point up an issue of considerable importance. Should a vital experience of regeneration be prerequisite to church membership and should ministers be required to affirm some inward call to preach before receiving ordination? The revivalists answered that such was as important as a fine education; without it a man's ministry would be sterile. A congregation without piety and conviction was a lost congregation. The conservatives were scarcely in a position to agree. Many had entered the ministry without ever undergoing a spiritual crisis; some had been guilty of immoral practices. What was important to them was high educational standards, doctrinal orthodoxy, and dignified services of worship. The lines dividing the two groups were now sharply defined, admitting little hope of reconciliation.

By the meeting of synod in 1741 the breaking point had been reached. The Scotch-Irish faction, clearly in the majority, offered a "Protestation" which declared that the revivalists had forfeited their right to membership in the synod and should be expelled unless they would agree to submit to all directives of synod. The revivalists then withdrew, the remainder proceeding to expel the New Brunswick Presbytery; American Presbyterianism was now formally rent asunder. In 1745, this Presbytery, joined by the Presbyteries of New York and New Castle, organized the Synod of New York, which came to be known as the "New Side." As for the "Old Side" Synod of Philadelphia, it proudly nursed its wounds and continued as before.

Unquestionably, the "Old Side" suffered most from the schism. Had they been able to provide sufficient clergy, they might have made considerable gains among the great mass of Scotch-Irish settlers who were making their homes in Pennsylvania and in Virginia's Shenandoah Valley. But they were unable to meet the challenge. The fact that they had a high percentage of mediocre or morally unfit clergy further weakened their efforts. During the period of schism the Synod of Philadelphia made virtually no gains; by 1758 its clerical membership had dropped from twenty-seven to twenty-three, and its lay strength had also sharply declined.

The situation in the "New Side" camp was almost the exact opposite. Through the dynamic Christo centric preaching of the revivalists, hundreds were brought to a spiritual crisis and won to the church. Young and vigorous ministers and laymen gave leadership to a rapidly growing movement and proved beyond all doubt that revivalism was a tremendously effective force. During the thirteen years of its independent existence, the Synod of New York made notable gains in New York, New Jersey, and Pennsylvania, and increased its clergy from twenty-two to seventy-three. In addition, it conducted a flourishing missionary effort in the South.

One of the most rewarding of the "New Side" missionary campaigns took place in eastern Virginia. In Hanover County, where a number of laymen headed by Samuel Morris had become dissatisfied with the Anglican Church's ministry, a spontaneous revival broke out about 1740 and soon spread to other communities. When attendance at the Anglican churches dropped at an alarming rate, the authorities attempted to suppress the movement but to no avail. In 1743, William Robinson, a minister from the New Brunswick Presbytery, arrived in the area after a successful preaching mission in the valley of Virginia. He preached with such power that the dissenters of Hanover County decided to embrace Presbyterianism. In doing so they invited new opposition from the colonial government which was necessarily committed to the Anglican establishment. This eventuality seems not to have dissuaded other Presbyterian revivalists from conducting "unlawful meetings," and so the visits of itinerant preachers continued.

The most distinguished of these missionaries to Virginia was Samuel Davies (1723–1761). Ordained in 1747 by the Presbytery of New Castle, he was commissioned that very year to undertake evangelistic work in Hanover County. Upon his arrival there he secured from the court a license to hold services at four meeting houses in the vicinity of Hanover. But when he tried to obtain a license for his friend and fellow minister, John Rodgers, it was denied; this was even more remarkable in the light of the fact that in the autumn of 1747 Davies was licensed to preach in three additional places. Certainly Davies' irenic disposition, which prompted him never to attack the Established Church, helped to mitigate governmental opposition. But an even more important factor was his ability to convince the court, against the arguments of the prosecuting attorney, Peyton Randolph, that the government had no legal right to ban dissenting bodies. He thus struck a powerful blow for religious liberty.

In a host of ways Davies made his influence felt. He, more than any other man, was responsible for the organization of the Presbytery of Hanover in 1755, the first southern presbytery with the exception of the independent presbytery in South Carolina. He brought the Gospel to the Negroes, giving them special attention and winning many to communicant membership. In the political realm he actively supported the British cause during the French and Indian War, largely because of his fear of Roman Catholicism and dictatorial government. By so doing he won the friendship of Governor Gooch of Virginia. After Davies departed in 1759 to become president of the College of New Jersey, the Presbyterian revival in Hanover County entered a period of decline.

Meanwhile, the tensions which had led to schism in the church had abated and the prospects for reunion seemed bright. Gilbert Tennent, once the arch foe of the orthodox, became one of the strongest proponents of reconciliation. His pamphlet entitled "The Peace of Jerusalem" was given wide circulation and proved to be a positive force toward union.

A Plan of Union was presented and adopted by both synods in 1758, bringing to an end the unfortunate estrangement. It provided that ministers should subscribe to the Confession, carry on professional activities in congregations other than their own only when invited, and give greater deference to the authority of church judicatories. It also provided that ministerial candidates should be examined as to their "experimental acquaintance with religion." Obviously, neither side had gained a significant victory.

Once again a united church turned to the task of expanding its missions. During the next decade Presbyterianism enjoyed a steady growth in almost all the colonies. In order to further stimulate this growth, every church in the denomination was directed in 1766 to take a collection for the "propagation and support of the gospel in such parts as cannot otherwise enjoy it." Marked gains were noted in the South, particularly in western North Carolina. Itinerant preachers such as William Robinson, Hugh McAden, and John Thomson were the first to evangelize in that region, but not until the coming of Alexander Craighead in 1758 was there a settled pastor. That year he assumed the leadership of Rocky River Church; three years later he became pastor of Sugar Creek Church. The work in North Carolina progressed so well that in 1770 the Presbytery of Orange was founded with seven ministers laboring within its bounds. Perhaps the principal value of this widespread missionary activity to the church at large was that it helped to bind the churches in the various colonies together and promote a spirit of unity. Every step toward cohesiveness would be a step toward fortifying the colonies to face the problems of the revolutionary era.

During the Great Awakening representatives of two smaller Scottish Presbyterian bodies made their way to America. The Reformed Presbyterians or Covenanters had formed a separate communion in the seventeenth century as an expression of hostility to episcopal polity and the supremacy of the king over the national Scottish Church. In 1751, John Cuthbertson arrived in Pennsylvania to minister to the people of this persuasion. He was joined by Matthew Lind and Alexander Dobbin in 1773. The following year they organized a presbytery. Meanwhile, members of the Associate Church, which had more recently been organized in opposition to lay patronage, began to arrive in the colonies; they organized their first presbytery in 1753. The two denominations united in 1782 to form the Associate Reformed Synod.

THE EDWARDEAN REVIVAL

The same forces which initiated the revival in the Middle Colonies were at work in the New England Awakening, which was inaugurated by Jonathan Edwards at Northampton, Massachusetts, in the fall of 1734. Edwards was uniquely prepared for his task. Born at East Windsor, Connecticut, in 1703, the son and grandson of Congregational ministers, he was reared by godly parents and inspired to follow their example. As a youth, he demonstrated extraordinary mental precocity and an unusual awareness of God in his life. He was educated at Yale, where he became deeply influenced by John Locke's *Essay on the Human Understanding.* Graduating in 1720, at the age of seventeen, he pursued graduate studies for two years, held a brief Presbyterian pastorate, then returned to Yale as a tutor. In 1727, he accepted a call to become assistant minister of the Congregational church at Northampton, Massachusetts, which was pastored by his grandfather, Solomon Stoddard.

At Northampton he soon gained a reputation for loving books and abstract ideas more than pastoral evangelism. He devoted thirteen hours a day to study, a fact which was clearly discernible in his carefully prepared sermons. Not long after his arrival, he married Sarah Pierpont, daughter of a Congregational minister in New Haven. She proved to be a person of gracious refinement, strong in her religious faith, and of inestimable help to her husband. Two years after Edwards' call to the church his grandfather died, leaving him in charge of one of the largest congregations in Massachusetts.

Edwards found the local citizenry to be "very insensible of the things of religion," having lapsed into the degeneracy of the times. The moral level was low and intemperance and other forms of vice were common, especially among the youth. The young minister felt that the growing trend toward Arminianism, with its high view of man, was at least partially responsible for the religious indifference of the people. Arminianism was breaking down the traditional emphasis on man's utter depravity. Men were becoming more sinful precisely because they were losing their awareness of sin. What they needed was something to convict them of sin and shock them out of their complacency. Thus, in his preaching he came to stress man's complete dependence on God. But unlike Calvin, who centered his theology on the omnipotence and sovereignty of God, Edwards based his on the unworthiness of man. Sin was the bitter foe to be combated; recognizing this, young Edwards put on the breastplate of righteousness and prepared to do battle.

The sermons could scarcely be characterized as sensational. Edwards' pulpit appearance was unassuming, his manner of preaching mild, his voice penetrating but not stentorian. It was the message itself and the complete sincerity with which it was delivered which pierced the heart like a flaming arrow. As early as 1733, it was noticed that young people were coming more regularly to church and were giving greater heed to the admonitions of their pastor. By 1734, a sense of anxiety, born of the fear of God's wrath, had gripped the townspeople; within six months three hundred persons had been converted and received into the church. In his

"Narrative of Surprising Conversions," published in 1737, Edwards spoke glowingly of the revival.

This work of God, as it was carried on, and the number of true saints multiplied, soon made a glorious alteration in the town; so that in the spring and summer following, anno 1735, the town seemed to be full of the presence of God: it never was so full of love, nor so full of joy, and yet so full of distress as it was then. There were remarkable tokens of God's presence in almost every house. It was a time of joy in families on account of salvation being brought to them; parents rejoicing over their children as new born, and husbands over their wives, and wives over their husbands. The goings of God were then seen in his sanctuary, God's day was a delight, and his tabernacles were amiable. Our public assemblies were then beautiful; the congregation was alive in God's service, every one earnestly intent on the public worship, every hearer eager to drink in the words of the minister as they came from his mouth; the assembly in general were, from time to time, in tears while the word was preached; some weeping with sorrow and distress, others with joy and love, others with pity and concern for the souls of their neighbors.[2]

The spirit of the revival soon spread into other communities such as South Hadley, Suffield, Green River, Hatfield, and Enfield. In Windsor and East Windsor, Connecticut, there was a general awakening. So the revival diffused itself through the Connecticut Valley and continued through successive years. It gained increasing momentum with the publication of Edwards' "Narrative." By 1740, the revival had generally shifted from the frontier regions to eastern New England and the first impulses from the Middle Colony revival were beginning to be felt. In June and July, 1740, Ebenezer Pemberton, minister of the Presbyterian Church in New York, preached a number of evangelistic sermons in Boston, and with great effect. The time was ripe for the arrival of George Whitefield.

The eminent evangelist, upon the completion of a heartening visit to Georgia, set out for Boston. He landed at Newport, Rhode Island, in September, 1740, and held meetings in the Anglican church. He then pressed on to Boston, which was tense with excitement and anticipation at word of his coming. At his first meeting he states that he preached to 4000 persons and on the following Sunday to 15,000. With the exception of Charles Chauncy of First Church, who opposed him in every way, he received the support of the city's leading ministers. But this in no way prompted reserve on his part in denouncing "unconverted Ministers." After censuring Boston for its spiritual lethargy, Whitefield went to Ipswich, Newbury, Hampton, Portsmouth, and back to Boston. He was welcomed by large crowds at each place with the exception of Newbury, where only one pulpit was made available for his use.

[2] Mode, *op. cit.*, 216.

In October, 1740, Whitefield visited Northampton and preached several times for Edwards. He later wrote that during one of the Sunday services

Dear Mr. Edwards wept during the whole Time of Exercise.—The People were equally, if not more affected, and my own soul was much lifted up towards God. In the Afternoon the Power encreased yet more and more. Our Lord seem'd to keep the good Wine till the last. I have not seen four such gracious meetings together since my Arrival . . .[3]

It is interesting to compare the ideas and methods of Edwards and White-field. While the former was collected and reserved, the latter was emotional and sensational. Both preached the love of God, but Edwards placed more stress on God's wrath while Whitefield emphasized man's hope. Their most emphatic agreement was on the supernatural nature of conversion and the necessity of a conversion experience. They saw no more important distinction in life than that between the regenerate and the unregenerate. The core of their religious thought was the doctrine of salvation.

Before he departed from New England, Whitefield visited Harvard and Yale and found that "their Light is become Darkness." Then he started south again, his destination Georgia. The work in New England had borne fruit in abundance. Between December, 1740, and March, 1741, the revival reached its highest intensity. Many an evangelist such as Edwards, Joseph Bellamy, and Eleazer Wheelock carried on an itinerant ministry for some weeks and won considerable numbers to a profession of faith. No single sermon made more of an impression upon its hearers than "Sinners in the Hands of an Angry God," preached by Edwards at Enfield, Connecticut, in July, 1741. It was scarcely typical of his preaching, though it was indicative of the direction which the revival was following. Taking as his text Deuteronomy 32:35, "Their foot shall slide in due time," he explained that the vengeance of God was threatened on the wicked unbelieving Israelites. They were always exposed to sudden, unexpected destruction, and when the appointed time came their feet would slide. "The pit is prepared; the fire is made ready; the furnace is now hot; ready to receive them; the flames do now rage and glow." Before he had finished his sermon, the congregation was so gripped by the sense of sin and fear of punishment that hysteria reigned and Edwards had to call for silence before he could proceed.

Jonathan Edwards was more than the leader of a revival; he was a philosopher and theologian in his own right and one of the most brilliant America has produced. In some respects he was a Puritan mystic who loved to speak of "sweetly conversing with Christ" or "being wrapt and swallowed up in God." He was never satisfied with a moralistic conception

[3] Quoted in E. S. Gaustad, *The Great Awakening in New England* (Harper, c. 1957), 28.

of piety. Religion to him was not so much morality as an experience of the reality of God, a feeling of divine joy and happiness. On the other hand, he looked upon God as a sovereign ruler who, in His wrath, holds the unconverted sinner over the pit of hell. Thus in Edwards' thought we find a combination of the immanent God who illumines the heart of man, and the transcendent God who strikes down the sinner.

Edwards' principal theological contributions lay in three areas in which he felt heresy was spreading. In regard to the will and human freedom, he took sharp issue with the Arminians who taught that man was free to accept or reject the influences of the Holy Spirit and was responsible for his own actions. Edwards also believed in man's moral responsibility, but was equally certain that God determines all things. The problem was how to explain away the inconsistency. His principal treatment of this subject was in one of his later essays on *The Freedom of the Will*, published in 1754. Following the lead of John Locke, he divided "mind" into the faculties of "understanding" and "will." "Will" is that "by which the mind chooses anything." When faced with several alternatives, a man's mind will respond to whichever seems to be most in harmony with his nature and his environmentally shaped likes and inclinations. These are the controlling factors over will, and they are determined by God. On any other basis freedom would be little more than arbitrary lawlessness. Even God does not exercise that type of freedom, for He must be consistent with His own nature or essence. For a person to do whatever he pleases without regard to his nature and history would be out of place in an orderly world.

Edwards' idea of inspiration had tremendous implications for the current awakening. While he was a friend of the revival he recognized in it a danger that people might look to a personal experience as the authority of revelation. He feared that if left unchecked it might develop into the kind of mysticism held by the Society of Friends. For Edwards, authority could be based only on the Bible, which is alone an infallible guide of faith and practice. The experience which comes to the believer at conversion is not inspiration but illumination. Illumination, unlike inspiration, reveals no new doctrine; it simply gives meaning to truth which is already contained in the Scriptures. And so when exuberance broke out among the people and they behaved in a strange fashion, declaring that they had been recipients of new truth, he warned them of the Devil who provokes enthusiasm and deludes men into thinking they have received a special revelation. There is a place for emotion, but only if it is born of the sincere joy which comes through the illumination of the Scriptures. This was consistent Calvinism.

One of Edwards' most important contributions to American theology was his idea of virtue and the Christian life. It is difficult to comprehend unless one understands that for him the universe is an emanation from God and that it possesses reality only to the extent that it partakes of the divine nature. He is willing to ascribe some independent existence to human souls, but this is only because his doctrine of man makes it necessary. In his *Nature of True Virtue*, written in 1755, he identifies goodness, in true Neo-Platonic fashion, with being or existence. The more existence a being has the more excellent it is. God, being infinite, has the most being and is therefore the most excellent. Virtue is good will toward being, or love for being, which in its fullness is God. Therefore our greatest love must be for God. Our delight must be in His happiness. The love which we hold for other beings ought to depend upon the degree to which they possess existence or partake of God's being. There can scarcely be any justification for loving the nonelect since they do not share in the divine nature.

It might seem that this concept would be destructive of evangelism, inasmuch as love would be involved in preaching to sinners, many of whom could be expected to be among the nonelect. But Edwards would have rejected this philosophy. He maintained that it is our highest goal in life to give glory to God and to do His will, and since His will is that we should spread the Gospel message, we must carry on the work of missions for the glory of God. To do it because of the satisfaction we might get would be selfish and to do it for our love of the unconverted would be unjust. Still no man knows whom it is God's intention to save; he can simply do as he has been commanded and leave the rest to providence. This idea had important implications for the nineteenth century Protestant attitude toward missions and toward the "heathen" and their conversion.

Despite Edwards' valiant battle to maintain the Calvinist faith and to save its intellectual respectability, he was fighting for a lost cause. There was too much uncertainty and adventure about life in America for the pioneer to bow to the dictum that everything had been predetermined. Arminianism seemed more in harmony with the optimistic spirit of the frontier and the democratic processes which pronounced man free and responsible at points that matter. At the same time, Calvinism of the Edwardean variety gave backbone and stamina to religion and continued to influence American theology for generations to come.

PROGRESS AND REACTION IN NEW ENGLAND

What was unique about the Great Awakening was that it touched every area of life. Urban dweller, rural settler, rich man, poor man, savant, illiterate—all felt the force of its power. Beginning as a frontier phenomenon, it gradually spread into the cities where it was advanced by both great and obscure. By 1741 and 1742 the revival had reached the peak of its influence. Ministers spoke feelingly of it as a means ordained of God for leading men to salvation and Joseph Sewall of Old South Church, Boston, was moved to comment:

God is pleas'd to pour out his Spirit upon his People, and then his Works of Grace are as the Light which goeth forth. Many ask the Way to Zion, with their Faces thitherward, and not a few declare God's Works of Grace towards them with rejoicing. Convictions and Conversions become more frequent and apparent. . . . Persons that were before quietly in their Sins and unconcerned, are so awakened that they can't stifle their Convictions nor conceal their Distress. . . .[4]

The most immediate and observable effect of the revival was the winning of converts; many estimates have been made as to its numerical results. Benjamin Trumbull, in his *History of Connecticut,* published in 1818, judged the number to have been between 30,000 and 40,000. But lacking definite information from primary sources, it is impossible to be precise. Certainly there was no mass movement of converted sinners marching up a "sawdust trail." Joseph Seccombe, minister of the church at Harvard, reported in 1744 that the revival had brought him a net gain of about twenty members per year. His experience was typical of perhaps the majority of ministers in New England.

More significant factors in judging the impact of the awakening were the quality of the religious experience and the level of public morals. Everywhere there were evidences of concern and repentance. There were more people in attendance at church services than before and more were remaining afterward to discuss personal anxieties with the minister. Numerous meetings for prayer and discussion were being held in private homes; such meetings often led to some renewed evangelistic effort in the community. Young people in particular were eager to participate in lay preaching and personal evangelism. The effect of these pietistic trends was to increase the sectarian ideal in the churches which based church membership on a voluntary act of commitment and a life of discipline. This would help to widen the gap between church and state and prepare Congregationalism for the acceptance of separatism during the period following independence.

Public morals also showed signs of elevation. According to the report of Thomas Prince, the assistant pastor of Old South Church, Boston:

In this year 1741, the very face of the town seemed to be strangely altered. Some, who had not been here since the fall before, have told me their great surprise at the change in the general look and carriage of people, as soon as they landed. Even the negroes and boys in the streets surprisingly left their usual rudeness . . . And one of our worthy gentlemen expressing his wonder at the remarkable change, informed me, that whereas he used with others on Saturday evenings to visit the taverns, in order to clear them of town inhabitants, they were wont to find many there, and meet with trouble to get them

---

[4] *Ibid.,* 57–58.

away; but now, having gone at those seasons again, he found them empty of all but lodgers.[5]

But if there was strength in the revival, there was also weakness. As it progressed, certain evangelists began to resort to sensational and offensive practices which cast embarrassment and reproach upon the movement. Shortly after the departure of Whitefield, the tempestuous Gilbert Tennent blew into New England to fan the flames of enthusiasm. For nearly three months he itinerated through Massachusetts and Connecticut, being greeted wherever he went by great crowds. At Boston he received a tremendous ovation. But his flamboyant mannerisms and his raucous rantings on hellfire and damnation themes gradually evoked the criticism of more sensitive spirits, who contributed mightily to his disparagement. No personality, of whatever age or sex, was exempt from his frightening tirades. His sermon "Early Religion Recommended," preached in 1757, might just as well have been delivered during his New England tour. It is addressed to children.

O consider, that you may never live till you grow big, for the most, by far, die when they are little, and this may be your case in a few days, in a few hours; haven't you seen coffins as short as yourselves, carried to the grave? And would it not be terrible for you to die unconverted, and to burn in hell forever? Your being young and little won't keep you from that bad place, and from the bad man, unless you be good yourselves before you die.[6]

It is interesting to note that Jonathan Edwards justified sermons of this kind on the ground that truth should not be concealed from children. By nature all are the children of wrath and those who have not been converted are subject at every moment to everlasting punishment.

The Reverend James Davenport had an even more riotous effect when, in 1741, he left his Long Island congregation and set out on an evangelistic tour of Connecticut. There was no dignity which he did not revile, no decorum which he did not upset. It was not long before reports of his "excesses" began to drift back to his congregation. He was accused of marching uninvited into the churches, conducting noisy and unrestrained revivals, and pronouncing as converted all who responded vociferously to his wild oratory. He led a reckless attack on all clergy who objected in the slightest to his untoward methods, referring to them as "letter learned rabbies, scribes and Pharisees, and unconverted ministers." Some pastors capitulated rather than face the wrath of their aroused congregations; others stood firm, refusing to be intimidated. At most of Davenport's meetings bedlam reigned as men fell to the floor screaming and women fainted. Finally, the authorities had had enough. In 1742, the General Assembly of

[5] Mode, *op. cit.*, 221.
[6] Quoted in G. M. Stephenson, *The Puritan Heritage* (Macmillan, 1952), 53.

Connecticut passed an "Act for regulating abuses and correcting disorders in Ecclesiastical Affairs," which provided that no nonresident of the colony could preach in any church in Connecticut without obtaining permission from its pastor. Davenport was then arrested and summarily ejected.

By this time New England Congregationalists had virtually split into two camps. On the one side were the "New Lights" or protagonists of the revival headed by Edwards; on the other were the "Old Lights" led by Charles Chauncy, pastor of First Church, Boston. Feeling over the issue of revivalism frequently ran so high that congregations split asunder. Chauncy, who might be described as a Puritan liberal, fired a salvo at the proponents of "enthusiasm" in 1742; the following year he launched a direct attack on Edwards in his work entitled *Seasonable Thoughts on the State of Religion in New-England*. Chauncy characterized the revival as a fresh outbreak of antinomianism, which had plagued Massachusetts during the seventeenth century. His argument did not go unheard.

When the churches of Massachusetts met in annual convention at Boston in May, 1743, they passed a resolution to the effect that it was highly improper for persons with little formal preparation to preach and that no person should be ordained as a minister at large. Almost two months later, a group of Boston ministers who favored the revival drew up a statement which declared that there had been a most gratifying resurgence of religion in many places, after a long period of flagging zeal. The awakening had assuredly been an asset. "But who can wonder, if at such times as this, Satan should intermingle himself, to hinder and blemish a work so directly contrary to the interests of his kingdom?" Apparently even the proponents of the revival had their reservations.

In the autumn of 1744, George Whitefield, though seriously ill, arrived at York, Maine, in response to repeated requests for his return. But this time he was met by strong opposition, inspired in large measure by Chauncy. Many ministers refused to admit him to their pulpits. The Harvard faculty, in a statement made in December, 1744, pronounced his itinerant ministry to be harmful to the peace and purity of the churches. They criticized him for preaching extemporaneously on the ground that such sermons have much repetition but little didactic value and represent a "most lazy manner of preaching." Still smarting from his frank observations concerning Harvard, they characterized him as an "uncharitable, censorious, and slanderous man." The Yale faculty was only too happy to concur. Whitefield never completely overcame the force of these attacks. During his last visits to New England he was welcomed cordially by the people, but the old spark was missing from his preaching. He died at Newburyport, Massachusetts, in 1770, still in the fold of the Church of England, and was laid to rest under the pulpit of the Presbyterian Church.

Meanwhile, opposition to the revival was mounting and at Northampton where Edwards continued the emphases of earlier years, the congregation was becoming increasingly dissatisfied with its minister. By 1748 there was an open rupture between Edwards and his people. Two immediate causes accounted for the dissension. The first was a badly handled case of discipline in which Edwards instituted proceedings against some of his young people for circulating "impure books." However justifiable his action might have been, its result was to alienate nearly all the young people in Northampton. But the principal cause of disharmony was his change of mind as to the propriety of admitting persons who had never been converted to the sacrament of the Lord's Supper. His grandfather, Solomon Stoddard, had favored the practice on the ground that it was one means of leading the sinner to a conversion experience. Edwards saw the sacrament as a "confessing ordinance" rather than a "converting ordinance," and therefore wished to restrict it to professing Christians who were members of the visible church. He also opposed the Half-Way Covenant, maintaining that the sacrament of infant baptism should be extended only to the children of converted parents.

In June, 1750, the angered members of the Northampton church voted to dismiss the pastor; several months later the town meeting decreed that never again should he be permitted to preach in the town. Thus a ministry of more than twenty years was ignominiously brought to an end. In the summer of 1751 he accepted a call to minister to a few English families and undertake missionary work among the Indians at Stockbridge. He discharged his duties with fidelity but not with distinction; his mind was more preoccupied with scholarship than with Indians. He devoted much of his time to writing important works on *Original Sin, The Nature of True Virtue,* and *The Freedom of the Will.* In 1757, his son-in-law, Aaron Burr, died suddenly and Edwards was invited to succeed him as president of the College of New Jersey, an institution which had shown sympathy for the revival. He accepted and entered immediately upon these duties. Some months later he fell victim to smallpox and died in his fifty-fifth year. His passing symbolized the end of the New England Awakening. The decades just ahead would witness a resurgence of rationalism, spiritual lethargy, theological controversy, and political upheaval.

THE REVIVAL AMONG THE BAPTISTS

New England Baptists were slow to become involved in the Great Awakening largely because prior to the revival most of their congregations followed Arminianism, and an evangelistic campaign rooted in Calvinistic theology was not to their liking. The practice of infant baptism among the revivalists also contributed to Baptist aloofness. Nevertheless, some Baptists withdrew from their congregations, voicing their opposition to Arminianism and cold formalism, and founded new churches. One such church was the Warren Avenue Church of Boston organized in 1748. It was not until the revival among the Congregationalists was in a state of decline that the Baptists derived any real benefit from it. In many cases Congregationalist laymen in churches where there was opposition to the revival established "Separate" or "Strict" congregations only to affiliate later with the Baptist movement. These newcomers to the Baptist fold did much to further the doctrines of Calvinism within the denomination. Most of the gains in membership were made during the latter half of the eighteenth century, and largely in those churches which accepted Calvinistic theology. Between 1740 and 1790, eighty-six new Baptist churches were founded in Massachusetts, to a considerable extent through the efforts of Hezekiah Smith. In Connecticut, there were about sixty churches by 1800. The pattern was the same throughout New England; by the end of the century the total number of Baptist churches in the region had risen to 325.

One of the most prominent Baptist preachers in Massachusetts was Isaac Backus (1724–1806). During the years 1756 to 1767 he traveled about 15,000 miles on missionary tours through New England. He and two fellow ministers, James Manning and John Gano, were instrumental in organizing the Warren Association at Warren, Rhode Island. An important aim of the Association was the promotion of religious liberty. Backus later served with distinction as its agent in the struggle for freedom.

The Middle Colony Baptists also felt the influence of the revival. In the Philadelphia Association, which leaned heavily toward Calvinism, there was a notable intensification of evangelistic efforts. However, the chief gains in membership were made not in the Middle Colonies, where the Presbyterians were most powerful, but in the South. There a moderately successful missionary program was launched by ministers sent out by the Philadelphia Association. Between 1743 and 1762 at least four churches were organized by these Regular Baptist missionaries along the Atlantic Coast as far south as Charleston, South Carolina. The response in northern Virginia was very encouraging. In 1766, these churches in the South withdrew from the Philadelphia Association and founded the Ketocton Regular Baptist Association.

The most significant advances in the South were made by the Separate Baptists, who stemmed from the revival in New England. Their principal leader was Shubael Stearns, a former "New Light" Congregationalist who had accepted the doctrines of believer's baptism and immersion in 1751. Three years later he led a small group of followers from New England to Frederick County, Virginia. When these wanderers expressed their desire to unite with the Regular Baptist Church at Opeckon Creek, they were greeted with hostility and so decided to continue their migration. For a time they sojourned in Hampshire County, then turned southward across the Blue Ridge, arriving in North Carolina in 1755. There they chose to settle in the Sandy Creek section of Guilford County, where they began at once to evangelize and even to ordain a lay-preacher. The first church was founded at Sandy Creek the year of their arrival with Shubael Stearns as pastor. Though poorly educated, his deep consecration and manifest sincerity convinced many that he was admirably suited for this task. He was an impressive figure in the pulpit and had the ability to draw from his listeners a variety of emotional responses.

Stearns received able support from his brother-in-law, Daniel Marshall, a former Presbyterian missionary to the Mohawk Indians, who had become a Baptist in 1754. Two years later he was ordained pastor of Abbott's Creek Church. An able evangelist, he preached widely in North Carolina and Virginia, winning hundreds of converts to the Baptist faith. The last years of his ministry were spent in South Carolina and Georgia.

From the mother church at Sandy Creek sprang a number of Baptist churches. By 1758, the congregations in North Carolina had organized themselves into the first Separate Baptist Association. That same year their missionaries at work in Virginia founded a Separate Baptist congregation in the western part of Halifax County. The Virginia group was fortunate in winning to its fold Samuel Harris, a prominent citizen who had served as a burgess, a county official, and a vestryman in the Anglican Church. He was ordained in 1760 and thenceforth rendered notable service to the Baptist cause in Virginia. Other preachers who traveled through the back country and conducted successful revivals were Dutton Lane, James Reed, and John Waller. The latter was active in the founding of eighteen churches and baptized more than 2000 persons into the Baptist faith.

Baptist success on the frontier must be attributed in considerable degree to the fact that the movement spoke to the poor and uneducated with clarity and power. Denominations of more conservative inclination, which insisted upon an educated ministry and dignified worship, could scarcely make an impression upon rude frontiersmen who could neither read nor write. What was needed was a simplified Gospel easily understood which, when preached with persuasive zeal, could strike deep into the hearts of the hearers and call forth a verdict. If many were won to the church in a moment of frenzied excitement brought on by a bombastic revivalist who had taken little time to instruct them in the obligations of their profession, it was to be expected. Under the circumstances, emotion was a more effective weapon than reason.

That Baptist ministers were able to develop rapport with these simple folk was not surprising; they shared a common heritage and environment. Coming mostly from the less-privileged classes, few who felt called to preach either expected or desired to receive formal training. In their eyes an educated clergy was for the most part an unconverted clergy; its function was to spin delightful homilies for the intellectual enrichment of affluent parishioners. Never would these men who had felt the call of God to preach allow their message to be "corrupted" by theological education. All they needed was enthusiasm and the will to serve; the Holy Spirit would do the rest.

Robert Semple, an early Baptist historian, commented thus on the sermonic presentations of Separate Baptists.

> Their manner of preaching was if possible much more novel than their doctrines. They had acquired a very warm and pathetic address accompanied by strong gestures and a singular tone of voice. Being often deeply affected themselves while preaching, correspondent affections were felt by their pious hearers, which were frequently expressed by tears, trembling, screams, shouts and acclamations.[7]

It was perhaps inevitable that unrestrained evangelical preachers should come into conflict with those who expressed their religion in a more subdued way and that the authorities should seek to suppress them. In every area of life the status quo seemed to be threatened by their preaching. As the movement grew in strength, claiming 10,000 adherents by 1776, opposition increased accordingly. It came not only from the respectable elements in society but from the riotous and irresponsible mobs who thought nothing of subjecting frontier ministers to ducking and stoning. Only rarely did a public official resort to illegal methods of brutality in the prosecution of his duty.

Most of the difficulties which the Baptists experienced in Virginia came as a result of their disregard for a law which required the licensing of dissenting ministers and meeting houses. Holding as they did to the complete separation of Church and State, they could not recognize any right on the part of the civil authorities to control their activities. Obviously it would have been impossible for lay preachers to register in any court even though they had made the effort. What was so infuriating to the officials was the refusal of ordained Baptist ministers to register or record their places of preaching. Recognizing the extreme difficulty of forcing the Baptists to comply with this law, they decided to make arrests on the charge of disturbing the peace. Between 1768 and 1776, almost fifty ministers were imprisoned. Such action proved to be no deterrent to their activities; most of them stood before the barred windows of their cells and preached to whosoever would give them a hearing. In every place where they were jailed the number of converts increased.

The phenomenal growth of the Baptists in Virginia led to the organization of the first Separate Baptist Association in that colony in 1771. During the next few years the Regular and Separate Baptists grew closer together and finally in 1787 joined forces. But with the outbreak of the Revolution membership began to decline, resulting in new losses. Not until the Second Awakening would the trend be reversed.

[7] Quoted in Brydon, *op. cit.*, II, 191.

THE COMING OF THE METHODISTS

As the period of the first great colonial awakening drew to a close, a movement which had infused new life into English Protestantism was introduced to America. While it had originated within the Anglican Church, it had departed radically from Anglican thought in emphases. Its stress was upon conversion instead of baptism, upon personal religious experience rather than formal communicant membership in a church institution. Its aim was to combat the skepticism and immorality of the times and revive the power of the Gospel within the hearts of men.

The founder of the movement, John Wesley (1703–1791), was influenced as a child principally by his father, an Anglican clergyman, and by his mother who was of Puritan background. During his student days at Oxford, he resolved to prepare for holy orders and to lead a strict and devout life. He and his brother Charles became deeply involved in the activities of the Holy Club, a society which met regularly for study, meditation, and prayer, and contributed to the relief of the poor. Some years after his ordination to the priesthood in 1728, Wesley accepted an offer to serve as chaplain for the Society for the Propagation of the Gospel in Georgia. On his voyage to the colony in 1735 he was impressed by the serene lives of a band of Moravians and by their calmness in the face of a raging storm. That he found nothing of the same spirit in his own life troubled him greatly. After his return to England in 1738, he associated himself with Peter Böhler and a small company of Moravians in London. At a meeting on May 24, 1738, which featured the reading of Luther's preface to the *Epistle to the Romans,* Wesley felt his "heart strangely warmed." It was the turning point in his life. That June he sailed for Germany in order to imbibe the pietistic spirit of Halle and Herrnhut.

In 1739, Wesley returned home and joined forces with George Whitefield, who had only recently arrived from Georgia. The two men began to hold open-air services which were well attended and were notably successful in bringing about conversions. Though opposition to their activities soon developed within the Anglican Church, both Wesley and Whitefield regarded themselves as loyal members of that communion to the time of their death. The fact that Methodism finally emerged as a separate denomination can be explained by pointing to fundamental differences of opinion as to the nature of the church, the use of lay preachers, and the administration of ordination.

While Wesley made no original contributions to theology, the doctrines which he emphasized placed a peculiar stamp upon the movement. He built his religious thought around the doctrinal and moral authority of the Bible, which he believed to be infallible and inerrant in all its parts. Like Jonathan Edwards, he stressed the doctrine of the fall of man and original sin, refusing to believe in man's natural worth and ability. The deity of

Jesus Christ and his vicarious atonement, by which he died on the cross to save men from their sins, held a central place in his system. But when it came to the question of salvation, Wesley adhered to Arminianism and assigned to man a certain share in working out his own salvation.

In Wesley's thought salvation is not merely a gift received through the power of the Holy Spirit at conversion. It is the Christian life itself, a present reality. It is a continuing escape from sin and the unceasing attainment of holiness. The persistent presence of the Holy Spirit, however, is needed if the Christian life is to be maintained. Wesley drew a sharp contrast between the man who was truly religious and the man who was merely moral. A person who lived a pure and upright life, but did not depend on Christ alone for salvation, was the farthest person from the Kingdom of God. But there was always hope for the man who recognized his sin and his need of divine grace. Once a man had been converted he should be vividly conscious of the Spirit's work within him, and that awareness should express itself in joy, enthusiasm, and devotion. If these qualities were not present, it was unlikely that the man had been converted. One of the best ways one could give evidence of his conversion would be to renounce the usual pleasures and pursuits of society, such as card playing, dancing, gambling, and attendance at the theater. The influence which this idea would have upon evangelical Protestant conceptions of morality throughout the nineteenth century in England and America would be prodigious.

Almost a decade before the arrival of Wesley's first official missionaries, Methodist societies had been planted in America. Perhaps as early as 1760 Robert Strawbridge, a local preacher from northern Ireland, settled on Sam's Creek in Frederick County, Maryland. There he founded a society and erected a log meeting house. Strawbridge soon began an itinerant ministry which took him into Delaware, Pennsylvania, and Virginia, preaching and organizing classes of converts. About the same time another group of Methodists landed at New York; by 1765 a society was meeting in the home of Philip Embury. The following year the little group was fortunate in obtaining the services of Captain Thomas Webb, who had been licensed by Wesley to preach. As a speaker he was forceful and persuasive and won so many converts that the society was obliged to erect a stone chapel in order to house them.

In 1769, two English local preachers, John King and Robert Williams, reached America. King introduced Methodism into Baltimore, while Williams carried on an itinerant ministry in Virginia. Upon his arrival in southern Virginia, Williams discovered that a revival was already under way in Dinwiddie and Chesterfield Counties and was being conducted by two clergymen of the Anglican Church. The first and most important, Devereux Jarratt, had been influenced as a young man by the sermons of Whitefield and Presbyterian revivalism in Virginia. Convinced that his services would be of greater value to the Anglican Church than to the Presbyterian, he went to England for episcopal ordination. During his sojourn there he became much impressed by the preaching of Wesley and Whitefield and resolved to emulate them. He returned to Virginia in the summer of 1763 and assumed the rectorship of Bath Parish in Dinwiddie County. Jarratt's preaching was of an evangelical type, intensely emotional and appealing. Soon his church was packed with people from far and near who desired to hear his persuasive sermons. He was associated in his work with Archibald McRoberts, a somewhat younger clergyman of revivalist tendencies, who became rector of Dale Parish in Chesterfield County in 1769. Because of popular demand, Jarratt began to hold services in other parishes despite the opposition of the clergy. When necessity dictated, he preached out of doors. Eventually he extended his ministry even to parishes in North Carolina, establishing religious clubs or societies wherever he went.

The labors of Jarratt indirectly paved the way for the introduction of Methodism in Virginia. When Robert Williams arrived in Dinwiddie County in 1773, he received a warm welcome from the Anglican clergyman, who was happy to assist in setting up the societies and class-meetings proposed by Wesley. The fact that Methodism was still regarded as part of the Established Church proved to be of immeasurable benefit to the new movement during its early years in the colony. Sheltered by the Anglican Church, it suffered none of the hardships which came to the Baptists. The result was that Methodism spread quickly in the areas where Jarratt had been at work. In fact, Jarratt actually encouraged his followers to affiliate with the new societies, an action which he later came for a time to regret.

By 1775, the Methodist revival in the South was fast approaching its peak. Jarratt, whose full account of the revival was later made public in Francis Asbury's *Journal*, was convinced that the awakening would have both salutary and lasting effects. Jesse Lee, a young convert, observed:

I have been at meetings where the whole congregation would be bathed in tears; and sometimes their cries would be so loud that the preacher's voice could not be heard. Some would be seized with trembling, and in a few moments drop on the floor as if they were dead; while others were embracing each other with streaming eyes, and all were lost in wonder, love, and praise.[8]

At the Methodist Conference of 1777, a meeting of Methodist preachers first organized in 1773, it was reported that 4449 persons were members of the societies in Virginia as opposed to 100 four years before.

In the meantime Wesley had commissioned two men, Richard Boardman and Joseph Pilmoor, to serve as official representatives in the Middle

---

[8] Quoted in W. W. Sweet, *Methodism in American History* (Abingdon, 1954), 76.

Colonies. Landing in October, 1769, Boardman took over the work in New York, while Pilmoor served for a time in Philadelphia and then went on an extensive missionary tour through the Middle Colonies and the South. Other official appointees were Francis Asbury and Richard Wright in 1771, Thomas Rankin and George Shadford in 1772, and James Dempster and Martin Rodda in 1774. Of these, the most important were Francis Asbury (1745–1816) and Thomas Rankin, his successor, who administered the entire work in America. Within a decade Asbury would emerge as the guiding genius of the denomination. By the opening of the Revolution in 1775, the total membership of colonial Methodism had risen to 3148; of these only 764 lived north of Mason and Dixon's line. In the South, the movement would continue to flourish during the period of hostilities, especially because of its reputation for patriotism which it shared with the Established Church in Virginia. In the North, where Methodists were identified with the unpopular Anglican Church and thought of as Tories, the societies suffered heavy losses. Not until they became an independent national denomination would they advance again in that area.

The full impact of the Great Awakening upon American life can scarcely be appreciated through a study limited to religious institutions, important though these may be. Clearly, the revival established an evangelistic pattern which would be followed again and again on the frontier and even in the cities. It helped to mold a theology for the American environment and to transform immigrant denominations into indigenous bodies. But it did much more. It fostered a progressive democratization of religion by diminishing sectarian insularity and strengthening the ideal of one common humanity. Politically, it proved indirectly to be of assistance to those groups, notably in the South, which were opposed to establishments. More significantly, it served to tie the colonies together in a new way. The names of Edwards, Tennent, and Whitefield became symbols of a growing interdependence in the colonies and a wider sense of community. In short, the revival helped to break down localism and thus support those forces which would give rise to a new nation.

9

The Aftermath of the Revival

IF THE GREAT AWAKENING PLAYED AN IMPORTANT ROLE IN THE GROWING democratization of American religion, it figured just as prominently in the upsurge of a new humanitarian impulse. In every section of the country there were evidences of a deeper concern for man, a wider commitment to his amelioration. The idealism of the times found expression in sundry causes and movements dedicated to the spiritual, intellectual, or physical advancement of Indians, Negro slaves, orphans, college students, and other favored persons. In some cases these movements stemmed directly from the revival effort in America; in others they traced their origins to pietistic or humanitarian strains planted within the denomination in its embryonic stage. There were even instances in which they were promoted by liberal or secular forces which were somehow caught up and swept along in the fast-moving currents of reform. It was ironic that the humanitarianism of the Awakening, God-centered as it was, should have contributed to the rise of doctrines which emphasized man and his good works. But it was also inevitable. The restless, optimistic spirit of the frontier channeled the course of American thought in that direction.

THE RESURGENCE OF INDIAN MISSIONS

In New England, where missionary work among the Indians had virtually lain dormant since the death of John Eliot in 1690, reawakened in-

79

terest in the evangelization of the aborigines was manifested as early as the 1730's. In 1734, John Sargeant, a tutor at Yale, was chosen by the Commissioners for Indian Affairs to undertake missionary work among the Housatonic Indians, a small tribe dwelling in western Massachusetts. The following year he was ordained at Deerfield and labored with the Indians until his death in 1749. Under his guidance a new settlement named Stockbridge was founded; it was built after the pattern of an English colonial town and boasted a small school for the training of Indian children. Through his effective work, which included the translation of parts of the Bible into the vernacular, Sargeant led 129 natives to receive baptism and 42 to enter into communicant membership. He was succeeded by Jonathan Edwards and later by his own son. After the Revolution, the Stockbridge Indians removed to the central part of New York State and thence to Indiana.

One of the most successful missionaries to the Indians was David Brainerd (1718–1747). In 1739, shortly after his conversion, he enrolled in Yale College to study for the ministry. A man of great mental powers, he won high honors for his scholarship. Unfortunately, an indiscreet remark that one of the tutors was as "destitute of grace as this chair" led to his expulsion in 1742, an act which was strenuously opposed by some of the clergy. That same year he was licensed to preach and appointed missionary to the Indians by the Scottish Society for Propagating Christian Knowledge. His first assignment took him to Kaunaumeek, between Albany and Stockbridge. In a letter written to the Reverend Ebenezer Pemberton, in 1744, he describes his technique in presenting the Gospel to the natives.

In my labours with them, in order to "turn them from darkness to light," I studied what was most *plain* and *easy*, and best suited to their capacities; and endeavoured to set before them from time to time, as they were able to receive them, the most *important* and *necessary* truths of Christianity; such as most immediately concerned their speedy conversion to God, and such as I judged had the greatest tendency, as means, to effect that glorious change in them. But especially I made it the *scope* and *drift* of all my labors, to lead them into a thorough acquaintance with these two things.—*First*, The *sinfulness* and *misery* of the estate they were *naturally* in; the evil of their hearts, the pollution of their natures; the heavy guilt they were under, and their exposedness to everlasting punishment. . . .—And, *secondly*, I frequently endeavoured to open to them the *fulness, all-sufficiency*, and *freeness* of that *redemption*, which the Son of God has wrought out by his obedience and sufferings, for perishing sinners; how this provision he had made, was suited to all their wants, and how he called and invited them to accept of everlasting life freely, notwithstanding all their sinfulness, inability, unworthiness, &c.[1]

[1] Mode, *op. cit.*, 527–528.

But despite the help of a Christian interpreter, the work came to naught; there were too few Indians in the area.

Brainerd was ordained by the Presbytery of New York in 1744, thereafter performing most of his missionary labors in Pennsylvania and New Jersey. He worked among the Indians at the Forks of the Delaware in Pennsylvania for a year, during that time making two journeys to the Susquehanna River. In none of these places did he meet with success. His most promising mission was at Crosswicks, near Trenton, New Jersey, where more than 130 natives were baptized Christians within the first year of its founding. Through the help of the Scottish Society for Propagating Christian Knowledge and of neighboring Presbyterian churches, Brainerd was encouraged to begin a new mission on a large tract of land at Cranbury, fifteen miles farther north. There he founded an Indian community with a church and an industrial school. Once this project was well under way he set out on another missionary tour through the Susquehanna Valley. In the summer of 1747 he was stricken with tuberculosis and was taken to Northampton, Massachusetts, where his fiancee, Jerusha Edwards, the daughter of Jonathan Edwards, endeavored in vain to nurse him back to health. That fall he died, only 29 years of age, and was succeeded by his brother John. Edwards, who had the highest regard for the young man, brought him posthumous fame by publishing his diary. It was widely read and probably more than any other work aroused American interest in the Indian missionary effort and later in home and foreign missionary undertakings.

In New England, Indians who were impressed by the revival often attended the parish churches, sometimes becoming communicant members. When James Davenport preached at Lyme, Connecticut, the Indians of the vicinity experienced a notable awakening. Nathanael Eells and Joseph Parks had similar results in their work among the Narragansett Indians at Stonington and Westerly. Some of their native converts became missionaries to other tribes in Rhode Island.

One of the outstanding Congregational missionaries to the Indians was Eleazer Wheelock (1711–1779). After several years of service as minister of Second Church in Lebanon, Connecticut, he turned his attention to founding an Indian Missionary School, which was maintained principally by subscriptions from the legislatures of Connecticut and Massachusetts. The institution eventually received the name of Moor's Indian Charity School, Joshua Moor having made a donation of a house and two acres of land about the year 1754. Whites and Indians alike were welcomed at the school, which graduated such distinguished future clergymen as Samson Occom, a Mohegan Indian, and Samuel Kirkland. In 1766, Occom and the Reverend Nathaniel Whitaker were sent to England and Scotland for the purpose of raising funds for the school. To the British, an Indian preacher was a curiosity worth seeing; they flocked to hear his sermons and to contribute to the cause which he represented. When the pair departed the country they had amassed a sum in the neighborhood of 10,000 pounds. A few years later Wheelock decided to transfer his school to New Hampshire, and a charter was obtained for a college, with about 40,000 acres of land as an endowment from Governor John Wentworth and others. By 1770, Dartmouth College had been founded at Hanover, New Hampshire. For some time, Moor's school was maintained there as a separate institution. Wheelock himself went to Hanover in August, 1770, and presided over the erection of a school building.

Samson Occom, after his graduation from Wheelock's school, served as a teacher in New London, Connecticut, and at Montauk, on Long Island. At the latter place he led a successful revival which resulted in many conversions among the Indians. He was ordained by Suffolk Presbytery in 1759. The closing years of his life were spent among the Indians near Utica, New York. Another graduate from Moor's Indian Charity School, Samuel Kirkland, also carried on an effective ministry among the natives. Upon his graduation from the College of New Jersey in 1765, he went on a missionary visit to the Seneca Indians in New York. The following year he was ordained to the Congregational ministry and appointed a missionary under the auspices of the Scottish Society for Propagating Christian Knowledge. He then settled in the midst of the Oneida tribe in central New York and labored among them until the Revolution suspended his activities. When the war came to an end, he resumed his mission and continued it until his death in 1808.

In addition to the Moravians, who maintained one of the best missionary programs for the Indians, the Anglican Society for the Propagation of the Gospel performed an exemplary work. Its best-known representative was the Reverend Henry Barclay, who was appointed missionary to the Mohawk Indians near Albany in 1735. Though he became rector of the church at Albany two years later, he continued to devote much time and attention to the 500 natives living in the vicinity. Most of them eventually accepted Christian baptism. When Barclay was called to Trinity Church, New York City, in 1746, John Ogilvie and later Henry Munro carried on the mission to the Indians with partial success.

THE CHURCHES AND THE NEGRO

Near the end of the seventeenth century the demand for Negro slaves in the colonies increased considerably, largely because of the diminishing supply of indentured servants. From 1714 to 1760 the number of Negro slaves in America jumped from 58,850 to 310,000. That relatively few slaves were to be found in the North was not due to Yankee disapproval of the institution but rather to the realization that it was for the most part economically impractical. Only on the great livestock farms of southern

Rhode Island were slaves to be found in considerable numbers. This circumstance, however, was no deterrent to the slave trade, into which many a New England entrepreneur ventured with the thought of becoming wealthy. In the Middle Colonies, where crops were diversified, slave labor was seldom satisfactory. In the South, however, where many workers were needed on the large tobacco, rice, and indigo plantations, slavery developed with unfailing regularity.

In view of the fact that several English courts had declared in the latter part of the seventeenth century that baptized slaves must be freed, many American slaveowners approached the question of evangelizing their slaves with extreme caution. When several of the colonies passed legislation to the effect that baptism did not confer the right to freedom, greater efforts were made to convert the Negroes. But little systematic work was carried on among them prior to the advent of the Great Awakening.

The Anglican Church, through its Society for the Propagation of the Gospel, was the first in the colonies to devote much attention to the Negro. Numerous missionaries, catechists, and schoolmasters sent to America were exhorted to work for his conversion. In 1741 the society raised more than 2000 pounds to promote this activity. The Associates of Dr. Bray, an organization formed by admirers of Commissary Bray, founded schools for Negroes in Philadelphia in 1758, and in 1760 in New York, Newport, Rhode Island, and Williamsburg, Virginia. These schools were in operation as late as 1775. Two other societies which functioned under the auspices of the Church of England and cooperated with the Society for the Propagation of the Gospel were the Society for Promoting Christian Knowledge and the Society for Promoting Christian Learning. They provided missionaries for the conversion of slaves and distributed religious literature among them. As for the institution of slavery, the Church of England seems to have taken no position against it as being incompatible with Christianity.

It was the Society of Friends which led the first noteworthy attack on the system of human bondage, though the Mennonites of Germantown were the first to make a public protest against slavery. By the opening of the eighteenth century, the Quaker community began to issue pronouncements to the effect that Friends should not purchase slaves. A most forceful agitator in this regard was the Quarterly Meeting of Chester, Pennsylvania, which made its first protest in 1711. Within a few decades the entire slave trade was under attack, being opposed by such leaders as William Burling, Benjamin Lay, Ralph Sandiford, and William Southby. One of the principal proponents of reform was the Quaker mystic and humanitarian, John Woolman (1720–1772). The passions of his life were to reconcile Indians with whites and to improve the status of the Negro. Much of his time was spent in working for the abolition of the slave trade. His *Journal* teems with illustrative material on his struggle against slavery. In a conversation with a colonel of the militia, while traveling through Virginia in 1757, he observed that "men having power too often misapplied it; that though we made slaves of the negroes, and the Turks made slaves of the Christians, I believed that liberty was the natural right of all men equally." Woolman was ably supported in his mission by Anthony Benezet of Philadelphia, the son of a French Huguenot, author of a number of anti-slavery publications, and sponsor of a school for Negroes. Due largely to their influence, the Philadelphia Yearly Meeting in 1758 repudiated slavery and in 1776 terminated all connection with Friends who refused to emancipate their slaves. Yearly meetings in the South were generally less bold, being content to urge their members to offer Christian instruction to those held in bondage. The request frequently went unheeded.

With certain notable exceptions, New England Congregationalists made few efforts to Christianize the Negro. Early in the eighteenth century Cotton Mather wrote in favor of their conversion, and a few local churches decried the institution of slavery, but few regarded it as a real problem. The most vigorous opponent of slavery in New England was Samuel Hopkins, the eminent theologian of Newport, Rhode Island. In 1769, he persuaded his slave-holding and trading communicants to go on record against human bondage. Among Presbyterians no direct action against slavery was taken prior to the Revolution, though individual ministers such as Samuel Davies did what they could to evangelize Negroes as well as whites and receive them into the church. In a number of instances, Baptist churches in Virginia and North Carolina admitted Negroes to church membership. The Lutherans for the most part provided religious instruction for slaves without opposing the system which held them bound. On the whole, neither clergy nor laity seemed vitally concerned over the welfare of the Negro during the colonial period. Ministers themselves, among them George Whitefield, Jonathan Edwards, and Ezra Stiles, frequently held slaves and saw nothing immoral in the practice. The religious condition of the Negro at the opening of the Revolution was deplorable.

PHILANTHROPIC ENTERPRISES

The humanitarian impulse which accompanied the Great Awakening bore fruit in a number of worthy projects for the benefit of the needy. Philanthropy was very much in evidence in almost every colony, and every denomination did what it could to solicit funds both in Europe and America. There were times when the competition between solicitors was so great that only those persons with exceptional public appeal could hope to secure a donation. Colleges, elementary schools, missions, and orphanages—all profited from the benevolent spirit of the age.

Apart from Michael Schlatter's charity schools and Eleazer Wheelock's school for Indians, perhaps the best-known philanthropic enterprise in eighteenth century America was George Whitefield's Orphan House near Savannah, Georgia. Before leaving England in 1738 on his first trip to America, Whitefield had raised 13,000 pounds for the poor of Georgia and for charity schools. Upon his arrival in Georgia he at once opened a school for children in Savannah. Gradually he envisioned an orphanage which might care for children of deceased immigrants; the thought so constrained him that he sailed for England that very year to raise funds. By January, 1740, he was back in Savannah, taking possession of a 500 acre tract ten miles from the city which he named Bethesda or House of Mercy, and arranging for the construction of a sixty foot long, two story high orphanage. It was completed early in 1741. Many of the funds raised for this purpose were obtained in the colonies through Whitefield's personal efforts. His ability as a solicitor is clearly indicated in the following account by Benjamin Franklin, who was by no means an indiscriminate philanthropist:

I did not disapprove of the design, but, as Georgia was then destitute of materials and workmen, and it was proposed to send them from Philadelphia at a great expense, I thought it would have been better to have built the house here, and brought the children to it. This I advis'd; but he was resolute in his first project, rejected my counsel, and I therefore refus'd to contribute. I happened soon after to attend one of his sermons, in the course of which I perceived he intended to finish with a collection, and I silently resolved he should get nothing from me. I had in my pocket a handful of copper money, three or four silver dollars, and five pistoles in gold. As he proceeded I began to soften, and concluded to give the coppers. Another stroke of his oratory made me asham'd of that, and determin'd me to give the silver; and he finish'd so admirably, that I empty'd my pocket wholly into the collector's dish, gold and all. . . .[2]

Unfortunately, Whitefield had little understanding of business and was almost constantly in financial difficulty; throughout his later years he spent practically everything he had to maintain his dream. His domineering manner and lack of tact combined to bring him into further embarrassing situations, especially when he attempted to force orphans who were not destitute to enter his asylum against their will. Finally, he was obliged to tour the colonies to seek candidates for his institution.

Whitefield had the hope that Bethesda would become more than an orphanage and in 1764 he developed a plan to establish a college there. The Georgia legislature approved the plan but the home government referred the petition for a charter to the Archbishop of Canterbury who insisted that the college become a Church of England institution. Unwill-

---

[2] B. Franklin, *Autobiography* (Collier, c. 1937), 101–102.

ing to accept such terms, Whitefield decided to found an academy; but it never became recognized as anything more than an orphanage offering vocational instruction.

CONTRIBUTIONS TO EDUCATION

In no area did the Great Awakening yield a richer harvest than that of formal education. The period witnessed an unusual proclivity for the founding of academies and colleges, particularly in the Middle Colonies. Presbyterians were most active in the establishment of new institutions. During the 1740's several academies were founded by graduates of William Tennent's Log College. At Fagg's Manor, Chester County, Pennsylvania, Samuel Blair established a school which provided a sound classical education; the curriculum emphasized the study of Latin, Greek, and Hebrew. Among those who went forth from the school to assume important positions in the church were Samuel Davies, missionary in Virginia and President of the College of New Jersey, James Finley, John Rodgers, and Robert Smith. Samuel Finley founded a school of the same type at Nottingham, Pennsylvania, near the Maryland border. Its best-known graduate was Dr. Benjamin Rush, eminent physician and founder of Dickinson College. Still another academy, Pequea in Lancaster County, Pennsylvania, was opened by Robert Smith; one of its distinguished graduates was John McMillan, one of the first Presbyterian ministers to settle in western Pennsylvania and a founder of Jefferson College.

Closely connected with the revival was the founding of the College of New Jersey. In March, 1745, certain ministers of the New York Presbytery took steps to found in the Middle Colonies a college sympathetic to the revival. But it was not until the following year that they were able to obtain a charter. Jonathan Dickinson was elected first president of the College of New Jersey, with Caleb Smith as tutor. The action was timely inasmuch as the Log College became defunct with the death of William Tennent in 1746. Classes began in May, 1747, in Dickinson's home at Elizabethtown, New Jersey, with eight or ten students. When Dickinson died that autumn, the college was moved to Newark, where it met in the home of its second president, Aaron Burr. In 1753, Samuel Davies and Gilbert Tennent went to England and raised more than 4000 pounds for the college, which by this time had obtained a new charter and had moved to Princeton. The college attracted not only New Side Presbyterians but New Light Congregationalists who objected to the conservatism of Harvard and Yale.

Though essentially a product of the Enlightenment, the founding of the University of Pennsylvania had a certain relationship to the revival. In 1740, Whitefield's supporters erected a great tabernacle 100 feet long to be used for his evangelistic services, inasmuch as it was not always practicable to meet out of doors. According to Benjamin Franklin: "Both house and ground were vested in trustees, expressly for the use of any preacher of any religious persuasion who might desire to say something to the people of Philadelphia. . . ." It was used by Whitefield and many other ministers connected with the revival. In accordance with a plan of Franklin, it was purchased and conveyed, in 1750, to the trustees of the Publick Academy in the City of Philadelphia. The school, which was founded for the benefit of poor children, was opened the following year. By 1755, the school had developed into a degree-granting college, which was nonsectarian in character. Finally, an act passed in 1791 designated it as the University of Pennsylvania.

In 1754, King's College in New York began operations under the presidency of the American Dr. Samuel Johnson and the institution was granted a royal charter. Trinity Episcopal Church had already donated a tract of land on the condition that the president of the school should always be a communicant member of the Established Church and that chapel exercises be conducted according to the usage of the Book of Common Prayer. These provisions brought forth a storm of protest from local dissenters, a circumstance which in no wise deterred the legislature from making appropriations to the school. The first building was erected in 1756. Under the leadership of Dr. Johnson, and later of the Reverend Myles Cooper, complete religious freedom prevailed at the college and it was declared that no person should incur any infringement of his academic rights because of his religious persuasion. After the Revolution, the name of the school was changed to Columbia College.

The founding of a college by the Dutch Reformed denomination was part of a larger movement to gain greater autonomy for the church in America. As in the case of the Presbyterians, many Dutch Reformed leaders realized the need of a judicatory to administer church affairs and a college for the training of ministers. In 1747, the authorities in the Netherlands granted permission for the colonists to form a coetus or subpresbytery responsible to the Classis of Amsterdam. But there was considerable disagreement among colonial churchmen over this action. Some preferred to remain completely subordinate to the Classis in Holland; others desired some independence and a native-trained ministry. The attempt of the latter faction to establish a chair of theology at King's College ended in failure. In the meantime there had been a rift in the Coetus with five conservative members who questioned independent church authority withdrawing in 1754 to form a Conferentie. The following year the majority remaining in the Coetus organized a classis and took steps to found an academy or college. But it was not until 1766 that the American Classis could obtain a charter for Queen's College in New Jersey. Meanwhile the Conferentie party, after attacking the introduction of preaching in English in New York, formally established themselves in 1764 into an Assembly Subordinate to the Classis of Amsterdam. Through the efforts of the Reverend John H. Livingston (1746–1825), a man as distinguished by piety as by scholarship, the unhappy division was brought to an end. Returning to New York in 1770, after completing his studies for the ministry at the University of Utrecht, he presented a plan of union satisfactory to the Classis of Amsterdam which was approved in 1772 by the American Classis and the Conferentie. It provided that the American body, though subordinate to the Classis of Amsterdam, should be substantially independent. Steps were also taken to implement the decision made in 1770 to found Queen's College at New Brunswick. Before much could be accomplished, the colonies were embroiled in war. When independence was gained, Dr. Livingston was elected first professor of theology. In the nineteenth century the name of the college was changed to Rutgers.

In New England, two colleges emerged as scions of the Great Awakening. The Baptists, having taken on new life, added numbers, and greater zeal for scholarship, became interested in the establishment of a college which would provide general training as well as preparation for the ministry. To that end the College of Rhode Island was chartered in 1764 and located at Warren. Its first president was James Manning, a graduate of the College of New Jersey. Like so many other colleges which grew out of the revival, it stood for full religious liberty; though Baptists were in charge of the institution, Protestants of all denominations might be invited to join its faculty. It was moved to Providence in 1770 and a few decades later was renamed Brown University. The second college, Dartmouth, was an outgrowth of Moor's Indian Charity School. Named after the Earl of Dartmouth, one of the school's benefactors, it was incorporated in 1769 by a charter granted by George III. While the college was predominantly under the control of Congregationalists, it soon became noted for its broad tolerance.

In Virginia the most significant educational advance was made by the Presbyterians. Hanover Presbytery, in 1774, took over the Augusta Academy and later reestablished it as Liberty Hall at Timber Ridge. Finally it was brought to Lexington where it was first named Washington College. Since the Civil War it has been known as Washington and Lee University. The same presbytery also organized Hampden-Sydney College in 1776, despite Anglican opposition. A charter for it was obtained in 1783. In North Carolina, a number of classical schools were founded after 1755 by graduates of the College of New Jersey. In 1771, an effort was made to expand the classical school at Sugar Creek, Mecklenburg County, into a college; but it was stymied by governmental opposition.

CHANGING PATTERNS IN THEOLOGY

The Great Awakening had focused attention upon man and his salvation, but it had left many questions unanswered. What was the meaning of sin, atonement, the divine decree, justification, and free will; and how were they related one to the other? Various schools of thought reflecting an age which was placing more and more stress upon man and his capabilities attempted to find answers to these questions. In doing so they either modified or denied the classical teachings of the Federal or Covenant theology.

Jonathan Edwards was followed by a group of disciples who labored to refute Arminianism, but each in his own way undermined the Calvinistic emphasis upon God and shifted it to man. Joseph Bellamy (1719–1790), a student of Edwards and a leader in the Connecticut phase of the revival, held to the Federal idea of original sin. But he believed also that sinful man has the ability to repent and should be exhorted to do so by his minister. Sin, though permitted by God, is a necessary means of achieving the highest good.

More important was Samuel Hopkins (1721–1803), close friend of Edwards and founder of the system known as Hopkinsianism. At the center of his system was the love, rather than the justice, of God. Like Bellamy, he believed that man has freedom and that salvation is through his volition. Sin, too, is a free choice and is by no means an imputation of Adam's initial disobedience. Nor has man lost his natural powers beyond that of an inclination to do the will of God. In the process of salvation, God performs the work of regeneration to which man responds in the act of conversion which takes place instantaneously. Through this act, God, for the sake of Christ, deals with the sinner as though he had never acted in disobedience. The death of Christ as an act of Atonement is not limited to the elect, as in Calvinism, but is for all men. Those who respond through conversion manifest their new state in works of holiness which grow out of "disinterested benevolence," or concern for the greatest welfare of all. They put away self-love which is the essence of human depravity and labor to attain the highest good for the largest number. Such persons, if they find it necessary, will be willing to accept the detrimental effects of evil in order to preserve others from greater evil or to achieve some worthy end. Hopkinsianism confronted men with this challenge: "Are you willing to be damned for the glory of God, and for the greatest good of the whole?" The implications of such a question for a missionary program are obvious.

Later exponents of the Edwardean theology or the New Divinity were Chandler Robbins, Stephen West, John Smalley, Jonathan Edwards the Younger, Nathanael Emmons, and Timothy Dwight. Emmons (1745–

1840) opposed the idea of the Covenant theology that God entered into a contract with Adam. The Deity established a "law of paradise" and arbitrarily determined that if Adam was disobedient to it mankind would become sinful. When Emmons went one step further and stated that God had put within Adam's heart an inclination toward evil, many opposed his teaching on the ground that it made the Deity directly responsible for sin. Timothy Dwight (1752–1817), President of Yale, insisted that God did no more than permit Adam to become disobedient. He believed in man's natural depravity as an inheritance from Adam.

Meanwhile a decidedly more liberal position was developing in sharp contrast to the theology of Edwards and his followers. Its roots may be traced to the teachings of the English Presbyterian theologian and arch foe of Federalism, John Taylor (1694–1761). In his *Scripture-Doctrine of Original Sin* he rejects the doctrine of original sin and maintains that since guilt is personal it cannot be transferred from one person to another. Likewise moral corruption cannot be inherited from the parent. Each person is born with the capacity to be either righteous or sinful; only by making evil choices does he become sinful. Though the great majority of New Englanders would have found this view distasteful, it caught hold in the Boston area where a reaction was building up to the revival and its Calvinistic concepts. One of its proponents was Jonathan Mayhew (1720–1766), a Bostonian with an inclination toward the rationalism of the Enlightenment who emphasized man's natural abilities and his essential goodness.

The chief representatives of Taylorism in New England were Samuel Webster (1718–1796) and Charles Chauncy (1705–1787). A strong opponent of the doctrine of original sin, Webster insisted that persons dying in infancy escaped eternal damnation because they were born into the world undefiled. Rather inconsistently, however, he also contended that all men need a Saviour; his theological antagonists took full advantage of this weakness. Chauncy, the anti-revivalist pastor of First Church, Boston, taught that men were not guilty of Adam's transgression, but as its consequence inherited mortality and a somewhat less perfect nature than was possessed originally by Adam. Chauncy was not certain as to the nature of this imperfection, except that it did not consist in moral depravity. He also proved himself to be a friend of Universalism in taking the position that ultimately all men would be brought to salvation.

By the end of the eighteenth century, the Edwardean School had emerged as the leading party in western Massachusetts and Connecticut and had made vast inroads among those Presbyterians who adhered to the New Side, anticipating a conflict which would promote schism in the Presbyterian Church in the nineteenth century. The new position became most influential in eastern Massachusetts, especially the Boston area. As the years passed, tension increased between these opposing wings of Congregationalism until finally they were split asunder.

While the churches were embroiled in theological polemic, a powerful philosophical force was steadily gaining strength; before the eighteenth century ended it would constitute the most significant challenge facing American Christianity. Since the seventeenth century Deism, which was the religious expression of the prevailing rationalism, had been making a considerable impact upon English intellectual life. The way had been prepared by such giants of philosophy as Newton, Spinoza, Hobbes, and Locke, who emphasized universal law, natural religion, man's innate ethical capacities, and revelation tested by reason. The Deists, a group which enjoyed considerable prestige within the Anglican Church in particular, stood for greater distrust of the supernatural in religion, greater faith in the sufficiency of man's reason, and greater trust in man's moral ability to live the good life. Gradually these views spread to the colonies where they first made themselves felt in the colleges. Throughout the eighteenth century the movement gained momentum in America, reaching its height during the last quarter, at which time it was nurtured more by French than by English influences.

Doctrines which stressed God's activity through nature and man's innate goodness had a certain natural appeal to the American mind; to certain groups of intellectuals and anti-revivalists they were highly gratifying. In the place of "enthusiasm" they could substitute reason, in the place of faith, good works. Many Deists maintained a nominal connection with the church without adhering to its doctrines, as in the case of George Washington. Others, such as Jefferson and Franklin, exhibited an attitude of friendliness toward organized religion, without becoming communicants of any church. Franklin's opinion of orthodoxy is clearly seen in a letter written in 1790 to President Ezra Stiles of Yale.

As to Jesus of Nazareth, my opinion of whom you particularly desire, I think the System of Morals and Religion, as he left them to us, the best the World ever saw or is likely to see; but I apprehend it has received various corrupting Changes, and I have, with most of the present Dissenters in England, some doubts as to his Divinity, tho' it is a question I do not dogmatize upon, having never studied it, and think it needless to busy myself with it now, when I expect soon an Opportunity of knowing the Truth with less trouble.[3]

At its best, Deism was a champion of spiritual and intellectual liberation. Its power, like that of the Great Awakening, lay in its catholicity. That men developed a broader outlook and gained freedom from parochial opinions was due in large measure to its influence. Its passion was man and his betterment. If it was naive in its estimate of mankind, at least it erred in a positive direction. It envisioned an ideal society, ruled by reason, ennobled by benevolence, and blessed by freedom. There can be no doubt but that it played a profound role in the making of the revolutionary generation.

[3] Quoted in Sweet, *Religion in Colonial America,* 337.

Religion in the

Revolutionary Era

EXCEPT FOR THE GREAT AWAKENING, NO FORCES OF CONSEQUENCE HAD ACTED prior to the Revolution to break down the social, economic, and religious walls which divided the American colonies. Indeed, there seemed to be a profound horror of consolidation, tending to tear down any proposals for unification. So regnant was this feeling that the colonists, many of them loyal members of the Church of England, labored to prevent the introduction of the Anglican episcopate into America lest it begin a process of setting up a complete autocratic hierarchy with centralized authority. Because the Church of England had such a traditionally centralized organization, it never became a popular church in colonial America, even where it was established by law.

THE BACKGROUND OF THE REVOLUTION

Nevertheless, certain intellectual factors, as well as economic and political, helped to prepare the way for revolution and to bind the people, out of necessity, into a confederation. Among these were the idea of fundamental law and the natural rights of the individual as guaranteed by that law; the "social contract" idea that government is created by consent of the people; and the idea—taught by Calvin—that when there is oppression, the representatives of the people have the right to resist.

Three religious factors, in particular, had an important and direct bearing on the Revolution. The first was the Great Awakening. In this great revival, the American colonists discovered for the first time a common emotional and intellectual challenge. Intercolonial leaders such as Edwards, Whitefield, and Tennent did much to foster cooperation and union among various religious groups and to lessen racial and denominational tensions. This emphasis, together with an increasing shift of population throughout the colonies, helped to create a sense of rapport. By drawing many nominal adherents of the Anglican Church into the fellowship of the evangelical denominations the revival weakened the chain which bound the colonies to England. Since the Anglican Church was one of the principal links between England and her possessions, any noticeable decline in its strength was bound to have an effect on relations with the mother country.

A second contributing factor was fear of Anglican ecclesiasticism by evangelicals. Since colonial Anglicanism was hindered by its inability to administer confirmation and ordination in America, it was natural that from time to time some of its leaders would agitate for the establishment of an episcopate which would make these functions possible. The sending of a bishop to America might actually have been a step toward independence, for it would have whetted the American appetite for self-rule. But evangelical leaders, principally Congregationalists and Presbyterians, strongly objected to this attempt on the ground that it was another excuse for interference from the British government. Between the years 1766 and 1775 these two denominations held joint conferences to combat ecclesiasticism; the principal effect of their meetings was to promote a more favorable attitude toward intercolonial cooperation. While nothing came of the effort to establish an American episcopate, the discussion stirred up more discontent with England and its national church and thus indirectly contributed to the revolutionary cause.

A third factor was concern over the Quebec Act of 1774. In 1763 England had received the French dominions in Canada as part of the settlement of the Treaty of Paris which terminated the Seven Years' War. In return she had agreed to extend toleration to Roman Catholics. But eleven years later, when she included the Northwest Territory, a triangular area between the Ohio and Mississippi Rivers within the boundaries of the Province of Quebec, a storm of protest was raised. It seemed to many Protestants that Roman Catholic influence would be coming too close to New England and the Middle Colonies for comfort. The result was mounting tension culminating in revolt.

During the pre-revolutionary era the pulpit was the most important single force in the colonies for the shaping and controlling of public opinion. The minister was usually the best-educated person in the community, and his words were regarded as having considerable authority behind them, even when they dealt with political philosophy. When fired with zeal to preach independence and resistance to royal authority, he could exercise a tremendous influence over his congregation. In light of the fact that Congregationalist, Presbyterian, Dutch Reformed, and Baptist ministers were almost overwhelmingly on the side of the Revolution and that they were supported to a large extent by the Lutherans and German Reformed, one can understand the importance of the role played by the clergy in this tumultuous era.

The attitude of the ministry is well represented in the sermons of the period. The philosophy of John Locke is curiously blended with illustrations from the Old Testament. George III is reminded of the fate of Rehoboam, and communities which do not furnish their quotas of men and money to the patriot cause are reminded that the people of Meroz were cursed for similar faults. Compelled submission to the arbitrary acts of legislators who do not represent the people is contrary to the will of God and must be resisted. So the clergy stirred the minds of their people and fanned the flames of rebellion.

Edmund Burke, who understood the colonies as well as any Englishman, reported to Parliament that the Americans were largely Protestant dissenters from the Church of England. They had grown accustomed to the freest discussion of all religious questions, and this had brought about extreme individualism. The right of private judgment which they reserved for themselves in spiritual matters and the right to elect and dismiss religious leaders had been carried over into politics, a fact which accounted for their pronounced liberalism. But perhaps the most important factor in American patriotism was the conviction that from the outset God himself had guided their adventure in the new land. Fortified by a dream and a destiny, they could not be overwhelmed.

CHURCH ESTABLISHMENTS AND THE REVOLUTION

The Congregationalists

No religious body surpassed the Congregationalists in contributions to the revolutionary effort. The entire force of New England was thrown into the struggle, and this force was started and controlled largely by the clergy. One Loyalist from New York wrote to a friend in London that the New England ministers were wicked, malicious, and inflammatory; their pulpits were "converted into Gutters of Sedition" and they substituted politics for the Gospel. Perhaps the most outspoken of these ministers was Jonathan Mayhew of Boston, a vigorous opponent of the Stamp Act and the establishment of episcopacy in America. One of his best-known sermons, entitled "A Snare Broken," was preached in Boston on May 23, 1776. In it he said he had learned from the Bible "that wise, brave and virtuous men were always friends to liberty; that God gave the Israelites a king, or absolute monarch, in his anger, because they had not sense and virtue enough to like a free commonwealth."

The New England clergy had plenty of opportunity to preach on civil affairs on election days, days for "fasting and humiliation," and Thanksgiving days. The election sermon was especially important because it was preached before the governor and the colony's law-making body, and then was published. From their studies of Locke and Milton, the ministers taught that civil government was of divine origin and that rulers derived their power from God. But rulers are limited by law and must not transcend their rights. If they do so then the people have the right to resist. The clergy could, of course, find plenty of reasons why the people should resist the tyranny of England.

An example of their patriotism may be seen in a statement which was issued by the General Association of Connecticut on June 18, 1776.

Deeply impressed with a sense of the calamitous state in which our Land is involved: reduced by the arbitrary edicts of the British Parliament, and the cruel and inhuman methods used to enforce them to the sad necessity of defending by force and arms those precious privileges which our fathers fled into this wilderness quietly to enjoy: declared rebels by the British King and Parliament: not only the power of Britain, but a large army of foreign mercenaries, hired at a most extravagant price, employed to dragoon us into obedience or rather abject submission to Tyranny: our foreign trade almost annihilated: many of our towns ruined and destroyed: our children, our friends, our dearest connections called from our bosoms to the field of battle: and some of them captivated and enslaved by our cruel and insulting foes . . . deeply impressed with a view of these dire calamities, we are lead anxiously to enquire what sins and iniquities prevalent in our land have called down these heavy judgments of Heaven upon us.[1]

A most interesting election sermon was preached in 1774 by Gad Hitchcock, pastor of the church in Pembroke, Massachusetts. His principal thesis was that the people are the only source of civil authority and that where rulers have "evil dispositions" resistance is both lawful and necessary. Equally important was the election sermon preached by Jonas Clark of Lexington in 1781, for it sheds considerable light on the political theory of the day. "It remains," he said, "with the community, state, or nation, as a public, political body, at any time, at pleasure to change, alter or

---

[1] Quoted in E. F. Humphrey, *Nationalism and Religion in America, 1774–1789* (Chipman, 1924), 64.

even totally dissolve the constitution, and return to a state of nature, or to form anew, as to them shall seem meet. . . ."

When hostilities actually broke out, the New England clergy exercised great influence in raising volunteers. Presidents Samuel Langdon of Harvard and Timothy Dwight of Yale advocated revolution and then commended the war effort to their students. Many ministers joined the army as chaplains or as regular soldiers. In fact, it was quite common for a clergyman to become an officer of troops raised from his own congregation. The dynamic and forceful John Cleaveland of Ipswich, Massachusetts, is said to have persuaded his entire parish to enlist and then volunteered himself. David Avery of Windsor, Vermont, on hearing about the battle of Lexington, preached a sermon in which he called his congregation to arms. He then bade them farewell and marched away at the head of a score of volunteers, enlisting others as they went along the way. At Beverly, Massachusetts, Joseph Willard helped to raise two companies which he escorted into battle. There were undoubtedly many instances in which a zealous clergyman could win more recruits than a seasoned veteran of many campaigns. Those who could not go to war contributed much to the cause of independence through their writings and gave as liberally as their stipends would permit.

Representative of Congregational laymen in the revolutionary era was Samuel Adams (1722–1803). Educated at Harvard, where he had been trained in both theology and law, his thought was shaped largely by Puritanism and the natural-rights school of political philosophy. His democratic psychology was grounded in the New England town-meeting. He believed fervently in the sovereignty of the people and in their right to change their fundamental law, along with its interpretation and administration, whenever they desired. This was because of his liberal faith that the people were competent to judge their own good and conduct their own affairs.

The *multitude* I am speaking of, is the *body of the people*—no contemptible multitude—for whose sake government is instituted; or rather, who have themselves erected it, solely for their own good—to whom even kings and all in subordination to them, are strictly speaking, servants and not masters. . . . I am not of levelling principles: But I am apt to think, that constitution of civil government which admits equality in the most extensive degree, consistent with the true design of government, is the best.[2]

Through his vigorous support of the revolutionary effort he furthered the democratic ideals of his compatriots and gave added force to the doctrines being proclaimed from New England pulpits.

[2] Quoted in Parrington, *op. cit.*, I, 251.

The Anglicans

As an ecclesiastical organization the Anglican Church was, of all the denominations, most loyal to the English king. Yet out of its ranks came many of the most outspoken patriots, men who would give their very lives for freedom from the tyranny of that same ruler. Among the clergy there was a strong inclination at the beginning of the Revolution to remain loyal to the crown. This attitude is reflected in *A View of the Causes and Consequences of the American Revolution,* written by the Reverend Jonathan Boucher of Virginia and published in London in 1797. He wrote:

God forbid any of us should live to see the day when we may be convicted of the truth of King James' maxim—'No bishop, no king' and when this dominion, now the fair image of one of the best governments upon the earth, shall be so degenerate and mean as to become the ape of New England in her civil institutions, and therefore too likely to follow the same wretched model in what the people of New England call the platform of religion.[3]

Boucher seems to have felt that the establishment of political republicanism would mean the downfall of the Anglican Church. At any rate it would mean the end of establishment. The subsequent history of Virginia reveals that his fears were well founded.

There are very few Loyalist sermons dating from the war period now in existence. Because of national sentiment it was extremely hazardous for a Tory minister to preach his political convictions. In fact, Jonathan Boucher deemed it necessary to preach with loaded pistols lying before him on a cushion. During one service he was actually forced out of his church by a band of armed men.

In Virginia the majority of the clergy were Loyalist, though a substantial minority, perhaps one-third, were hostile to the English crown. Among the laity of Virginia, overwhelming support was on the side of independence with only a portion adopting the opinions of the Loyalist clergy. In the northern colonies, especially Massachusetts, Connecticut, and New York, the clergy were even more inclined toward loyalty to England than in the South. From New York the Reverend John Stuart wrote: "No class was so uncompromising in its loyalty as the clergy of the Church of England in this State; and they in consequence did not fail to experience the bitter effects of their own unwise resolution." The Reverend Charles Inglis of Trinity Church, New York, in his "Letters of Papinian," addressed to John Jay and the people of North America, attacked the revolutionary leaders in vehement tones: "You will find these pretended enemies of oppression the most unrelenting oppressors and their little fingers heavier

---

[3] Quoted in Humphrey, *op. cit.,* 23.

than the king's loins. . . . There is more liberty in Turkey than in the
dominions of the Congress." In New England, with the exception of Connecticut, most of the clergy were forced to flee; they took refuge in New
York, Canada, or England. Those that remained followed the dictates of
necessity and were known for their "peaceful submission and quiet deportment." Considering the fact that New England was the most zealous
of all the regions in waging the war for independence, mere refusal to
take a stand against the British could be viewed as a form of high treason.

No Tory minister in the colonies labored under greater difficulties than
the Reverend Samuel Seabury (1729–1796), subsequently to become
bishop of Connecticut. When the Revolution began, he was in charge of
the Westchester parish in New York and was busily engaged in turning
out a series of loyalist pamphlets under the pseudonym "The Westchester
Farmer." In these pamphlets, which were written in an unusually witty
and engaging manner, he attacked the Continental Congress and proposed
peaceful submission to Britain. Later, while in Connecticut, Seabury was
seized by a band of armed men and thrown into the New Haven jail on
a charge of authoring the pamphlets. After languishing in prison for a
month he was released for lack of evidence. Upon returning to New York
he was severely persecuted. Then, after the battle of Long Island in 1776,
he managed to escape to the British lines. He became a chaplain in the
king's army and was assigned to a regiment of American Loyalists.

All New York Anglicans, however, were not Loyalists. Dr. Samuel Pro-
voost, later to become first bishop of New York, fought on the side of the
Revolution; and it was Alexander Hamilton, a Church of England layman,
who refuted the arguments made by Seabury as the "Westchester Farmer."
Other New York Anglicans of patriotic renown were John Jay and Robert
Morris.

Philadelphia Anglicanism was more revolutionary than that of New
York. Two of its outstanding representatives were William Smith, Provost
of the College of Philadelphia, and Jacob Duché, rector of Christ Church.
Duché served as the first chaplain of the Continental Congress from 1774
to 1776, and during that time no preacher could have done more for the
cause of freedom. He is especially noted for his sermon, "The Duty of
Standing Fast in our Spiritual and Temporal Liberties," preached in Christ
Church on July 7, 1775. Strangely enough, when the British captured Philadelphia he went over to their side and later fled to England where he
became chaplain of an orphanage.

One of the most faithful leaders on the American side was the Reverend
William White of Philadelphia. At the time when the revolutionary cause
was closest to disaster he was offered the chaplaincy of Congress, which
he accepted even though he knew that it might cost him his life if the
British were victorious. He remained as chaplain until the close of the

war. His influence had much to do with the decisions of many clergymen to serve as army chaplains, and the fact that the Anglican Church contributed the third largest number of chaplains to the patriot side was at least partially due to his efforts.

It is significant that a large majority of Anglican laymen were patriots, while two-thirds of the signers of the Declaration of Independence were affiliated with the Anglican Church. In general, however, Anglican laymen were very much divided in their allegiance. In the Southern and Middle Colonies the majority were patriotic, while in New England they tended to side with the British. In the South, most Whigs belonged to the Church of England; in New England no outstanding Whig was an Anglican.

Unlike the Congregational churches which were free and independent, the Anglican Church in the colonies was in no position to give its formal allegiance to the fight for freedom. In fact, there is not a single official act which shows that it favored the patriotic side. For this it suffered greatly, probably more than any other denomination. Yet in all fairness it should be noted that the Anglican Church had no legislative body in America through which it could have expressed a patriotic sentiment. Its reputation was, of course, ruined by the large number of pro-British clergymen. Nevertheless, through many laymen as well as some clergy, the church made a contribution to American independence. One need only look at the names of a few of its distinguished members—George Washington, James Madison, Patrick Henry, John Marshall, Robert Morris, John Jay, and Alexander Hamilton—to be assured of that fact.

THE ROLE OF THE VOLUNTARY BODIES

The Presbyterians

It has been asserted that the "sturdy Republicanism" of the Presbyterians gave them "an influence over the course of the Revolution out of all proportion to their numbers." Many writings of Loyalist leaders have indicated the amount of support given by Presbyterians to the patriot cause. Joseph Galloway, a Pennsylvania Tory, said that the foes of the English government in 1774 were "Congregationalists, Presbyterians and smugglers." Concerning the composition of the Continental army he reported that one-fourth were natives of America, one-half were Irish, and the other fourth were English and Scottish. While it is certainly true that the Presbyterian Church took its stand in favor of independence, it is worth noting that as late as 1775 the Synod of New York and Philadelphia opposed a complete break with the mother country and claimed that "it is well known to you, (otherwise it would be imprudent indeed thus publicly to profess,) that we have not been instrumental in inflaming the minds of the people, or urging them to acts of violence and disorder." On the other hand, the Synod endorsed the Continental Congress as a body of representatives duly elected by the people and commissioned to secure and defend their natural rights. Such action was thoroughly in harmony with the Calvinistic theory of government.

British officials in the Middle Colonies, however, seemed to be thoroughly convinced that the Presbyterians were responsible in large measure for the political events of the time. John Hughes, the stamp distributor for Pennsylvania, reported in 1775 that bigoted Calvinists were "ripe for open Rebellion, when they poisoned the Minds of the people enough." The following year the Reverend Charles Inglis, an Anglican Loyalist in New York, accused the Synod of passing a resolution to support the Continental Congress in all its measures; he was probably referring to the statement issued in 1775. More malicious and unfounded was the report of missionaries of the Society for the Propagation of the Gospel in Delaware, who claimed at the outset of the Revolution that the war had been definitely planned by Presbyterians with the object of gaining their own religious establishment.

The first religious body in the colonies to accept officially the Declaration of Independence and identify itself with the revolutionary cause was the Hanover Presbytery in Virginia. In a statement directed to the Virginia Assembly on October 24, 1776, it declared that "we rely upon this Declaration, as well as the justice of our honorable legislature, to secure us the free exercise of religion according to the dictates of our consciences."

In 1778, when the British controlled Philadelphia, the Synod was held at Bedminster because Philadelphia was "in possession of the enemy." It would seem definite that the Synod considered itself on the side of the Continental army. Nor could Abigail Adams have been entirely wrong in her statement to her husband, John, that "the Presbyterian clergy are particularly active in supporting the measures of Congress from the rostrum, gaining proselytes, persecuting the unbelievers, preaching up the righteousness of their cause, and persuading the unthinking populace of the infallibility of success."

A considerable number of Presbyterians were leaders of the Revolution. Many were graduates of the College of New Jersey where they had first been exposed to the principles of freedom of conscience and government by the consent of the governed. Nine of the college's alumni became members of the Federal Constitutional Convention in 1787, and its president, John Witherspoon (1723–1794), a Scottish immigrant, was a memorable figure in political affairs. So prominent was he in the movement for independence that he was characterized by John Adams as an "animated Son of Liberty." A great proportion of the Presbyterian clergy in those days had come under his guidance, a circumstance which partially accounts for the fervid patriotism of those leaders.

Elected to represent New Jersey in the Continental Congress, Witherspoon began to agitate almost immediately for independence. In 1776 he signed the Declaration of Independence, being the only minister who was a member of the Continental Congress when that historic measure was enacted. His service in the Congress continued until 1783. In 1778 he signed the Articles of Confederation on behalf of his state. He was a member of the committee on foreign affairs, the board of war, the secret committee, and also the committees of finance and supplies for the army. In November, 1776, when the war was going badly for the Americans, he and two others went to the headquarters of General Washington to render assistance in reenlisting the soldiers whose terms had expired or were about to expire. It is not difficult to understand why the Reverend Jonathan Odell, the Tory satirist, who quit his parish at Burlington, New Jersey, and fled to the British lines in 1777, singled him out for this vitriolic attack in verse:

> Meanwhile unhappy Jersey mourns her thrall,
> Ordained by the vilest of the vile to fall;
> To fall by Witherspoon!—O name the curse
> Of sound religion, and disgrace of verse.
> Member of Congress, we must hail him next:
> "Come out of Babylon," was now his text.
> Fierce of the fiercest, foremost of the first,
> He'd rail at Kings, with venom well-nigh burst;
> Not uniformly grand-for some bye-end,
> To dirtiest acts of treason he'd descend;
> I've known him seek the dungeon, dark as night,
> Imprison'd Tories to convert or fright;
> While to myself I've hummed in Dismal tune,
> I'd rather be a dog than Witherspoon.[4]

The following passage from one of Witherspoon's sermons, however, reveals a very different man than that described by the prejudiced Odell.

You shall not, my brother, hear from me in the pulpit, what you have never heard from me in conversation; I mean railing at the king personally, or even his ministers and the parliament, and people of Britain, as so many barbarous savages . . . I do not refuse submission to their unjust claims, because they are corrupt or profligate, although probably many of them are so, but because they are *men*, and therefore liable to all the selfish bias inseparable from human nature. I call these claims unjust, of making laws to bind us in all cases whatsoever, because they are separated from us, independent of us, and have an inter-

[4] Quoted in W. W. Sweet, *Religion in the Development of American Culture* (Scribner, 1952), 20–21.

est in opposing us . . . This is the true and proper hinge of the controversy between Great Britain and America.[5]

George Duffield, chaplain to the Continental Congress and pastor of the Third Presbyterian Church, Philadelphia, was another outstanding leader. He was particularly noted for his direct and forceful sermonic presentations, with their pithy remarks, which prompted John Adams to observe in a letter to his wife that Duffield's "principles, prayer, and sermons more nearly resemble those of our New England clergy than any I have heard." The minister became chaplain to the army around New York during the summer of 1776, and remained with that body during the whole of that terrible campaign.

Perhaps the most romantic episode concerned James Caldwell of the Presbyterian church at Elizabeth, New Jersey. It is said that when the militia at the battle of Springfield ran out of wadding for their muskets, Caldwell hurried to his church and returned with an armful of Watts' Psalm Books, throwing them to the ground and crying out, "Now, boys, give 'em Watts! Give 'em Watts!" Caldwell and his wife were subsequently murdered by the British.

When the war finally drew to a close in October, 1781, Presbyterians rejoiced over the victory. The following year the Synod sent out a "Pastoral Letter" which spoke of "the general and almost universal attachment of the Presbyterian body to the cause of liberty and the rights of mankind." It then urged that prayers of thanksgiving be offered for the achievement of independence.

The Dutch Reformed

The Dutch Reformed Church was fundamentally on the side of freedom. Unfortunately, since its congregations were situated largely in areas where British might was most vigorous, the church suffered acutely from the war; many edifices were destroyed and the ministers were frequently driven from their homes. When the British captured New York, a number of the church buildings were desecrated; the Dutch ministers fled the city and their congregations were scattered.

The denomination set aside days of fasting, thanksgiving, prayer, and humiliation during the war period. Thus, in 1775, the General Synod recommended its churches in New York and New Jersey to set aside the seventh of May as a "day of solemn humiliation, with fasting and prayer." At the same time the church did what it could to further enlistments in the Continental army. Because of war conditions the synod did not meet in 1776 and 1777. After what the synod deemed a just and necessary war had been terminated, it deposed Domine J. C. Rubel for immoralities he was alleged to have committed and for being a Tory.

[5] Armstrong, Loetscher and Anderson, *op. cit.*, 86–87.

The German Reformed

In general the record of the German Reformed Church was patriotic. A number of the officers in the Continental army such as General Nicholas Herkimer, "the hero of Oriskany," and Baron Frederick William Von Steuben, a ruling elder in the Nassau Street Church in New York, were from its ranks. Many of the ministers also seem to have been staunch supporters of independence. At the outset of the war the Reverend John H. Weikel got into difficulty for preaching on the text, "Better is a poor and wise child, than an old and foolish king, who will no more be admonished." Michael Schlatter of Philadelphia was put in prison by the British for favoring the American cause, while William Hendel required armed guards to protect him from pro-British Indians while preaching in Lykens Valley, Pennsylvania.

Conversely, several German Reformed churchmen favored the British. The Reverend John Michael Kern of New York became a Loyalist because he thought that the colonies were not yet prepared for independence. He emigrated to Nova Scotia but at the close of his life returned to Pennsylvania, penniless and sick at heart. At the beginning of the struggle Dr. John Joachim Zubly of Savannah, Georgia, played a prominent part with the Sons of Liberty, armed citizens who harassed British officialdom up and down the country. He was even sent to the Continental Congress as a representative from Georgia. But he did not favor separation from England and used what influence he had to combat it. The result was that he soon lost his prestige and was banished from Savannah in 1777.

In 1775 the Pennsylvania Coetus directed that a day of "general fasting, repentance and prayer shall be held in all our congregations" on the last Wednesday in June. That same year the Reformed and Lutheran Churches joined in an appeal to the German citizens of New York and North Carolina, calling upon them to support the measures of Congress and the cause of American freedom. The Germans also helped to organize militia companies which were prepared to march wherever and whenever they were commanded.

The Lutherans

The German Lutherans were not well organized in America when the Revolutionary War began, and so their contributions must be measured in terms of the actions of various representative leaders. By all standards, the family of the Muhlenbergs was the most important of the Lutherans in America. Henry Melchior Muhlenberg, the father, had exercised a governing position over all the Lutheran churches from New York to Georgia. Though he maintained a standard of neutrality, his sons were patriots.

One of the sons, John Peter Muhlenberg, was a pastor at Woodstock,

Virginia, at the beginning of hostilities. The Sunday after he had heard the news of Bunker Hill he rose in his pulpit and told his congregation that "in the language of Holy Writ, there is a time for all things. There is a time to preach and a time to fight; and now is the time to fight." At the close of the service he removed his pulpit vestments and stood before the congregation in the uniform of a Virginia colonel. He later became a breveted major-general and took part in the battles of Brandywine, Germantown, and Monmouth. At Yorktown he was in command of the first brigade. In 1776 he was a member of the Virginia Convention, and later represented Pennsylvania in both the House and Senate of the United States.

Frederick A. C. Muhlenberg, his brother, was pastor of Christ German Lutheran Church in New York. When the British approached the city in 1776, he fled and became an assistant to his father. From 1779 to 1780 he was a member of the Continental Congress and was president of the Pennsylvania Convention which ratified the Federal Constitution. During the years 1789 to 1797 he was a member of the national House of Representatives and served as its first speaker.

While Lutherans were predominantly in favor of independence, some were loyal to the English crown. When the British captured New York the Reverend Bernard Hausihl remained in the city and proved himself to be a Tory. Upon the evacuation of the city by the English army, he and many of his congregation migrated to Nova Scotia and settled near Halifax. He later became a clergyman in the Church of England. In Georgia, the Reverend Christopher Triebner, a German immigrant, went over to the British side and at the close of the war moved to England.

The Baptists

Baptist congregations gave intense support to the movement for independence. Persecuted as they were under English law, they could not help but favor a cause which promised them full liberty of conscience. They generally supported the Revolution because they hoped for fairer treatment under the new government and because idealogically their democratic polity and compact theory of government harmonized more nearly with the principles which ruled the patriot side.

The Baptists suffered excessively at the hands of the British. When the English army took possession of Newport, Rhode Island, in 1776, they burned the Baptist meetinghouse and parsonage and imprisoned the minister. From that time Rhode Island Baptists worked actively for the Revolution, even though it meant uniting with the Congregationalists, who had once bitterly persecuted them. Isaac Backus, the Baptist historian, stated that in Massachusetts the Baptists were so completely united in the defense of their country that when the General Court of Boston passed an act in October, 1778, listing 311 men who were enemies of the government and should not be permitted to return, not a single Baptist was on the list.

In 1774, the Warren Association, composed of Baptist churches in New England, met under the leadership of Isaac Backus, President Manning of Rhode Island College, John Gano, and Morgan Edwards. Backus was sent to Philadelphia to petition the Continental Congress for full religious liberty. The attempt met with failure and the Baptists turned to the provincial congress of Massachusetts where once again their overtures were rejected.

The Baptists, nevertheless, did receive some recognition for their patriotic activities. In 1779, Samuel Stillman, pastor of the First Baptist Church of Boston, was commissioned to preach the annual election sermon. The principal thesis of his homily was that the foundation of civil society is the consent of the governed. Election should be free and often, and representation should be as equal as possible. The sacred rights of conscience are among the inalienable rights of mankind and can never be controlled by any human authority.

Virginia Baptists were particularly militant. In August, 1775, they issued an "Address" which stated that because of the oppression in America it was perfectly lawful to go to war, and that they ought to resist Britain because of her unjust invasion, her oppressive tyranny, and her repeated hostilities. Numerous Baptists responded by enlisting in the army. In Culpepper County, Thomas McClanahan recruited a company of Baptists and led them into service.

The Methodists

At the beginning of the Revolution Methodism was still new to America. In all the colonies there were only 19 preachers and 3148 members. In general this group was regarded as unpatriotic, thanks largely to the pronouncements of John Wesley. Until 1775 Wesley had disapproved of the repressive measures taken by the British government. But then he read Dr. Samuel Johnson's "Taxation No Tyranny," and was so convinced that he wrote "A Calm Address to the American Colonies," in which he condemned the colonists for their actions against the crown. This created rabid hostility to the Methodists which was not relieved when, in 1776, Wesley called John Hancock a felon and urged the Americans to lay down their arms.

Most Virginia Methodists hurried to the defense of the Established Church. A large proportion of their missionaries had only recently arrived from England and, of course, remained loyal. Leaders such as Martin Rodda and Thomas Rankin became pronounced Loyalists. Even Francis Asbury refused to take the oath of allegiance in Maryland and was forced to flee to Delaware where clergymen were not required to take the oath. Some were pacifists, as in the case of Jesse Lee. By 1778, every Methodist minister sent out by Wesley had left America, with the exception of Asbury, and he was in forced retirement. Methodists were frequently persecuted. During the years 1778 to 1780, few gains were made outside Maryland and Virginia where the Anglican Church was strong and not entirely opposed to the Methodist societies.

A number of Methodists refused to follow their English leaders and went over to the patriot side. Among the native preachers there were many patriots such as Freeborn Carrettson, Philip Gatch, and William Watters. But their contributions were not sufficient to relieve Methodism of the contempt which had been placed upon it. Despite all disabilities, however, the Methodist revival was carried forward in the South; by 1781 the membership throughout the country had risen to 10,539.

The Friends

Contributions of the Friends to the Revolution were relatively meager. With the exception of a minority who believed a defensive war to be justifiable, they opposed war because they felt it could not be justified by its results. At a time when feeling ran high and physical resistance was regarded as the only proof of loyalty, such a position practically amounted to treason. But a close examination of the facts will show that while the majority of Friends were opposed to war most of them tended to be anti-British. In 1765, fifty of them signed a non-importation agreement as a means of passive resistance. What the Loyalists counted on was the conservatism of the old Quaker families and the strong resolutions passed by the Quaker meetings against violent resistance to the civil authorities. Actually, about 400 members of the church were disowned for participating in the war efforts of the patriots, while only six were similarly disciplined for aiding the British. Friends were expelled not only for joining the army, but also for fitting out an armed vessel, making weapons of war, and even assuming a military appearance. The faction which held that armed resistance is justifiable broke with the orthodox group and founded the "Free Quakers" or "Fighting Quakers," a sect which lasted well into the nineteenth century. Among them were Thomas Mifflin, who subsequently became Quartermaster General and governor of Pennsylvania, and Nathanael Greene, who succeeded Mifflin as Quartermaster General. None was more famous than Betsy Ross, who made the first American "Stars and Stripes."

When the British, under General Howe, were in the vicinity of Philadelphia in 1777, a number of prominent Friends alleged to be pro-British were arrested and removed to Winchester, Virginia, where they were held in confinement throughout the winter. After the Continental army reentered Philadelphia in the spring of 1778, the Quaker residents became targets of malicious attacks inspired by feverish patriots. Their homes were ransacked, their farms despoiled, and their property seized when they refused to pay war taxes. School teachers were thrown into prison for refusing to take an oath of allegiance; others were kept in jail for months without being brought to trial.

In New England the Friends were treated with greater favor. Early in the war the Rhode Island Legislature passed an act which granted exemption from military service to persons who could prove they held membership in a Quaker meeting. But the misuse of the provision by unworthy persons soon led to its repeal. A new enactment provided that Friends, upon being drafted, might elect to pay for a substitute; if they refused to do so, their property would be confiscated. In view of the terrible hardships experienced by the revolutionaries in Rhode Island and the apparent Loyalist leanings of the Friends at Newport, such legislation seems to have been mild. In Massachusetts, where Friends were to be found in considerable numbers, the government adopted a policy similar to that of Rhode Island.

The Mennonites and Moravians

Most of the Mennonites in Pennsylvania, like the Friends, favored the American side, but refused to engage in hostilities. Only a few were Tories, and these emigrated to Canada at the close of the war. Their main division came over the question of whether they should pay the war tax. A group led by Christian Funk thought they should pay it; the majority, notwithstanding, felt otherwise, and Funk and his followers were forced to withdraw in 1776 and form a separate religious body. On the whole the Mennonites suffered little persecution, although they contributed nothing beyond a few supplies to the patriotic cause.

The Moravians furthered the revolutionary effort in various non-military ways, but were badly treated by both sides. They offered their buildings at Bethlehem to be used as hospitals for the Continental army and furnished the army with much-needed supplies. Some rendered noncombatant service, as in caring for wounded Continental soldiers. Probably their greatest service was rendered through their missions to the Indians. In the opening years of the struggle, David Zeisberger kept the Delawares from going to war with the settlers—a most important service in days when every man was needed to fight the British. During the course of the war Zeisberger and his associates were twice summoned to Detroit and accused of espionage, but they were able to prove their innocence. Their Indian converts, inspired by pacifist principles, did their utmost to dissuade hostile natives from going on the warpath as well as to warn settlers of planned attacks. Their motives were frequently misjudged by both sides; during the winter of 1781 they suffered terribly from exposure and lack of food, having been driven by the British from their homes. Finally they were granted permission to go back to their settlements along the Tuscarawas River in Ohio to gather food. Here the Christian Indians welcomed a company of American militia who, they supposed, had come on a friendly mission. Instead they were crowded into two buildings and ruthlessly slaughtered. Only two boys in the party of 96 escaped alive.

The Roman Catholics

The year 1776 found Roman Catholicism in America neither populous nor well organized. But its adherents supported the Revolution wholeheartedly in the hope that they might gain more toleration, since only in Maryland and Pennsylvania did they enjoy anything approximating religious liberty. As the war advanced, their influence grew, especially after the Roman Catholic countries of Spain and France had recognized the United States.

Father John Carroll, later archbishop, worked, though unsuccessfully, with a committee of Congress in an effort to win the French Canadians to the cause of independence. Among the Roman Catholic signers of the Declaration of Independence and the Constitution were Thomas Fitzsimmons, Daniel Carroll, and Charles Carroll of Carrollton. A number of Roman Catholic volunteers enlisted in the army and navy. Several Roman Catholic regiments were organized, including "Congress' Own," the Catholic Indians from St. John, Maine, and the Catholic Penobscots. There were also a number of Roman Catholic officers who came from Ireland, France, and Poland to give their services to the cause of liberty.

Only a few Roman Catholics were Tories. In Philadelphia, a Roman Catholic regiment was recruited in 1777–1778, while General Howe and his troops occupied that city. It was commanded by Lieutenant Colonel Alfred Clinton, then a member of St. Mary's parish.

On July 4, 1779, the French minister and first diplomatic representative to the United States, Conrad Gérard, invited the American officials in Philadelphia to attend a *Te Deum* in St. Mary's Church to celebrate the third anniversary of American independence. When the news of the surrender at Yorktown reached Philadelphia, the French minister again invited the Congress to attend a service of thanksgiving in the Roman Catholic church. These actions did much to place Roman Catholics in a favorable light and to establish their prestige among the American people. It is thus understandable that in response to a letter of congratulations from the Roman Catholics, President Washington should have written of their part in the struggle for independence: "I presume your fellow-citizens will not forget the patriotic part which you took in the accomplishment of their revolution."

While the American churches can scarcely be held responsible for the precipitation of the revolutionary conflict, there were elements within them which fostered the national desire for liberty. There was a "religious temper" in America which bred discontent with the former order. Not only did the majority of church bodies in the colonial period have polities which favored democracy or republicanism, they experienced a higher degree of religious liberty than was to be found in any other country of the world. Where religious liberty is found in part, a demand for political freedom will come in like manner. The Christian churches supported the cause of independence, not because they hoped to profit from it in a materialistic way, but because of their profound conviction that every man has the right to live in freedom and worship his Maker according to the dictates of his own conscience.

The Churches in a Period

of Reorganization

WITH THE SURRENDER OF LORD CORNWALLIS AT YORKTOWN IN 1781, AMERI-can independence had at last been achieved. An American nation, however, waited to be born out of the conflict and confusion which characterized the opening years of autonomous rule. At the completion of independence, America was thirteen rather than one; the Articles of Confederation had, to be sure, established a loosely knit confederacy, but its power was in name only. The spirit of localism, forgotten for a time in the flush of revolutionary idealism, was once more abroad in the land. It manifested itself in a collection of sovereign states, dedicated primarily to the advancement of their own interests and loyal to the confederation only so far as it seemed advantageous. During this period which preceded the establishment of a stronger Federal government, a score of liberal ideas which had been brought to light during the Revolution saw fruition in the acts of various state legislatures. These revealed a developing process of democratization which would be carried forward in the Federal Constitution and the Bill of Rights. One of the forces which played a fundamental role in the democratic process was that of organized religion.

RELIGION AND THE STATE

The Movement toward Church Disestablishment

Before the ink could dry on the Declaration of Independence, agitation had arisen in certain colonies to bring to an end the favors enjoyed by the established churches. In Virginia, where more than half of the population was identified with dissenting bodies, a movement of protest against state support of the Anglican Church had for some years been gathering momentum. Baptists and Presbyterians in particular had showed steady determination to strike at the roots of a system which had resulted not only in inequity but intolerance and persecution. They were joined in this sentiment by many an Anglican layman who had grown tired of the widespread corruption in his church. Such a person was James Madison, who wrote to a college classmate in 1774: "Union of religious sentiments begets a surprising confidence, and ecclesiastical establishments tend to great ignorance and corruption; all of which facilitates the execution of mischievous projects. . . ." This philosophy was embraced by a number of political leaders in Virginia, among them Patrick Henry, Thomas Jefferson, and George Mason.

In June, 1776, the House of Burgesses sat as a constitutional convention at Williamsburg and adopted a Declaration of Rights, which was principally the work of George Mason, though amended by James Madison. It provided complete religious freedom, but did not abolish the establishment. The only religious body which petitioned the convention for religious liberty was the Baptists. In return for such a favor, the petitioners promised that they would "gladly unite with their brethren and to the utmost for their ability promote the common cause."

The following October, the first republican legislature of Virginia, the General Assembly, convened at Williamsburg. Nine petitions against the establishment were presented during the meeting; of these, several originated with the Baptists, while one came from the Lutherans and another from Hanover Presbytery. The Presbyterian statement was representative:

In this enlightened age, and in a land where all of every denomination are united in most strenuous efforts to be free, we hope and expect our representatives will cheerfully concur in removing every species of religious as well as civil bondage. Certain it is, that every argument for civil liberty gains additional strength when applied in the concerns of religion; . . .

We would also humbly represent that the only proper objects of civil government are the happiness and protection of men in their present state of existence, the security of the life, liberty, and the property of the citizens, and to restrain the vicious and to encourage the virtuous, by wholesome laws equally extending to every individual; but that the duty which we owe to our Creator, and the manner of discharging it, can only be directed by reason or conviction, and is nowhere cognizable but at the tribunal of the Universal Judge.[1]

The memorial was referred to the Committee on Religion, of which Thomas Jefferson was chairman. Despite Jefferson's sympathy for it, he was not able to lead his committee to any agreement and the matter was turned over to the Committee of the Whole House upon the State of the Country. In December the Assembly passed an act which made it incumbent for no man to attend or support in any fashion a church not of his choice. Jefferson regarded the legislation highly significant since for all practical purposes it spelled the doom of the establishment.

The ensuing decade witnessed the passage of several important pieces of legislation in the direction of disestablishment. In 1779, the payment of salaries to the Anglican clergy was officially discontinued, though in actuality no payments had been made since 1776. Then, in 1780, the Assembly granted dissenting ministers the right to officiate at marriages on the condition that they obtain a license. About the same time considerable support was given by Episcopalians, Methodists, and certain Presbyterians to a proposal that the Christian faith be pronounced the established religion and that certain taxes be divided among the several denominations. The Baptists strenuously opposed the idea. After several years of debate, the issue came to a head in the 1784–1785 session of the General Assembly. James Madison, whose ideas ran counter to those of Patrick Henry on this point, authored a "Memorial and Remonstrance Against Religious Assessments" in which he argued that payments to any denomination from the public treasury would be in violation of the principle of religious liberty. Henry had strong public support for his religious assessment bill and for a time it appeared that it would become law. Even George Washington and John Marshall were inclined to favor the bill. But passage of the legislation was delayed, giving Madison a much-needed opportunity to win over the electorate and so defeat the bill. In this campaign he received invaluable help from Baptists and Presbyterians who saw that the establishment of Christianity would necessarily be unfair to some citizens and so inconsistent with full religious freedom. The General Committee of the Baptists, in a statement on the assessment bill, declared "that no human laws ought to be established for this purpose, but that every person ought to be left entirely free in respect to matters of religion. . . ." The Hanover Presbytery took an identical position, which was later approved by the Convention of the Presbyterian Church in Virginia.

The way was at last prepared for more decisive legislation in the cause of freedom. Thomas Jefferson's Bill for Establishing Religious Freedom, first presented in 1779, was taken up once more and adopted by the As-

---

[1] Quoted in A. P. Stokes, *Church and State in the United States* (Harper, c. 1950), I, 376–377.

sembly in December, 1785. Jefferson regarded it as one of the most significant achievements of his life and directed that after his death it be recorded on his marker. It provided

That no man shall be compelled to frequent or support any religious worship, place, or ministry whatsoever, nor shall be enforced, restrained, molested, or burthened in his body or goods, nor shall otherwise suffer, on account of his religious opinions or belief; but that all men shall be free to profess, and by argument to maintain, their opinions in matters of religion, and that the same shall in no wise diminish, enlarge, or effect their civil capacities.[2]

The bill was circulated widely and undoubtedly had considerable influence in winning religious freedom in other parts of the new nation.

Other legislation directed toward the complete separation of church and state soon followed. In 1787 the General Assembly repealed an act which had incorporated the Protestant Episcopal Church, without at the same time interfering with the right of that church to continue to hold property which had been granted it through the action of the state. Not until 1802 did the General Assembly repeal all laws relative to the Protestant Episcopal Church. At that time it was enacted that whenever a glebe should become vacant, the Overseers of the Poor might sell it and use the proceeds for the relief of the poor or for any other secular purpose agreeable to a majority of the voters. This act of course had nothing whatsoever to do with property owned privately by the churches or with the church edifices and grounds immediately surrounding them. The Episcopal Church challenged the act and carried the matter into the courts; after long and involved litigation the state Court of Appeals, in 1840, ruled in favor of the state. The separation of church and state in Virginia was complete.

Other southern states soon followed the lead of Virginia and terminated their official connections with the Anglican Church. Maryland's constitution of 1776 guaranteed full religious freedom to all Christians but did not confer all political rights upon Jews until 1826. In North Carolina, where the Anglican establishment was grossly unpopular, the Halifax Congress met from November 12 to December 18, 1776, and adopted a constitution which provided that there should be no establishment of any particular church but restricted the holding of civil office in the state to persons who affirmed "the truth of the Protestant religion." South Carolina's first constitution, adopted in March 1776, made no mention of religion; its second constitution, adopted two years later, established Protestantism without favoring any specific denomination. The Episcopal Church was permitted to retain whatever property was in its possession. Then, in 1790, South Carolina adopted another constitution which recog-

2 *Ibid.,* I, 393–394.

nized no establishment of any kind. At the outset of hostilities with Britain, Georgia abolished the establishment and in its first constitution in 1777 guaranteed freedom of conscience to all. A later constitution, adopted in 1789, declared that "all persons shall have the free exercise of religion, without being obliged to contribute to the support of any religious profession but their own."

New York was the only state north of the Mason and Dixon line where anything like an Anglican establishment had prevailed. The connection between church and state was terminated by the constitution of 1777, and religious liberty was extended to all citizens. It was decided that property granted by authority of the king prior to October 14, 1775, should remain in the hands of its possessors, thus preserving the holdings of the several churches. In 1784 the legislature repealed all acts which had conferred special favors upon the Episcopal Church.

The situation in New England, where Congregationalism was established, was far different. Since the establishments there had been overwhelmingly on the side of independence, the severance of political ties with England had little bearing on their future status. Naturally the clerical leaders and prominent laymen of Congregationalism were anxious to preserve the status quo and exerted what influence they had, which was considerable, to maintain the establishment. The inherent conservatism which prevailed in a state such as Connecticut led to the retaining of the old royal charter with some necessary amendments; Connecticut had no state constitution for more than forty years after independence had been declared. Under such circumstances it was relatively easy for the Congregational clergy to retain their position of dominance and to wield exceptional power in the government. For several decades no non-Congregationalist could be chosen to sit in the upper house.

In the meantime the forces of dissent had been rapidly gaining strength so that by the opening of the Revolution they numbered perhaps one-third of the population of Connecticut. Baptists and Methodists were especially vigorous in agitating for full religious freedom and the complete separation of church and state. Aided by a general spirit of tolerance, they could not help but make some impression on the standing order. In 1784, a Toleration Act was adopted; it provided that persons who belonged to dissenting churches might obtain certificates granting them permission to pay their church tax to their own denomination. After the turn of the century, a concerted effort to bring the establishment to an end was begun by Baptists, Methodists, Unitarians, Universalists, Friends, and most Episcopalians. These were allied with the Republican party in opposition to the Federalists, who were supported by the Congregationalists. By 1817, the Republicans had built up enough strength to win at the polls and introduce a more liberal influence in the state government. The following year, 1818, a constitutional convention assembled at Hartford and drew up a constitution. It stipulated that "no preference shall be given by law to any Christian sect or mode of worship." Lyman Beecher, the eminent Congregationalist minister, has recorded his impressions on that fateful day which brought disestablishment.

. . . It was as dark a day as ever I saw. The odium thrown upon the ministry was inconceivable. The injury done to the cause of Christ, as we then supposed, was irreparable. For several days I suffered what no tongue can tell *for the best thing that ever happened to the State of Connecticut.* It cut the churches loose from dependence on state support. It threw them wholly on their own resources and on God. . . . They say ministers have lost their influence; the fact is, they have gained. By voluntary efforts, societies, missions, and revivals, they exert a deeper influence than ever they could by queues and shoe buckles, and cocked hats and gold-headed canes.[3]

In New Hampshire the struggle over the question of establishment was somewhat less bitter. The first state to adopt a constitution (January 5, 1776), it included no provision concerning religion; Congregationalism, however, remained the established faith. A second constitution, adopted in 1783, empowered the legislature to authorize the "several towns, parishes, bodies-corporate, or religious societies within this state, to make adequate provision at their own expense, for the support and maintenance of public protestant teachers of piety, religion and morality," but permitted citizens to refrain from making payments to support teachers of another religious persuasion. During the ensuing years mounting antagonism toward the maintenance of an establishment, spurred on by the Baptists, led to the enactment of more liberal policies. Finally, in 1817, on the recommendation of Governor William Plumer, the legislature placed all churches in the state on essentially the same legal basis, bringing to an end the Congregational establishment.

Despite strong liberal forces which were operative in Massachusetts during the revolutionary era, the Bay State was the tardiest in achieving disestablishment. Its first constitution, adopted in 1780, contained a Declaration of Rights which was authored principally by John Adams. The Declaration recognized the right of every man to worship God according to the dictates of his own conscience, "provided he doth not disturb the public peace, or obstruct others in their religious worship." At the same time it authorized the government to make provision "for the institution of the public worship of GOD, and for the support and maintenance of public Protestant teachers of piety, religion, and morality." Dissenters, however, might have the privilege of earmarking their religious tax for the support of teachers belonging to their denomination.

As the years passed, the Congregationalists, weakened by the Unitarian

[3] *Ibid.*, I, 418.

schism and subsequent litigation over rights to the establishment, felt ever more sharply the blows being struck by Baptists and other dissenters in favor of the separation of church and state. Finally, in 1831, the state legislature approved a bill of disestablishment which was ratified in a constitutional amendment two years later. With that act the last American establishment passed quietly into history.

Religion and the Formation of the National Government

From the time the First Continental Congress assembled in September, 1774, religious leaders had been active in the process of creating a Federal government. Practically every denomination was represented in Congress, some even by clergy. Without dealing directly with the question of establishments, the Congress exhibited its high regard for the Christian religion by maintaining a chaplain, designating certain days for humiliation, fasting, and prayer, sending Christian missionaries to labor among the Delawares, and appropriating funds for Dr. Wheelock's Indian school. One of the first acts of Congress after the Articles of Confederation went into effect in March, 1781, was to direct the publication of an American edition of the Bible. It was produced by Robert Aitken of Philadelphia and officially endorsed by the Congress. At no point did the Congress indicate the slightest inclination toward effecting a separation between religion and the state.

In the decade which spanned the issuance of the Declaration of Independence and the ratification of the Federal Constitution, the campaign for religious liberty in the several states expanded to national proportions. The Declaration, though expressive of the natural rights philosophy, was also a Christian document, emphasizing man's duties to God and to his neighbor. It is true that it makes no reference to the church, but this is not surprising in the light of the fact that few church establishments in the colonies were imposed by the British government. Nevertheless, dissident groups such as Baptists and Episcopalians in New England, Baptists and Presbyterians in the South, and Roman Catholics throughout the colonies had every intention of doing what they could to achieve religious liberty, civic status, and eventually disestablishment. This attitude would be reflected in the debate concerning the Federal Constitution.

During the half decade following 1781, it became increasingly obvious that Congress could never build a strong united America with the powers vested in it by the Articles of Confederation. In all important matters authority was reserved for the several states; the Congress could not even levy taxes or regulate commerce. A series of tariff wars between the states brought on an economic depression; markets were flooded with paper money which became virtually worthless; the country was encumbered with a war debt amounting to about forty-three million dollars. Unless a way to improve the situation could be found the nation would have to expect a series of popular uprisings, such as that led by Daniel Shays in Massachusetts in 1786. The way seemed to lie through a strong central government.

The calling of the Constitutional Convention to meet at Philadelphia in May, 1787, gave evidence of the widespread demand to seek a solution to the vexatious problems facing the nation. As in previous conventions and congresses, the interests of the various denominations were well represented. There were nineteen Episcopalian delegates, eight Congregationalists, seven Presbyterians, two Roman Catholics, two Friends, one Methodist, and one Dutch Reformed. During the debates which accompanied the preparation of the Constitution, little attention was given to the question of religion. Article VI contains the only direct reference to religion in the body of the document. It provides that "no religious test shall ever be required as a qualification to any office or public trust under the United States." When this article was discussed in the state ratifying conventions, considerable differences of opinion appeared. Some favored it on the ground that the use of religious tests might lead to an infringement of personal rights. A second group favored it but felt that it should be made stronger through the addition of a Bill of Rights which would guarantee religious liberty and provide for disestablishment. A third party was unalterably opposed to it since it would permit non-Protestants to hold public office; such a circumstance they deemed highly dangerous to the welfare of the state. Apparently the framers of the article thought it best to leave the religious issue to the states. They had no fear that they had left the door open for the creation of a national religious establishment since there were so many denominations in the United States that it seemed none could ever attain a position of dominance.

The chief protagonists among the denominations for a Bill of Rights were the Baptists and Presbyterians. As dissenters, they could not approve the Constitution unless they had some assurance that religious establishments would be abolished. Nevertheless, the members of the Constitutional Convention knew that they could not deal with such an issue too directly without losing the support of the states that were still committed to their Congregational or Episcopal establishments. The result of this policy of non-action was that strong opposition to ratification was engendered among many Baptist, Presbyterian, Lutheran, Reformed, and other non-established bodies. Of these, the Baptists were the most vocal in their stand against ratification. Had the opposition to ratification not centered in the rural and interior areas where communication was more difficult, it seems likely that the proponents of the Constitution would have had to face a long and agonizing struggle. As it was, nine months passed before the necessary number of states adopted the instrument, and in some of them the margin of victory was slim.

After ratification of the Constitution, the matter of a Bill of Rights was taken up again. By this time eight states had adopted such bills and support for additional guarantees of rights on a national level was mounting steadily. James Madison was the guiding spirit of the movement in Congress. The First Amendment to the Constitution in the Bill of Rights, adopted by Congress in 1789 and ratified two years later, was pertinent to religion. It provided that

Congress shall make no law respecting an establishment of religion, or prohibiting the free exercise thereof; or abridging the freedom of speech, or of the press; or the right of the people peaceably to assemble and to petition the Government for a redress of grievances.

The purpose of the amendment was not to work hardship upon Christianity, but rather to discourage rivalry among the various denominations for governmental favors and to prevent any national establishment, whether of a denominational or interdenominational character. The effect of the article was not to protect Americans from religion but to insure the vitality and strengthening of religion; the experience of its framers was that state support tended to further complacency and thus render a denomination's efforts ineffectual.

RELIGIOUS DECLINE IN THE POST-REVOLUTIONARY ERA

The period immediately following the Revolution witnessed a progressive deterioration of spiritual zeal. The protracted conflict, which had begun in the North and gradually enveloped the entire country, had been fought with cruelty and frequent disdain for even the rights of non-combatants. All the evils which ordinarily follow after war became manifest. Nor was the religious situation enhanced by liberal tendencies which had already crept into organized religion. Before Lexington and Concord, a strong reaction had asserted itself against the revivalism of the Great Awakening. The tide of revolt from Congregational orthodoxy in New England was rising; and not only Unitarianism and Universalism, but Deism also, discovered numerous advocates throughout the country. During the course of the war these views won new support due partially to European influence introduced by French officers. Samuel Hopkins insisted that untold harm had been done to orthodoxy in Newport, Rhode Island, by the presence of Allied troops during the Revolution. But it seems highly doubtful that many of these forces were even acquainted with the work of such radicals as Voltaire.

Whatever the case, Deism gradually but steadily won favor in America, at first primarily among the educated classes and finally among the masses of the people. In the two decades following the Revolution, few colleges did not succumb to the new intellectual fever. Lyman Beecher, describing Yale College during the 1790's, wrote: "That was the day of the infidelity of the Tom Paine school . . . most of the classes before me were infidels, and called each other Voltaire, Rousseau, D'Alembert. . . ." The statement might have applied equally to classes from Dartmouth to the University of Georgia. To be fashionable was to be radical, as many a student testified in his mistaken attempt to imitate that anticlerical society, the Bavarian Illuminati. Everywhere morals declined and discipline lagged, though not so badly as the horrified orthodox clergy imagined. It was a period of transition, even upheaval, and if a devil-may-care attitude was common among the college generation, it was at least symbolic of the times. That Yale's graduating class of 1800 numbered only one church member was perhaps not so much a sign of irreligiosity as of a definite break with the past and a desire to build a new world.

To the orthodox ministry, persons of Deistic inclination were atheists, infidels, and agents of the prince of darkness. They stormed and raged against the "heretics" and charged them with committing every imaginable crime against society. Among conservative New Englanders, nothing too contemptuous could be said of Thomas Jefferson; he was the embodiment of all they held to be insidious both in politics and religion, a Francophile who could be expected to breed Jacobin radicalism.

Other favorite whipping boys of the Protestant clergy were Ethan Allen (1737–1789) and Thomas Paine (1737–1809). Allen, erstwhile officer of the Continental Army and hero of Ticonderoga, published, in 1784, a work entitled *Reason the Only Oracle of Man*. It amounted to a searching criticism of revealed religion as opposed to the new religion of Nature. Allen charged that the clergy possessed no truth which could not be gained through the normal processes of reason and that their idea of God was riddled with inconsistencies. The doctrines of original sin and the atonement of Christ he found to be utterly untenable. What was so shocking to the orthodox was the vulgar and unrestrained fashion in which Allen presented his arguments. When his untimely death was announced five years later, they saw in it the hand of Providence. Ezra Stiles observed in his diary: "13th Inst. died in Vermont the profane and impious Deist General Ethan Allen, Author of the Oracles of Reason, a Book replete with scurrilous Reflections on Revelation.—'And in Hell he lift up his Eyes being in Torments.'"

Even more universally despised was Thomas Paine. His completion of the *Age of Reason* in 1793 marked the beginnings of Deism as a popular movement in America, especially since the book was circulated in almost every community. Contrary to the allegations of his enemies, Paine was no atheist. He believed in God and found Him to be revealed "in the immensity of creation" and "the unchangeable order by which the incomprehensible whole is governed." But he refused to accept what he held to be the superstitious concepts of organized religion such as the Bible as the word of God or Jesus Christ as the saviour of men. His creed was simple.

> I believe in one God and no more; and I hope for happiness beyond this life.
> I believe in the equality of man; and I believe that religious duties consist in doing justice, loving mercy, and endeavoring to make our fellow-creatures happy.
> The world is my country, to do good my religion.[4]

Few Americans were able to read the work with dispassion; more often than not they misunderstood it and then promptly condemned its author for positions which he did not take. Many uncontented with mere acrid rebuttal resorted to defamation of character. Representative of this latter group was Uzal Ogden, an Episcopal clergyman who, in 1795, published an *Antidote to Deism*. After disputing Paine's arguments he charged that his unfortunate identification with infidelism was due to the fact that "the refulgent light of Divine Revelation, gave too much pain to his *reddened* Eyes of intemperance, and therefore in hope of obtaining ease, closed them against the sun-beams of the gospel."

Paine's work was carried on by Elihu Palmer, an ex-Baptist minister unfrocked for heresy. His work entitled *Principles of Nature*, published in 1802, represented an attempt to carry Deism to the masses; instead it aroused such a reaction among intellectuals who were afraid of popular causes that it hastened the movement toward an earlier death. Druidical and Theophilanthropist societies remained in the towns and cities, but they were symbols of an age which was fast drawing to its close.

In the meantime the churches had been feeling the chilling effects of religious indifference. Attendance at services of worship had declined noticeably and many congregations were averaging no more than four or five new members a year. In many parts of the South, Sunday became a day of "riot and drunkenness." The Presbyterian General Assembly of 1798 noted with apprehension "a general dereliction of religious principles and practice among our fellow citizens . . . and an abounding infidelity, which in many instances tends to atheism itself." Six years later Lyman Beecher, in similar fashion, decried the fact that "irreligion hath become in all parts of our land, alarmingly prevalent. The name of God is blasphemed; the bible denounced; the sabbath profaned; the public worship of God is neglected; intemperance hath destroyed its thousands; and is preparing the destruction of thousands more. . . ."

Conditions were no better on the frontier. The wild and reckless existence which faced the pioneer was a natural deterrent to inhibition, an invitation to moral laxity in the form of drunkenness and debauchery.

---

[4] *Ibid.*, I, 322.

Besides, the material concerns of the settler were necessarily so great that there seemed to be little time for cultivating the spiritual life. Nor did the inroads of Deism encourage churchmanship. According to the report of a pioneer in Kentucky around the turn of the century, half of the state's inhabitants subscribed to Deism. Robert Davidson, historian of Presbyterianism in Kentucky, declared that "worldly mindedness, infidelity, and dissipation threatened to deluge the land, and sweep away all vestiges of piety and morality. The rising generation was growing up in almost universal ignorance of religious obligation." What was needed to stem the tide of spiritual diffidence was a revival of dynamic faith, a resurgence of religious vitality which could appeal to the heart as well as the mind. Such a revival would soon be forthcoming in the Second Awakening.

DENOMINATIONAL ADJUSTMENTS TO A CHANGING ORDER

The changes which took place in the political order through the achievement of American independence gave rise to numerous challenges and opportunities for the forces of organized religion. Some of the denominations, having been bound tightly to ecclesiastical authorities in England, found that the severance of political ties necessitated a fresh appraisal of their positions. Other religious bodies which had already attained full or partial autonomy discovered the advisability of making certain structural changes by way of adjustment to a society in rapid transition. All saw the need to rethink their programs, though to varying extent, and to energize their institutions.

The Episcopalians

The Church of England in America faced the opening of the national period in a sorry and uncertain condition. In the states north of Maryland a large percentage of the clergy were representatives of the Society for the Propagation of the Gospel and, being Loyalists, soon departed the country. Henceforth the denomination could count on no support from the Society, a circumstance which had serious effects. In the South the loss of special privileges through disestablishment and the potent opposition of lower-class dissenters contributed to widespread defections to other denominations and the subsequent weakening of the church. Deism also took its toll. Even so, the Episcopal Church at the close of the revolutionary era was the fourth largest denomination in the United States.

The story of the reorganization of the church centers around the work of three clerical leaders: William Smith in Maryland, Samuel Seabury in Connecticut, and William White of Pennsylvania. William Smith (1727–1803), a clergyman whose patriot sympathies had been mixed with semi-loyalist tendencies, had assumed the rectorship of Chester Parish,

Maryland, in 1779. The following year he convened an assembly of three clergymen and a number of laymen to discuss the status of the churches. At that meeting they denominated themselves the Protestant Episcopal Church, a name which was officially adopted at a second convention held at Annapolis in 1783. The convention of 1783 adopted a "Declaration of Certain Fundamental Rights and Liberties," in which it was affirmed that the Protestant Episcopal Church in Maryland had a legal right to all property held by the established church inasmuch as they were one and the same. After adopting a framework of ecclesiastical polity, the convention proceeded to elect William Smith first bishop of Maryland. That he was never consecrated to this office was regarded by many as a stroke of good fortune for the church since Smith had a reputation for insobriety.

In other parts of the country there was a similar concern over securing bishops; the life of the church literally depended on the establishment of an American episcopate. The movement to obtain a bishop for New England began with a secret meeting of ten clergymen in Connecticut in March, 1783. These men commissioned either Jeremiah Leaming or Samuel Seabury to go to England for episcopal consecration. Leaming declined on account of his advanced years, but Seabury (1729–1796) accepted; four months later he arrived in London. To his dismay he discovered that the English bishops would not proceed with his consecration until he could show that the state of Connecticut held no objection to his election and until he would agree to take an oath of allegiance to the English crown. The first requirement posed no difficulty, but it was inconceivable that a cleric who pledged his political loyalty to England could preside over an American diocese. Reluctantly, Seabury traveled northward to Scotland where he was greeted warmly by the non-juring bishops. These men were the successors of those bishops who in 1688 had refused to take the oath of allegiance to William and Mary and had subsequently lost their political standing. On November 14, 1784, the Scottish bishops met at Aberdeen and conferred episcopal consecration on Seabury. He returned to America the following June and shortly thereafter ordained four men to the diaconate during the first convocation of his clergy. Outside of Connecticut Seabury encountered moderate criticism. There was no question as to the validity of his consecration; some, however, felt that it had been obtained from a schismatic church. Others were antagonistic to him because of his loyalist stand during the Revolution. He was clearly not the man to weld the church together as a national body.

The times were calling for such a man as William White (1748–1836), rector of Christ Church, Philadelphia. He had received his education at the College of Philadelphia and after serving as assistant minister at Christ Church, under Jacob Duché, succeeded to the rectorship in 1777. During his service as chaplain of the Continental Congress, he proved himself to be not only a patriot but a man of moderation and deep understanding.

He belonged to the low church party in the denomination which emphasized the rational aspects of Christianity and the comprehensive nature of the church. They believed in the historic episcopate but did not hold the authority of bishops in too high esteem. This philosophy helps to explain White's pamphlet entitled "The Case of the Episcopal Churches Considered," published anonymously in 1782. Its principal thesis was that there was an immediate need for a national organization and that since there was little prospect of securing a bishop in the near future the churches should call a convention composed of both clerical and lay delegates in equal numbers. The pamphlet further proposed that a committee of clergy, selected by the convention, be empowered to administer ordination and discipline, and that the country be divided into three districts with annual assemblies. A general convention would be called triennially.

In keeping with White's suggestions, an informal meeting of clergy and laity was held at New Brunswick, New Jersey, in May, 1784. Here arrangements were made for a meeting with wider representation to be convened in New York in October. A few days after the New Brunswick meeting, William White presided over a convention of Pennsylvania clergy and laity in Philadelphia. This body declared its independence from all foreign authority, affirmed its power to regulate its own affairs, and enjoined a threefold ministry of bishops, presbyters, and deacons, and a liturgy in conformity with that of the Church of England. The group which met five months later in New York was widely representative of American Episcopalianism. It adopted a set of resolutions similar to those of the Pennsylvania convention and recommended the calling of a General Convention to meet in Philadelphia during September, 1785. In the meantime the state conventions were expected to elect bishops to be seated at the General Convention. The result was that William White, Samuel Provoost, and David Griffith were chosen to become bishops of Pennsylvania, New York, and Virginia respectively.

Sixteen clergymen and twenty-four laymen, representing seven states, were present at the opening of the Convention. The New England churches, dissatisfied that greater powers were not reserved for the episcopate, sent no delegates. They may also have been reluctant to participate in a meeting where antagonism was felt toward their bishop. The principal task of the Convention, over which William White presided, was to frame a constitution, revise the liturgy, and, if possible, arrange for the consecration of bishops-elect White, Provoost, and Griffith. Only the work of revising the liturgy was not completed at this meeting. An Ecclesiastical Constitution, largely the product of White's fertile mind, was submitted to the churches for ratification, and an appeal was sent to the English bishops that they confer episcopal orders upon the men chosen by the state conventions. As soon as all matters could be settled to the satisfaction of the English bishops and Parliament had passed the necessary act of permission, White and Provoost sailed to England. They were consecrated in Lambeth Chapel on February 4, 1787. For reasons of indigence and ailing health, Griffith could not make the trip; he never received consecration. Nevertheless a milestone had been reached. With three bishops now in America, the canonical number required for the consecration of other bishops, there could no longer be any question as to the ability of the church in the United States to perpetuate itself. The next step was to achieve cooperation among the three bishops. This was a task which required delicate maneuvering, especially because of the enmity between Seabury and Provoost; and it was fortunate that the church could rely upon the tactful and composed efforts of Bishop White. When the General Convention met in July, 1789, Seabury was present; two months later, at its second session, delegates from the New England states joined the assembly and signed a revised constitution which provided for a separate House of Bishops. The accomplishments of this General Convention were little short of extraordinary. Not only did it achieve the unity of the church, but it adopted a constitution and a set of canons and authorized a revised Book of Common Prayer. It set a course which the church would follow for decades to come.

The years between 1789 and 1811 witnessed a quiet and gradual resurgence of strength in the Episcopal Church. The episcopate was extended through the consecration of Thomas Claggett of Maryland in 1792, Robert Smith of South Carolina in 1795, and Edward Bass of Massachusetts and Rhode Island in 1797. James Madison had received consecration as bishop of Virginia in ceremonies at Lambeth in 1790. These bishops moved generally with extreme caution; Americans were still unused to bishops and regarded them with suspicion, fearing that they might attempt to usurp power from the lower clergy and laity. Not until the episcopate of John Henry Hobart, which began in 1811, would the bishops accustom themselves to doing much more than ordaining and confirming.

The Methodists

Until the close of the Revolution the Methodist movement in America remained identified with the Anglican Church, being simply a part of the "Wesleyan Connection." In the words of Jesse Lee, the first Methodist historian, "We were only a religious society, and not a church; and any member of any church, who would conform to our rules and meet in a class, had liberty to continue in their own church." Before the war could come to an end, however, some of the southern preachers took steps to form an independent church. At a conference held at Fluvanna, Virginia, in May, 1779, they decided to establish themselves into a presbytery and ordain ministers so that the people might be provided with the sacraments. The older men ordained themselves, then proceeded to the ordination of others who had been called to the ministry. For a time it appeared that there might be a schism between the southern preachers and the northern faction which remained loyal to Francis Asbury, whom they regarded as Wesley's agent in America. Earlier that year the northern group had met at Kent Circuit, Delaware, and recognized Asbury as their rightful leader. In their view his authority extended to all American Methodists. Fortunately the two groups were able to draw together and reconcile their differences; the southern wing recognized Asbury as General Assistant and agreed to abstain from administering the sacraments.

After the restoration of peace, Wesley began to reestablish connections with his brethren in the United States, with the view of resuming full authority over them. He had not the slightest intention of forming a separate church in America; at the same time he seems to have sensed that the American leaders would exercise greater authority than before, with or without his approval. In the most conciliatory fashion he exhorted them to remain faithful to the Methodist doctrine and discipline and give heed to the directions of Francis Asbury. Knowing that their most pressing need was to secure ministers who could administer the sacraments, he at length determined to ordain preachers for the United States. He was aware that such action would be contrary to the canons of the Church of England but justified his decision on the ground that in the ancient church at Alexandria presbyters had ordained bishops. Wesley still adhered to the episcopal form of government; he was convinced, however, that when the circumstances dictated, ordination by presbyters was scripturally valid. He therefore invited his friend, Dr. Thomas Coke (1747–1814), a presbyter in the Church of England, to receive ordination as a superintendent at his hands; he arranged simultaneously for the ordination of two other men as presbyters. In July, 1784, at the Conference at Leeds, Wesley appointed Coke, Richard Whatcoat, and Thomas Vasey to ministerial service in America. The following September he and James Creighton, a presbyter in the Church of England, ordained Whatcoat and Vasey first as deacons and then as elders and Coke as superintendent. The three men departed almost at once for their new posts.

When Coke and his two associates arrived in New York on November 3, 1784, they bore a letter from Wesley stating his desire that Coke and Asbury serve as joint superintendents and that the Methodists follow certain prescriptions which he provided for their guidance.

I have accordingly appointed Dr. Coke and Mr. Francis Asbury to be joint superintendents over our brethren in North America; as also Richard Whatcoat and Thomas Vasey to act as elders among them, by baptizing and administering the Lord's Supper. And I have prepared a liturgy, little differing from that of the Church of England (I think the best constituted national church in the world), which I advise all the traveling preachers to use on the Lord's day in all the congregations, reading the Litany only on Wednesdays and Fridays, and praying extempore on all other days. I also advise the elders to administer the Supper of the Lord on every Lord's day.[5]

The liturgical work, which included the form for ordaining superintendents, presbyters, and deacons, together with twenty-four articles of religion, was entitled *The Sunday Service of the Methodists in North America, With Occasional Services.*

Eleven days after landing in New York, Coke met Asbury for the first time at Barratt's Chapel in Delaware. At that meeting Asbury proposed that a General Conference be called for the purpose of passing judgment on Wesley's recommendations. Coke agreed to the suggestion and Freeborn Garrettson, a Methodist preacher, was "sent off like an arrow" to summon the ministers to a conference at Baltimore on December 24, 1784. That such a meeting could be called testified to the spirit of independence steadily developing among American Methodists; certainly Wesley had not planned for it and even Coke had some misgivings about the action.

The "Christmas Conference" marks the nascence of Methodism as a separate denominational entity. First among several important decisions made at the conference was the resolution to organize as the Methodist Episcopal Church, the name being suggested by John Dickins. After the reading of Wesley's letter, Asbury refused to accept his appointment as superintendent. But when the assembly of nearly sixty preachers unanimously elected him, with Coke, to the office, he acceded and was ordained to his position of responsibility. From that time until his death in 1791, Wesley's authority over the newly founded denomination was merely nominal. After 1785, Coke spent relatively little time in the United States where he usually felt ill at ease being a loyal British subject. Asbury, now in practical command, began to refer to himself as "bishop"; there was some opposition to this at first, but it was not long before the title became fixed.

Another contribution of the "Christmas Conference" was the adoption of a form of government and discipline. The organization was highly centralized, basic units being those of the circuit and the conference. Both it and the discipline were patterned after the system followed in England. In the matter of doctrine, the Conference approved the Twenty-four Articles of Religion, which Wesley had adapted from the Thirty-nine Articles of the Anglican Church. It added, however, another article concerning the rulers of the United States. Wesley's *Sunday Service* and *Hymns* were also officially endorsed. As if these accomplishments were not sufficient for their zeal, the Conference laid plans for the establishment of a college to be called Cokesbury, in honor of the superintendents, and located at Abingdon, Maryland. The college opened in 1787, but after eight auspicious

[5] Mode, *op. cit.*, 322.

years its building was destroyed by fire and no efforts were made to re-build it.

During the next few years the Methodists made encouraging advances in all parts of the country. In 1785, seven new circuits were founded in the southern states; the following year the first preachers were sent to Kentucky. The year 1789 witnessed the appointment of Jesse Lee to Stamford Circuit in Connecticut, the first to be organized in New England. Contrary to predictions, Methodism thereafter developed steadily in that area. Throughout the nation, however, the denomination experienced during the last half decade of the century the effects of the general spiritual declension. It was further weakened by its first schism. In 1792, James O'Kelly, a prominent preacher in Virginia, proposed to the Conference that preachers dissatisfied with their appointments to circuits be allowed to appeal to the Conference for a different position. When this proposal was rejected, he and some of his followers withdrew and eventually organized a denomination called the Republican Methodists, which grew to a membership of several thousand. It later merged with the New Light or Christian movement.

The Congregationalists

Probably no religious body in America faced the national period with more privileges and more internal weaknesses than the Congregational. At the close of the Revolution it was the largest denomination in the country with its strength centered predominantly in New England. In that section its leaders enjoyed high prestige both in society and government and were able to maintain the benefits of establishment in Massachusetts, Connecticut, and New Hampshire. The blessings of temporal prosperity, unfortunately, contributed to a spirit of phlegmatic complacency which unfitted the denomination to meet the challenges and opportunities presented by a burgeoning society. Adjustment to the new national government constituted no problem; adjustment to a newly conceived national task was another matter. Failing to develop a broad outlook upon the work at hand, the Congregationalists sentenced themselves to remain essentially a sectional body during the formative stage of the country's history and to play a relatively minor role in the building of the West.

A second problem which plagued the denomination was the growing cleavage between the unitarian and trinitarian wings of the churches. Unitarianism was particularly strong in eastern Massachusetts, especially in the area of Boston, while the more conservative position flourished in western Massachusetts and Connecticut. As the two factions grew steadily farther apart, the latter was drawn closer to the Presbyterianism prevalent in the northern tier of the Middle Atlantic states. Many Congregationalist leaders of the Edwardean tradition, among them Jonathan Edwards the

Younger and Timothy Dwight, endeavored to effect an intimate association between the two denominations. They emphasized the slight differences between Presbyterian polity and the consociationism of Connecticut
Congregationalism.

When state associations similar to those of Connecticut were proposed
for Massachusetts in 1803, the prominent Edwardean theologian, Nathaniel Emmons, who had trained more than a hundred men for the ministry,
came out in opposition to the plan. He insisted on the democratic character of Congregationalism which placed the full power of church government in the hands of the membership and permitted no higher judicatory
to override their decisions. He maintained that "Association leads to Consociation; Consociation leads to Presbyterianism; Presbyterianism leads to
Episcopacy; Episcopacy leads to Roman Catholicism; and Roman Catholicism is an ultimate fact." This philosophy of separatism and individualism which ran counter to the more aristocratic Puritan conceptions of
the seventeenth century was well received in Massachusetts and eventually became standard in Congregationalism. However worthwhile the
philosophy may have been, the effect was to make it difficult for Congregationalists to unite for any project on a national level. The consequences
of such a view for an effective missionary program in the West are all too
obvious.

The Presbyterians

Since the founding of the first presbytery in 1706, American Presbyterians had been independent of European judicatories. Nevertheless, the
rapid strides made by the denomination, which was the second largest in
America, called for some reorganization which would enable the church
to function more efficiently. Between the years 1758 and 1788, the Presbyterian clergy increased from 96 to 177 and several new presbyteries were
added. In 1781, the Synod of New York and Philadelphia organized the
Presbytery of Redstone in southwestern Pennsylvania; the Presbytery of
South Carolina was constituted in 1784 and the following year the Presbyteries of Abingdon, Lexington, and Transylvania, in Kentucky, were
established. The principal growth of Presbyterianism during this period
was in the South and West.

Even before the outbreak of the Revolution certain leaders in the
church had seen the advisability of making some alterations in the denominational structure. To continue governing the church as a whole
through the overgrown undelegated synod was clearly absurd if not impossible. Thus, in the thinking of prominent churchmen such as John
Witherspoon and John Rodgers, the time was at hand to consider the
formation of a more adequate system. At the meeting of synod in 1785,
Witherspoon and nine other ministers were appointed to formulate a sys-

tem of general rules for the government of the synod and its presbyteries and to report at the next meeting. An overture to constitute a national judicatory known as the General Assembly was also brought before the assemblage. At the meeting of 1786, a committee chaired by Dr. Rodgers brought in a plan to create sixteen presbyteries, four synods, and a General Assembly. Affirmative action was taken only on the matter of the presbyteries. The committee appointed to draft a system of polity and discipline made its report; and after some debate, a new committee under the chairmanship of Witherspoon was appointed to reconsider the matter. This committee was in session during September and produced an entire book on the subject entrusted to them. The work was printed under the title *Draught of a Plan of Government and Discipline* and was submitted to the presbyteries.

At the meeting of synod in 1787 some amendments were made to the proposed plan; again it was printed and sent to the presbyteries for approval. In the midst of discussion concerning the plan of government, the synod was shocked to receive a request from the Presbytery of Suffolk on Long Island that their union with the synod be dissolved since their "situation renders it inconvenient to maintain the union." A committee headed by Dr. Rodgers was commissioned to meet with the leaders of that presbytery and, if possible, dissuade them from their intention of withdrawal. To incur such a loss at this critical time would be indeed serious. But the Presbytery of Suffolk decided to maintain its union with the synod and a devastating split was thus averted.

The year 1788 proved to be one of decisive action among American Presbyterians. At the meeting of synod, the Form of Government and the Book of Discipline were adopted as the Constitution of the Presbyterian Church in America, together with the Westminster Confession of Faith which had been amended to conform to the American principle of the separation of church and state. It also adopted the amended Larger Catechism, the Shorter Catechism, and the Westminster Directory for the Worship of God. The latter work was an almost complete revision of the older English Directory and liturgically decidedly inferior to it. These standards could be amended only by approval of two-thirds of the presbyteries. The synod then directed its own dissolution and the creation of four synods and sixteen presbyteries under the national governance of the General Assembly.

On May 31, 1789, at the very time the first United States Congress under the Federal Constitution was meeting at New York, the General Assembly convened at Philadelphia. John Witherspoon served as its presiding officer. Quite appropriately, the Assembly appointed a committee chaired by Witherspoon to draft a suitable address to President George Washington, to which Washington graciously responded. These mutual felicitations symbolized the advent of a new era which Presbyterians knew they could face with self-confidence now that their reorganization had been made complete.

The years following the Revolution witnessed a growing trend toward theological conservatism within the Presbyterian denomination. Everywhere the church had felt the effects of Deism, not only in its liberal centers but also in traditionally orthodox areas. At the College of New Jersey, the idealistic Edwardean theology had been replaced by the Scottish philosophy of natural realism or common sense. When the reaction set in after the war, leaders such as Witherspoon endeavored to lead the church to a position of formal orthodoxy and were supported notably by those Scotch-Irish immigrants who had arrived since 1760. In many ways the new movement was as much a reaction to the Great Awakening as to Deism, inasmuch as it found its basis in rationalism rather than in an electrifying religious experience. From this conservative reaction sprang the Old School Presbyterianism which stood strongly for strict adherence to the doctrine and polity of the church during the early decades of the nineteenth century.

The Baptists

Probably no denomination greeted the national period with more eager anticipation than the Baptists. Their long and hard-fought campaign for religious liberty had been brought to a successful conclusion even in Virginia and Massachusetts where they had suffered the most for their faith. With the removal of whatever stigmas had been attached to their communion, they made rapid gains from Maine to Georgia. In Virginia they led all other religious bodies in numerical strength; throughout the nation they stood in third place.

While Baptist polity did not seem to warrant a national organization, the spirit of the times led them in that direction. As they began to see the values of union in government, they came to a greater appreciation of cooperation between the churches. Already several voluntary associations such as the Philadelphia Association had been organized in different parts of the country. From 1751 to 1799, forty-nine such associations came into existence. They had no more than advisory powers, but they made their influence widely felt and with most helpful effects. The tendencies toward union went further in Virginia than elsewhere. Between the years 1784 and 1799, Virginia Baptists organized the General Committee, which was composed of delegates from four associations. Its most important contribution was to guide the union between Regular and Separate Baptists which took place in 1787, giving rise to the United Baptist Churches of Virginia. For a time the General Committee enjoyed national prestige among the Baptist churches. Apparently the Committee regarded itself as a spokesman for American Baptists, judging from a report which they sent to George Washington in 1788 concerning the Constitution.

. . . Convinced, on the one hand, that without an effective national government the States would fall into disunion and all the subsequent evils; and, on
the other hand, fearing that we should be accessory to some religious oppression, should any one society in the Union predominate over the rest; yet, amidst
all these inquietudes of mind, our consolation arose from this consideration—
the plan must be good, for it has the signature of a tried, trusty friend, and if
religious liberty is rather insecure in the Constitution, 'the administration will
certainly prevent all oppression, for a WASHINGTON will preside.' . . .[6]

The Baptist zeal for independence prevented the Committee or any similar organization from developing into a permanent national governing
body. But during the decades to come the Baptists would discover that
through cooperation on a national level they could render more effective
service; they were not remiss in rising to the occasion.

The Dutch Reformed

The unhappy schism which had rent the Dutch Reformed Church into
Coetus and Conferentie had been healed only three short years before the
outbreak of war. Under the terms of the settlement, union with the church
in Holland was still affirmed, but many rights and privileges such as the
ordination of ministers were granted to the church in America. When the
Revolution came to an end, the clergy reconsidered the church's status
and many were in agreement that a national organization should be developed. The first step was taken in 1784 when the judicatories changed
their names from General Body to Synod and Particular Bodies to Classes.
Four years later the Synod created a committee to adapt the standards
of the church as approved by the Synod of Dort in 1618 to American use
and to translate the articles of doctrine into English, since that language
was being used increasingly throughout the denomination. Their work,
which was adopted by Synod in 1792, provided for a General Synod entirely independent from Holland and conventional in character. After the
organization of this Synod, in 1794, the old one became a Particular Synod,
composed of delegates of classes. In 1867, the Dutch Reformed Church
changed its name to the Reformed Church in America.

The German Reformed

The movement toward nationalization in the German Reformed Church
went forward at a somewhat slower pace than in the Dutch Reformed
Church. In 1771 its leaders declined an offer to unite with the Dutch Reformed denomination, preferring in many cases to merge their congregations with Lutheran bodies and denominate them Evangelical Churches.
German interdenominational cooperation was evidenced also in the es-

[6] Quoted in Stokes, *op. cit.*, I, 76⁊.

tablishment of Franklin College at Lancaster, Pennsylvania, in 1787, named in honor of its chief benefactor, Benjamin Franklin.

By 1789 the German Reformed Coetus reported to its parent Classis in Holland that the time had come to form an independent national organization. Receiving no reply, the American churchmen adopted a declaration of independence in 1791. The following year the Coetus appointed a committee to prepare a Synodical constitution. In 1793 the first Synod of the German Reformed Church convened at Lancaster and adopted a system of church government. Two years later a new edition of the Heidelberg Catechism was published in German; not until 1810 was it issued in English. By the latter date it was apparent that the denomination could not long continue as an essentially German-speaking church. It was rapidly being assimilated into the American environment.

The Lutherans

Through the work of Henry Melchior Muhlenberg the Lutheran Church in America had gradually taken on a semblance of organization during the colonial period. The first stage in the process was reached in 1761 when the Ministerium of Pennsylvania, an annual assembly for the German and Swedish clergy, was brought into being. Gradually a synodical constitution was formed and in 1781 it was formally approved under the title "The Evangelical Lutheran Ministerium in North America." Ordination was made a definite function of that body, which was composed only of ministers. After a decade of experience it seemed advisable to make certain changes in the organization. The new constitution of "The Evangelical Lutheran Congregations in Pennsylvania and Adjacent States," as the body was now called, admitted lay delegates to the annual meetings. It provided that only two officers, a president and a secretary, should be elected each year at the synodical meeting by the pastors and lay delegates. A further provision declared that "all ordained ministers are equal in regard to rank and title, excepting the officers spoken of before; they have therefore in their congregations no other superintendents but these officers, and these only in so far as this Constitution renders it incumbent on them to impart their views and advice to ministers. . . ."

Additional synods were organized in New York in 1786, North Carolina in 1803, and Ohio in 1818. The Synod of Maryland and Virginia and the Synod of Tennessee were founded in 1820. These bodies were established in response to a felt need for more regional assemblies which could recruit, train, and ordain ministers and to conduct whatever enterprises were for the good of the churches in a given area. At the same time a national union movement was in the process of development. In 1818 the Ministerium in Pennsylvania passed a resolution calling for union among the various synods. The result was the organization of the General Synod in

1820 at Hagerstown, Maryland, with four synods represented. This General Synod was given large advisory powers and was authorized to plan missionary and educational programs on a national level. It would prove to be a highly effective force in welding together the heterogeneous elements which made up American Lutheranism.

The Moravians

Among those denominations that maintained ties with European religious bodies prior to the Revolution, the Moravians alone remained dependent upon the centralized authority in Europe after the completion of American independence. In 1769, the General Synod at Marienborn had ruled that Moravian congregations in Britain and America were to be regarded as subordinate to it and that they were to be controlled by boards known as Provincial Helpers. This principle was reaffirmed by the General Synod which met at Herrnhut in 1782. The fact that the Moravians were dominated by European ideas and practices proved decidedly detrimental to their progress in a new nation. Nor did the establishment of a seminary at Nazareth, Pennsylvania, in 1807, for the training of Moravian ministers greatly improve their situation. Finally, in 1847, the Americans were permitted to elect their own executive board, but it was not until 1857 that the American church was granted a constitution which enabled it to form the "Provincial Synod of the American church, North," an ecclesiastical body which enjoyed some real measure of independence.

The Friends

The founding of a national government had little effect on the organization of the Society of Friends in America. Their polity was congregational and democratic, and though they retained connections with the parent body in England they were autonomous. At the London Yearly Meeting of 1784, ten Friends from America were in attendance. Their presence, however, testified only to their fraternal spirit and their desire for spiritual fellowship with their English brethren. Save for the spreading of their work to the West, no important changes took place in the Quaker community until the early decades of the nineteenth century.

The Roman Catholics

At the close of the Revolutionary era Roman Catholicism in America found itself in a relatively strong position. Many Roman Catholics had done yeoman service in the struggle against England and this had done much to elevate their general prestige. Then too, the spirit of liberty was abroad in the land, a sentiment which proved beneficial to the Roman

Catholic minority. Nevertheless, devout churchmen could scarcely face the national era with giddy optimism. They had serious problems, most of which were internal. There were less than thirty priests to minister to a Roman Catholic population of more than 24,000, centered largely in Maryland and Pennsylvania. These priests, formerly Jesuits, were now serving as secular priests, their order having been suppressed by Pope Clement XIV in 1773. The effect of this action had been to cast a pall of discouragement over the American clergy. Prior to the Revolution they had been under the jurisdiction of Bishop James Talbot, the Vicar-Apostolic in London. With the outbreak of hostilities the bishop refused to take any further responsibility for his charges in America, having just previously appointed Father John Lewis as Vicar-General. The American clergy realized that a bishop was necessary for the proper functioning of the church. Yet they were hesitant to do anything about it since American opinion at the time was unfavorable to bishops and they did not wish to take any action which would diminish their popularity. What was needed most was a man of deep insight who would give leadership and direction to the movement. That man was to be found in Father John Carroll.

John Carroll (1735–1815) belonged to one of the old aristocratic Roman Catholic families of Maryland. His cousin, Charles Carroll, was the only Roman Catholic signer of the Declaration of Independence. John Carroll had been educated in France, where he became a member of the Jesuit order. For a time he lived in England but returned to this country just before the advent of war to begin a mission at Rock Creek, Maryland. During the Revolution he served the Continental Congress as a member of the committee on Canada. To many he seemed the most logical choice to attempt the consolidation of American Catholicism. Carroll would have liked to have been consecrated bishop, but the papacy was reluctant to establish an episcopate in the United States for diplomatic reasons; and many American Catholics shared this view, fearing that such an establishment might lead to the loss of some of their powers of local church government. Thus Carroll was granted only the title of Prefect Apostolic, with episcopal powers as soon as the status of the church was known. He held the office from 1784 to 1789.

Throughout this period he was troubled by problems of discipline of the clergy and the practice of lay trusteeship. In New York, where Carroll had appointed Maurice Whelan, a Capuchin priest, pastor of the congregation, resentment was aroused over Father Whelan's poverty at preaching. With the arrival in 1785 of Father Andrew Nugent, who possessed splendid oratorical gifts, a large faction in the congregation desired to oust Whelan and obtain the services of Nugent. The trustees who were in control of the property and strongly pro-Nugent refused to pay Whelan's salary. Despite many attempts on the part of Carroll to settle the matter favorably for Whelan, the Capuchin finally gave up the struggle and left the congregation under the care of Nugent. Later the congregation divided over Nugent and when Carroll suspended him the recalcitrant priest refused to leave. The matter finally had to be settled in civil courts.

It was obvious that episcopal powers were needed to avert schism in the church and this was now recognized by Rome. The American priests, being granted the right to choose their bishop, met at Whitemarsh, Maryland, and elected John Carroll. He sailed for England and was consecrated Bishop of Baltimore by the Vicar-Apostolic of London on August 15, 1790. Among the first important events of his episcopate were the calling of the first national synod of the church in 1791 and the founding of Georgetown College and St. Mary's Seminary in Maryland the same year.

The problem of lay trusteeship did not cease after Carroll's elevation to episcopal rank. Roman Catholic laymen had accustomed themselves so long to the privilege of conducting their own parochial affairs that they were hesitant to relinquish it. Especially was this true of the ownership of church buildings, the titles to which were in the hands of the parish trustees. These officials were reluctant to surrender to their bishop the right to hold the property and in this they were supported by civil law which recognized the local congregation as owner of its church building. The circumstances were such that Bishop Carroll could do little more than concede the right of trusteeship to the laity, at least for the time being. During the early nineteenth century, debate on this issue would rise to gigantic proportions.

Another serious problem which faced Carroll and his successors was that of staffing the parishes with adequate clergy. After the Revolution it was difficult to secure English priests for work in America. The great influx of priests was from France, where life had been difficult for the clergy in the secularized order which followed the French Revolution. At first Carroll was glad to see them come, for they were men of piety, intellect, and culture. Though their efforts were largely ineffective, due partially to opposition on the part of Irish congregations, some of them rose to high offices in the church. But this was merely a temporary arrangement. The real future lay with the Irish priests who in the early part of the nineteenth century began to enter the United States in large numbers.

The establishment of the first Roman Catholic congregation in Boston in 1788 was encouraging. By this time New Englanders were somewhat more favorably disposed toward Roman Catholics because of their role in the Revolution. At first the majority of Roman Catholics in New England were French, but by the turn of the century the Irish were in the position of dominance. For a number of years the Boston congregation was torn by a feud between its French and Irish members. The trouble was brought to an end only with the coming of Father Francis Matignon, a wise and understanding French priest. Not only did he restore peace to the congregation, but he also won the respect of many Protestants. Even better known was Father John de Cheverus, a French refugee who came to Boston in 1796. Working closely with Father Matignon, he brought considerable prestige to his church. He stood high in the Protestant community and frequently accepted invitations to preach in Protestant churches. In 1808, he became the first Roman Catholic bishop of Boston.

By the opening of the nineteenth century, steady gains made by the church rendered it necessary to make some changes in organization. Upon the recommendation of Bishop Carroll, Pope Pius VII, in 1808, raised Baltimore to metropolitan status, with Carroll as archbishop, and erected the four episcopal sees of Boston, New York, Philadelphia, and Bardstown, Kentucky. The church was at last becoming equipped to meet the challenge of an expanding America.

THE RISE OF NEW DENOMINATIONS

Around the turn of the century two German groups which had been nurtured in pietism emerged as independent denominations. They represent the fruits of the German phase of the Great Awakening which came relatively late due to the tardiness of the arrival of German-speaking evangelists. Only in the most indirect way did they profit from the influence of revivalists such as Whitefield and Tennent, whose preaching was directed to the English-speaking segments of the population.

The United Brethren in Christ

The movement which culminated in the founding of a new denomination, the United Brethren in Christ, began with the arrival in America of Philip William Otterbein (1726–1813), a minister of the German Reformed Church. Born and educated in Germany, he came to Lancaster, Pennsylvania, in 1752, as a missionary to the German people there. He subsequently held pastorates at Tulpehocken, Pennsylvania; Frederick, Maryland; and York, Pennsylvania. His preaching was strongly pietistic, and though he never became a popular orator he was held in affection by his people. In 1774, Otterbein was called to the Second Reformed Church of Baltimore where there had recently been bitter strife among members of the congregation, the faction which called Otterbein having withdrawn to form a new church. During this pastorate, Otterbein became an intimate friend of Francis Asbury, so much so that when Asbury was consecrated Superintendent in 1784 he requested that the German Reformed minister be invited to participate in the service. Asbury's influence can be seen in Otterbein's organization of class meetings and his appointment of lay leaders to assist the pastor in his work. Even the semi-annual conference, with the presentation of reports by the classes, became a regular feature of the program. Most of the German Reformed ministers and churches in Maryland together with several in Pennsylvania attended the conferences; for the time being, however, there was no withdrawal from the German Reformed Church.

Meanwhile, certain leaders not identified with the Reformed Church had become interested in Otterbein's movement and affiliated with it. The most important of these was Martin Boehm, who had been a Mennonite. His fervid evangelical preaching had endeared him to Otterbein and the two became mutual admirers. After 1789, the Mennonite influence in the movement became stronger while enthusiasm for denominational connections steadily waned. Finally, in 1800, Otterbein, Boehm, and eleven others met in conference and formally launched a new church which they denominated the United Brethren in Christ. The church, fashioned after the pattern of Methodist polity and doctrine, chose Otterbein and Boehm to be its first bishops. During the first decade of the nineteenth century the church carried on a successful missionary program in Ohio, Indiana, and Kentucky, necessitating the establishment in 1810 of a conference west of the Allegheny Mountains. In 1815 the first General Conference of the United Brethren Church was held at Mount Pleasant, Pennsylvania.

The Evangelical Association

In 1790, Jacob Albright (1759–1808), a Pennsylvania-born businessman of German ancestry, was suddenly converted to Christianity through the efforts of Adam Riegel, an independent lay preacher. Soon after his conversion Albright announced his adherence to the Methodists. As he grew in the spiritual life he felt a call from God to preach to the Germans of Pennsylvania; in 1796 he began to preach in the eastern counties of Pennsylvania but soon extended his ministry to Maryland and Virginia, where he preached in German to those who could not understand English, which was spoken by Methodist preachers. In 1800, Albright organized several classes, which looked upon him as their spiritual leader. Three years later, at a general meeting of the society, he was consecrated as a minister by the imposition of hands by two of his younger associates. The first Annual Conference, composed of all officers of the society, was held in 1807. On that occasion the conference adopted the name "The Newly Formed Methodist Conference" and elected Albright as bishop. Two years later the conference approved a discipline based on the doctrine and polity of the Methodists. With the first meeting of the General Conference in 1816, the denomination, by then known as the Evangelical Association, had accomplished its national organization. The nineteenth century would witness its expansion westward until its center of activity would be located west of the Alleghenies.

Western Expansion and the

Second Awakening

IT WAS THE SAGE EMERSON WHO NOTED THAT "EUROPE EXTENDS TO THE Alleghenies, while America lies beyond." His observation was instructive. That vast area which stretches from the eastern mountains to the great plains was the crucible in which Americanism was fashioned and endowed with its most distinctive character. In the Middle West, the first part of America to be cultivated by English-speaking settlers since the advent of the national era, a new pattern was developing almost wholly independently of the eastern models which looked to Europe for their inspiration. Though Spanish and French adventurers had sailed up its arbor-framed rivers and traversed its rolling or flat terrain, the stamp of Old World culture left but a faint impression upon the land, and this was virtually obliterated by the ponderous tread of the American frontiersman. On the frontier this scion of individualism and progress carved out a new civilization, wild and crude according to urban standards, yet founded upon the dignity of man and his infinite perfectibility. He could face the future for in it all things were possible.

As time passed, the congested cities of the East looked increasingly toward the West, instead of predominantly to Europe. The very political, economic, and spiritual destiny of the nation seemed to depend on the events which transpired on the burgeoning frontier. Statesman, businessman, churchman—each in his own way could recognize the strategic importance of the West. It was through western expansion that the mighty nation, the affluent society, the Kingdom of God in America was to be achieved. Those who saw the vision most clearly and responded most vigorously became architects of the new civilization, the moving spirits in the great American essay.

In the time it takes a new generation to rise to manhood, the United States evolved from an infant republic huddled between the ocean and the first range of western mountains to an adolescent nation unrestrained by any natural barrier east of the Rockies. According to the terms of the Treaty of Peace with Great Britain in 1783, the territorial holdings of the United States were extended to the Mississippi. To persons of conservative inclination it was doubtful whether it would ever be fully settled; even the eastern seaboard had not completely succumbed to the onward press of civilization. Nevertheless, the increase of population from about three million at the end of the war to four million in 1790, in a society plagued by economic depression, dictated the establishment of new communities and the steady thrust of the frontier westward.

When the Revolution ended, the only settlements in the Ohio Valley were in western Pennsylvania, Kentucky, and Tennessee. North of the Ohio River the aborigines were in almost complete possession. In the region south of the Ohio, pioneering was farther advanced. A steady wave of settlers was pouring into the wilderness and transforming it into a cultivated garden. Many who originated in Virginia and the Carolinas came by way of the Cumberland Gap. More frequently they sailed down the Monongahela to the Ohio. Others came through Maryland or southern Pennsylvania. In 1787 alone more than 900 boats carried 18,000 newcomers, 650 wagons, and 12,000 animals down the broad Ohio River into the old Southwest. By 1790 there were 50,000 or more in the Kentucky settlements and probably 120,000 living west of the Appalachians. Favorable economic conditions had a special attraction for dwellers in the South, where the full effects of the depression had been experienced. During the next few years the populations of Maryland, Virginia, and the Carolinas would shrink appreciably as their former citizens trekked across the Blue Ridge into Kentucky and Tennessee. In 1792, Kentucky was admited to statehood; Tennessee followed four years later. Thereafter, the roll call of new states would proceed in rapid order: Ohio, 1803; Louisiana, 1812; Indiana, 1816; Alabama, 1817; Illinois, 1818; Mississippi, 1819; Missouri, 1821. By 1829 nine of the eleven new states were situated west of the Alleghenies and contained more than a third of the nation's population.

The enactment of the Northwest Ordinance of 1787 for the government of the Northwest Territory provided a tremendous impetus to western settlement. It provided that in this vast region between the Mississippi, the Ohio, and the Great Lakes there should be full religious freedom and no slavery or involuntary servitude other than in the punishment of crimes. Unquestionably, these provisions helped to induce certain religious groups such as anti-slavery Friends to make their homes in that region. In 1788 a settlement was founded at Marietta, along the Muskingum River in southeastern Ohio, by the Ohio Company. The immigrants were among the first of a mass of New Englanders who would push through the valley of the Mohawk into the Northwest Territory. Occupation, however, was not accomplished without bloodshed. The natives, aroused by the invasion of their lands by whites, took to the warpath, murdering and pillaging until they were repulsed in August, 1794, at the battle of Fallen Timbers, by the forces of General Anthony Wayne. During the next decade settlers from Virginia, Maryland, Kentucky, New Jersey, and New England flocked into the Scioto Valley and the Miami country of Ohio. A large number of migrants from Connecticut poured into the Western Reserve in northeastern Ohio. By 1800 the increase of population justified the partition of the Northwest Territory. The Ohio section retained its old name, the region to the West being christened Indiana Territory. In 1812, the inhabitants of Ohio numbered more than 250,000.

During the 1780's New Englanders, pushing westward in large numbers to escape overcrowding, high prices, and the Congregational establishment, or to build a more liberal social order, began to settle in western New York. By 1793 the Mohawk Turnpike running westward from Albany was opened as far as Utica. Most of the land in this area was purchased by speculators, some of them organized into companies, who in turn sold their purchases to settlers. Many of the speculators were connected with English and Dutch business houses and had such abundant wealth that they could erect entire communities on the frontier in record time. In this way export centers came to be established on Lake Ontario, the Genesee River, the Seneca River, and the Cohocton River. By 1800 a mass shift of population was under way, bringing the number of inhabitants in western New York in 1812 to 200,000. More than two-thirds of these pioneers were from New England.

Similar circumstances prevailed in the Southwest, where more than 220,000 persons had made their homes in Kentucky and more than 105,-000 in Tennessee by 1800. These states filled so quickly that the transition from frontier to civilized community was accomplished virtually overnight. Land was cheap and most settlers found that after three or four years of successful harvests it was possible to enjoy the basic necessities of life together with a few frills. The rapid influx of pioneers, however, did not transform society in the Southwest from rural to urban. As late as 1800, Lexington, Kentucky, the largest city in the West, numbered only 1795 inhabitants; towns such as Louisville, Frankfort, Nashville, and Knoxville had populations which stood at less than 500. Farming was the principal occupation and the chief product corn, which could be fed to cattle and hogs or concentrated into whisky. The marketing of large herds of cattle and hogs and the exportation of whisky soon brought a modicum of prosperity to the frontier.

Diplomatic considerations played a significant role in the settlement of the West. The presence of the Spanish and later the French in the Mississippi Valley and the Spanish in Florida was regarded by both the national government and the settlers on the frontier as a definite threat to American expansion. In the eyes of Jefferson and many others the designs of the Corsican Bonaparte had to be frustrated at all costs. Thus the proposal of Talleyrand in 1803 to sell the whole of Louisiana for about fifteen million dollars was accepted with due dispatch by American diplomats Robert Livingston and James Monroe. Not only did the purchase more than double the area of the United States, it removed a political menace from the Mississippi Valley, provided land on which the repulsed Indian tribes could be resettled, and opened the way for unlimited colonization in the West. The Louisiana treaty involved the nation in a dispute with Spain over the possession of West Florida; the matter was not settled until 1819, when the whole of Florida was purchased by the United States. Americans now enjoyed undisputed control over the Southwest and the geographical prerequisites to becoming a great power.

With the outbreak of the War of 1812, western expansion slackened and for a time was virtually halted. The frontier was aflame with tensions and conflicts brought on by economic depression resultant from England's blockade and Jefferson's embargo policy, Indian uprisings under the leadership of Tecumseh and his brother, The Prophet, and British attacks in the regions of the Great Lakes and the Mississippi Valley. Mere mention of the names Tippecanoe, Detroit, Lundy's Lane, Ft. Mims, and New Orleans will suffice to demonstrate the significance of the West in the tumultuous period of the War of 1812. By 1814 two facts emerged to the everlasting comfort of American patriots: the future of the United States as an independent nation was assured, and the way was clear for a new era of westward expansion.

The quarter century which followed 1815 witnessed the opening of two regions, the Lake Plains and the Gulf Plains, to pioneers. The settlement of these areas would continue until 1850, when populating the eastern half of the continent would be complete. In the North the Indians were driven from Indiana, Illinois, and Michigan so that by 1821 this territory was ready for the reception of white settlers. Into these lands which abounded in forests of hardwoods, prairies, and grasslands came swarms of newcomers from the East. Perhaps a majority traveled over the mountains on the new National Road, which by 1818 extended to Wheeling, and from there down the Ohio River. From Louisville and Shawneetown they made their way northward through Indiana and Illinois. As one traveler on the National Road observed in 1817: "Old America seems to be breaking up and moving westward. We are seldom out of sight, as we travel on this ground track, towards the Ohio, of family groups before and behind us." After 1825, the Erie Canal became the most important route to the West.

During the same quarter century another deluge of immigrants poured into the Gulf Plains from the seaboard states of the South Atlantic. Their migration was due largely to the depleted soil caused by unwise agricultural procedures. In Alabama and Mississippi they sought rich soil for the cultivation of cotton and corn. By the end of 1819, 200,000 people were living in the Gulf Plains and producing one-half the nation's cotton.

THE CHURCHES ON THE FRONTIER

The rapid colonization of the West created unique problems for organized religion. If the future of America depended upon what took place beyond the Appalachians, then the building of the Kingdom of God in America rested upon the ability of the churches to make an impact on frontier society. It was not simply a matter of sending ministers to care for relocated communicants; primarily it involved the conversion of countless persons who did not belong to any church and who gave little evidence of a desire to be so affiliated. The work of frontier evangelism was arduous, but for those who could meet the challenge the rewards were impressive. Those religious bodies which were best able to accommodate themselves to the conditions of the frontier emerged as the largest in the nation.

The Congregationalists and Presbyterians

From the standpoint of numerical strength, leadership, and prestige, the Congregationalists were by all odds the most important denomination in the country at the dawn of the national era. But no communion was less prepared to face the problems of the frontier. Several factors account for this unhappy circumstance. In the first place, the preservation of the establishment in New England served to infect Congregationalists of that area with an attitude of superiority and self-centered complacency. More serious, however, was the parochial viewpoint of the Congregational leaders who were so engrossed in the glories of New England that in their myopia they failed to see the possibility of a great nation extending to the Pacific. If the denomination had been able to render an adequate ministry to the 800,000 persons who, between 1790 and 1830, migrated from southern New England to frontier territory, it would undoubtedly have continued as one of the largest religious bodies in the country. Failing to do this, it consigned itself to a minor role on the western frontier.

While settlers from New England had established a community at Marietta, Ohio, as early as 1788, it was not until December, 1796, that the first Congregational church was founded there. The earliest Congregational church to be established in the Western Reserve was that of Austinburg, which was instituted in 1801. For a time, various Congregational missionary societies organized in Connecticut, Massachusetts, and New Hampshire raised funds for the support of frontier missions. These efforts bore fruit chiefly in Vermont, which had been settled almost wholly by New Englanders. In Ohio, where settlers were highly mixed in origin, the way was more difficult and it was not long before cooperation with the Presbyterians seemed desirable.

In the meantime, Presbyterianism had been planting itself firmly in the West. Inasmuch as the Scotch-Irish, who represented the last important emigration from Europe prior to the Revolution, had founded communities up and down the frontier by 1760, the Presbyterians had a natural base of operations from which to work. In 1766 the Synod of New York and Philadelphia sent the Reverends Charles Beatty and George Duffield on a mission of exploration into the Indian country west of the mountains. Some years before, Beatty had been the first Protestant clergyman to visit the Pittsburgh area while on duty with the army as a chaplain. These men were the first Presbyterian ministers to visit the valley of the Ohio. The following year they reported to the synod that "they found on the frontiers numbers of people earnestly desirous of forming themselves into congregations" and that "they visited the Indians at the chief town of the Delaware Nation, on the Muskingum, about one hundred and thirty miles beyond Fort Pitt." Before the Revolution terminated missionary operations, the synod sent out several other ministers to serve for brief or extended periods in southwestern Pennsylvania. The first permanent ministers in the area, arriving between 1776 and 1781, were John McMillan, Thaddeus Todd, James Power, and Joseph Smith. Each was responsible for two churches, but the demands for their services were so great that it was common for them to travel many miles through the wilderness to preach to unchurched pioneers. The founding of the Presbytery of Redstone in 1781, the first presbytery to be organized west of the Alleghenies, came about largely because of the efforts of these men. By 1801 three presbyteries had been constituted in western Pennsylvania; the following year they were placed under care of the new Synod of Pittsburgh.

About the same time Presbyterian congregations were being formed among the Scotch-Irish settlers who had migrated from western Virginia and North Carolina into Kentucky and Tennessee. In 1783, the Reverend David Rice, a native of Hanover County, Virginia, visited Kentucky with the thought of making it his place of residence. He preached frequently and apparently with such effectiveness that after his return to Virginia he received a call from 300 persons to assume a pastorate in Kentucky. October, 1783, found him once again in Mercer County, Kentucky, where he accepted the call and shortly thereafter organized a Presbyterian church at Danville, the first to be founded in the state. He later established churches at Cane Run and Salt River and erected edifices at each of these places. In 1785 the Synod of New York and Philadelphia ordered the establishment of the Transylvania Presbytery, the second to be founded west of the Alleghenies. At its first meeting in October, 1786, Rice was elected moderator.

Apart from the schism brought on by Adam Rankin, who had become pastor of the church at Lexington in 1784, Presbyterianism in Kentucky enjoyed steady development. Rankin had been dismissed from the presbytery in 1792 for contending that he was the "subject of extraordinary Divine Revelation" and for his adamant stand against Watts' psalms. After being received the following year into the ministry of the Associate Reformed Church, he organized his admirers into congregations. By 1818 most of these churches had become defunct. In the meantime, the arrival of the Reverend James McGready in 1798 to take charge of three congregations in Logan County gave considerable impetus to Presbyterianism. By 1802 the denomination had received so many communicants that it was necessary to establish the Synod of Kentucky, which consisted of the Presbyteries of Transylvania, West Lexington, and Washington. An additional presbytery, embracing the churches on the Cumberland, was organized that same year. It numbered among its six ministers James McGready and William McGee, prominently known in the West because of their leadership in the Second Awakening.

Dr. Samuel Doak was the first minister to settle in Tennessee, having arrived in 1777. Soon after his coming he founded the Salem Presbyterian Church, which was the first Protestant church to be organized in the state. Within a decade twenty-three Presbyterian churches had been erected in Tennessee. When the Presbytery of Abingdon was constituted in 1785, these churches were included within its bounds. Then, in 1810, they were attached to the Synod of Kentucky, and finally to the newly-formed Synod of Tennessee in 1817. The first Presbyterian work in Alabama was begun in 1807, when the Reverend Robert Bell was sent to minister to the new settlements in the neighborhood of Huntsville. But it was not until 1820 that Alabama Presbytery was constituted. In Mississippi, the oldest extant Presbyterian church was organized near Natchez in 1807 by the Reverend James Smylie. The Mississippi Presbytery was organized in 1816.

Presbyterianism in Ohio began in 1790, when the Reverend David Rice founded the Cincinnati-Columbia Presbyterian Church. Its first pastor was James Kemper. In 1798 the Washington Presbytery was organized, including in its jurisdiction churches in Kentucky and northwest of the Ohio. The Synod of Ohio was constituted in 1815. Within a decade presbyteries would be established in Indiana and Illinois.

Of profound importance to the development of Presbyterianism and Congregationalism in the West was the Plan of Union of 1801. For some decades the two denominations had gradually been drawing together in cooperative activity. The trend had begun with the adoption by Connecticut Congregationalists of the Saybrook Platform in 1708 and had moved forward during and after the Great Awakening through the frequent interchange of ministers. Between the years 1766 and 1775, when agitation for the establishment of an American episcopate was most keenly felt, representatives of the associations of Connecticut and the Synod of New York and Philadelphia met in annual conventions to oppose its occurrence. Considerable progress in interdenominational relations was made in 1791 when the General Association of Connecticut and the Presbyterian General Assembly each agreed to send delegates to the meetings of the other body. From 1794 to 1827 these delegates were granted full membership and enjoyed the privilege of speaking and voting in the meetings. The Congregational General Association of Vermont entered into a similar relationship with the Presbyterian General Assembly in 1809; the General Associations of New Hampshire and Massachusetts followed suit in 1810 and 1811 respectively.

During the great revival of 1798–1801, the Presbyterians sent missionaries into the frontier regions of central and western New York, where they encountered Congregational ministers who had recently arrived from New England. Leaders of both denominations sensed the futility of competition and began to explore the possibilities of a joint effort in the West. In 1800, Jonathan Edwards the Younger, then president of Union College, proposed a Plan of Union while seated as a Presbyterian delegate to the General Association of Connecticut. The following year the Plan was adopted by both the General Association and the General Assembly; it was later approved by the other New England associations. According to the terms of the agreement, it was possible for Congregationalists and Presbyterians to form themselves into one congregation which might be connected with both denominations yet could conduct its local government as the majority of its members preferred. The church might call as its pastor a minister of either denomination, who would retain his affiliation with either the presbytery or association. Should difficulty arise between the pastor and his congregation the matter would be referred to the presbytery or association of which the minister was a member or to a council composed of equal representatives of each denomination. A Presbyterian minister might appeal his case all the way to the General Assembly, but the final court of appeal for a Congregationalist clergyman was the male communicants of the church. Elders from Presbyterian churches were invited to sit as delegates in meetings of Congregational associations, while Congregational churches were given representation in the presbyteries through the seating of committeemen.

The Plan of Union was first put in operation in central and western New York. Though Congregationalists from Connecticut were predominant in this section only a few years passed before they had become almost completely absorbed into Presbyterianism. At the same time they preserved many of their Congregational usages. In 1808 the Middle Association of New York Congregationalists became an integral part of the Presbyterian Synod of Albany, while retaining its Congregational character. The same situation prevailed in the Western Reserve and other areas of Ohio, where early Congregational churches were almost uniformly received into local presbyteries. Likewise, in Indiana, Illinois, Missouri, Kentucky, and Tennessee, the combined efforts of Congregationalist and Presbyterian missionaries resulted in the establishment of Presbyterian churches. For example, the churches of Springfield (now West Zanesville), Clinton, and Waterford, Ohio, which had formed the Muskingum Association in 1809, united with the Lancaster Presbytery just seven years later. Not until the 1830's did a growing estrangement between Congregationalists and Presbyterians lead to the establishment of many separate Congregational churches in the West. By this time Congregationalists were becoming more denominationally minded and less willing to share the fruits of their labors with another religious body. Old School Presbyterians were also becoming more fearful of the alliance for doctrinal and social reasons. The so-called "Presbygational" system was impracticable inasmuch as it brought together two autonomous denominations with distinct and often dissimilar doctrines and practices and subjected them to the impossible maintenance of a two-sided structure. That both sides abrogated the Plan of Union prior to the outbreak of the Civil War was hardly surprising.

Despite the cooperative activity of Congregationalists and Presbyterians on the frontier, neither denomination was able to keep up with the impressive gains made by Methodists and Baptists. By 1850 the Congregationalists who, at the close of the Revolution, had ranked first among the American churches had fallen to fourth place among Protestants with 197,000 members. The Presbyterians, with a membership of 487,000, had dropped from second to third place. Many reasons have been advanced to explain this declension. Among the Congregationalists, lack of a national view and policy undoubtedly was a contributing factor. As for the Presbyterians, probably the chief consideration was their inability or unwillingness to adapt their polity and practices to the needs of the frontier Their repudiation of emotional excesses in revivalism, of which the Baptists and Methodists made such efficacious use, seriously weakened their effectiveness among backwoodsmen. Presbyterian insistence upon an educated ministry meant that fewer men could qualify for missionary labors, and even though the Presbyterians used a circuit system they still could not supply enough ministers to meet the demand. To make matters worse, the work of the Presbyterian missions was hindered by the spirit of contention existing between the Old and New School wings during the early decades of the nineteenth century and by the resultant schism of 1837. However, the assertion that the Presbyterian cause was weakened due to the reserve of frontier ministers in working among other than those of Presbyterian background is not in keeping with the facts. These ministers evangelized whomsoever they could.

The Episcopalians

Until the close of the War of 1812 the Protestant Episcopal Church in the United States was engaged principally in efforts to overcome the shock sustained by its losses in the Revolution. Although the church underwent a complete reorganization, it was difficult to convince Americans that the Episcopal Church was anything other than an English institution. With the withdrawal of the Methodists the church was left with virtually no activities on the frontier. Besides, its lack of popularity with the masses placed it in a disadvantageous position. It was a time of general discouragement and gloom.

The picture began to change with the elevation of John Henry Hobart (1775–1830) to Assistant Bishop of New York in 1811. During the second year of his episcopate, he went on a 2000-mile tour of his diocese, visiting 33 parishes and confirming 1100 persons; the result was a general quickening of the life of the church. When he first took office Hobart had only two diocesan missionaries; nineteen years later there were fifty. The bishop made it his annual duty to visit a large part of his diocese and, when the occasion warranted, to consecrate new churches. By 1830 the number of parishes in western New York had risen to fifty-three, the rapid increase necessitating the creation of a second diocese in New York eight years later. Nearly every important town in the state had an Episcopal church and a settled ministry.

The founding father of the Episcopal Church west of the Alleghenies was Philander Chase (1775–1852), first Episcopal Bishop of Ohio. Graduate of Dartmouth College and convert to the Episcopal Church, he took training for holy orders and, after his ordination as deacon in 1798, was assigned to missionary work in central New York. In 1805, he went to New Orleans where he was the first Protestant minister to found a church. After another short pastorate at Hartford, Connecticut, he became a free-lance missionary in Ohio in 1817. The following year the Diocese of Ohio was organized, and at a later convention Chase was elected bishop. During the early years of his episcopate, his principal concerns were the raising of funds for his destitute diocese and the founding of Kenyon College (which will be treated in a later chapter). Despite significant contributions, his dictatorial methods in the administration of Kenyon College led to rebuke by the diocesan convention of 1831 and his immediate resignation. Four years later he was elected first Bishop of Illinois. In this post Chase devoted himself chiefly to the founding of Jubilee College, but in this he was only moderately successful. His death in 1852 cut short a work which was still far from accomplishment.

Throughout the West the progress of the Episcopal Church was painfully slow. At the Ohio convention of 1820 it was reported that there was no Episcopal minister in Indiana, Tennessee, Illinois, or Missouri, and probably none in the territories. Only a few modest efforts had been made in Kentucky and Louisiana. In 1835 Jackson Kemper was consecrated a missionary bishop with authority over all states and territories which as yet enjoyed no diocesan organization. By this time, however, it was too late to make any significant impression upon the religious pattern in the West. Statistics reveal that in 1850 the Episcopal Church had 90,000 communicants but had fallen from fourth to seventh place among Protestants in numerical strength. The factors which hindered the growth of Congregationalism and Presbyterianism were also operative in the Episcopal Church. Moreover, the fact that the Episcopal clergyman was attached so completely to his parish as to rule out any wide practice of itineracy emphasizes the relative impotence of the church in ministering to the religious needs of frontier society.

The Baptists

Among the new stream of immigrants that flooded Kentucky and Tennessee after the Revolution were large numbers of Baptists who had been forced by economic depression to leave their homes in the East. The greater majority originated in Virginia or North Carolina and belonged to the lower middle class. Their principal goal was to find inexpensive but fertile land on which they could settle and raise crops. Harassed in the East by the former Anglican establishment, they also sought freedom in the new land to worship God according to their convictions. There was an aura of democracy about them which was diffused osmotically in their social and political mores and in their practice of religion. Their preachers were of similar rank and station, for the most part theologically untrained farmers who had felt a call to preach, a call which could not be impeded by the rigors of formal education. Unencumbered by ecclesiastical organization, they could move easily among the frontier settlements and preach wherever they could gather a congregation. Their sermons were of the people and for the people and they spoke to the condition of the frontiersman in a way which could never be matched by the cultivated clergyman from the East. Their non-professionalism endeared them to rustics who had a natural abhorrence for a trained and salaried ministry. Preachers were of two classes, licensed and ordained. Licensing was the first step taken by a local church in recognition of one who felt called to preach. When he was called to the pastorate of a congregation he was granted ordination.

An excellent example of the Baptist farmer-preacher was John Taylor. Born into a poor Virginian family of Anglican background, he was won after great spiritual struggle to the Baptist faith. In 1784 he moved to Woodward County, Kentucky, and settled on Clear Creek. There he labored as a successful farmer and pastor of the Clear Creek Baptist Church for nine years. He was active in the founding of seven other churches in Kentucky and still more in western Virginia and North Carolina and Tennessee. His *History of Ten Baptist Churches,* published in 1823, gives an illuminating picture of Baptist activities on the frontier.

There were instances in which an entire congregation moved with its pastor to the West, as in the case of the Gilbert's Creek Church in Kentucky. When the congregation of the Upper Spottsylvania Church in Virginia learned that their pastor, Lewis Craig, planned to move to Kentucky, the majority decided, in 1781, to accompany him. On the long trek over the mountains they maintained their unity as a congregation and conducted worship with unfailing regularity. It is said that when they heard the report of Cornwallis' surrender, while stopping at Abingdon, Virginia, they greeted the news with a celebration that could be heard miles away. They arrived at Gilbert's Creek in December and on the following Sunday met for worship "around the same old Bible they had used in Spottsylvania."

Both Regular and Separate Baptists were to be found among the early frontier settlers. A sizeable majority of the Kentucky preachers had been Separate Baptists in the East, insisting that the Bible alone should serve as the basis of their beliefs; for some unknown reason most of them became identified with the Regular Baptists after their arrival in the West. By the end of 1785 there were eleven Regular and seven Separate Baptist churches in Kentucky. Earlier that year an attempt had been made at South Elkhorn to organize a union association. But the minority of Separate Baptists refused to join when they learned that the majority favored the adoption of the Philadelphia Confession, an action contrary to their anti-creedal views.

The first Baptist Association west of the Allegheny Mountains was born in September, 1785, when representatives of six Regular Baptist churches met at the home of pastor Craig and formed the Elkhorn Association. Its center of operation was central Kentucky. A month later the Regular Baptist churches in the western settlements organized the Salem Association. The Separate Baptists followed suit in 1787 with the establishment of the South Kentucky Association. In 1800 representatives from the Elkhorn and South Kentucky Associations met and agreed on a plan of union which featured a compromise between the tenets of Calvinism and Arminianism and revealed the preference of frontier Baptists for a mild form of Calvinism; it became effective in 1801. By this time there were 5110 Baptist communicants in Kentucky organized into six associations. Within two years the membership climbed to 10,380, a phenomenal growth due in large measure to revivalistic zeal. By 1820, when Baptist membership in Kentucky reached 31,689, there was still a noteworthy trend upward.

By 1780 several Baptist ministers and their congregations had left Virginia and North Carolina and had settled in the Holston section of eastern Tennessee. In less than a year half a dozen churches had been founded in that area, justifying the formation of the Holston Association in 1786. This association comprised both Regular and Separate Baptists and held as its platform the Philadelphia Confession of Faith; apparently this arrangement was not opposed by the Separate Baptist element. In 1802 the Tennessee Association was founded by the churches in the southern part of the territory. By 1809 combined membership in the two associations was 2679.

Baptist activities in southwestern Tennessee began to develop about 1790 and within half a decade five churches had been organized in the Cumberland country. These in turn formed themselves into the Mero Association which by 1801 included eighteen churches and about 1200 communicants. This association was beset by internal conflict brought on by Joseph Dorris, a troublesome minister who pastored the church at Head of Sulphur Creek. Being unable to remove him from the association because of his powerful connections, the members finally dissolved the association and, in 1803, formed themselves into the new Cumberland Association, into which they refused to receive Dorris or his church. Three years from that time thirty-nine churches and about 1900 communicants were affiliated with the association. By 1809 the Red River, Elk River, and Concord Associations had been brought into existence.

North of the Ohio River, Baptist activities were under way as early as 1789 when a number of Baptist laymen from New England and the Middle States founded a settlement on the Little Miami and began to hold worship services. A year later the Reverend Stephen Gano organized a church there, the first of the Baptist denomination to be planted in the Northwest Territory. In 1797 four Baptist churches in the general region of Cincinnati organized the Miami Association. By 1812 the Associations of Scioto Valley, Redstone, Muskingum, and Mad River had been similarly organized. The total number of Baptist communicants in Ohio that year was about 2400. In Indiana the first Baptist church had been organized at Silver Creek in 1798; a decade later the Wabash Association was constituted. Baptist churches were organized in Illinois by 1796 and in Missouri by 1804. Mississippi and Louisiana received their first Baptist immigrants from South Carolina and Georgia. A church was organized near Natchez while Mississippi was still under Spanish rule, but it was not until the territory was ceded to the United States that any significant progress was made. In 1806 the Mississippi Baptist Association was organized. Six years later the first Baptist church was founded in Louisiana.

Baptist successes on the frontier may be attributed to several noteworthy factors. First and foremost was the simple but efficient manner in which they carried on their labors. Unimpeded by ecclesiastical machinery, they could gather congregations and found churches, wherever it seemed practical; and since the preachers did not have to depend upon their churches for support, it was perfectly feasible to establish a church even if there were not more than a dozen members. The very democracy of such an arrangement had appeal for the man on the frontier. To be sure there was organization. Most of the churches held monthly business meetings; all provided rules for administration and discipline in addition to their constitutions or covenants. If church records of the period seem to reveal a superabundance of disciplinary action, it was due to the general roughness and lack of decorum which characterized frontier society. Insobriety, brawling, adultery, and stealing were perennial problems which required a solution, and they were tackled with vigor by Baptist preachers and lay leaders. Discipline was frequently meted out to both white and Negro members for conduct unbecoming a professing Baptist. Strictness of discipline, however, seems not to have detracted from the church's popularity. Indeed, the Baptists were successful not only in holding their own members but in winning unchurched pioneers to the faith. Perhaps this was because of their ability to translate religion into the language of the common man—to confront him with simple alternatives such as doubt or faith, sin or righteousness, hell or heaven. In any case, their growth was phenomenal; by 1855 they stood second among Protestants in numerical strength throughout the nation with a total membership of 1,105,546.

The Methodists

At first sight, it might appear that the highly centralized and regulated Methodist system would have little appeal to the democratically inclined frontiersman. Certainly its episcopal polity was singled out by Baptist competitors to bear the brunt of their attacks. This liability was nevertheless overcome by the effectiveness of the circuit system and the local organization. Circuit riding, a method introduced by Wesley to meet the religious needs of a shifting English population, proved to be an ideal solution to the problem of maintaining a reasonably adequate frontier ministry. The founder and one of the main representatives of the circuit ministry in America was Francis Asbury. For forty-five years he traveled back and forth across the country, supervising the work of the church and performing a variety of services. His ministry established a pattern which became normative on the frontier. Prior to 1796 all the preachers met in an annual conference at which they would submit reports of their year's work and receive their assignment for the following year. By 1796, however, the denomination had grown to such an extent that it was necessary to divide the country into six annual conferences, one of which served the territory west of the mountains. In 1792 the position of presiding elder was created, a post which called for the oversight of the circuits and circuit riders in a given district. The presiding elder might even organize new circuits between annual conferences.

Circuits established in newly settled areas always covered a wide territory, sometimes requiring six weeks to make the rounds. A 500-mile trip to cover fifteen to twenty-five preaching stations was not thought to be unusual. When a circuit rider came to a settlement which he deemed ripe for conversion, he preached to the people in barn, tavern, or whatever place was available. If possible, he organized a class of a few believers and appointed a class leader to guide their spiritual progress during his absence. Members who felt a call to preach and demonstrated some ability in public speaking were encouraged to apply to the presiding elder for a local preacher's license which entitled them to deliver sermons and organize classes. Thus the means was provided for a vital ministry to the unchurched as well as to professing Methodists. While it was not necessary for the minister to receive formal college training, the Methodists were not opposed to education and encouraged their men to read as widely as possible. By 1816 the General Conference directed the annual conferences to offer a course of study for all ministerial candidates and to appoint the presiding elders to supervise the course. This was the nascence of Methodist theological education.

A typical representative of the itinerant ministry was Peter Cartwright (1785–1872). Converted at a Kentucky camp meeting in 1801, he was licensed as a Methodist preacher the following year and ordained a deacon in 1806. The high quality of his performance led to his appointment six years later as presiding elder of the Wabash District, which was composed of three circuits partly in Illinois and partly in Kentucky. His work required him to cross the Ohio River sixteen times each year. His sermons, which were of a variety common to Methodist frontier preachers, were vigorous and intense and usually of a doctrinal nature. The main theme was sin and salvation, with an emphasis on the general atonement of Christ and man's free will and personal responsibility for his actions. Cartwright's preaching was practical and was presented on a level easily understood and appreciated by his hearers. Through it he won many converts to the church.

The first regularly commissioned circuit rider west of the mountains was sent to the Yadkin Circuit in western North Carolina in 1782. A year later the Holston Circuit was established in eastern Tennessee. In 1784 the first Methodist preacher was sent to the Redstone region in southwestern Pennsylvania. The Kentucky Circuit was founded in 1786. So rapid was the Methodist advance on the frontier that by 1789 there were three circuits in Kentucky, four in Tennessee, and three on the upper Ohio. The first circuit in Ohio was erected by John Kobler in 1798 to care for the religious needs of the many settlers who were flooding the Ohio country after the close of the Indian wars. By the opening of the nineteenth century there were more than 2400 Methodists in Tennessee and Kentucky, 257 in the Northwest Territory, and 60 in the lower Mississippi Valley. During the previous decade Bishop Francis Asbury traveled many times across the mountains to counsel circuit riders, hold conferences, and act in matters of administration. His *Journals* reveal a life of courage and devotion to the cause of missions. In them he speaks of swimming his horse across raging rivers, of his concern to avoid hostile Indians, and of the poverty of his preachers, whom he found to be "indifferently clad, with emaciated bodies." Asbury frequently traveled 100 miles in two days, reaching his destination in a state of exhaustion. Between the years 1800 and 1808 the Western Conference was under the supervision of William McKendree (1757–1835), one of the ablest of the frontier leaders and subsequently a bishop.

The opening decade of the new century witnessed such spectacular gains in the Methodist camp that at the General Conference of 1812 the three new Conferences of the Ohio, the Tennessee, and the Genesee were constituted. The Ohio and Tennessee Conferences had been formed out of the older Western Conference. The division was necessary not only to care for the many new circuits being formed in Tennessee and Ohio but also for those being organized in Indiana, Illinois, and the territory running southward along the Mississippi. At that time there were nearly 19,000 Methodist communicants in Kentucky and Tennessee alone.

During the War of 1812 the church suffered a loss in membership, as did all denominations, due to the rising tide of irreligion brought on by conflict. With the end of the war, however, Methodists entered a new period of rapid growth. By 1824 seventeen Conferences had come into existence; six more were added in 1832. Eight years later the number stood at thirty-four, including the Liberia Mission Conference. It was becoming increasingly apparent that the Methodist circuit riders were performing an efficacious work in American society. By 1855 the national membership of Methodism was 1,577,014, making the Methodists the largest Protestant body in the United States.

The Friends

The first Friends Meeting established west of the Alleghenies was at Westland in southwestern Pennsylvania. This was made possible by action of Hopewell Monthly Meeting in Virginia in 1782. After 1787 large numbers of Friends moved into the Northwest Territory from Pennsylvania, Maryland, Virginia, the Carolinas, and Georgia. One principal motivating factor behind the Quaker migration was the desire to dwell in a territory where slavery was forbidden. Within a few years there were almost no Friends left in Georgia and South Carolina. Substantial numbers left North Carolina and the exodus from Virginia was so great that the Virginia Yearly Meeting ceased to function. The result was that the South lost some of its finest citizens to Ohio and Indiana.

In 1796 George Harlan and his family moved to the Ohio region, the first Friends to settle in that area. They were soon followed by other family groups from Virginia and North Carolina who opened a meeting for worship in 1799. About 1800 Quaker settlements were founded west of the Ohio River and by 1801 the Concord Monthly Meeting had been established. From the Miami Valley, where Friends founded the Miami Monthly Meeting in 1803, the Friends pushed westward into Indiana and organized the Whitewater Quarterly Meeting in 1820. By 1845 there were 18,000 Friends in Ohio and 30,000 in Indiana. Nevertheless, the Friends failed to make significant gains on the frontier largely due to the fact that they remained essentially a static and exclusive body and thus made little impact on the outside world.

The Roman Catholics

Before the end of the eighteenth century certain Roman Catholic refugee priests were being sent across the Alleghenies to serve the long-overlooked French settlements at Vincennes and Kaskaskia. Others were being sent to minister to the newly formed Roman Catholic communities in Kentucky, whose citizenry had originated largely in Maryland. An appointment in the West was regarded as at once a challenge and a remarkable opportunity by many of the French priests who had encountered indifference or opposition on the Atlantic coast. Special efforts were made even in France to enlist the interest of the French clergy, and a statement was circulated which read: "We offer you: No salary; No Recompense;

No Holidays; No Pension. But: Much Hard Work; a Poor Dwelling; Few Consolations; Many Disappointments; Frequent Sickness; a Violent or Lonely Death; an Unknown Grave." French priests did not fail to respond to the challenge.

In 1792, Stephen Badin, a seminarian, and Father Benedict Joseph Flaget emigrated from France to America. Badin was ordained in Baltimore the following year, the first Roman Catholic seminarian to receive holy orders in the United States. He was thereupon assigned to missionary work in Kentucky, where by 1800 he presided over half a dozen log chapels. Several priests assisted him in this activity, the most able of whom was Charles Nerinckx, a Belgian priest who arrived on the frontier in 1805. Meanwhile, Father Flaget had reached Vincennes in December, 1792, and had found the log church to be "open to the weather and almost tottering." The spiritual condition of the congregation was abysmal. Only twelve of the nearly 700 nominal Roman Catholics could be persuaded to "approach holy communion during the Christmas festivities." A similar situation prevailed in all the Roman Catholic missions of the West, to which priests were being sent to reactivate the virtually defunct institutions of religion. Gradually the church regained its lost strength, and by 1808 the number of its adherents living west of the Alleghenies had increased to such an extent that a new diocese was erected at Bardstown, Kentucky. Father Flaget became its first bishop.

Certainly the most colorful priest on the frontier was Dmitri Gallitzin. A Russian prince and son of the Russian ambassador to the Netherlands, he had been reared in the Orthodox Church. Later his mother was converted to Roman Catholicism and the son soon followed her example. He came to the United States shortly after his conversion, with letters of introduction to Bishop Carroll. Determining to serve the church as a priest, he was given theological training and ordained in 1795. Four years later the bishop appointed him priest to a community of German and Irish Catholics living in what is now Cambria County, in western Pennsylvania. There this consecrated priest, known to his parishioners as Father Smith, ministered until his death in 1840.

When Bishop Flaget arrived at Bardstown, there were only six priests to minister to the six thousand Roman Catholics living in Kentucky and Tennessee. As in the case of Protestant ministers, the bishop and his priests were obliged to ride circuit in order to meet the needs of the laymen. Some assistance came from the Dominican Fathers, who had been in Kentucky since 1806 and had founded a college and novitiate. By 1815 there were ten priests and nineteen churches in Kentucky alone, with a Roman Catholic population of 10,000. In addition, Bishop Flaget was responsible for all the faithful dwelling in Ohio, Indiana, Illinois, and as far north as Detroit. He gained some relief when John Baptist David was appointed his coadjutor in 1817. Four years later Ohio was erected into a diocese, with the episcopal seat in Cincinnati. The Dominican Father Edward D. Fenwick was chosen first bishop.

With the purchase of Louisiana in 1803, 15,000 Roman Catholics of French and Spanish descent came under the government of the United States. For the time being the Holy See placed them under the care of Bishop Carroll, an impossible task considering his already burdensome duties. In 1812 he arranged for the appointment of William du Bourg as Administrator Apostolic of Louisiana and the Floridas. Three years later du Bourg became bishop of the Diocese of New Orleans. In 1827 the northern part of this diocese was separated from New Orleans and formed into the Diocese of St. Louis. Its first bishop was the Reverend Joseph Rosati.

THE RESURGENCE OF REVIVALISM

Just before the close of the eighteenth century the disturbing conditions which had brought religious life in the new nation to a low ebb were gradually replaced by forces which promoted a revival of faith. These forces were not essentially different from those which had given rise to the Great Awakening; they were born of a general reaction to spiritual diffidence and manifested themselves in a response to a felt challenge. The prestige of French rationalism had suffered crippling defeat through American indignation over the Reign of Terror. With its passing there was ushered in a new age of romantic idealism, an age of the common man, of popular democracy and crusading evangelism. America's spiritual recovery began with the Second Awakening.

The Revival in the East

As early as 1786 signs of a forthcoming revival were abroad in the South. At Hampden-Sidney College and later at Washington College, both Presbyterian institutions in Virginia, there was an awakening among the student body and a number of decisions to enter the ministry. Many of the men who sought ordination eventually went to the West where they rendered valuable service to Presbyterianism.

The presence of Methodist evangelists in New England after 1790 was probably a contributing factor to the general awakening which took place in that part of the country. But the way was prepared chiefly by the doctrine and preaching of evangelical Congregationalists in the Edwardean tradition. When the revival broke out in the 1790's, it failed to engender the widespread excitement which had accompanied the Great Awakening. Nor did it produce any princes of the pulpit such as Whitefield. But its effects were unquestionably more permanent than those of the earlier revival. In 1791 an awakening took place at North Yarmouth, Maine; the next year it was extended to Lee, Massachusetts, and East Haddam and Lyme, Connecticut. Year by year the revival increased in strength until reaching its full flowering in 1799. A remarkable transformation took place at Yale College where Timothy Dwight, after becoming president in 1795, used his full capacities to win students to an acceptance of the evangelical faith. Through forceful lecturing and preaching he led them to serious consideration of the vital issues of religion and served up satisfying answers to questions grounded in naturalistic philosophy. His appeal lay in his ability to meet the student on his own ground and to speak eloquently and persuasively enough to stir the heart as well as the mind. Due largely to his influence Yale College experienced a notable revival in 1802, a phenomenon which was repeated in subsequent years. Other colleges such as Amherst, Dartmouth, and Williams had similar awakenings.

The theology of the revival reflected the new spirit of democracy. It stood for the sovereignty of God, but departed from Calvinism in its emphasis upon the work of man. The Arminian tendencies of Unitarianism and Methodism undoubtedly influenced the change which was demanded by the spirit of the times. In any case, the classic doctrine of divine election was relegated to the background and men were assured that all who sought salvation might find it through a vital faith and works of righteousness. This activistic emphasis would become more prominent in American evangelicalism as the nineteenth century progressed, expressing itself in the home and foreign missions movement, the founding of church-related educational institutions, and a host of humanitarian and philanthropic organizations.

The Revival on the Frontier

The frontier phase of the Second Awakening was manifestly different from that of the East. It was characterized by frenzied excitement and emotional outbursts, even by physical aberrations. On the other hand, it could be, and frequently was, dignified and orderly, especially in the older and more settled communities where there was naturally a larger measure of decorum. As it was conducted by Presbyterians and Congregationalists, it did not differ radically from the revival in the East. Inasmuch as it presented a Gospel which was Calvinistically interpreted, offering salvation to the elect alone, its range of influence was decidedly limited. The masses had little enthusiasm for such an "undemocratic" theological system and were suspicious of the educated clergy who preached it. As conducted by Methodists and Baptists, however, the revival touched the lives of thousands who would otherwise have remained unmoved. Its offer, presented mainly on an emotional basis, was salvation for all who would accept it in faith. It attracted so many people that it was frequently necessary to hold the great revival meetings out of doors in order to accommodate the surging throngs. Ironically, these outdoor meetings which Methodists and Baptists operated with such success were initiated by Presbyterians, who later repudiated them because of their emotional excesses.

The father of the Second Awakening in the West was James McGready, a Presbyterian minister of Scotch-Irish parentage. While serving in Orange County, North Carolina, he had initiated a revival which resulted in the conversion of twelve men, one of whom was Barton W. Stone. Though McGready's contemporaries usually found him to be ugly and uncouth, Stone was impressed by his "coarse tremulous voice" and his earnestness and zeal for the salvation of souls. Later, in South Carolina, he was accused of "running people distracted." The opposition became so intense that he moved to Logan County, Kentucky, where, in 1796, he became pastor of three congregations located on the Gasper, Red, and Muddy Rivers. There his techniques of vigorous preaching, diligent pastoral work, and the promotion of special days for prayer and fasting resulted in a spiritual awakening. In May, 1797, the Logan County revival broke out in the congregation, at Gasper River. Gradually it picked up strength in spite of opposition, and by the time of the sacramental service at Red River in June, 1800, it had reached its height. For several days meetings were held at the Red River Church with the emotional pitch of the congregation rising steadily with each service. At the observance of the Lord's Supper on Sunday many fell to the floor crying, "What shall I do to be saved?"

Reports of this rather unusual event circulated widely and evoked considerable excitement. Some were horrified by the emotionalism of the services while others saw in them an important technique for the conversion of sinners. When announcement was made that the next sacramental service would be held in July, persons from all over the country flocked to Gasper River. Present at these meetings, which in all probability constituted the first camp meetings to be held in America, were the brothers William and John McGee, Presbyterian and Methodist ministers respectively. They participated in the revival which went on day and night and which was received with such spontaneous enthusiasm that "no person seemed to wish to go home." In the spring of 1801 Barton W. Stone, now a Presbyterian minister, made a long journey across the state of Kentucky to inquire into the nature of the revivals. His description of one of the camp meetings is most instructive.

There, on the edge of a prairie in Logan County, Kentucky, the multitudes came together and continued a number of days and nights encamped on the ground, during which time worship was carried on in some part of the encampment. The scene was new to me and passing strange. It baffled description. Many, very many, fell down as men slain in battle, and continued for hours together in an apparently breathless and motionless state, sometimes for a few moments reviving and exhibiting symptoms of life by a deep groan or piercing shriek, or by a prayer for mercy fervently uttered. After lying there for hours they obtained deliverance. The gloomy cloud that had covered their faces seemed gradually and visibly to disappear, and hope, in smiles, brightened into joy. They would rise, shouting deliverance, and then would address the surrounding multitude in language truly eloquent and impressive. With astonishment did I hear men, women, and children declaring the wonderful works of God and the glorious mysteries of the gospel. Their appeals were solemn, heart-penetrating, bold, and free. Under such circumstances many others would fall down into the same state from which the speakers had just been delivered.[1]

Upon returning to his congregations of Concord and Cane Ridge in Bourbon County, Stone gave a full report of what he had seen and heard. The people were profoundly stirred and within a few months another revival broke out at Cane Ridge.

The Cane Ridge camp meeting of August, 1801, proved to be the colossus of camp meetings in Kentucky. People flocked from all parts of the surrounding country, even from Ohio, to attend what promised to be a truly remarkable occasion. The ministers who gathered at Cane Ridge confessed that they had never seen anything like it. Some calculated that 20,000 people were present; one placed the figure as high as 25,000. But when one considers that at this time there were not more than a quarter of a million persons scattered throughout the state, the figure seems somewhat high. The meeting, which had been set up under the auspices of the Presbyterians, turned out to be an interdenominational enterprise with Baptist and Methodist preachers joining enthusiastically in the proceedings. Preaching stands were set up in various parts of the area and crowds pressed around them to hear the fiery-tongued evangelists pour out their impassioned appeals for hardened sinners to become "washed in the blood of the Lamb." By Sunday the confusion had grown so great that denominational distinctions were laid aside and lead tokens to admit persons to the service of communion were passed out to 750 people with no questions asked about church affiliation.

The meeting was accompanied by extraordinary outbursts of feeling on the part of the participants. William Burke, a Methodist preacher, claimed that as he preached the word of God hundreds fell prostrate before him, writhing in agony. Others would occasionally rush to their feet and proclaim the wonders of redemption in stentorian tones that would cause the most fearless frontiersman to tremble. Little children also were affected by the surging tide of emotion and, according to reports which were probably highly exaggerated, would at times exhort the crowds to

[1] Quoted in L. W. Bacon, *A History of American Christianity* (Scribner, 1900), 234.

accept Christ as their merciful Saviour. James B. Finley, reared a Presbyterian and later to become a Methodist minister, attended the proceedings out of curiosity, determined not to be carried away by the
emotionalism of religious fanatics. After a short time he found that his
heart was pounding with excitement and his knees were becoming soft as
jelly. When he could stand it no longer, he rushed into the woods, then
finally made his way to a tavern where he fortified himself with a shot of
brandy. For hours he was captivated by thoughts of guilt and fits of crying. The next day toward evening he knelt in the woods to pray and experienced such an emotional seizure that he fell prostrate to the ground.
Friends carried him to shelter; when he awoke he felt a wonderful sense
of release and went home shouting, weeping, and laughing, completely
unable to control his emotions.

The revival blew hot and cold. In the Presbyterian camp it was greeted
with mingled feelings of approbation and contempt. The Presbyterian
General Assembly of 1805, while giving faint praise to the revival, observed also that "God is a God of order and not of confusion; and whatever tends to destroy the comely order of his worship is not from him, for
he is consistent with himself." The commissioners may well have been
influenced by the reports of such anti-revivalist ministers as John Lyle,
who, while on a visit to Cumberland Presbytery, in Tennessee, in 1805,
prepared a rather unsympathetic description of a camp meeting. In it, he
speaks of one of the more recent manifestations of the nervous epidemic,
a phenomenon known as "the jerks."

The heads of the jerking patients flew, with wondrous quickness, from side
to side, in various directions, and their necks doubled like a flail in the hands
of a thresher. Their faces were distorted and black, as if they were strangling,
and their eyes seemed to flash horror and distortion. Numbers of them roared
out in sounds the most wild and terrific. . . .
The people camped in waggons and tents around the stand. I retired to the
Rev. William M'Gee's. The people who lodged here appeared engaged in singing, conversing, leaping and shouting. They appeared much like a drinking
party when heard from the other room; but when I drew nigh, found their
language and rejoicings were of a religious kind.[2]

The Baptists and Methodists had no such reservations. With or without
the "jerks" and other abnormal manifestations, they used the techniques
of the camp meeting to the limit of their capacities. To such leaders as
Bishop Asbury the camp meeting became Methodism's harvest time. As
the years passed there was less cooperation with Presbyterians until the
revivals came to be characterized by denominational exclusiveness. Even

[2] Armstrong, Loetscher, and Anderson, *op. cit.*, 113.

the hymns revealed a growing spirit of sectarianism, as in this favorite of Methodist evangelists:

> The *world*, the *Devil* and *Tom Paine*
> Have try'd their force, but all in vain,
> They can't prevail, the reason is,
> The Lord Defends the Methodist.

Between the years 1800 and 1804 the revival spread like wildfire through Kentucky, Tennessee, Ohio, western New York and Pennsylvania, the old South, and western New England. The chief agency for its promotion was the camp meeting, which became so popular that by 1811 there were some 400 to 500 held in the United States, according to an estimate of Bishop Asbury. Long after other denominations gave them up, the Methodists continued to hold annual camp meetings, principally with the thought of adding significantly to the list of new communicants. The spontaneous nature of the meetings was lost and they became highly formalized, usually lasting four days and running according to a rigidly prescribed plan. By the 1840's their peak of popularity had passed in the trans-Allegheny West and the revivals gradually diminished. One factor in their decline was the frequency with which they were held in contiguous areas. Another was their bad reputation which unfortunately grew worse with the passage of time. The trend from henceforth was toward the indoor revival.

To critics of the revival, the principal weakness of the movement lay in its emphasis on an appeal to the emotions rather than to the intellect. Conversion brought on through the "pressure of artificial excitement" could lead only to backsliding as soon as the spirit of the occasion had grown dim. Certainly many conversions proved to be impermanent. Objection was also raised to the immorality encouraged by a system which brought persons of both sexes into close proximity and fanned the flames of emotion until they reached white heat. It was sometimes alleged that the immoralities of the camp meeting were of the most base variety and that "there were more souls made than saved" while they were being conducted. But such charges have little basis in fact. That behavior at the camp meetings was boisterous, and manners crude, are indisputable facts. Under the circumstances, one could scarcely have expected otherwise.

To understand the tremendous effect of the revival one must bear in mind the social conditions which prevailed. Here was a population, whose temper was particularly susceptible to intense excitement, transplanted into a wild region where there were few social restrictions due to convention or civil law. Although they had originated in a culture which recognized the necessity of at least formal religion they had torn themselves free from its control and were living in careless disregard of religious values. Suddenly they were convicted with a sense of their culpability before God. This was accomplished not through a settled preaching ministry which gradually and regularly planted seeds of Christian thought within their minds, but through an intensive revival campaign which lasted for days. As multitudes of people were pressed together, engaged in the task of contemplating momentous truths which were being communicated through impassioned repetition, there was bound to be a good deal of tension which would have to be released. This explains the sudden outcries, hysterical weeping and laughter, faintings and trances. In such a tense group only one or two incidents would be necessary to send the entire crowd into a state of frenzy. Multitudes would fall prostrate to the earth, "spiritually slain." Some would lie motionless, unable to utter a syllable. Some could speak but found it impossible to move. Others leaped like madmen over the benches and tree stumps, then rushed from sight into the forest crying "Lost! Lost!"

But there were leaders in the revival who appealed to the reason as well as to the emotions and who measured their success not by the professions of faith made at the altar but by the quickening of the spiritual life and the elevation of community morals. Dr. George A. Baxter, president of Washington College in Virginia, observed while on a trip through Kentucky in 1801:

. . . A profane expression was hardly ever heard. A religious awe seemed to pervade the country. Upon the whole, I think the revival in Kentucky the most extraordinary that has ever visited the church of Christ; and, all things considered, it was peculiarly adapted to the circumstances of the country into which it came. Infidelity was triumphant and religion was on the point of expiring. Something extraordinary seemed necessary to arrest the attention of giddy people who were ready to conclude that Christianity was a fable and futurity a delusion. This revival has done it. It has confounded infidelity and brought numbers beyond calculation under serious impressions.[3]

Equally enthusiastic was the Reverend David Rice, who reported to the Presbyterian Synod of Kentucky in 1803:

. . . Drunkards, profane swearers, liars, quarrelsome persons, etc., are remarkably reformed. . . . A number of families who had lived apparently without the fear of God, in folly and in vice, without any religious instruction or any proper government, are now reduced to order and are daily joining in the worship of God, reading his word, singing his praises, and offering up their supplications to a throne of grace. . . .[4]

[3] Quoted in Bacon, op. cit., 237.
[4] Ibid., 237–238.

That such apparent transformation of character was short-lived among many persons converted at the revivals must be freely conceded; on the other hand, many others demonstrated lasting moral improvement as a result of their experience. With all its excesses, the revival was thus religiously constructive and left a positive influence for good that would not be effaced from American society for years to come.

13

The Great Missionary

Enterprise

THE PEACE OF GHENT, WHICH OFFICIALLY RANG DOWN THE CURTAIN ON THE most doubtful military victory in American history, demonstrated to the world that the future of the United States as an independent nation was assured. More than that, it presaged the rise of a powerful nationalistic spirit which for a time eclipsed the older sectionalism of the East. The breeding ground of nationalism was in the West. It beckoned to all classes and conditions of men, from all states and countries, who believed in America, "the land of the free and the home of the brave." As Americans looked out upon a West which had been so wondrously nationalized through the Louisiana Purchase, they dreamed a dream. They saw that their "manifest destiny" was the conquest of the entire continent, that one day the standard of the Republic would fly over that gigantic sweep of territory which plunged westward to greet the ocean. The accession of Florida, Texas, Oregon, and California, was the dream translated into reality. It was perhaps the most optimistic period in our national life. The favorite theme of orators was the glorious future of the country.

264

Even the highly nationalistic decisions of Chief Justice Marshall and the celebrated Monroe Doctrine reflected the spirit of the age.

It is hardly surprising that the new spirit of nationalism should also have made an impact upon organized religion. Many clergymen of insight saw that the center of population was fast moving westward and that in time the strength of the country would lie west of the Allegheny Mountains. They thus became convinced that the churches would have to develop strong missionary programs if frontier society was to be won to Christian ideals and practices. Their motivation included but was not dominated by any mere sentimental affection for the frontiersman or evangelical zeal for his conversion. They regarded missions as the means whereby the West, the nation, and ultimately the world might be redeemed from the disastrous effects of immorality, skepticism, and materialism. The urgency of this task was clearly recognized in the report of the Reverend J. Van Vecten, a clergyman of the Dutch Reformed Church, in a report to the American Home Missionary Society in 1829.

. . . . The strength of the nation lies beyond the Alleghany. The centre of dominion is fast moving in that direction. The ruler of this country is growing up in the great valley: leave him without the gospel, and he will be a ruffian giant, who will regard neither the decencies of civilization, nor the charities of religion. The tide of population will not wait till we have settled every metaphysical point of theology, and every canon of church government. While we are deliberating, the mighty swell is rising higher and higher on the sides of the mountain.[1]

Various theological and philosophical forces also helped to prepare the way for the great missionary enterprise. One of the more important was renewed emphasis upon the dignity and worth of man. The Unitarian and Universalist movements which blossomed in the declining years of the eighteenth century found man to be a noble work of God rather than a morally depraved being who could do no good thing without divine election. Coupled with the natural rights philosophy and Jeffersonian individualism, both popular ideologies of the period, the concept of the worth of man tended to awaken more interest in the question of human advancement and thus indirectly aid the cause of missions. More direct support came from the Arminian doctrine of God's infinite love and mercy for all sinful men, which was being presented by the burgeoning Methodist denomination. If God's plan of salvation extended to all men, then all men ought to have the opportunity to accept it. Such an opportunity could come only through the extension of missions. Equally if not more influential was the disinterested benevolence of a theology authored

[1] Quoted in W. B. Posey, *The Presbyterian Church in the Old Southwest, 1778–1838* (John Knox, 1952), 111.

by New England Congregationalist Samuel Hopkins. He believed that since God wills the greatest good for the greatest number, the true Christian will sacrifice his personal interests for the greater good of the whole. To many serious-minded persons this constituted a call to dedicate their lives to mission work among the "heathen," whether in the United States or abroad. When these ideas were charged with the electric excitement of the Second Awakening, the American missionary movement sprang to life.

THE HOME MISSIONS MOVEMENT

The most immediate and vital missionary concern of many Christian leaders in the era which followed the War of 1812 was the conversion of America, which in three decades would push its borders to the great Pacific. By 1844 expansionist sentiment, despite considerable opposition in the East, reached a new peak. It was enhanced a year later with the annexation of Texas and by the acquisition of the Oregon Territory, running north to the 49th parallel, in 1846. The year 1846 also witnessed occupation of California and the outbreak of war with Mexico. In 1848, the Mexican Cession brought California, Nevada, Utah, Arizona, and parts of New Mexico, Colorado, and Wyoming within the territory of the United States. The Gadsden Purchase of 1853 added nearly 30,000 square miles in southern New Mexico and Arizona. While these newly acquired territories afforded a real challenge for missions, so did the vast area of the Louisiana Purchase which was steadily being filled with settlements. The challenge did not go unanswered.

State and National Missionary Societies

The predominant missionary societies on the frontier were operated by Congregationalists and Presbyterians; Baptists and Methodists made relatively little use of such agencies even after they had been founded. Among New England Congregationalists there had been little interest in the West for its own sake or as part of a growing nation; the spirit of sectionalism held too firm a grip on the life of the people. And yet the prospect of hundreds of citizens moving westward and being cut off from the social institutions of the old Northeast was more than they could bear. In Connecticut where the exodus reached staggering proportions, plans were made to provide the settlers with the ministrations of the Gospel according to Congregationalism. As early as 1798, the Missionary Society of Connecticut was called into existence, its chief purposes being to convert the Indians and promote Christianity in the new settlements. During its first year of operation, six missionaries went to preach to new communities in Vermont, New York, and Pennsylvania. One of the pioneer missionaries was Joseph Badger who, between the years 1802 and 1806, founded the first churches in the Western Reserve. He and his associates were often treated as *persona non grata* upon their arrival in communities where large segments of the population originated outside New England. The Congregational establishment and the Federalist politics of New Englanders were highly unpopular among the more democratically and individualistically inclined settlers who feared that the Congregational missionaries had aristocratic designs upon the West. Their influence was thus restricted almost entirely to their own people.

Other societies, somewhat weaker than that of Connecticut, were founded in Massachusetts (1799), New Hampshire (1801), Rhode Island (1801), Vermont (1807), and Maine (1809). They were supported by auxiliary organizations such as the Boston Female Society for Missionary Purposes and the Female Cent Institution, and were encouraged by such missionary-minded clergymen as Samuel Hopkins. A great impetus was given to the cause of missions when the Missionary Societies of Massachusetts and Connecticut, together with the Philadelphia Bible Society and the Philadelphia Missionary Society, commissioned Samuel J. Mills, a recent graduate of Andover Theological Seminary, and John D. Schermerhorn of the Dutch Reformed Church to attempt extensive missionary tours. During 1812 and 1813 they traveled through Ohio, Indiana, Kentucky, and Tennessee and down the Mississippi to New Orleans, gathering data on the religious conditions and opportunities in each area. Their report, published in 1814 under the title *Correct View of that Part of the United States which Lies West of the Alleghany Mountains*, drew the attention of many Easterners to the importance of home missions. Mills made another journey in 1814 and 1815, accompanied by Daniel Smith, and brought back vital information concerning the religious needs of the people in the Mississippi Valley.

At the close of the War of 1812 the new nationalistic spirit seemed to call for a program of home missions on a national level. The most important of these new national agencies was the American Home Missionary Society, founded in 1826 in New York by 126 delegates from the Presbyterian, Congregational, Dutch Reformed, and Associate Reformed denominations. From the outset the work of the Society flourished; during its first year it employed 169 missionaries. By 1833 it numbered 606 missionaries among its employees and 801 congregations and missionary districts. For a decade or more the Society suffered from the withdrawal of the Old School Presbyterians in 1837 because of the Society's alleged theological errors and practical indiscretions. By 1850, however, it had fully recovered and was able to employ 1065 persons for missionary labors.

The work of the American Home Missionary Society was centered largely in the areas north of Virginia, Kentucky, and Tennessee. Its failure in the South and Southwest may be explained partially by the fact that most of its missionaries originated in states north of Maryland and had a natural bias against functioning in regions where slavery was practiced. Another factor was that the missionaries had a preference for work among people of like experience rather than among those who had been reared in a different social and religious setting.

The Society's program called for the organization of churches in new settlements as quickly as possible and for the subsidization of churches whose poverty rendered impossible the support of a minister. Such churches might apply to the Society for aid. If the application was approved, the Society provided one-fourth of the minister's annual support, calculating that sum to be four hundred dollars and its own share therefore to be one hundred dollars. Since a missionary was not permitted to supplement his income through additional employment, it was difficult for him to remain in the field, especially if he had a family. The Society's niggardly policy in this respect was counterbalanced by generosity in another. In 1859, a Swedish Lutheran pastor testified that although his denomination was not affiliated with the Society he was granted financial assistance with no questions asked concerning his denominational connections.

Most of the agents of the Society went out one by one, each being assigned to a given field of responsibility. Stephen Peet, for example, went to Wisconsin under the auspices of the Society in 1837; he not only established new churches and supplied them with ministers, but was instrumental in founding Beloit College and Chicago Theological Seminary. Samuel H. Willey organized a Presbyterian church in San Francisco in 1850 and became one of the founders of the University of California. George H. Atkinson founded Congregational churches in Oregon and Washington and helped introduce wheat-growing in the eastern part of those territories.

On the whole, missionaries sent out by the Society had little respect for their Baptist and Methodist competitors, regarding them as untutored and incompetent. Flavel Bascom, a Yale graduate who came to Illinois as a missionary in 1833 and six years later became superintendent of Home Missions in that state, mentions in his *Autobiography* a sermon he heard from a rustic evangelist.

. . . . He commenced by saying that his text was a passage which had come to his mind while the Brother was speaking, viz. "we have this treasure of the Gospel in earthen vessels" &c. This passage, said he, teaches man's impotency to keep the commandments of God. Having thus expounded it, he never referred to it again, but commenced an indiscriminate quotation of passages from the Genesis to Revelations and back again, with apparently no connection between them except that some word in one verse would serve as a catch-word to remind him of another. Thus he went bellowing and blowing through the Bible shedding no more light upon the passages quoted, than the roar of artillery does upon our declaration of independence.[2]

Disrespect between the two sides was, however, quite mutual. Peter Cartwright, the Methodist circuit rider, had harsh words for young missionaries sent out "to civilize and Christianize the poor heathen of the West." He singled out a "fresh, green, live Yankee from down East," who had just completed his college training and had been employed by the Home Missionary Society to direct the light of the Gospel upon the darkened areas of the West. Having been educated to believe that Methodist preachers were nothing more than a crude, illiterate collection of boors, he longed for the chance to demonstrate his superiority and hurl "us poor upstart preachers in the West, especially Methodist preachers, into the shades of everlasting darkness." Yet in spite of misunderstandings, rivalries, and clashes over doctrinal and social questions, the frontier manifested a certain unity and unusual tolerance. An attitude of forbearance and cooperation was made mandatory by the very want of resources and accommodations which plagued frontier society. On the other hand, when a proposal was made in Illinois in 1840 that Christians disband their organizations and affiliate with a new sect called "Unionists," there was good thinking behind the reaction of a certain deacon. He was opposed to the union on the ground that he did not believe in "being united all to pieces."

Denominational Missions

While the Presbyterians were officially connected with the American Home Missionary Society, they never gave that organization their undivided support. As early as 1802 the General Assembly had created a Standing Committee of Missions to plan for religious cultivation of the expanding population and the spreading frontier. In 1816 this committee evolved into the Board of Missions, which was renamed the Board of Domestic Missions after the establishment of the Board of Foreign Missions in 1837. The most notable change in policy after 1816 was the abandonment of the circuit-riding system in favor of the subsidization of small churches so they might enjoy the services of resident pastors. With a new impetus to mission work the Presbyterian Church grew to such an extent that by 1828 it had become established in most states east of the Mississippi and in Missouri, Oklahoma, Arkansas, and Louisiana, west of the Great River. Like many denominations developing in the Southwest, Presbyterians favored the extension of American influence in territories

[2] Quoted in W. W. Sweet, *Religion on the American Frontier. The Congregationalists* (Chicago, 1939), 258.

held by Mexico, believing that their accession would open the door to the Protestant evangelization of the Roman Catholic residents.

The effectiveness of Presbyterian mission work was curtailed between 1817 and 1837 by the struggle of Old and New School factions over the organization and procedure of home missions. The Old School side maintained that the missionary enterprise should be conducted wholly under the auspices of church-controlled agencies. The New School wing was active in winning approval of Presbyterian participation in the interdenominational American Home Missionary Society. Until the division of 1837 each group supported its favorite agency, thus contributing to a general confusion which detracted from Presbyterian success on the frontier.

In 1802 Baptists in Boston established the Massachusetts Baptist Missionary Society "to promote the knowledge of evangelic truth in the new settlements within these United States." The Lake Baptist Missionary Society was founded at Pompey, New York, five years later. In 1825 it merged with the Baptist Domestic Missionary Convention of the State of New York to form the Baptist Missionary Convention of the State of New York. This body sent missionaries to New Jersey, Pennsylvania, Ohio, Michigan, and Wisconsin. In 1817 the General Missionary (Triennial) Convention of the Baptist Denomination in the United States, which had been organized in 1814 largely through the efforts of Luther Rice, also began to send missionaries to preach in the new western settlements. Between 1813 and 1815, Rice had gone on extended tours, raising funds and laying the groundwork for a missionary program in the West.

One of the outstanding leaders in the Baptist missions movement was John Mason Peck (1789–1838), a convert from Congregationalism. In 1818, under the auspices of the Triennial Convention, he organized a church in St. Louis, then devoted several years to the establishment of Bible societies and schools in Illinois, Indiana, and Missouri. With the assistance of Jonathan Going, a pastor in Worcester, Massachusetts, he helped to found the American Baptist Home Mission Society in 1832. This society eventually extended its ministrations to persons living beyond the borders of the United States. During its first year it placed more than fifty missionaries in New York, Ohio, Michigan, Indiana, and Illinois. Perhaps the most colorful of these missionaries was Ezra Fisher, who founded churches in Indiana, Illinois, and Iowa. Attracted by the Far West, he journeyed to Oregon in 1845 and returned with carefully prepared recommendations as to what the church might do in that region. He spent the remaining years of his life as pastor of small churches.

The Methodists, though among the earliest to carry the Gospel to the frontier, were relatively late in forming missionary societies. Interest, however, was aroused by the work of John Stewart, a freeborn mulatto, among the Wyandot Indians of Ohio in 1816. The program evolving there was taken over in 1817 by the Ohio Conference but required considerable support from the churches in the East if it was to be continued. Nathan Bangs, Presiding Elder of the New York District, envisioned the possibilities of building a great missionary organization which might minister not only to the Indians but to all races and classes of men. Due to his efforts and those of the managers of the Methodist Book Concern in New York, the Methodist Missionary Society was established in 1819 and given full approval the following year by the General Conference.

The Methodist Missionary Society cooperated with the Annual Conferences in the creation of new mission fields and the recruitment of an itinerant ministry. Thus in 1829 the Illinois Conference founded three missions and appointed a committee chaired by Peter Cartwright to estimate the cost of their support. Two years later the Conference organized a missionary district and appointed Jesse Walker, one of the most distinguished missionaries in the West, to superintend its three missions. By 1836 there were 110 missionaries serving in 109 Conference missions.

Though the Episcopalians were somewhat tardy in entering the home missions movement, in 1821 they organized the Domestic and Foreign Missionary Society of the Protestant Episcopal Church. In 1835 it was declared that all communicants of the church were members of the society. That same year the General Convention inaugurated the policy of electing missionary bishops for territories which as yet had no full ecclesiastical organization. Jackson Kemper was the first clergyman chosen to preside over the advance of the church in the Northwest; Francis Hawks was elected to perform a similar function in the Southwest. Hawks declined consecration and three years later Leonidas Polk was elected Missionary Bishop of Arkansas. In that year the first Episcopal missionaries entered Texas. Under the influence of the Oxford Movement in England, a group of young men from General Theological Seminary in New York went to Wisconsin in 1841 where they established a semi-monastic community and began to train theological students. By 1850 the church had begun missionary work in California.

ANTIMISSIONISM

The initial efforts of Luther Rice and John Peck on behalf of Baptist missions had encountered little opposition on the frontier. Indeed, the western communities made impressive contributions to the cause and set up auxiliary organizations for missions. By 1820, however, it was obvious that a reaction was in progress. Individual churches and later associations in Indiana and Illinois were taking action not to support either Baptist home or foreign mission societies. Within a year this attitude had spread so widely in the West that few persons or churches dared to oppose it.

Congregations were expelled from associations simply for trying to justify the activities of the mission boards.

A number of factors account for this amazing transformation. Perhaps the most popularly accepted explanation was that missionary organizations were contrary to the Scriptures. Since no ecclesiastical body other than the church was sanctioned by the Bible, the evangelization of the unconverted would have to be accomplished solely through the agency of the church. But there was also a theological reason behind the opposition. The Arminian teachings of a general atonement and human free will had proved disturbing to many Baptists who adhered to a hyper-Calvinist position. Such persons concluded that missions were unnecessary since God needed no human help to bring his elect to salvation; those who were of the non-elect could not be saved through all the preaching in the world. It was an affront to the Deity to assume that missionaries could change the ordered pattern of events.

Antimissionism was also grounded in a practical objection to authority. Many Baptists feared that the evolution of a strong missionary society would carry with it increased centralization of power. They contemplated the prospect of missionary agents sending undesirable men to the frontier and placing them in churches where they were not wanted. They could even imagine a day in which the congregations would be totally dependent upon some national denominational agency with their autonomy being dissolved into nothingness. Besides, the average frontiersman was suspicious of the better-educated professional minister usually sent out from the East. He preferred the farmer-preacher without benefit of education or salary. John Taylor typified this spirit in his attack on Luther Rice, whom he referred to as a "modern Tetzel," who worked primarily for the sake of financial gain. "Tetzel's great eloquence, and success in getting money, alarmed first Martin Luther, and afterwards the chief of the States of Germany. Our Luther by his measures of cunning in the same art of Tetzel may alarm all the American Baptists." Undoubtedly such attacks were motivated to a considerable extent by jealousy on the part of the farmer-preachers who were apprehensive over the possible success of their competitors. Although they received no salary, they experienced a certain gratification at being able to hold power and influence over others. This fact was revealed in the answer given by one of them when being questioned as to his reasons for opposing the missionaries. "Well, if you must know, Brother Moderator, you know the big trees in the woods overshadow the little ones; and these missionaries will be all great men, and the people will all go to hear them preach, and we shall all be put down. That's the objection."

When word was circulated that the churches would be taxed for the support of missionaries assigned to them, opposition burst out in full flame. The Apple Creek Anti-mission Association in Illinois was founded in 1830 largely as a result of this fear of taxation. Its constitution provided that no missionary preacher should have the privilege of speaking before the association. Two years later the Sugar Creek Association was organized in Indiana. According to article fourteen of its constitution:

Any church suffering their members to unite with any of the Mission Conventions, Colleges, Tracts, Bible, Temperance, &tc. Societies, and failing to deal with their members, shall be considered guilty of such violation of the principles of the union, that the Association when put in possession of a knowledge of such facts shall punish such Churches as being not of us.

Similar action was taken by scores of Baptist churches and associations, particularly those situated in the West, between 1820 and 1840. Many congregations were torn asunder by the strife. It has been estimated that by 1846 there were 68,068 antimission Baptists in America. Of these, two-thirds made their homes in the states of Kentucky, Tennessee, Alabama, Mississippi, Ohio, Indiana, Illinois, and Missouri. Significant numbers were found also in western Virginia, North Carolina, and Georgia.

Antimissionism expressed itself chiefly through two denominational groups. The first, known as the Two-Seed-in-the-Spirit Predestinarian Baptist, was organized in the 1820's by Elder Daniel Parker, a preacher in southeastern Illinois. He developed a theory of the two seeds in Eve, imparted by God and Satan, which produce good and bad people. God predestines those who are to be saved and rejects those who are to be lost. Neither missions nor ministers are needed by God to bring about the salvation of His elect. The second group, denominated the Primitive Baptists, came into being in 1835, when the Chemung Association in New York State broke with all associations which had missionary societies on the ground that the practice had no precedent in New Testament times. They were somewhat less extreme in their views and did not oppose evangelistic preaching as long as it was not part of an organized missionary program.

Among the most vocal of the opponents of missions were John Taylor, Daniel Parker, and Alexander Campbell. Taylor's pamphlet entitled *Thoughts on Missions*, published in 1819, contained an angry attack upon the missionaries; in it he charged that their primary object was to get money and that their methods were like those of the horse leech which sucks blood from its victims. Equally unrestrained was Daniel Parker of Illinois who in 1820 published a thirty-eight page pamphlet entitled *A Public Address to the Baptist Society*, in which he was sharply critical of the Baptist Board of Foreign Missions. His principal fear seems to have been that the mission boards would eventually destroy the democratic structure of the church. Between 1813 and 1830, when Alexander Campbell was affiliated with the Baptists, he attacked missions for the reason that they lacked scriptural authority. His arguments were circulated through his periodicals called the *Christian Baptist* and the *Millennial Harbinger,* begun in 1823 and 1829 respectively. He later changed his mind in regard to missions and came out strongly in their behalf.

INDIAN MISSIONS

From the beginnings of American colonization there seems to have been a feeling on the part of white settlers that they had some moral and spiritual responsibility toward the natives whom they intended to dispossess of their lands. This benevolent attitude was, however, almost always eclipsed by the tendency to exploit the hapless aborigines. With the drive again to the frontier which had virtually come to a standstill during the Revolution, the process of pushing the Indian westward began anew. By 1789 the Oneida, Tuscarora, and Cayuga tribes of New York had given up their lands in return for cash settlements, annuities, and reservations. Between 1802 and 1806 the Cherokee, Choctaw, and Chickasaw Indians lost millions of acres in central Georgia, southern Tennessee, and Mississippi Territory, and were forced to live in restricted areas. Meanwhile, in the Northwest, Governor William Henry Harrison of Indiana Territory was gaining cessions from the Kickapoo, Wea, and Delaware tribes. Due to further accessions from the Kaskaskia, Sauk, and Fox tribes, the United States held control of eastern Michigan, southern Indiana, and most of Illinois by the end of 1807. The next step was to dominate the Lake Plains. In 1826 the government gained large tracts of land in Indiana which had formerly belonged to the Potawatomi and the Miami Indians. Six years later the Winnebago moved out of Wisconsin bound for the Far West. In 1831 the Choctaws and Chickasaws, having been persuaded to cede their remaining lands in Georgia and Alabama, set out for new homes in Arkansas. When the Cherokees of Georgia resisted removal, they were forcibly ejected by the state authorities in 1838. This policy of removal was supported by many highly respected churchmen who were seemingly unmoved by its obvious injustice. For the time being the only future for the Indian appeared to lie west of the Mississippi River.

The painful experiences of Indian wars on the frontier combined with the revival of missionary interest early in the national era persuaded many Christian leaders of the necessity of Indian missions. It occurred to them that the conversion of the natives might be a peaceful way of solving a difficult problem and that it might be a potent means of furthering the Kingdom of God in America. In the northern part of the country, considerable interest had been aroused in the Indians who, about 1795, withdrew from New England and settled in northern and western New York. The Northern Missionary Society of the State of New York, organized in 1800, sent representatives to work among the Oneidas. The Massachusetts

Missionary Society began missionary activities among the Wyandottes in 1811. About the same time the Connecticut Missionary Society sent out emissaries, one of whom carried the Gospel to the Ojibways in northern Michigan. Baptist missionary societies in New York and Massachusetts cooperated in 1807 to support a representative among the Tuscaroras in western New York. Various yearly meetings of the Friends carried on Indian missions in the Northwest Territory. The Moravians began a mission on the White River in Indiana in 1799 which lasted but seven years.

In 1823 the Methodists opened a mission among the Potawatomies on the Fox River in northern Illinois; in little more than a decade the work had been extended to include the New York tribes and the Winnebagos and Western Chippewas in Wisconsin. Jesse Walker of the Illinois Conference thus describes his mission to the Potawatomies:

. . . . In the spring of 1825, together with five white families, I proceeded to the mouth of Fox river, shortly after which I had a most satisfactory council with five chiefs of said tribe. We immediately built cabins for the accommodation of the families. I opened a school, into which I received fourteen Indian children; but finding that the school was not located on Indian land, I proceeded up Fox river about thirteen miles, selected a situation, and am now preparing to remove to it, which I will accomplish as soon as possible. . . .[3]

In 1820 Isaac McCoy (1784–1846), an outstanding leader of Baptist Indian missions, founded an Indian school at Fort Wayne, Indiana. Two years afterward he established a mission near what is now Niles, Michigan, and named it Carey in honor of the eminent Baptist missionary to India. Remarkable results accompanied his ministry there. Eleazer Williams of the Protestant Episcopal Church carried on a fruitful mission after 1823 among the Oneidas in Wisconsin. Successful too were the priests sent out by Bishop Fenwick of the Roman Catholic Diocese of Cincinnati to the Indians in Michigan and Wisconsin. They established schools and ministered in countless ways to the natives. Perhaps the most influential was Frederic Baraga, a Slavic immigrant, who founded missions in Michigan and Wisconsin. He later became vicar apostolic of the area and finally first Bishop of Sault Ste. Marie-Marquette.

In the South and Southwest important Indian mission work was undertaken by both Protestants and Roman Catholics. The Moravians of North Carolina sent a mission to the Cherokees in Georgia in 1801; it flourished until the forcible removal of the tribe brought its activities to an end. In 1804 the Presbyterians established a school for the Cherokees under the leadership of Gideon Blackburn; the Baptist Triennial Convention entered the field thirteen years later. In 1817 Cyrus Kingsbury founded a mission in Tennessee under the auspices of the American Board of Commissioners

---

[3] Quoted in Sweet, *Religion in the Development of American Culture*, 149.

for Foreign Missions. It featured a fine school and Christian literature in the vernacular. The following year the Board planted a mission among the Choctaws. By 1830 the American Board was conducting missions for the Cherokees in Tennessee and Arkansas, the Choctaws and Chickasaws in South Carolina and Georgia, and the Creeks and Osages in Arkansas and Missouri. In the 1820's the southern conferences of the Methodist Church sent emissaries to the Creeks in Georgia, the Cherokees in Alabama, and the Choctaws in Mississippi. The Baptists began their missions among the North Carolina Cherokees in 1818.

West of the Mississippi a number of interesting missionary projects were initiated prior to the Civil War. Ever since the celebrated explorations of Lewis and Clark in 1804 and 1805 Americans had looked with eagerness to the opening of the Pacific Northwest. To the various denominations this new territory afforded a decided evangelistic challenge. In 1834, Jason Lee (1803–1845), by appointment of the Methodists, made a hazardous overland journey to the Willamette Valley of Oregon and, with the help of later reinforcements, established several missions in that area. When the work among the Indians proved fruitless, the missionaries turned their attention to the religious needs of white settlers who shortly thereafter began to arrive in the Oregon country.

The nascence of mission work in the Pacific Northwest under the auspices of the American Board of Commissioners for Foreign Missions was in 1836, when Marcus Whitman, a physician, and his wife, and the Reverend and Mrs. Henry H. Spalding, all Presbyterians, were appointed its agents to the Oregon territory. Whitman established his headquarters at Waiilatpu among the Cayuses in what is now Washington, while Spalding took up work among the Nez Perces at Lapwai, about 125 miles away. Two years later the first Protestant church west of the Rockies was founded with Spalding as pastor and Whitman as elder. By 1846 the Oregon mission had three stations and eight workers. The two leaders not only trained the Indians in religious subjects but taught them new methods of agriculture. For a time their efforts were rewarded with phenomenal success. Then, in 1847, a rumor was started among the Cayuses that Dr. Whitman was responsible for a series of epidemics then prevalent. The result was an Indian attack upon the mission, during which Dr. and Mrs. Whitman and twelve other persons were massacred. The Oregon mission was closed and not until 1871 did Spalding return to the Nez Perces.

The American Board of Commissioners for Foreign Missions also inaugurated a missionary program among the Sioux or Dakotas in Minnesota and North and South Dakota. In 1835 Thomas S. Williamson, a physician, led a party of missionaries into Sioux territory and founded a mission among them near the present site of Minneapolis. They were assisted in this endeavor by the brothers Samuel W. and Gideon H. Pond, who had come to work among the Sioux in 1834 as free-lance missionaries. The most distinguished ministry in this area was performed by Stephen R. Riggs, who arrived in 1837 and joined Williamson in founding schools and churches.

The labors performed by Roman Catholic missionaries west of the Mississippi were most important. In 1823, Bishop Du Bourg of Louisiana and the Floridas requested the Jesuits, whose order had been restored by Pius VII in 1814, to care for the spiritual welfare of the Indians living along the Missouri River and its tributaries. At Florissant, near St. Louis, they erected a school for Indian boys which was under the direction of Charles Felix Van Quickenborne. Other missions were established among the Osage Indians in Kansas and the Potawatomies in Iowa and Kansas. Most famous of the Jesuit missionaries to the Indians was the Belgian, Pierre-Jean De Smet (1801–1873). At the request of the Indians dwelling in the Columbia region, Father De Smet set out in 1840 on a missionary journey to the Oregon country where he founded missions among the Flatheads, Kalispels, and Coeur d'Alenes. Farther to the northwest, in Alaska, Russian Orthodox missionaries had begun the work of evangelization as early as 1794. The most important religious activities prior to Alaska's purchase by the United States were carried on by John Veniaminoff, a priest who arrived in the Aleutian Islands in 1824; he later moved to Sitka, the capital, and was made bishop.

NEGRO MISSIONS AND CHURCHES

During the colonial period several Protestant denominations had developed missionary programs for the Negroes. These were continued and augmented after national independence had been won. The great majority of Christianized Negroes affiliated with the Baptist and Methodist churches, largely because they held the greatest emotional appeal. It has been estimated that of the 468,000 Negroes in the South who were church members in 1859, 215,000 were Methodists and 175,000 were Baptists. The next most popular denomination among southern Negroes was the Disciples of Christ.

As early as 1787 the Methodist General Conference exhorted its preachers to evangelize the slaves and win as many as possible to church membership. Within a decade the number of Negro communicants stood at 12,218. Methodist missions to the slaves increased significantly during the nineteenth century so that by 1851 there were ninety-nine missionaries devoting full time to that work. In the South, Baptist churches were either composed of whites and Negroes or were wholly Negro in membership. Negro Baptists were most numerous in Maryland and Virginia. Many Presbyterian ministers gave considerable time to the instruction of Negroes in the faith and reserved a special place for them in their churches in order that they might worship at the same time as the whites. Several denominations set up schools and colleges to educate the Negro. Prominent among these were Avery College and Asmun Institute (later Lincoln University) in Pennsylvania, Berea College (biracial) in Kentucky, and Wilberforce University in Ohio.

Much of the work of Negro missions was carried on by Christian members of the Negro race. The very effectiveness of their ministry dictated that they be used increasingly in the missionary cause and that whites restrict their activities to founding and managing Christian schools. Some Negro preachers were able to raise large congregations. For example, Henry Evans, a free Negro and a Methodist licensed preacher living in Fayetteville, North Carolina, worked as a shoemaker during the week and preached to a good-sized congregation on Sundays. A well-known Negro Presbyterian preacher in North Carolina was John Clavis who had received some training at Princeton and in 1801 served as an itinerant minister for the General Assembly. He preached to both whites and Negroes until Negro ministers were denied that function through action of the state legislature in 1831.

While thousands of Negroes belonged to white congregations, there was a growing demand on the part of Negroes during the late eighteenth and early nineteenth centuries for churches of their own. Here was a way by which they might enjoy some measure of freedom to conduct their affairs as they desired without interference from the socially dominant whites. It afforded them a degree of dignity. In the South it was customary for a white congregation to sponsor a Negro church and to practice general supervision over its activities whenever supervision was advisable. There are records of an independent Negro Baptist church in South Carolina as early as 1775. Others were soon founded in Petersburg and Richmond, Virginia. During the early decades of the nineteenth century, Negro Baptist congregations were organized in Boston, New York, Philadelphia, Ohio, Illinois, and Louisiana. Several Negro Methodist congregations came into existence at the close of the eighteenth century, but they soon organized themselves into Negro denominations.

The Negro church performed a social function of which a mixed or white congregation would have been incapable. It presented a gospel of hope, with an emphasis upon the loving Father who leads His suffering children through every vicissitude of life and rewards them with a glorious life beyond the grave. It would be difficult to overestimate the sense of security this gospel could nurture in the experience of one whose life in the work-a-day world was continually beset with frustration and despair. It held a light before his weary eyes and encouraged him to carry on. The preaching was often poor and frequently the product of Biblical eisegesis, but it spoke to the condition of its hearers. Many Negroes, like Indians, carried primitive superstitious beliefs with them into the church and assimilated them into their religion. On the other hand, the gradual elevation of moral standards among Negroes as the result of Christian influence testifies to the effectiveness of the missionary program. That many entered the church only slightly concerned about the heavy obligations incumbent upon them and intellectually unequipped to grasp the heart of the Christian faith in no wise detracts from the accomplishment. Mass conversion frequently serves only to shift the problems from outside to inside the church; what is important is that the convert be impelled in a new direction. Such was the case in the Negro churches.

A growing racial consciousness among Negroes led to a demand for independent denominations. It was based purely on social and anthropological considerations rather than upon theological differences. In 1787 two free Negro Methodists, Richard Allen and Absalom Jones, founded in Philadelphia the Free African Society. Four years later this group voted to adopt a form of church polity based on that of the Protestant Episcopal Church. Absalom Jones became their pastor and eventually received ordination. Allen, however, adhered to Methodism and in 1792 founded the Bethel African Methodist Episcopal Church, which was consecrated by Bishop Asbury. In Baltimore the Reverend Daniel Coker, a former Negro slave, opened an "African School" for the training of Negro boys and girls. A similar movement took place in Wilmington, Delaware, where Peter Spencer and William Anderson established an African church in 1805.

In 1816 delegates from several Negro congregations met in Philadelphia and organized the African Methodist Church of the United States of America. It was later renamed the African Methodist Episcopal Church. This body adopted, with the exception of one portion, the Discipline of the Methodist Episcopal Church and elected Daniel Coker as its first bishop. When he declined the honor, Richard Allen was elected and consecrated in his place. The new denomination made notable strides under his leadership, organizing new churches and creating additional circuits and conferences. In 1817 the denomination formed a discipline of its own based on that of the Methodist Episcopal Church; it was adopted by the congregations. The doctrinal standards were the same as those of white Methodists. Perhaps the church's most distinguished clergyman was Daniel Alexander Payne who, in 1863, arranged for the denomination to purchase Wilberforce University. He became president of the University, the first Negro in the United States to hold such an office. By 1860 the church's membership was estimated to be about 20,000.

Another denomination, the African Methodist Episcopal Church Zion, sprang from the Negro membership of the John Street Church of New York City. In 1796 the Negro communicants withdrew, with the permission of Bishop Asbury, and formed their own congregation. From this parent body missionaries went forth into other cities to organize Negro congregations. By 1821 the church's leaders were ready to create a denomination separate from the Methodist Episcopal Church and named the African Methodist Episcopal Church in America. The name Zion was added in 1848. James Varick was elected the first bishop in New York in 1822. In doctrine and polity the church followed essentially the standards of the Methodist Episcopal Church. Its membership by 1860 is reported to have been in the neighborhood of 6000.

THE FOREIGN MISSIONS MOVEMENT

The same forces which prompted the rise of home missionary interest, when combined with certain other distinctive forces, gave a powerful impetus to the development of foreign missions. Toward the end of the eighteenth century stirring reports of the missionary accomplishments of the English Baptist cobbler, William Carey, in India, were brought to America and circulated through such religious periodicals as the *Arminian Magazine*, the *Evangelical Magazine*, the *Connecticut Evangelical Magazine*, and the *Panoplist*. The news was greeted with a sense of admiration, but more profoundly by the realization that America would have to act quickly if the world was to be won to Christ through its example and preaching.

To American Protestants it seemed quite clear that God had chosen them to be the political and religious teachers of the entire human race. The fact that every day more and more Europeans were heeding the call to come to America, the land of opportunity, testified to their recognition that in the United States lay the hope of the world. Events in Europe seemed to bear this out with increasing clarity as the nineteenth century progressed. From the French Revolution to the Revolutions of 1848, the European pattern appeared to be one of upheaval and convulsion ending in reaction and authoritarianism. During the same period American republicanism was nurtured in an ordered and reasonable society which was benevolently and without violence enlarging its borders to include Texas, Oregon, and California. The keynote of American history was progress—the upward climb to a higher order of civilization which might in turn be shared with the less fortunate nations. William R. Williams enunciated this idea with clarity in an article written in 1836.

Our Heavenly Father has made us a national epistle to other lands. See that you read a full and impressive comment to all lands, of the power of Christian principle, and of the expansive and self-sustaining energies of the gospel, when left unfettered by national endowments, and secular alliances. The evangelical character of our land is to tell upon the plans and destinies of other nations.[4]

[4] Quoted in J. R. Bodo, *The Protestant Clergy and Public Issues* (Princeton, 1954), 241.

Two events occurred toward the middle of the nineteenth century which helped to strengthen this conviction. With the annexation of Upper California by the United States in 1846, the Protestant nations of England and America had at least partial control of the four coast lines of the two northern hemispheres. It appeared to many that God was thus linking the United States with Asia and that through mutual contacts of the people of both continents, the Christian faith was destined to gain influence in the Orient. Also heralded as significant in America were Britain's military losses in the early phases of the Crimean War and its final indecisive victory (1854–1856). At the time it was interpreted by Americans as a sign that Britain was beginning a gradual decline. America, as Britain's joint defender of Protestantism, would now have to take a larger degree of responsibility. This challenge could be met only if America were first Christianized itself. Thus the home and world missionary enterprises came to be fused in the minds of American people. An able statement of this view appeared in the *Home Missionary* for February, 1855.

The West is a part of the world, a part very necessary to those who wish to save the heathen; . . . The world is to be converted at the West. . . . No one can tell how soon China or even Japan may be begging at our doors for the Word of Life. . . . How can these demands be met? If we should be so far faithless to our own country and kindred, as to give only a feeble support to religion at home, so that throughout large regions it must maintain an ineffective war with the powers of darkness, then where is the spirit, and whence can the resources come that will carry on to successful results these costly foreign enterprises? Impossible! The church must be strong throughout America, or it will never be able to push its triumphs around the world. We need the West![5]

New England seamen who had participated in the increasing American trade with the Orient, together with tourists who had visited the Far East, helped to spark the foreign missions movement by their exotic tales of life on that distant continent. When these were added to the accounts of English missionaries, American interest in foreign missions mounted steadily. In 1806, Samuel J. Mills (1783–1818), a young Congregationalist who during the course of the Second Awakening had felt called to become a foreign missionary, matriculated at Williams College. A group of the students, inspired by Mills' spiritual zeal, began to hold meetings with him near a remote haystack and eventually pledged themselves to the work of missions. Most of them later enrolled in Andover Seminary where they met other persons with similar inclinations. In 1810 some of this group, calling themselves the Brethren, requested the Congregational General Association of Massachusetts to establish a missionary program and to send them as its first missionaries. The result was the formation in

[5] Mode, *op. cit.*, 40.

that same year of the American Board of Commissioners for Foreign Missions. Two years later Adoniram Judson, Gordon Hall, Luther Rice, Samuel Newell, and Samuel Nott, Jr., set sail for India as agents of the American Board. En route to the Orient in different ships, Judson and Rice became convinced that the truest principles were held by the Baptists; upon arriving in Calcutta they and their wives were immersed in the Baptist church there.

The conversion of Judson and Rice afforded a powerful challenge to American Baptists to get behind the work of foreign missions. In order that he and Judson might receive adequate support from the homeland, Rice returned to America and toured the country organizing local missionary societies. Then in May, 1814, the General Missionary Convention of the Baptist Denomination in the United States of America for Foreign Missions was founded in Philadelphia. American Baptists continued to work under this Convention until the southern Baptists withdrew in 1845.

Meanwhile, the American Board had been establishing missions in Ceylon and the Hawaiian Islands. Particularly interesting is the story of Henry Obookiah, a young Hawaiian who, having been tutored in Connecticut, decided to become a missionary to his own people. A Foreign Missions School was established at Cornwall, Connecticut, to train him and like-minded persons for work in the Pacific. Obookiah's life was cut short by typhus fever before he could complete his studies, but three of his classmates were successful in winning King Kamehameha II to Christianity and in starting a revival in the Sandwich Islands. Before 1860 the American Board had extended its missionary program to include stations in China, Greece, Syria, and South Africa.

In 1811 the American Board requested the Presbyterian General Assembly to found a similar board with which it might cooperate. Instead, the Assembly decided to commend the Board to its churches for support. The Board responded by appointing a number of Presbyterian ministers and laymen to its membership. In 1817 the Presbyterian, Dutch Reformed, and Associate Reformed denominations established the United Foreign Missionary Society, which announced as its purpose the spreading of "the gospel among the Indians of North America, the inhabitants of Mexico and South America, and in other portions of the heathen and anti-Christian world." Nine years later the society terminated its activities and turned over its property to the American Board. In 1837 the Old School Presbyterian Church organized its own Board of Foreign Missions which carried on a missionary program in Africa, India, Siam, China, and South America.

The Missionary and Bible Society of the Methodist Episcopal Church was founded in 1819, but its early activities were confined to the United States. By the 1830's, however, it was sending missionaries to Liberia and South America. In 1821, the Protestant Episcopal Church organized its

Domestic and Foreign Missionary Society and initiated missionary programs in West Africa, China, and Greece. The Lutherans founded in 1837 the Foreign Missionary Society of the Evangelical Lutheran Church in the United States. Also, with the separation of the Baptists, Methodists, and Presbyterians into northern and southern denominational units, there came about a schism in the various boards of missions; after that time the southern churches supported their own denominational societies.

While the earliest missionaries seem to have entered upon their foreign assignments with no thought of accomplishing more than the conversion of the "heathen," as the nineteenth century wore on more attention was given to missions as a means of imparting the American way of life. Certainly this idea was prominent in the mind of Samuel J. Mills as he contemplated the future contributions of graduates of the Foreign Missions School at Cornwall. As he saw it, these men would "civilize" as well as "Christianize" their islands. In Hawaii, for example, the program of missions was a door which opened the way to commerce and finally to political control by the United States. Before the nineteenth century drew to its close, the foreign missions enterprise would have proved itself an unusually important, if sometimes unconscious, ally of American imperialism.

14

Christian Contributions

to Education

ONE OF THE IMPORTANT BY-PRODUCTS OF THE AGE OF DISINTERESTED BENEVO-
lence was a passion for learning. Up and down the country church leaders,
especially those of the Congregationalist, Presbyterian, or Episcopal persuasions, were recognizing that sound education was one of the prerequisites to a Christian America, that only through training could the
citizenry adequately prepare themselves for their divine mission to the
world. The dearth of educated ministers alone dictated the immediate
necessity of acquiring additional institutions for their preparation. And yet
even if the need were met, a larger problem loomed ahead. A mighty
nation was rising in the West, virtually untouched by Christian learning
and therefore potentially an obstacle to the fulfillment of America's
destiny. There was only one answer—by means of colleges, seminaries,
Bibles, tracts, religious journals, and Sunday Schools, the boundless
energies of the West must be kept from reprobate purposes and turned
to Christian endeavors. The task was urgent, the response swift.

THE FOUNDING OF THEOLOGICAL SEMINARIES

As early as 1784 the Dutch Reformed Church established a professorship of theology which had no connection with any college. This action is usually interpreted as constituting the first Protestant theological seminary in the United States. John Henry Livingston, who was appointed to the professorship, began teaching in New York in 1785. In 1810, he moved to New Brunswick, New Jersey, where the seminary was intimately connected with Queens College. It has since come to be known as the New Brunswick Theological Seminary. The first permanently located theological institution founded on a complete plan was established by orthodox Congregationalists at Andover, Massachusetts, in 1807. It came about as the result of Harvard College's steady drift toward Unitarianism, culminating in the appointment of a Unitarian to the Hollis Professorship in 1805. As a guard against "heresy," all members of the seminary faculty were required to subscribe to the famous Andover Creed. The motivation for seminary founding was therefore based not only on the desperate need for ministers but on the demand that their training be in harmony with the views of their denomination.

In 1816 the Congregationalists founded their second seminary, Bangor Theological Seminary, in Maine. A conservative wing of the church established Hartford Theological Seminary in 1834. The Presbyterians opened their first seminary at Princeton in 1812, their second at Auburn, New York, in 1818, and their third, Union Theological Seminary, at Richmond in 1824. New School Presbyterians were responsible for the birth of Union Theological Seminary in New York in 1836. The Protestant Episcopal Church entered the seminary movement with the founding of General Theological Seminary in New York in 1817. Six years later the church opened an additional seminary at Alexandria, Virginia. The Lutherans established Hartwick Seminary at Otsego, New York, as their first training school for clergy in 1816. The Lutheran Seminary at Gettysburg was founded a decade later. At Carlisle, Pennsylvania, the German Reformed Church founded its first theological school in 1825. Divinity schools in connection with Harvard and Yale Universities were established in 1816 and 1822 respectively.

Despite the suspicion of an educated ministry exhibited by Methodists and Baptists during the early decades of the nineteenth century, both denominations established seminaries prior to 1840. The reasons for this action lay in the increased demand by the laity, particularly those with education and wealth, for a clergy that could command their respect, and in the competition presented by Congregationalists and Presbyterians, chiefly in New England. The establishment of Newton Theological Seminary in Massachusetts by the Baptists in 1825 and a seminary by the Methodists at Newbury, Vermont, in 1839 (later removed to Boston), represents the first efforts of these denominations to alleviate their educational deficiency.

On the frontier informal theological schools were established first by the Presbyterians. The most prominent was John McMillan's school in southwestern Pennsylvania which flourished during the latter decades of the eighteenth century and graduated a large percentage of the Presbyterian clergy in the early West. The first true Presbyterian seminary in the West was Western, established at Pittsburgh in 1827; the second was opened at Hanover, Indiana, in 1830, and was later moved to Chicago where it was renamed McCormick Theological Seminary. Lane Theological Seminary, founded at Cincinnati in 1832, was operated under the Plan of Union and thus constituted a Presbyterian-Congregationalist institution. Congregationalists were instrumental in the founding of Oberlin Theological Seminary in 1835, after a student rebellion at Lane. The first Episcopal theological school in the West was Bexley Hall, established in 1824 in connection with Kenyon College.

THE CHURCH COLLEGE MOVEMENT

Early in the national period a number of forces combined to influence an unprecedented wave of college building under the auspices of American churches. To some extent it constituted a reaction to the trend of establishing state universities and secularizing older institutions which had formerly been under church management. A powerful blow had been struck in favor of private colleges with the decision of the Supreme Court in 'the famous Dartmouth College case in 1819. By defending the right of Dartmouth College to remain a privately controlled institution, it strengthened the position of other similarly governed schools and encouraged the establishment of additional ones. Further incentive to found new colleges in the West came through heavy speculation in land. Financiers would buy up many acres of cheap land, lay it out in towns and set aside several sections for a college. This was done largely because they regarded a college as a distinct asset to a community and knew that it would attract settlers and thus increase the value of all their holdings.

More immediate causes of the college-building program were the desire to train candidates for the ministry, the competition between denominations, and the fear of ascending Roman Catholic power. The first factor was operative primarily among Presbyterians, Congregationalists, and Episcopalians, who concerned themselves with an educated clergy. Neither Baptists nor Methodists regarded their earliest colleges first and foremost as schools for ministerial training. That they organized colleges at all was due partially to their resentment over Congregational and Presbyterian competition on the frontier. In some circumstances Methodist and Baptist laymen matriculated at Congregational or Presbyterian colleges and were eventually lost to the parent denomination. The only reasonable protection was to acquire their own colleges. Concern over the phenomenal increase in Roman Catholic population through immigration during the 1830's and 1840's led to a further demand for the establishment of church colleges. Lyman Beecher, distinguished president of Lane Seminary, helped to spark this demand in his series of lectures entitled *A Plea for the West*, published in 1835. It was his conviction "that the conflict which is to decide the destiny of the West, will be a conflict of institutions for the education of her sons, for purposes of superstition, or evangelical light; of despotism, or liberty." He was perhaps referring to the systematic efforts of the Jesuit order to found Christian colleges, an activity which he viewed with trepidation.

A considerable boost to the educational movement was given by the American Education Society, organized in 1815. Though its leadership was overwhelmingly Presbyterian and Congregationalist, it remained relatively free from sectarianism. One of its most important services was to secure scholarships for young men who desired to enter the ministry but who did not possess adequate financial resources. It also gave vigorous support to the campaign for new colleges and seminaries. In 1818 the Protestant Episcopal Church created its own Education Society, a step which was shortly thereafter taken by Baptists, Methodists, and other Protestant communions.

The achievements of the churches in the area of college building prior to the Civil War were no less than astounding. During the eighty years between 1780 and 1860, the number of colleges in the United States increased from nine to 173 which survived and perhaps four times that number which became defunct. While a few of these were public institutions, most were operated by the several denominations. The Presbyterians, who had traditionally emphasized education, controlled forty-nine colleges which extended from Princeton in the East to Pacific University in the West. The Congregationalists, motivated by a similar conviction, operated twenty-one colleges located principally in New England and the Middle West. During that same period the Roman Catholics founded fourteen institutions, the Episcopalians eleven, the Lutherans six, the Disciples of Christ five, the German Reformed and Universalists four each, the Friends and Unitarians two each, and the Dutch Reformed and United Brethren one each. The Baptists, who had only four colleges in 1830, increased that number to twenty-five by 1860; in the same time interval, the Methodists founded their first thirty-four institutions of higher learning. These colleges were staffed mainly by ministers; their presidents were always members of the clergy.

Among the colleges established primarily by Presbyterians were Transylvania in Kentucky, 1783; Blount College (later the University of Tennessee), 1794; Jefferson, 1802, and Washington, 1806, which united to become Washington and Jefferson in western Pennsylvania, 1869; Wabash College in Indiana, 1834; and Davidson College in North Carolina, 1838. Several of the colleges developed from academies which had been founded earlier, as in the case of Jefferson College which was an outgrowth of the academy established at Canonsburg in 1794. Of the fourteen permanent colleges which were founded west of the Alleghenies between 1780 and 1829, seven were organized by Presbyterians and one by the cooperative efforts of Presbyterians and Congregationalists. Only four were established by the state, and these could trace their beginnings to Presbyterian influence. It would be difficult to overstate the positive good which the institutions accomplished in settling the frontier.

It was in Kentucky that the Presbyterians encountered the greatest difficulty in maintaining control of their schools. Transylvania Seminary, founded in 1783 under the leadership of Caleb Wallace, a Presbyterian minister, opened two years later in the home of David Rice near Danville. Some years after the school's removal to Lexington in 1788, the Presbyterians withdrew support because a Baptist minister with Unitarian ideas had been elected to the presidency. Transylvania Presbytery then took steps to found a school under its immediate direction. Through a subscription campaign, to which such notables as George Washington, John Adams, and Robert Morris contributed, enough funds were raised to open the Kentucky Academy at Pisgah in 1797. Its avowed purpose was "the promotion of Science, Morals, and Religion." The following year the Academy and Transylvania Seminary merged to form Transylvania University, an action taken largely because of economic necessity. As the school increased in prosperity, Presbyterian representation on the board of trustees declined. In 1818 the board elected Horace Holley, a Unitarian minister of unusual ability, to the presidency. After a decade in office he was forced to resign due to the mounting opposition of orthodox Presbyterians. Meanwhile the Synod of Kentucky determined to found an institution under its control. The result was the establishment of Centre College at Danville in 1823. By act of the state legislature a year later the college came under the full control of the Synod of Kentucky.

Like the Presbyterians, the Congregationalists were early in founding academies which developed into colleges, especially in the Northwest Territory. Representative of these was Marietta, established in 1790; it later became Marietta College. In the East, Amherst College was founded in 1821, principally to offer pre-theological training. Many of its graduates went on to Andover or other seminaries. In the West, the Congregationalists cooperated with the Presbyterians in founding Western Reserve University in 1826. Much of the Congregational college building on the frontier was accomplished through the efforts of men devoted to the cause of missions. In 1829 there arrived in Illinois seven Yale theological students who called themselves the "Yale Band." That same year they established Illinois College and organized a number of churches. One of the band, Theron Baldwin, helped to found the Society for the Promotion of Collegiate and Theological Education at the West and for twenty-seven years served as its secretary. Iowa College, founded at Davenport, Iowa, in 1847, grew out of the work of eleven students from Andover Seminary, who were known as the "Iowa Band" and who came to the territory in 1843. The college moved to Grinnell in 1860 and was later renamed Grinnell College.

The Baptist program of education called for the establishment of a denominational college in each state. Waterville College (later Colby College), founded in Maine, in 1820, was the first such institution. The following year the Columbian College (subsequently George Washington University) was organized as a nonsectarian institution at Washington, D.C.; its founding, however, was due in considerable measure to the efforts of the Baptist leader, Luther Rice. The father of Baptist higher education in the West was John Mason Peck. In 1827 he organized in his home at Rock Spring, Illinois, the Rock Spring Seminary. After five years it was moved to Upper Alton, where it was chartered and renamed Shurtleff College in 1835. Another Baptist school, The Granville Literary and Theological Institution, was founded in 1832 at Granville, Ohio. It became a college in 1845, and in 1856 was renamed and expanded into Denison University.

During the 1830's the following colleges began to operate under the auspices of the Methodist Church: Wesleyan University in Connecticut (1831); Randolph-Macon College in Virginia (1832); Dickinson College, founded originally by Presbyterians in 1783, in Pennsylvania (1833); Allegheny College, also established originally by Presbyterians in 1815, in Pennsylvania (1834); McKendree College in Illinois (1834); Emory College in Georgia (1836); and Indiana Asbury University (later DePauw University) in Indiana (1837). The principal intent of their founders was to provide an adequate education for Methodist laymen.

Of the eleven colleges established by Episcopalians prior to the Civil War, three in particular deserve mention. Geneva, later Hobart College, was founded at Geneva, New York, in 1822, in connection with a theological seminary which was shortly thereafter discontinued. Washington, later Trinity, College was opened at Hartford, Connecticut, in 1823. The following year Kenyon College was founded in Ohio, largely through the efforts of Bishop Philander Chase, who raised funds for the institution in England.

Relatively few of the many colleges founded before 1860 have survived due to an overabundance, poor location, and physical disasters. Most of them were able to attract not more than 200 students annually; largely dependent on student fees, it was difficult for them to secure either an adequate faculty or suitable equipment. What they lacked in resources, however, they made up in devotion. Certainly they contributed much both to organized religion and to the enrichment of personality.

THE CHURCHES AND PUBLIC EDUCATION

Prior to the second quarter of the nineteenth century the preponderance of elementary and secondary schools in the United States were privately endowed or supported. Where public schools were in existence, there was usually a strong sectarian influence, as in the case of Congregationalism in the New England schools. After 1825, however, the trend was definitely toward the secularization of public education. The giant in this movement was Horace Mann (1796–1859), under whose leadership Massachusetts developed in 1837 a system of secular schools under state control. It was Mann's hope that the schools might give instruction in the basic principles of Christianity, without becoming sectarian. This philosophy was accepted not only in Massachusetts but in many other states with public school systems. According to Mann's own statement,

. . . . In every course of studies, all the practical and perceptive parts of the Gospel should have been sacredly included; and all dogmatical theology and sectarianism sacredly excluded. In no school should the Bible have been opened to reveal the sword of the polemic, but to unloose the dove of peace.[1]

While some of the Protestant clergy were in agreement with the educational philosophy of Horace Mann, others felt that Bible reading unaccompanied by sound teaching of Christian doctrine would hardly be satisfactory. In its place they suggested the creation of a Protestant parochial educational system. The Presbyterians especially favored the idea. In 1845 the Synod of New Jersey viewed with concern the coming generation "of irreligious and infidel youth, such as may be expected to issue from public schools." Its members proposed that each taxpayer be permitted to designate the agency or denomination to which his school tax should be applied. During the following decade more than 250 Presbyterian parochial schools were organized throughout the nation. But with steady improvement of public education and increasing difficulty in raising funds for parochial education, the Presbyterian program became almost entirely defunct within a period of thirty years. Only Roman Catholics and Lutherans were able to achieve successful parochial school systems on a wide scale.

THE SUNDAY SCHOOL MOVEMENT

In 1780 Robert Raikes, a philanthropist who lived in Gloucester, England, initiated an interesting educational experiment. On Sundays he

[1] Quoted in Stokes, *op. cit.*, II, 56.

gathered a number of indigent children whose parents could not afford to send them to school and gave them elementary education as well as specifically religious instruction. By 1785 William Elliott, a Virginia philanthropist, had founded a school on the same pattern in Accomac County. A second school, in Hanover County, was founded by Bishop Asbury a year later. In 1790 the Methodist Conference held at Charleston, South Carolina, took action to organize and promote Sunday Schools. But the schools were not very well attended, the teachers became discouraged, and finally the venture was abandoned.

At the outset of the national era the Sunday School movement began to develop in full force. In most cases these schools, while promoted by Christians, were administered independently of the church organizations. During the last decade of the eighteenth and the first quarter of the nineteenth centuries Sunday Schools were organized and operated mainly by societies and unions. The first organization of this kind had its origin in Philadelphia in 1790 and was known as the First Day or Sabbath School Society. It brought instruction to more than 2000 pupils during the first decade of its existence. In 1804 the Union Society was organized to provide for the education of the poor female children of Philadelphia. Other large cities such as Pittsburgh, Boston, New York, Albany, Hartford, Baltimore, and Charleston soon followed suit.

The spirit of nationalism, which fostered so many cooperative enterprises among American Protestants, contributed to a growing demand for a Sunday School movement on a national level. The result was the organization of the American Sunday School Union in May, 1824. It was strictly an enterprise for laymen, for its constitution provided that no clergyman could be an officer or manager of the society. The Union was supported by all of the major denominations and by many of the smaller ones as well. Its principal function at first was to publish lesson materials which contained nothing offensive to any of the evangelical churches. This made it possible to set up schools in communities where no single denomination was strong enough to maintain a school of its own. In this way the interdenominational school became normative. Such schools were frequently taught by men who held distinguished positions in public life. Among their number were members of Congress, governors, judges, and college presidents. Chief Justice Marshall was at one time Vice President of the Union; before he became President, William Henry Harrison taught a class in Ohio. As a supplement to the Sunday Schools there were Bible classes which were usually taught by a minister or outstanding layman. It was not unusual to find as many as 500 persons in one Bible class. In many areas there were separate classes for men and women.

The Sunday Schools afforded a splendid opportunity for women to serve the church by teaching the young. The Union also provided several publications primarily for the use of mothers, and there were maternal societies meeting weekly to discuss the rearing of children. Undoubtedly this woman's movement within the church was a forerunner of the broader movement which would develop later in the century to call for equal rights for women in other fields.

By a resolution adopted in May, 1830, the Union pledged itself to the establishment of Sunday Schools in the Mississippi Valley. Within three years more than 4000 schools were founded. In many cases schools were established before there was a settled ministry and congregations to support them. The Union was also able to carry on a vigorous program in the South since its missionaries and agents were instructed to remain silent on the subject of slavery.

The early Sunday Schools had four grades: infant, in which the alphabet and words of one syllable were mastered; elementary, in which words of two and three syllables were spelled; Scripture, in which portions of the Bible were read; and senior, in which there were readings from both testaments. At first the schools offered a combination of secular and religious instruction. However, as public schools improved and the Sunday School was gradually taken over by the church, the teaching became distinctively religious in character. In 1827 the Methodist Episcopal Church organized its own Sunday School Union. The Unitarian Church developed its Sunday School Society the same year, and in 1830 the Lutheran Church founded a Sunday School Union. Within a dozen years a majority of the Protestant denominations recognized promotion and care of the Sunday School as part of their church activities.

THE SPREAD OF CHRISTIAN LITERATURE

Since the rock foundation of Protestant faith was the Bible as the inspired Word of God, one does not find it too amazing that the various denominations should have concerned themselves with the challenge of its universal circulation. The spiritual destitution of the West made the task urgent. During the first decade of the nineteenth century some work of this kind was carried on by state Bible societies such as those of New York and New Jersey. These did much to awaken interest in a national organization. The chief incentive, however, came from Samuel J. Mills, who made extensive tours through the West in 1812 and subsequent years and reported that on the frontier Bibles were notably scarce. Not only did he aid in the formation of Bible societies in Ohio, Indiana, and Illinois, he paved the way for the convention which organized the American Bible Society on May 11, 1816. The purpose of the society was to circulate Bibles "without note or comment" and in the "version in common use" in all the nations of the earth. Its officers were connected with the leading evangelical churches and included such prominent citizens as John Jay, John Quincy Adams, and Daniel Webster.

From its inception the Society met with notable success and the number of auxiliaries connected with it increased from year to year until about thirty years after its founding there were some 1200 auxiliaries in the various states and territories. Systematic efforts were made to place the Bible in every home which did not possess a copy. For a time Bibles were also circulated among French Roman Catholics in New Orleans, without objection from their bishop. In Central and South America, the Society made an especially vigorous effort to bring the Bible to the people. By and large the Society enjoyed happy relations with the various denominations until 1835. In that year Baptist leaders requested aid in the publication of the "Bengalee Scriptures" for their Indian missionaries. When it was discovered that in this version the Greek word for "baptize" was translated into the word meaning "immerse," the Society refused to contribute on the ground that it could not support any sectarian position. The Baptists then formally withdrew from the Society and organized the American and Foreign Baptist Bible Society.

A kindred organization was the American Tract Society, founded in New York in 1825. Its purpose was to spread the doctrines of evangelical Protestantism throughout the land. Since the Society was interdenominational in character, it could enunciate only those doctrines which were acceptable to all Protestants. Its ouput was tremendous and was indicative of generous financial support. Some of the more important publications were the fifteen volume *Evangelical Family Library* and the twenty-five volume *Religious Library*. The Society also published a paper, the *Christian Messenger,* which soon enjoyed wide circulation; and it cooperated with Temperance, Bible, Missionary, and Sabbath societies in printing and circulating their literature. Among the Society's publications were devotional works, biographies, histories, and classics such as Bunyan's *Pilgrim's Progress.* Tracts offered such inviting topics as "The Evils of Excessive Drinking," "The Ruinous Consequences of Gambling," and "Divine Songs for Children." They were distributed by colporteurs who went where there were no organized churches or stationed themselves at docks to present tracts to immigrants as they landed. Such an organization proved to be a powerful weapon for the dissemination of Protestant doctrines.

Of particular value in promoting several missionary programs were the missionary periodicals. In 1800 the Connecticut Missionary Society began publication of the *Connecticut Evangelical Magazine* and for fourteen years used it as an organ for the dissemination of missionary information as well as for theological discussion. Its announced purpose was "to comfort and edify the people of God and to interest the pious mind by exhibiting displays of the grace and mercy of God." The Massachusetts Missionary Society published the first edition of its *Massachusetts Missionary Magazine* in 1803; the name was changed to the

Missionary Herald after 1820. One of the most popular magazines, the *Panoplist,* was first issued in 1805 for the purpose of attacking the Unitarian position. In 1815 it merged with the various Congregational missionary periodicals in New England and was published as the *Panoplist and Missionary Magazine.* Presbyterians also were early to enter the field of missionary journalism with the publication of *The General Assembly's Missionary Magazine or Evangelical Intelligencer.*

Religious journals of a more general nature flooded the market in the years between the Revolution and the Civil War. By 1840 the number of religious publications stood at 850, 250 of which originated on the frontier. Only about half of these were denominational in character. The Presbyterians and Universalists led the field in denominational publications. In the establishment of the Methodist Book Concern in New York in 1789, however, the Methodists were first to found an official press. They were also the first to issue an official publication, the *Methodist Magazine;* this periodical, which made its appearance in 1818, was later named the *Methodist Review.* The fact that every Methodist circuit rider served as a circulating agent helps to explain why the *Christian Advocate and Journal,* founded in 1826, enjoyed within three years what was then a phenomenal circulation of 25,000. By 1824 the Baptists had formed what became the American Baptist Publication Society, just as many other denominations had formed similar organizations. It would be difficult to overemphasize the contribution made by such religious publications in the molding of American thought. They represented one of the primary means of bringing Christian education into the home and influencing the lives of thousands in a positive way.

15

Conflicts in Religious

Thought and Practice

WHILE AMERICANS WERE ABLE TO COOPERATE IN A SCORE OF INTERDENOMINA-
tional spiritual enterprises during the opening decades of the nineteenth
century, the heterogeneity of their religious institutions and life became
more apparent as the century progressed. This was true both in the eastern cities and on the western frontier. One of the forces which promoted
this trend was a strong sectarian spirit, encouraged by diverse interpretations of the Bible. Another powerful force was the individualistic character of the age which nurtured an attitude of nonconformity and
self-reliance and often manifested itself in liberal theologies which stood
adamantly against churchly or Biblical authoritarianism. By the 1830's
and 1840's a series of social and political tensions had combined with the
above-mentioned religious forces to create irreconcilable differences between various factions in the churches. In some cases permanent parties
with opposing emphases emerged within a denomination; in others the
way led to open schism.

THE RISE OF UNITARIANISM AND UNIVERSALISM

From the middle of the eighteenth century an increasing array of liberal ideas were making their appearance in New England to the decided detriment of Calvinist influence. Interestingly enough, the movement stemmed no more from liberal emphases among the clergy than from prosperous business and professional men to whom the harsh doctrines of Calvin had become increasingly distasteful. Such persons did not withdraw from the Congregational churches in large numbers; they simply refused to take their doctrines seriously. Those who did leave affiliated mostly with the Episcopal Church, and largely for aesthetic reasons. The King's Chapel parish in Boston became, in 1785, the first church in America to declare itself Unitarian. It stood for the unity of God but denied Trinitarianism as an explanation of the Godhead, and therefore dropped all references to the Trinity in its new form of liturgy. Meanwhile, many Congregational ministers in eastern Massachusetts, particularly those who had opposed the revival, began to espouse a rational and practical religion devoid of Trinitarian concepts. The estrangement between them and their orthodox colleagues became steadily more pronounced after the inception of the nineteenth century.

With the election of a liberal candidate, Henry Ware, to the Hollis professorship of Divinity at Harvard in 1805, the conflict was launched. It led to the establishment of Andover Seminary by the orthodox and the publication of the *Panoplist* which, under the editorship of Jeremiah Evarts, sharply attacked the Unitarian position. A great furor was raised when a pamphlet on *American Unitarianism,* written by the English Unitarian, Thomas Belsham, appeared in Boston in 1815. According to a critical review of the pamphlet, published by Jeremiah Evarts, the Boston liberals held to the mere humanity of Christ. In reality they held to an Arian or supernatural position, while rejecting the doctrine of the Trinity. While the tempest blew hot and cold, the Boston liberals became more enamored with the term "Unitarian," and gradually began to apply it to their own distinctive ideas. The debate had brought Congregationalism to the verge of schism.

The inevitable separation came after a famous sermon by William Ellery Channing (1780–1842), minister of the Federal Street Church in Boston. He was raised by stern Calvinistic parents and attended Harvard College. After graduation from Harvard, he was much influenced by Samuel Hopkins, the Edwardean theologian. As a pastor, Channing became increasingly inclined toward non-Trinitarianism. When, in 1819, he was invited to preach the ordination sermon of Jared Sparks as minister of a Unitarian society in Baltimore, he took as his subject "Unitarian Christianity." In the introduction to the sermon he exalted reason as being able to perceive revelation and to interpret the Bible. He rejected the doctrines of the Trinity and Christ's twofold nature, as well as the orthodox concept of the atonement. He said, "We believe that Jesus is one mind, one soul, one being, as truly one as we are, and equally distinct from the one God." According to this theology, Christ was a pre-existent rational creature of God. As such he could not be a Saviour in the orthodox sense. To Channing, man might win salvation through the exercise of his moral faculties. God, who is immanent in man, has endowed him with a knowledge of right and the ability and free will to realize it.

The sermon, which was given national publicity, soon came to be regarded as the platform of the Unitarian movement. The Unitarian revolt fanned into full flame and by 1825, 125 churches had formed themselves into the American Unitarian Association. Prior to this time the orthodox wing of Congregationalism had brought suit before the courts in an attempt to prevent the Unitarians from gaining title to church property originally held by Congregationalists. In the famous Dedham case, decided in 1820, the Massachusetts Supreme Court ruled that church property was vested in the voters of the parish rather than in the communicants. Thus the property in more than sixty parishes was transferred to the Unitarians. But the greatest loss to Congregationalism was in intellectual leadership. According to Lyman Beecher, who remained loyal to Congregationalism,

All the literary men of Massachusetts were Unitarian. All the trustees and professors of Harvard College were Unitarians. All the elite of wealth and fashion crowded Unitarian churches. The judges on the bench were Unitarian, giving decisions by which the peculiar features of church organization, so carefully ordained by the Pilgrim fathers, had been nullified. . . .[1]

By the 1830's a left-wing movement was developing within Unitarianism, equipped with a theology which Channing regarded as frankly humanistic. It was intimately associated with a group of New England savants, mostly Unitarian clergymen, who founded the Transcendental Club. Through Coleridge and Carlyle they became remarkably impressed with German culture and influenced by the Kantian philosophy which held forth an intuitive faith stripped of dogmatism and enlightened by reason. Among these literati, the shining star was Ralph Waldo Emerson (1803–1882). Born in Boston, he was educated at Harvard and was ordained to the Congregational ministry in 1829. After three years of service at Second Church, Boston, he resigned his charge because the congregation was unwilling to discontinue the communion service or alter it to omit the elements of bread and wine. He subsequently made his greatest contributions as a philosopher and essayist.

Since Emerson's idea of God bordered on pantheism, there was no

---

[1] *Ibid.*, I, 763.

place in his idealistic system for evil as an ontological reality, and thus no need for a Saviour to free men from bondage to sin. He believed that God incarnates Himself in every man just as He did in Jesus, and reveals Himself progressively from within. Each person must develop his own religion, for if a man bases his faith upon someone else's knowledge of God, he gets "wide from God with every year this secondary form lasts." While many Unitarians wanted to stand upon the truth of Scripture and reject the historic creeds of the church, Emerson's theology was neither scriptural nor creedal. To him the final religious authority was the revelation of reason and right within the mental and moral constitution of a human being. "In the soul let redemption be sought." Such philosophical theology, repudiating as it did the supernatural foundation of Christianity, was antagonistic both to Congregationalism and the Channing type of Unitarianism. It was an example of American Transcendentalism at its best, seeking to comprehend eternal truth through the intuitions of the soul.

More liberal than Emerson was Theodore Parker (1810–1860). After graduating from Harvard, he became pastor of a church in the Boston area. His principal contribution was to spread the ideas of German Biblical criticism and idealistic philosophy through Unitarianism. For Parker religion was nothing more than morality, the love of man responding to the love of God. It was the truth of his words rather than his divine nature which made the teachings of Jesus authoritative. This humanistic teaching evoked a storm of protest from more conservative Unitarians and Parker soon found that many pulpits were closed to him. For half a century Unitarianism was torn by controversy over these conflicting theologies. Some efforts were made to adopt a creedal statement, but all were doomed to failure.

A second emerging denomination often popularly associated with Unitarianism was Universalism. At its inception it gave credence to the principal evangelical doctrines omitting only the concepts of limited atonement and eternal damnation and punishment. The origin of the movement in America may be traced to Massachusetts in 1770 and the arrival of John Murray, formerly a member of Whitefield's London tabernacle. By 1779 he had organized a Universalist congregation at Gloucester; later he was called to the pastorate of the First Universalist Society in Boston. Another type of Universalism sprang up in Philadelphia where Elhanan Winchester, a Calvinistic Baptist minister, founded the Society of Universal Baptists in 1785. Five years later a national convention of Universalists met in Philadelphia and adopted articles of faith and a plan of church government.

More than any other man, Hosea Ballou (1771–1852) set the theological standard for Universalism in America. Having shed the influences of his Baptist past, he published a *Treatise on the Atonement* in 1805 which clearly revealed his acceptance of Unitarian doctrines. He soon won recognition as the leader of the Universalists and henceforth the denomination remained in fundamental theological agreement with the Unitarians. The church gained many adherents from the Baptists in particular, but found some success among other communions as well. Though sharply opposed by orthodox Protestants, Universalism prospered in Ohio, Indiana, and Illinois. In 1833, its General Convention, a delegated body with advisory powers, adopted a revised constitution. After 1866 the Convention served as an authoritative body.

LIBERAL TRENDS IN CONGREGATIONALISM

The liberal forces which had aided the rise of Unitarianism also exercised an influence on those who remained within the Congregational fold. As the Calvinistic emphasis on a limited atonement for the elect alone gradually broke down, there arose in its place the doctrine that Christ died for all men. With the new theology came a more optimistic view of man and his possibilities. Among the thinkers who promulgated a more liberal teaching within Congregationalism, the names of Nathaniel W. Taylor and Horace Bushnell are conspicuous.

Nathaniel W. Taylor (1786–1858), Congregational pastor in New Haven and first professor of Didactic Theology in Yale Divinity School, began his work with the intention of supporting the Calvinistic character of Congregationalism which had come under vigorous attack by Unitarians. He considered that he belonged to the school of Jonathan Edwards, though he departed from the great master in certain areas. His goal was to restate the older Calvinistic concepts so that they would be consistent with a practical revivalistic theology. In this activity, which resulted in the construction of the New Haven theology or Taylorism, he was associated with Lyman Beecher, then pastor at Litchfield, Connecticut.

As Taylor interpreted Calvinism, man's moral depravity is his own act, "consisting in a free choice of some object rather than God, as his chief good;—or a free preference of the world and of worldly good, to the will and glory of God." Men sin as soon as they become moral agents since it is a part of their nature to do so; what Taylor never explained was how Adam's first sin occasioned universal sinfulness in his progeny. In any case, he made men fully responsible for their moral condition. He taught further that all men would persist in sinning until they were converted through the power of divine grace. Their salvation depended upon their free agency to accept or reject the Gospel. No irresistible force would bring them into a state of salvation against their wills. The result of this teaching was that it incurred the displeasure of both orthodox Congregationalists and Unitarians, and the more Taylor tried to show that his position was not inconsistent with Calvinism the more intense the dispute grew. In 1833 the conservatives called for the establishment of a union composed of orthodox pastors, "for the defense of the truth and the suppression of heresy." This organization was instrumental in the founding of Hartford Seminary the following year. Its first president was Bennet Tyler, one of Taylor's most vigorous critics. In the long and oft-times bitter debate between the opposing sides, the orthodox received the support of the Old School Presbyterians of the Middle Atlantic states, who were experiencing a similar conflict within their own denomination. Had Congregationalism possessed the necessary ecclesiastical machinery and form of government, doubtless there would have been a series of heresy trials culminating in schism. Under the circumstances, there were merely doctrinal schisms within local congregations.

A prime exponent of the later New Haven theology was Horace Bushnell (1802–1876). Much of his conditioning came from his home life and through the influence of his father who was an Arminian. He entered Yale Divinity School at the very time the struggle over New Haven theology was at its height. Already prejudiced against orthodox Calvinism, he soon came to the conclusion that the system of his teacher, Nathaniel Taylor, was equally unsatisfactory. He could see logic in it, too much perhaps, and this constituted his chief difficulty with it, for Bushnell was concerned with life rather than logic. That in the end he decided not to attack orthodox Calvinism but simply to ignore it was due in considerable degree to this attitude of mind.

In his first book, *Christian Nurture,* published in 1847, Bushnell developed a new theory in Christian education. Before his time, children reared in orthodox Congregational homes were taught to think of themselves as morally depraved until they were gripped by a datable conversion experience. The most momentous event in a young person's life was his decision at a revival meeting to renounce sin and accept Christ. Rejecting the idea of total depravity, Bushnell insisted that a child is susceptible to good even though he is plagued by sinful tendencies from his birth. Christians should therefore refrain from emphasizing the datable conversion experience and raise their children as part of the household of faith so that there should never be a time in their lives when they thought they were anything but Christians. This attack on the revivalistic pattern of conversion brought on a counter-attack in which Bushnell was accused of discounting the special agency of the Holy Spirit in man's conversion and reducing Christianity to a form of religious naturalism. The pressure became so great that Bushnell's church in Hartford finally withdrew from the Association. But the new idea could not be effaced; rather, it became instrumental in inaugurating a distinctly different philosophy of religious education.

Of like importance to theology was Bushnell's view of Christ and his atonement. In *God in Christ* (1849), he represented Christ as the expression of God in finite form, the revealer of the divine nature. In *Vicarious Sacrifice* (1865), he held that Christ came into the world to manifest the mercy, patience, and compassionate love of God. Men are saved not by the sacrifice of Christ as an act of propitiation to God but by a living spiritual union with their Lord, through whose suffering they come to know and respond to God's redemptive love. Though widely criticized at the time, by 1900 this idea had fairly permeated liberal Protestant thought.

SCHISMS IN THE EAST

During the early decades of the nineteenth century, an increasing demand for greater freedom in theology and church polity led to a number of schisms which were felt most acutely in the East. They are of interest not so much because of the number of members involved, which in most cases was slight, but because they reflect the individualistic temper of the age.

The Freewill Baptists

During the colonial period several Arminian Baptist groups had appeared in America, particularly in New England; among them were the General Six-Principle Baptists and the Original Freewill Baptists. The most important Arminian group, the Freewill Baptists, originated in New England in 1780. Benjamin Randall, their founder, had been converted in 1770 and had united with a Congregational church. By 1776 he had become convinced of the validity of believers' baptism and had shifted his allegiance to the Baptist denomination. But the extreme Calvinism held by the congregation to which he belonged prompted him to affiliate with a newly founded Arminian Baptist church in New Hampshire. In 1779 he received ordination and organized a Free Baptist church at New Durham, New Hampshire. During the years 1781–1792, he conducted a series of evangelistic tours which bore fruit in the founding of about fifteen churches. For the purpose of binding them together he organized Quarterly and Yearly Meetings, which usually became occasions for mass evangelism. By the time of Randall's death in 1808 there were 130 congregations with a combined membership of about 6000. The mantle of leadership then fell upon John Colby of New Hampshire, who planted churches in Rhode Island, New York, Pennsylvania, Indiana, and Ohio. In 1827 the General Conference of Freewill Baptists was established, composed of delegates from the Yearly Meetings. Contrary to traditional Baptist practice, the Conference was given authority to discipline Yearly Meetings and Associations. After 1830 the denomination enjoyed a period of rapid growth; by 1845 it numbered some 60,000 communicants. In

1841 the Conference adopted a Constitution and By-Laws and reaffirmed Arminianism and the practice of open communion.

The Hicksite Friends

The opening decades of the nineteenth century witnessed heightening discontent within the normally placid community of Friends due to the penetration of certain divisive external influences. Many Friends, especially those living in urban areas, had become intrigued with the doctrines of English evangelicals and had accepted the concepts of the full authority of Scripture and the depravity of man. These ideas ran counter to the traditional Quaker emphasis on religion as an inner experience and the Inner Light as the saviour of all men. Those Friends who adhered to the old position looked with concern upon their neighbors who seemed to be conforming not only to alien doctrines but to the worldliness of society.

One of the arch opponents of the new emphasis was Elias Hicks (1748–1830) of Long Island, a man of keen intellect unrefined by formal education. While he did not question the value of the Bible as a guide in spiritual matters, he refused to accept its full authority for faith and practice. For him the final authority was the Inner Light. He rejected the orthodox doctrine of original sin, not because he did not believe in man's fall, but because he believed that every person was as pure and sinless at birth as Adam was before his fall. There was thus no place in his thinking for an orthodox doctrine of the atonement. He preferred to think of Christ as the spiritual revelation of God, communicated inwardly to man, without the aid of Scripture or clergy. In no sense was he Unitarian in his thinking, as has sometimes been charged.

Matters came to a head in 1823 when the Philadelphia Meeting for Sufferings adopted a statement of faith which was thoroughly evangelical. It was later presented to the Philadelphia Yearly Meeting where it was recorded in the minutes without being adopted. In 1827 the Hicksite party, having failed to gain control of the Philadelphia Yearly Meeting, withdrew and founded their own Philadelphia Yearly Meeting. Similar schisms took place shortly thereafter in New York, Ohio, Baltimore, and Indiana, where the Hicksites were in the majority. Since about fifty per cent of the Friends left the orthodox camp in what proved to be a permanent schism, the division must be judged the most serious that has occurred among American Friends.

The Methodist Protestants

The exercise of arbitrary power in the Methodist Church, which led to the withdrawal of James O'Kelly and his followers, contributed to a further reaction in the early nineteenth century. In the age of popular Jacksonian democracy and the rise of the common man which followed the presidential election of 1828, many voices were raised in behalf of church reform. A group of Methodist reformers met at Cincinnati in 1823 and called for a wider democracy in Methodism. Their views were presented to the General Conference of 1824, but to no avail. That same year the reformers, whose movement was now chiefly centered in Baltimore, began publication of a new periodical entitled *The Mutual Rights of the Ministers and Members of the Methodist Episcopal Church.* Some of its contributors and supporters who dared to attack the authoritarianism of the episcopal system soon found themselves expelled from the church. By 1828 the General Conference was besieged by requests for the readmission of the expelled ministers and for lay representation in the Conference. When both petitions were denied, the reformers took steps to organize independent churches and conferences. In 1830 they met in convention at Baltimore and established the Methodist Protestant Church. According to the terms of the constitution, the presiding officers of their conferences were to be known as "president" rather than "bishop." By 1834 fourteen conferences had been created, with a total reported membership of 26,587. The greatest strength of the denomination was in the East; on the frontier the problem of authoritarianism had scarcely created a ripple on the smooth waters of Methodism.

The Church of God

The founding of the Church of God, in 1825, grew out of a revival which John Winebrenner, a German Reformed clergyman, conducted among the Germans of Pennsylvania. The only requirement for membership in the church was regeneration. There was no creed but the Bible. Similar churches were founded in surrounding communities, and these organized themselves into the General Eldership of the Church of God in 1830. By 1845 three elderships had been established, and these were brought under the General Eldership of the Church of God in North America. Arminian doctrines were commonly accepted and the ordinances of baptism, the Lord's Supper, and foot washing were made obligatory.

The Christian Reformed Church

In 1822 five ministers of the Dutch Reformed Church seceded from their communion "on account of Hopkinsian errors of doctrine and looseness of discipline" and founded the True Reformed Dutch Church. Within two years they had organized a General Synod composed of the Classis of Hackensack, New Jersey, and the Classis of Union, New York.

By 1859 the denomination numbered twenty-six congregations. Meanwhile, in 1834, a group of congregations in the Netherlands had withdrawn from the Established Church in protest to a growing doctrinal latitudinarianism. Many of these dissidents emigrated to the United States during the late 1840's and settled in western Michigan. For some years they associated themselves with the Dutch Reformed Church, but finally becoming dissatisfied with what they alleged to be doctrinal laxity and un-Reformed practices, they withdrew in 1857 and founded the Christian Reformed Church which took as its standards the Belgic Confession, the Heidelberg Catechism, and the Canons of Dort. In 1882 another group seceded from the Dutch Reformed Church and affiliated with the Christian Reformed Church because the denomination refused to denounce freemasonry and all secret societies. Seven years later most of the remnant of the True Reformed Dutch Church also merged with this body.

THEOLOGICAL CONFLICTS ON THE FRONTIER

During the opening decades of the nineteenth century, religion on the frontier manifested a decidedly anti-Calvinist bias. Much opposition came from the Methodists who were strong apologists for free grace and individual responsibility. For years the fires of theological polemic were kept burning by such personalities as Peter Cartwright and Parson William G. Brownlow for the Methodists, Thomas Cleland and Frederick Augustus Ross for the Presbyterians. On the whole the debate went rather badly for Calvinism. Concepts of an aristocratic God who determines all things in His creation were not in accord with the democratic and optimistic ideas of the frontier mind. But this was a period of individualism also, and no single expression of religion could meet the varied needs and interests of backwoodsmen. The result was that on the frontier the older denominations had to face the competitive force of various Presbyterian schismatic bodies which for one reason or another had withdrawn to form new ecclesiastical groupings. These bodies enjoyed wide popularity, for their message and program spoke with power to the condition of their contemporaries.

The Cumberland Presbyterians

The younger and more democratically inclined elements among the Presbyterian clergy in Kentucky and Tennessee had utilized revivalistic techniques and had preached modified Calvinistic doctrines with some effectiveness during the Second Awakening. Unhappily, their apparent success had only served to widen the gap between the revivalistic and anti-revivalistic factions within Presbyterianism. The revival party saw that strict adherence to Presbyterian doctrine and practice would lead to permanent losses on the frontier. A rigid presentation of the "God of inexorable decrees" would prove revolting to persons who had accustomed themselves to the fullest independence. Equally disturbing was the high educational standard for ordination, which caused the ministerial supply to be sharply curtailed. The same high standard was responsible for the inability of available ministers to preach in a manner which could be comprehended by the untutored members of their churches.

In order to find at least a partial solution to these problems, the Transylvania Presbytery lowered the educational requirements for the ministry in 1801 and received four men as exhorters and catechists. At its next meeting the Presbytery licensed three of them to preach before three of its congregations which had no regularly ordained minister. Five members of the Presbytery objected strenuously to this action. The following year, by order of the Synod of Kentucky, the judicatory was divided into the Transylvania and Cumberland presbyteries. The new Cumberland Presbytery almost at once licensed additional catechists, bringing the number to seventeen. Since the General Assembly offered no certain reproof for the licensing of candidates without college training, the practice continued. Most of these preachers proclaimed doctrines which were decidedly Arminian in character.

Trouble arose when the Synod of Kentucky, at the insistence of the anti-revivalists, appointed a committee in 1804 to investigate the proceedings of Cumberland Presbytery, particularly regarding the licensing of those who lacked the educational prerequisites set by the church. This action was vigorously denounced by the presbytery. When synod's committee arrived for the meeting of presbytery in December, 1805, they were greeted with conspicuous hostility by the revival group. During the investigation it was brought out that the presbytery, without mentioning the fact in its minutes, had allowed its candidates to subscribe to the Confession of Faith only "so far as they deemed it agreeable to the word of God." When the committee of synod decided to reexamine each candidate, the Cumberland Presbytery refused to give its permission on the ground that it alone held the right to perform that task. The committee nevertheless ruled that the candidates could render no ministerial services until they had submitted to further examination and directed five members of Cumberland Presbytery to appear before synod and face charges of error or contumacy. Presbytery resisted this directive, and at its next meeting the Synod dissolved Cumberland Presbytery and attached its churches to Transylvania Presbytery.

Stunned and embittered by what they believed to be a peremptory act, the members of the now dissolved presbytery appealed in vain to the General Assembly of 1807 and 1808 to overrule the synod. A final appeal, addressed to the Synod of Kentucky in 1809, was answered by an exhortation to submit to synodical authority. Some members of the presbytery did obeisance; the remainder, namely Finis Ewing, Samuel King, and Samuel McAdow, met in February, 1810 and organized an independent Cumberland Presbytery, which became the nucleus of the Cumberland Presbyterian Church. The doctrinal standards of the new church revealed a sharply modified position on election and predestination in favor of Arminianism. During the next few decades, the Cumberland Presbyterians, through their use of the circuit system and revivalistic techniques, spread rapidly through the South and Southwest. In 1829 their first General Assembly met at Princeton, Kentucky. By 1835 the church numbered nine synods, thirty-five presbyteries, and 75,000 communicant members. Its phenomenal growth continued through the period of the Civil War.

The New Light or Christian Movement

In reality, the founders of the New Light movement were not the first to adopt for themselves the name "Christian." The Republican Methodists, under James O'Kelly, referred to their denomination as the "Christian Church" in 1794, after their secession from the Methodist Church. In 1801 another "Christian Church" was founded in New England by two Baptist preachers, Abner Jones and Elias Smith, who had grown dissatisfied with orthodox Calvinism. They repudiated all standards save the Bible. But unquestionably the most significant of the "Christian" movements was that which emerged under the leadership of Barton Warren Stone (1772–1844). As a young man in North Carolina he had come under the influence of New Light Presbyterianism and had been converted by a constraining message of the grace and love of God. He prepared himself informally for the Presbyterian ministry and was awarded a license to preach. During 1796 he itinerated through Tennessee and Kentucky and finally settled down as supply minister at Cane Ridge and Concord. The following year he presented himself for ordination to the Transylvania Presbytery, despite the fact that he was having serious difficulties with the doctrine of the Trinity as a Biblical concept. Presbytery approved his ordination and allowed him to affirm his acceptance of the Westminster Confession only "as far as I see it consistent with the Word of God." Stone never came to accept a truly Trinitarian position; he later rejected the doctrine of the vicarious atonement in favor of the more rationalistic idea that Christ was sent to reconcile men to God.

When the wave of revivalism spread from Logan County to Cane Ridge, Stone became one of its enthusiastic supporters and rejoiced at the way in which it fostered rapport among members of various denominations. As a result of the revivals Stone and certain other Presbyterian ministers, among them Richard McNemar, John Thompson, Robert Marshall, and John Dunlavy, came to doubt the doctrines of election and limited atonement. In 1803 the Synod of Kentucky charged McNemar and Thompson with teaching Arminian doctrines and proposed to bring them to trial. The five above-mentioned ministers strongly opposed this contemplated action, declared the Bible to be the final norm of doctrine, and seceded from the Synod of Kentucky. After several futile efforts on the part of Synod and General Assembly to reclaim them, they were placed under suspension and their pulpits declared vacant.

In the meantime, the five schismatics had met and organized the independent Springfield Presbytery, which was probably not a true presbytery since there is no mention of officers or lay members. By January, 1804, they thought it well to publish a pamphlet entitled *An Abstract of an Apology for Renouncing the Jurisdiction of the Synod of Kentucky,* in which they argued for the Bible as the sole basis of doctrine. A few months later they reached the conclusion that the whole Presbyterian system of theology and polity was inadequate to bring about the desired unity of Christians. Thus they decided to dissolve their presbyterial organization in June, 1804, and made known that fact in a document called "The Last Will and Testament of the Springfield Presbytery," the outwardly whimsical character of which has often obliterated the serious intentions of the authors. It was accompanied by an address which closed with these words: "We heartily unite with our Christian brethren of every name, in thanksgiving to God for the display of his goodness in the glorious work he is carrying on in our Western country, which we hope will terminate in the universal spread of the gospel, and the unity of the church."

The members of the disbanded presbytery met in June, 1804, and adopted the name "Christian" as an expression of their anti-sectarian convictions. But Stone alone remained with the movement; McNemar and Dunlavy were converted by the Shakers, while Marshall and Thompson returned to the Presbyterian fold. Undaunted by these losses, the new church, which stood for the independence of each local congregation, proclaimed its democratic principles to a frontier society that heard and responded. By 1827 the Christian Church numbered nearly 13,000 communicants, the greater majority residing in Ohio, Kentucky, Tennessee, and Indiana. A trend toward the practice of immersion among Christians made the movement more attractive to Baptists and there were many cases in which entire Baptist congregations withdrew from their associations to affiliate with the Christian Church.

The Campbellites or Disciples of Christ

At the same time that followers of Stone were promoting their cause in Ohio and Kentucky, there was evolving farther to the East a similar movement with which they would eventually merge. The pioneer of this nascent entity was Thomas Campbell (1763–1854), a Scotch-Irish Seceder Presbyterian minister who arrived in the United States in 1807. After receiving his education at Glasgow, he conducted a school in County Armagh and pastored a church which was affiliated with the hyper-conservative Anti-Burgher division of the Seceder Presbyterians, a group which opposed the appointment of ministers to their parishes by lay landlords and rejected oaths of allegiance to the established church. Despite his strict environment, Campbell became a scholar with broad interests and learned to despise the trivialities which rent asunder the Christian community. In this he was influenced considerably by the congregational principles of the Independent Church at Rich Hill, by the warm evangelicalism of Rowland Hill and J. A. Haldane, and by John Locke's *Letters Concerning Toleration.* Upon his arrival in America he affiliated with the Associate (Seceder) Synod of North America and was assigned to a circuit in southwestern Pennsylvania which fell under the jurisdiction of the Presbytery of Chartiers.

It was not long before Campbell was in difficulty with his presbytery. Refusing to abide by what amounted to a close communion rule, he invited all Christians to participate in the communion, regardless of their denominational connection. Charges were filed against him in presbytery and he was adjudged worthy of censure. He appealed to the Associate Synod basing his argument upon the Scriptures. The Synod removed the stigma of censure but advised the liberally inclined clergyman to withdraw lest he find himself in further difficulty. Campbell accepted their advice and became a free-lance minister in the area which he had served earlier. For nearly a year he journeyed from one community to the next, preaching in private houses as opportunity afforded. His central theme was the sole authority of Scripture and the unity of Christians. In August, 1809, he and his followers organized the Christian Association of Washington; the motto of this informal society was "where the Scriptures speak, we speak; where the Scriptures are silent, we are silent." In no sense did its members regard their organization as a church. It was rather an independent society which sought to achieve reform within the Christian community. That others might know of these purposes, Campbell prepared a *Declaration and Address,* which the association ordered published in September, 1809.

October, 1809, witnessed the arrival in southwestern Pennsylvania of the remainder of the Campbell family. Alexander Campbell (1788–1866), the son, was destined to become the genius of the new movement. While a student at Glasgow, he had come under the same evangelical influences which had challenged his father and these had brought him to the point of withdrawal from the Seceder Church. After joining his father, he enthusiastically took up the study of the Scriptures in the original languages and preached frequently in private houses. During this period Thomas

Campbell applied to the Presbyterian Synod of Pittsburgh to be received as a minister, but upon investigation the Synod declined to grant his request inasmuch as his theological views were not in full harmony with the Confession of Faith. Several months later, in May, 1811, the Christian Association organized itself into an independent church which was named Brush Run Church. A new denomination based on congregational principles had thus been born. Thomas Campbell was elected elder; Alexander Campbell was licensed to preach; and four deacons were chosen. The following year Alexander was ordained to the ministry.

From its incipience the church observed the Lord's Supper weekly. When the question of baptism was raised, it was agreed after careful study that immersion was the only mode justified by Scripture. This decision brought the church into closer relations with the Baptists; after numerous conferences, in which the differences between the two groups in the matter of baptism and the Lord's Supper were discussed, the Brush Run Church applied for admission to the Redstone Baptist Association in the autumn of 1813 and was duly received. This nominal connection with the Baptists continued until 1830.

The dozen or more years which followed the union witnessed the steady rise of Alexander Campbell as the movement's recognized leader, while his father busied himself with a private school at Cambridge, Ohio. To Alexander fell the task of building a definitive theology and polity for the guidance of his associates. In certain respects Campbell's thought was not in agreement with that of the Baptists. A cardinal feature of his theology was that with the coming of Christ the entire law had been abrogated; the principles of morality contained in the law were still in force, but only because they were necessary to any covenant between God and man. Such practices as observing the Sabbath and holy days and paying tithes belonged to the Old Testament and should not be accepted on that basis by Christians. Christ introduced a completely new covenant, with its own institutions and ordinances. Campbell found no connection between baptism and circumcision, as did dispensationalists who desired to show that infant baptism was the Christian fulfillment of a Hebrew practice. The ordinance of baptism was provided for the washing away of the sins of penitent believers and thus had no value for infants. Campbell's emphasis on baptism brought him into conflict with many Baptists who regarded the ordinance merely as a public sign of an accomplished act.

In order that his ideas might be widely disseminated, Campbell began to publish a paper in 1823 which was significantly entitled the *Christian Baptist*. While its goal was to achieve the union of all Christians, its effect was to precipitate a withdrawal from the Baptist communion. Through preaching and debate, Campbell enjoined a return to the "ancient order of things" and inspired reform movements in numerous churches. As orthodox Baptists scored the Campbellite reforms, the reform elements began to withdraw from the Baptist churches and organize congregations of their own. This process was greatly abetted by the evangelistic appeal of Walter Scott, a Scottish immigrant and friend of Campbell's who looked more to reason than to emotion to support his message. Between 1826 and 1830 the defection from the Baptist churches grew apace. In Kentucky several thousand persons were won to the newly separated bodies whose members called themselves Disciples. In some cases entire Baptist associations dissolved and joined the unorganized movement.

In 1824 Campbell and Barton Stone met for the first time and immediately recognized that their programs had much in common. Though differences existed among the Disciples and Christians, the intervening years brought a deepening sense of unity. In 1831 and 1832, leaders of the two groups held several conferences, the outcome of which was the decision to unite. Due to the nature of their church polity, merger could be accomplished only by the vote of individual congregations. This was done with amazing alacrity, largely because of the effective and persuasive work of the leaders. Nevertheless, a number of Christian churches in the West and a majority of those in the East refused to enter the union. These continued their independent existence under the name Christian Connection Church, which constituted a coalition of the New Light remnant, the Republican Methodists, and the New England Christians.

The Disciples of Christ or Christians, the two names being used interchangeably, began with 20,000 to 30,000 communicants; by 1850 they numbered about 118,000, having made phenomenal gains on the frontier. They founded Bacon College in Kentucky in 1836 and Bethany College in what is now West Virginia in 1840. At their first national convention, held at Cincinnati in 1849, the American Christian Missionary Society was organized as their first cooperative endeavor in missionary work. The objection that such a society found no warrant in Scripture went unheeded; the trend toward formal organization had begun.

The Oberlin Theology

With the installation of Presbyterian-Congregationalist Charles G. Finney (1792–1875) as Professor of Theology at Oberlin Seminary, Ohio, in 1835, orthodox Calvinism, already much maligned on the frontier, was subjected to another blow obliquely delivered. Finney's theology reflected the current American passion for the achievement of perfection. During his earlier career as a successful evangelist and pastor in New York, he gave himself to a careful study of the Bible which resulted in the conviction "that an altogether higher and more stable form of Christian life was attainable, and was the privilege of all Christians." The attainment of this goal did not involve emancipation from wrong choices or sinful thoughts; rather, it implied complete trust and dedication and the experience of Christ's love in all its fullness. During a revival which broke out at Oberlin in 1839, believers were exhorted to strive for the attainment of Christian perfection and to lead a holy life.

Such idealism was in full accord with the transcendentalist spirit of the age, without at the same time being grounded in any humanistic philosophy. Its roots were perhaps as deeply imbedded in Methodist sanctification as in the free agency concepts of the New Haven Theology. Certainly the Oberlin Theology placed its first emphasis on human dependence upon God's gift of sanctification. That its proponents developed an increasing taste for the doctrine of natural ability was doubtless due to their desire to maintain an identification with New School Presbyterianism. Finney regretted this compromise which, in his opinion, minimized faith and exalted works, and in subsequent years retreated to his old position. In the meantime, his graduates were being denied admission to presbyteries and congregational associations because of their "unscriptural" views. Not until the great revival of 1858 would the prejudice against Oberlin graduates show signs of abatement.

OLD AND NEW SCHOOL PRESBYTERIANISM

Just as the spirit of sectionalism became increasingly characteristic of American life in the restless tempestuous era which followed 1830, so did a growing sectarianism typify the decline of the sense of community between and within the denominations. New sects arose amid the welter of confusion and emotionalism, while older communions bled from the wounds inflicted by bitter schisms. Among the latter, the Presbyterians were the first to succumb to the forces of estrangement.

Almost from the outset, the Plan of Union had evoked dissension among Presbyterians with varying theological emphases. The strong winds of New England Congregational theology which surged through the Plan of Union churches on the frontier seemed to orthodox Presbyterians of the Scotch-Irish tradition like the hot breath of Satan. They viewed with trepidation the steady penetration of the New Haven Theology into Presbyterianism and envisioned the decay of traditional Federalist Calvinism. As early as 1826 Ashbel Green, orthodox editor of the Presbyterian *Christian Advocate*, crossed swords with Eleazer Fitch, champion of Taylorism. But after the delivery of Nathaniel Taylor's famous sermon, "Concio ad Clerum," preached to the Connecticut clergy in 1828, Old School Presbyterians rose up in arms. Taylor had mutilated their doctrine of original sin.

Early in 1829 Albert Barnes, youthful pastor of the Presbyterian church at Morristown, New Jersey, preached a controversial sermon entitled "The

Way of Salvation." In it he held that a sinner is not "personally answerable for the transgressions of Adam," which was the same as denying the federal doctrine of imputed guilt. The sermon was given wide publicity the following year, and the First Presbyterian Church, Philadelphia, extended a call to Barnes to assume the pastorate; at that time the retiring pastor of the church, James P. Wilson, publicly defended Barnes. Despite heavy opposition from Ashbel Green, George Junkin, and other Old School members of presbytery, Barnes was installed as pastor of one of the most historic and prominent churches in the denomination. In 1831 he was charged with error, particularly in regard to the doctrine of original sin, and adjudged guilty by the presbytery. The case was carried to the General Assembly that year, which body pronounced some of Barnes' teachings objectionable but advised the presbytery to drop the matter. Barnes continued to expound his anti-federalist views and in 1835 George Junkin brought charges of heresy against him before presbytery. When Barnes was acquitted, Junkin appealed to Synod, which found him guilty and suspended him from the ministry. Finally the case went to the General Assembly of 1836 which found in favor of the defendant, much to the indignation of the Old School men. It was apparent that the New School forces in the General Assembly were highly powerful.

Another case which raised the ire of the orthodox was that of Lyman Beecher (1775–1863). After a successful ministry at a Congregational church in Boston, he moved to Cincinnati in 1832 to assume the presidency of Lane Theological Seminary, a Plan of Union enterprise. He was received as a member of the Presbytery of Cincinnati over the protest of its moderator, Joshua L. Wilson. In 1834 Wilson filed charges against Beecher before the Presbytery which alleged that he was heretical in regard to the doctrines of original sin, human ability, and the regenerative activity of the Holy Spirit. Beecher was acquitted. Wilson appealed to the Synod of Cincinnati and once again Beecher won acquittal, but he was requested to publish a "concise statement" of his views on those points of doctrine concerning which he was somewhat suspect. His *Views in Theology*, published in 1836, was so carefully worded as to confuse the most ardent heresy hunter. Meanwhile, in 1833, Edward Beecher, President of Illinois College, and two of his professors, William Kirby and J. M. Sturdevant, were arraigned before the Presbytery of Illinois for promulgating Taylorite doctrines. All three were acquitted. These decisions, instead of achieving peace, only incited the orthodox to search more diligently for evidence which might enable them to drive their theological opponents from the Presbyterian denomination. The orthodox were further helped by the shift of Princeton Seminary from a moderate position to the Old School side. About the same time (1836) the New School men founded Union Theological Seminary in New York, an institution which was independent of the control of General Assembly. Doubt-less this action had some influence on the decision of the Princeton faculty to support the Old School.

The tension between Old and New School wings was heightened by questions of polity and order. Orthodox Presbyterians were discontent with the Plan of Union inasmuch as the churches organized under it could not be adequately disciplined and controlled by Presbyterian judicatories. New School adherents, many of whom had been reared in Congregationalism, insisted that the Plan of Union churches had rendered important and effective service and were invaluable to Presbyterianism. As for interdenominational agencies such as The American Board of Commissioners for Foreign Missions and the American Home Missionary Society, the Old School party concluded that it would be best for Presbyterians to withdraw their support from them and found their own denominational boards which would come under the authority of the General Assembly. They did what they could in the General Assembly of 1836 to gain a favorable decision in this matter, but the New School majority stymied their efforts. With determination, the orthodox began to regroup their forces for an offensive attack the following year.

Still another cause of intra-Presbyterian tension was the slavery issue. It was of minor importance at this time inasmuch as the Abolitionist campaign had only recently started operations. The New School party, however, was strongest in areas where Abolitionism was most rapidly becoming influential, and undoubtedly its members were, on the whole, more aggressively opposed to slavery than those of the Old School. The latter endeavored to keep the slavery issue from being debated on the floor of General Assembly for fear that it might divide their own party. New School men were thus a constant menace to the internal harmony of the orthodox wing, since they might attempt to lead the church to an unequivocal stand against slavery at any time. Their removal from the church would be a decided boon to the Old School interests.

As early as 1835 certain members of the Old School wing circulated through the denomination an "Act and Testimony" which warned of the "prevalence of unsound doctrine and laxity in discipline." At the General Assembly of 1837, the orthodox, now merged with the moderates, were in a majority and armed with a strategy to rid themselves of their opponents. The result was that the Plan of Union was abrogated by the Assembly and the four synods of Western Reserve, Utica, Geneva, and Genesee, which had been organized under the Plan of Union, were read out of the church. General Assembly then voted to terminate cooperative activities with various interdenominational societies and created the Board of Foreign Missions to supersede the Western Foreign Missionary Society, which had been organized by the Synod of Pittsburgh in 1831. The boards of Education and Domestic Missions were awarded full responsi‑ bility for functions which had formerly been shared with the American Education and Home Missionary societies.

In August, 1837, the New School party met at Auburn, New York, voted to apply for readmission to the General Assembly the following year, and drew up the "Auburn Declaration," which defended their theological tenets. At the General Assembly of 1838 commissioners from the ex‑ scinded presbyteries applied for seating but were refused. They promptly adjourned to another place of meeting and formed themselves into a General Assembly. The schism was complete; four-ninths of the original denomination or some 102,000 persons now constituted the New School Presbyterian Church. With the exception of the Synod of Eastern Ten‑ nessee and several southern presbyteries the preponderance of New School membership was in the North. In a number of cases synods and presbyteries were rent asunder. During the remaining years before the Civil War the New School gradually became more dissatisfied with the Plan of Union and in 1852 established church boards to assume control of its home missions and official publications. That same year the Congre‑ gationalists abrogated the Plan of Union. Theologically, the continued drift toward liberalism predicted by the orthodox never materialized. The New School did not return to federal doctrines but, through the work of Henry B. Smith (1815–1876), of Union Seminary, who, according to Philip Schaff, made "Christ the central point of all important religious truth and doctrine," was guided in a somewhat more conservative direc‑ tion. Certainly it became rigorously moral and considerably stricter in its application of discipline.

The Old School Presbyterian Church, which began its separate exist‑ ence with some 126,000 communicants, was declared by the courts to be the legal successor of the older denomination. As the years passed it be‑ came progressively less rigid in the extent to which it required subscrip‑ tion to its doctrinal standards. Its chief theologian was the Princeton scholar, Charles Hodge (1797–1878). He gave the federal theology a central place in his system and held to the verbal inspiration of the Bible. Hodge taught that while the covenant of grace is universal it becomes efficacious only in the elect who are given by the Father to the Son. At the same time he revealed a slightly more liberal train of thought in allowing for some error in the ideas of the Biblical writers and insisting upon the salvation of all who die in infancy. His work paved the way for a less polemical spirit in Old School theology.

THE UNITED PRESBYTERIANS

While the majority of Presbyterians were feeling the effects of es‑ trangement a smaller group of American Presbyterians were drawing together after a long period of schisms. The Associate Reformed Synod, brought about by a union of the Covenanter and Associate groups in 1782, had not completely healed the schism of these Scottish Presbyterian immigrants. The remnant of the Associate group continued its independent existence and after 1801 was known as the Associate Synod of North America. Meanwhile, the Associate Reformed Church was encountering difficulty in retaining its unity. During the 1820's the denomination was split by the withdrawal of the Synod of Carolina and the Synod of the West to become independent synods. This had occurred largely because of a feeling of isolation on the part of these synods and a conviction that too much power was being exercised by the Synod of Pennsylvania. After the schism many of the churches in the East affiliated with the Presbyterian Church, which was then undivided. In 1855 the Associate Reformed Synod of New York united with the Synod of the West to form the Associate Reformed Church of America. This body in turn merged with the Associate Synod of North America at Pittsburgh in 1858; the united body which numbered almost 55,000 members took as its name the United Presbyterian Church of North America. The merger did not come about through growing doctrinal harmony, for neither group had departed from Calvinistic orthodoxy. It was effected through a mutual resolve to allow the spirit of unity to overrule their differences, which concerned only intricate details.

GERMAN REFORMED THEOLOGY

With the progress of Old and New School Presbyterian thought, there developed simultaneously another school of theology in the German Reformed Church. It was nurtured in the Mercersburg (Pennsylvania) Theological Seminary which was founded at Carlisle in 1825 and ten years later removed to Mercersburg. The principal proponents of what would be called the Mercersburg Theology were Frederick A. Rauch (1806–1841), John W. Nevin (1803–1886), and Philip Schaff (1819–1893). Of these, Nevin stands out with greatest distinction. Formerly a Presbyterian, he had been educated at Princeton Seminary but had veered from its strict Calvinism. He was particularly influenced by the experiential emphases of the German theologian, Friedrich Schleiermacher. After a period of teaching at Western Theological Seminary, he was called to Mercersburg in 1840.

The Mercersburg theologians stressed the centrality of the person of Christ in salvation and His mystical presence in the Lord's Supper. All believers are members of Christ and constitute a mystical body with Him. This body is the holy, catholic, and apostolic church which remains one through all the centuries and never changes although the character of its life and dogma may be altered. Thus no formal theological expression of the church's belief must necessarily be final. The church may modify its doctrines as it advances in Christian awareness. The Mercersburg theologians also called for a return to a higher view of the sacraments and the liturgy, and for this were accused of Romanizing tendencies. They were subjected to heresy trials in 1845 and on two other occasions, but each time were acquitted with almost complete unanimity. With their sense of high churchmanship and mystical sacramentarianism they constituted the Reformed counterpart to the Neo-Lutheran Movement in Germany and the Oxford Movement in England. A terrific furor was raised by their teachings and in certain instances led to a loss in church membership. The denomination, however, emerged from the conflict bearing no significant wounds.

DIVERGENT PARTIES IN THE EPISCOPAL CHURCH

Prior to the opening decades of the nineteenth century American Episcopalianism was dominated by the low-church party, which emphasized the Protestant factor in the church and stressed the authority of the Bible, salvation by faith alone, and the individualistic subjective nature of religion. During the early period, however, the high churchmen also joined in these emphases, but refrained from many cooperative endeavors with Protestants and from participation in humanitarian causes. With the consecration of John Henry Hobart as Assistant Bishop of New York in 1811 the high-church party came into greater prominence. Hobart's work, *The Principles of the Churchman stated and explained, in distinction from the corruptions of the Church of Rome and from the errors of certain Protestant sects,* published in 1819, helped to elicit interest in the movement. According to him, the churchman holds to justification by faith in Christ; the three-fold order of bishops, priests, and deacons; and the bread and wine of the Holy Communion as symbols. He rejects the doctrines of total depravity and election to reprobation, transubstantiation and sacrifice in the mass, and auricular confession. "The Churchman is distinguished by the great stress which he lays on the sacraments, ordinances, and ministrations of the Church. . . . He would think that he hazarded his salvation if he refused or neglected to receive these means and pledges of the divine favor."

These tenets frequently caused Hobart to take stands which were highly unpopular and which at times led to bitter controversies. He used every power within his means to keep his clergy and laity from participating in extradenominational activities, being convinced that they tended to detract from loyalty to one's own communion. He was strongly opposed to cooperation with the American Bible Society and did what he could to discourage evangelistic gatherings such as prayer meetings and revivals on the ground that they led to confusion and hyperemotionalism. For the most part he gave enthusiastic support to denominational organizations and helped to found such agencies as the Protestant Episcopal Society for the Promotion of Religion and Learning in the State of New York, the New York Bible and Common Prayer Book Society, the Protestant Episcopal Tract Society, and the New York Protestant Episcopal Sunday School Society. Yet he ordered disbanded a society of his clergy known as the Protestant Episcopal Clerical Association largely because he distrusted the evangelical party which made up the majority. The clergy acceded to his directive; but instead of the matter thereafter being dropped, a series of pamphlets critical of Hobart were issued. On the whole, however, Hobart was successful in getting his way without unusual difficulty and in magnifying the position of high churchmanship.

Prominent among the evangelical or low-church bishops were Alexander Viets Griswold (1766–1843) of the Eastern Diocese (New England), and Richard Channing Moore (1762–1841) of Virginia. Griswold's election to the episcopate in 1810 placed him in the position of administering what was really four dioceses, none of which alone could support a bishop. His efforts in the area of church extension were so effective that by 1818 the number of communicants in his diocese had doubled. During the 1820's the bishop was distressed to note a growing antagonism between high churchmen and evangelicals under his pastoral care. He refused to take sides publicly, though his personal preference lay heavily with the evangelicals. On one or more occasions he was critical of a parish for using the communion table as if it were an altar and for displaying candles and flowers in the sanctuary. When the Oxford Movement, which called for a return to high churchmanship, broke out in England, Griswold commented with dry wit:

I am well aware that there is a new sect lately sprung up among us called Puseyites, or Low Papists, who have, chiefly in England, written and preached and published much against the Reformation, and are endeavoring to bring back into the Church of England many of those superstitious mummeries and idolatrous practices, for protesting against which so many of her pious bishops and other ministers have been burnt at the stake.[2]

The Diocese of Virginia, at the time of Bishop Moore's elevation in 1814, was in critical condition. For two years it had been without a bishop and the number of its clergy had declined to half a dozen. Within two years after his consecration, however, Bishop Moore could report that he had confirmed 750 persons and had provided clergy for twenty vacant parishes. Moore was a true evangelical. He encouraged prayer meetings and gave his full approval to societies whose aim was to develop personal religion.

[2] Quoted in J. T. Addison, *The Episcopal Church in the United States, 1789–1931* (Scribner, 1951), 94.

His attitude toward interdenominational associations was favorable, and he served as president of the Virginia branch of the American Bible Society himself. In one of his addresses he observed: "We stretch forth the right hand of fellowship to all who in sincerity call upon the Lord Jesus Christ; we expect to meet in heaven with Christians of all denominations; and while we labor in our department, we wish prosperity to all the Saviour's friends." As regards morals, there was a Puritanical side to his nature. In 1818 he persuaded his convention to approve a resolution which was critical of horse-racing, dancing in public, gambling, and frequenting the theater.

By the late 1830's the conflict between high churchmen and low churchmen, which for a few years appeared to be receding, was beginning to flare up again. The most immediate cause of mounting tension was the Oxford Movement, which was achieving a revival of high churchmanship in England. The movement had arisen out of a reaction to the rather cold and negative Protestantism, repressive to the emotions, which then found sanction among low churchmen in the Anglican Church. It was part of a broad European reaction against democracy in government, pure rationalism in philosophy, and individualism and theological liberalism in religion. Influenced as it was by romanticism, it looked to the past and glorified it. The principal leaders of the movement, which had its formal origins at Oriel College, Oxford, in 1833, were Edward B. Pusey, Richard Hurrell Froude, and John Henry Newman. Newman, the chief spokesman for the group, believed that what was most needed was a revival of the Catholic character of the Church of England. The true church he found not in Roman Catholicism, at least not until the 1840's, but in the primitive church of the Greek fathers. He was convinced that the Anglican Church was most in harmony with the primitive Greek Church, and that it served as a *via media* between Protestantism and Romanism.

In 1839 Bishop Moore of Virginia, troubled by the significance the Oxford Movement was acquiring in America, cautioned his convention to guard themselves against "a revival of the worst evils of the Romish system." Two years later Bishop Charles McIlvaine of Ohio, another prominent evangelical, charged the Anglo-Catholic party with rejecting such doctrines as justification by faith and advised them to return to Rome which was their true home. On the frontier Bishop Jackson Kemper, though a moderate high churchman, warned his associates against "the blasphemies of Rome." At General Theological Seminary, where it had been rumored that Roman Catholic doctrines and practices were being taught, the trustees conducted a full investigation which failed to confirm the truth of the reports. At the General Convention of 1844 it was apparent that the evangelicals were decidedly in the majority; nevertheless, by 1855 about thirty of the clergy had followed the example of Newman and had united with the Roman Catholic Church. One clergyman, John Murray Forbes, became a Roman Catholic in 1849, but gradually became dissatisfied with his decision, reentered the Episcopal Church in 1859, and eventually became dean of General Seminary.

After 1840 there were signs that even the high churchmen were dividing into two camps. The old high-church party, which centered largely in the East, held to a sacramental conception of the church and emphasized apostolic succession, and yet showed little interest in ceremonialism. The new high-church party, largely an English import which found its greatest influence in the Middle West, was strongly ritualistic. With such a rift, widened further by an aroused evangelical party, it seemed as if the Episcopal Church were about to split asunder.

That schism in the church did not materialize is due to a marked degree to the efforts of William A. Muhlenberg (1796–1876). After his ordination in 1820 and a period of service as a pastor and an educator, he spent some time in England, where he became acquainted with Newman and Pusey. Though he held them in highest respect, he found it impossible to agree with their precepts. Instead, he developed his own system, which he called "Evangelical Catholicism." It was essentially a combination of evangelical doctrines with Anglo-Catholic forms and practices. In 1847 Muhlenberg became rector of a new parish in New York, the Church of the Holy Communion, whose edifice was built through the generosity of his wealthy sister. There he began a series of activities which anticipated the "institutional churches" of a later era. His wide religious and social concern led him to found the first successful order of deaconesses in American Episcopalianism, the Sisterhood of the Holy Communion, and to establish St. Luke's Hospital.

Muhlenberg's most significant contribution to the preservation of unity within the denomination was made through his authorship of the so-called "Muhlenberg Memorial" which was presented to the House of Bishops in 1853. Its object was to suggest to the bishops

the practicability, under your auspices, of some ecclesiastical system, broader and more comprehensive than that which you now administer, surrounding and including the Protestant Episcopal Church as it now is, leaving that Church untouched, identical with that Church in all its great principles, yet providing for as much freedom in opinion, discipline, and worship, as is compatible with the essential faith and order of the Gospel.[3]

Muhlenberg saw no reason why the high- and low-church parties could not exist side by side in the one united church provided a larger measure of freedom were granted. He even favored the ordination of men outside the denomination who desired episcopal orders, if they would abide by

[3] *Ibid.*, 178.

certain doctrinal, administrative, and liturgical requirements set by the church. When he saw that this proposal was not likely to be approved, he modified it to such an extent that it suggested merely that there should be wider latitude in liturgical usage. Surprisingly, the "Muhlenberg Memorial" received its greatest support from evangelicals rather than from high churchmen. That few of its suggestions were adopted seems less remarkable, especially in view of their highly controversial nature. Succeeding years gave evidence of heightened tension between the two parties and a steady gain in influence on the part of the high churchmen.

16

Immigration and the Changing

Religious Scene

THE THREESCORE AND TEN YEARS WHICH CULMINATED IN THE GREAT AMER-
ican Civil War witnessed an eight-fold increase in the country's population. That it rose from nearly four million to more than thirty-one million
in such a relatively short interval was due partially to a high rate of birth
and a reduced death rate, but above all it could be attributed to a tidal
wave of immigration which transformed the character of American society. The mass invasion was prompted by no official policy of the national
government, though considerable encouragement was given by businessmen who sought laborers and by several Middle Western states which
hoped to improve their general position by attracting settlers in increasing
numbers. It was prompted by adverse economic conditions and unfavorable political and social developments in Europe and spurred on by a
dream of life in a free nation where land was cheap, salaries relatively
high, and opportunities unlimited.

From 1790 to 1815 only about 250,000 immigrants arrived in the United
States: but after the Napoleonic Wars, immigration at once increased in

volume, rising markedly in the 1830's and soaring to phenomenal heights by the late 1840's and 1850's as a deluge of settlers poured into the ports of New York, New Orleans, Boston, Philadelphia, and Baltimore. By 1860 the foreign-born residents in the United States numbered 4,136,000 or nearly one-eighth of the total population. These newcomers were not readily assimilable in American society; they tended to form themselves into segregated communities where they could preserve their Old World customs and ideologies. To settled Americans their manners seemed strange, their conduct suspicious. That they constituted a menace to the American way of life seemed perfectly plausible to many who feared that which was different. Immigration was thus shadowed by unusual tensions which on occasion flared openly in acts of violence nurtured in the bosom of rabid bigotry.

The Irish were among the most conspicuous in the mass immigration of the 1830's and 1840's. In South Ireland, which was predominantly Roman Catholic, the people had been humiliated and exploited by English absentee landlords who milked their profits and by a hated English government which forced them to pay tithes to the Church of England. Disease, famine, and revolutions besides persuaded almost one million Irishmen to emigrate to America by 1845. That same year the potato crop, upon which the poor had come to depend for their sustenance, failed, striking a mortal blow to Irish economy. During the following winter thousands died of slow starvation, while millions were evicted from their homes by their English landlords. In panic, every Irishman who could muster the necessary funds crowded aboard American and Canadian vessels in order to flee the country. Thousands died of plague at sea; those who finally arrived in America were more often than not completely destitute and obliged to become common laborers in the cities of the East. Between 1841 and 1855 nearly 1,600,000 persons, practically one-fifth of the entire Irish population, migrated to the United States. More than half settled in New York, Pennsylvania, and Massachusetts, where their influence was strongly felt in New York City, Brooklyn, Philadelphia, and Boston. These cities soon became leading centers of Irish Roman Catholicism.

Hard on the heels of the oppressed Irish came a flood of German immigrants, whose number had reached 1,301,136 prior to the outbreak of the Civil War. While the crest was not reached until the 1850's, emigration on a large scale began two decades earlier. Many of the troubles which prompted their departure were similar to those which plagued the Irish. In Bavaria and the Rhineland, the peasantry suffered severely from the effects of crop failure and the demands of their landlords. A potato blight plus the misfortune of a scanty wine crop made the winter of 1846–1847 particularly rigorous, and the fear of starvation paralyzed many a village. This peril, coupled with the fact of impossible tax burdens and enforced military service, led thousands to seek transportation to America. The political difficulties of 1830 and the oppressive measures which followed the short-lived liberal revolution of 1848 also provided incentive for emigration, but to a lesser degree and chiefly among intellectuals. Many Germans of Roman Catholic, Lutheran, Reformed, or Jewish persuasion settled in the coastal cities. Others followed the Erie Canal and the Great Lakes to Albany, Buffalo, Cleveland, Chicago, and Milwaukee or took the overland route to the Ohio River cities of Cincinnati and Louisville. Others came by way of the Mississippi River to St. Louis. A large percentage became farmers in New York, Pennsylvania, or the Middle Western states of Ohio, Illinois, Iowa, Missouri, and Wisconsin.

During the 1850's nearly 73,000 persons entered the United States from Denmark, Sweden, and especially Norway. The Scandinavian countries also had experienced the rigors of famine and poverty, powerful incentives to escape to a more productive land. But there were other factors such as discontent with the authoritarian established church and compulsory military service. The greater majority arrived in the United States via the St. Lawrence River and the Great Lakes and settled in Illinois, Wisconsin, Minnesota, and Iowa. Their religious affiliation was preponderantly Lutheran. In addition to the Scandinavians, there was a continued migration of Englishmen and Canadians into the country. In California, the settlement of 50,000 Chinese prior to the Civil War constituted the first noteworthy immigration from Asia.

ROMAN CATHOLICISM IN AN ERA OF GROWTH
AND TENSION

It was fortunate for Roman Catholicism that in the decades immediately prior to the great Irish and German immigration the church had been able to solve certain internal problems and to make massive strides in the realm of organization and missionary outreach. One of the most vexing problems had been that of Trusteeism. Since 1785 the hierarchy had been plagued by congregations which contended that through their trustees they held the right to administer their own affairs, even to call the pastor of their choice. In the South, the forces of Trusteeism were frequently allied with those which opposed the appointment of French clergy to the parishes. Archbishop Ambrose Maréchal of Baltimore, who enjoyed no favor among the Roman Catholic Irish of Norfolk, Virginia, and Charleston, South Carolina, was repeatedly ignored by obstinate clergy and rebellious laity. Certain malcontents in the South plotted to form a church independent of Maréchal's control. This eventuality was obviated by the erection of two new dioceses at Charleston and Richmond in 1820 and the appointment of two Irishmen to occupy the episcopal seats. Bishop John England of

the Charleston diocese did much to curb the powers of the trustees by
devising a constitution which nominally preserved their rights but which
actually reserved ultimate authority for the episcopate.

In Philadelphia, where the conflict over Trusteeism had been long and
hard fought, Bishop Francis Kenrick felt obliged, in 1831, to place St.
Mary's Church under an interdict; while it remained in effect no priest
could perform churchly functions in that parish. The trustees were soon
brought to submission and henceforth the authority of the episcopate was
not challenged. Bishop John Hughes of New York encountered similar
difficulty in 1839 with a board of trustees which had expelled from the
Sunday School a teacher appointed by the bishop. He was finally able to
persuade the laity of the unlawfulness of such action, and at the next election for trustees a board favorable to the bishop was elected.

Among the more important agencies which advanced the cause of the
church were the religious orders. In 1806 the long-suppressed Society of
Jesus was slowly reviving in the United States; with its splendidly trained
ministry it was able to make a noteworthy contribution in the field of education. Orders of women such as the Ursulines, the Carmelites, and the
Religious of the Sacred Heart devoted themselves to teaching the young.
In 1808 Elizabeth Bayley Seton, a convert to Roman Catholicism, founded
the Sisters of Charity, the first religious community for women to be organized in America. The following year she established a school for girls
at Emmitsburg, Maryland. To her belongs credit for setting up the first
completely free parochial school in this country and staffing it with members of her order. The parochial school system became one of the most
effective means of cultivating the faith of immigrant children and helping
them to adjust to their new environment. To meet the needs of indigent
children, the Sisters of Charity founded St. Joseph's Orphanage in Philadelphia in 1814, the first Roman Catholic institution of its kind in America.

Two Roman Catholic bishops in particular stand out as having given
creative and inspired leadership to the church. The first, John England
(1786–1842), Bishop of Charleston, understood the mind of his American
coreligionists as did perhaps none of his colleagues. He saw that if his
faith was to spread in the country it would have to rid itself of the charge
of being a "foreign religion" by so adapting its outward character as to
appear indigenous. In order that his cause might be brought before the
public, he founded the *United States Catholic Miscellany* in 1822, the first
American Roman Catholic weekly newspaper. Bishop England traveled
regularly through his extended diocese which included the Carolinas and
Georgia, performing his episcopal functions and giving direction to a host
of new enterprises. He was a prolific writer and an eloquent lecturer who
employed his skills to enhance the prestige of his communion in the popular mind.

The second important leader was Bishop, later Archbishop, John

Hughes (1797–1864) of New York. Forceful and dynamic, he was also stubborn and headstrong, and his career in the episcopate might be described as vigorously polemical. Though plagued by Trusteeism, he found ample time to carry on a series of debates with Protestant leaders over such questions as the private interpretation of the Bible, civil and religious liberty, and the separation of church and state. Though the debates were seldom edifying, they at least served to sharpen the issues on which Protestants and Roman Catholics were divided. Unfortunately, they also contributed to the growing spirit of contention and strife which sallied forth under the banners of nativism.

Hughes is best known for his role in the public school question. An ardent foe of public education, he contended that only in the parochial schools could a Roman Catholic child receive an adequate education from the point of view of the church. So strong were his convictions in this regard that he adopted the maxim "The school before the church." He was instrumental in developing a fine parochial system in New York which would serve as a model to be followed in other dioceses. By 1840 there were 200 Roman Catholic parish schools in the United States, a goodly number of them west of the Alleghenies.

In New York City the educational needs had been met by the Public School Society, founded in 1805, and by various charitable and denominational organizations. Each organization had received state funds which were apportioned on the basis of enrollment. Because of abuses, the state terminated that arrangement in 1824 and henceforth provided funds for only the Public School Society and a few nonsectarian groups. In 1840 the Roman Catholics under Bishop Coadjutor Hughes opened fire on the Public School Society, charging that it was really a Protestant enterprise and demanded that part of the school funds be earmarked for Roman Catholic parochial education. Ironically, Hughes' campaign contributed indirectly to the strengthening of the public school concept of education. The New York legislature, determined to end the harassment by ecclesiastical leaders, reaffirmed the principle that no state funds should be appropriated for sectarian purposes and created a city board of education to develop a public school system. The Public School Society conducted schools for another decade and then turned over its property to the city. During the next twenty-one years nine other states banned public aid to sectarian schools.

As the Roman Catholic population climbed steadily, Protestant leaders who had conceived of the United States as a Protestant nation became more and more concerned. To be sure their anxieties did not crystallize immediately. During the 1820's there was only a mild concern over Roman Catholic competition, expressing itself in more determined missionary efforts. Nowhere was the right of Roman Catholics to propagate their faith questioned or denied. But the attitude began to change when reports from the West told with increasing frequency the story of Roman Catholic progress. One such report was written from Missouri in March, 1829, by a correspondent of the *Home Missionary*. His warning that "the Jesuits are making rapid strides here in their usual way, building chapels, school-houses, and establishing nunneries," aroused the fears of many readers of the article. In the decade which followed 1825 at least 5000 Irish Roman Catholic immigrants entered the country each year. Not only did they bring with them their Old World customs, but their progress in American-ization seemed painfully slow, a circumstance which served to enhance the fears of the Protestant clergy as to the foreign nature and connections of the Roman Catholic Church.

Meanwhile, several Roman Catholic missionary societies had been founded in Europe to promote the church's program among emigrants to America. The Society for Propagating the Faith had been organized at Lyons, France, in 1822; in less than thirty years it raised the unusually large sum of nine million francs for missionary work in the United States. Other noteworthy societies were the Leopold Foundation, founded in Vi-enna in 1828, and the Ludwig Mission, established in 1838 by Louis I of Bavaria, both of which adopted as their special project the conversion of the West to Roman Catholicism. Samuel F. B. Morse, inventor of the tele-graph, was entirely persuaded that the Austrian society was the agency of a subversive plot to overthrow American democracy by means of Roman Catholic infiltration. He published a book in 1835 entitled *Foreign Con-spiracy Against the Liberties of the United States*. In it he charged that the Roman Catholic Church was a political organization and that it pro-mulgated certain political conceptions which were wholly opposed to democratic principles. Prominent among them was the doctrine that the pope is supreme in temporal as well as spiritual matters. As proof of his claim, he cited the existence of the Papal States and the pronouncements and practices of pontiffs since the Middle Ages. He maintained further that Europe's Roman Catholic despots had become so alarmed over the growth of democratic principles that they had determined to undermine them by changing the American character through immigration. They hoped to accomplish their ends also by sending the most oppressed and ignorant citizens so that America would finally become a dumping ground for riffraff.

Tension reached the breaking point in 1834 in Massachusetts when a young woman who had been dismissed from the employ of the Ursuline Convent at Charlestown began to circulate lurid stories of life in the con-vent. Public indignation over what was later proved to be a completely untrue account conjured up by a mentally unbalanced person was aggra-vated by the anti-Roman Catholic preaching of Lyman Beecher and many of his fellow clergy. A hastily formed mob descended upon the convent and burned it to the ground. At a mass meeting of Protestants in Boston the action was condemned, but so widespread was the belief that there was immorality in the convents that such a distinguished minister and historian as Robert Baird could insist that the convent "was not destroyed because it was a Roman Catholic institution . . . had it been a Protestant one it would, under the same circumstances, have shared the same fate." After 1836, when the *Awful Disclosures* of Maria Monk were published, in which she alleged she had been forced to become mistress to a priest in a convent in Montreal, tons of scandalous literature were dumped upon the American market. That the stories were demonstrably false did not interfere with their appeal to those who wanted to believe the worst. The effect of this literature was to encourage the few atrocities which were committed during this turbulent era against Roman Catholic citizens and their property.

While one wing of Protestant opinion stood militantly opposed to Roman Catholicism, there were many Protestants whose thought on the subject was more liberal. Thus John Leland, a Baptist with Jeffersonian and Jacksonian sympathies, wrote in 1836 concerning the Roman Catholics: "Should they by fair persuasion . . . increase their number above all other sects collectively, in that case they must of right have the rule; for no man who has the soul of an American will deny the maxim, that 'the voice of the majority is the voice of the whole.'" Eleven years later a Presbyterian minister in Ohio, W. C. Anderson, had the temerity to question the existence of a foreign plot to overthrow the government. He wrote, "Our country is safe enough, if we instruct the whole people, and especially the immigrant portion of them . . . in the true principles of government, teach them the difference between intelligent liberty and mere licentiousness, place in their hands the Bible and the constitution of the Republic. . . ."

It was tragic that opposition to Roman Catholicism became a national issue, giving rise to the Native American party in 1837, an organization which sought to curtail immigration and require aliens to live in the country twenty-one years before becoming eligible for citizenship. In 1849 a "patriotic" society known as The Order of the Star-Spangled Banner was organized in New York; its function was "to place in all offices of honor, trust, or profit, in the gift of the people, or by appointment, none but native-born Protestant citizens." From this group sprang the Know Nothings, who gained control of several state legislatures in 1854 and 1855 and ran Millard Fillmore for the presidency in 1856 but without success. By this time the movement had largely spent its force, and Americans were too absorbed in questions of slavery and the maintenance of national unity to give it much attention.

Despite the efforts of some to render Roman Catholicism odious to the rank and file of Americans, the church continued to flourish. One of its most eloquent champions was the convert Orestes Brownson, erstwhile

Presbyterian, Universalist, and Unitarian who, after a career of espousing socialistic causes and Transcendentalist principles, found his way into the Roman Church in 1844. Through the publication of *Brownson's Quarterly Review*, he proved himself to be an able spokesman for at least some of his coreligionists and helped to stimulate the interest of intellectuals in the church.

By 1850 dioceses had been erected in almost every city of considerable size; ten years later the Roman Catholic Church, with 3,100,000 adherents, constituted the largest single denomination in the United States. More encouraging to the hierarchy was the decision of the national government in 1848 to open diplomatic relations with the Papal States, which included an extensive territory in central Italy. It was undoubtedly influenced to some extent by the liberal policies pursued for a brief time by Pius IX after his election as pope in 1846. But involved debate with the papal authorities over the maintenance of a Protestant church in Rome, largely for the benefit of the American delegation, together with reports of increasingly reactionary policies by the pope, gradually soured any enthusiasm Americans might have had for the mission. It was terminated by Congress in 1867.

A telling sign of the church's advance was the First Plenary Council or assemblage of the nation's hierarchy, which was held at Baltimore in May, 1852. Of the thirty-two bishops present, only nine were native-born. The council issued twenty-five decrees which dealt with such themes as parochial schools, administration of the church's property, and the standardization of discipline, but it ignored fundamental issues such as slavery. The chief significance of the council was that it voiced the church's recognition that its problems were no longer purely provincial, but national.

THE GERMAN PROTESTANT BODIES

Several decades before the high tide of German immigration transformed the character of American Lutheranism, a serious controversy arose within the denomination as to the theological and liturgical course which the church ought to pursue. The rising confessional party contended that the church should demand rigid adherence to the Augsburg Confession and the other symbolical books of the Lutheran tradition and that the German language should be retained in the service. The "American Lutheran" party, a minority group, favored a modification of the confessions and practices of historic Lutheranism so as to bring the church into a wider conformity to the American religious environment. This liberal wing was headed by Samuel S. Schmucker (1799–1873), a professor at Gettysburg Seminary and a moving spirit in the founding of both the seminary and Pennsylvania College. Though originally conservative in theological outlook, he gradually turned to a more liberal position. Thus at a time in which religion in the United States was being characterized more by denominational exclusiveness, Schmucker was moving toward a broad and tolerant viewpoint and a desire for greater unity among the various communions. In his "Fraternal Appeal to the American Churches," published in 1838, he urged the churches to reunite on "the apostolic basis." He and his associates not only favored modification of the confessions, but free worship as opposed to liturgical worship, and the use of revivalistic techniques. American Lutheranism, however, was not in harmony with the spirit of the times or the ideologies of a majority of German immigrants and therefore lost much of its influence in the councils of the church.

The trend toward confessionalism became more pronounced throughout the 1840's and 1850's as a mass of German immigrants began to arrive in the Middle West. Most of these settlers came via the Mississippi River and landed at St. Louis. The first group, which reached Missouri in 1839, had originated in Saxony and had gained a reputation for fervid pietism coupled with rigid Lutheran orthodoxy. They had left Saxony in protest to the pure rationalism which prevailed in official church circles there. The leadership of this band soon fell to a young pastor, Carl F. W. Walther (1811–1887). From the outset he was faced with unusual problems. Many of the people soon became disconsolate, finding themselves virtually penniless in a strange land, and wished that they had remained at home. It was Walther who guided his coreligionists to more positive considerations and gave them hope to go forward. After a few years as pastor of the congregation at St. Louis, he turned to journalistic pursuits and began to publish, in 1844, a paper called *Der Lutheraner* in order to answer attacks made upon the church and to propagate Lutheran doctrines and ideologies. The publication not only focused attention on Walther's work but stimulated interest in the doctrinal views of Missouri Lutherans. By 1845 German immigration had increased to such an extent that efforts were made to form a new synod. The organization was effected two years later, in Chicago, where Walther was elected first president of the German Evangelical Lutheran Synod of Missouri, Ohio and other States, popularly known as the Missouri Synod. All the symbolical books, which were regarded as "the pure and uncorrupted explanation and statement of the Divine Word," were adopted as standards by the synod. The new synod placed a high value on education under ecclesiastical auspices and soon established a system of parochial schools, colleges, and seminaries. Other confessional synods organized about the same time were the Buffalo Synod (1845) and the Iowa Synod (1854).

Another source of Lutheran confessionalism in America was to be found in the Scandinavian immigration which began toward the middle of the century. The first group of Norwegian Lutherans to arrive in the United

States settled in Illinois in 1834. Most of them had been influenced in the homeland by the pietistic revivalism of Hans Nielsen Hauge, a lay evangelist who opposed the clergy of the established church. Illinois and Wisconsin soon became the chief centers of Norwegian Lutheranism. By 1853, under the leadership of Herman Amberg Preus, The Synod of the Norwegian Evangelical Lutheran Church of America was organized. Preus helped to guide the church toward orthodoxy and away from Hauge's type of evangelism. Meanwhile, a number of the low-church wing among the Norwegians had founded the Evangelical Lutheran Church of America in 1846, largely on the initiative of a follower of Hauge, Elling Eielsen. This body was committed to the use of revivalistic techniques and insisted upon "proof of conversion" for admission to communicant membership.

Swedish Lutherans founded their first church in the United States at Andover, Illinois, in 1850, under the pastoral leadership of Lars Paul Esbjörn, advocate of temperance reform and outspoken critic of church establishments. Esbjörn and his members united with the Northern Illinois Synod when it was organized in 1851 as a district of the General Synod. Gradually the Scandinavian element became dissatisfied with the General Synod because of the liberalism which was part of its makeup and in 1860 Esbjörn, Tuve N. Hasselquist, and several other ministers withdrew their membership from the Synod and formed a new body which they denominated The Scandinavian Evangelical Lutheran Augustana Synod of North America. The membership, which was predominantly Swedish, elected Hasselquist to be first president. That same year a college and seminary were founded at Chicago. While the denomination stood for strict orthodoxy, a strong current of pietism coursed through its ranks and inspired some notable social service projects.

The growth of Lutheran confessionalism was due not only to the entrance of orthodox immigrants but to conservative trends among the older settled congregations which belonged to the General Synod. By 1850 there was a definite cleavage between the American or "New" Lutherans and the "Old" or orthodox Lutherans in the Synod. The liberals, headed by Samuel Schmucker, did what they could to halt the steady march to power of the conservatives. They endeavored to present in an unfavorable light their strict doctrinal orthodoxy, their inclination toward liturgical forms, and their exclusiveness. In 1855 Schmucker published a document called the "Definite Synodical Platform." Its purpose was to provide a theological foundation for Lutheran synods in America. In order that it might be fairly representative of clerical opinion, Lutheran ministers in both eastern and western synods were consulted. The Platform proved to be essentially a revision of the Augsburg Confession, those articles which recognized private confession and absolution and taught the real presence of Christ in the communion being omitted. Schmucker was disappointed by the reception given his work. Charles Porterfield Krauth, the theological leader of the conservatives and one of Schmucker's former students, staunchly opposed the document; and one by one the district synods of the General Synod rejected it. "American Lutheranism" had suffered a crushing defeat and a powerful blow had been struck on behalf of the historic faith as presented by the framers of the Augsburg Confession.

Within the several synods, however, the conflict continued until the flames of dissension stifled unity and brought on schisms wrought in rancor and bitterness. The most serious of these came with the secession of the Ministerium of Pennsylvania from the General Synod because of opposition to the decision of the General Synod in 1864 to admit the Franckean Synod, a body which had never formally adopted the Augsburg Confession. Two years later the Ministerium invited those synods which held to the Confession to join in the formation of a new general body "on a truly Lutheran basis." Thirteen synods responded by sending representatives to a convention held at Reading, Pennsylvania, in December, 1866. The outcome of this meeting was the formation of the General Council of the Evangelical Lutheran Church of North America, which held its first convention the following year. It was not long before the General Council surpassed the General Synod in numerical strength.

The large German immigration to the Middle West also had a salient effect upon the German Reformed Church. This denomination had been split asunder in 1824 when the Classis of Ohio withdrew from the Eastern Synod and formed the Western Synod so as to be able to ordain its own ministerial candidates. Most of the churches were too poor to assume the expense of sending them to Pennsylvania for examination and ordination. When the Eastern Synod later granted its classes the privilege of ordination, it invited the Western Synod to resume its former status. Nothing came of the overture at that time, but as the heightened problems of ministering adequately to the increasing tide of German immigrants seemed to call for a concerted effort, the two synods grew closer together. At last, in 1863, they were united into a General Synod, which met triennially.

DEVELOPMENTS IN JUDAISM

At the opening of the national era the future of Judaism in the United States seemed auspicious. Many Jews, among them the financier, Haym Salomon, had served the patriot cause in time of war; when peace was restored to the land Jews were accorded the full rights of citizens, except in Maryland where they were not eligible to hold public office until 1825. By the end of the eighteenth century the Ashkenazic Jews, whose origins were in Germany and Poland, were beginning to outnumber the more aristocratic Sephardic Jews of Spanish and Portuguese origins. Because of a difference in ritual and in the pronunciation of Hebrew, the two groups grew apart, especially as the Ashkenazic element increased. Finally separate congregations were organized, in Philadelphia in 1802, and in New York in 1825. Cincinnati also, in 1825, could boast a new congregation which followed the Ashkenazic ritual.

During the latter part of the eighteenth century, revolutionary movements opened the way for fuller civil liberties for Jews in western Europe. Young Jews in particular began to imbibe the exhilarating intellectual atmosphere and glory in their new-found freedom. The effect on synagogue life in both Europe and America would be tremendous. At first minor changes were made in the synagogue worship, introducing sermons and prayers in the vernacular and organs and choirs, much to the dismay of the orthodox. Then changes in the Jewish theological climate were noticeable as certain scholars began to react to Biblical authoritarianism. In 1843 a group of Jewish liberals in the German city of Frankfurt-am-Main organized themselves into the Frankfurt Society of the Friends of Reform and issued the following declaration:

> First, we recognize the possibility of unlimited development in the Mosaic religion. Second, the collection of controversies and prescriptions commonly designated by the name Talmud possess for us no authority from either the doctrinal or the practical standpoint. Third, a Messiah who is to lead back the Israelites to the land of Palestine is neither expected nor desired by us; we know no Fatherland but that to which we belong by birth or citizenship.[1]

This manifesto evoked a storm of dissension within Judaism which was magnified during the coming decade. After 1848 a conservative reaction set in and many of the German liberals migrated to the United States.

Reform movements appeared also in America early in the nineteenth century. In 1824, a band under the leadership of the journalist, Isaac Harby, founded the Reformed Society of Israelites in Charleston, South Carolina. Portions of the service were in English, sermons were preached by the laity, and the congregation worshipped with heads uncovered. When a new synagogue was erected in 1841, it was equipped with an organ. The impulse for reform became stronger after 1836 with the advent of Jewish mass immigration from Germany. Between 1840 and 1860 the Jewish population climbed from about 15,000 to 150,000. A high percentage of the Jews who arrived in this period were prosperous and well educated; several learned rabbis who had been regularly ordained were in their company. Gradually the liberals began to form congregations which they called temples. Har Sinai in Baltimore was the first (1842), followed by Emanuel in New York, and Sinai in Chicago. The real founder of the Reform movement in America was Isaac Mayer Wise (1819–1900), a German-speaking rabbi from Bohemia. After assuming the spiritual leader-

---

[1] Quoted in D. Philipson, *The Reform Movement in Judaism* (Macmillan, c. 1931), 122.

ship of a congregation at Albany in 1846, he introduced minor reforms. He later intensified this program in his temple in Cincinnati, to which he had been called in 1854. Three years later he published his *Minhag America*, a modernized prayer book.

Although the Reform movement was relatively successful in the United States, it developed not without vigorous competition. In 1829 Mikveh Israel congregation in Philadelphia called to its ministry Isaac Leeser (1806–1868), who sympathized with Reform Judaism in some respects but was more conservative in many of his views. He preached in English and made a translation of the Scriptures into that language without sacrificing his essential orthodoxy. He published the *Occident* from 1843 to 1868, a paper which was regarded as the chief competitor to Wise's weekly, the *American Israelite*. The first Sunday School for Jewish children was founded in 1838 by Rebecca Gratz, a member of Leeser's congregation. As the century wore on the counterreaction of Mikveh Israel and other conservatively minded congregations to Reform principles became more emphatic and led to permanent cleavages in American Judaism.

There was, nevertheless, at least one effort to create unity among the various Jewish factions. In 1843 a group of German Jews in New York founded the Independent Order of B'nai B'rith (Sons of the Covenant) to promote fellowship along cultural and philanthropic lines. The order developed rapidly in the United States and made important contributions to educational and social welfare work, principally in the great urban centers. Happily, it provided a meeting-ground where Jews with varied religious convictions could labor for a common purpose.

17

The Emergence of Religious Cults and Movements

IF AMERICAN RELIGION EXHIBITED ANY COMMON CHARACTERISTIC DURING that delightfully naive though turbulent era which preceded the Civil War, it was that it refused to be average. Every man aspired to be a nonconformist, and in no area did his hope bear more evidence of fruition than in religion. Truth seemed always contiguous, available to anyone who would reach out and grasp it. That it should have presented itself in variant and conflicting forms was troublesome only to rationalists, and the Age of Reason was dead. What most Americans craved was truth, in whatever form, that could warm the heart, fire the imagination, and point the way toward a life of bliss, whether in heaven or on earth. Where restlessness and dissatisfaction with the status quo were most pronounced there was most often a tendency to become identified with indigenous cults and movements which sprang up in fertile soil and offered escape from the stark realities of the work-a-day world to a dream land of perfection. This tendency was magnified by the rising tension over slavery, states rights, and nativism, which gripped the country during the three decades of unrest and upheaval antecedent to sanguinary war.

334

The frontier in particular was a natural breeding ground for bizarre cults and utopian societies which desired some virgin retreat, unblemished by social iniquity, to which they might repair and build their paradise. Rural areas in New England, Pennsylvania, and the Middle West received a goodly representation of dissident groups, but it was in central and western New York that eccentric opinion and unconventional behavior reached their height. This "Burnt" or "Burned-over" District, so named because it had been swept so often by the fires of revivalism, had been settled by New Englanders generally sensitive to religious influences but with a penchant for nonconformity. From the time of settlement the region was characterized by unusual deviations from doctrinal orthodoxy, clerical exhibitionism, egregious conduct, and frequent change of denominational affiliation. The extravagant emotionalism which accompanied the revivals held in that area gave rise to claims of prophetic gifts and infallible revelations from God, which were well received by a superstitious and credulous people. As revivalism, fed by the impassioned preaching of Charles Grandison Finney, climbed to the height of its influence in the decade which followed 1825, so mounted the tension and excitement. The products were anti-Masonry, millennialism, spiritualism, Mormonism, and a score of fervent and often rabid causes which brought on interdenominational conflict and almost constant debate between enthusiasts and conservatives within a given communion. The latter, who belonged predominantly to the educated class which had moved more recently into the area from New England and eastern New York, tended to favor progressive social movements and spent their energies in the support of Bible societies, Sunday School unions, and temperance and Sabbath-observance campaigns.

THE MORMONS OR LATTER-DAY SAINTS

Central-western New York was the birthplace of the most peculiarly American religious movement to originate prior to the Civil War. The holy history of Mormonism deals with North America; its exodus was across the American plains to a promised land in Utah. Joseph Smith (1805–1844), its founder, was a fitting product of the paroxysmal erratic society of New York's Burned-over District. He had been brought to Palmyra in 1816 by his destitute family who had emigrated from Vermont in the hope of finding better economic conditions. The Smiths, who were barely literate, eked out an existence by keeping a village shop; like many of their neighbors they frittered away much of their time hunting gold when the moon was in its proper phase. They were a childlike people who half-expected to confront a miracle at every turn and were as surprised by the ordinary as by the grotesque. Religiously, they were nomads who sampled the wares of one denomination after another without committing themselves permanently to any.

Joseph Smith, though the recipient of little formal education, read without difficulty. An imaginative youth, he was attracted to treasure hunting and the search for glasslike objects called "peek stones" which, according to popular rumor, enabled their owner to locate stolen or lost articles. As he grew older he became captivated by the revivals which were sweeping the area and one day in 1820 reported a vision which culminated in his conversion. Three years later he professed to have been visited in his room by the angel Moroni who told him of a hidden book written on gold plates which gave an account of the former inhabitants of North America. But according to Smith's testimony, it was not until September, 1827, that he was permitted to remove the plates from the hill in which they were buried and translate them. These plates, which were written in "Egyptian, Chaldiac, Assyric, and Arabic" characters, were sealed in a stone box which also contained two stones provided to help Smith with the work of translation. No other person was permitted to examine the plates, and so for three years he dictated his translations, while shielded by a curtain, to four persons who assisted him on various occasions. The *Book of Mormon* was published in 1830 at Palmyra, together with a testimony by three witnesses to the genuineness of the plates, which had been removed by Moroni after completion of the translation.

The subject of the *Book of Mormon* is what is purported to be American history from the time of original settlement to the fifth century after Christ. The first to arrive were the Jaredites, who had been driven from the Tower of Babel; these eventually destroyed themselves through incessant civil strife. Then came the Lamanites or American Indians, a people of warlike nature. When God's chosen people, the Nephites, located in America, the Lamanites warred against them for centuries until by 384 A.D. only a few Nephites, among them Mormon and his son Moroni, were left. Moroni gathered the records of his tribe and deposited them for safe-keeping in a hill in western New York until a true prophet should arise to disinter them.

For many years non-Mormon scholars have speculated concerning the origin of this enigmatic book. In style and vocabulary it frequently reveals a remarkable similarity to the English of the King James Version of the Bible. Many of its concepts are Biblical. A long-famous theory attributed the authorship of the historical sections of the work to a Presbyterian minister named Solomon Spaulding, who had prepared an imaginative account of the origin of the American Indians. Another theory credited Sidney Rigdon, a Campbellite Baptist minister who later became a follower of Smith, with the authorship. Neither explanation seems satisfactory. There is no part of the work which could not have grown out of Joseph Smith's own experience. Where it departs from Biblical thought and style, it reflects the cultural, political, economic, and social ideas of his contemporaries, even to a suggestion of the anti-masonic movement of the period. The work would appear to have been composed in western New York in the years immediately following 1826. For all his imagination, Smith was probably a genuine and sincere man who expressed with both logic and emotion the prevailing ethos of his time.

The year in which the *Book of Mormon* was published witnessed the organization of six persons into the Church of Jesus Christ of Latter-day Saints, at Fayette in Seneca County. Among the increasing number of converts were Parley Pratt and Sidney Rigdon, two Campbellite ministers from Ohio. The latter, an exceptionally able man, was no doubt instrumental in the decision to remove to Kirtland, Ohio, in 1831. At Kirtland they set up a communistic type of community, purchased large tracts of land, erected their first temple, and founded a bank. During this period, in which Joseph Smith taught that the present world order was drawing rapidly to its close and that after the day of judgment the Mormon Saints would inherit the earth, the church won to its fold a future leader, Brigham Young (1801-1877). When the Kirtland bank failed during the Panic of 1837, lawsuits were filed against Smith and Rigdon for infractions of the banking laws; hastily the majority of Mormons departed for Missouri where they settled in Caldwell County. An antagonistic populace, fearing that the Mormons would soon buy up all the land, began to persecute them. Smith and Rigdon retaliated by organizing a band of guerillas which warred on the state militia. When Smith and his leaders were arrested, most of their followers fled to Illinois. Smith escaped in 1839 and rejoined his coreligionists across the Mississippi.

From 1840 to 1846 the Mormons made their home at Nauvoo, Illinois, situated along the great river which separated them from the wrathful Missourians. It was here that Joseph Smith enjoyed his highest success. In return for their support of the Whigs in the election of 1840, the city of Nauvoo was granted a charter which conferred unusual powers upon the mayor and aldermen. Smith was, of course, the first incumbent of the mayoralty. The Nauvoo Legion or militia was organized with Smith as lieutenant general, and a charter was obtained for a university which never did more than award a few honorary degrees. During this period Mormon missionaries in England won to the Mormon faith many converts among the factory workers. These persons emigrated to Nauvoo, and by 1845 the city was the largest in the state, numbering about 15,000. Smith was so encouraged by the turn of events that he ran for the Presidency of the United States in 1844, pledging himself to abolish slavery, free criminals from prison, and perform any number of services for the benefit of the oppressed. But his star was already beginning to wane. In July, 1843, he announced to his closest associates that he had received divine authorization to practice polygamy. When word of this teaching was spread among the non-Mormon citizens, tempers soared and a group of incensed townspeople began publication in 1844 of the *Nauvoo Expositor*, in which they publicly attacked Smith for immorality. When the Mormon authorities arrested the editors and destroyed their presses, the state militia and civilian mobs were pitted against the Mormons. Joseph Smith and his brother Hyrum were arrested and placed in the jail at Carthage. On June 27, 1844, an enraged mob descended upon the jail and shot the brothers in cold blood.

A contest for power began at once among the would-be successors to Smith. Smith's family seceded from the main body of Mormons, insisting that Joseph had never taught polygamy, and led a minority group to Iowa where they formed the Reorganized Church of Jesus Christ of Latter-day Saints. Another group followed James J. Strang, an eccentric who reported receiving a divine appointment to succeed Smith, to Wisconsin and later to the Beaver Islands in Lake Michigan. In 1850, Strang announced that it had been revealed that he was to become Prophet and King of the Kingdom of God on earth, a kingdom independent of the United States. This monarchy suddenly came to an end in 1856 when angered non-Mormons attacked the kingdom and mortally wounded Strang.

The majority of Mormons took as their leader Brigham Young, a convert from Methodism. It was he who led the group in its great trek to the West. By February, 1846, most of the Mormons were in Iowa; in July of the following year they reached the Great Salt Lake, where they established their State of Deseret as an autonomous political entity. At that time Utah was under the control of Mexico, but in 1848 it became the property of the United States under the terms of the Mexican Cession. Upon hearing this news the Mormons called a convention and sent a resolution to Congress requesting admission to statehood; the request was denied. In 1850, Congress created the Territory of Utah and President Fillmore named Young as territorial governor. The Mormon administration eventually proved unsatisfactory to the Federal Government, and in 1857 Young was replaced by a non-Mormon. When an army troop which was escorting the new governor approached Salt Lake City, the Mormons supposed that it had been sent to kill their leaders. They promptly raised a militia which harassed the army and sabotaged military shipments. At the height of the tension in 1857 some Mormons massacred a party of settlers on their way to California. Within a year tempers cooled and the Mormons accepted a "Gentile" governor; in actuality Brigham Young continued to govern the territory. He was an able and efficient administrator who directed a highly successful cooperative community.

RELIGIOUS COMMUNAL SECTS

The half century which followed the ratification of the Constitution witnessed the rise of a number of communal sects dedicated to the estab-

lishment of an ideal order along religious lines. While their roots were
in the left-wing movements of the Reformation which advocated withdrawal from a sinful society, they were more directly an outgrowth of
revivalism, which emphasized salvation. It was only natural that persons
converted at a revival should have felt an inclination to associate with
persons of like experience. Where the inclination was strong enough it
led on occasion to the formation of religious communities which sought
to emulate the faith and practice of Christians in apostolic times. Almost
all the sects interpreted the Bible literally and were pietistic in their emphases. Most believed that by the collective ownership of property they
could best prepare themselves for the establishment of a perfect social
order when Christ came again on earth. The most practical motivation
for entrance into such a community was poverty; many destitute persons
found that they could considerably strengthen their economic position by
banding together in a cooperative enterprise. While the greater number
of these groups originated in Europe, having constituted a reaction to
the failure of European revolutionary movements to achieve a more perfect society, some were distinctively American. Few attracted a large
number of adherents, however, and most eventually became defunct.

One of the earlier communal movements was that of the Shakers, officially known as the Millennial Church or the United Society of Believers.
The founder, Ann Lee (1736–1784), had united in 1758 with a society
in England known as the Shaking Quakers, whose vexation over their
own sins caused them to shake. Shortly thereafter she claimed to be the
recipient of heavenly visions and prophesied "in tongues." Because of
this gift, Mother Ann, as she was known to her followers, began to hold
religious services which were marked by dancing, singing, speaking in
tongues, and bodily contortions. In 1774, Ann Lee and eight of her disciples emigrated to America and soon established their headquarters at
what is now Watervliet, New York. The first organized Shaker society
was founded in 1787 at Mount Lebanon, also in New York. By 1794 eleven
communities in New York and New England had adopted the Shaker way
of life, the economic foundation of which was communism.

The Shaker movement prospered most on the frontier, especially in
Ohio, Kentucky, and Indiana, where it profited from the influence of the
Second Awakening. Union Village, Ohio, became its chief center in the
West. The Shaker missionaries, who after 1805 often competed with those
of the evangelical denominations in winning converts, were usually well
received in the West, though there were some cases of persecution. Members of the Shaker communities won a reputation for industry and the
accumulation of wealth. But they gained notoriety for their extremes in
advocating celibacy on the ground that sex was the source of all sin, in
rejecting the sacraments of orthodox Protestantism and the inspiration of
the Bible, and in exalting Ann Lee as the person through whom the Christ
Spirit was exhibited a second time. As a result the orthodox churches on

the frontier united in opposing Shakerism. While the sect flourished for a time, so that by the Civil War it numbered some 6000 members dwelling in nineteen different communities, it gradually lost its religious character and became virtually absorbed in economic interests, a factor which contributed to its breakdown. By the end of the nineteenth century it was almost extinct.

In doctrine and practice, the Rappites were similar to the Shakers. Their founder, George Rapp (1770–1847), was a German peasant farmer of pietistic leanings who was persecuted in the homeland because of his refusal to adhere to the established church. He and three hundred of his pietist followers migrated to America in 1803 and 1804 to seek religious freedom and founded a communal settlement named Harmony in western Pennsylvania. The community prospered under Rapp's administration and year after year the fertile soil yielded an abundant harvest. But the settlers were dissatisfied because the land and climate were not suitable for vine and fruit culture, and in 1815 they moved to Indiana and founded New Harmony near the mouth of the Wabash. The settlement, which soon boasted the largest population in the territory, came to be known for its vineyards and orchards and for its saw, woolen, and grist mills. New Harmony became a model community of simple but neat dwellings, whose inhabitants worked with diligence and practiced love and charity. All persons were required to confess their sins to Father Rapp and to settle peaceably differences between them and their neighbors. Since one of their chief tenets was that Christ would soon come again, the Rappites endeavored to gain as much wealth as possible so that when the Lord arrived they might place it at his disposal. They held all property in common and practiced celibacy, looking forward to the imminent return of Christ.

After a decade in New Harmony, Rapp decided to lead his flock back to Pennsylvania; in arriving at his decision he had considered the prevalence of malaria in the area and the possibility of better markets farther East. Robert Owen, a social reformer in Scotland, purchased the Rappite property and initiated in New Harmony an experiment in socialism which attracted many radical and irreligious intellectuals, but which proved to be a failure. Rapp and his people returned to western Pennsylvania and founded a settlement named Economy on the banks of the Ohio. As always, they were preeminently successful. It was apparent, however, that by this time economic interests had outweighed the theological in importance. After Rapp's death in 1847 the community entered a period of decline which ended with the absorption of the group into the larger American environment.

Another pietistic sect was the Amana Society or Community of True Inspiration. It was founded in Germany by Michael Krausent, Christian Metz, and Barbara Heinemann, who rejected the state church and accepted the Bible as their only guide. In 1843 the members emigrated to the United States and organized a community called Ebenezer, near Buffalo, New York, in which property was held in common. During the next three years 800 additional members of the sect arrived from Germany, making it necessary to establish four villages. Finally the problem of living space became so acute that in the 1850's the community moved to Iowa. After the Civil War it began a gradual process of dissolution.

Among the several American experiments in Christian socialism, the Hopedale Community near Milford, Massachusetts, was one of the most prominent. It was founded and nurtured by a Universalist minister, Adin Ballou (1803–1890), who about 1840 became convinced that it was the duty of Christ's disciples to work for the consummation of the kingdom of heaven on earth. To that end he invited like-minded persons to join him in the formation of an ideal community. Within a year some thirty individuals had accepted his invitation and adopted a constitution for "Fraternal Communism." The community was organized like a corporation, each adult member being a stockholder with voting privileges at all meetings. The officers were chosen by the membership; it was their duty to see that each person had employment suited to his abilities and was paid a fixed salary based upon a 48-hour week. By 1851 nearly 200 people were living in the community, having assented to live by the religion of Jesus Christ as a prerequisite to membership. As an expression of the movement of social reform which was then sweeping the country, Hopedale sought to banish intemperance, profanity, slavery, capital punishment, war, and all acts known to be in violation of God's will. Then, after a decade of relatively successful community living, the desire for economic gain gradually forged ahead of the dream of a utopian order; in 1856 the community was dissolved and its members went their several ways.

Similar to Hopedale was the experiment at Brook Farm, nine miles from Boston. Its founder, George Ripley (1802–1880), was a leading member of the famous Transcendental Club and minister of a wealthy Unitarian church in Boston. He resigned his pastorate in 1841 and devoted himself to the formation of a small community designed to promote cultural values in a fully egalitarian order. The atmosphere was intellectually invigorating and attracted a number of savants who offered brilliantly taught courses in literature and the sciences. As at Hopedale, every member was a shareholder and participated in the election of the association's officers. The same wages were paid for all labor performed during a work week of 48 hours. Every member was entitled to send one child to the community school without payment of tuition. Social life was pleasant, featuring lectures, plays, dances, picnics, and boating parties on the Charles River. Among the distinguished persons who participated in the movement were Nathaniel Hawthorne, Isaac Hecker, and Charles A. Dana. Most of Ripley's friends in the Transcendental Club, Emerson, Thoreau, Margaret

Fuller, and Bronson Alcott, demonstrated mild interest in the venture but assumed little more than the role of spectators. For four years Brook Farm achieved notable success in the intellectual realm; from the standpoint of economic profit, it left much to be desired.

In 1845 the membership voted to model the community after the principles of the French socialist, François Fourier. He taught that society should be divided into small units or "phalanxes" of 1600 people living in a large "phalanstery" at the center of an area three miles square. Each person would be assigned labor for which he was best fitted. When the movement was brought to America, Brook Farm embraced it with some enthusiasm and was reorganized into a phalanx. The majority of Transcendentalists promptly disassociated themselves with the movement, the vision of a great cultural center vanished, and the *raison d'être* of the community was reduced to a passion for numbers and profits. Factiousness and strife soon marred the serenity of the utopian order, and within a decade the experiment lapsed into oblivion.

A most interesting attempt to adjust sex relations to perfectionist ideals was initiated by John Humphrey Noyes (1811–1886), founder of the Oneida Community. Noyes was born into a respected New England family. After graduating from Dartmouth in 1830, he came under the influence of Charles G. Finney's revivalism and decided to enter the ministry. He attended Andover Theological Seminary and Yale Divinity School and was licensed to preach by the Congregational association at New Haven. His license was revoked when it was learned that he taught the possibility of attaining perfection in this life. The next few years witnessed the strengthening of his perfectionist convictions and his resolution to form a type of communistic society which might help to establish the Kingdom of God on earth. In 1843 he founded the Putney Corporation or Association of Perfectionists at Putney, Vermont. It bore the obvious mark of Fourierism, but was distinguished also by its founder's radical religious and social concepts. Noyes received great notoriety for advocating "complex marriage," a system whereby every woman in the community was the wife of every man and every man was the husband of every woman. All sex relations, however, had to be regulated and quotas were set for the number of offspring to be produced in any given year. Opposition to this practice became so intense on the part of the villagers that in 1848 Noyes and his followers removed to Oneida, New York.

At Oneida, the community enjoyed extraordinary economic success, particularly through the manufacture of traps for capturing game. Its development of canning industries led to increased profits which were considerably enhanced when the enterprising members added the manufacture of sewing silk and silverware. In doctrinal and social matters Noyes exercised the absolute sway of an oriental potentate. While the group achieved a reputation for industrious and responsible citizenship, their repudiation of monogamy brought them into conflict with their neighbors. They were also criticized for their doctrine that the second coming of Christ had taken place at the end of the Apostolic Age and that through communion with Christ all sin might be overcome. By the 1870's opposition to the community had become so pronounced that the system of "complex marriage" was repudiated in 1879, and the following year the community was reorganized as a joint-stock company under the name Oneida Community Ltd. Noyes spent the remainder of his life in Canada.

THE MILLERITES OR ADVENTISTS

The late 1830's and 1840's witnessed a renewed emphasis upon premillennialism in the American revivalistic sects. This doctrine taught that the earth was in a steady process of moral deterioration and that Christ would soon come again to reign for a thousand years of peace. It was based upon a literal reading of the Book of Daniel and the twentieth chapter of Revelation. Since the teaching was most popular in time of trouble, it is not difficult to understand why its prestige should have been magnified during the period of economic stress which followed the Panic of 1837. Almost all the successful evangelists of the day preached the imminent return of Jesus Christ.

The principal exponent of premillennialism was William Miller (1782–1849). Born in western Massachusetts and raised in Washington County, New York, he served for a time as sheriff at Poultney, Vermont, and as an army captain in the War of 1812. After the war he settled on a farm at Low Hampton, New York; during a local revival in 1816 he was converted from his deistic persuasion and became a member of the Baptist Church. Shortly thereafter he began a thorough study of the Bible which continued for fourteen years. During this study he became absorbed in the Biblical prophecies of the last things, particularly those related to the millennium; on the basis of his investigations he concluded that Christ would come again about 1843. In 1831 he gave lectures in northern New York and western Vermont on the advent of Christ and two years later was licensed as a Baptist preacher. His lectures were published in 1838 under the title *Evidence from Scripture and History of the Second Coming of Christ, About the Year 1843*. Within a year the work had received nationwide publicity and numerous disciples had appeared to lend support to the movement.

While giving a series of lectures in Massachusetts in 1839, Miller met a Baptist minister in Boston, Joshua Himes, who was won to Adventism and subsequently became the publicity agent for the movement. Under Himes' direction, periodicals such as the *Midnight Cry* and *Signs of the Times* were circulated widely and won many converts. During the summers of

1842 and 1843 more than 100 camp meetings were held in the United States to prepare the people for the advent of Christ. Miller's dramatic appeals alone would have been enough to electrify whole communities. On one occasion he gave a moving description of the coming event.

. . . . Behold, the heavens grow black with clouds; the sun has veiled himself; the moon, pale and forsaken, hangs in middle air; the hail descends; the seven thunders utter loud their voices; the lightnings send their vivid gleams and sulphurous flames abroad; and the great city of the nations falls to rise no more forever and forever! At this dread moment, look! The clouds have burst asunder; the heavens appear; the great white throne is in sight! Amazement fills the Universe with awe! He comes!—He comes!—Behold the Saviour comes!—Lift up your heads, ye saints—He comes! He comes! He comes![1]

Despite the active condemnation of the movement by ministers of many denominations, thousands turned to Adventism, and by 1843 there were perhaps 50,000 persons who believed that the time of Christ's coming was near at hand. With the dawning of that keenly anticipated year and the appearance of a brilliant comet in the heavens between February 28 and April 1, the tension mounted, for the second coming was expected to occur sometime between March, 1843, and March, 1844. As the year waxed and waned, expectancy was turned into disappointment, and with the passing of the spring equinox in 1844 a gray pall of gloom settled over the Millerites.

Some of Miller's associates, undaunted by the failure of their leader's calculations, made a further study which prompted them to set another date, October 22, 1844, on which fell the Jewish Day of Atonement. As the day approached, hundreds of believers made their final preparations for the long-heralded event. Believers were almost constantly gathered for prayer, both for themselves and for the salvation of the unconverted. Fervid preaching was much in evidence, for the time was short and there were many to be redeemed. Scores of persons abandoned their secular vocations in order to devote themselves wholly to religious pursuits. Joseph Marsh, pre-millennialist editor of the *Palladium* reported a "deep searching, sanctifying influence of the truth. . . . The Lord is evidently doing up his last work. . . . A few days more and our faith will be lost in vision." On the appointed day the Millerites congregated in churches and homes to await the coming of Christ. But the day passed into history without the momentous event, and great was the disappointment among the faithful throughout the land

A majority of the disillusioned Adventists gradually found their way back to their parent churches, though some, feeling betrayed, were permanently lost to the church. Miller and many of his followers were never-

[1] Quoted in A. F. Tyler, *Freedom's Ferment* (Minnesota, c. 1944), 73.

theless convinced that while an error in calculation had been made, the second coming would take place very soon. Numerous individuals of revivalist leanings were inclined to agree. Such persons withdrew from the older communions and formed themselves into organizations which stressed the pre-millennialist view. In 1845 a general conference of Adventists was held at Albany, New York, to effect a loose organization and to adopt a declaration of principles. It proved impossible, however, to maintain a united Adventist movement. As early as 1844 a small group in Washington, New Hampshire, had begun to observe the seventh-day Sabbath. From this body sprang the Seventh-day Adventists, who developed a denominational organization in 1860. Their principal leader and theologian was Mrs. Ellen G. White who, for more than seventy years, gave direction to the movement. Other schisms brought about the formation of the Advent Christian Association in 1861, which denied that immortality is inherent in mankind, and the Life and Advent Union in 1863, which taught that there will be no resurrection of the wicked. The Church of God (Adventist) was formed in 1865 by persons who denied the inspiration of Mrs. White.

SPIRITUALISM

Excitement over the Millerite movement had scarcely subsided before the cult of Spiritualism appeared on the American scene. Swedenborgianism, which had arrived from Sweden early in the century, had prepared the way for its coming by emphasizing a tangible spirit world where human beings might grow toward perfection. Its appeal to the non-orthodox lay in the fact that it harmonized liberal theologies with the scientific and sociological conceptions of the period and brought the supernatural close to nature. In America it was frequently linked with mesmerism, which sought to reveal the laws of the spirit world by means of the trance. The practice of clairvoyance came to be regarded by many as a magic key that could unlock the mysteries of the world beyond. Perhaps it might be possible to communicate with the spirits of the dead. Prominent leaders in the American adaptation of Swedenborgianism were George Bush, professor of "occult therapy" at New York University, and Andrew Jackson Davis, self-styled clairvoyant and interpreter of Emanuel Swedenborg.

The thought of making contact with departed spirits held wide appeal for persons of varied background and character, and nowhere was this more true than in the Burned-over District of New York. In March, 1848, the family of John D. Fox was disturbed by strange nocturnal rappings in their home at Hydesville, not far from Palmyra, New York. Fox's daughters, Margaretta and Katie, convinced that the rappings were caused by spirits, devised a system of communication with them. It was not long before the Fox sisters were conducting public seances, and so convincingly that Horace Greeley was led to observe that "it would be the basest cowardice not to say that we are convinced beyond a doubt of their perfect integrity and good faith." Though an investigating committee later discovered that the girls produced the rapping sounds with their toe joints, this in no wise diminished the faith of the general public. Professional mediums throughout the country did a lucrative business through the holding of seances which featured not only rappings but the appearance of unexplained writings and the moving of tables as if by magic. The educated as well as the ignorant were attracted to these bizarre gatherings. Perhaps the most useful convert to the movement was Robert Dale Owen, long known for his agnosticism, who published several books which added to the popularity of spiritualism. Interest ran high throughout the 1850's, but with the outbreak of the Civil War it quickly subsided. Not until the latter part of the century did the movement achieve a national organization.

18

Evangelism and Social Reform

FROM HIS VANTAGE POINT AT THE MIDDLE OF THE NINETEENTH CENTURY, THE historian Emerson Davis reflected thus on the half century which had just elapsed: "There has been . . . a more perfect development of the benevolent spirit of the gospel in the souls of men than has been known at any previous time since the age of the apostles." Granted that the statement was somewhat hyperbolic, it was nonetheless expressive of the prevailing ethos in this time of uncritical idealism. The national impulse to achieve a perfect society characterized by benevolence and good will was inspired primarily by that wave of revivals which began with the Second Awakening and mounted with increasing intensity after the opening of the Finney revivals in 1826.

Two evangelists in particular bridged the gap between the Second Awakening and the resurgence of revivalism. Lyman Beecher (1775–1863), a famous Congregational and Presbyterian divine, had from the beginning of his ministry in 1799 preached with a powerful persuasiveness which gripped the hearts of his hearers and impelled them to a change of character. Homiletic fame won him promotion from his little church at East Hampton, Long Island, to a larger congregation at Litch-field, Connecticut. In his hands, revivalism became a powerful defensive weapon for evangelical churches which had been harassed by liberal doc-trines and weakened by the effects of declining spiritual zeal. He saw that through revivalism society could be morally improved and made ready for the millennium. To that end this bellicose evangelist conducted a one-man campaign against sin, attacking a host of social ills, running here and there to confound skeptics, and doing it all with phenomenal success. A somewhat different type of evangelism was exhibited by Asahel Nettleton (1783–1844), a Connecticut Congregationalist. His evangelistic campaigns in Connecticut and New York were reminiscent of the strongly intellec-tual revivalism once practiced by Edwards. No spellbinder in the pulpit, his greatest appeal was among small groups with whom he could converse simply and convincingly about God's redemptive love. His signal triumphs were in the small towns; in cities such as New York he was a colossal fail-ure. Conservative and retiring, he possessed neither the interest nor the ability to become a leader in mass evangelism and after 1826 his place in the evangelistic firmament was taken by one who was in almost every re-spect his opposite, Charles G. Finney.

ANTE-BELLUM EVANGELISM

More than any commanding figure of his time, Charles Grandison Fin-ney (1792–1875) united within his person the clerical and scholarly pat-terns of New England religion with the lay and pietistic emphases of the frontier. He was the greatest evangelist of the ante-bellum era, first in a line of professional revivalists. Born in Connecticut and raised in Oneida County, in the Burned-over District of New York, he typified the restless and religiously capricious spirit of the frontier. His parents practiced no formal religion and there were few church adherents among their neigh-bors. After graduation from secondary school in Warren, Connecticut, he taught school and worked in a law office, during which time he was highly uncertain as to his religious convictions. It was not until 1821, when he was approaching his thirtieth birthday, that he was converted to Chris-tianity. This conversion came after months of inward struggle and fervent prayer, culminating in an intense emotional experience. Finney later re-ported that on that occasion Jesus stood before him as if in real life and he was seized by the power of the Holy Spirit.

The Holy Spirit descended upon me in a manner that seemed to go through me, body and soul. I could feel the impression, like a wave of electricity, going through and through me. Indeed it seemed to come in waves and waves of liquid love . . . It seemed like the very breath of God. I can recollect dis-tinctly that it seemed to fan me, like immense wings. . . .[1]

[1] Quoted in B. A. Weisberger, *They Gathered at the River* (Little, Brown, c. 1958), 92.

In this state he experienced his justification by faith and found peace with God.

Determined to become a minister, Finney went under the care of St. Lawrence Presbytery in 1822. He proved to be something of a problem to his ministerial advisors, however, refusing to heed their advice that he attend Princeton Seminary and insisting upon independent theological study. Although the Presbytery finally licensed him to preach in 1824, it did so with some reservations as to his theological position. He rejected the doctrine of election, being convinced that the atonement was for all men rather than for a chosen few, and leaned in the direction of perfectionism. After twelve years in the Presbyterian ministry, during which time he was frequently under attack by members of the Presbyterian denomination, he withdrew and adopted Congregationalism.

As a revivalist Finney was without question one of the greatest, and his most permanent influence was felt in the central and western part of New York. His most useful implement was emotion. It is said that while he was conducting a revival at Antwerp, New York, during the early days of his ministry, Finney spoke so forcefully that the congregation was gripped by shock. Men and women began to fall from the benches crying for mercy. The evangelist wrote later that had he been armed with a sword in each hand he could not have cut them down as fast as they fell. Nearly the entire assemblage was on its knees or prostrate within minutes after the first shock came upon them. Finney was so successful in winning converts during the opening of his revival campaigns in 1826 that he soon became a peripatetic evangelist, conducting revivals in Philadelphia in 1827, New York in 1829, and Boston in 1831. Wherever he went, congregations were held spellbound by his searching hypnotic eyes and his stentorian voice, which he employed with theatrical effect. Plain-speaking and fearful of ostentation, he spoke extemporaneously with straight-forward conviction to the common man and yet with such logic that the educated were awed by his homilies. Lyman Beecher, Asahel Nettleton, and others attacked him for his methods, which included use of the "anxious bench," the "inquiry room," and the "protracted meeting," Nettleton going so far as to suggest that the fruits of his preaching would be envy, malice, anger, and evil speaking.

Opposition on the part of disaffected clergy could not diminish Finney's popularity. During the 1830's his star climbed steadily into the firmament as he toured the East, holding remarkably successful revivals at Rochester, Auburn, Buffalo, Providence, Boston, and New York City. For a time he contented himself with the obligations of a settled pastorate in New York, but by 1835 he was off again, this time to a professorship at Oberlin and the amplification of his perfectionist ideas. Even then he found time to conduct periodic revivals in the East and in England. It would be difficult to estimate the number of persons influenced by his ministry; conservatively, it ran into the tens of thousands.

There were other important stars in the galaxy of evangelists. The champion leader of revivals among the Baptists was Jacob Knapp (1799–1874). Indefatigably energetic, for twenty-five years he stormed up and down the country lashing his congregations, provoking his enemies, and stirring up controversy. During the early 1830's the principal scene of his labors was upstate New York; the remainder of the decade found him dividing his energies between New York City, Brooklyn, Baltimore, and the Mohawk Valley of New York. By the 1840's he had extended his circuit to include Providence, Boston, Washington, and Chicago. He was a man of uncommon oratorical skills and won wide popularity in the face of marked criticism. Other well-known evangelists of the period were Congregationalists Edward Norris Kirk and Joshua Leavitt, Baptists Francis Wayland and Jabez Swan, Presbyterians Albert Barnes and Nathaniel Beman, and Methodist John Newland Maffitt. The majority of these revivalists achieved their greatest success in the cities. Urban evangelism was a powerful force in the thirty years which preceded the Civil War.

Immediately following the economic collapse of 1837, revivalism entered a lean period, a situation which was not improved during the Mexican War. The evangelist was accepted as a permanent fixture on the national scene, but there were temporarily fewer revivals while the attention of the people was fixed upon economic and political matters. Even Finney found his audiences to be somewhat less enthusiastic than before. And in 1851 the New York Congregationalist journal, the *Independent*, bewailed the dearth of evangelical zeal and found cause to "mourn over the desolations of Zion, and to hang our harps upon the willows." Among the foes of the revival this condition was greeted with rejoicing. In the most thoroughly revivalistic churches, namely the Baptist, Methodist, Congregational, and Presbyterian, there had long been a dissenting group which felt that evangelists of the Finney school were too much in conformity with the humanistic tendencies of the age. In the Lutheran Church the anti-revivalist German confessionalists were sharply at odds with their more liberal and "enthusiastic" brethren who opposed liturgical worship. Unitarians as well had been troubled by an evangelistic wing in their denomination, sparked by George E. Ellis and Frederic Dan Huntington, which affirmed a supernatural salvation from sin through Jesus Christ. Other opponents of revivalism included high-church Episcopalians and German Reformed advocates of the Mercersburg Theology.

Despite the various forces which combined to diminish evangelistic returns in the 1840's, American revivalism was by no means dead. It had established itself as a permanent feature of urban religious life and was simply awaiting the providential moment to break out again in full flame. In the fall of 1857 there were obvious signs of stirrings in the spiritual realm, the first being weekly gatherings of laymen for prayer in New York City. These meetings, inspired by Jeremiah C. Lanphier, were so popular that by October they were being held daily. About the same time the stock market crash brought on mass hysteria and a popular feeling that the crisis was a divine judgment on a sinful order. The hour had come for national repentance and an outpouring of the Holy Spirit. Thus began a revival distinguished by its urban character and lay leadership.

By February, 1858, multitudes were jamming their way into the daily prayer meetings; two months later twenty such meetings were being held in New York alone. Reports of these remarkable sessions were disseminated by the New York newspapers and the telegraph. Similar meetings soon began to spring up in Chicago and Philadelphia and it was not long before every large city had regular gatherings for prayer. These services were highly informal; any person might lead in prayer or song according to his inclination, though it was customary to place a time limit on each presentation. They were conducted on an interdenominational basis and received considerable support from local units of the Young Men's Christian Association. Gradually the movement gathered strength in the smaller cities and towns and rural areas until the nation was caught in the full sweep of revivalism. Surprisingly, it received support from Episcopalians, Old School Presbyterians, Unitarians, and Universalists, who were ordinarily suspicious of "enthusiasm." So universal was the attractiveness of the movement that virtually no opposition was raised to its activities. Once again the giants of evangelism came into the limelight. Finney, Knapp, Kirk, and many others were besieged with more invitations to speak than they could possibly accept. But a new generation of evangelists was also coming before the public eye. The brilliant successes of Edward Payson Hammond in New England and the already assured status of Henry Ward Beecher in Brooklyn bear evidence of that truth. All in all, the awakening of 1858 was a positive force in the direction of spiritual vitality and moral reform which continued in effect through the Civil War.

THE IMPACT OF CHRISTIAN PERFECTIONISM

The revival of 1858 bore powerful indications of the influence of perfectionism, which held that through God's grace a relative attainment of the Christian goal was possible for believers in this life. As early as the 1830's such teachings had emerged in the Oberlin Theology and in the platforms of the various utopian sects. Another important source of perfectionist concepts was the Methodist doctrine of sanctification. It was grounded in Wesley's teaching that through the reception of Christ's saving love, men are gradually empowered to perform the works of God and purify their hearts from sinful impulses. Not until after 1825, however, was the doctrine emphasized in American Methodism, and then it was spoken of as an instantaneous work. Phoebe Palmer, wife of Methodist physician Walter Palmer and sponsor of devotional meetings for women in New York City during the 1830's, did much to popularize the teaching through her book, which was entitled *The Way to Holiness* (1851). Perfectionism received another boost through the revivals of the Methodist evangelists John Newland Maffitt, James Caughey, and William Taylor. It gained intellectual respectability through the support of such giants of Methodism as Matthew Simpson, preacher extraordinary; Nathan Bangs, publishing agent; George O. Peck, church editor; and Abel Stevens, clergyman and denominational historian. With such impressive endorsement the movement finally filtered down to the parish level and holiness revivals broke out in many parts of the country. In the Genesee Conference of western New York certain advocates of holiness gave voice to the charge that their ministerial colleagues who were lukewarm on the subject of sanctification were worldly and theologically liberal. After several ministers of the holiness group had been expelled from the church for unchristian behavior, several thousand dissatisfied perfectionists withdrew from the denomination in 1860 and founded the Free Methodist Church.

The decade which followed 1850 witnessed a rising tide of perfectionist preaching in the major Protestant denominations. Few non-Methodists adopted the Wesleyan view, but most churchmen were in substantial agreement on the need for individual holiness. Undoubtedly this zeal for Christian improvement was one of the forces which instigated the great revival of 1858. To the champions of perfectionism the revival seemed to presage the coming conversion of the nations and the establishment on earth of the Kingdom of God. This conviction increased steadily in American evangelical Protestantism throughout and beyond the Civil War. Perfectionism flourished primarily in urban areas, where the social problems and the individual frustrations presented a peculiar challenge to those who believed that Christianity could "work" to the betterment of mankind. To persons thrown into the impersonal environment of the city and tortured by the loneliness of the crowd it was comforting to discover in a revival service a sense of belonging and to learn that the perfection of one's life made a difference to society. This "practical" Christianity made a profound impression on the plain people and inspired them to labor to the full extent of their capacities for the evangelization of the community, the nation, the world.

MOVEMENTS OF SOCIAL REFORM

It was natural that where there were revivals there should also be reform; it was the means whereby the Kingdom of God was to be achieved in America. During the earliest decades of the nineteenth century, revivalistic fervor expressed itself chiefly through the work of Bible, tract, missionary, and Sunday School societies. As the century progressed interest in peace, prison reform, poor relief, temperance, the proper observance of the Sabbath, and a host of other moral and social problems steadily mounted in the American Protestant milieu until social reform became the absorbing passion of Christians who embraced revivalism. But not all Protestants could enter with equal enthusiasm into every phase of social reform. The more Biblically legalistic and theocratic thinkers, particularly those of the Calvinistic tradition, were apt to place their emphasis upon personal reform as a panacea for social evils. Thus the cause of poverty was laziness, want of ability, pride, insanity, and intemperance; through moral improvement the disease could be remedied. The prerequisite to such improvement was evangelism and Christian education. On the other hand, Christians of perfectionist and millennialist inclinations as well as liberal Unitarians and Friends tended to go a step further and identify themselves with such social causes as the abolition of slavery.

The Peace Movement

Prior to the Revolutionary War the principal anti-war agitation had stemmed from the Society of Friends. At the opening of the national era a number of irenic-spirited gentlemen, among them Dr. Benjamin Rush, urged the government to initiate a movement for peace. Nothing came of it, but when the War of 1812 drew to a close peace efforts began anew. In 1815, David Low Dodge, a New York merchant of Presbyterian persuasion, published a book entitled *War Inconsistent with the Religion of Jesus Christ*. That August he and thirty others formed a peace society, the chief activity of which was to distribute literature on the subject of their interest. The year 1815 also witnessed the founding of the Massachusetts Peace Society in the home of William Ellery Channing. Many clergymen affiliated with the society and Thomas Jefferson accepted honorary membership. Shortly thereafter several other state societies were born.

It was largely through the dedicated efforts of William Ladd, Yankee entrepreneur, that the various state societies unified their programs through the organization of the American Peace Society in 1828. The official organs of the society were the *Harbinger of Peace,* the *Calumet,* and the *American Advocate of Peace.* Among the solutions to war proposed by the society were arbitration and an international court or congress. By 1838 the Peace Society was torn by internal conflict. That year William Lloyd Garrison and a number of assertive followers who were disappointed over the national organization's failure to endorse non-resistance in all circumstances created a new association called the New England Non-Resistance Society. Neither body was supported to any significant extent by the American public. About the time of the Mexican War there was a certain flurry of interest. Theodore Parker urged his fellow citizens to take no part in the conflict and James Russell Lowell pronounced it to be nothing more than murder. Under the leadership of Elihu Burritt a last valiant effort was made in 1846 to persuade the American Peace Society to condemn all war. Failing in this, Burritt left for England where he founded the League of Universal Brotherhood and masterminded four international peace conferences between 1848 and 1852. With the opening of the tumultuous 1850's, however, the peace movement in the United States rapidly declined in the face of mounting tension over slavery. Some of the more extreme reformers were beginning to think that war might be necessary in order to destroy the great evil of human bondage. Not until the termination of the War Between the States would the movement for peace be revived.

The Temperance and Sabbath Crusades

During colonial times the use of alcoholic beverages had not been considered as a particular problem in society. It was not until the Revolutionary era that the ravages of drinking became apparent. In 1784 the matter was brought before the public by the eminent physician, Benjamin Rush, in a pamphlet entitled *An Inquiry into the Effects of Spiritous Liquors on the Human Body and Mind*. With the advent of the Second Awakening many a revivalist cited the work to enforce his arguments against intemperance and then went on to urge sobriety for moral and spiritual reasons. Lyman Beecher, upon reading Rush's publication, was so impressed that he became a leader of temperance reform. Soon local societies began to spring up all over New England and the Middle Atlantic states, later coalescing into state societies to fight the "sin of drunkenness." The Congregationalist, Presbyterian, and Methodist denominations gave general support to the movement, though there were instances in which individual clergymen refused to cooperate. Peter Cartwright, on the frontier, reported that one congregation was split over the matter, a minority group following their inebriated preacher out the door of the church. Even those groups which emphasized temperance seldom held any brief for abstinence.

The formation of the American Society for the Promotion of Temperance in 1826 reflected the moral concerns of the current wave of revivalism. With the exception of the Lutherans and Episcopalians, who at the time were little involved in the revival effort, most of the major Protestant denominations officially endorsed the temperance crusade. A sister organization, the United States Temperance Union, came into existence in Philadelphia in 1833; three years later it merged with the older society, forming the American Temperance Union. About this time dissension began to appear in the national organization. A number of the delegates desired to ban only strong drinks and to exempt beer and wine from the general condemnation. But their will did not prevail and the forerunners of the prohibition movement came increasingly to dominate the scene.

Subsequent disunity spelled the general declension of the cause during the late 1830's.

With the formation of the Washington Temperance Society in Baltimore in 1840, the temperance movement entered a new phase. A band of reformed alcoholics pledged themselves to total abstinence and the reclamation of inebriates. Their success was astounding; there were more than a thousand adherents in Baltimore before the end of the first year. The movement spread like wildfire, claiming perhaps a hundred thousand drunkards within three years. Its best-known leader was John B. Gough, himself a convert from drink, who made hundreds of addresses and persuaded thousands to sign temperance pledges. All over the country "experience meetings" were held in churches, schoolhouses, and halls, at which three or four reformed drunkards would testify. Gradually, however, the Washingtonian movement dissolved and its work was taken over by more religiously centered organizations.

Nor was the temperance movement confined to Protestants. In 1849 Father Theobold Mathew, fresh from a temperance crusade in Ireland, arrived in America to begin an extensive speaking tour of the country. It was estimated that within a period of two years he persuaded 500,000 Roman Catholics to take a pledge of total abstinence. Joseph Cretin, first Roman Catholic Bishop of St. Paul, Minnesota, was a firm advocate of the temperance cause and a determined foe of frontier saloons. When the Minnesota legislature passed a law regulating liquor he directed that the cathedral bell be rung as a sign of approbation.

Meanwhile, the older temperance societies, having experienced a resurgence of strength, began to urge the passage of legislation which would curtail the sale of intoxicants. A Massachusetts law of 1838 forbade the sale of hard liquors in any quantity less than fifteen gallons, the intention being to end tavern abuses. A storm of protest went up and two years later the law was repealed. During the decade which followed 1840 several states adopted local-option laws; in 1851 the first state-wide prohibition law was enacted in Maine, largely through the efforts of a Quaker merchant, Neal Dow. Within four years every northern state legislature except that of New Jersey had enacted some form of temperance legislation. By 1860, however, the American public had lost interest in the cause and by 1868 Maine alone had prohibition legislation still in effect. But temperance reform had made considerable progress, especially in the rural areas which remained relatively untouched by immigrants who favored the use of intoxicants. It would receive a new impetus in the era which followed the Civil War.

With the liberalizing tendencies which had appeared late in the eighteenth century, there was a noticeable decline in the strict observance of the Sabbath. Especially was this evident on the frontier. Home mission-

aries reported frequently that their charges neglected the proper observance of the Lord's Day. One missionary in Ohio sent word in 1808 that
he had spoken regularly on the need to conduct oneself with decorum on
the Sabbath. Perhaps the situation there was not unlike that which Peter
Cartwright discovered in southern Kentucky, where Sunday was apparently reserved for horse racing, hunting, fishing, card playing, and dancing. Yet there were evidences of strong Sabbatarianism in the West.
According to the records for 1816 of the Congregational Church of Madison, Ohio, "This church considers the collecting of hay or grain on the
Sabbath; attending to any part of the business of making sugar; the visiting of friends, except in cases of sickness; the prosecuting of journeys on
that day, without special necessity, a violation of Christian duty." In 1839
the South District Baptist Association of Illinois resolved "that this association deeply deplores the neglect of the Lord's day, by too many members of our churches, and for this reason do earnestly urge a more strict
observance of the same."

Of particular concern to Sabbatarians was the transportation of mail on
Sunday. Between 1810 and 1815 numerous religious organizations passed
resolutions against the practice and petitioned Congress to pass prohibitive legislation. The controversy was intensified in 1825 when a law was
enacted requiring all post offices where mail was delivered on Sunday to
remain open the whole day. It led to the founding of the General Union
for Promoting the Observance of the Christian Sabbath three years later.
Though the organization sent frequent petitions to Congress its activities
were without success and its membership and influence gradually declined.

By 1843 there was a revival of interest in Sabbath reform and in that
year was born the American and Foreign Sabbath Union. The reports of
Justin Edwards, during his seven-year tenure as secretary, claimed remarkable progress. They mentioned that the transportation of mails on
the Sabbath had been discontinued on a number of routes and that about
forty railroads had terminated train service on that day. "The communities through which they pass, and whose right to the stillness and quiet
of the day had for years been grossly violated by the screaming and rum-
bling of cars in time of public worship, are now free from the nuisance,
and are permitted to enjoy their rights and privileges without molestation." In the long run, however, the Sabbath crusaders were doomed to
failure. One mighty force against them was the steady increase of immigration from Europe and the concomitant "Continental Sabbath," which
was decidedly opposed to the Puritan concept of the day. This institution
provided for worship on Sunday mornings and for amusement in the afternoons and evenings. Then, during the Civil War, when Christians of various lands and creeds intermingled as never before and it was not always

possible to observe the Sabbath when in the field, the force of the Sabbath tradition tended to break down. The Sabbatarians, to be sure, continued their fight, but it was a losing battle. The forces of secularization were slowly surmounting the power of orthodox Protestantism.

Miscellaneous Problems of Morals

Evangelical reform penetrated every area of life and peeked into every dark corner to ferret out "sin" and destroy it. Among many abuses which evangelicals hoped to correct are three of special interest. The first concerned the practice of dueling, which was beginning to disappear by the opening of the nineteenth century. Lyman Beecher, in his *The Remedy for Duelling*, published in 1809, focused attention on the evil. "The duellist," he said, "is a murderer." To cast a vote for such a person was a sin against God and society. In response to the rising tide of protest against dueling Connecticut made the practice illegal in 1818; Virginia followed suit a year later. Several other states, notably those in the South, passed similar legislation prior to the outbreak of the Civil War.

Also under the attack of evangelicals was the theater, regarded by many revivalists as a competitive institution. Henry Ward Beecher, who regarded it as "the gate of debauchery, the porch of pollution," observed in his *Lectures to Young Men*, published in 1856: "It is notorious that the theatre is the door to all the sinks of iniquity." Evangelists ranted and railed about the theater, praying for its destruction and conversion into a place of worship. Other favorite targets of their venom were gaudy apparel, card playing, and dancing.

Another problem which elicited the wide support of evangelists was the reform of wayward girls. In 1830 a Presbyterian minister, John R. McDowell, established a Magdalen Asylum in New York for such girls who desired to return to righteous living. He issued his *Magdalen Report* in 1832 and began publication of *McDowell's Journal* a year later. Both the *Report* and the *Journal* contained such offensive accounts of prostitution and houses of ill fame in New York that he was censured by his communion and his periodical pronounced an aggravation by the Grand Jury. A much more effective organization was the American Female Moral Reform Society, founded in 1834 and operated by women. Through its efforts a wide-scale attack was made on prostitution and some progress was made in the reclamation of delinquent girls. The year 1834 also witnessed the establishment of the Young Men's Moral Reform Society of New York. Toward the end of the decade, however, the movement bore increasing signs of neglect; the Panic of 1837 contributed to the loss of financial support, but more important, the public was growing tired of lurid reports and disgusted with the reformers who authored them.

The Humanitarian Impulse

With the steady rise of immigration, the increasing centralization of the population in urban areas, and the uncertainties of employment in an emergent industrial economy, the problem of the poor became more acute. Through Puritan eyes the condition was the result of moral depravity and could be corrected through conversion. Protestants who embraced this view early in the nineteenth century thus saw no need for social reform apart from that which would come automatically through the Christianization of the individual. The philosophy was adequately expressed by John Brooks in a letter to Charles G. Finney in 1830, in which he spoke of plans to help the poor in Salem, Massachusetts.

The object is to raise up Local missionaries to visit and read the Scriptures, and preach to the *poor* in our own neighborhood. Brethren and Sisters are to join— each to visit etc. to a certain number of Families once in two weeks and meet for prayer, searching the Scriptures and make reports to a Superintendent weekly. Every member *must work or quit*. No honorary members.[2]

After the devastating effects of the Panic of 1837, certain evangelists began to realize that a new approach was needed to the problem of urban poverty. Edward Norris Kirk, for example, suggested in 1842 that "when men love their neighbors as themselves, the causes of poverty will be sought out, and the remedy applied as far as possible." More than a decade later the editors of *The Independent* called for "low rents, commodious, cleanly, healthy buildings, upon the most approved plan of lodging-houses," and urged city churches to give more heed to the working class. In 1851, Stephen Colwell, influential Presbyterian layman, took an even more positive approach to the problem in his anonymously published work, *New Themes for the Protestant Clergy*. He took to task the older program of organized benevolence and advocated the passage of social legislation for the protection of the working man. The response to his effort was bitter invective delivered by conservatives from all parts of the country.

The Christian community, nevertheless, made some advance in the pre-Civil War era in understanding the social problem, notably in its recognition that society itself could be at least partially responsible for contemporary social evils. Implementation of this discovery was essentially limited, however, to social welfare projects. During the 1840's, Phoebe Palmer played a prominent part in the establishment of Hedding Church by the Methodists, a mission to the poor in the slums of New York; she was also active in The New York Female Assistance Society for

---

[2] Quoted in C. C. Cole, Jr., *The Social Ideas of the Northern Evangelists, 1826–1860* (Columbia, 1954), 111.

the Relief and Religious Instruction of the Sick Poor. More important was her contribution to the establishment in 1850 of the Five Points Mission, a precursor of the settlement house. It featured a chapel, schoolrooms, and twenty apartments which were available to those who had no means of support and were willing to abide by the rules of the mission. Within a few years similar institutions were operating in other cities as well as New York.

In this age of evangelical compassion there was born in the United States an organization which concerned itself with the spiritual development of young men. The Young Men's Christian Association had been founded in London in 1844 by George Williams, a young clerk; its purpose was to improve "the Spiritual Condition of Young Men in the Drapery and other Trades." The first association in the United States was founded in 1851 in Boston, where the way had been prepared through the work of Edward Norris Kirk with young men at the Mt. Vernon Church of that city. During the next year ten more associations came into existence; by 1861 the number of American associations had climbed to two hundred. Their principal activities included conducting prayer meetings, Bible classes, and mission schools, giving courses of sermons and lectures, and maintaining libraries and reading rooms. In 1854 and 1855 international conventions were held at Buffalo and Cincinnati. The work of the Y.M.C.A. was closely integrated with that of the evangelical churches and was everywhere supported by leading ministers. It figured prominently in the revival of 1858, becoming noted for its union prayer meetings.

One popular outlet for the expression of humanitarian zeal was prison reform. Its motivation was the moral renovation of the prisoner and the salvation of his soul. The restoration of the criminal to responsible citizenship was the avowed purpose of the Philadelphia Society for Alleviating the Miseries of Public Prisons, founded in 1787. To that end its members provided Sunday services and schools for the inmates and furnished Bibles for every cell. Resident chaplains and visiting clergymen ministered to the needs of the unfortunates, while philanthropists, particularly those of the Society of Friends, agitated for the improvement of conditions in the prisons and the abolition of cruel forms of punishment and imprisonment for debt. After the War of 1812 renewed interest in prison reform led to the establishment of new penal institutions such as that at Auburn, New York, which was based on the philosophy that inmates could best rehabilitate themselves through communal labor. At Philadelphia's new penitentiary, erected in 1829, prisoners were isolated and encouraged to read and meditate upon the Bible. The Boston Prison Discipline Society of 1825 and the New York Prison Association of 1845 exemplified the desire of humanitarians to elevate the morals of imprisoned criminals.

Reformers were equally interested in the rehabilitation of young delinquents. The House of Reformation in South Boston, managed by an Episcopal clergyman who encouraged the boys to conduct their own student government, was typical of the contemporary "houses of refuge" and reformatories. The pre-Civil War period also found public-spirited citizens engaged in activities for the benefit of the handicapped. Thus Thomas H. Gallaudet founded a school in Hartford for the education of deaf-mutes, Samuel G. Howe organized a school in Boston for the blind, and Dorothea Dix of Massachusetts championed state-supported hospitals for the mentally ill.

Despite considerable opposition from most of the clergy, women entered more freely into the activities of the churches as the nineteenth century progressed and thus contributed to the broader movement which called for equal rights for women in other fields. They participated freely in Bible, tractarian, and Sunday School work and poured themselves into the ministry of poor relief, penal, and anti-slavery societies. Regarded by men as socially inferior, it was only through determination and persistence that they found a place in the movement for reform. Horace Bushnell spoke for the conservatives when he said: "God made the woman to be a help for man, not to be a wrestler with him. . . . But if to all our present powers of strife and faction we are to add a race of factious women, there will not be left enough of feeling and rest to make life tolerable or allow virtue to breathe." But the future belonged to the forces that favored women's rights. In the generation antecedent to the War Between the States perhaps a score or more of distinguished ladies added lustre to the feminist movement. Among them were the educators, Emma Willard and Mary Lyon; the author and editor, Margaret Fuller; the physician, Harriot K. Hunt; the anti-slavery agitators, Sarah and Angelina Grimké and Lucretia Mott; the temperance leaders, Susan B. Anthony and Elizabeth Cady Stanton; and that missionary and humanitarian extraordinary, Phoebe Palmer. Much of their support came from Quakers, Transcendentalists, and perfectionists who consistently worked for the attainment of democratic ideals and principles. In 1848 the first Woman's Rights Convention was held at Seneca Falls, New York; beginning in 1850, such conventions were held annually. The movement, which demanded equality with men before the law and in society, steadily gathered momentum until, for a time, the Civil War diverted attention to other interests.

During the thirty-five years which preceded the Civil War singular changes were wrought in the character of American Protestantism. Most obvious was the increased function of the laity in the program of the churches, whether through participation in prayer meetings or leadership in humanitarian causes. Since the emphasis among lay Protestants fell upon conversion and the practice of righteousness, there was understandably less concern on their part for denominational differences and the finer points of doctrine. What was important was that people be "saved" and perfected, and this could best be accomplished through interdenomi-national cooperation sparked by mutual understanding and love. To a generation steeped in pietism, to have dogma without love was to be "a noisy gong or a clanging cymbal." Nor could the rigors of Calvinism speak to the spiritual condition of a romantic age. The call was for a warm, vibrant, emotional religion which spoke of the free grace of God and the infinite perfectibility of man. To be sure, orthodoxy did what it could to stem the tide of the new revivalism, but its seed fell upon rocky ground. The pattern had been set for the development of a liberal and socially centered faith during the remainder of the nineteenth century.

19

The Churches and the Slavery Controversy

IN THE SEVENTY-FIVE YEARS WHICH MARKED THE NASCENCE AND DECAY OF American unity, unquestionably the most serious problem vexing the American public was that of Negro slavery. Though slavery was one of the oldest and best-established institutions in American society, it had never been free from attack by humanitarians both within and without the camp of organized Christianity. For those who believed fervently in the equality of men before God slavery was an ugly blot upon the record of a nation conceived in liberty and destined to become a ray of light in a weary world. For those who viewed the institution as economically productive and vital to the fiscal well-being of the community it was a glorious provision of God defended by Scripture. It was perhaps inevitable that as conviction on both sides mounted tension should have increased—that the issue should have become the subject of national debate which contributed to bitter conflicts over states' rights versus federalism, the admission of new states into the body politic, colonization of free Negroes, and abolitionism. Into this debate the churches entered with an ardor born of spiritual conviction and environmental stimuli, making pronounce-

362

ments which bore evidence of their own disunity. The fruits of fervor were friction and ultimately schism as American churchmen followed the crusader's path to sanguinary war.

THE SLAVERY ISSUE TO 1830

The post-revolutionary popularization of deism, the natural rights philosophy, and humanitarianism had profound implications for the slavery issue. Thomas Paine's affirmation that Africans had a "natural and perfect right to freedom" made a deep impression upon the American public and found support even in the South. Benjamin Franklin, Thomas Jefferson, and a host of political leaders argued strenuously against slavery on the basis not only of natural rights but of God's justice. Various states took legislative action against slavery. In the northern states, where there was but a fraction of the number of slaves in the South, legislation was finally enacted; by 1787 Rhode Island, Vermont, Massachusetts, Connecticut, New York, New Jersey, and Pennsylvania had either abolished slavery or provided for its gradual abolition. The Northwest Ordinance of 1787 excluded slavery forever. In the South several states either prohibited the further importation of slaves or placed restrictions upon their importation. While the national Constitution was silent on slaveholding, the Congress provided for the abolition of the slave trade in 1808.

During this period a number of abolition societies made their appearance. The first, The Society for the Relief of Free Negroes Unlawfully Held in Bondage, was organized in Philadelphia in 1775 and reorganized as an abolition society in 1787. Similar organizations were founded in New York (1785), Maryland (1790), Virginia (1791), Connecticut (1791), New Jersey (1792), and Delaware (1794). At least part of the incentive for these societies came from the challenging work by Thomas Clarkson entitled *Essay on the Slavery and Commerce of the Human Species,* published in 1786 in England, and William Wilberforce's militant stand in Parliament on behalf of abolition. By 1794 the movement had become national when what came to be known as The American Convention for Promoting the Abolition of Slavery and Improving the Condition of the African Race was held. Half of its delegates were from southern states. The principal work of this organization, which met almost annually until 1829, was to plan for the education of Negroes, petition for the abolition of slavery in the District of Columbia, and publicize the natural rights philosophy of the Declaration of Independence.

The Churches and Slavery

During the colonial period the Society of Friends had taken the lead in opposing slavery. It was thus fitting that the first petition to the new

Congress against the institution, delivered in 1790, should have been authored by Quakers. The Yearly Meetings of 1819, 1823, and 1824 sent similar memorials to the national government. One of the most vocal of the
Quaker opponents of slavery was Benjamin Lundy, founder of "The Hu-
mane Society" at St. Clairsville, Ohio, in 1815. Through his periodical,
The Genius of Universal Emancipation, first published in 1821, his views
gained a wide hearing. Lundy favored the abolition of slavery by the
Congress in all territories and districts under its control and the colonization of Negroes in countries other than the United States. He thus gave
full support to the American Colonization Society. In 1822 the Friends in
Pennsylvania, Ohio, and Illinois voted to assist Negroes who had escaped
from the South.

After the Revolution the Methodists were the first denomination, other
than the Society of Friends, to adopt an antislavery position. At the
Christmas Conference, held in Baltimore in 1784, it was voted to expel,
after suitable warning, members who bought and sold slaves. Local
preachers were directed to emancipate their slaves, and a plan was drawn
up for all Methodists to follow in granting freedom to those whom they
held in bondage. Members who did not comply with the directive within
one year were to be excluded from the church. The only exceptions made
were for members who resided in states where manumission was illegal.
This was the most positive and forceful action which the denomination
would take on the subject prior to the Civil War. Yet within six months
the regulation was suspended because of its extreme nature. A reaction
set in and the following year Bishop Coke narrowly escaped injury at the
hands of a Virginia mob because of his pronounced antislavery views. The
judicious Asbury was more guarded in his statements and thus avoided
open strife. Both men eventually came to the point of advising slaves to
obey their masters. Another attempt was made in 1796 to force communicants to emancipate their slaves, but it too failed. From that time the
emancipation rule proved more difficult to enforce, especially because
the southern states were beginning to prohibit manumission. Still there is
evidence that prior to the passage of such legislation many slaves were
granted freedom by their Methodist owners.

After the opening of the nineteenth century there was a growing conservatism in the pronouncements of the church. In 1804 the general conference reiterated its stand against slavery and directed its ministers to
preach to slaveholders on the matter. Members who did not live in North
Carolina, South Carolina, or Georgia were to be expelled for selling or
purchasing slaves, except under certain carefully defined conditions. In
1808 the church rescinded its action prohibiting church members to hold
slaves. Eight years later the general conference adopted a "Compromise
Law" which provided only that slaveholders living in states where manumission was legal were not eligible to hold office in the denomination.

Antislavery agitation appeared also among Baptists at the opening of the national era. As early as 1787 the Ketocton Association in Virginia pronounced slavery to be in violation of the law of God and appointed a committee to work out a plan for gradual emancipation. But when the plan was formed, the committee's report created such a furor in the churches that the association quietly tabled the matter. Two years later, however, the General Committee adopted the following resolution presented by the antislavery leader, John Leland.

Resolved, That slavery is a violent deprivation of the rights of nature, and inconsistent with a republican government, and therefore recommend it to our brethren, to make use of every legal measure to extirpate this horrid evil from the land; and pray Almighty God that our honorable legislature may have it in their power to proclaim the great Jubilee, consistent with the principles of good policy.[1]

Generally the Baptist associations refrained from endorsing the resolution and advised their members to act according to their consciences; one association even requested the General Committee not to become involved in the slavery question. The following year the committee tabled the matter.

When the Elkhorn Association in Kentucky appointed a committee in 1791 to seek the inclusion of an abolition clause in the state constitution, such a controversy broke out in the congregations that the plan had to be abandoned. Nevertheless, abolitionist preachers furthered the cause of manumission and formed emancipation parties in the churches. In 1805 the association warned its ministers not to interfere in the slavery issue, but the advice went unheeded. Two years later an abolitionist society called the Friends of Humanity Association was organized. It refused to admit slaveholders into the membership of its churches. The Friends of Humanity movement became particularly strong in Illinois under the leadership of James Lemen, an admirer of Thomas Jefferson. In Indiana this group later became involved in the activities of the "Underground Railroad" which helped runaway slaves escape to the northern states or Canada. The greater majority of Baptists throughout the country, however, took a much more compromising position in the hope of maintaining unity and peace.

The earliest important official Presbyterian action on the slavery question was taken by the Synod of New York and Philadelphia in 1787. That body called for the gradual abolition of slavery and the immediate education of the Negro in order that he might be fitted for a responsible role in society. Slaveholders were exhorted to grant their slaves the time and means to procure their freedom. Resolutions passed by the General Assembly in 1793 and 1795 reveal a deep concern over slavery but at the

[1] Quoted in Stokes, op. cit., II, 136.

same time a general reluctance to alienate the proslavery faction in the church. After two decades of avoiding action, the Assembly of 1815 declared that the buying and selling of slaves was "inconsistent with the spirit of the Gospel" but remained silent on the matter of abolition.

The year 1818 witnessed the adoption of a significant resolution by the General Assembly. It declared slavery to be "a gross violation of the most precious and sacred rights of human nature" and "utterly inconsistent with the law of God," and urged all Christians "as speedily as possible to efface this blot on our holy religion, and to obtain the complete abolition of slavery throughout christendom, and if possible throughout the world. . . ." In the meantime slaveholders were encouraged to educate their servants and advised not to treat them with cruelty. In evaluating the importance of this resolution it should be noted that it was adopted at the last session of the Assembly. At earlier sessions the proslavery commissioners had devoted their energies to the case of George Bourne, a staunchly antislavery minister who had conducted himself in such a bellicose fashion as to convince his presbytery that he was worthy of deposition from the ministry. The case was finally carried to the General Assembly of 1818, where the proslavery forces made every effort to win an endorsement of his deposition. Once having gained their ends they retired, leaving the floor to the opponents of slavery, who promptly proceeded to pass the resolution.

Other denominations also made antislavery pronouncements during this period. The Reformed Presbyterians in 1800 ruled that no slaveholder could belong to their communion. Congregationalists and Unitarians were almost wholly opposed to slavery. Indeed, Congregational Andover Seminary became a center of the antislavery movement. The Roman Catholic and Protestant Episcopal churches, however, took no official action on slavery at this time.

The Colonization Movement

While there was a conviction among many of the Protestant clergy that slavery was a social and moral evil, it did not include the reception of the Negro into American society on equal footing with the white membership. They were convinced that after emancipation the Negro would continue to represent a despised and rejected racial minority and that his presence would upset the social equilibrium of the nation. The thought of amalgamation was too revolting for consideration. Archibald Alexander, Princeton theologian, put it this way:

. . . the whites and blacks in this country, by no human effort, could be amalgamated into *one homogeneous mass* in a thousand years; and during this long period the state of society would be perpetually disturbed by many contending factions. Either the whites must remove and give up the country to the coloured people, or the coloured people must be removed; *otherwise the latter must remain in subjection to the former.*[2]

The answer for many seemed to lie in the return of the Negro to Africa. This idea had been introduced in 1776 by Samuel Hopkins, the Rhode Island Congregationalist and ardent proponent of the "disinterested benevolence" theology. He was not only the first to advocate Negro colonization but was also one of the first antislavery ministers in the United States.

By 1815 the number of free Negroes living in America had climbed to the neighborhood of 200,000; approximately half of them were located in the border states of Delaware, Maryland, Virginia, and North Carolina. For the purpose of transporting these free Negroes to Africa and helping them to build a new life, a group of clergymen and laymen from the Middle Atlantic states organized the American Colonization Society on January 1, 1817. The first communion to give official endorsement to the movement was the Presbyterian Church, whose General Assembly stated in 1818 that "we exceedingly rejoice to have witnessed its origin and organization among the *holders of slaves*" and expressed the confidence that others would support it with equal zeal. Within the first half decade of the society's history it was endorsed by the Baptist General Convention, the Methodist General Conference, and the General Convention of the Protestant Episcopal Church. The General Synod of the Dutch Reformed Church took similar action in 1825.

It was not long after its founding that the society, under the management of Ralph Gurley, a Presbyterian licentiate, was able to put into effect a program for the founding of Liberia. The first emigrant ship, carrying 89 Negroes, arrived at Sierra Leone in March, 1821. The enterprise was supported by grants from the national government and from certain states as well as by private philanthropy. During the 1820's it found favor not only among future abolitionists such as William Lloyd Garrison and Arthur and Lewis Tappan but among southern slaveholders such as Henry Clay and John Randolph. The motivation behind its support was diversified. Many supported it because they believed it would afford an entree to the conversion of Africa. Many felt a genuine desire to elevate the Negro race but believed that it should be done cautiously and under ideal conditions. Others thought that the removal of the Negro would relieve a heightening social problem, check the rapid increase of the Negro population, and restore unity to the nation.

By 1830 the society was encountering insuperable difficulties. Poverty and disease in Liberia had soured Negro colonists on the venture, while northern philanthropists had discovered that the financial burden was greater than the benefits and that southern slaveholders were not so much

[2] Quoted in Bodo, *op. cit.*, 113.

interested in emancipation as in ridding their communities of free Negroes. The society's effort to maintain a middle-of-the-road position had only fostered dissension; the South thought it was abolitionist and the North thought it was not abolitionist enough. Thus with the 1830's the society began to decline in importance and the slavery issue became essentially a concern of abolitionists and advocates of slavery.

In view of the changes in the economic situation in the South from 1790 to 1830, it seems not at all surprising that any voluntary program of emancipation was doomed to failure. Slavery, which had appeared to be a gradually dying institution around the end of the eighteenth century because of its relative unprofitability, suddenly took on new value with the invention of Whitney's cotton gin in 1792 and the development of a cotton market in England where raw materials were needed for expanding spinning and weaving industries. Cotton was the main staple raised in the Lower South, and plantation agriculture once again became profitable. Between the years 1814 and 1855 the production of cotton in the great Cotton Kingdom which extended from the Atlantic to the Gulf states rose from 150,000 to 4,500,000 bales. Since slaves were indispensable in such an economy and a valuable commodity which brought up to $2000 per person by 1860, any thought of emancipation was quickly forgotten. From 1800 to 1860 the number of Negro slaves rose from almost 900,000 to nearly 4,000,000.

With the application of Missouri for statehood in 1818 the debate over slavery in the national arena became bitter. It happened that up to that time free and slave states had entered the Union in pairs, making a balance in the Senate if not in the House. Fearing that if slavery were permitted in Missouri the rest of the Louisiana Purchase territory would follow suit, northern leaders proposed a restrictive amendment in the bill of admission. This Tallmadge amendment was beaten but only after heated debate. Finally the matter was settled in 1820 through the acceptance of the Thomas amendment, usually known as the Missouri Compromise, which modified the terms of the bill proposing the admission of both Maine and Missouri. The amendment provided that Missouri be admitted without restriction over the matter of slavery, but that the institution be prohibited in the Louisiana Purchase territory west and north of the southern boundary of Missouri. Maine was admitted as a free state. Thus the balance of free and slave states was maintained, while the sectional tension heightened.

THE ABOLITIONIST MOVEMENT

In 1829 a young Massachusetts printer, William Lloyd Garrison (1805–1879), joined forces in Baltimore with Benjamin Lundy, a well-known anti-slavery agitator who had begun publication of *The Genius of Univer-*

sal Emancipation eight years earlier. It was not long before Garrison broke with Lundy over the latter's advocacy of colonization and eventual manumission and returned to Boston to launch a vigorous campaign for the immediate release of slaves. The first issue of his famous *Liberator* appeared on January 1, 1831. In it he affirmed that since slavery was a sin it should be brought at once to an end and Negroes granted their full rights. Garrison recognized that in order to win his objective he would have to destroy the prestige of the Colonization Society. This he attempted to do by showing that the high hopes which its clerical supporters had for the settlement in Liberia were to no avail and that Liberia had more "wars, rum, and tobacco" than evangelization. Although this attack won for him the hostility of the clergy, it made a growing impression on the general public in the North. Beginning with the 1830's more and more churches closed their doors to colonizationist lecturers because their ministers feared that the membership might object. At the same time Garrison also encountered opposition in many churches, which led him to remark: "I have been almost as cruelly opposed by ministers of the Gospel and church members as by any other class of men."

In 1832 Garrison's followers organized themselves into the New England Anti-Slavery Society. A year later the movement became national with the birth of the American Anti-Slavery Society at Philadelphia, which announced as its purpose the conversion of all Americans to the philosophy that "Slaveholding is a heinous crime in the sight of God, and that the duty, safety, and best interests of all concerned, require its *immediate abandonment* without expatriation." One of the early converts was the poet John Greenleaf Whittier, who thereafter worked against slavery with indefatigable zeal. Soon antislavery societies began to spring up throughout the North and Middle West. By 1836 there were 250 auxiliary antislavery societies in thirteen states; two years later the number stood at 1006. These societies sent memorials to the Congress favoring abolition of the interstate slave trade and the abolition of slavery in the District of Columbia and the territories of the United States and urged the churches to excommunicate slaveholders. Gradually the movement spread to the churches, several of which organized their own antislavery societies on a state or regional level.

Much of the strength of the abolitionist movement came from those evangelicals of perfectionist leanings who figured prominently in the current resurgence of revivalism and the program of social reform. Among this group was Theodore Dwight Weld (1803–1895), one of the most effective agents of the American Anti-Slavery Society. While a student at Hamilton College, he had heard Charles G. Finney preach at Utica, New York, and had decided to dedicate his life to the ministry. Before going to seminary, however, he attended the conferences called by Arthur and Lewis Tappan, New York philanthropists, which resulted in the nationalizing of the abolition movement. Weld became an arch foe of slavery, and upon removing to Lane Seminary in Cincinnati in 1833 he determined to make the school a center of abolitionism.

The newly founded Lane Seminary, over which Lyman Beecher presided as chief executive, attracted numbers of Finney's converts interested in social reform as well as a group of southerners who wished to improve the status of the Negro. These young men established an antislavery society and operated schools and Sunday Schools for the benefit of Negroes living in Cincinnati. They became so involved in fraternization with the Negro that the trustees, fearing that reports of radicalism at Lane would lead to the loss of public support, banned the activities of Weld and his party. Northern abolitionists came to the defense of the student agitators, but Beecher upheld the action of his trustees, referring to radical abolitionists as "he-goat men who think they do God service by butting everything in the line of their march." In this regard Beecher represented a large segment of the Protestant clergy which was opposed to radicalism in any form; this group could adhere to the principles of colonization but despised Garrison and all his works.

Seeing that the die was cast, a majority of the Lane students withdrew and matriculated in 1835 at the new Oberlin Seminary, made possible by the Tappan brothers and their associates. They were surprised that Charles G. Finney, now professor of theology, greeted them with only mild enthusiasm; Finney had been vigorous in his abolitionism. What troubled the teacher-evangelist was that the same fate might befall Oberlin that had overtaken Lane, and he urged his charges to devote themselves to philanthropy and social reform which would eventually lead to the ruination of slavery. The Tappan brothers became angered over what seemed to them to be a compromising position and withdrew their financial assistance. Despite Finney's somewhat modified abolitionism, Oberlin soon won the reputation of being the chief center of abolitionism in the West. Its graduates fanned out, preaching antislavery doctrines and winning converts in western Pennsylvania, western New York, Ohio, and Michigan, until these areas became citadels of abolitionism stronger than New England. This was particularly the case after 1836. Among the prominent associates of Weld in the struggle against slavery were James G. Birney, formerly a southern slaveholder and organizer of the Kentucky Anti-Slavery Society; Beriah Green and Elizur Wright, Jr., of Western Reserve College in Cleveland; and Angelina Grimké, who came northward from Charleston, South Carolina, with her sister Sarah, and presently became the wife of Theodore Weld.

By the mid-1830's the reaction to abolitionism in the North was fully under way. Northern moderates who disliked slavery and had worked for colonization deplored the campaign for immediate abolition as a threat to peace. Charles Hodge, the eminent Princeton theologian, spoke for this group in an article published in 1836 in the *Biblical Repertory* in which he argued that abolitionism would foster antagonism among southerners and promote dissension among those in the North who were sympathetic to the Negro's cause. Continued abolitionist pressure could lead only to "the disunion of the states and the division of all ecclesiastical societies in the country." He did not find slavery condemned as sinful in the Scriptures, nor could he discover any evidence that Christ or the apostles had called for its abolition. Nevertheless it was his hope that through the gradual improvement of the Negro the institution of slavery would be finally brought to an end.

As the abolitionists continued their aggressive polemics, verbal counterattacks were followed by physical force, prompted by businessmen who feared a loss of trade with the South and workingmen who were concerned over the possible economic competition of free Negroes. Mobs in the North and Middle West broke up meetings of abolitionist societies and threatened their leaders. Weld was pelted with rotten eggs and stones in Ohio; Lewis Tappan's home in New York was wrecked; and Garrison was dragged through the streets of Boston with a rope around his body. After Lydia Child, the gifted historical novelist, published her *Appeal in Behalf of that Class of Americans Called Africans* in 1833 it took years before she could regain her popularity. In Alton, Illinois, the abolitionist editor, Elijah P. Lovejoy, was murdered in 1837 by a band of fanatics. These events seemed only to fortify the determination of the abolitionists and to win new adherents to their cause. Prominent among the new converts were Wendell Phillips, Gerrit Smith, and Salmon P. Chase. One of the outstanding abolitionist leaders was the brilliant mulatto and former slave, Frederick Douglass, who won for himself an education in Massachusetts and became a popular lecturer and newspaper editor.

As the 1830's drew to a close, Garrison, reacting to the pressure of persecution, became rabid and irresponsible in his attacks on those who disagreed with him. Moderate abolitionists and churchmen became as much the targets of his scathing abuse as did slaveholders. He denounced the churches for their corruptions, condemned the Constitution as "a covenant with death and an agreement with hell," opposed participation in politics, and prophesied the political dismemberment of the Union. By 1839 he had decided to drive from the American Anti-Slavery Society all who had opposed him in any way. In this he was successful, and the non-Garrisonians, headed by Weld, Stanton, and Birney, withdrew and formed themselves into the American and Foreign Anti-Slavery Society. Neither organization from that time exercised much influence in American life. Weld's group spent much of its energy in trying to persuade the national government to abolish slavery. Their new periodical, *The National Era,* became an effective instrument for this purpose. They founded the Liberty Party and in 1840 and 1844 ran James G. Birney for the presidency.

Though Birney was unsuccessful in each instance, a much heavier vote in his favor in 1844 than in 1840 indicated a swing toward abolitionism which would continue to the opening of the Civil War.

At the opening of the 1840's Protestant Christians in the North were divided into three groups regarding the question of slavery. On the far left were the decided minority of immediate abolitionists who were willing to sacrifice the Union for the sake of Negro freedom. On the far right were the conservatives who stated all sorts of justifications for slavery in order to preserve peace and the Union. In the middle was the party of evangelicals who wished to show love to slaveholders but did not feel they could neglect their antislavery sentiments. As the decade progressed many of these persons, recognizing the increasing determination of the southern proslavery defense and the indecisiveness of their own position, began to lean more toward abolitionism. Their changing attitudes helped to point up the fundamental conflicts in the churches and prepare the way for schism.

Francis Wayland (1796–1865), Baptist minister and president of Brown University, was representative of this group. In his book entitled *Limitations of Human Responsibility,* published in 1838, he had taken the position that though slavery was a moral evil the state had the right to preserve it if it so desired. The principal function of abolitionist societies was to stir up strife and contention. By 1842 his thought had undergone a metamorphosis. While he still believed that Christian charity should be shown to slaveholders, he thought it imperative to instruct them in their Christian duty to remove the social evil from their communities. At this point he saw no necessity for violence. The passage of the Fugitive Slave Act of 1850, however, prepared him to take a step closer to abolitionism. To Wayland and many others of similar conviction a law that required all citizens to cooperate with the authorities to apprehend runaway slaves and return them to their owners stood in violation of all morality. It evoked a storm of protest in the North and many abolitionists responded by breaking it at every opportunity. Antislavery agitation in the North mounted steadily after Harriet Beecher Stowe in 1852 touched the hearts of the public through the pathos and emotion of her *Uncle Tom's Cabin.* Within five years one-half million copies had been sold and Simon Legree became a fixed symbol of cruelty in northern imagination. In the South the work was anathema.

When Stephen A. Douglas sponsored the Kansas-Nebraska bill in 1854, which provided for the right of the territorial legislatures to admit or prohibit slavery, evangelicals of the Francis Wayland variety were provoked to anger which was greatly magnified after the bill became law. The subsequent fighting in "bleeding Kansas" between proslavery and antislavery forces only strengthened their conviction that the act had been fundamentally wrong. The famous Dred Scott decision of the Supreme Court in 1857, in which the court ruled that a Negro slave held by his master in free territory was not entitled to freedom, raised a furor throughout the North. Moderate evangelicals were convinced that the time for charity and patience was over. Southern Christians had not the slightest intention of terminating slavery and northern churchmen who thought otherwise were only fooling themselves. Thus those who for so long had been opponents of radicalism now stood in the camp of immediate abolitionism. They came not to bring peace but a sword with which to amputate the gangrenous member of American society and purify the nation for its divine mission to the world. Even the preservation of the Union was too high a price to pay for perpetuating oppression. *The Independent,* a Congregational paper, expressed the views of a score of denominational organs when its editors declared in 1854:

Do what we will, we can not now get rid of slavery without *suffering.* . . . a Christian nation that in this age has voluntarily given itself to the crime of oppression must suffer the judgments of heaven. . . . Slavery will go down. . . . But the law of divine retribution is now arrayed against us, and will work itself out.[3]

The die was cast for war.

THE SOUTHERN DEFENSE

It was not until southerners discovered that slavery was economically advantageous that they gave any real attention to its defense on moral and religious grounds. The first signs of a revival of proslavery thought occurred during the 1820's when a conservative reaction to the natural rights philosophy and compact theory of government became noticeable among southern intellectuals. The Missouri debates of 1820 were marked by attacks of Congressmen from the South upon the Declaration of Independence as an instrument which taught the false doctrine that all men are created equal. It was also asserted that the Congress had no power on the basis of the Constitution to legislate on the matter of slavery. From time to time, however, the proslavery argument took a more positive bent. Some argued that the institution offered the best possible basis on which two races, one of which was manifestly inferior to the other, could live in one society. Probably the most important statement on the subject during the early 1820's was by Dr. Richard Furman, a Baptist minister in South Carolina. He chose to debate the issue on moral grounds, insisting that men who are bound by "ignorance and error" cannot be free and that true liberty consists not in name but in reality.

Southern reaction to the activities of the American Colonization Society also accounts for part of the proslavery defense of the 1820's. Slaveholders

[3] Quoted in T. L. Smith, *Revivalism and Social Reform* (Abingdon, c. 1957), 209.

were only too happy to cooperate in ridding the land of free Negroes and surplus slaves, but the trend of society toward gradual emancipation could not receive their blessing. They counterattacked with the affirmation that slavery was a positive good both for the Negro and the white. The entrance of Garrison and his radical abolitionists into the debate intensified the ardor of the South. Here was a group which threatened not only the economic stability but the entire social structure of the southern communities and dared, with New England legalistic righteousness, to pronounce southerners, who valued their religious life, depraved sinners. Abolitionists were not only dangerous radicals but meddlesome and ungentlemanly boors. From that time southern intellectuals treated slavery as a divine institution sanctioned by the Scriptures.

The most significant work of a southerner on the slavery question was by Thomas R. Dew, professor of history, metaphysics, and political law at William and Mary College. In his *Essay on Slavery*, published in 1832, he attempted to answer those persons in the Virginia legislature who sought the gradual abolition of slavery. He maintained that the institution was as old as the human race and had been held in honor even among the Jews. It marked "some benevolent design" and was "intended by our Creator for some useful purpose." In addition, it had the added benefit of tending to reduce the number of wars by introducing ignorant natives to cultured society, in which they might be trained for productive labor and fitted to enjoy a standard of living higher than they could have ever attained in their former habitat. Slavery also elevated the status of women and provided them with greater physical security than they had prior to their entrance into bondage. The institution benefited white society by focusing attention upon the high value of freedom and by fostering a deeper sense of equality among whites through the assignment of the Negro to all menial tasks. It was obvious that his idea of democracy was classical Greek rather than Jeffersonian, and that he visualized a citizenry devoted to government and education, freed from the necessity of physical labor.

Much of the moral justification of slavery originated with the southern clergy, who examined the institution in the light of Biblical teaching. From the Old Testament was drawn the argument that God had decreed slavery and had sanctioned it among the Jews since the time of the patriarchs. Moreover, the Levitical Law provided that unbelievers taken captive might be held as slaves to the end of their lives. From the New Testament was drawn the argument that since Christ had come to fulfill rather than to destroy the law, the institutions of his time did not stand under condemnation. Nor did the apostles teach anything other than the proper submission of a slave to his master. This being the case, the relation between master and slave could not in itself be sinful. Only cruel treatment by an unjust master could justify such a charge.

When clergymen in the North countered with the objection that the proslavery argument was based upon literalism rather than upon the spirit of the Bible, the leading Old School Presbyterian minister in the South, James Henley Thornwell, replied that what they advocated against literalism was rationalism and that nothing could stand more in opposition to the plain teaching of Scripture. In a report to the Synod of South Carolina in 1851 he defined the relation of the church to slavery. The purpose of the church was to obey the revealed word of God; this did not include becoming "a moral institute of universal good, whose business it is to wage war upon every form of human ill, whether social, civil, political or moral . . ." On this basis the church had no right to preach the extermination of slavery. What the church could say was that both slave and master ought to perform their obligations one to the other in a way consistent with Scriptural exhortation. In a world cursed by sin, slavery might prove to be a necessary evil whereby human progress could be achieved. The Christian should accept this circumstance but should treat his slaves as immortal spirits rather than brutes and should do his best to expose them to the benefits of Christian civilization and culture. That the argument failed to impress northern abolitionists was not surprising; what was important was that it solidified the differences between the opposing parties. In so doing, it too helped to prepare the way for schism and holocaust.

DENOMINATIONAL SCHISMS

In an age which was not averse to schism it was improbable that abolitionists and slaveholders could long remain within the same denominational camp. The very confidence of each in the righteousness of his cause militated against it. For a few anxious decades both sides strove valiantly to preserve an uneasy peace; eventually, however, the tensions became too great and the largest Protestant denominations were torn by schism.

The Methodists

The Methodist Episcopal Church was among the first to be rent asunder. In 1834 the first Methodist Anti-Slavery Society was organized in New York City under the leadership of LeRoy Sunderland. Similar societies were founded a year later in the New England and New Hampshire Conferences. With abolitionist influence becoming stronger in Methodist pulpits in the North, it was inevitable that a contest for control of the General Conference would soon take place. At the time a majority of Methodist officials favored moderate views as a means of preserving unity in the denomination and were perfectly willing to join forces with proslavery southerners to restrain the heavy-handed dealing of northern radicals. At the meeting of the General Conference in 1836, held in Cincinnati, two delegates were censured for having given lectures in the city in favor of abolitionism. The body further resolved that it held no sympathy for "modern abolitionism" and did not intend to interfere in the matter of slavery. This resolution did not have the hoped-for effect of calming the storm; instead, Methodist abolitionists throughout the North rose in protest. In 1837 a number of antislavery men tried to get some resolutions in favor of abolition passed by the New England Conference, but the bishop ruled that such resolutions could not be introduced since they were unrelated to the business of the conference. Refusing to be silenced, the petitioners began holding their own antislavery conventions and publishing abolitionist literature. Some conferences, on the other hand, followed exactly the directions of the General Conference and a few went as far as to refuse to admit abolitionists.

Despite the heavy pressures brought against them by denominational executives, the antislavery forces made some inroads in the regional conferences and slightly strengthened their position among the laity. At the General Conference of 1840, meeting in Baltimore, the bishops asked for a ruling as to whether their practice of refusing to admit resolutions which were unrelated to the regular business of the conferences was legitimate. The Conference ruled that they were justified in so doing, thus frustrating once again the efforts of the antislavery forces. For the next three or four years abolitionism was at a low ebb. The movement had been torn by dissension within its ranks and left weakened and ineffectual; the churches had largely repudiated its philosophy. Through the minds of Methodist abolitionists ran thoughts of secession, and many individuals actually did withdraw from the denomination. Thus in 1841 a small group of Methodists in Michigan organized themselves as the Wesleyan Methodists and within two years gathered a membership of more than a thousand. The following year a group of dissatisfied Methodist abolitionists met at Albany, New York, and decided to secede from the church because of its aristocratic government, its refusal to ban slaveholders from its membership, and its lack of charity in dealing with dissenting ministers. In May, 1843, the group convened at Utica and formally established the Wesleyan Connection, the Discipline of which specifically prohibited slaveholding and the use of intoxicating beverages. The new denomination, which at the outset numbered 6000 communicants, was divided into six conferences. Its polity provided for the seating of lay delegates in the conferences and for the election of a president in each conference by its membership.

Moderates in the Methodist Episcopal Church now began to recognize that their efforts to avoid schism had been futile; the price of northern-southern union was northern division. In order to prevent a larger exodus from the denomination many decided to take a more favorable look at abolitionism. The result was that by 1844 the antislavery party in the General Conference had gained mightily in strength. It was apparent from the outset that the central issue before the conference, which met in New York, was slavery. The first problem facing the body was the appeal of Francis A. Harding, a minister of the Baltimore Conference, who had been suspended by his conference for refusing to emancipate certain slaves that had come into his possession through marriage. After five days of debate the General Conference sustained his conviction, an act which definitely revealed a trend toward abolitionism. More troublesome was the case of Bishop James O. Andrew of Georgia, who had come into the possession of some slaves through bequest and marriage. The antislavery delegates insisted that he should manumit his slaves or resign from office; the southern delegates replied that the bishop had broken no regulation of the church and that the General Conference had no constitutional right to suspend him. The northern members then countered with the statement that improper conduct was certainly a legitimate ground for dismissal. Eleven days of heated debate transpired before the conference reached a decision, days in which certain northern conferences threatened to withdraw from the church if the bishop were permitted to retain his office. The vote was almost two to one against Bishop Andrews.

With dispatch the southern proslavery delegates prepared for secession. Bishop William Capers of South Carolina proposed the organization of two equal and coordinate General Conferences, one having jurisdiction over Methodists in the slave states, the other administering Methodism in the free states. The work of foreign missions and publications would be conducted jointly. This proposal led to several committee studies which culminated in the presentation of a Plan of Separation. It was a most amicable agreement, the work of Christian gentlemen, providing for the equitable distribution of property, the refraining from activity in territory under the jurisdiction of the opposite conference, and the right of ministers to choose between the two denominations. Some delegates opposed the plan, being convinced that it could contribute only to friction and conflict, but in the end it was approved by an overwhelming majority. The day after the adjournment of the General Conference the southern delegates held a meeting; the principal goal of this was to arrange for a convention composed of representatives from the southern conferences to meet at Louisville, Kentucky, on May 1, 1845. Approval of this plan was easily obtained from the southern conferences and the convention was held on schedule. Delegates from thirteen conferences declared their independence from the General Conference and formed themselves into the Methodist Episcopal Church, South. The following year the first General Conference of the new denomination convened at Petersburg, Virginia;

its Discipline was almost identical with that of the northern church and so continued until the adoption of a new rule on slavery by the northern body in 1860.

Meanwhile, northern Methodists reacted with mixed emotions to the action taken by their delegates at the General Conference of 1844. Many doubted the wisdom of the separation, while others questioned the constitutional right of the General Conference to dissolve the union. Besides, an unfriendly attitude toward the southern conferences was rapidly developing among northern Methodists who were becoming less disposed to cooperate in any way with the secessionists. When the next General Conference of the Methodist Episcopal Church convened in 1848, the Plan of Separation was virtually repudiated and the body resolved that "this General Conference does not consider it proper at present to enter into fraternal relations with the Methodist Episcopal Church, South." Thus the Conference of 1848 repudiated the work of the very same body four years previously, an action which led to increased bitterness between Methodists North and South.

Peter Cartwright's warning in 1844 that one result of schism would be competition and strife in the border states was prophetic. Each side began at once to strive for greater influence in the areas of Kentucky, Missouri, western Virginia, and Maryland, even to the extent of employing physical coercion. Congregations, torn by dissenting factions, were undecided as to their ecclesiastical allegiance, and for a time confusion was king. The contest over property rights was especially heated. Failure of the southern church to gain its share of the Methodist Book Concern properties brought on three involved lawsuits. As for the New York branch of the Book Concern, the Federal court in New York ruled in favor of the South. The Federal court in Ohio, however, awarded the Western Book Concern property to the northern denomination. Southern churchmen appealed the decision and finally in 1854 the Supreme Court of the United States rendered a unanimous decision in favor of the South. The matter was settled with a division of the property, but thenceforth relations between the two churches became progressively strained.

The Baptists

Since 1814 the Triennial Convention had administered the missionary activities of northern and southern Baptists alike; after 1826, however, it concerned itself primarily with foreign missions. In 1832 the work of home missions was placed under the care of the American Baptist Home Mission Society, there being at this time a trend among Baptists away from one central organization to administer the total program of the denomination. Signs of tension between northern and southern Baptists began to appear soon after the establishment of the Home Mission Society. Southerners protested that its primary attention was being directed toward those areas which had received a heavy emigration from New England and the Middle Atlantic states and that the needs of the southern states were being disregarded. Some southern leaders favored the organization of a separate convention, but their efforts came to naught.

What brought sectional tension to the breaking point was the issue of slavery. Until 1840, when the American Baptist Anti-Slavery Convention met in New York, there was relative peace. But fear that this organization of radical abolitionists might gain control of the missionary societies prompted the Alabama Baptist Convention to withhold funds from these agencies until they could be assured that they were free of abolitionist influence. The officers of the Triennial Convention replied that southern Baptists had no need for concern inasmuch as they had no right to take any action in regard to slavery. At the Triennial Convention in 1841 in Baltimore, the southern delegates took steps to insure their promised security. As they saw it, the principal single threat to their cause was Elon Galusha, vice president of the Board of Foreign Missions and abolitionist leader who had recently supported a resolution condemning slavery at an antislavery convention in London. On their objection and with the aid of northern moderates, Galusha was removed and Richard Fuller of South Carolina was appointed to the office. Beyond this the gathering was characterized, outwardly at least, by serenity. This accomplishment was due largely to the careful maneuvering of the moderates, who managed to keep any discussion of slavery from the floor of the convention.

To many of the northern delegates the compromising disposition of the moderates made for unsatisfactory conditions. Some of these men, who were in the abolitionist camp, began efforts in 1842 to persuade a few of the foreign missionaries to adhere to the Anti-Slavery Convention rather than to the Triennial Convention for their support. Then, in 1843, the antislavery forces met in Boston and organized the American and Foreign Free Baptist Board of Foreign Missions. Their action was promptly condemned by the Baptist Board of Foreign Missions, which was responsible for the Triennial Convention's missionary funds.

Despite the persistent antislavery agitation of Baptist abolitionists, it was apparent at the Triennial Convention of 1844, held in Philadelphia, that the moderates were still in control. Francis Wayland, who was representative of this irenic group, was chosen president. After considerable debate, in which the South Carolinian clergyman, Richard Fuller, figured prominently, the Convention resolved "That in co-operating together as members of this Convention in the work of Foreign Missions, we disclaim all sanction, either express or implied, whether of slavery or of antislavery, but as individuals we are perfectly free both to express and promote our own views on these subjects in a Christian manner and spirit." The Mission Society, meeting in Philadelphia at the same time, passed a similar

resolution of neutrality but also appointed a committee to consider the
friendly dissolution of the organization.

Southern Baptists reacted justifiably with suspicion. Soon the good faith
of the officers of the Board of the Home Mission Society was put to the
test when the Georgia Baptist Convention proposed the appointment of
a slaveholder as a missionary to the Cherokees. The proposal was rejected.
Another case brought before the Foreign Mission Board was answered in
the same way. It was obvious that abolitionist influence was having a
marked effect on both boards. Southern churchmen were incensed over
what seemed to them not only discrimination but illegal action, and the
Alabama State Convention was moved to send the following ultimatum
to the Foreign Missions Board.

. . . . Resolved, That our duty at this crisis requires us to demand from the
proper authorities in all those bodies to whose funds we have contributed, or
with whom we have in any way been connected, the distinct, explicit avowal
that slave-holders are eligible, and entitled, equally with non-slave-holders, to
all the privileges and immunities of their several unions; and especially to receive any agency, mission, or other appointment, which may run within the
scope of their operations or duties.[4]

The answer of the board was polite but forthright and incisive. It insisted
that in the thirty years of the board's history no slaveholder had, to its
knowledge, applied for missionary service. Since the board sent out no
domestics or servants, it would not be possible for a missionary to take
slaves with him, even though it might be morally acceptable for him to
hold them. "If, however, any one should offer himself as a missionary,
having slaves, and should insist on retaining them as his property, we
could not appoint him. One thing is certain, we can never be a party to
any arrangement which would imply approbation of slavery."

Without further ado the southern state conventions and auxiliary foreign missionary societies formally seceded from the national body and,
prompted by a suggestion of the Home Mission Society, the Virginia Foreign Missionary Society called for a convention to be held at Augusta,
Georgia, in May, 1845. At this convention the southerners organized themselves into the Southern Baptist Convention. Nearly 300 congregations
were represented by delegates from Maryland, Virginia, North Carolina,
South Carolina, Georgia, Alabama, Louisiana, and Kentucky. Almost no
spirit of bitterness pervaded the assemblage; their action was motivated
by the sincere conviction that northern and southern Baptists could work
best through separation. The announced purpose of the convention was
to cooperate in the promotion of foreign and home missions without interfering in any way with the independence of the local churches. Prior

[4] Quoted in Stokes, *op. cit.,* II, 169.

to the Civil War the convention met biennially. Southern Baptists took a significant step forward in 1859 when they established the Southern Baptist Theological Seminary at Greenville, South Carolina. The institution was later removed to Louisville, Kentucky.

With the completion of the schism the churches of the North moved ahead with new energy. Rather than follow the southern trend toward a centralized denominational body, they elected to follow the older "society" method of organization. Thus the Triennial Convention, renamed the American Baptist Missionary Union, continued to function primarily as a foreign mission society. Other organizations were the American Baptist Home Mission Society and the American Baptist Publication Society.

The Presbyterians

New School Presbyterianism, though somewhat more inclined than Old School Presbyterianism toward the abolitionist cause, labored conscientiously to preserve denominational peace and unity. It was apparent at the New School General Assembly of 1839 that the leaders were trying to dodge the responsibility of taking an official stand on the question of slavery; all the Assembly was willing to do was to refer the matter to the lower judicatories for action. By 1846 it was not so easy to bypass the issue, especially since four synods and twenty-nine presbyteries had overtured for a strong repudiation of slavery. The Assembly finally passed a resolution to the effect that slavery was "an unrighteous and oppressive system, and is opposed to the prescriptions of the law of God," but it did little more than exhort the membership to do what they could to remove the evil from their midst.

Abolitionists, though in agreement with the general position taken by the Assembly, were dissatisfied that it did not provide for the expulsion of slaveholders. The New School Presbytery of Ripley, in Ohio, was concerned to the extent of withdrawing from the denomination and forming the Free Presbytery of Ripley in 1847, which body refused to admit slaveholders to its membership. That same year the presbytery organized an additional presbytery, the Free Presbytery of Mahoning, its ministers being schismatics from the Old School Church. By 1848 there were three presbyteries in the Free Church, and these united to form the Free Presbyterian Synod of Cincinnati, or the Free Church Synod of the United States. Since this orthodox body had been established largely as a protest against slavery, with the termination of the despised institution it lost its reason for existence and gradually the congregations filtered back into the denominations from which they had withdrawn.

Meanwhile the New School Assembly became more stringent in its condemnation of slavery, pressured as it was by increasing abolitionist sentiment both in New England and the Middle West. In 1850 it resolved that the "holding of our fellow-men in the condition of slavery, except in those cases where it is unavoidable, by the laws of the State, the obligations of guardianship, or the demands of humanity, is an offence in the proper import of that term . . ." Three years later the Assembly requested its churches in the slave states to provide complete information as to the slaveholding status of their members. When the Presbytery of Lexington, in Kentucky, replied that its membership held slaves on principle and by desire, the Assembly soundly condemned this philosophy and thus paved the way for schism.

The New School Assembly of 1857, after protracted debate, adopted resolutions exhorting the membership to repudiate the doctrine that slavery is "an ordinance of God" and is "Scriptural and right." Indignant over this action, the southern commissioners prepared to withdraw. A call went out to the southern churches to form a General Assembly in which the question of slavery would not be discussed. Six synods and twenty-one presbyteries responded and thus was born the United Synod of the Presbyterian Church, with 15,000 communicants.

The Old School Presbyterians, with one-third of their membership in the South, tended to be very diplomatic in their dealings with slaveholders while at the same time not favoring slavery. Perhaps they would have taken no action at all had it not been for a vociferous minority of abolitionists who protested the general practice of tabling all memorials on the subject of slavery. In 1845 the General Assembly, by a vote of 168 to 13, resolved that it could not "denounce the holding of slaves as necessarily a heinous and scandalous sin" since the institution was condoned by Scripture. Nevertheless, it did exhort Presbyterian masters not to treat their slaves merely as property, but as "human beings, rational, accountable, immortal." This action was reemphasized in 1849, when the General Assembly resolved

that in view of the civil and domestic nature of this institution, and the competency of our secular Legislatures alone to remove it . . . it is considered peculiarly improper and inexpedient for this General Assembly to attempt to propose measures in the work of emancipation.[5]

The man who engineered these pronouncements was Nathan L. Rice, "fencewalker" extraordinary, who was determined to guide the church along a middle course and so preserve union. He and his party shaped the policy of the Old School denomination, thus explaining the fact that schism was avoided until the outbreak of civil war.

During the critical decade which preceded 1860 a malcontent abolitionist minority was in almost constant conflict with the Old School moderates. In the 1840's the antislavery forces in the synods of the Middle

[5] *Ibid.,* II, 174.

West became sufficiently powerful to organize a seminary which they hoped would become the abolitionist answer to moderate and conservative Princeton. Dr. E. D. MacMaster, professor in this New Albany Seminary in Indiana and an ardent abolitionist, was one of Nathan Rice's chief ideological antagonists. Through the financial help of Cyrus McCormick, who favored slavery, and the maneuvering of Rice the institution eventually came under the control of the General Assembly and was removed to Chicago in 1859 where it was subsequently renamed McCormick Theological Seminary. In this way the church frustrated the plans of abolitionists.

That other denominations remained unplagued by schisms over slavery was due to several factors. In the case of Congregationalists and Unitarians it can be explained partially by the fact that their membership was largely in the antislavery North. The Friends, both in the South and North, were very largely opposed to slavery and therefore had no reason to divide. In the Episcopal Church no definite action was taken on slavery; the church did not favor entanglement in political questions, especially when it was engrossed in the high- low-church controversy. Lutherans made a sharp separation between the sacred and the secular and refrained from involvement in a political matter, while the Disciples of Christ eschewed social reform in favor of personal evangelization. The Roman Catholic hierarchy was unfavorably disposed toward slavery, but believed that its termination should be gradual and according to due process of law. Accordingly, the church had nothing official to say about the matter. The only schism which these churches experienced, therefore, was the political separation necessitated by war. When the conflict drew to its close their reunion was natural and spontaneous.

20

The House Divided

IT WAS THAT ASTUTE POLITICIAN, WILLIAM H. SEWARD, WHO PROPHESIED IN 1858 the advent of "an irrepressible conflict between opposing and enduring forces." The New York senator, soon to become Lincoln's Secretary of State, was certain beyond all doubt that the nation could not long endure half slave and half free. Compromise was merely vain and ephemeral strategy to escape the hard responsibility of decision. Yet responsibility would have to be faced and the verdict would have to be decisive. No section of the country was more cognizant of this verity than the South. Harassed by mounting pressures conjured by northern radicals and perfectionists, southern leaders found that the once ugly thought of secession began to take on a certain luster. Assurances from mammon-hungry businessmen who feared the loss of lucrative trade and placid churchmen who thought any compromise better than disruption sounded hollow in their ears. They saw all too clearly that the price of a preserved union would be the surrender of their institutions, their values, their way of life.

Since the admission of California as a free state, southern power in the national legislature was at best tenuous. Apprehensive capitalists in the North were solidifying their position through economic marriage with the West, thus preparing for the possible severance of ties with the South; with increasing security they showed themselves more amenable to an antislavery position. Even the two largest Protestant communions had be-

384

come disillusioned by apparently hopeless differences and had split asunder. A tall lanky Kentuckian, upon his initiation into the Presidency of the United States, plucked "the mystic chords of memory" and implored Americans everywhere not to "break our bonds of affection," but few heeded his pensive plea. As the guns at Sumter signaled the end of uncertain peace, each side, convinced of the righteousness of its cause, took up arms for a great crusade. Only after four seemingly interminable years of sanguinary conflict did the awesome silence of Appomattox announce the rebirth of a united nation.

THE GREAT CRUSADE

Few wars in modern history have received such overwhelming approval from religious institutions as the Civil War. In both North and South the churches threw the weight of their support behind their respective governments and made available their full spiritual resources for the waging of a conflict which they believed to be under divine control.

The Churches North

Organized Christianity in the North greeted Lincoln's call for defenders of the Union with enthusiasm; ministers preached their young men into the army and fervently prayed that God might bless the Yankee cause. The Methodist Episcopal New York Conference spoke for many of its sister denominations when it resolved in March, 1861:

That we do here and now declare our earnest and entire sympathy with the cause of our country in this conflict, and our purpose to use all means legitimate to our calling to sustain the Government of the United States in defence and support of the Constitution and the nation's welfare.[1]

The General Congregational Association of Connecticut called upon all citizens to do everything in their power to suppress "this wicked rebellion" and banish the system of slavery from the land. Baptists throughout the North gave their unqualified endorsement to the national government, but Baptists in the border states were divided in their sympathies.

By the time the Old School Presbyterian General Assembly met in Philadelphia in 1861, ten states had seceded from the Union. It was apparent to the commissioners that the church's conciliatory policy in regard to slavery was now useless as an instrument to avoid schism. Dr. Gardiner Spring, pastor of the Brick Church in New York and a conservative on the issue of slavery, was asked to prepare a resolution on the national crisis. He had been noted for his efforts with southern leaders to preserve peace

[1] Quoted in Stokes, *op. cit.*, II, 203.

and unity and could be expected to author a most judicious statement. Being now convinced, however, that war could not be averted, he thought that the church should declare its loyalty to the Union and so stated that philosophy in his resolution. Dr. Charles Hodge protested that it was not within the province of the Assembly to decide "to what government the allegiance of Presbyterians is due," but he was overruled and the since-famous Spring Resolutions were passed. The second of these affirmed

. . . That this General Assembly, in the spirit of that Christian patriotism which the Scriptures enjoin, and which has always characterized this Church, do hereby acknowledge and declare our obligations to promote and perpetuate, so far as in us lies, the integrity of these United States, and to strengthen, uphold, and encourage, the Federal Government in the exercise of all its functions under our noble Constitution: and to this Constitution in all its provisions, requirements, and principles, we profess our unabated loyalty.[2]

Southern Presbyterians of the Old School, recognizing that their political loyalties must belong to the Confederacy, quietly withdrew and took steps to form a new denomination.

In view of the traditional Lutheran position on the relationship between church and state, the Lutheran attitude toward secession is particularly interesting. The General Synod in 1862 dispatched a committee to deliver to President Lincoln resolutions which condemned "the rebellion against the constitutional government of this land" as "most wicked in its inception, inhuman in its prosecution, oppressive in its aims, and destructive in its results to the highest interests of morality and religion." Thus its criticism of southern Lutherans was not over the slavery issue but over the commitment of "treason and insurrection." By this time most of the southern synods had terminated their affiliation with the General Synod.

With the formation of the Confederacy, it became necessary for the Protestant Episcopal Church to divide because of conflicting political allegiance. The church had not become embroiled in the slavery controversy and consequently little ill will had developed between its northern and southern dioceses. At the General Convention of 1862 the roll call included the southern dioceses, just as if no schism had occurred. Several strongly worded resolutions condemning the "rebellion" were tabled and a committee of nine was appointed to draft suitable resolutions. These, which were approved by the House of Deputies, affirmed the loyalty of the Episcopal Church to the Union and disapproved secession but included no word of condemnation for those who had seen fit to give their allegiance to the Confederacy. The Convention was irenically patriotic.

While the Society of Friends had been highly vocal in its repudiation of slavery, its pacifist sentiment made it difficult for its membership to

---

[2] Armstrong, Loetscher, and Anderson, op. cit., 211–212.

support the war. Indeed, when the federal government resorted to conscription in 1863, most Quakers declared themselves to be conscientious objectors. Some refused to pay taxes since part of the funds would be used for war purposes. After considerable pressure from Friends and other pacifists, Secretary of War Edwin M. Stanton proposed that they be permitted to pay a commutation fee which would be used for freedmen relief; this was soundly rejected by the conscientious objectors. In the conscription law of February, 1864, provision was made for objectors to do hospital work or care for liberated Negroes. Most Friends, Mennonites, Dunkers, and other pacifists were willing to perform humanitarian service and were thankful that the government made this possible.

The Roman Catholic Church in the North, never vocal on the subject of slavery, followed traditional church practice in giving its support to the established government. Archbishop John Hughes expressed the point of view of his communion in a letter written to Simon Cameron, Lincoln's first Secretary of War, in October, 1861.

The Catholics, so far as I know, whether of native or foreign birth, are willing to fight to the death for the support of the constitution, the Government, and the laws of the country. But if it should be understood that, with or without knowing it, they are to fight for the abolition of slavery then, indeed, they will turn away in disgust from the discharge of what would otherwise be a patriotic duty.[3]

Archbishop John Purcell demonstrated his espousal of the Union cause in 1861 by directing that the American ensign be flown from the spire of his cathedral.

Northern Jews, who had been sympathetic but not active in the campaign against slavery, supported the federal government with unanimity and some 6000 served in the Union army. In November, 1862, General U. S. Grant, annoyed by Jewish peddlers, ordered all Jews expelled from his Department. A protest was sent to President Lincoln and Grant was forced to rescind his directive.

Individual clergymen in various communions rendered important services for the government. In 1861 Archbishop John Hughes went to Europe at the request of Mr. Lincoln to win good will for the United States. He interviewed Napoleon III of France, was present at a canonization of martyrs in Rome, and laid the cornerstone of a new Roman Catholic university in Dublin. During his eight-month tour he gained many friends for the Union cause. After the northern victory at Gettysburg, Henry Ward Beecher, the inimitable orator of Plymouth Church, Brooklyn, visited England and addressed mass meetings at Liverpool and Manchester in behalf of the United States; he was more entertaining than persuasive.

[3] Quoted in Stokes, *op. cit.*, II, 225.

The services of John McClintock, Methodist pastor of the American chapel in Paris during the war years, were more effectual. He was widely known for the eloquence of his pro-Union appeals, both written and oral. At home, Matthew Simpson, bishop of the Methodist Episcopal Church and trusted friend and adviser of Mr. Lincoln, made a series of powerful addresses on the Union in many of the northern cities and was employed by the government on several missions of a confidential nature. His patriotic lecture entitled "Our Country" held audiences throughout the North spellbound.

The Churches South

At the outset of hostilities most of the major denominations issued statements of allegiance to the Confederacy. The Southern Baptist Convention, representing some 600,000 communicants, spoke the sentiments of many southern communions in its resolution of May, 1861.

. . . . Resolved, That we most cordially approve of the formation of the Government of the Confederate States of America, and admire and applaud the noble course of that Government up to the present time. . . . Every principle of religion, of patriotism, and of humanity, calls upon us to pledge our fortunes and lives in the good work.[4]

It was fitting that the churches should have backed the government with such enthusiasm inasmuch as they had admittedly been in large measure responsible for the secession.

After the Old School Presbyterians in the South had withdrawn from the northern body, they began at once to plan for the creation of their own General Assembly. This Assembly of the Presbyterian Church in the Confederate States was formed in December, 1861, at a meeting of commissioners from southern synods in Augusta, Georgia. The able theologian and educator, Benjamin M. Palmer, who had been an ardent protagonist of secession, was elected first moderator. At this meeting the Assembly adopted a statement by James H. Thornwell, which attempted to defend the southern position on Christian grounds. Once having affirmed that slavery was an institution whose propagation or abolition was in the hands of the state and not the church, it went on to characterize slavery as "kindly and benevolent," a gift of God without which "we are profoundly persuaded that the African race in the midst of us can never be elevated in the scale of being." The following year the "Narrative of the State of Religion," presented before the Assembly stated: ". . . All the Presbyterial narratives, without exception, mention the fact that their congregations have evinced the most cordial sympathy with the people of the

---

[4] *Ibid.*, II, 242.

Confederate States in their efforts to maintain their cherished rights and institutions against the despotic power which is attempting to crush them." In 1864 this Assembly merged with the Assembly of the United Synod of the Presbyterian Church (New School), thus uniting a majority of Presbyterians in the South. After the war the denomination changed its name to the Presbyterian Church in the United States.

Early in 1861 Protestant Episcopal bishops Leonidas Polk of Louisiana and Stephen Elliott of Georgia issued a call for southern bishops and other diocesan representatives to meet at Montgomery, Alabama, on the third of July. At this meeting, which was attended by four bishops, it was agreed that an independent church would have to be organized. In October, 1861, a larger gathering at Columbia, South Carolina, which included ten bishops, adopted a constitution for the Protestant Episcopal Church in the Confederate States of America. By the middle of September, 1862, ratification was complete. The only changes made in the standards of the church were in the statements and prayers related to the state. Bishop Polk, who accepted a major general's commission and was killed fighting for the Confederacy, expressed the general attitude of his coreligionists when he said: "We fight for our hearth stones and our altars; above all we fight for a race that has been by Divine Providence entrusted to our most sacred keeping."

Southern Lutherans, whose principal strength was in Virginia and the Carolinas, broke with the General Synod early in the war. Virginia seceded in 1861, with North and South Carolina following in 1862. Lutheran leaders met in May, 1862, and planned for the organization of a southern church. A year later they established the General Synod of the Evangelical Lutheran Church in the Confederate States of America. They adopted the *Southern Lutheran*, which had been founded in 1861 in South Carolina, as their official organ.

Roman Catholics in the South gave loyal support to the Confederacy, avowing that their brethren in the North were no longer their countrymen. Bishop Augustin Verot, of Savannah, defended slavery as not being "reproved by the law of nature or by the law of the Gospel" and declared that southerners were fighting for justice and freedom. Roman Catholic priests blessed the standards of southern regiments and offered prayers for their victory in arms. In October, 1862, Pope Pius IX addressed letters to Archbishop Hughes of New York and Archbishop John Odin of New Orleans urging them to exhort their people and statesmen "that with conciliated minds they would embrace peace and love each other with uninterrupted charity." President Jefferson Davis, in a gracious manner, reechoed the pontiff's sentiments in his reply the following year.

Conscientious objectors in the South received somewhat less lenient treatment than those in the North, probably because the dearth of men was more acute. Members of the pacifist denominations, however, such as the Society of Friends, the Dunkers, or the Mennonites were permitted, according to a conscription law of October, 1862, to receive exemption from military service by paying $500 or providing a substitute.

In April, 1863, several months after the issuance of Mr. Lincoln's Emancipation Proclamation, Baptists, Methodists, Presbyterians, Episcopalians, Lutherans, and other denominations in the South united in the publication of "An Address to Christians throughout the World," which was signed by ninety-six ministers. It pronounced the recent proclamation "a suitable occasion for solemn protest on the part of the people of God throughout the world."

THE MINISTRY TO COMBATANTS

The soldier in the field did not want for attention in the area of religion. At the outset of the conflict the War Department, recognizing the need of ministering to the spiritual life of its personnel, authorized the appointment of regularly ordained ministers as chaplains, the quota being one per regiment. Ministers who volunteered for such service were given the rating of private. After some experience with this type of ministry the government realized that chaplains were more desperately needed in the hospitals than among the men in camp. The result was that in May, 1862, Congress approved the appointment of chaplains to the permanent hospitals. Most of these clergymen won the admiration and respect of the men in uniform, but there were always a few reports of indolent and unconcerned chaplains who rendered little spiritual assistance to the sick and wounded and thus brought discredit to their profession. In one instance an actor represented himself as a clergyman in order to gain the $100 per month stipend of a chaplain. Determined to halt any further misrepresentations in this direction, Congress passed an act in July, 1862, which required all candidates for the chaplaincy not only to be regularly ordained men of good standing in their communion, but to present credentials from denominational representatives certifying their worthiness for the office. The various denominations cooperated wholeheartedly in supplying chaplains, the Methodist churches providing about 500. It was not uncommon for a chaplain to organize a regimental church or to conduct protracted revival meetings should the men be kept long in camp. One chaplain of an Indiana regiment won forty-eight persons to the regimental church after a revival. Chaplains performed a variety of services which included counseling homesick or frightened young soldiers, writing to their families, comforting the sick, and burying the dead.

The work of the chaplains was greatly enhanced through the activities of several charitable institutions founded for the benefit of the northern soldier. One of the more important of these was the United States Sanitary Commission, established in 1861 under the leadership of a Unitarian minister, Henry Bellows. Its principal function was to care for the sick and wounded and for their dependents. At one time some 500 representatives of the commission served in field hospitals, provided food for the soldiers, and drove ambulances.

Another valuable work of mercy was performed by the United States Christian Commission, which grew out of a meeting of Y.M.C.A. delegates in 1861. It distributed among the soldiers books and other reading materials, mostly of a moral and religious nature, and opened libraries and reading rooms in hospitals and camps. In the year 1864 alone the organization supplied the men of the army and navy nearly six million "knapsack books" such as Newman Hall's *Come to Jesus,* more than a million Bibles, eleven million tracts, and nearly a million hymnbooks and psalmbooks. Novels and other secular reading materials were much in demand and were furnished gladly by the Commission. The common experience of commission workers was that practically nothing was so desperately desired by the men in uniform as something to read. To come into possession of a book was a soldier's rare delight; it was also an effective booster of morale. The "commission" which each agent carried with him for presentation to military commanders reflects the versatile character of the services performed.

His work will be that of distributing stores where needed, in hospitals and camps; circulating good reading matter among soldiers and sailors; visiting the sick and wounded, to instruct, comfort, and cheer them, and aid them in correspondence with their friends at home; aiding Surgeons on the battlefield and elsewhere, in the care and conveyance of the wounded to hospitals; helping Chaplains in their ministrations and influence for the good of the men under their care; and addressing soldiers and sailors, individually and collectively, in explanation of the work of the Commission and its delegates, and for their personal instruction and benefit, temporal and eternal.[5]

The Commission, which was operated solely by volunteer workers, was generously supported by the churches and thus enabled financially to render a far more effective service than might otherwise have been possible.

Though the central offices of the American Bible Society were located in New York City and the institution received its sustenance largely in the North, its Board of Managers determined that each Confederate as well as each Union soldier should be supplied with either a Bible or a New Testament. One of the heart-warming stories to come out of the war concerns the decision of Federal officers to allow shipments of Bibles to pass through northern lines into territory held by the Confederates. By virtue of this "Truce of God" some 300,000 Bibles, Testaments, and single Gospels came into the hands of southern fighting men. Only in a few cases

[5] *Ibid.,* II, 231.

were shipments held as contraband of war. The Bible Society also provided southern soldiers held in northern prison camps with Bibles.

As in the case of the Union army, Confederate military personnel were fairly well supplied with chaplains and missionaries who performed similar duties. Some ministers, among them Brigadier General William N. Pendleton, Lee's chief of artillery, became line officers and served with distinction. The Methodist and Protestant Episcopal churches furnished some 300 chaplains, while a proportionately fine record was maintained by the Baptist, Presbyterian, and Roman Catholic communions. Many of the South's leading clergymen made regular visits to the Confederate troops, notably those in the West, and conducted revivals among them. It has been estimated that as many as 150,000 soldiers may have been converted during such meetings. Known converts were Generals William J. Hardee, John B. Hood, and Joseph E. Johnston.

Perhaps no military organization in history fought with greater assurance that God was on its side than did the Confederate armies. Their most beloved commanders, Episcopalian Robert E. Lee and Presbyterian Thomas J. "Stonewall" Jackson, believed fervently that their victories were the Lord's doing. These and other officers welcomed chaplains and civilian clergy into their camps with enthusiasm and did everything within their power to aid their ministry. Stonewall Jackson frequently used rest periods for conducting great camp meetings and General Pendleton officiated at services and preached each Sunday to his men. The most hardened veterans appeared regularly at church services and revival meetings and participated in prayer meetings which were often conducted by itinerant ministers and circuit riders. One of Mr. Lincoln's informants was concerned that the southern soldiers were "praying with a great deal more earnestness" than the Union troops. The most successful of the revivals broke out at Orange Courthouse, Virginia, during the winter of 1863–1864. A soldier from North Carolina writing about it in March, 1864, observed: "We have preaching almost every night. Our Brigade has constructed a very neat and very comfortable log house as a Chapel and we have preaching in it almost every day."

Religious reading materials were furnished the men in arms in ample quantity by the churches and interdenominational societies. Tract societies published and distributed such varied titles as A Mother's Parting Words to Her Soldier Boy, Are You Ready to Die, and Sinner, You are Soon to be Damned. Much more popular were the religious periodicals such as the Army and Navy Messenger, issued by the Evangelical Tract Society, and denominational papers published by the Baptists, Methodists, and Presbyterians. Besides the Bibles passed through the northern lines by the American Bible Society, there was a source of supply from England. It was not always dependable, however, since in order to make delivery it was necessary for the ships to run the northern blockade. This circumstance caused Confederate printers to publish Bibles in large quantities for the first time. These printers were assisted in their work by Bible societies, which were founded in several of the states. The work of these organizations was unified with the formation of the Confederate States Bible Society in March, 1862. The Y.M.C.A., particularly its Richmond branch, performed an invaluable service by providing and distributing food for the sick and wounded and delivering packages sent by friends and relatives. It also presented lectures on religious themes and opened a reading room in Richmond for the use of military personnel.

NORTHERN PROGRAMS FOR NEGROES AND CONFEDERATES

Those northern Christians of perfectionist and humanitarian inclination who had agitated for the immediate emancipation of the Negro were naturally disappointed when, at the opening of the war, the government took no prompt action to secure his freedom. Many were highly critical of the Lincoln administration. Their heroes were Generals Benjamin F. Butler and John C. Frémont, probably the most incompetent officers in the Union army. Early in the war Butler declared that all slaves coming into his camp in Virginia were contraband of war; his position was approved by the War Department and strengthened by the passage of a confiscation act by Congress in August, 1861. Soon afterward Frémont, in Missouri, ordered the forfeiture of all property, including slaves, in the possession of disloyal citizens who lived within the territory under his command. Lincoln believed Frémont's action to be premature and therefore overruled it; by so doing he brought upon himself a tirade of abuse from northern radicals who were aroused to "righteous indignation." Lincoln, however, and many of his supporters favored a program of gradual emancipation and colonization which did not include immediate abolition.

Nevertheless, the government did take steps toward the abolition of slavery. In April, 1862, the Congress provided for the manumission of the 3000 slaves in the District of Columbia and for the compensation of their former owners. An additional law, passed two months later, excluded slavery from the federal territories. After long and serious reflection Mr. Lincoln, believing that the issuance of an act of liberation would be effective in weakening the Confederacy, released a preliminary proclamation on September 22, in which he pronounced all slaves living in territories disloyal to the United States to be free as of January 1, 1863. When New Year's Day arrived, the President issued the final Emancipation Proclamation. It did not, of course, apply to the border states or to those areas of the Confederacy then occupied by Union forces. It was not until the Thirteenth Amendment went into effect in December, 1865, that slavery was abolished in all states and territories of the United States.

Each legal step toward emancipation was greeted with increasing approval by northern liberals, whether within or outside the church. The Protestant churches in New England and the Middle West were especially vocal in their appreciation. Anti-abolitionists, on the other hand, viewed the process as ruinous to northern unity and as dangerous to the well-being of society; the result would be the introduction into the social order of a people culturally unprepared to live as equals with the whites. The reaction of the Confederacy to the northern program for emancipation needs no comment.

As the war progressed and Union troops penetrated deeper into southern territory, large numbers of slaves deserted to their lines and many enlisted in the army and served courageously. Concern for the education of these people led to the founding of philanthropic organizations such as the American Missionary Association, the United States Commission for the Relief of National Freedmen, and the Boston Educational Commission, which, in turn, founded schools for Negroes and staffed them with teachers. Fifty or more schools were established in Virginia in 1863, with many Negroes acting as assistant teachers. In the same year the Congress incorporated the Institution for the Education of Colored Youth, to be located in the District of Columbia.

The American Missionary Association, a chief agency through which the churches ministered to the recently emancipated Negro population, founded schools at Hampton and Norfolk, Virginia; Washington, D.C.; Cairo, Illinois; and New Bern, North Carolina. By 1864 the society had 250 representatives working among the Negroes; within three years the number had increased to 528 and the organization had embarked upon a program which embraced the entire South.

Denominational associations also carried on work among the Negroes. By 1862 the American Baptist Home Mission Society was conducting a program of education for freedmen in the District of Columbia and certain southern states. The following year the Society instituted a Freedmen's Fund, considerable support for which came from abolitionist Baptists in New England. Most of the Protestant denominations in the North either organized their own Freedmen's societies or contributed to local Freedmen's Relief Associations which were begun during the winter of 1861–1862 in Boston, New York, and Philadelphia. These associations sprang up in every section of the North and West until there were literally hundreds of them. While their purposes were exemplary, there was much overlapping in their activities and inefficiency in their administration. Attempts to unify these agencies were without success until the formation of the American Freedmen's Union Commisssion in 1866.

If the northern churches were benevolently disposed toward the Negro, their feeling did not always extend to their defeated brethren in the South. It was recognized all too clearly by northern churchmen that southern preachers had played a leading role in the movement toward secession and that some of them were more dangerous than a company of Confederate soldiers. Antagonism toward the southern churches was highly evident in the treatment shown to ministers and congregations by Union troops in occupied territory. The southern churches paid a heavy price for their deep commitment to the Confederate cause. In a number of cases Union officers attempted to dictate to southern ministers concerning the conduct of their services. When the Episcopal Church in the South changed the Prayer Book in 1862 so that its intercessions were for the Confederacy rather than for the United States, General Benjamin Butler interpreted this as an act of hostility toward the United States. As southern communities fell under the control of northern commanders, Episcopal rectors were often arrested and sent north as prisoners and their churches were closed. In Alabama, Bishop Richard Wilmer and his clergy continued to read the prayers for the Confederacy; Federal officers retaliated by closing the parish churches and stationing armed guards at the entrances. But the bishop had the last word; he wrote a letter of protest to President Lincoln, who promptly ordered the ban on the churches rescinded.

Not all the churches in the Southland were as fortunate as the Episcopal in Alabama. At the Pohick Church in Virginia, where Washington had once been in attendance, Union soldiers desecrated the walls and destroyed the pews. Over the protest of Bishop Augustin Verot, Federal troops erected breastworks on the site of the Roman Catholic cemetery in Savannah. A church at Hardeeville, North Carolina, was torn down by troops under the command of General Sherman, and the lumber was used to build temporary shelters for the soldiers. Congregations also suffered considerably at the hands of occupation forces. In Vicksburg and Natchez women communicants of the Episcopal Church were banished for walking out of services at which the clergy were forced to read the prayer for the President of the United States.

A case which attracted wide attention was that of Samuel B. McPheeters, a Presbyterian minister in St. Louis, whose congregation was sharply divided in its political sympathies. McPheeters had discreetly refrained from the discussion of political topics in the pulpit and had thus preserved the peace, if not the purity, of the church. Then one of his communicants presented a child for baptism, to be named after the Confederate General Sterling Price, who was particularly despised by Unionists in the state. When McPheeters performed the rite as requested, the northern sympathizers in the congregation complained to the provost-marshal general of the Department of the Missouri that their minister's loyalty to the Union was not without question. General F. A. Dick, in an order issued in December, 1862, banished Dr. and Mrs. McPheeters from the military district because of "unmistakable evidence of sympathy with the Rebellion." The minister went straight to Washington and appealed to Mr. Lincoln, who directed that he be permitted to return to Missouri. Still McPheeters was not permitted to practice his office until a second communication from the President in December, 1863, made it plain that the military were not to interfere in ecclesiastical affairs.

What Mr. Lincoln did not know at the time was that the War Department had, on several occasions, directed its commanding generals to seize control of certain southern churches and turn over their operation to ministers loyal to the Union. In many cases the pro-Confederate clergy had already retired with the southern troops leaving a city without a ministry. Such was the situation in New Orleans after its capture in 1862; more than forty churches in that city found themselves without pastors. Sometimes the chaplains with the forces of occupation would commandeer a vacant church edifice and use it for their services; there were instances in which a congregation would be invited to join in worship with the soldiers. When this situation became known to the officials of the northern churches, they recognized that here was an opportunity to further their missionary program. Through the cooperation of military commanders, they could place Unionist ministers in southern pulpits without fear of their being forcibly removed.

The Methodist Episcopal Church, South, felt most acutely the burden of an unwanted "missionary" program conducted by northern Methodists. The program was made possible by a directive of Secretary of War Stanton to Federal commanders in the Departments of Missouri, Tennessee, and the Gulf, issued in November, 1862. It ordered them to turn over to Bishop Edward R. Ames, a northern Methodist, "all houses of worship belonging to the Methodist Episcopal Church, South," in which a Unionist clergyman "who has been appointed by a loyal Bishop" does not serve as minister. These orders were soon expanded to include three other Departments, the Methodist churches which were assigned to Bishops Osmon C. Baker, Edmund S. Janes, and Matthew Simpson. In the meantime, Bishop Ames made a tour of the South which resulted in placing a number of northern ministers in the southern churches. Probably the best known of these missionaries was John P. Newman, who was appointed in 1864 to superintend all Methodist work in New Orleans. That same year the Methodist Missionary Board in New York City voted a sum of $35,000 to be expended for missions in the South. Confederate churchmen deplored this invasion of northern ministers, whom they feelingly described as church robbers; one minister, John Hagan of Missouri, protested to Mr. Lincoln, who was most embarrassed to learn of the Secretary of War's order concerning the disposition of southern Methodist churches, especially in the light of his own handling of the McPheeters case. When Lincoln wrote Stanton for an explanation, the Secretary of War hastily modified his orders, making them null and void for areas loyal to the Union. Military commanders nevertheless were always able to find ways of circumventing the order, and the system, which was conveniently defended by northern churchmen on the basis of Scripture, was continued.

Indeed, the War Department issued orders in 1864 to the effect that Baptist churches in southern occupied territory were to be turned over to the American Baptist Home Mission Society if they were not already pastored by a minister loyal to the Union. Similar directives applied to the recently united Presbyterian Church in the Confederate States and to the Associate Reformed Presbyterian Church. Thus before the tragic war could be brought to an end, the forces which would prevail during the dark years of Reconstruction were already at work in the South. Being covered by the cloak of self-righteousness, it was relatively easy for them to justify their aggressions; after all, they believed themselves to be on the side of God.

THE WAR AND VITAL RELIGION

The natural concomitants of war are demoralization and spiritual decline, and the War Between the States was no exception. Urban centers in particular suffered from the chaotic upheaval which accompanied the preparation for, and waging of, hostilities. In many cases the churches were weakened by the diversion of their interest and energies to the temporal and the mundane. As the pursuit of spirituality was placed in the background, it became more difficult to sustain Christian institutions and generally there was a decrease in church membership.

There were, however, compensations. If the public in the North was less attracted to the ordinances of formal religion than in normal times, its proclivity for charitable enterprises increased. Not only did people give generously to enterprises conducted for the benefit of the soldiers; they gave freely to the work of home and foreign missions. There was also a marked deepening of tone in the public addresses of the period, indicating a fuller awareness of the sovereignty of God as supreme governor of the nations. The conflict itself was regarded as a mighty work of the Lord for the chastisement and purification of a sinful society. In the hour of judgment the Divine Ruler was "trampling out the vintage where the grapes of wrath are stored."

Toward the end of the war a revived interest in religion began to be in evidence throughout the United States. Church periodicals reported a growing wave of revivalism which bore fruit in a gradual increase in church membership and a heightened sense of Christian responsibility. The Y.M.C.A. performed an invaluable service for both the veteran and the man without military experience and was in such demand that new branches were opened in many cities. With the climb in church attendance the building of edifices for worship began anew. The return to religion, however, was not sufficiently dynamic to ward off the evil influences which accompanied the war. Intemperance had once again become a major problem for society, while selfishness and greed brought a moral desolation which would grip the nation for decades to come.

In the South, the churches continued as the chief builders of morale throughout the war. From their pulpits was sounded the call to crusade for righteousness and the invocation for divine assistance. A great host looked to the churches for the promise of victory and when the victory came it was to the churches that they congregated to offer their prayers of thanksgiving. The worshipping civilian was as much in evidence as the praying soldier. Henry H. Tucker, a clergyman in Georgia, initiated a movement whereby all citizens of the Confederacy, regardless of their whereabouts, were to kneel each day at one o'clock and pray for the victory of southern arms. Another plan summoned all the women of the South to engage in similar prayers on December 1, 1862, and to repeat them monthly until the final triumph had been secured. It was not uncommon for churches to conduct daily prayer meetings. The government also arranged for days of thanksgiving and for times of fasting and prayer; probably the most widely observed of these was the day of prayer set by President Jefferson Davis for April 8, 1864. In the face of increasing adversity and military setbacks, thousands of persons hoped that the spiritual power released by manifold fervent prayers might lead to an improved condition. Many scoffed at such attempts to win the divine favor, but the 5000 persons in Richmond who flocked to the New Richmond Theatre in April, 1864, to invoke the blessing of God thought otherwise.

There was, nevertheless, a strong element of secularism running through southern society which was heightened by the distractions of war. As in the North, the presence of moral laxity and religious indifference as growing perils in the Confederacy was all too evident. As the dark hours of defeat were superseded by the black years of Reconstruction, a sense of futility and despair beclouded the once serene countenance of a romantic and gallant South. The carefree days of southern adolescence were over; ahead lay the grim shadows of poverty and social turmoil as an embittered and chastised people struggled for their redemption.

Denominational Consolidation

and Expansion

AS VICTORY BELLS PEALED THE GOOD TIDINGS OF PEACE AT APPOMATTOX, there was born a new period which would witness the nascence of modern America. Whatever the justice of the Confederate cause, the war had demonstrated with finality that the Union would be preserved. This irrefutable fact having been recognized, a sorely castigated people turned to the sobering task of binding up their wounds and rebuilding their society upon the residue of the old order. That there was frequently more passion than reflection in the accomplishment of this task was not remarkable in view of the radical and unrestrained elements in power, whose ruling motivations were vengeance and greed and whose legacy was heightened sectional ill will.

The post-war generation seemed to be gripped by an insatiable lust for power coupled with an arrogant self-righteousness and self-esteem. In every section of the nation enormous amounts of energy were released in programs of personal and social aggrandizement. White Southerners, trampled under the heavy boot of Reconstruction, struggled valiantly to regain status in government and to avoid economic catastrophe; their former slaves, dazzled by the splendiferous glare of freedom, seized upon every opportunity to find position and prestige in a time of rapid social transition. In the North the phenomenal development of machine-industry and the accelerated rise of great urban centers testified to the kaleidoscopic changes which were taking place in American life. Beyond the broad Missouri, armies of intrepid adventurers hastened westward to conquer the last frontier. This was an age of social naivete, reckless speculation, unbounded assurance, flamboyant taste, and deficient morals. Its first love was "bigness," its measure of value economic. It believed in God, but its faith was in man and in the bright tomorrows in which all things were possible.

THE CHURCHES AND RECONSTRUCTION

With the assassination of the Civil War President any hope that the South might have had for considerate treatment quickly faded into oblivion. Mr. Lincoln had favored a policy of forgiveness toward the defeated enemy and the return, as soon as practicable, of the seceded states into the Union. Andrew Johnson, his successor, shared the same philosophy, but he was almost wholly lacking in patience and political acumen and was unable to master the various factions in the Congress. Radical Republicans, determined to work their vengeance upon a hated South, were disappointed by Johnson's nonvindictive spirit and were determined to make an example of him. They held him responsible for anti-Negro legislation passed by the newly organized southern state governments. By April, 1866, they had sufficient strength in the Congress to pass over his veto a civil rights act which conferred citizenship upon Negroes born in the United States and gave them the same legal rights as white citizens.

After the fall elections of 1866 the Radicals were clearly in the majority in both houses of the Congress, a circumstance due in large measure to public reaction to a series of defamatory speeches by Johnson. The next Congress placed the South under the control of five military districts and decreed that the southern states should be entitled to representation in the national legislature only after satisfying certain requirements, among them the establishment of Negro suffrage and the adoption of the Fourteenth Amendment, which was designed to bar from public office those ex-Confederates who had been federal or state officials prior to the war. Thus began the chaotic period of rule by greedy northern Carpetbaggers, turncoat Scalawags from the South, and misguided Negroes who were swept into positions for which they had no fitness. For a time the Ku Klux Klan, a movement of southern terrorists, sought by violence to rid the South of government by Northerners and Negroes, but its efforts proved ineffectual and by 1872 it had almost completely disappeared. Not until

1877 were the last federal occupation forces withdrawn from the South. In the meantime, the nation had suffered the embarrassment of the Johnson impeachment trial and the corruptions of Grant's administration.

The Post-war Politics of the Northern Churches

There was little unanimity among northern churchmen as to the punishment deserved by the South. Henry Ward Beecher, writing in 1865 about a proposed visit to Fort Sumter, declared: "If any man goes supposing that he accompanies me on an errand of triumph and exultation over a fallen foe, he does not know the first letter of my feelings." On the other hand, his bombastic successor to the editorship of the *Independent*, Theodore Tilton, could speak of Richmond as "Babylon the Great, Mother of Harlots and Abominations of the earth" and rejoice over its ruin. Perhaps most northern churchmen would have preferred to take an intermediate position.

Since the majority of church members loyal to the Union believed the war to have been fought in order to purge the nation from the sin of slavery, they favored a strict and unwavering policy in forcing the South to make the needed reforms. Some, knowing Lincoln's conciliatory nature, privately regarded his demise as a divine act; Ralph Waldo Emerson was convinced that "what remained to be done required new and uncommitted hands." As the problems of southern adjustment became intensified the northern churches veered to the side of the Radicals and began to turn against President Johnson. When Schuyler Colfax, Speaker of the House of Representatives, informed an audience just before the opening of the Congress in 1865 that it would be the national legislature rather than the President that would determine the future of the South, he was complimented by Bishop Ames of the Methodist Church.

Republican pastors regularly used their churches as preaching stations for the advocacy of Negro suffrage and strict measures for "rebels." This was all the more remarkable inasmuch as at that time several northern states withheld voting privileges from the Negro. William G. Brownlow, Governor of Tennessee and minister of the Methodist Church, spoke for radicals in the South when he said: "The Devil is in the people of the South and in the man at the White House in particular. If we are to have another war, I want a finger in that pie. I want your army to come in three divisions, the first to kill, the second to burn, and the third to survey the land into small parcels and give it to those who are loyal in the North."[1] As for the defeated Confederate leaders, there was generally little of a critical nature said of military commanders such as General Lee; the vehement attacks of northern churchmen were reserved for Jef-

[1] Quoted in W. E. Garrison, *The March of Faith* (Harper, 1933), 22–23.

ferson Davis. The editor of the *Independent* spoke with what he felt to be true objectivity when he wrote concerning the ex-President of the Confederacy: "On whatever charge he may be tried, let his trial be dignified, passionless and impartial, and after the sentence let the death penalty be solemnly executed." When impeachment proceedings were instituted against President Johnson, Henry Ward Beecher came to his defense and in so doing brought upon himself the wrath of his own congregation; eventually he was forced to recant. The New England Conference of the Methodist Episcopal Church, during its sessions at Boston in March, 1868, deplored the actions of the President which had "compelled his impeachment for high crimes and misdemeanors," while the Methodist General Conference, in session at Chicago two months later, appointed an hour for prayer that "corrupt influences" might not be permitted to halt the President's conviction. That in the end the impeachment failed by a narrow margin was scarcely the fault of the churches.

Northern Church Activities in the South

It was the sincere conviction of northern church members that the southern churches had become so depraved that only with the help of northern missionaries was there any hope of their being cleansed. To such a task the North had been summoned by God; His agents were the churches and the radical elements in the Republican party which favored a strict policy of Reconstruction. With a deep assurance of the righteousness of their cause northern missionaries moved into the South to convert the "apostates." Southern churchmen, however, did not regard themselves as fit subjects for conversion and greeted the invaders with bitter invective and scorn. Without the presence of Federal bayonets the position of the northern missionaries, like that of Carpetbaggers and Scalawags, would have been untenable indeed. The editor of a Baptist paper revealed a keen insight into the problem when he observed in October, 1865: "Let the military be withdrawn and the union men will be slaughtered like sheep by these unhung traitors."

Actually the northern churches tended to lose interest in converting white Southerners after the first blush of Reconstruction fervor and settled down to the work of educating the Negro. The Methodist Episcopal Church did take possession of a number of churches which had been under the control of its southern counterpart, but these were returned to their original owners by President Johnson as soon as he heard of their occupation; this action gained for him the antipathy of northern Methodists. On the whole, the conversion of white Southerners was a much more serious concern of religious journalists than of the rank and file of church membership.

Post-war Denominational Adjustments

It was natural that at the close of the war some efforts should have been made to reunite the denominations which had divided into northern and southern branches. In the Methodist Episcopal Church there was some agitation for a merger with Methodists in the South on the condition that the former Confederates would profess loyalty to the government and repudiate slavery. But there was widespread opposition to this proposal among northern Methodists, and in the South it was greeted with suspicion. When the matter was broached again in 1869 the southern bishops replied "that the conduct of some of your missionaries and agents who have been sent into that portion of our common country occupied by us, and their avowed purpose to disintegrate and absorb our societies, that otherwise dwelt quietly, have been very prejudicial to that charity which we desire our people to cultivate toward all Christians, and especially those who are called by the endeared name Methodists." There were a number of exchanges of fraternal delegates in the years immediately following, but there was no merger.

Among the Baptists there were likewise efforts at reconciliation, and during the post-war era northern Baptist societies carried on work in the South. The leaders of the Southern Baptist Convention, however, voted in 1879 to continue their independent status, while at the same time seeking to improve relations with their northern brethren. This decision was in part a reflection of sectionalism; nevertheless it must also be recognized that Baptists in the South favored a stronger denominational system. As the years passed sectional differences, rather than abating, seemed to become more deep-seated, even though northern and southern Baptists maintained amicable relations with one another.

The first five years after the war marked a schism in the Old School Presbyterian Church and a merger with the New School denomination. The schism resulted from dissatisfaction on the part of Presbyterians in the border states over the General Assembly's refusal to seat commissioners who had not complied with the order of General Rosecrans that they take the oath of allegiance to the United States. When the complainants issued a "Declaration and Testimony" stating their grievances and were subsequently disciplined by the Assembly, the Synods of Kentucky and Missouri were rent asunder and the dissenters eventually affiliated with the Assembly of the Presbyterian Church in the United States.

Meanwhile, Old and New School Presbyterians in the North had been entertaining the possibility of reunion. Events of the past quarter of a century had demonstrated that the New School exercised stricter church discipline and closer adherence to the Presbyterian standards than the Old School had expected. During the same period, Old School leaders had grown more conciliatory in their attitudes toward the New School. In 1866, the Old School Assembly, meeting in St. Louis, proposed the creation of a joint committee of thirty to discuss reunion; to this suggestion the New School Assembly gave hearty approval. At the two Assemblies of 1869 the committee presented a plan of reunion "on the doctrinal and ecclesiastical basis of the common standards" which was referred to the presbyteries for consideration. These judicatories voted overwhelmingly for the union and it was consummated in 1870. The willingness of the Old School to merge may be explained in part by the loss of its most conservative elements in the southern schism of 1861. There were powers in the church which would have preferred a union with southern Presbyterians rather than with the New School in the North, but the prevailing forces did not permit any significant movement in that direction. Nor did southern Presbyterians wish to unite with their northern brethren. The result was the merger of Old and New School to form the Presbyterian Church in the United States of America.

The reunion of northern and southern Episcopalians was achieved without difficulty. At the General Convention of 1865 delegates were sent from Texas, North Carolina, Tennessee, and the border states, and a Kentuckian was reelected President of the House of Deputies. The General Convention also approved the election and consecration of Bishop Richard Wilmer of Alabama by southern bishops during the war, provided he would promise to abide by the doctrine and discipline of the church. The House of Bishops issued a resolution in gratitude for "the return of peace to the country and unity to the Church," in which the Deputies were happy to concur.

Denominations such as the Congregational and Unitarian had no problems of reunion to face inasmuch as their membership was predominantly in the North, and there was consequently no schism. Roman Catholics and Disciples of Christ had never recognized ecclesiastical cleavages in their communions and with the termination of political conflict their reunions were spontaneous. In Lutheranism, however, the schism remained unhealed for many years.

THE CHURCHES AND THE NEGRO

The principal concern of organized religion during the era of Reconstruction was the education and social advancement of the freedman. Through sudden political upheaval he had been thrust into a society which granted him a liberty for which he had not been adequately prepared; without the paternalistic guidance of white masters a life of freedom often produced more bewilderment than confidence. True, many a warm relationship between master and slave was perpetuated after emancipation, but the burdensome problems of readjustment rendered it impossible for the white southerner to assume much responsibility for the Negro. It was the northern churches more than any other group of institutions that took the freedman in hand and ministered to his economic, intellectual, moral, and spiritual needs. The results were phenomenal by any standard.

Church Missions Among the Negro

One of the most important of the organizations which carried education to the Negro was the American Missionary Association, a nondenominational society supported mainly by Congregationalists. It offered schooling from the elementary grades through college and maintained theological seminaries to train Negro ministers. Some of the institutions of higher learning which owed their establishment to its labors were Atlanta University in Georgia (1865), Fisk University in Tennessee (1866), Talladega College in Alabama (1867), and Hampton Institute in Virginia (1868). Though chartered by the Congress in 1867 and supported principally by the government as a nondenominational institution, Howard University in Washington, D.C., grew out of a missionary meeting held in 1866 at the First Congregational Church in the nation's capital. The university, which reflected a Christian philosophy of education, was the recipient of considerable funds from the American Missionary Association, many of which were earmarked for Howard's School of Religion. After 1872 the Association directed most of its funds to secondary and higher education for the Negro, the southern state governments having provided satisfactorily for the elementary education of Negro children. By 1913 the Association was contributing to the work of sixty-five schools with an enrollment of more than 12,000 students.

The greater proportion of Negro college graduates during the first half century after emancipation found their way into the ministry or teaching. Among the latter group the most distinguished was Booker T. Washington. Born a slave, he was educated at Hampton Institute and for a time was a member of its faculty. He was later called as chief administrator of the normal school at Tuskegee, Alabama; during his incumbency the institution gained the reputation of being one of the finest schools for Negroes in the country.

A vigorous educational program was also conducted by the several denominations. The Methodist Episcopal Church founded and maintained twenty-six schools through its Freedmen's Aid Society, while the women of the church operated sixteen homes for the education of girls in domestic subjects. It joined with the Colored Methodist Episcopal Church in the maintenance of Paine College, an institution for Negroes in Augusta, Georgia. The American Baptist Home Mission Society founded several secondary schools and colleges; one of the most notable was Spelman College for women. This latter institution also received aid from the Women's American Baptist Home Mission Society.

The official agency of the Presbyterian Church in the U.S.A. was the Board of Missions for Freedmen which, by 1914, was contributing to the maintenance of 136 schools. After 1890 the denomination employed Negro missionaries to found Sunday Schools in the South; by the opening of the First World War some 3000 of these schools were in operation. The best known of the several institutions founded by the Protestant Episcopal Church was Bishop Payne Divinity School, at which more than half of all Negro clerics in the denomination received their training. Other agencies active in the work of Negro missions were the Board of Freedmen's Missions of the United Presbyterian Church and the Lutheran Board for Colored Missions. The Society of Friends was noted for its Penn School on St. Helena Island off the coast of South Carolina as well as for its Sunday School program.

During the fifty years following the Civil War, Roman Catholic missions among the Negroes were on the whole not as effective as those of Protestants; there was nevertheless some progress. The second Plenary Council of the American hierarchy in 1866 appealed to the bishops to make the spiritual and intellectual advancement of freedmen one of their major concerns. An important work was carried on after 1871 by the Society of St. Joseph, whose headquarters were in England. In 1887 it founded a seminary in Baltimore for the education of missionaries; six years later its representatives in the United States were formed into an independent order named St. Joseph's Society of the Sacred Heart. Orders of women also performed an important service as witness the case of the Catherine of Siena Congregation of Dominican Sisters, which founded a school in Kentucky for Negro children in 1877. Other leading agencies of the church were the Commission for Catholic Missions Among the Colored People and Indians, created by the hierarchy after the Third Plenary Council in 1884, and the Catholic Board for Mission Work Among the Colored People, founded in 1907.

To a lesser extent ministrations to the Negro stemmed from southern sources. The Methodist Episcopal Church, South, renewed its activities in the area of religious education for the Negro immediately after the war and planned for the establishment of separate Negro congregations. In 1865 the Alabama Baptist Convention affirmed that the "condition of our colored population appeals strongly to the sympathy of every Christian heart and demands, at the hands of all who love the Saviour, renewed exertions for their moral and religious improvement." This body further suggested the organization of Sunday Schools for the freedmen and an improved ministry of preaching to them. The Protestant Episcopal Bishop of North Carolina cited in his pastoral letter the illiteracy and inexperience of the former slaves and urged the establishment of Negro congregations and schools to ward off the danger of the freedmen falling into the clutches of designing persons who were determined to destroy the South.

The fears of the Episcopal bishop were amply justified. Unscrupulous Carpetbaggers taught the Negro that Christianity and Republicanism were synonymous and so identified politics with religion that the freedmen thought it perfectly proper to hold political rallies in the church. Negro congregations in many areas were used by northern politicians as agencies through which political control of the Negro might be achieved. Colored ministers, along with Carpetbaggers and Scalawags, were swept into federal and state offices by the votes of newly franchised Negroes. Under such unenlightened and corrupt administration, many of the southern states approached the verge of bankruptcy; financial support which would ordinarily have been given to the churches was made impossible due to inordinate taxation.

The Negro Churches

Of the 4,441,830 Negroes in the United States in 1860 perhaps 520,000 or 11.7 per cent were church members. At that time the membership of the two foremost independent Negro Methodist bodies was 26,000. During and after the war the trend among Negroes was to withdraw from the white denominations and unite with existing Negro communions or form new denominational structures. In 1863 the African Methodist Episcopal Church initiated work in Virginia, while the African Methodist Episcopal Zion Church inaugurated missionary programs in North Carolina and Louisiana. After the termination of hostilities, both communions developed rapidly in the South, partially through the transfer of members from the Methodist Episcopal Church, South. During the period of Reconstruction this latter body lost more than half of its colored membership. White Methodists in the South encouraged the freedmen to develop their own congregations and in 1866 adopted a plan for the formation of separate Negro conferences as well as congregations. It was provided that when two or more annual conferences were formed they should be organized into an independent denomination. Thus, with the full approval of the Methodist Episcopal Church, South, its Negro communicants were organized in 1870 into the Colored Methodist Episcopal Church. This was a relatively small body, since the greater proportion of Negro Methodists in the South had already affiliated with the African Methodist Episcopal Church or the African Methodist Episcopal Zion Church. Negro members of the Methodist Episcopal Church living in southeastern Virginia organized themselves into the Zion Union Apostolic Church in 1869; twelve years later it was reconstituted as the Reformed Zion Union Apostolic Church.

The Negro proclivity for separate denominations was also evident in other communions. After the Civil War colored Baptists in Virginia withdrew from the white churches and created their own organization; by 1867 these churches formed the Virginia Baptist State Convention. Churches or missions had been founded in almost every community in Virginia by 1880. This same process was eventually repeated in all the southern states. The next step was the formation of regional and national bodies such as the Northwestern and Southern Baptist Convention in 1864, the Consolidated American Baptist Missionary Convention in 1866, the Baptist Foreign Mission Convention of the United States in 1880, and the American National Baptist Convention in 1886. In 1893 the greater majority of Negro Baptists became affiliated with the National Baptist Convention. The democratic organization of the Baptist churches together with the popular appeal of baptism by immersion were powerful factors in winning Negroes to that persuasion and help to account for the fact that in the postwar period Baptists came to surpass Methodists in numerical strength.

Negro withdrawals from the Presbyterian Church in the United States were so overwhelming that between the years 1861 and 1916 the colored membership declined from 31,000 to 1322. In the Cumberland Presbyterian Church the Negro communicants formed separate congregations which were organized into presbyteries in 1869. Five years later there was brought into existence the General Assembly of the Colored Cumberland Presbyterian Church. In the Protestant Episcopal Church there were few Negroes and these made no attempt to form an independent body, but they were frequently set apart in their own parishes. Roman Catholicism in the South suffered from a marked defection of Negroes, many of whom affiliated with Protestant denominations. During the next fifty years the church made some gains in this area, but as late as 1906 little more than one per cent of Negro church members were Roman Catholic. In 1916 almost ninety per cent of those Negroes who held church affiliation were identified with the National Baptist Convention, the Colored Methodist Episcopal Church, the African Methodist Episcopal Church, the African Methodist Episcopal Zion Church, and the Methodist Episcopal Church. Of these, nearly two-thirds were associated with the National Baptist Convention.

According to the *Yearbook of American Churches for 1959* the four leading Negro denominations were the National Baptist Convention, U.S.A., Inc. with 4,557,416 members; the National Baptist Convention of America with 2,668,799 members; the African Methodist Episcopal Church with 1,166,301 members; and the African Methodist Episcopal Zion Church with 761,000 members. In addition to these denominations there were some thirty other Negro communions and a large Negro membership in racially mixed denominations. Probably not more than ten per cent of all Negro church members would be found in denominations other than the

Baptist or Methodist. Roman Catholic gains among the Negroes in the years which followed the First World War are worthy of consideration but it seems unlikely that there were more than half a million Roman Catholic Negroes in the United States by 1959.

Negro Religion

Unlike the Negroes of South Africa who divided into hundreds of separate denominations, American Negroes developed no new denominational types of major significance. They preferred to follow those basic structures with which they had become familiar during their period of slavery, leaning heavily on Baptist and Methodist doctrine and polity. In fact, they were divided into fewer denominations than were the whites. Their general conformity to the religious practices of the whites was evident in their services of worship and in the organization of their churches. The order of worship and the character and function of the sermon were patterned after the standard practice in America, particularly those of the evangelical, low-church variety. Negro churches also adopted such well-accepted institutions as Sunday Schools, youth groups, societies for women, and mid-week prayer meetings. Church-affiliated organizations of this kind not only served the cause of spiritual growth but filled a social need for a people which enjoyed few if any other outlets for social expression.

What was unique about the Negro's religion was its highly emotional character. Never was this more apparent than in his revivals, which elevated the soul and charmed the senses. Preaching was unusually dramatic, often eloquent; at its best it possessed the happy faculty of telescoping the Biblical past with the decisive present so that Biblical characters seemed contemporary. Theology was uncomplicated and the emphasis fell upon the doctrines of sin and salvation through the free grace of Jesus Christ for all who would accept it. Singing played a dominant role in any Negro service; indeed, through music, particularly the music of the "spirituals," Negro Protestant Christianity made its most original contribution.

Though American Negro religion was dynamic and manifested concern for social problems, the Negro churches were not, on the whole, as vitally interested in foreign missions as the white churches and generally confined their activities to colored peoples in Africa, the West Indies, or Guiana. This situation can be explained partially by the fact that since the Civil War Negro churches have become necessarily absorbed in the task of confronting Negro Americans with the Gospel and educating them in the Christian life. These churches have also been faced with the task of serving as primary agencies for the Negro's cultural and social advancement. Despite their relative poverty, which has made it difficult to finance an effective missionary program, their qualitative performance has been encouraging and has undoubtedly made an impact on the people of their race.

THE CHALLENGE OF THE FRONTIER

A cartographer charting the bounds of the American frontier in 1865 would have drawn a line southward from the western border of Minnesota, making it bulge westward to include portions of Nebraska and Kansas, and terminating it in central Texas. He would have shown that east of this line there was still much unoccupied land and that west of it there were settled districts in the Willamette and Columbia valleys, in the areas near San Francisco and San Diego, and in the Mormon country of Utah. Most of the territory west of the line, however, represented frontier territory inhabited only by Indians and wild life. Yet within a quarter of a century this vast region would virtually be conquered for white civilization and carved into states and territories.

One of the factors which speeded the white penetration of the West was the Homestead Act, passed by Congress in 1862. It offered free lands of 160 acres to citizens or those who were in the process of attaining citizenship on the condition that they would settle on the land and improve it for five years; by 1883, 26,000,000 acres had been granted under the terms of this act. Unquestionably, the completion of a transcontinental railroad line by 1869 provided additional incentive for western travel, as did other lines which began to operate within the next fifteen years. The subjugation of hostile Indians also helped to prepare the way for new settlements in the West. Nor should the economic attractions of the frontier be underestimated. The discovery of precious metals in the mountainous areas brought a flood of prospectors into New Mexico, Arizona, Nevada, Idaho, western Montana, and eastern Oregon and Washington. The Comstock Lode in Nevada yielded a fortune in silver and gold. As hundreds of adventurers moved into the West, boom towns grew up like mushrooms with their common characteristic at first being lawlessness. During this same period cattle raising in the area east of the Rockies became an important industry and attracted many for whom ranching offered a challenge and opportunity for a successful career. But gradually the cattle kingdom gave way to farming and settled communities.

The increase in population was phenomenal. Between 1870 and 1890 Idaho's population multiplied by six, Montana's and Wyoming's by seven, Colorado's by ten, and Washington's by fifteen. In 1867 Nebraska won statehood, while Colorado followed in 1876; in 1889 and 1890 North and South Dakota, Montana, Washington, Idaho, and Wyoming entered the Union. Utah gained entrance in 1896. In 1889 the government opened the section of Indian Territory known as Oklahoma to settlers and the following year organized it into a territory. Thus by 1890 the frontier had become a part of history and the era of rapid geographical expansion had come to an end. There were, of course, other territorial gains. Most important to the political and military security of the United States was the purchase of Alaska in 1867 and the annexation of Hawaii by Congress in 1898. These territories, however, failed to attract settlers in significant numbers.

Church Extension

Burgeoning settlements in the West presented the churches with new challenges and opportunities. In areas such as the mining camps, where men were rough and profane, the ordinances of religion were generally ill received and it was not uncommon for missionaries to be run out of town. In the more settled agricultural centers religion was usually welcomed as a stabilizing influence and chambers of commerce in the new cities supported the establishment of churches. To meet a growing need the denominations organized boards and agencies to inaugurate religious programs in promising areas and to found churches wherever possible. Thus the Methodist Church Extension Society was organized in 1864, the Congregational National Council in 1865, and a number of similar denominational agencies after 1870. During the 1860's Protestant organizations of this type raised and spent an average of about two million dollars per year; by the 1870's the figure had climbed to three million and by the 1880's it had reached the four million mark.

Until 1890 the principal interest of the extension societies was the occupation of new territory and the development of new churches. Basically the churches followed the line of the railroads. Sharp-witted leaders of the American Baptist Home Mission Society persuaded the management of the Union Pacific and Central Pacific Railroads to set aside lands for their free use in every town served by these lines. Chaplain C. C. McCabe, who served from 1868 to 1884 as assistant secretary of the Methodist Church Extension Society, rode the trains from town to town establishing churches or superintending their erection. To the claim of the prominent freethinker, Robert G. Ingersoll, that the churches were "dying out all over the land," McCabe countered with the boast that the Methodists were building more than one church a day and expected soon to raise it to two.

The Methodists, Baptists, and Presbyterians were the most successful of the older denominations in meeting the demands of the frontier. Church extension officials in the Methodist Episcopal Church made it their principal task in the three decades which followed the Civil War to plant Methodism in the prairie and Rocky Mountain regions. To their amazement they often discovered that before they could found a new church in some recently established community, a Methodist settler had already gathered a congregation and was acting as a local preacher. In such cases the chief function of the Church Extension Society was to give financial assistance. The American Baptist Home Mission Society inaugurated church extension work in Colorado, the Dakotas, Wyoming, and Idaho by 1864 and in the Washington Territory by 1870. In some areas where there was not sufficient population to justify several churches belonging to different denominations, the Society either entered into comity agreements with other communions or arranged for the establishment of federated or union churches. Where the church preserved its denominational connection, the Baptist mission society rendered much-needed financial assistance. Most of the Baptist congregations were poor and consequently far behind the Methodists and Presbyterians in building edifices. The merger of Old and New School Presbyterians led to the creation of the Board of Home Missions in 1870. During the next thirty-year period this board was responsible for the organization of 3688 new churches. A separate Sustentation Committee was appointed by the General Assembly of 1871 to provide fiscal help for needy churches and to guide them toward financial independence.

The Congregationalists had laid the groundwork for missionary advance at their Albany Convention of 1852, which was the first meeting of a Congregational body on a national level since the Cambridge Synod of 1648. Besides repudiating the Plan of Union with the Presbyterians the delegates took a positive step forward in planning a revitalized campaign for winning the West. A call for $50,000 to aid in building churches in the Middle West was answered by gifts totaling more than $60,000. In 1853 there was organized the American Congregational Union, later the Congregational Church Building Society, which was assigned the task of erecting church edifices and parsonages. After the Civil War the denomination entered so vigorously into the work of church extension that by 1882 there were Congregational missions or churches in every western state or territory.

In 1859 the Protestant Episcopal Church divided the vast unorganized territory in the West into two missionary jurisdictions, the Northwest and the Southwest. Joseph C. Talbot became bishop of the former, while Henry C. Lay assumed episcopal responsibilities for the latter. Talbot, who referred to himself as "Bishop of All Outdoors," was in charge of the Territories of Nebraska, the Dakotas, Wyoming, Colorado, Utah, and Montana, which comprised 750,000 square miles. Oregon was already united with Washington into a separate missionary jurisdiction, and California had been erected into a diocese. By 1865 the work had progressed to the extent that it seemed advisable for the General Convention to divide the Far West, exclusive of California, into five missionary jurisdictions: Arkansas and Indian Territory; Nebraska and Dakota; Colorado,

Montana, Idaho, and Wyoming; Nevada, Utah, Arizona, and New Mexico; and Oregon and Washington. By 1890 Nebraska, Arkansas, and Colorado had been organized into dioceses. Inadequate financial support of the missionaries and the difficulty in obtaining ministerial volunteers seriously hampered the work; the church, nevertheless, enjoyed fairly steady growth through much of the western territory.

The Disciples of Christ, nurtured on the frontier, were quite at home in the work of western church extension. They grew relatively strong in almost all the western states and territories and exceptionally powerful in Kansas, Oklahoma, and Oregon. By 1893, Disciples of Christ congregations had been gathered also in Arizona, Colorado, Montana, New Mexico, Utah, and Wyoming, largely through the efforts of the American Christian Missionary Society, which had been founded by the denomination in 1849. Since this body was charged with the responsibility of both home and foreign mission programs prior to 1875, it was relatively ineffective until the creation of a separate agency for foreign missions that year released it for full service on the home scene. It was not until the 1880's, however, that the church extension program of the Disciples came into full swing with the organization of a committee on church extension in 1884. Four years later the committee was made into the Board of Church Extension. This body purchased strategic sites and assisted in the erection of churches.

The principal strength of the Roman Catholic Church in the Far West during the two decades following the Civil War was in those states and territories which had a heavy Spanish population. As early as 1850 the holy see had erected the vicariate of New Mexico into the Diocese of Santa Fé; three years later San Francisco was made an archiepiscopal see. Nebraska, Kansas, and Colorado were placed under the jurisdiction of a Vicar Apostolic of the Indian Territory. The chief centers of Roman Catholicism in the Pacific Northwest were the Archdiocese of Oregon City and the Diocese of Nesqually in Oregon; in this area the growth of the church was relatively slow. By the opening of the twentieth century, however, the accessions in the Far West had been such as to justify the creation of the following dioceses: Helena (1884), Omaha (1885), Sacramento (1886), Cheyenne and Denver (1887), Fargo and Sioux Falls (1889), Salt Lake (1891), Boise (1893), and Tucson (1897).

Missionary Leaders on the Frontier

The history of missions is to a large extent the story of heroic figures who have braved the unknown in order to share their dynamic faith with other men. In the taming of the American West there emerged certain leaders of outstanding importance who made an imperishable mark upon the new society. Such a man was the Presbyterian missionary, Sheldon

Jackson (1834–1909). Prior to the Civil War he had labored among the Choctaws in Indian Territory and had pastored a church in Minnesota. At the conclusion of the war he was appointed "superintendent of missions for Western Iowa, Nebraska, Dakota, Montana, Wyoming, and Utah." A human dynamo, he traveled unceasingly from place to place in his vast territory of responsibility planting churches and ministering in countless other ways. It was not long before he extended his missionary activities to Colorado, New Mexico, Arizona, and Nevada. He even founded a religious periodical entitled *The Rocky Mountain Presbyterian*. In 1877 he visited Alaska and was so overwhelmed by the educational and spiritual needs of this new frontier that he devoted much of the remainder of his life to its cultivation. In this enterprise he was associated with Mrs. Amanda McFarland, the first woman missionary in Alaska. His missionary achievements won for him such recognition in Washington that he was appointed General Agent of Education in Alaska for the Government of the United States; in this capacity he did much to relieve the suffering of the Eskimos in the North. His church later honored him by electing him to the moderatorship of its General Assembly.

Another leading Presbyterian minister in the Far West was Samuel H. Willey, who came to California in 1849. He was one of the principal agents in founding the College of California and later became a moving spirit in establishing the state university. Equally valued for his services was Thomas Fraser, who served as synodical superintendent of the Synod of the Pacific from 1868 to 1887. During his superintendency the number of Presbyterian churches within his jurisdiction rose from 57 to 158.

In the Protestant Episcopal Church the name of Bishop Daniel Sylvester Tuttle stands out significantly. He was chosen by the House of Bishops in 1866 to become "Missionary Bishop of Montana with jurisdiction in Idaho and Utah." The young Easterner had never been West and his trip by railroad and stage through hostile Indian country was a harrowing experience. Upon his arrival in Montana, he found the mining towns of Helena and Virginia City to be "eminently excitable, unruly, defiant, without fear of God or man." At Virginia City he met a Roman Catholic priest and a Methodist minister, but as yet there were no Baptist or Presbyterian missionaries. In the face of overwhelming obstacles he began to hold services, and it was not long before ten persons were in attendance at divine worship. Still, after eight months of hard work not a single person was willing to be confirmed. Patiently he continued ministering to the people and gradually won their full confidence. After establishing clergy at Helena and Virginia City in 1869, he made Salt Lake City his base of operations and founded there St. Mark's Hospital and Rowland Hall, a school for girls. When he left Utah and Idaho in 1886 to become Bishop of Missouri, he left behind him two parishes, thirteen organized missions, twelve clergymen, and nearly a thousand communicants. Tuttle eventually became Presiding Bishop of the Protestant Episcopal Church.

Space does not permit a full recital of missionary contributions on the frontier. One may only mention such leaders as Joseph A. Benton, the Congregational missionary who was identified with Pacific Theological Seminary, at Oakland, California, from 1869 to 1892, and Joseph Ward, the father of Congregationalism in the Dakotas and founder of Yankton College in 1881. Among the Baptists one thinks of Ezra Fisher, who organized churches and schools in Oregon until his death in 1874.

MISSIONS AMONG THE INDIANS

In 1860 there were possibly 225,000 Indians scattered throughout the West. The greater majority, in return for gifts of food, clothing, and supplies from the national government, stayed within their preserves and maintained the peace. With the rapid influx of white settlers after the war and the government's decision to remove the Indians to less desirable lands, there began a period of almost incessant conflict between the natives and the whites which lasted until 1886. The situation was temporarily improved after President Grant set up a Board of Indian Commissioners in 1869 to administer government expenditures for the Indians, but the destruction by white hunters of the buffalo herds which were so vital to the native economy caused hostilities to flare up again. When the conflict finally drew to a close, the Indians had been so decisively defeated that they had no choice but to accept a life of dependence on reservations provided by the national government. By 1910 the 265,683 Indians living in the United States were widely scattered and frequently were in relatively small units; about half were dwelling in Oklahoma, Arizona, New Mexico, and South Dakota.

Christian missions among the Indians were at best difficult. Since the natives were divided into many tribes which spoke different dialects, no one missionary could expect to reach a great number. The problem was heightened by the Indian's reluctance to adapt himself to settled community life, by his lack of initiative, and by his vacillating nature. The churches, nevertheless, sent hundreds of missionaries to the Indian tribes; these persons not only brought the Gospel to the natives but helped them adjust to a new way of life in a society dominated by white men. By 1914 probably forty per cent or more of the Indians were nominal Christians or at least subjected to Christian influence. It has been estimated that of the approximately 400,000 Indians living in the United States in 1950, twenty-eight per cent were Protestant, twenty-eight per cent Roman Catholic, and forty-four per cent either pagan or uncommitted. In all likelihood this estimate is too generous on the side of Christian commitment.

Protestant Missions

During the quarter century which followed the Civil War, no Protestant denomination was more successful in its work among the Indians than the Methodist Episcopal Church, South. Rather than place the Indians living in the Indian and Oklahoma Territories in a separate ecclesiastical jurisdiction, the church formed a mixed conference known as the Indian Mission Conference. By 1893 it numbered some 2000 white members and nearly 11,000 Indian members, some pure bloods, others mixed bloods. In that same year more than 1000 persons were won to the 160 churches in the conference. The church also maintained five schools in this region, the most important of which was the Harrell Institute.

At the close of the Civil War the American Baptist Home Mission Society had only two active missions left among the Cherokees, Shawanos, and Delawares in the Indian Territory. The Southern Baptist Home Mission Board had only four missionaries still engaged in the work of Indian missions. In 1880, Almon C. Bacone, a missionary sent out by the Northern Baptists, founded a school to serve the five tribes in the Indian Territory. John D. Rockefeller, Sr., was one of the principal donors to the school. The following year Southern Baptists established the Levering Mission Manual Labor School for the Creeks in the Indian Territory. Mission stations were opened among the Blanket Tribes, the Gaddoes, and Wichitas in 1887, the Kiowas in 1892, the Comanches in 1893, the Cheyennes in 1895, and the Arapahoes in 1898. During the twentieth century additional missions were undertaken among the Crows in Wyoming and the Navajos in New Mexico.

Throughout the Far West there were evidences of Presbyterian mission work. After the death of Henry Spalding in 1874, Miss Sue McBeth carried on his program among the Nez Percé Indians in northern Idaho. She and her sister Kate founded a school for the training of a native ministry at Kamiah, which later was removed to Lapwai; by 1893 twelve graduates of this school had been ordained to the Christian ministry. In 1899 James M. Cornelison founded the Tutuilla Mission near Pendleton, Oregon, for the evangelization of the Cayuses and Umatillas; fifty years later the church which he established on the reservation numbered 100 communicants. In Arizona, an important mission to the Pimas was begun by Charles H. Cook in 1870. The following year he opened a school for thirty-five Indian pupils which was subsequently named Cook Indian Training School. The First Pima Presbyterian Church of Sacaton was organized in 1889. Cook, who learned the Indian language, enjoyed the full confidence of the natives and was thus able to win more than 100 to Christianity.

In 1871 the General Convention of the Protestant Episcopal Church directed its Board of Missions to create a Commission on Indian Affairs, while the House of Deputies appointed a committee to work with the

Commission in protecting the rights of the Indian. On that occasion there was also set up a missionary jurisdiction named Niobrara, which included the reservations in South Dakota and western Nebraska; five Indian and three white clergymen were then laboring in the area. Two years later William Hobart Hare was consecrated Bishop of Niobrara. By 1900 Bishop Hare was in charge of Indian missions on ten reservations which included ninety congregations, 3200 communicants, and twenty-one clergymen. There were four industrial boarding schools also under his jurisdiction. In 1885 Bishop W. D. Walker of North Dakota, at the request of the Chippewa Indians in the Turtle Mountains, founded a school among them.

The twentieth century witnessed both a trend upward in the Indian population and a heightened interest on the part of the churches in Indian mission work. In 1951 thirty-six Protestant denominations were engaged in such missionary programs, largely through the media of mission stations, mission schools, hospitals, and churches.

Roman Catholic and Eastern Orthodox Missions

Roman Catholicism also extended its influence among the Indians during the post Civil War era. The Benedictines in particular performed noteworthy service among the Indians in Minnesota, the Dakotas, and Oklahoma. In 1889 Katharine Drexel donated a large sum to Indian missions and established the Sisters of the Blessed Sacrament for Indians and Negroes. The Jesuits inaugurated a mission among the Alaskan Eskimos in the 1880's, while the Franciscans of Cincinnati founded a mission for the Navajos in Arizona in 1898 and a few years later assumed responsibility for some of the old missions in New Mexico. The Brothers Minor conducted programs among the Chippewas and the Ottawas. In 1874 the Bureau of Catholic Indian Missions was founded at Washington, D.C. Its main purpose was to coordinate the church's efforts for the natives and to represent the Roman Catholic position in regard to the Indian before the national government. None understood more fully the mind of the Indian or were more eager to defend him against exploitation by the whites than the missionaries. They were usually among the best qualified to negotiate treaties between the government and the natives. Father Pierre-Jean De Smet, for example, was sent as the official emissary of the United States to present peace terms to the Sioux in 1868. He was the only commissioner who dared to go into the Indian camp. De Smet and others like him were often the only persons who could prevent an Indian outbreak or restore peace once war had been declared.

Since the opening of the twentieth century the Roman Catholic Church has extended its missionary program to Indians living on eighty-one reservations. While it has experienced some success in evangelizing the natives, neither it nor the Protestant churches have been able to train an adequate indigenous leadership. Relatively few Indians have shown any interest in entering the ministry. In 1950 the Roman Catholic Church estimated its Indian membership at 95,000.

From the time the able and industrious John Veniaminoff arrived in the Aleutian Islands in 1824, the Russian Orthodox Church had maintained missions in Alaska. By 1860 it was reported that some 4700 Indians had received baptism. The transfer of Alaska to the United States in 1867 in no wise prompted the church to curb its missionary activities in this promising area. The church did, however, create an independent bishopric at San Francisco in 1872 and placed Alaska under its jurisdiction. In 1900 the Orthodox Missionary Society inaugurated a missionary program in Alaska. But gradually the Orthodox Church lost ground to Protestants and Roman Catholics.

22

Americanism and the

Immigrant Faiths

A DEEPENING SENSE OF AMERICAN NATIONALISM AND OF AMERICA'S REDEMP-
tive mission in the years which followed the Civil War contributed to a
more favorable attitude toward unrestricted immigration. The majority of
immigrants after the Revolution had been farmers and workingmen from
the British Isles, Germany, and later the Scandinavian countries. By 1880
there were 6,680,000 foreign-born persons living in the United States;
among these were about 2,000,000 Germans, 1,855,000 Irish, 717,000 Canadians, 664,000 English, and 440,000 Scandinavians. For the most part the
newly arrived aliens took up farming; many were attracted to the Upper
Mississippi Valley where by 1880 a larger percentage of immigrants were
living than in any other region of the nation. Assimilation of these people
was not difficult inasmuch as they had descended from the same stock as
the Anglo-Saxon people. The influx from northern and western Europe,
which was greatly encouraged by under-populated states, reached its crest
in 1882 and henceforth declined.

It was prophetic that in 1882, the year in which immigrants first ap-

419

peared in significant numbers from eastern and southern Europe, Congress passed its first important restrictive legislation. As the years passed the multitudes from Russia, Austria-Hungary, Italy, and other countries along the Mediterranean continued to increase until in 1896 they were arriving in greater numbers than those from northern Europe. There were many reasons for this heavy immigration, among them being overpopulation in the mother country, persecution of Jews in Russia beginning in the 1880's, the inauguration of direct steamship service between Mediterranean and American ports, and the lure of employment in recently opened mines and factories. These later immigrants could not be assimilated quickly into the American environment. They were inclined to group themselves together in relative isolation, perpetuating for as long as they could their Old World customs and native dialects. The greater majority of Russians, Poles, Slavs, Magyars, Greeks, and Italians provided the manual labor necessary to the phenomenal development of industry during the last third of the nineteenth century. Most of these factory workers had received little if any education and exhibited only a modest inclination toward learning.

On the Pacific Coast, Chinese coolies had been in such demand during the 1850's and 1860's that shiploads were imported to provide cheap labor. By 1880 more than 100,000 had arrived in America. They were resented by white laborers because of their competition for jobs, their low standard of living, and their unfamiliar customs. Mounting antagonism toward the Chinese during the 1870's led to the placing of legislative curbs on Chinese immigration. The arrival of numerous Japanese immigrants early in the twentieth century caused further concern which resulted in additional discriminatory legislation in the Webb Act of 1913 and the exclusion of all immigration from Japan in 1924.

The immigration statistics for the period following the Civil War are little short of phenomenal. During the thirty-five years between 1865 and 1900 no less than 13,500,000 aliens arrived on these shores, a figure surpassing by more than a million the total population in 1830. And this was slight when compared with immigration in the opening decades of the twentieth century. This tidal wave of newcomers effected certain significant changes in the makeup of communities in a number of sections. The assertion of Donahoe's Magazine in 1889 that "Boston is no longer the Boston of the Endicotts and the Winthrops, but the Boston of the Collinses and the O'Briens" was impossible of refutation. That very year the Irish held the reins of government in sixty-eight cities and towns in Massachusetts. New York City was the world's principal melting pot with two and one-half times as many Jews as Warsaw, twice as many Irish as Dublin, and as many Germans as Hamburg. Chicago could boast that as far as Czech, Pole, and Canadian immigrants were concerned, it led New York.

During the opening decades of the twentieth century it became increasingly apparent that popular enthusiasm for immigration had cooled. Organized labor in particular raised its voice in protest against unrestricted immigration which was creating excessive competition for jobs. In 1917 a literacy test was enacted as a prerequisite to admission to the country. The most restrictive legislation, however, was enacted in 1924; the Immigration Act fixed the quotas at 2 per cent of the foreign-born of each nationality counted in the census of 1890 and excluded all Japanese. Thus one of the major forces influencing American social change was curbed.

Organized religion in the United States bore the obvious marks of the impact made by mass immigration. Some religious bodies experienced an appreciable gain in membership, while some expressions of religion appeared for the first time on the American scene. Those bodies most affected by the tidal wave of immigration were the Lutheran, Roman Catholic, Jewish, and Eastern Orthodox.

THE LUTHERANS

Between 1870 and 1910, Lutheran church membership in the United States rose from less than 500,000 to almost 2,250,000 so that in numerical strength the Lutheran churches were elevated to third place among Protestant denominations. This gain had been made possible largely through heavy German and Scandinavian immigration. At the conclusion of the Civil War, the influx of Germans, temporarily reduced, increased once more until in 1882 more than 250,000 arrived in America. Thereafter the German immigration dropped sharply, reaching low ebb in 1898 when only 17,000 settlers arrived.

More than 1,750,000 Scandinavians emigrated to America from 1870 to 1910; approximately half originated in Sweden, while one-third came from Norway and one-sixth from Denmark. Scandinavian immigration reached its peak in 1882, when more than 100,000 arrived. Toward the end of the century there was a decline in the number of immigrants, largely because of the economic recession. But the number swelled again as prosperity returned at the opening of the twentieth century until in 1903 some 77,000 arrived. After that time there was a sharp decline in the number of new settlers. The main stream of Scandinavian immigration poured into the Upper Mississippi Valley, with its rich farm lands. Minnesota became their chief center with a Scandinavian population of more than a million by 1910. Others settled in Wisconsin, the Dakotas, Illinois, Michigan, and Iowa. The greater majority had come from a Lutheran background but were theologically more liberal than many Germans. Numbers of them were happy to be beyond the reach of the established churches, and once in America they departed from their Old World religious heritage. In some cases this resulted in free-church tendencies within American Lutheranism; in others it led to affiliation with non-Lutheran denominations or with no church at all.

Reorganization in the Scandinavian Bodies

With the formation of the Augustana Synod in 1860, Scandinavian Lutheranism in America set out in a new direction. The trend in the Swedish and Norwegian churches of the Synod was to favor unqualified subscription to the Augsburg Confession, to attach greater importance to the work of the laity, to stress the personal religious experience, and to give a pietistic interpretation to the Christian life. These emphases were most prominent in the ministries of such leading Augustana Lutherans as Tuve Hasselquist, Erland Carlsson, O. C. T. Andren, and Eric Norelius. During the first decade of the Synod's existence attention was directed principally toward the establishment of a theological seminary and the development of churches in unorganized fields.

In 1870 the Norwegian element in the Augustana Church, having for some time been concerned over the preponderance of the Swedes in the Synod and having desired a fellowship which would be dominantly Norwegian, withdrew and promptly divided into two denominational bodies, the Norwegian Danish Augustana Synod and the Conference of the Norwegian Danish Evangelical Lutheran Church in America. That same year the Swedish group, not desiring to erect a nationalistic church in the United States, merged with the theologically conservative General Council of the Evangelical Lutheran Church of North America. The next twenty-five years witnessed such a marked numerical growth that the Synod found it necessary to shift responsibility for such important tasks as church extension to the regional conferences. By 1880 the conferences had become so vital to the work of the church that the Synod created a synodical council of representatives from the conferences whose purpose was to plan for the meetings of the Synod and to perform whatever additional tasks might be assigned to it. The conference organization was officially approved by the Synod in 1894; thereafter the conferences functioned much as district synods. In 1894 the denomination also gave evidence of its Americanization by changing its name to the Evangelical Lutheran Augustana Synod of North America.

One of the larger Norwegian Lutheran bodies was the Synod for the Norwegian Evangelical Lutheran Church in America, organized in 1853 by persons who favored a strict interpretation of doctrine and rigid adherence to the ritual and procedure of the Norwegian Church. They frowned on lay participation in the conduct of evangelistic meetings and were decidedly opposed to the Norwegian Lutheran group headed by Elling Eielsen. About one-third of the Norwegian Synod withdrew in 1887 because of dissension over the doctrine of predestination and formed the Anti-

Missouri Brotherhood. This action stemmed from an earlier controversy over the Missouri Synod's strict interpretation of predestination. The Anti-Missouri Brotherhood merged with the Norwegian Danish Conference and the Norwegian Augustana Synod in 1890 to constitute the United Norwegian Church. This became the largest of the Norwegian bodies, with a membership in 1910 of more than 250,000.

Danish Lutheran immigrants founded two new denominations before the end of the nineteenth century. The Danish Lutheran Church in America, organized in 1872, claimed to be a branch of the established church in Denmark. Another denomination was created in 1896 by a union of secessionists from the Norwegian Danish Conference and the Danish Lutheran Church in America; it took as its name the United Danish Lutheran Church in America. It was by far the largest organization of Danish Lutherans in the country.

Home Missions in the West

With the mass influx of European Lutherans and the presence of increasing numbers of American Lutherans in the West, bodies such as the General Synod and the General Council were faced with the challenge to extend their influence beyond the Mississippi. Since their churches were zealous for missions and generous in their benevolences, it was possible to put into operation a highly effective program of church extension. The General Council organized English and German mission boards, sending out missionaries especially to those areas in the Northwest where there was a heavy concentration of Lutherans. In 1871 the General Council created the Indiana Synod and twenty years later founded the English Synod of the Northwest, the latter having jurisdiction over English missions extending from Wisconsin to Washington. The Pacific Synod was formed in 1901 from the western part of the English Synod.

The older and less theologically conservative General Synod, through its Board of Home Missions and its Board of Church Extension, also had a vigorous western missionary program. In the forty-year period following the Civil War its membership more than tripled. These gains necessitated additional synodical organization which was provided in the creation of the Kansas Synod in 1868, the Nebraska Synod in 1871, and the Rocky Mountain Synod and the California Synod in 1891. A special effort among immigrant Germans led to mergers with the German Wartburg Synod which had withdrawn from the Central Illinois Synod in 1872, and with the German Nebraska Synod established in 1890. For a time pastors were brought from Germany to minister to the German-speaking congregations; in 1883 a German Seminary was established in Chicago. Gradually, however, the German element became thoroughly assimilated into the American environment and by 1910 not more than one-tenth of the congregations belonging to the General Synod employed German in their services.

The Missouri Synod

Possibly the most dynamic of all the Lutheran bodies was the strictly orthodox Missouri Synod. This denomination, which held to the infallible character of the Scriptures and full acceptance of the Lutheran confessions, carried its message with indefatigable zeal to German immigrants during the last half of the nineteenth century and with such success that by 1890 its number of communicants had risen to 293,211. Until 1917 its official name was The German Evangelical Lutheran Synod of Missouri, Ohio, and Other States; in that year it dropped the word "German" from its name. In 1947 the denomination changed its title to The Lutheran Church—Missouri Synod.

As a result of negotiations begun by the Joint Synod of Ohio, the midwestern synods, Missouri, Ohio, Illinois, Wisconsin, and Minnesota, organized a federation in 1872 known as the Synodical Conference. It was intended to represent a more rigid type of Lutheran confessionalism than that of the General Council, just as that of the General Council was more rigid than that of the General Synod. The president of the Conference, Dr. C. F. W. Walther, regarded this federation as a positive step toward Lutheran unity. He was therefore all the more disappointed when a controversy over the doctrine of predestination led to the withdrawal of the Joint Synod of Ohio in 1881 and the Norwegian Synod in 1882. The Missouri Synod had insisted that predestination to salvation is not due to God's foreknowledge of faith in man, but that faith and perseverance are part of God's decree. The leaders of the Ohio party attacked this teaching as Calvinistic and then removed themselves from the fellowship of the Missouri Synod.

In 1872 The English Evangelical Lutheran Conference of Missouri was organized for the benefit of English-speaking Lutherans in Missouri. The movement had been initiated by several theologically conservative pastors who had moved to Missouri from North Carolina and Tennessee and who desired to maintain services in the English language. In 1887 these congregations requested admission to the Missouri Synod as a separate English District. Upon advice of the Missouri Synod the congregations retained their independent character and in 1890 organized themselves into The English Evangelical Lutheran Synod of Missouri and Other States. As the years passed the German and English groups grew closer together, largely because of the trend toward the use of English in the German Synod. Finally, in 1911, the two denominations merged. By 1925 not more than half of the Synod's congregation employed German in any services of worship.

MISCELLANEOUS ACCESSIONS THROUGH IMMIGRATION

While the majority of German immigrants having a Protestant background united with Lutheran bodies, there were several thousand who formed an alliance based on both Lutheran and Reformed principles. As early as 1840 such an organization, known as the *Kirchenverein des Westens,* had appeared in Missouri; by the end of the Civil War it had congregations in Indiana, Illinois, Ohio, Wisconsin, and Iowa. In 1877 the *Kirchenverein* united with several other similarly minded groups to form the Evangelical Synod of North America.

Among the non-Lutheran Protestant denominations which were relatively successful in gaining converts from German and Scandinavian immigrants were the Methodists, Baptists, and Congregationalists. During the 1840's the Methodists, chiefly through the work of William Nast, had inaugurated a missionary program for the German communities in Ohio. German Methodist congregations were formed and by 1864 German conferences had been set up. In 1907 there were ten German conferences embracing a membership of about 64,000. The Methodists were likewise able to form a Danish-Norwegian Conference in 1907 and to gather a sizeable number of Swedish congregations.

In the twenty-year period prior to 1860 the American Baptist Home Mission Society won a considerable number of German immigrants to the Baptist position and organized them into churches. Rochester Theological Seminary even created a German Department in 1854, headed by Dr. Karl August Rauschenbusch, father of the eminent Walter Rauschenbusch, to train a ministry for these churches. Eventually the German Baptist churches were grouped into conferences. Notable gains were also made among the Scandinavians. As early as 1848 a Norwegian Baptist church was organized at Indian Creek, Illinois; by 1882 there were thirty Danish-Norwegian churches. The first Swedish Baptist congregation was gathered in 1852 at Rock Island, Illinois; within thirty years there were 104 churches organized in a Swedish Conference. In 1855 the first Danish Baptist church was founded in Patten County, Illinois.

The Congregationalists sought actively to minister to newly arrived Germans and Scandinavians. Before 1860 they had founded several churches among the Germans in Iowa, but their principal gains in the Middle West were not made until the 1870's and 1880's. During those decades churches were organized in the northern tier of states between the Mississippi and the Rocky Mountains. By 1911 there were more than 13,000 communicants in the German Congregational churches.

The Reformed Church in America, so named after 1867, gained a number of accessions through the Dutch immigration which increased markedly after 1846. A high percentage of these settlers located in the Middle West. The greater majority held strictly to Calvinism and looked to the

Classis of Holland, Michigan, to set a proper example of orthodoxy. Another Reformed body, the Hungarian Reformed Church in America, was created in 1904 by the many Hungarians of Reformed background who had only recently come to America. Most of the churches in the denomination united with the Reformed Church in America in 1922; a minority declined to merge and formed the Free Magyar Reformed Church in America. The Presbyterian Church in the U.S.A. also won a number of adherents from among the Hungarian Reformed. As for immigrants from the British Isles, one may cite the Welsh Calvinistic groups, who organized along Presbyterian lines and established a General Assembly in 1869. This group finally abandoned the use of Welsh in its services and in 1920 united with the Presbyterian Church in the U.S.A. A more unusual group was the Plymouth Brethren, which first appeared in the United States about the middle of the nineteenth century. It had risen in England and Ireland during the 1820's as a protest against any union between church and state and stereotyped forms of worship. Though officially opposed to sectarianism, the members divided into eight bodies after their arrival in the United States.

THE ROMAN CATHOLICS

Prior to the Civil War the principal accessions to Roman Catholicism were through the great Irish immigration, which witnessed the arrival of nearly two million Irish to these shores. As late as 1882 the British Isles provided as much as 27.7 per cent of the immigrants, but it was clear that the peak of Irish immigration had long since passed. Henceforth the Roman Catholic Church would have to look to central, eastern, and southern Europe for its chief gains. During the last decades of the nineteenth century a rather heavy German immigration swelled the ranks of the church in America. After 1900, however, the accessions from Italy, Austria-Hungary, and Poland proved to be more important. A large migration of French Canadians into the United States added significantly to Roman Catholic strength in New England and northern New York, while the entrance of more than 100,000 Mexicans into the Southwest by 1900 had the same effect.

Church Extension

In June, 1908, Pope Pius X declared that the church in America was no longer under the jurisdiction of the Congregation de Propaganda Fide and was consequently no longer to be regarded as missionary territory; it was now on a par with other great national bodies such as those in France and Italy. Considering the impressive numerical gains made by the church during the preceding half century the pronouncement does not seem surprising. In 1865 the Roman Catholic membership in the United States was approximately 3,000,000 or 9.65 per cent of the total population. By 1900 the church had a membership of 12,000,000 or 15.78 per cent of the whole. Roman Catholics constituted 18.76 per cent of the population in 1930, with an enrollment of 23,000,000; by 1958 the figures had risen to 35,846,-477, or 21 per cent of the country's population. The greatest gain percentagewise was from 1865 to 1900. As the gain has slackened considerably since 1900 and particularly since 1930, one may conclude that the numerical gains of the church were due overwhelmingly to immigration.

The church, nevertheless, suffered serious losses through "leakage" to other denominations or the secularization of the immigrant. In rural areas, notably in the South and West, where there was often no priest, numbers of Roman Catholics were permanently lost to the church. Nor was this condition corrected to any significant extent during the first half of the twentieth century; in 1953 about 26 per cent of all counties in the United States had no resident priest. The greatest losses, however, were incurred in the urban areas which attracted the largest numbers of immigrants, especially in the metropolitan districts of the East. Manifold reasons may account for this situation: an insufficient number of priests to minister to the personal needs of the immigrant, the impersonal nature of parishes in the big cities, preoccupation with economic concerns, and the attractions of secularism. In any case, the defections were substantial; some embraced Protestantism, but many more completely neglected the ordinances of religion.

The Roman Catholic Church made every effort to keep up with the immigrant, establishing dioceses as quickly as growth in population warranted them. Since the greater proportion of Roman Catholic immigrants settled in the cities of the East, the church was faced with the task of creating ecclesiastical organizations for these burgeoning communities at the same time the westward movement of population called for aggressive efforts on the frontier. Between 1865 and 1940 a number of new dioceses were erected in the East, among them the dioceses of Harrisburg and Scranton (1868), Ogdensburg and Providence (1872), Trenton (1881), Syracuse (1886), Altoona (1901), and Camden and Paterson (1937).

Missionary activities both in the cities and on the frontier were greatly strengthened by the arrival of priests, lay brothers, and nuns from abroad, the major part of whom came from Ireland, Germany, France, and Belgium. One of the most dedicated orders was the Benedictine sisters of St. Walburg's Convent at Eichstätt who, after coming to the United States in 1852 and founding a home at St. Mary's, Pennsylvania, founded houses in various parts of the country. The order, which was later organized into the Congregation of Saint Scholastica, was devoted to teaching. German Benedictines and Franciscans founded houses in Oregon, New Jersey, and Ohio, while a group of German Carmelites arrived in 1882 and established themselves in Texas, Louisiana, and New Mexico. From Italy came several groups of missionaries to labor in chosen fields. The Jesuits of the province of Naples, for example, were sent to Colorado and New Mexico in 1867 to conduct missions for both Indians and European immigrants. Twenty years later the bishop of Piacenza organized the Pious Society of the Missionaries of St. Charles Borromeo to train missionaries for the Italians in America. In 1888 the society obtained a church in New York City and was soon operating in a number of dioceses. The Lazarist provinces of Barcelona and Poland dispatched missionaries to the United States to work among Spanish and Polish immigrants. There were even a few instances in which clerics born and educated abroad were appointed to episcopal responsibilities in America. Thus from 1870 to 1872 Ignatius Persico, an Italian who had been Vicar-Apostolic of Agra, India, served as bishop of Savannah.

In addition to the regular Roman Catholic immigrants, the church faced a unique challenge in the arrival of thousands of members of the Uniate churches. These bodies had for centuries adhered to their Eastern Catholic rites and customs but had recognized the Roman pope as supreme pontiff. With services in a different language, married parish priests, the giving of communion in both kinds to the laity, and the administration of confirmation immediately after baptism, they differed widely from Latin-rite Roman Catholics. The Ruthenians, largely from the Austro-Hungarian Empire, began to arrive in significant numbers after 1880, there being about 400,000 by 1908. Separate churches were organized for these persons and a bishop was appointed in 1907. Roumanian Uniates arrived in fairly large numbers after 1900; they, too, had their own priesthood.

New Dogmas and Practices

Possibly no pontificate in history saw more signal developments in Roman Catholicism than that of Pope Pius IX, who governed the church from 1846 to 1878. The period of his reign was marked by the political unification of Germany and Italy, popular revolutions, and the rise of evolutionary theory. During the first few months of his rule Pius IX won the reputation of being a liberal because of his reforms which included greater freedom for the press, the appointment of laymen to papal offices, and the adoption of a constitution for Rome. The liberal revolutions of 1848, however, permanently soured the pope on democratic movements and henceforth his reign was characterized by conservative acts and pronouncements. In December, 1864, he issued the famous *Syllabus of Errors,* in which he listed under eighty headings what he felt to be the principal errors of his time. The following were among the propositions to be condemned: that Protestantism is acceptable to God as a form of the

Christian religion; that socialism, communism, secret societies, and Bible societies should be permitted; that church and state should be separated; that the civil power should have complete control over public education; that the state should have jurisdiction over marriage and divorce; and that the church should accept liberalism and modern conceptions of society. The document brought considerable embarrassment to the hierarchy in the United States inasmuch as it reflected views which were decidedly unpopular among Americans; and therefore, it served to lessen what prestige the church had been able to gain through persistent effort.

In the realm of doctrine, a rising attitude of devotion to the Virgin Mary, sparked by Catherine Labouré's reported vision of Mary in 1830, had led to the definition of the Immaculate Conception by Pius IX in 1854 as a dogma of the church. It emphasized that from the moment of her creation Mary had been "immune from all taint of original sin." Henceforth, devotion to the Virgin increased among Roman Catholics in the United States and in other parts of the world. The trend continued into the twentieth century and on November 1, 1950, Pope Pius XII proclaimed the bodily assumption to heaven of the Virgin Mary as a dogma to be accepted by all communicants.

Another trend during the pontificate of Pius IX was toward ultramontanism (beyond the mountains), a view which suggested that the church should look to the Holy See in Rome for its final authority. Pius IX had been able to strengthen the papal position through his proclamation of the Immaculate Conception in 1854. By the 1860's the time seemed ripe for a definition of papal infallibility. To this end he summoned a general council of the church, the first since the Council of Trent in the sixteenth century, to meet at the Vatican late in 1869. The principal question before the bishops was that of papal infallibility. Many were reluctant to give their approval to such a definition, thinking it inopportune. The members of the American hierarchy recognized that its passage could prove injurious to Roman Catholicism in the United States by fomenting anti-Catholic prejudice. But when the matter came to a vote in 1870, only two bishops replied in the negative. One of these was Bishop Edward Fitzgerald of Little Rock, Arkansas; and he accepted the doctrine as soon as it was proclaimed. The doctrine, as promulgated by the pope in the document known as *Pastor aeternus*, declared that

it is a dogma divinely revealed that the Roman Pontiff, when he speaks *ex cathedra,* that is, when in the discharge of the office of pastor and doctor of all Christians, by virtue of his supreme apostolic authority he defines a doctrine regarding faith or morals to be held by the universal Church, by the divine assistance promised to him in blessed Peter, is possessed of that infallibility with which the divine Redeemer willed that His Church should be endowed for defining doctrine regarding faith or morals: and that therefore such definitions of the Roman Pontiff are irreformable of themselves, and not from the consent of the Church.[1]

Those recalcitrants who refused to accept the dogma formed themselves into Old Catholic bodies, which were strongest in Switzerland and Holland. From these sprang four American denominations with a combined membership of about 90,000 in 1950. They were the American Catholic Church; the American Catholic Church, Archdiocese of New York; the North American Old Roman Catholic Church; and the Old Catholic Church in America.

The Church and Americanism

A perennial fear of many non-Roman Catholic Americans was that the church was essentially a foreign power which, if allowed to expand without limitation, would bring to an end the American way of life. Many American bishops, acutely conscious of this attitude, did everything possible to disabuse the public of the idea that Roman Catholics were un-American. Their task was admittedly difficult. There was a cohesiveness which cemented together the various national groups which arrived in the country and it was frequently difficult to persuade them that they were now Americans rather than Germans, Poles, or Italians. The German resistance to Americanization was particularly evident. In 1890 the Archangel Raphael Society in Germany, organized in 1871 to aid German immigrants, sent a memorial through its secretary, Peter Cahensly, to the pope. It suggested that the national groups in America should have their own churches, parochial schools, priests, and bishops, since millions had been lost to the church through its failure to provide them. The American hierarchy as well as the public in general opposed the plan, arguing in favor of a homogeneous church. Their arguments against Cahenslyism were so impressive that Rome decided in their favor. Another source of conflict was the contention of Polish Roman Catholics that they should have full control of all property purchased and maintained by them. Failing to receive satisfaction in this, they seceded from the church and founded the Polish National Catholic Church at Scranton, Pennsylvania, in 1897. Its first synod was held in 1904. The only body of considerable size in this country to withdraw from the Roman Catholic Church, it numbered some 250,000 communicants in 1950.

That the Roman Catholic Church in the post-Civil War era was vitally concerned over the achievement of a strong national denomination and the Americanization of its membership was evident in its official pronouncements and acts. At the Third Plenary Council of Baltimore in 1884, a national gathering of the hierarchy, the priesthood was directed to refrain

[1] Quoted in K. S. Latourette, *A History of Christianity* (Harper, c. 1953), 1095.

from making public statements on political issues. At the same time steps were taken to provide the church with a leadership scholarly and astute enough to win the respect of intellectuals. One of the Council's most constructive decisions was to found the Catholic University of America at Washington, D.C. This institution, which opened in 1889, provided graduate school training for persons who wished to pursue advanced studies.

Possibly no member of the clergy contributed more to the Americanization of the church than Isaac Thomas Hecker (1819–1888). Founder of the Missionary Society of St. Paul the Apostle or the Paulists in 1858 and editor of the *Catholic World,* he had been a convert from Protestantism and upon entering the priesthood had sought to develop a program for the conversion of Protestants. He recognized that in order to accomplish this he would have to make Roman Catholicism attractive to persons of Protestant persuasion by Americanizing it. He had no desire to detract from papal authority, but he did want to remove the stress from unqualified obedience and dependence and place it on independent thinking and personal initiative. Through Walter Elliott's biography of Father Hecker, published after his death, these ideas gained wider publicity. Archbishop John Ireland, writing of Hecker in the preface to the biography, called him the ideal American priest and supported his contention that a different kind of churchmanship was needed to meet the problems of the modern age. "His was the profound conviction that in the present age, at any rate, the order of the day should be individual action—every man doing his fair duty and waiting for no one else to prompt him."

Clearly the most distinguished member of the American hierarchy in the fifty-year period following 1870 was James Gibbons (1834–1921), Cardinal Archbishop of Baltimore. After his ordination in 1861, he rose rapidly in the councils of the church and by 1868 was consecrated Vicar-Apostolic of North Carolina. In 1877 he became Archbishop of Baltimore and nine years later was created a cardinal, the second American to receive that honor. Judicious in temperament and broad in sympathy, he sought out men of all classes and persuasions and fraternized with non-Roman Catholics more than any member of the hierarchy ever had before. In 1893 he opened with prayer the World Congress of Religions at Chicago. Cardinal Gibbons was American to the core and championed the separation of church and state, even though he recognized that from the standpoint of Roman Catholic philosophy it was not ideal. He seized every opportunity to defend democratic institutions and to express his love for the American way of life. More than anything else he wanted a virile and unified Roman Catholicism, thoroughly assimilated into the American environment; his life was dedicated to the achievement of that goal.

Associated with Cardinal Gibbons in his mission were such prominent American churchmen as the well-known John Ireland (1838–1918),

Bishop, and later Archbishop, of St. Paul. Archbishop Ireland spoke for the group in a sermon before the Catholic Congress in 1899. He said: "The Church of America must be, of course, as Catholic as even in Jerusalem or Rome; but as far as her garments assume color from the local atmosphere, she must be American. Let no one dare paint her brow with a foreign tint or pin to her mantle foreign linings." Pope Leo XIII, astute diplomat that he was, allowed some of the opinions of Gibbons and Ireland to pass without condemnation, though to pacify the conservatives he removed Bishop John Keane from his Catholic University rectorship. By 1899, however, he concluded that drastic measures must be taken. In January of that year he issued the papal letter *Testem benevolentiae*, addressed to Cardinal Gibbons. The immediate occasion for the letter was the French translation of Father Elliott's biography of Isaac Hecker, which created the impression that Father Hecker exemplified a new and worthier type of Roman Catholicism. Leo XIII condemned that kind of Americanism which thought the church should harmonize itself with modern theories and abrogate its right to determine all questions of a doctrinal and moral character and that the individual should be allowed greater initiative in the development of his spiritual life.

. . . We cannot approve the opinions which some comprise under the head of Americanism. If, indeed, by that name be designated the characteristic qualities which reflect honor on the people of America . . . or if it implies the condition of your commonwealths, or the laws and customs which prevail in them, there is surely no reason why We should deem that it ought to be discarded. But if it is to be used not only to signify, but even to commend the above doctrines, there can be no doubt but that our Venerable Brethren the bishops of America would be the first to repudiate and condemn it, as being especially unjust to them and to the entire nation as well. For it raises the suspicion that there are some among you who conceive of and desire a church in America different from that which is in the rest of the world. One in the unity of doctrine as in the unity of government, such is the Catholic Church, and, since God has established its centre and foundation in the Chair of Peter, one which is rightly called Roman, for where Peter is there is the Church.[2]

The letter was at once clear and final; with its issuance an era of liberalizing tendencies and wide fraternization came to an end.

The School Question

Since the days of Bishop Hughes in New York, Roman Catholics had sought public support for schools in which their religion would be taught. Failing in this, they turned to the creation of a parochial school system which could guarantee the children of the faithful an education deemed

[2] Mode, *op. cit.,* 486.

satisfactory by the church. Ordinarily the parochial school was housed in the church building, a most unhappy situation. Many church leaders after the Civil War began to agitate for a national school policy. At the Third Plenary Council of Baltimore, held in 1884, certain constructive principles were laid down. The hierarchy decreed that "near each church, where it does not exist, a parochial school is to be erected within two years from the promulgation of this Council, and is to be maintained *in perpetuum,* unless the bishop, on account of grave difficulties, judge that a postponement be allowed." While the laity were exhorted to support these schools it was specifically directed that no parent be denied the sacraments for not heeding the exhortation.

In the meantime, a new campaign had begun to secure public funds for the maintenance of Roman Catholic schools. Bishop John B. Purcell of Cincinnati directed a statement to the people of the United States in 1876, in which he demanded that Roman Catholics be tax exempt so far as taxes for the maintenance of non-Roman Catholic schools were concerned. Being unsuccessful in this, the church presented several plans whereby the Roman Catholic schools might be recognized as part of the public school system and thus obtain public funds. One operated in Poughkeepsie, New York, from 1873 to 1898. The local board of education leased the parochial schools from the parishes and staffed them with nuns who taught both religious and secular subjects. Better known was the plan put into effect in Faribault, Minnesota, a town with a heavy Roman Catholic majority, from 1891 to 1893. While in many respects it was similar to the Poughkeepsie plan, it provided for religious instruction only after school hours.

Conservatives in the church, who favored a strong and separate parochial school system, looked with horror upon the Faribault Plan. They saw it as part of Archbishop Ireland's plan to Americanize the church and they wanted no part of it. A great controversy was touched off in 1891 when Father Thomas Bouquillon, Professor of Moral Theology at the Catholic University, published a pamphlet in which he maintained that the state has the right to educate its citizens and to set academic and other requirements for its schools. The pamphlet aroused a storm of protest and the issue was carried to Rome. Much to the surprise of the conservatives, the Congregation of Propaganda, then responsible for the direction of the church in America, ruled in 1892 that the Faribault Plan was acceptable. When Monsignor Satolli, the newly appointed first Apostolic Delegate to the church in America, arrived on the scene in 1893, he was somewhat tactless in interpreting this decision to the archbishops meeting in New York; and the Pope had to intervene with a further statement of the papal position. For some years thereafter the trend seemed to be in the direction of Father Bouquillon's views. The American Federation of Catholic Societies, assembled at Buffalo in 1906, pronounced that the secular instruction in Roman Catholic schools, though not the religious teaching, should be sustained by public school funds, and that so far as secular subjects were concerned, parochial schools should be under the inspection and ultimate regulation of the state. Protestant sentiment continued to oppose the use of tax money for sectarian educational purposes and regularly combated Roman Catholic efforts to gain appropriations from public funds.

The Anti-Roman Catholic Reaction

The growth in numerical strength and influence of the Roman Catholic Church in the decades immediately following the Civil War occasioned in many non-Roman Catholic minds a fear which found expression in various organizations. Since the Nativist agitation during the 1830's and 1840's, there had been considerable thought given to the possible political pretensions of the papacy; the issuance of the Syllabus of Errors, therefore, followed by the pronouncement of papal infallibility served only to convince many Americans of the anti-democratic character of the Roman Catholic Church and its incompatibility with American institutions. These statements, which were an embarrassment to many Roman Catholic leaders in the United States, proved to be effective weapons in the hands of those who were antagonistic toward the Roman Church.

Religion figured in the presidential campaign of 1884, when James G. Blaine, whose mother was a Roman Catholic, ran on the Republican ticket against Grover Cleveland, a Democrat and son of a Presbyterian minister. Neither man had a past which was unimpeachable and it was not long before the campaign fell to the level of mud-slinging. Since the outcome of the election seemed to depend in large measure upon New York's electorate, a special effort was made to win the votes of the Roman Catholic Irish in that state. Perhaps Blaine would have carried the state had it not been for an ill-chosen pre-election remark made by the Reverend Samuel Burchard in a speech on behalf of Blaine. He labeled the Democrats as the party of "rum, Romanism and rebellion," and so angered the Roman Catholic citizenry that many shifted their votes to Cleveland, who carried the state by a narrow margin and won the election.

The most vigorous anti-Roman Catholic organization in the closing decades of the nineteenth century was the American Protective Association, founded in Iowa in 1887. Its chief goals were to curb immigration and to frustrate Roman Catholic efforts to win public funds for parochial school purposes. During the Panic of 1893, when jobs were scarce, the association was able to convince a large segment of the American populace of the advisability of placing decided limits on immigration. Indeed, its own membership had climbed to the 70,000 mark by that year, a witness to its growing influence. When Monsignor Satolli, the first Apostolic Delegate to the Roman Catholic Church in the United States, arrived in 1893, it was popularly believed that he was a diplomatic representative to the government; the A.P.A. took full advantage of this belief and used it as a talking-point against the Roman Catholic Church. In politics, it almost always supported the Republican Party since Irish leadership had won the Roman Catholic voters almost completely to the Democratic cause. Its undoing came in 1896 with an attempt to prevent the nomination of the Methodist, William McKinley, as the Republican choice for the presidency on the ground that he was under Roman Catholic influence. The association split on this issue and lost strength which it was never able to regain.

Another wave of anti-Roman Catholic propaganda was released during the five years following 1908. It stemmed no doubt from reaction to the nation-wide publicity given the first American Catholic missionary congress, held in 1908 in Chicago, and the appointment of two additional American cardinals. Anti-Roman Catholic fanatics began the publication of *The Menace,* a false and bigoted sheet designed to convince the public that Roman Catholicism was the enemy of American civilization. Despite its manifestly unworthy character, circulation exceeded 1,400,000 by 1914. The following year there was a revival of the Ku Klux Klan in Georgia; this organization devoted much of its activities to prejudicing the public against Roman Catholicism. During World War I there was a decline in anti-Roman Catholic agitation due largely to the fact that the energies of its leaders were being spent in other causes. By the opening of the 1920's, however, the tension appeared again, this time leading to more unfortunate incidents than before.

THE JEWS

The post-Civil War era witnessed the emergence of German Jews as the dominant group in the American Jewish community. This had come about through heavy German Jewish immigration during the two decades prior to the war. After 1871 immigration from Germany declined inasmuch as Jews in that country were now being granted civil and political equality. From that time the bulk of Jewish immigrants came from eastern Europe. Polish, Roumanian, and Russian immigration began in the 1860's and reached tremendous proportions in the 1880's mainly because of Russian persecution. As a result of the fearful pogroms, communities migrated *en masse* with more than 20,000 Jews entering the United States annually. During the 1890's the Russians inaugurated their policy of wholesale Jewish expulsions; the greater majority of the exiles turned to America. It has been estimated that between 1881 and 1900 approximately 600,000 Russian and Roumanian Jews entered the United States, raising the total Jewish population to more than a million. There followed an additional wave of persecutions, the Russian Revolution, and a series of Jewish massacres, which led to the migration of nearly a million more Jews to this country. Within a generation America had one of the highest concentrations of Jews in the history of the world. At the close of 1957 the membership of Jewish congregations in the United States was approximately 5,500,000. Possibly fifty per cent were affiliated with the Orthodox wing, with the Conservative branch being slightly smaller than the Reform.

Developments in Reform and Conservative Judaism

The years immediately following 1865 witnessed the full assimilation of Reform Judaism into American life. A high percentage of German Jews, though frequently poor and untutored upon their arrival in America, found ways to advance themselves, and many entered business or the professions. With rising social prestige there came the desire to pattern one's religious institutions after the pattern of the community. Reform Judaism therefore took on much of the character of an upper-middle class Protestant church, with most of the distinctively Jewish features removed. In an era in which theological liberalism was making an impact on organized religion, some Jews went beyond and consequently outside Reform Judaism by presenting their faith purely in humanistic ethical terms. One such person was Felix Adler (1851–1933), the son of a rabbi, who rejected the distinctive tenets of Judaism and founded the Ethical Culture Society in 1876 in order "to assert the supreme importance of the ethical factor in all relations of life, personal, social, national and international, apart from any theological or metaphysical considerations."

Until his death in 1900, Isaac Mayer Wise remained the acknowledged leader of Reform Judaism in America. For some years prior to the Civil War this distinguished rabbi had dreamed of establishing a college for the education of rabbis. He nevertheless recognized that his dream could not be realized until a union of congregations to support such an institution could be effected. Such a movement began in 1871 and for the next two years various conferences were held for the purpose of achieving a union of Jewish congregations. Finally, at a convention held in Cincinnati in 1873 arrangements were made by the Reform congregations to establish the Union of American Hebrew Congregations. The Union's first council met in Cleveland the following year and unanimously voted to establish a theological college to be known as Hebrew Union College. In 1875 the institution opened in Cincinnati with Rabbi Wise as its president.

A more radical reformer than Wise was David Einhorn (1809–1879), who had arrived from Germany in 1855. It was largely under his influence that the theoretical basis of American Reform Judaism would be crystallized. Following in the steps of the German reformers, Einhorn maintained that the dispersion of the Jews had not been brought about because of their sins but because of the divine will that they bear testimony to their faith before the nations. He and some other leaders felt it advisable to delete those passages in the Jewish prayer book in which petitions were offered to God for the return of the Jews to Israel. At a conference of eastern Reform rabbis in Philadelphia in 1869 an announcement was issued that "the messianic aim of Israel is not the restoration of the old Jewish state . . . but the union of all the children of God."

The standards of Reform Judaism in America were finally fixed at a conference assembled in Pittsburgh in 1885. In some respects they were more radical than those of the Reform movement in Germany. They provided for the rejection of all Mosaic laws concerned with ceremonialism which could not be harmonized with modern civilization, affirming that Judaism was a "progressive religion, ever striving to be in accord with the postulates of reason." "We consider ourselves no longer a nation but a religious community, and therefore expect neither a return to Palestine, nor a sacrificial worship under the administration of the sons of Aaron, nor the restoration of any of the laws concerning the Jewish state."

In 1889 Rabbi Wise organized a Central Conference of American Rabbis, composed of Reform spiritual leaders. Through its activities and achievements the Reform congregations of America were brought closer together, but in no sense did it interfere with the autonomy of each congregation. It published treatises on important subjects affecting Judaism and in 1894 adopted the Union Prayer Book as the form of worship common to all its American congregations.

The crystallization of the Reform position prompted conservative leaders to initiate counteraction. Rabbi Sabato Morais (1823–1897), successor to the eminent Isaac Leeser in Philadelphia, founded the Jewish Theological Seminary Association in 1885 with the help of other leaders of conservative persuasion, and began to hold classes in New York. The purpose of the seminary was to train for the ministry those Jews who were "faithful to Mosaic Law and ancestral traditions." That the institution did not flourish was due to the fact that six of the eleven congregations which participated in its founding affiliated with the Reform movement before the end of the century. With the arrival of thousands of immigrants from eastern Europe, however, Conservative Judaism was infused with a new energy which would be released through such institutions as the Jewish Theological Seminary.

The Influx from Eastern Europe

Unlike Judaism in Germany, Judaism in eastern Europe remained uninfluenced by the Reform movement. Where it felt the impact of liberal ideas it expressed them in nationalist and socialist movements without relating them to religious concepts and practices. Indeed, within the sphere of religion there was an assiduous adherence to orthodoxy and tradition quite unknown to German Judaism. It was inevitable that when this group finally confronted in the United States their Americanized German Reform brethren feeling should have been intense. The upper-class Reform Jews often looked askance at poverty-stricken East-European immigrants, who, if they had nothing else, possessed the determination to preserve their cultural heritage unblemished by compromise. The Orthodox immigrants, on the other hand, viewed their Reform counterparts as hypocrites who had renounced all that was specifically Jewish in order to blend into the American cultural pattern. Gradually the tension was overcome through an increasing willingness on the part of well-established Jews to help their less fortunate coreligionists and by a growing tendency on the part of the newcomers to adjust to their surroundings and become assimilated into the American environment.

In 1888 Rabbi Jacob Joseph, a prominent preacher and scholar, was brought to New York as part of a plan to place religious life under the authority of the community. Rabbi Joseph was expected to serve as chief rabbi in this enterprise which was intended to bind together the 130 synagogues for Jews from East Europe already established in New York. Actually, only a small percentage of them became involved in the venture; the non-cooperating congregations made the situation worse by attacking the plan and finally it had to be abandoned. It was apparent that while the older immigrants could be held to the Old World traditions, the young were rapidly becoming Americanized and were slipping away from the religion taught by imported Orthodox rabbis who spoke in a foreign tongue. The process of Americanization was greatly abetted by the Sunday or Sabbath schools operated by the established synagogues.

Efforts were, of course, made by Orthodox leaders to provide an educational system which would check the defections to liberalism. Schools such as the *hadarim* and the Talmud Torahs were founded for teaching the Bible, Hebrew, and the prayer book. Many of these schools, which were conducted after public school hours, developed into excellent institutions. In 1896, Rabbi Isaac Elchanan Theological Seminary was founded in New York; it later developed into Yeshiva University. Despite the untiring zeal of Orthodox leaders, they were unable through education to halt the mounting losses. Relatively few Jewish children received any training in the synagogue schools, and those who did were likely to depart from the traditions of their fathers when they reached the age of maturity. The seriousness of the problem was recognized by both established and immigrant Jews, who were deeply concerned over the large numbers of East-European Jewish young people who were rejecting all religion in favor of radical philosophies. They saw that some positive action had to be taken at once.

At this juncture the older established Conservative element began to draw closer to the East-European Orthodox groups in the hope that their association would be mutually advantageous. Rabbi Henry Pereira Mendes of New York, one of the founding fathers of the Jewish Theological Seminary, tried to strengthen the position of Conservative Judaism by allying it with Orthodoxy; in 1898 he led in the establishment of the Union of Orthodox Jewish Congregations. Shortly thereafter, Cyrus Adler of the Smithsonian Institution proposed the restoration of the Jewish Theological Seminary, then practically defunct, as an institution to train English-speaking rabbis for the East-European immigrants; it would adhere to the ancient traditions but would keep its students informed concerning the findings of modern scholarship. Jewish philanthropists considered the proposal sound and contributed half a million dollars to the venture.

Solomon Schecter (1847–1915) was the logical choice for the presidency. The Roumanian-born scholar, who had been a product of both Talmudic and secular schools, had acquired for himself an enviable reputation as a student of the Biblical texts and had settled at Cambridge University. A man of broad interests, he hoped for a revival of Orthodoxy but not at the expense of rejecting modern scholarship. Upon arriving in 1901 to assume the duties of president, he at once made arrangements to bring to the faculty distinguished Orthodox scholars of East-European and German background. In spite of all this, the East-European immigrants did not on the whole support the institution, preferring to remain aloof. Nor would they recognize the seminary as having any authority to ordain rabbis.

The association with the East-European Orthodox proved to be most unsatisfactory to the Conservatives. The Union of Orthodox Jewish Congregations soon fell under the complete control of the former, and in 1902 the East-European Orthodox rabbis founded their own rabbinical society, the Union of Orthodox Rabbis. Neither of these organizations, however, was supported by a majority of Orthodox congregations. In the meantime, the Conservative movement enjoyed a period of vitality and growth, and in 1913 Schecter gathered sixteen congregations to form the United Synagogue of America. This newly founded wing of Judaism stood midway between Orthodoxy and Reform, recognizing the authority of Jewish religious and ritual law and emphasizing the importance of the Hebrew language, but also accepting the findings of historical criticism when demonstrated beyond reasonable doubt.

Despite the tendency of second-generation immigrants to adopt a modified Judaism or none at all, the steady influx of newcomers from East Europe until the 1920's assured the preservation of traditional customs and practices. Of the approximately 3,400,000 Jews in the United States in 1917, possibly eighty per cent were of East-European extraction. The majority of these new settlers continued to speak in Yiddish and maintain Yiddish newspapers and periodicals. Indeed, until the great immigration was curbed by restrictive laws, more Yiddish was spoken on the East Side of New York City than in any other place in the world. In areas where there was a high concentration of immigrant Jews an abundance of kosher shops testified to the solidarity of the traditional faith. At the same time the Orthodox synagogues revealed an increasing accommodation to the American environment which became more pronounced as the twentieth century advanced. Services were more formal and sermons were in English. In some cases Orthodox congregations became Conservative. Reform temples were still predominant among affluent Jews, but the Reform movement grew slowly after 1900. Not until 1940 would there be a decided trend upward in the numerical strength of Reform Judaism.

THE EASTERN ORTHODOX

The same mass movement which brought thousands of Orthodox Jews to the United States was responsible for the arrival of additional thousands of Christians representing the Eastern Orthodox churches. The bulk of these immigrants, which were by no means as many as the Jews, arrived between 1880 and 1920. Their principal purposes in coming were to escape the effects of poverty, revolutions, and wars. The churches to which they belonged were as ancient as Christianity, being planted in areas in which the Gospel was first preached. Since 1054 they had not been in communion with the Western Church, having refused to recognize the pope as their supreme head and having differed with the Western Church on certain points of doctrine and practice. While they were one in dogma and practice, taking as their authority the Scriptures, the decrees of the seven ecumenical councils of the ancient church, and the traditions, they were organized for the most part along national lines and therefore looked to different patriarchs for their leadership. When their adherents began to arrive in the United States they tended to perpetuate their national alignments.

The Russian Orthodox

While Russian Orthodoxy had made some impression on the Pacific Coast and in Alaska prior to the Civil War, it was not until 1876 that a Russian Orthodox church was founded in New York and not until the 1880's and 1890's that any noteworthy immigration of Orthodox Christians to America began. During this period Russian parishes were established in New York and Chicago. In 1905 the episcopal see in San Francisco was transferred to New York and made an archdiocese; under the archbishop were two vicar bishops, one in charge of Alaska, the other responsible for the Syrian Mission with headquarters in Brooklyn.

Late in the nineteenth century the Russian Orthodox Church won a number of adherents among immigrants from Austria-Hungary, who had formerly belonged to the Uniate churches. The churches, located in territory where the influence of the Roman Catholic Church was strong, had been persuaded to recognize the supremacy of the pope but were permitted to retain their own bishops, liturgy, and practices. Upon coming to America, the communicants of these churches found they were required to use the Roman Catholic liturgy and function under the jurisdiction of Roman Catholic bishops. After 1891 a considerable number of these churches withdrew and were received into the Russian Orthodox Church.

The history of the Russian Church in America after the communist revolution reflected the uncertainty and turmoil of life in Russia. Prior to the Revolution of 1917, the Holy Synod of Russia, under whose jurisdiction the churches in America had been placed, provided them with an annual allotment of $77,850 besides an additional contribution of $1481 for purely missionary purposes from the Missionary Society of Russia. These benefits were now terminated. In 1919 the American clergy held a Sobor or council at Pittsburgh and pronounced the church in the United States to be "temporarily autonomous." Nevertheless, when Patriarch Tikhon of Moscow, while in prison, appointed Metropolitan Platon in 1923 to be administrator of the church in America, the appointment was accepted. At an All-American Sobor held in Detroit in 1924, Metropolitan Platon was confirmed, even though this body once again pronounced the church in the United States to have temporary autonomy. This action of the All-American Sobor was repudiated by an organization headed by Russian emigré bishops known as the Synod of Bishops Outside Russia; it claimed to exercise full control over all Russian churches outside the bounds of the Soviet Union. This organization had appointed Metropolitan Platon to the American Church in 1921 and for this reason had ever since claimed jurisdiction. In 1926 Platon withdrew from the Synod of Bishops and supported the action of the Sobor of 1924, which ruled the church in America to be independent. The Synod of Bishops then sent several bishops to this country, and these men founded parishes for those who refused to follow Platon. Between 1935 and 1946 the two bodies merged under one metropolitan; in the latter year, however, the All-American Sobor, meeting in Cleveland, voted to terminate relations with the Synod of Bishops and to reaffirm its independence. It remained by far the largest of the Russian Orthodox bodies, having in 1957 a membership of 755,000; its official name was the Russian Orthodox Greek Catholic Church of America. The smaller body, known as the Russian Orthodox Church Outside Russia, had in 1955 a membership of 55,000. Other Russian communions carrying on activities in the United States were the Eastern Orthodox Catholic Church in America and the Russian Orthodox Catholic Church, Archdiocese of the Aleutian Islands and North America.

The Greek Orthodox

The largest of the Eastern Orthodox communions in America by 1957 was the Greek Archdiocese of North and South America, with 1,150,000 communicants. While a church of that persuasion had been organized in New Orleans as early as 1867, it was not until the period between 1890 and 1914 that a substantial immigration from Greece swelled the ranks of the Greek Orthodox Church in the United States. At first the newcomers were largely single men or married men who had left their families behind them. As they became permanent residents, and especially as they were joined by their families, they felt the need for Orthodox religious services. Upon their application to the appropriate religious officials a number of priests were dispatched to this country and soon congregations were organized in the larger cities. In 1908 the Patriarchate of Constantinople gave the Holy Synod of Greece authority over the American churches, with the thought that these churches should be organized into a diocese. No complete church organization was effected, however, until 1918, when Bishop Alexander was sent to America as first bishop and synodical delegate.

In 1922 the Patriarchate of Constantinople once again placed the American churches under its aegis and the same year, by a synodical and patriarchal act known as the Founding Tome of 1922, erected the Greek Archdiocese of North and South America; Bishop Alexander was promoted to the rank of archbishop and four bishoprics were established in his archdiocese. Later that year the Second General Convention of the Archdiocese of America met in New York and adopted a constitution for the church which was ratified by the Patriarchate of Constantinople. In 1930, due to certain internal strife within the church, a new archbishop, The Most Reverend Athenagoras, was appointed for America. When Archbishop Athenagoras was elected Patriarch of the Greek Orthodox Church in 1948, he was succeeded by Archbishop Michael.

The Smaller Orthodox Bodies

Other Eastern Orthodox communions in the United States are the Roumanian, the Serbian, the Syrian, the Ukrainian, the Carpatho-Russian, the Albanian, and the Bulgarian. The first Roumanian church in this country was organized in Cleveland in 1905. By 1918 enough congregations had been formed to warrant the erection of a diocese; the first diocese was established at Youngstown, Ohio. In 1929 the Roumanian churches in the United States united with those in Canada to form the Roumanian Orthodox Episcopate of America. Serbian immigrants, who began to arrive in substantial numbers after 1890, worshipped at first in Russian churches. Not until 1894 was their first congregation organized at Jackson, California. The Serbian Patriarchate of Yugoslavia gave its approval in 1921 to the establishment of a diocese of the United States and Canada, but did not appoint its first bishop until six years later. The headquarters of the Serbian Orthodox Church were located at St. Sava's Serbian Monastery at Libertyville, Illinois. Originally the Syrian churches, composed of immigrants from Syria, Lebanon, Egypt, Palestine, and Iraq, were under the general oversight of the Russian Orthodox Church. When this relationship came to an end in 1927, the Syrian congregations split into five groups, each giving recognition to a different bishop. In 1934 the Patriarch of Antioch, seeking to bring unity to these parishes, appointed a vicar to create the Syrian Antiochian Orthodox Church. It was established as an archdiocese and in 1936 received its first Metropolitan-Archbishop, who took up residence in New York.

In their native country, the Ukrainians had been principally Uniates; they had given their allegiance to the Roman pope in return for the right to maintain their own liturgical system and their accustomed practices. When Ukrainian priests began to arrive in America during the latter decades of the nineteenth century, they found that the Roman Catholic hierarchy would not concede their right to marry or to conduct services according to the Eastern liturgy. In 1891 a number of Ukrainian priests and congregations placed themselves under the jurisdiction of the Russian Church. They found little satisfaction in this connection either; finally in 1927 they seceded from the Russian Church and founded the Ukrainian Orthodox Church of America. This new body, which was governed by an administrator, looked to the Patriarch of Constantinople for final authority. Its first bishop was consecrated by the Patriarch. Since 1950 the church has been independent of Constantinople in matters of administration.

Closely related to the Ukrainian Church is the American Carpatho-Russian Orthodox Greek Catholic Church. Communicants of this denomination trace their origins to dissatisfaction with their position as Uniates. Like the Ukrainians, to whom they were racially akin, they began to break with Roman Catholicism after coming to America and to affiliate with the Russian Church. This relationship also proved eventually to be unsatisfactory. In 1937 an independent, self-governing denomination was organized and a bishop was consecrated the following year by the Patriarch of Constantinople.

Among the smaller foreign-language Orthodox communions in America are the Albanian Orthodox Church and the Bulgarian Orthodox Church. It was not until after the First World War that the Albanian Church was formed in this country and provided with a bishop who has kept in close connection with the Holy Synod of Albania. The Bulgarian Church was established in 1909 as the Bulgarian Orthodox Mission; in 1938 a bishopric was erected in New York City.

In addition to these foreign-language bodies, three native American

bodies were formed during the twentieth century. The Apostolic Episcopal Church was founded in 1925 with the consecration of a former Anglican priest as bishop by three Chaldean bishops. It was completely
autonomous and its services were conducted in English according to the
rite of the Eastern churches. In 1947 it merged with a group which had
withdrawn from the Old Catholic Church of America. The second of
these bodies was the Holy Orthodox Church in America, organized in
1934 for the purpose of spreading Orthodoxy among English-speaking
peoples. The third, the American Holy Orthodox Catholic Apostolic Eastern Church, was instituted in 1932 as a self-governing body giving allegiance to no patriarchate.

Though the Eastern Orthodox communions have a hierarchical organization, most have made use of democratic practices. There has been a
place for lay leadership in church councils and laymen have had a voice
in the appointment of parish clergy. While there has been little cooperation between the various Eastern Orthodox bodies in the United States,
these communions have encouraged the assimilation of their communicants into American life; at the same time they have felt that the American public can be greatly benefited by sharing with them the rich heritage
of the Christian East.

The Armenians

Though not an Orthodox body, since it denies the doctrine of the two
natures of Christ and the decrees of the early church councils, the Ar-
menian Church of North America, Diocese, is in many respects similar
to the Eastern Orthodox bodies. It is in communion with the ancient Ar-
menian or Gregorian Church, which is hierarchical in that all clergy must
be episcopally ordained, but democratic in that the clergy are elected to
their several offices by the people. In order to escape the persecution of
the Turks during the last decade of the nineteenth century and during the
First World War period, thousands of Armenians fled to this country. As
early as 1889 a bishop was sent to minister to the few Armenians already
in America; two years later he organized a church at Worcester, Massachusetts. With the marked influx of refugees after 1894 it was necessary
to form the parishes into a missionary diocese. In 1903 the bishop was
elevated to the rank of archbishop. The church is under the jurisdiction
of the Catholicos of Etchmiadzin, Armenia; in 1957 it had fifty churches
with a membership of 101,199.

THE ASIATIC FAITHS

Because of barriers raised by the American government the number of
Asiatics in the United States has never been large. The second half of

the nineteenth century witnessed the arrival of more than 100,000 Chinese on the West Coast, where they were at first welcomed as inexpensive laborers. However, when white laborers began to compete with them for jobs, anti-Chinese feeling arose and the result was violence. Discriminatory immigration laws (rescinded, 1943) prohibited reception of Chinese immigrants. About the turn of the century there was a sharp increase in Japanese immigration, so that by 1910 there were 72,157 Japanese in the United States. Anti-Japanese sentiment also developed, particularly on the West Coast where the Japanese were most numerous. As in the case of the Chinese, the problem was remedied by the passage of discriminatory legislation.

Many Protestant leaders viewed the arrival of Asiatics, few of whom were Christian, as a unique missionary opportunity. As early as 1852 William Speer, a Presbyterian missionary who had served in Canton, began a mission among the Chinese of San Francisco. By 1870 similar activities had been started by the Baptists, Methodists, and Congregationalists. Despite a vigorous missionary effort the number of conversions was small; in 1900 probably not more than two per cent of the Chinese population had been converted to Christianity. The first mission for the Japanese was founded in 1877 in San Francisco. By 1913 there were forty-three Japanese churches in California, with a combined membership of 2430. Nevertheless, the influence of Buddhism remained strong, particularly among the Japanese. In 1898 the first Young Men's Buddhist Association was established at San Francisco. Seven years later the first Buddhist house of worship was erected in the same city. The year 1914 saw the organization of the Buddhist Mission of North America, a body which was incorporated in 1942 under the name of Buddhist Churches of America. This denomination teaches the philosophy of Mahayana Buddhism or the way of salvation through a power other than one's own. It affirms that through the grace of Amida Buddha men shall be saved. In 1957 there were 10,000 adherents of organized Buddhism in the United States; most of these were Japanese or Japanese-Americans. The head of the denomination holds the title of bishop superintendent, apparently a concession to western titles. Indeed, the entire organization bears the mark of American practice. The process of adaptation will undoubtedly continue to the extent that is deemed necessary in order to hold the allegiance of a membership thoroughly assimilated into the American environment.

Christian Idealism in

National Life

TO THE REPRESENTATIVE AMERICAN CHURCHGOER DURING THE DECADES IMME-
diately following the Civil War, religion was first and foremost a matter
of integrity and respectability. He might be careless in his orthodoxy,
slovenly in his worship, and indifferent in his attitude toward social ills;
but he was anxious not to be denied a reputation for piety, charity, and
unimpeachable conduct. He wore his religion much as he did his Prince
Albert coat; it was a thing of pride, a symbol of status pointing to his
dignity as a man. In theory he knew himself to be a sinner for this was
the pronouncement of orthodoxy, but he never allowed formality to stand
in the way of practice. Orthodoxy was his profession; activism was his
life. If the two elements suffered from incompatibility this did not concern him, for logic was not his forte.

Reared in the burgeoning optimism of an environment surrounded by
new physical, social, and intellectual frontiers, he recognized no end to
opportunity and no limits to success. Whether on the broad western frontier or in the teeming cities of the East or even in some distant clime,
society would be better, more Christian, because of his presence. Grad-

446

ually, but not imperceptibly, the Kingdom of God was growing among men. The task of his generation was to hasten its fulfillment. Thus into every darkened corridor of life that could be reached by pietism he carried his idealistic gospel. He patronized a multiplicity of causes which crusaded against sin, blissfully neglecting the complex and demonic forces which contributed to public corruption and social upheaval. He supported the church as a cause worthy of his backing and regarded his Sunday attendance as being as much a favor to his pastor as a benefit to his soul.

Perhaps this representative churchgoer could not or would not see that his complacency was contributing to the secularization of organized religion. But never in his country's history had the church been stronger in membership and weaker in spiritual effectiveness. Theology, debilitated by the defensive warfare of orthodoxy with science, was in a state of disintegration save for the doctrine of man's perfectibility, which suffered from an acute case of elephantiasis. God was conceived as being so immanent that He became a naturalized American, while religion became a social activity, a form of cultural amusement. Exhibitions of religious idealism were still much in evidence by the turn of the century, but leadership by the churches in this regard was less apparent. More and more the morals of the people were being molded by secular rather than by ecclesiastical agencies.

Meanwhile, organized religion was becoming equated with humanitarianism and expended its energies in collecting pennies from Sunday School children for Indian missions in the Southwest, holding church suppers for the benefit of settlement houses in the slums, and delivering Thanksgiving baskets to neighborhood unfortunates. It was all most commendable; none were more aware of that fact than the donors. That it provided no positive answers to the complex problem of man's separation from God and from his neighbors seemed not to have been a vital issue, if indeed it was recognized at all by the average churchman in the Victorian period.

CHURCH LIFE IN THE VICTORIAN ERA

The last half of the nineteenth century witnessed significant changes and trends in the character and position of the American churches. First and most obvious was the phenomenal gain in membership; whereas sixteen per cent of the population were church affiliates in 1850, thirty-six per cent were so related in 1900. Everywhere there were signs of prosperity and expansion in the churches. Where once there was a simple frame meeting house there stood now a majestic edifice of brick or stone, testifying to the affluence of its congregation. Robed choirs, strengthened by professional singers, marched with dignity to their stations in the chancel, accompanied by the swelling chords of great organs; and ministers, increasingly conscious of worship as a fine art, devoted more attention to conducting their services "decently and in order." Even the camp meeting was beginning to reflect the new formalism with a trend toward undemonstrative services mixed with lectures on semi-religious or secular themes presented in comfortable auditoriums. Religion seemed to be increasingly in the grasp of professionals who dispensed their wares with all the mechanical coldness of an automat. To many this was symbolic of progress, but it was a progress unknown to the apostolic church.

Possibly the most amazing trend was the growing influence of laymen in the Protestant denominations. As the churches became larger business enterprises, their physical control fell more and more under the jurisdiction of boards of trustees composed of businessmen. Denominations on the national level gave increasing recognition to laymen, as in the case of the Methodist Episcopal Church, which in 1872 introduced lay representation into the General Conference. Many of the denominations invited laymen to accept administrative positions in their national offices, while prominent businessmen frequently served as treasurers of denominational societies. The trend toward administration was felt even by the clergy, who were encouraged to add the function of business executive to their already staggering burdens. The majority of clergy who held high posts in their denominational headquarters could not easily be distinguished from lay executives in private industry; deans, district superintendents, stated clerks, synodical presidents, and bishops found that administrative prowess was considered as essential to effective leadership as education and piety.

Trends in Public Worship

One of the most obvious concomitants of church formalism was a rising interest in liturgy. This was most evident in the so-called liturgical churches such as the Episcopal and the Lutheran, but it was apparent also in other denominations. In some cases there were sharp conflicts over questions of worship, leading to schism. The Protestant Episcopal Church had experienced the rivalries between high-church and low-church parties for some decades, but never was the debate so heated as in the decade following the Civil War. Aggressive young priests who had become enamored of the Oxford Movement had been introducing forms and ceremonies into their services for which there was no provision in the Prayer Book. Evangelicals feared that the adoption of "Roman Catholic practices" would eventually destroy the Protestant character of the church. At the General Convention of 1868 they tried in vain to secure the passage of canons condemning the ritualism of the high-church party. They failed again at the next Convention three years later. So disappointed was Bishop

George Cummins, an evangelical and Assistant Bishop of Kentucky, over this failure that he and several other evangelicals seceded from the church in 1873 and founded the Reformed Episcopal Church. This event stirred the denomination, and at the General Convention of 1874 a canon was passed disallowing the elevation of the elements in the Eucharist, the use of incense, and the display of a crucifix in the church. By this means the Convention hoped to avert any further schism. Evangelicals were, of course, unhappy over the introduction of the English Society of Saint John the Evangelist or the Cowley Fathers, founded in 1865, into the American church and were highly incensed when the first indigenous monastic order, the Order of the Holy Cross, was approved in 1884. But on the whole tension between the high- and low-church parties was beginning to subside and leaders on both sides were adopting a more comprehensive view of the church. In 1892 a revised edition of the Prayer Book, with added prayers and canticles, was approved.

While liturgical developments in the Episcopal Church tended to nurture controversy, among American Lutherans they promoted union. The *Church Book* of 1868, adopted by the General Council, and the "Washington Service" of 1869, approved by the General Synod, constituted a marked improvement over earlier liturgies, but were not wholly satisfying as common standards of worship. In 1885 a joint committee representing the United Synod of the South, the General Synod, and the General Council undertook the task of preparing a "Lutheran Order of Service." This Common Service was completed in 1888 and was approved at once by the three cooperating bodies; it was adopted later by the Joint Synod of Ohio and the English Synod of Missouri. The joint committee then turned to the preparation of an English translation of Luther's Catechism, a common book of ministerial acts, and a common book of hymns. The collection of hymns was included in the *Common Service Book with Hymnal*, published in 1917. That same year the Missouri Synod approved a liturgy patterned after the Common Service.

The Reformed tradition also shared in the effects of the liturgical movement. As early as 1855 a Presbyterian minister, Charles W. Baird, published *Eutaxia, or the Presbyterian Liturgies: Historical Sketches*. At the same time this volume was awakening interest in worship among the Presbyterians, the Mercersburg theologians were advocating a revival of liturgy in the German Reformed Church. In 1857 Baird produced *A Book of Public Prayer*, based on the prayers of the Reformers; the following year the German Reformed Church published *A Liturgy, or Order of Christian Worship*. Out of the movement to achieve greater dignity in worship, which gradually built up strength during the remainder of the nineteenth century, came the Presbyterian *Book of Common Worship*, approved by the General Assembly of 1906 for voluntary use by the churches.

Knights of the Pulpit

The growing interest in liturgics late in the nineteenth century in no wise detracted from the glory of the American pulpit. It was the age of homiletical oratory, when knights of the pulpit could hold thousands enthralled as they fought all manner of evil with the sharp sword of rhetoric. To many congregations the portions of the service preceding the sermon were still the "preliminaries"; their purpose was to lead the worshipper to the climax of the service, the sermon. In the large cities congregations vied with one another for the distinction of having the most popular and sensational preacher. To be able to hold an audience spellbound became a standard criterion of ministerial success.

Few American clergymen could hope to compete for publicity with the nationally known Henry Ward Beecher (1813–1887), who dominated the pulpit of Plymouth Church, Brooklyn, from 1847 to the end of his life. Through a long pastorate he came to be recognized as the most creative personality and one of the greatest oratorical geniuses of the American pulpit. Crowds pressed into his acoustically perfect edifice each Sunday to thrill to the power of his preaching. He had the happy faculty of being able to present the most advanced thought of his generation in language easily understood by ordinary men and to stamp it indelibly, by means of word pictures, upon their minds. Uncompromising in his attacks on social evils and sterile orthodoxy, he made many enemies, and an unfortunate scandal concerning his personal life temporarily jeopardized his career. His successor, Lyman Abbott (1835–1922), less eloquent and more conversational in his preaching style, was none the less effective and won fame for his Sunday-evening lectures on current topics. The logical development in his sermon outlines and their down-to-earth practical character were suggestive of his earlier career in law.

One of the most unforgettable preachers of all time was the saintly Phillips Brooks (1835–1893). After his graduation from Harvard he served briefly and unsuccessfully as a teacher, then prepared himself for the ministry of the Episcopal Church at the Theological Seminary at Alexandria, Virginia. During a ten-year ministry at two churches in Philadelphia he acquired a reputation for impassioned discourses which seemed to flow from his being. His preaching was not of a type which called attention to itself; it was always straightforward, though poetic, and in its rapid delivery thrust deftly like a rapier into the heart. Brooks could not have given a more apt description of his own homiletic gifts than he did in his famous Yale Lectures on Preaching in 1877, in which he defined preaching as "truth through personality." Called by Trinity Church, Boston, in 1869, he soon became the city's favorite son and his church was regularly packed with persons who went away uplifted by his presence and charmed by the music of his voice. It was impossible for him to fulfill all the demands for his time. He devoted his summers to travel, mostly in Europe, and became a familiar guest in many of England's greatest churches. Though decidedly lacking in administrative skills, he was acclaimed Bishop of Massachusetts in 1891, the culminating honor of his full and useful life. On the occasion of his unexpected death in 1893 an entire city in mourning bore testimony to the majesty of his being.

Easily the most popular preacher during the last decades of the century was Thomas DeWitt Talmage (1832–1902). This scintillating Presbyterian orator, who held important pastorates in Philadelphia, Brooklyn, and Washington, D.C., was noted for his clever selection of trick texts which might be lifted out of context and made the basis of some popular homily. His florid rhetoric was the antithesis of Brooks' simple eloquence but perfectly matched Talmage's flair for sensationalism. He seemed oblivious to the currents of modern thought and quite unaware of the social implications of the Gospel. He preached an old-fashioned religion of salvation for the sinner and offered his parishioners a faith centered in "Mother, Home, and Heaven." His messages were highly comforting to the complacent respectability of the Victorian age, especially to the middle and upper classes which swallowed them with gusto and immediately called for more. It is possible that the eminent evangelist, Dwight L. Moody, was alluding to Talmage when he declared in 1899: "I am sick and tired of this essay preaching. I am nauseated with this silver-tongued orator preaching. I like to hear preachers, not windmills."

Other contemporary knights of the pulpit worthy of mention are Matthew Simpson, Methodist bishop and orator extraordinary, who died in 1884; David James Burrell of the Marble Collegiate Dutch Reformed Church, New York, whose homilies were warmly evangelical and studded with well-chosen illustrations; Washington Gladden, socially minded Congregational preacher of Columbus, Ohio; and George A. Gordon, able philosopher, theologian, and pastor of Old South Congregational Church, Boston.

The Revival of Perfectionism

The spiritual stagnation and moral lethargy which followed the Civil War were sources of concern to discerning churchmen throughout the nation. To Methodists, whose doctrines of instantaneous perfection were related to their calling to win converts and establish holiness, the religious inertia and cold formalism of the time were particularly distressing. In 1870 the bishops of the Methodist Episcopal Church, South, saddened over this depressing state of affairs, called for "an increase of inward, genuine, scriptural holiness." "Nothing is so much needed at the present time, throughout all these lands," they observed, "as a general and powerful revival of scriptural holiness." In the North, Methodist leaders proposed to revive a spiritually sick church by organizing a camp meeting for the promotion of holiness. To this end the National Association for the Promotion of Holiness was founded at Vineland, New Jersey, in 1867. Though the movement was sponsored chiefly by Methodists, it was interdenominational in character and before long was national in scope. Holiness associations were established in different sections of the country, being supported by many of the evangelical denominations. These associations were brought into close harmony through the First General Holiness Assembly, which met in Chicago in 1885. This body adopted a clearly stated doctrine of entire sanctification as part of its Declaration of Principles. Meanwhile, the holiness revival continued to sweep through the nation, sixty-seven national camp meetings having been held by 1887.

The holiness movement did not pass without criticism from leaders in organized Protestantism, many of whom were identified with the Methodist Church. In 1878 the editor of the *Methodist Quarterly Review* attacked the holiness associations not only for their program but for their theology, which he found to be inconsistent with that of Wesley. Others objected to them as schismatic enterprises calculated to destroy the unity of the church. Most of the associations recognized that there was at least a modicum of truth in the charges and hastened to repudiate those minorities in their midst which were promoting schism. They also deplored the conditions in the churches which gave rise to such tendencies. But they were powerless to prevent the infiltration of philosophical and scientific concepts which were drawing many educated Methodists away from traditional theologies to a Social Gospel which frankly regarded the holiness approach as tragically irrelevant to the problems of the time. It was perfectly natural that advocates of holiness, finding themselves frequently ignored or rejected, should have retreated into their increasingly exclusive fellowship and shut out the rest of the world. During the last decade of the nineteenth century many of the holiness groups organized themselves into separate denominations.

The most important holiness body to emerge during this period was the Church of the Nazarene which grew out of the union of three smaller sects. In 1907 the Church of the Nazarene, founded at Los Angeles in 1895, united with the Association of Pentecostal Churches of America organized in New York in 1895. These two uniting bodies adopted as their name the Pentecostal Church of the Nazarene. In 1908 this denomination merged with the Holiness Church of Christ, an organization whose principal strength was in the South. The word "Pentecostal" was officially deleted from the name of the denomination in 1919; henceforth it was known as the Church of the Nazarene. This action was taken in order to disassociate the church from certain Pentecostal groups of more recent origin, which practiced glossolalia, or speaking in tongues. Doctrine and polity in the Church of the Nazarene closely followed the pattern of the

Methodist church. The capstone of the theological system was sanctification as a second work of grace by the Holy Spirit. In 1957 the church's membership stood at 281,646. Other noteworthy groups were the Metropolitan Church Association, originally organized in 1894 under the name of the Burning Bush movement, and the Missionary Church Association, an interdenominational body established in 1898 on the platform of sanctification, premillennialism (the belief that the second coming of Christ will antedate the tl.ousand years of peace prophesied in the book of Revelation), and healing. The principal strength of the holiness movement was in rural areas of the Middle West and South, though it was to be found in all parts of the country. Its source of membership was to a considerable extent from the lower social and economic classes who felt a sense of dissatisfaction with the current order and who registered that feeling at least partially by disassociating themselves with churches which they deemed worldly.

THE RESURGENCE OF REVIVALISM

Since the Great Awakening of the eighteenth century, revivalism had been established as a permanent and characteristic feature of American Protestantism. For the most part its effectiveness had depended upon the personal persuasiveness of eminent clergymen who could hold thousands enthralled by the prowess of their oratory. This circumstance changed during the great revival of 1857–1858, a spontaneous movement virtually free of professional evangelists and directed by laymen. Perhaps its main contribution to future revivals was to train a force of lay evangelists, among them Dwight L. Moody, for subsequent service. Revivalism was temporarily eclipsed by secular and materialistic interests brought on by war, and challenged by the flood tide of immorality and corruption which accompanied and followed the conflict. America, in the post Civil War era, was ripe for another upsurge of revivalistic zeal. It was not long in coming. Practically all the evangelical churches and colleges felt its power and, to the end of the century, most reserved a certain period annually in order to hold revivalistic meetings designed to generate piety and enthusiasm.

The Moody Revivals

Dwight Lyman Moody (1837–1899), possibly the greatest evangelist since the days of Wesley and Edwards, was reared in poverty in New England and at the age of seventeen began work in a Boston shoe shop. About this time the young man made his decision to become a Christian and dedicated his life to the work of personal evangelism. In 1856 he moved to Chicago where he became a successful shoe salesman and a consecrated member of Plymouth Congregational Church. He rented four pews and filled them each Sunday with friends whom he invited as his guests. Constantly seeking some new avenue of service, he recruited a Sunday School class of urchins in a slum section of the city. Thus he moved from one experience to another, bringing the Gospel to the despised, the despondent, and the forgotten, and preparing himself in the school of life for a wider evangelistic mission. It was not long before he was operating his own non-denominational mission Sunday School. At the outset of the Civil War he gave up his business and devoted his time henceforth to evangelistic enterprises. For several years he served with the United States Christian Commission, ministering to the wounded on battlefields or in hospitals. As the war drew to a close, Moody redirected his vast energies to his Sunday School, which soon graduated into a church under Congregational auspices with Moody himself acting as a lay pastor. He organized Bible-study groups, prayer meetings, and missions, and even found time to serve as president of the local Y.M.C.A. Meanwhile, he was building a reputation as a powerful speaker with a "passion for souls."

Events moved swiftly after 1871. By this time Moody had joined forces with Ira D. Sankey, a Methodist layman with a divine gift for religious song, who would become an indispensable part of his campaigns and set a standard for revival music which would be followed for years to come. On Moody's third trip to England in 1873, this time with Sankey, he began a two-year revival which won thousands to an acceptance of Christ. There was opposition from staid Britons who disliked Moody's brusque manners and from conservative Scots who viewed Sankey's portable organ as a work of the Devil, but they could not prevent the two evangelists from winning their way into the hearts of the British people. In 1875 Moody and Sankey returned to America in triumph; that October they held their first important series of meetings in Brooklyn and took the city by storm. Philadelphia and New York were next, with equally impressive results. The country was still in the throes of a financial depression brought on by the Panic of 1873, and the widespread feeling that this condition was related to the national spiritual lethargy provided incentive for the revival. From 1876 to 1879 they campaigned in Chicago, Boston, the smaller cities of New England, Baltimore, St. Louis, and San Francisco. It was their practice not to accept an invitation unless the evangelical ministers of a city were united in the desire that they come. Every campaign was organized to the finest detail, with publicity going out weeks before Moody's revival. Persons converted at the meetings were shepherded into smaller inquiry rooms where they met with trained workers and were directed to some local church. Through these campaigns Moody reached literally millions. Unlike many earlier revivalists who used hyperemotional techniques to win converts, Moody appealed in a simple and straightforward manner to the reason as well as the emotions. Speaking once of feeling as a basis for religion, he declared: "I wish that word were banished from the inquiry room. I thank God I have a better foundation for my faith than feeling."

In his theology Moody was thoroughly orthodox. He believed in a God who sent unconverted sinners to hell and a Bible which was infallible in all its parts. He did not, however, place equal emphasis on all teachings of the Scriptures. Such theology as he had was simple and naive and could be summarized under the following points. All men are weighed down with original sin, and without the blood of Jesus Christ to redeem them will surely be cast into the fiery pit of hell. There is hope for them only if they repent and are converted to faith in Christ before they die. God longs for each lost sinner to come to Him in the arms of faith; to prove it He sent His son to die on the cross in order that all men might be saved. The only really important calling in life is to point men to this way of salvation, to tell men of the limitless love of God. At the very center of his theological system was God's love, and he preached it as few Christians had preached it before. Moody would have been horrified at the thought that his movement in any way contributed to a trend away from orthodoxy, but ultimately it did have that effect. For in his zeal to proclaim the love of God he neglected other aspects of dogma so that many came to believe that Moody's simple teaching was the whole Gospel. Thus he contributed to a decline in theological interest and indirectly gave comfort to those forces which were promoting liberalism.

In his declining years Moody, with the full cooperation of Sankey, devoted much of his energies and funds gained through the sale of the famous Moody and Sankey *Gospel Hymns* to education. He founded a seminary for young women in 1879 at Northfield, Massachusetts, and two years later opened the Mount Hermon school for boys, located in the same vicinity. In 1889 he established in Chicago the Bible institute which later bore his name; it became a prominent center for the training of evangelical Christian workers.

Moody's Successors

For a full generation after the Moody revivals a series of lesser revivalists, among them Sam Jones, Gypsy Smith, R. A. Torrey, J. Wilbur Chapman, and William A. Sunday followed in the steps of the great master. Chapman and Torrey had each won the approval of Moody. During the first decade of the twentieth century both led revival campaigns in New York, Boston, and Philadelphia, and went on world evangelistic missions. Chapman, who was a graduate of Lane Seminary, served from 1903 until his death in 1918 as a representative-at-large for the Evangelistic Commission of the Presbyterian Church. Reuben A. Torrey was something of an oddity in the world of revivalism as he had been educated at Yale and Leipzig in historical criticism of the Bible and ordained a Congregational minister and yet had adhered to the strictest theological conservatism. He became superintendent of the Moody Bible Institute.

Several of the revivalists who gained prominence between 1890 and 1920 won much of their popularity through the use of theatrical stunts, novel or eccentric practices, and flamboyant sensational preaching. Samuel P. Jones, a Methodist preacher from the South, became famous particularly in the Middle West by presenting his messages in the language and style of the southern hill country and providing fabulous entertainment for city dwellers unaccustomed to the jargon and nuances of thought peculiar to his locality. Rodney (Gypsy) Smith, an English-born revivalist, made capital of the fact that he had been born a gypsy and attracted crowds who came out of curiosity to see him and his daughter who often appeared with him in native costume as a singer. As the result of a revival held in Boston in 1906, he is said to have won 2550 "decisions" for Christ. By this time it was becoming customary to judge an evangelist's success by the number of "decision cards" turned in at the close of his series of meetings.

Undoubtedly the most accomplished showman among revivalists was William (Billy) A. Sunday (1863–1935). While pursuing a career as a professional baseball player in the National League, he was converted at the Pacific Garden Mission in Chicago. He gave up his profession and became an assistant secretary in the Y.M.C.A. In 1893 he joined the organization of J. Wilbur Chapman, assuming the position of "advance man" or agent in charge of arrangements. This work gave him invaluable experience which he would later use to good effect as an independent evangelist. In 1895 he received his first opportunity to conduct a week-long revival in Iowa; from that time he was on his own. The next ten years found him steadily building up strength and moving from towns into large cities. Between 1914 and 1919 he conducted revival meetings in Pittsburgh, Philadelphia, Baltimore, Boston, Los Angeles, Washington, and New York; in the latter city he claimed 98,000 converts. Sunday was known for his lack of propriety in speech and his pulpit gyrations. On the platform he could be expected to hurl chairs at "the Devil," roll up his sleeves and shake his fists at all manner of sinners, and run and slide across the stage in an impersonation of some reprobate trying to gain heaven by the same means a ball player might try to gain home plate. Every vaudeville star recognized him as something of a threat. After 1909, he was ably supported by Homer Rodeheaver, a master of the "singfest" and as expert as Sunday in persuading people to "hit the sawdust trail" and take their stand for God. Sunday, who was a thoroughly conservative Presbyterian as far as matters of theology were concerned, emphasized the doctrines of sin and salvation so dear to the heart of every revivalist, but he was unquestionably at his best when attacking "booze," dancing, and tobacco. His message was sincere even though his presentation of the Gospel was somewhat one-sided. He lived in a delightfully naive world which failed to recognize the complexities of modern life and supposed all ethical decisions involved simple choices between blacks and whites. By 1920 his age had drawn to a close; the jazz age loomed just ahead.

RELIGIOUS EDUCATION AND CULTURE

During the half century which followed the War Between the States more Americans in proportion to the total population reaped the benefits of education and culture than ever before. Elementary education had progressed to such an extent that between 1870 and 1910 the number of persons over ten years of age who were unable to write had fallen from 20 to 7.7 per cent. The general education of the populace was further enhanced through the steady improvement of communications which put them into closer touch with current events. New forms of adult education in an age which craved self-improvement helped to spread learning and culture throughout the land. The churches gave vigorous support to the educational movement and in a variety of ways exerted their influence in training the American mind along religious lines. In some cases they developed entirely new institutions to carry out that important task.

The Sunday School

The third quarter of the nineteenth century witnessed an attempt on the part of the Sunday School to develop a clearer conception of its task. Its leaders realized that Christian education involved more than the memorization of selected portions from the Bible or catechism. The result was the overthrow of the catechetical method of Bible study. In 1872 the Fifth National Sunday School Convention meeting in Indianapolis approved a plan for uniform lessons. According to this system, each participating school would study the same lesson simultaneously in all classes. Within three years the International Uniform Lessons were being used in nineteen countries. One of the chief advantages of the system was that it made possible the publication and distribution of Bible materials at a nominal cost and unified the work of the schools to such an extent that teachers could cooperate in the preparation of the lesson and superintendents could better supervise the program of the entire school. But there were also manifest weaknesses in the curriculum. It neglected the principle of grading whereby each lesson is prepared specifically for a single age group. Being an interdenominational project, it failed to treat denominational doctrines and thus was regarded as unsatisfactory by certain communions which stressed dogma. Failure to relate the lessons to the Church Year proved an irritant to liturgical bodies such as the Episcopal and Lutheran, both of which eventually developed their own lesson materials.

Toward the end of the nineteenth century the churches began to take cognizance of the new scientific spirit and method which were being felt in the fields of education and psychology. Following the leadership of such recognized philosophers of education as Johann Pestalozzi and Friedrich Froebel, the public schools began to place the child at the center of the curriculum and to use the best approved methods of educational science for his training. This trend in secular education was soon felt in the demand of the churches for a richer curriculum suited to the needs of the pupils. As early as the 1870's the Reverend Erastus Blakeslee had succeeded in producing a graded series of lessons with separate materials for the different age groups. These lessons exerted a powerful influence in causing the International Lesson Committee to make fundamental changes in accordance with the growing demand for a graded curriculum.

In 1908 the Twelfth International Sunday School Convention (the movement had become international after the Fifth National Sunday School Convention of 1872) meeting in Louisville, Kentucky, authorized the preparation of a closely graded series of lessons, with separate study materials for each grade or year. While these lessons, which first appeared in 1910, were devoted primarily to the study of the Bible, by 1912 some use of church history was made in the curriculum. This innovation was strenuously opposed by Southern Baptists and Southern Presbyterians, who refused to accept other than Biblical materials. In 1913 the Presbyterian Church in the U.S.A. rejected the lessons because of certain liberal views in the lesson helps which eliminated belief in the miraculous and the supernatural origin of the Scriptures. Finally, it produced its own Westminster Graded Series, graded by departments. After the reorganization of the International Lesson Committee in 1914 the Uniform Lessons were modified. While a common passage of Scripture was still used, separate captions and helps were provided for the Primary, Junior, Intermediate, Senior and Young People, and Adult. Later the committee permitted the Primary and Junior departments to study different passages from the Bible. This series came to be known after 1918 as the International Improved Uniform Lessons.

Another institution of learning, though independent of the Sunday School, was the Daily Vacation Bible School, founded in New York by Robert Boville, a Baptist minister, in 1901. Originally intended for poor children in the slums, it offered the opportunity to engage in worship, study, and play. By 1907 the Vacation School had become a national enterprise.

Programs for Youth

The closing decades of the nineteenth century were marked by a heightened interest in providing special programs of worship, study, and recreation for young people, apart from the formal activities of the Sunday School. Such programs were designed to afford young people above the age of twelve greater opportunity for self-expression. The greatest impetus to the movement was given by Dr. Francis E. Clark, who organized the first Christian Endeavor Society in the Williston Congregational Church of Portland, Maine, on February 2, 1881. It was a self-managed society of young people which provided worship and instruction and invited each person to participate in the program. Clark's idea caught the attention of church leaders throughout the country and in other lands, and within six years more than 7000 societies had been formed with a membership approaching 500,000. By the opening of the new century this international nondenominational organization had become the chief agency to unify youth activities in the evangelical churches. Its international conventions were spectacular events, characterized by radiant enthusiasm and conducted on a high spiritual plane; they frequently attracted more than 50,-000 delegates.

Meanwhile various denominations were developing their own youth movements, partly because of their dissatisfaction with the nondenominational program. Some, however, allowed their local societies of Christian Endeavor to continue alongside their own youth organizations. In 1889 several Methodist young people's groups merged to form the Epworth League, a movement recognized and promoted by Methodists, North and South. Two years later the Baptist Young People's Union was founded; the Lutherans organized their Luther League in 1895. Christian Endeavor leaders looked with disapproval upon this trend toward denominational organization, but once having begun it continued unabated, much to the detriment of Christian Endeavor.

The Chautauqua Movement

Adult education for Christian leadership was a primary concern of the churches during the era which followed 1865. A principal attraction to adults desirous of self-improvement was the traveling lecturer who toured the country speaking on various phases of the Christian life. Most prominent among these lecturers was Russell H. Conwell, a Philadelphia clergyman, who delivered his popular lecture entitled "Acres of Diamonds" some 5000 times between the years 1868 and 1913. A most important new educational device was developed in 1874 when John H. Vincent, minister and later bishop of the Methodist Church, and Lewis Miller, an Ohio manufacturer, took over an unused camp-meeting ground at Lake Chautauqua, New York, and organized a two-week summer assembly for the training of Sunday School teachers. It soon blossomed into an all-summer assembly with courses and lectures on all manner of themes. Prominent scholars and preachers from all over the country attracted thousands of eager middle-class adults who sat enthralled at their feet. Chautauqua presented many and varied opportunities for those who wished to study. In 1878 the Chautauqua Literary and Scientific circle developed a four-year reading course and enrolled 8000 adults who agreed to follow at home the prescribed reading program. By 1882 the institution was chartered as a university empowered to offer correspondence courses; the following year the Chautauqua School of Theology was offering non-resident courses for ministers, one of the best of which was William Rainey Harper's course in Hebrew. No institution in American history had so effectively blended religion and culture and presented them in such a palatable form. In 1903 the Redpath Lyceum Bureau founded a traveling Chautauqua which brought culture and entertainment to the nation's towns and villages; it was so well received that a number of companies were encouraged to present similar programs and in this way Chautauqua became known to millions of Americans.

The Religious Press

At the close of the Civil War the unquestioned leadership in the field of religious journalism belonged to Beecher's *Independent*, a nominally Congregational paper founded in 1848 which, since 1863, had been under the editorship of Theodore Tilton. Its main feature was Beecher's sermons, but a number of editorials and articles on cultural and social topics were also included. The increase in religious publications between 1865 and 1870 exceeded the gains made in the secular press, the number of religious periodicals rising from around 300 to 407. One of the best known of the newer publications was the *Christian Union*, founded by Henry Ward Beecher in 1866 and renamed the *Outlook* in 1893. After World War I it became increasingly secular in character and declined in popularity. Thenceforth the leading non-denominational weekly was Charles Clayton Morrison's *Christian Century*, founded in 1884 and reestablished in 1908. Its liberal theology and idealistic principles contributed much to the shaping of Protestant thought in the twentieth century. Of the religious dailies, the finest piece of journalism was the *Christian Science Monitor*, noted for its objectivity in reporting. In addition, there were hundreds of denominational papers and magazines which were issued in great abundance but were frequently of lower quality. As the twentieth century progressed, religious periodicals faced mounting competition from secular newspapers and magazines and, being unable to keep up with the expansion in production and advertising, suffered a proportionate loss in circulation.

MOVEMENTS OF REFORM

American morals in the Victorian period were conspicuous for the wide disparity between the attitudes professed by the nominally religious and respectable and the actual conduct which could be observed in the social order. If Americans were reluctant to criticize the fastidious principles of the time, they were somewhat less hesitant to ignore them. After the Civil War there was a deplorable laxity of morals in both private and public life. Business was controlled by railway magnates, steel kings, and coal barons who relentlessly fought for power and amassed huge fortunes at the expense of the public. William H. Vanderbilt, wealthy railroad entrepreneur, spoke for many contemporary executives when he declared, "The public be damned!" The times were marked by fraudulent schemes, reckless speculation, unscrupulous practices intended to ruin business competitors, and the forming of monopolies. Bitter financial struggles like that between Cornelius Vanderbilt and his opponents, Daniel Drew and Jay Gould, for control of the Erie Railway Company were the order of the day. Yet Drew could act as a moving spirit in the founding of Drew Theological Seminary and Vanderbilt could contribute heavily to the establishment of Vanderbilt University and recognize no impropriety in their actions. Not even the churches were wholly free from corruption; in 1868 a scandal over fraudulent practices plagued the Methodist Book Concern even though the matter was glossed over and ultimately suppressed.

In the area of politics, particularly during the Grant administration, corruption was rampant on national, state, and local levels. The nation was shocked when it became known in 1873 that the Crédit Mobilier, the construction company for the Union Pacific Railroad, had provided free shares for a number of Congressmen as an inducement to avoid inquiring into the corporation's affairs. Many cities were controlled by political machines, the most infamous of which was the "Boss" Tweed ring in New York, which pocketed public moneys running into the millions of dollars. Though Tweed was finally brought to justice, his corrupt Tammany organization held power in the city for years. The churches seldom raised a prophetic voice against political corruption, but individuals such as the Reverend Charles H. Parkhurst, a Presbyterian pastor in New York, whose exposures of Tammany were instrumental in its overthrow in 1894, made salient contributions to the campaign for good government. The International Reform Bureau, established in Washington by Dr. Wilbur Fisk Crafts in 1895, proved to be a valuable agency in furthering the passage of reform legislation by the Congress.

If the majority of American churchmen were indifferent to the financial and political corruption of the era, their concern over worldly amusements was serious to the point of being devastating. To puritan and perfectionist thinkers, it was difficult to conceive of greater moral perils than dancing, attending the theater, gambling, smoking, and drinking; and many a leader brought vehement criticism upon institutions which offered facilities for these pursuits. Even local chapters of the Y.M.C.A., institutional churches, and settlement houses were scored for providing their memberships with some kinds of amusements. The Methodists registered their disapproval of "worldly" amusements in 1872 by prohibiting dancing, card-playing, and attendance at the theater. A few liberally minded ministers, among them Washington Gladden, questioned the wisdom of removing these matters from the realm of individual preference, but they were shouted down by the conservatives.

The Sabbath Question

The increase of immigration was a social phenomenon which had its effects on the moral codes and on religion as well as upon economic life. In urban centers in particular, Protestant Christians were concerned to see the newcomers ignore old-fashioned Sabbath observance in favor of a day of relaxation and amusement. To the strait-laced, the Germans with their "Continental Sunday," the Irish, Italians, and Poles with their Catholic Sunday, and the Jews with their holy day on Saturday, constituted a threat to the American way of life. The epitome of moral degeneration was to spend one's Sunday evening in a German beer garden. Ministers decried the fact that the public more and more purchased Sunday newspapers, frequented ball parks and other amusement centers, went on excursions, or simply stayed at home, but they were unsuccessful in halting the trend. During the 1880's several states either relaxed or repealed their Sabbath blue laws. The Women's Christian Temperance Union, the American Sabbath Union, the International Sabbath Association, and the Sunday League of America all exerted what influence they could to keep the Sabbath day holy. From 1887 to 1889 they campaigned for the passage of national legislation which would curb interstate commerce as well as postal and military activities on Sundays, but in this they were without success. When the World's Fair opened in Chicago in 1893 the issue was raised again; after much agitation by the churches it was decided that the exposition grounds might be opened as a park but that the machinery should not be operated on Sunday. The First World War struck a decided blow to the forces for Sabbath observance since it was necessary to keep a number of war plants in operation on Sundays and to maintain other activities vital to national defense. From that time only an occasional pronouncement was made in protest over the secularization of Sunday.

Temperance and Prohibition

Between 1860 and 1880 the capital investment in the liquor industry climbed from 29 million dollars to 190 million dollars, testifying to a sharp increase in the consumption of alcoholic beverages after the war. The rise in liquor consumption was most evident in the cities where saloons, which offered free lunches to those who purchased liquid refreshment, became favorite gathering places for the workingman, especially for the immigrant laborer. Some employers and a few labor unions such as the Knights of Labor denied employment or admission to the union to those who used intoxicants or were involved in their sale. Most Protestant churches in urban areas maintained societies dedicated to total abstinence. In the Roman Catholic Church the Catholic Total Abstinence Union was active, while the hierarchy at the Third Plenary Council of Baltimore in 1884–1885 directed priests to exhort all Roman Catholic liquor dealers to "choose a more honorable way of making a living." In 1888 the Methodist Episcopal Church established a permanent Committee on Temperance and Prohibition. The purpose of these organizations was to promote voluntary abstinence.

Simultaneously a movement was developing which sought prohibitive legislation to curb the liquor traffic. The National Prohibition Party, organized in 1869, was sworn to "the total prohibition of the manufacturing, importation and traffic of intoxicating beverages." It was never effectual on a national level but was successful in many local elections. Many towns, through local option, refused to grant licenses to liquor dealers; and by 1898 New Hampshire, Vermont, Kansas, and North Dakota had joined Maine in the passage of state-wide prohibitive legislation. The most effective campaign against liquor, however, was waged by the Women's Christian Temperance Union, the first chapter of which was formed in 1873 at Hillsboro, Ohio. The following year the movement was organized along national lines. During the early years of its existence a determined membership organized crusades against the saloons; they would march boldly into the "dens of iniquity," hold prayer meetings for the benefit of patrons, and in some cases persuade the saloonkeeper to pour his product into the gutter. After the election of Miss Frances E. Willard, formerly dean of women at Northwestern University, to the presidency in 1879, the W.C.T.U. devoted much of its energies to agitating for temperance education in the public schools and inducing children to sign temperance pledges. The organization, which had the full support of the churches, became highly influential in shaping public opinion and made its presence felt in the political arena. When the Republicans and Democrats refused to include a prohibition plank in their 1884 platform, the W.C.T.U. shifted its support from the Republican to the Prohibition Party and thus contributed to the first defeat the former party had suffered in a presidential election since 1856. Its strength was, of course, most evident in the rural areas.

The campaign against liquor took on a new vitality with the creation of the Anti-Saloon League of America in 1895. The League was all it claimed to be: "the churches organized to fight the saloon." But it must be said that a great measure of its strength came from the Methodists and Baptists, who were determined to destroy the liquor interests at all costs. Lutherans, Episcopalians, and Roman Catholics, while sympathetic to moderation in drinking, could not bring themselves to support total abstinence or prohibition. From 1903 to 1916 the Anti-Saloon League, under the militant leadership of dry-boss Wayne B. Wheeler engineered an intensive drive to organize the anti-liquor interests for political action. The result was that eight southern states had adopted state-wide prohibition by 1915, and by 1916 six western states had taken the same course. In states which did not have state-wide prohibition the local option movement enjoyed considerable popularity, but in general local prohibition was more acceptable in rural areas than in the large cities. By 1914, 47 per cent of the country's population lived in communities where prohibition was in force. The previous year Congress passed the Webb-Kenyon bill making illegal the shipping of liquor to areas which had prohibition laws, and the initial action was taken toward the preparation of a Federal prohibition amendment. With the entrance of America into World War I, anti-German sentiment was directed against the many breweries and distilleries owned by persons of German background and thus helped to prepare the way for the passage of the Eighteenth Amendment prohibiting the manufacture, transportation, or sale of intoxicants. The Amendment became a part of the Constitution on January 16, 1919, having been ratified by every state save Connecticut and Rhode Island. The following year the Volstead Act defined illegal beverages as those containing more than half of one per cent of alcohol.

The Feminist Movement

To a considerable extent the feminist campaign during the latter decades of the nineteenth century for broader rights in society was linked with the movement for temperance and prohibition, many of its leaders being active in the W.C.T.U. The left wing of the movement was headed by Susan B. Anthony, Elizabeth Cady Stanton, and Lucy Stone, and was principally concerned with gaining the suffrage and other civil rights. A more conservative element found greater edification in clubs than in caucuses and devoted their energies to the formation of women's organizations which advanced culture and encouraged young ladies to attend college. That many women were able to make significant contributions to organized religion was due in large measure to the invaluable training they received in these organizations. Most churches refused to endorse woman suffrage but allowed women to work in church societies, a circumstance which brought certain prestige and standing to the movement. Nevertheless, there were instances in which ministers were disciplined for permitting women to speak in their churches. Quite independently of the churches, organizations such as the National Woman Suffrage Association and the American Woman Suffrage Association continued to advance their common cause; by 1896 four western states and territories had granted the franchise to women. The exceptional patriotic activities of American women during World War I further broke down opposition to their receiving the vote, and the Nineteenth Amendment to the Constitution, which prohibited voting restrictions on the basis of sex, was ratified in 1920. While women entered more freely into the professions after that time, only a few denominations were willing to grant them ordination and many were reluctant to place them in any position of ecclesiastical leadership other than that of women's activities.

CHALLENGES TO ORTHODOXY

To the uncritical observer the American theological scene at the close of the Civil War appeared to be unruffled by doctrinal dissension. Orthodoxy was in the saddle and its continued status seemed assured. In 1865 the Congregationalists held a National Council at Boston, their most important convention since the Cambridge Synod, and approved the "Burial Hill Declaration," the first statement of faith endorsed by a national Congregational council since 1648. It affirmed "our adherence to the faith and order of the apostolic and primitive churches held by our fathers, and substantially as embodied in the confessions and platforms which our synods of 1648 and 1680 set forth or reaffirmed." In 1866 the Lutheran General Synod, long doctrinally suspect by other Lutheran bodies, took a step toward confessional conservatism by formally receiving "the Augsburg Confession as a correct exhibition of the fundamental doctrines of the Divine Word and of the faith of our Church founded upon that Word." Such confessional unanimity developed in the South that in 1886 the conservative Tennessee Synod was willing to merge with the General Synod South and the Holston Synod to establish the United Synod in the South.

It was not long, however, before orthodoxy in many of the denominations was challenged by a variety of intellectual forces which fostered more liberal concepts. As a result some communions modified their theological position to provide greater latitude of thought, while others intensified their efforts to preserve the purest orthodoxy. The process was accompanied by impassioned debate and hard-fought heresy trials.

Darwinian Evolution

Charles Darwin's revolutionary *Origin of Species,* published in 1859, made little impact upon the American consciousness, except among scientists, until after the Civil War. By 1870, however, it was attracting a good deal of attention. Its principal thesis was that through a process of natural selection more complex species developed from simpler species. A later work of Darwin, published in 1871 under the title *Descent of Man,* applied the evolutionary thesis more directly to *homo sapiens.* Evolution came most vividly before the attention of Americans through the writings of the English philosopher, Herbert Spencer, who attempted to present a philosophical interpretation of evolution. The first impulse of churchmen and scientists alike was to reject the new theory. It seemed to contradict the Biblical teaching of God's creative activity, to deny man his distinctive character as a personality whose existence was conferred by divine fiat, and to imply that the Scriptures were lacking in plenary inspiration.

The 1870's witnessed a concerted effort on the part of evolutionists to harmonize their doctrine with the tenets of Christianity. John Fiske argued in his *Outlines of Cosmic Philosophy,* published in 1874, that "evolution is God's way of doing things," but Charles Hodge insisted that "a more absolutely incredible theory was never propounded for acceptance among men." About the same time the well-known Scottish evangelical, Henry Drummond, was touring the country with Dwight L. Moody, trying to show that evolution was compatible with dynamic, Christ-centered religion. The visit of Thomas Huxley in 1876, however, evoked the wrath of conservatives all over the country, especially since his lectures provided material which the agnostic, Robert G. Ingersoll, used in his attacks on the Christian religion. Mark Hopkins, eminent pedagogue, denounced evolution in a series of lectures at Princeton Theological Seminary as "essentially atheistic."

But if there was criticism there was also compromise. James McCosh, President of Princeton College, thought it feasible to regard evolution as the method used by God for the continuance of creation. Henry Ward Beecher gave his full support to the new teaching, describing himself as a "cordial Christian evolutionist." Lyman Abbott, in his *Theology of an Evolutionist,* published in 1897, spoke of evolution as part of the providence of God and suggested that it belonged to the divine plan for progress in history. From that point it was a short step to the position that sin was rooted in man's baser origins, but would eventually die out as men rose to a higher level of existence. History became the record of progress, the events which registered the steady improvement of the race and pointed to its ultimate sanctification. Scientists joined with liberal theologians in pointing out the essential agreement which existed between the Bible and the new theories and showing how evolution had strengthened rather than weakened their faith. At the 1884 meeting of the American Association for the Advancement of Science, one geologist who had formerly been critical of Christianity reported that "the agreement between Genesis and geology demonstrated the divine origin of the Bible." Throughout the remainder of the century, evolution held a prominent place in discourses from the pulpit and the warfare between science and religion continued to be a favorite topic among lecturers. The rank and file of the church membership, together with the vast majority of the clergy, however, took their stand against the new doctrines and condemned them as destructive of the truth. This opposition was markedly strong in the South, where the state legislatures of Texas, Tennessee, Arkansas, and Mississippi passed laws outlawing the teaching of evolution in the public schools. In seven other states similar legislation was rejected.

Trends in Biblical Studies

A major development in the post-war era was the introduction of Biblical higher criticism, which involved a scientific literary-historical study of the Scriptures. During the 1880's the writings of Julius Wellhausen, a leading German scholar in the Old Testament field, came to be known in the United States. Wellhausen's theory held that one might be able to reconstruct the history of the development of Biblical concepts by dating the books of the Bible. Through this methodology he discovered an evolution of thought in the Old Testament, starting from primitive polytheistic origins and progressing to ethical monotheism. Many Americans, however, reacted unfavorably to the assertion that the Pentateuch or Torah had not been authored by Moses and that there were at least two Isaiahs; they feared such teachings would detract from the Old Testament's authority. In the New Testament field similar critical studies were being made by Ferdinand Christian Baur of Tübingen, while the publication of the critical edition of the New Testament Greek text by English scholars Westcott and Hort in 1881 focused attention on New Testament criticism. There was also a growing tendency to prefer the synoptic gospels over the Gospel according to John as historical sources and to neglect the Christ of Christian dogma in favor of a very human and historical Jesus of Nazareth. These views touched off a period of protracted and heated controversy in orthodox churches which lasted well into the twentieth century.

Mounting interest in Biblical studies led to a demand for a more authoritative English translation of the Scriptures. To this end a joint committee of English and American scholars prepared a revision of the classic King James Version, introducing few changes in style and text but utilizing the best findings of scholarship. The New Testament was issued in 1881, the Old Testament in 1885. On the whole the American committee was somewhat dissatisfied with the work, being of the opinion that there should have been further changes in style and text. They therefore continued their labors, the result of which was the American Standard Edition published in 1901. By this time the movement toward modern speech translations had begun; the first of these, by Richard F. Weymouth, was issued in 1902.

The New Theology

Long before the Civil War a battery of intellectual forces originating on the European continent had begun to beat against the walls of theological conservatism; the effect was most noticeable in the decades after 1865. From the German philosopher-theologian, Friedrich Schleiermacher (1768–1834), came the idea that religion is based on intuition or feeling and that one finds the living God through an awareness of dependence upon the universe. The basis of authority was shifted from the Bible to the experience of the believer; salvation came not through conformity to a creed but through altruistic love shown to one's fellow man, the supreme example for this being Jesus. Philosophically, American thought was being shaped by the idealism of Georg W. F. Hegel (1770–1831) and Rudolf Lotze (1817–1881), which was reinterpreted for Americans by Josiah Royce (1855–1916) at Harvard, and George Trumbull Ladd (1843–1921) at Yale. Idealism, which was radiantly optimistic, taught that the universe was inherently rational and that the irrational would eventually be overcome by reason. In like manner, goodness would triumph over evil. A third creative force was found in the thought of a German theologian, Albrecht Ritschl (1822–1889). For him religion was intensely practical, its purpose being to cultivate the sense of values inherent in man. God has shown what man might become in Jesus Christ and it was therefore the task of religion to point men toward Jesus, who was divine because he realized in his life the highest truth and goodness. Ritschl's views were mediated to America by Adolf von Harnack, the renowned historical theologian who taught the Fatherhood of God and the brotherhood of men, but rejected the deity of Jesus Christ.

The closing decades of the nineteenth century witnessed a growing effort on the part of certain American thinkers to evaluate and adapt these concepts to form a theology which stressed the immanence of God in the world and the progressive moral improvement of man. Most of these theologians developed systems which were avowedly compatible with evolution and reflective of the new trends in Biblical criticism. Among the important works which shaped the direction of the new theology were *The Evidence of Christian Experience*, published by Lewis F. Stearns (1847–1892), the Bangor Seminary theologian, in 1891; *An Outline of Christian Theology*, issued in 1898 by the Colgate University scholar, William Newton Clarke; and *Christian Theology in Outline*, also published in 1898 by William Adams Brown of Union Seminary, New York. Somewhat more popular studies were George A. Gordon's *Ultimate Conceptions of Faith* (1903) and Washington Gladden's *Present Day Theology* (1913).

Concepts of God and revelation in the new theology bore the obvious imprint of idealistic philosophy. God was not so much a transcendent deity as a God who enters into His creation, manifesting Himself in nature, in history, and in the mind and heart of man. Lewis Stearns found Him ever working in the world, progressively achieving His purposes through natural processes. As for revelation, it was a dynamic encounter with God as He speaks through Christ to the individual soul. Stearns was thus quick to reject any external authority such as the Church or the Scriptures as infallible; the only standard of authority was the Christian consciousness. William N. Clarke found in the Scriptures a progressive revelation of God which culminated in Jesus Christ.

The liberal view of Jesus was well represented by William Adams Brown, who was influenced by Ritschl. His emphasis fell upon the Jesus of history who, through his deeds of mercy, his words of wisdom, and his magnetic personality, directed men to dedicate themselves to the service of that God with whom he enjoyed full communion. In Jesus men could capture their truest insight into the meaning of God and could find an example worthy of emulation. In a certain sense the man from Nazareth was the Son of God, but little attention was given to the ontological significance of such a statement or to the problems of the Virgin Birth or the two natures of Christ. There was place for an Atonement, but not in the orthodox sense of propitiating a just and wrathful God. Rather, Christ offered himself as a living sacrifice in order to show men the love of God and lead them into the larger life of reconciliation with their heavenly Father. Christ did not come to rescue men from eternal torments in hell, but to inspire them to long for the abundant life in God.

As for the concept of man, most liberals regarded him as potentially a son of God; the principal difference between Jesus and other men was that Jesus more fully realized the potentialities of men than any other. Newman Smyth (1843–1925), a Connecticut Congregationalist pastor, dwelt at length on the possibilities of man's moral progress. He dismissed the traditional ideas of the fall and original sin, suggesting that if there was a fall it was merely the tendency at times to slip backwards. What was important was the "unmistakable evidence of progress" in human history and man's inevitable advance to the realization of "creative and redeeming love." George A. Gordon found the essential nature of man to be divine, and moral progress to be the key to history. "Under the august pressure of the universe inhumanity is dying; the campaign of the Infinite in history is slow, but it is finally fatal to lies, lust, and all brutality." To men of this theological persuasion, the Kingdom of God would not be achieved so much by a divine cataclysmic event as by the dedicated serv-ice of human beings in the area of social relationships. By following the high example set for them by Christ, men might themselves realize the Kingdom of God on earth. Thus eschatology came to be identified with social ethics.

Denominational Reactions and Adjustments

No matter how much they may have wished it, American churchmen could not retrace their steps to an earlier and more ideal age, resting con-tentedly in the hard-won decisions of their forefathers; the new theology, evolution, and Biblical criticism were established facts which refused to go unnoticed. As denominational leaders confronted them and made their decisions for and against, controversy swept the churches; in some cases the issues were so hotly contested that ministers were brought to trial for heresy and disciplined by their communion. In no denomination was the conflict waged more fiercely than the Presbyterian, U.S.A. In 1874 Profes-sor Francis L. Patton of Northwestern (later McCormick) Seminary pros-ecuted Dr. David Swing, a Presbyterian pastor in Chicago, before the Chicago Presbytery on charges that there were implications in his teach-ings not in harmony with the Confession of Faith. Presbytery acquitted the defendant, but when Patton announced his intention to appeal to Synod, the irenically disposed Swing decided to withdraw from the church.

Much more publicity was given to the case of Dr. Charles A. Briggs, Professor of Biblical Theology at Union Seminary in New York. As early as 1870 Briggs had departed from the traditional view of Biblical inspira-tion; he became an advocate of Biblical criticism and a keen student of German theology. In 1881 and 1882 he clashed with Princeton conserva-tives A. A. Hodge and Benjamin B. Warfield over the question of verbal inspiration of the Bible which Briggs rejected, and over Mosaic author-ship of the Pentateuch which Briggs denied. When he sharply criticized the doctrine of the inerrancy of the Bible in an inaugural address deliv-ered at Union Seminary in 1891, his opponents decided to take action. He was prosecuted before the Presbytery of New York for heresy, and when that judicatory dismissed the case, it was appealed to the General Assembly of 1892. The latter body ruled that Presbytery would have to retry the case. Once again the long-suffering professor was acquitted, and the case was carried again to the General Assembly. The Assembly of 1893 decided against Dr. Briggs and suspended him from the ministry. In 1899 he received priest's orders in the Protestant Episcopal Church. As for Un-ion Seminary, it separated from the General Assembly in 1893 and there-after remained an independent institution.

Another famous case concerned Professor Henry Preserved Smith of

Lane Seminary in Cincinnati. In a public address delivered in 1891, he attacked the doctrine of verbal inspiration and for this was brought to trial by the Presbytery of Cincinnati and found guilty of heresy. He appealed his suspension from the ministry all the way to the General Assembly but without success. He then became a Congregationalist. When Arthur Cushman McGiffert, Union Seminary church historian, published in 1897 *A History of Christianity in the Apostolic Age,* which was criticized by some as containing teachings incompatible with the Westminster Confession, the matter was brought to the attention of the General Assembly of 1898. That Assembly advised Dr. McGiffert to recant or withdraw from the Presbyterian ministry. The next Assembly referred the case to the Presbytery of New York, which showed little willingness to convict the professor of heresy. Dissension in the Presbytery over the case, however, prompted Dr. McGiffert to withdraw from the church in 1900 and become a Congregationalist. In this way Presbyterianism lost some of its ablest scholars.

At the same time, newer theological attitudes were making inroads in the denomination to such an extent that in 1889 the General Assembly received overtures from fifteen presbyteries calling for a revision of the Westminster Confession. Most of the discussion centered around the doctrines of reprobation, "elect infants," and limited atonement. The presbyteries overwhelmingly approved a revision and the Assembly of 1890 appointed a committee to work out suggested alterations. The committee presented its revision proposals in 1892, but not a single one was adopted. Not until 1900 was the issue raised again and another committee appointed to attempt revision. In 1902 the committee presented a "Brief Statement of the Reformed Faith" which was approved, but not as part of the church's constitution. The following year final approval was given to two additional chapters to the Confession ("Of the Holy Spirit" and "Of the Love of God and Missions"), and to the doctrines that Christ's atonement is for all men and that all dying in infancy receive salvation. The trend was definitely toward emphasis on God's love for men.

Like the Presbyterians, Congregationalists also developed progressive and conservative wings which clashed over doctrine. In 1885 the Board of Visitors of Andover Seminary instituted proceedings against five instructors for nonconformity to the Andover creed and later dismissed the seminary's president. The matter was carried to the Massachusetts Supreme Court, which overruled the Board of Visitors. During this period the trend throughout the church was for greater latitude of doctrinal expression. In 1883 a committee appointed by the National Council presented a short and concise creed, evangelical in tone, which was freely adopted by many local churches as their standard of faith. This creed omitted the doctrine of predestination so prominent in many of the older symbols. In 1913 the National Council adopted as part of its constitution the Kansas City Creed, a compact statement of faith which emphasized direct communion between God and the believer and the right of private judgment.

Baptists were, on the whole, cautious about accepting the new theological trends and most rejected them overwhelmingly. There was in the North, however, a wing which espoused highly liberal concepts. It centered at the University of Chicago, which opened in 1892 under the presidency of William Rainey Harper (1856–1906). One of its most liberal professors was George B. Foster, a student of Ritschl and Harnack, who was dismissed from the Chicago Baptist Ministers' Conference in 1909 because of alleged radical views. To offset the radical influence of the Divinity School of the University of Chicago, Illinois Baptists founded Northern Baptist Theological Seminary at Chicago in 1913 for the training of a conservative ministry.

While the Disciples of Christ were not on the whole prone to accept the new theology, there were some instances of liberalism in their midst. One of the prominent cases was that of Dr. R. L. Cave, a pastor in St. Louis, who denied the Virgin Birth and bodily resurrection of Jesus. When, in 1889, he tried to persuade his congregation to adopt these principles, the people opposed him; as a consequence, he resigned. In 1892 a lively debate took place in Chicago between J. W. McGarvey and H. L. Willett over Biblical criticism, the latter, dean of the Disciples Divinity House, standing in its defense. A bitter fight was waged against Dr. Willett, but without success; higher criticism had won an assured place within denominational scholarship.

Though Methodism seldom exhibited a proclivity for heresy trials and generally permitted wide freedom in the area of doctrine, it became briefly involved in two unfortunate cases. In 1904 Professor Borden P. Bowne, the most distinguished member of the faculty of Boston University, was brought to trial by his conference for heresy. Following in the steps of Lotze, Bowne taught a system known as Personalism, which regarded "personality as the active ground of the world" and the Supreme Self as immanent in the human self. His peers failed to convict him. About the same time the bishops refused to confirm H. G. Mitchell as a professor of Old Testament in Boston University School of Theology because of his acceptance of higher criticism. The matter was finally carried to the General Conference of 1908, which pronounced in favor of Mitchell. That same year the bishops were relieved of the responsibility of investigating reported cases of heresy in the seminaries.

Because of its involvement in questions of ritual, the Protestant Episcopal Church did not become engrossed in the controversy over liberalism until the final quarter of the nineteenth century. The liberal or broad church movement was influenced considerably by intellectual currents in England. Frederick D. Maurice of King's College, London, though not a true liberal, rejected the doctrines of the substitutionary atonement and eternal punishment of the wicked and seems to have inspired liberalism in others; while the Cambridge scholars, Westcott, Hort, and Lightfoot, gave incentive to the scientific study of the Bible. In the United States, the first evidence of liberalism appeared at the American Church Congress, an assembly of churchmen held at New York in 1874 for the free discussion of various topics of interest. It was supported by such liberally inclined clergy as Bishop T. M. Clark of Rhode Island, Phillips Brooks, William Reed Huntington, and Edward A. Washburn. Huntington gave apt expression to the group's feeling when he said that "the theologians must learn to look upon the naturalists as their allies rather than their antagonists. . . ." The church was, nevertheless, slow to adopt new views. In 1884 R. Heber Newton of New York was directed by his bishop to desist from giving lectures on higher criticism in his church. Six years later Howard MacQueary published *The Evolution of Man and Christianity,* in which he reserved the right to interpret the Resurrection and the Virgin Birth differently from the creed; he was suspended from the ministry. As a result of lectures delivered in 1905, in which he expressed disbelief in the Virgin Birth, Algernon S. Crapsey of Rochester, New York, was also suspended from his ministerial office. During the next fifteen years there was an abatement of theological controversy due largely to the growing spirit of comprehensiveness in the church. Not until the 1920's would the doctrinal controversy break out again in full force.

While the penetration of higher criticism into the Roman Catholic Church caused serious internal strife in Europe, its effect was considerably less in the United States. There was little of the bitter controversy which surrounded the labors of such Roman Catholics as Alfred Loisy, Louis Duchesne, and George Tyrrell, who were modernists in their respect for science, historical criticism, and democratic principles. That the hierarchy considered their ideas dangerous to the church is evident in the fact that after the accession of Pius X to the pontificate in 1903, their works were officially condemned. The use of historical methodology in Biblical study was not without support among American priests, being championed by such able scholars as John Zahm of Notre Dame and Thomas O'Gorman of Catholic University. They were encouraged in this by Leo XIII's policy, enunciated in 1883, of encouraging historical research. Their thought was not to question dogma but to use the findings of science in support of the church's program. Thus Zahm maintained that the evolutionary view of transmutation of species was more devout than the idea of God's immediate creation in six days; few American Catholics, however, were willing to espouse his cause. Leo XIII's critique of "Americanism" in 1899 struck a heavy blow at the liberal movement in the United States, still in its infant stage. The *coup de grace* came with the issuance of Pius X's encyclical *Pascendi Domini gregis,* in 1907, in which the pontiff specifically condemned modernism and directed that professors tainted with that heresy be dismissed from their posts. In 1910 it was decreed that all ordinands and professors be required to take an oath disavowing modernist views. The result was that ideas not in harmony with the official teachings of the church were suppressed and their authors disciplined.

The Conservative Rebuttal

In the Protestant world the theses of liberal theologians went not un-challenged. Many a theological school, especially those in the Calvinist tradition, produced scholars who were sharply critical of the new currents in religion and clung rigidly to the doctrine of the plenary inspiration of the Bible. Among the leaders in this camp were the Presbyterians A. A. Hodge, Francis L. Patton, and Benjamin B. Warfield, and the Baptists John A. Broadus and Asahel Kendrick. At the Niagara Bible Conference, which opened in 1876 and continued to meet annually until the end of the century, conservatives regrouped their forces for a frontal attack on the new theology. Their leaders were A. J. Gordon, Arthur Pierson, C. I. Scofield, and James Gray. At the meeting in 1895 the conference formu-lated its famous "five points of fundamentalism" or necessary standards of belief. They were the inerrancy of Scripture, the Virgin Birth of Jesus Christ, the substitutionary theory of the atonement, the physical resurrec-tion of Christ, and his imminent bodily return to earth. These doctrines were taught as essential at such conservative centers as Moody Bible In-stitute in Chicago and Los Angeles Bible Institute. In 1909 two wealthy Californians, Lyman and Milton Stewart, financed the publication of twelve small volumes entitled *The Fundamentals: A Testimony to the Truth,* nearly three million copies of which were circulated among min-isters and laymen in the United States and abroad. The effect was to stir up a militant antagonism toward liberalism which would reach its height in the decade which followed the First World War. By that time the new theology would have grown old and about to be replaced by theologies which dealt more positively with contemporary issues.

24

Social Religion in

Modern America

ONE OF THE MARVELS OF AMERICAN LIFE IN THAT RESTLESS EBULLIENT ERA which spanned the administrations of Grant and McKinley was the extraordinary growth of the big cities. In 1870 little more than one-fifth of the country's population lived in urban areas; by 1890 the percentage had risen to one-third and by 1900 it had reached the 40 per cent mark. There were 547 communities in the latter year with a population of more than 8000 as opposed to 141 in 1860. This drive toward the city continued apace until 1910, when it was somewhat offset by a trend to the suburbs. By this time, however, the age of the metropolis had dawned, in which the cities reached out and irresistibly drew the surrounding communities into the vortex of urban life. Thus the New York area, unified under one government in 1898, enjoyed a growth of population from 1,174,779 in 1860 to 4,766,883 in 1910. Philadelphia, Boston, and Baltimore could not compete with that record, but they did uncommonly well. Most remarkable was the growth of cities in the Middle West. Chicago, which ranked eighth among American cities in 1860, stood in second place by 1890, with a population of more than a million. St. Louis, Cleveland, and Detroit also grew rapidly during this period. It was apparent that the United States was rapidly changing from a predominantly rural to an urban society.

Multifarious forces contributed to this development. First, but by no means foremost, was the vast immigration from northern Europe in the years immediately following the Civil War, and after 1880 from eastern and southern Europe. But whether from Europe or from the American farm the influx into the cities was made feasible principally through the rise of great industrial corporations, which by 1919 were employing 86 per cent of all wage earners and were producing more than 87 per cent of the total value of products. Merely a cursory study of the development of the railroads and the oil, iron and steel, and electrical industries during this period will bear witness to the surging might of industrial America. This power was concentrated in the large cities and in the hands of a relatively few financiers and industrial leaders who became fabulously wealthy and remained in that state through the use of high-handed, sometimes ruthless, tactics. Until Congress passed regulatory laws they were in a fair position to control the nation's economy by the use of price-fixing agreements, trusts, and monopolies.

Rural life was profoundly affected by the trend toward industrialization and urbanization. Economically the country became increasingly dependent on the city and the farmer fell ever more to the mercies of middle men who determined the prices he might receive for his wheat, corn, or cattle. With the decided trend upward in agricultural production after 1865 came a proportionate decrease in prices, and many farmers found it impossible to remain solvent. The Granger organizations, Farmers' Alliances, and Populist movement in the closing decades of the century testified to the discontent of the farmer and his effort to gain economic justice; none was conspicuously successful. The rural situation was further beclouded by the drift of population to the cities, leaving some rural areas virtually paralyzed. Between 1880 and 1890, the population in 800 out of 1424 townships in Illinois and 755 out of 1316 townships in Ohio suffered a decline in population. In almost any section of the country it was not extraordinary to find villages in a state of deterioration, the neighboring farms abandoned, the church closed, and the academy dismantled. By 1900 the situation was critical.

Nor did the trend toward urban life result in a social panacea. The visitor to a typical East Coast city in 1890, New York for example, would have walked through traffic-congested, litter-strewn streets lined by bleak narrow structures in which "cliff-dwellers" carried on their lonely existence in a fellowship of unconcern. He might have inspected the grimy tenements, breeding grounds for disease and crime, or he might have looked into the steaming sweatshops where refugees from eastern Europe labored long and dangerous hours for a mere pittance. There

were unquestioned advantages in the city: the latest of modern con-
veniences, better communication, more adequate cultural facilities,
greater educational opportunities; but there were also hazards and a host
of new social problems to be resolved.

Organized religion sought in varied ways to minister to the social needs
of the time, its motivation being shaped by numerous forces past and
present. Always to be considered was the activistic spirit of the churches,
the desire to be doing something for the Kingdom of God. Never was this
activism more prevalent than in a generation which was coming to
believe more and more in the innate goodness of man and his infinite
perfectibility. Certainly a most important factor was the triumph of mass
evangelism, which nurtured not only a personal faith but a passion to
defeat sin wherever it might appear, whether in the form of individual
indiscretions or social evils such as poverty. Another factor was the
mounting interest in the new disciplines of psychology and sociology,
which sought to deal scientifically with society's problems. Christians
were by no means one in their approach to contemporary issues. Some
adhered to the old pattern of ameliorating social evils by fighting sin
and practicing charity; some advocated a complete reconstruction of
economic and political organization along socialistic lines; others were
dissatisfied with the present social structure but were more conservative
in their advocacy of change.

THE GOSPEL OF WEALTH

To many the unprecedented fiscal opportunities of the Gilded Age
seemed to confirm the view that unrestricted personal initiative would
lead to rewards commensurate with acumen and industry as well as to
maximum economic stability. If they sought theological support for this
conviction, they were most likely to find it in the doctrine of God's
providence. The most representative apologist for this philosophy was
Andrew Carnegie, who presented it in a manner clearly reminiscent of
Charles Darwin. As Carnegie propounded the theory in 1889, where there
was free competition in business it was inevitable that there should be a
higher standard of living. The process would of course involve painful
social readjustment, as the weak gave way before the strong, but the
survival of the fittest was the law of life. His concept was rephrased in a
somewhat more Christian way by Bishop William Lawrence of Massachusetts, who preferred to think of wealth coming only to the "man
of morality." Clearly Mr. Rockefeller seems to have had no doubts that
his tremendous resources were a gift from God. Similarly, but much more
arrogantly, G. F. Baer of the Philadelphia and Reading Railroad observed
in 1902: "The rights and interests of the laboring man will be protected
and cared for not by labor agitators but by the Christian man to whom

God in His infinite wisdom has given the control of the property interests of this country." The greater percentage of the American clergy, while concerned over the problem of mass poverty, were careful to avoid any pronouncements which might be interpreted as attacks on *laissez faire* capitalism. Denominational periodicals frequently dealt with poverty as the price of sin and prescribed evangelism as the remedy. Russell H. Conwell, the most popular lecturer of the day, told his audiences that "money is power and you ought to be reasonably ambitious to have it. You ought because you can do more good with it than you could without it."

The Fruits of Philanthropy

During the years of revolutionary economic and social change, a striking transformation was taking place in the churches. Membership in the large Protestant bodies was becoming almost exclusively the property of administrators, professional men, businessmen, white-collar workers, and farmers. While at one time denominations such as the Methodist, Baptist, and Disciples prided themselves on their ministry to the poor, they could now note with satisfaction that they were becoming churches with status, with soaring budgets made possible by millionaire communicants.

Many of the industrial leaders who amassed vast fortunes through their skill and initiative were vigorous workers in their several denominations. The briefest of lists would have to include such names as John D. Rockefeller, Baptist; Cyrus McCormick and John Wanamaker, Presbyterian; and Jay Cooke and W. H. Vanderbilt, Episcopalian. Dozens of others contributed heavily to favorite religious projects which ran the gamut from erecting stately granite edifices to endowing chairs in church-related colleges. The result was that many churches became moderately wealthy and some, as in the case of Trinity Church, New York, even owned property in slum areas.

With increasing affluence came a demand for external splendor. Gothic and new Romanesque structures embellished with beautifully designed stained-glass windows, which the Puritans once regarded as works of the devil, became standard in Protestantism. Especially admired were windows depicting Biblical scenes and saints of the church, previously repudiated as idolatrous. As for music, the pipe organ was an absolute necessity. Some congregations patterned their churches after existing models in England or on the Continent, while others sought to outdo them through the achievement of more solid construction and greater beauty. According to the census report of 1890, church property in the United States was valued at 670 million dollars. In all fairness to the churches, however, it should be pointed out that as their property values increased so did their benevolence budgets.

Church-related colleges also entered into an unprecedented building program made possible by the gifts of philanthropists, and a number of new institutions sprang into being. Leading universities such as Cornell, Stanford, and Duke, as well as such prominent women's colleges as Vassar orginiated through the munificent gifts of wealthy industrialists. Among the many new professorships established through endowment was the one created by the Baptist manufacturer, John P. Crozer, at Bucknell. After his death his heirs founded Crozer Theological Seminary at Chester, Pennsylvania, in his memory. John D. Rockefeller gave a fortune to the University of Chicago which amounted to some 78 million dollars by the time of his demise. It was not long before every denominational college in the country, as well as the type without church affiliation, was looking for some grand benefactor who would solve all its financial woes. Few had any serious qualms about accepting money originally gained by questionable means and such a respected paper as the *Independent* could observe in 1868: "We need all the Jay Cookes we have and a thousand more. We want them because they are a help to the present age; because they use their money for patriotic, benevolent and Christian purposes."

The Impact of Business upon Religion

As churches and colleges looked increasingly to business for support, they came to interpret their own activities more frequently from the standpoint of a business enterprise and to emphasize administration and finances as never before. Successful ministers of large city churches were expected to have all the skills of an oil magnate, while college presidents gave up teaching in favor of administration and fund raising. College boards of trustees, once controlled by ministers, came to be dominated by industrialists and financiers who were often more interested in administration and promotion than teaching. The result was that budget items for administrative functions increased proportionally at a higher rate than those for purely didactic purposes.

In the local churches efficiency came to be as highly regarded as evangelism; in order that the church might function most effectively in the business sense, successful businessmen were elected with greater frequency to the lay boards and accorded more responsibility in the administration of congregational affairs. At denominational conventions there was a tendency to treat the communication of the Gospel much as a corporation might treat the promotion of its product and to devote considerable time to the discussion of church efficiency. An aura of professionalism and machine-like perfectionism settled over the churches, leading to the charge from many quarters that organized religion was becoming more concerned with goals than souls.

A natural concomitant of the growing propensity for efficiency was an interest in church organization and polity. Throughout the denominations there was a strong feeling that with sounder organizational structure and a more careful system of controls the ministry of the churches could be made more effective. Possibly no religious body responded more readily to this concept than the northern Baptist. Between 1881 and 1912 the Baptist Congress, an organization which developed out of the Baptist lay social unions, met annually for the discussion by clerical and lay delegates of problems and opportunities before the Baptist churches. Though it had no power to legislate for the denomination or to transact business, it performed a valuable service by bringing together the leading men of the churches and by formulating organizational standards for recommendation to the congregations. A trend toward greater unity among northern Baptists began in 1896, when the American Baptist Missionary Union, the American Baptist Home Mission Society, and the American Baptist Publication Society advocated the creation of a Commission on Systematic Beneficence to coordinate the work of the various societies. This commission, duly appointed, studied the possibility of merging the societies, but no positive action was taken until 1907 when the three general societies met together and made arrangements for the formation of a national body which could coordinate their activities. The Northern Baptist Convention was legally incorporated at Chicago in 1910. Its announced purpose was to give "expression to the opinions of its constituency upon moral, religious and denominational matters, and to promote denominational unity and efficiency in efforts for the evangelization of the world." A similar trend toward more centralized organization might be noted among Presbyterians, U.S.A. In 1908 the Executive Commission of the General Assembly was organized to carry on the interim work of the Assembly; in 1915 commissions on synodical and presbyterial levels were authorized. After extensive administrative reorganization in 1923, the work of the Executive Commission and several other organizations was committed to a newly founded General Council.

THE CHURCHES AND LABOR

During the 1850's American labor began to experiment with what later came to be a powerful weapon for bargaining with capital: the union. While there were only some 300 unions in the country at the close of the Civil War, the movement developed rapidly during the next few years. One of the most important unions was the Knights of Labor, founded as a secret society among the garment workers of Philadelphia in 1869. After it became a national organization in 1878 most of its esoteric features were dropped and business was conducted publicly. At the height of its popularity in the mid 1880's its heterogeneous membership of both skilled and unskilled workers climbed to 700,000. Easily the most influential union of its time, it was dedicated not only to the furtherance of workers' rights but to the advancement of education and morality. Unfortunately, it became increasingly involved in a series of disastrous strikes which contributed to its disintegration. Somewhat more conservative was the American Federation of Labor, a trade-union founded in 1886, which preferred collective bargaining over strikes as a means of negotiating with management.

In September, 1873, the nation entered a period of financial depression, hastened by the failure of the leading banking firm, Jay Cooke and Company. Five years would pass before the return of normal conditions. Drastic wage cuts brought labor unions into conflict with capital, but the unions were notably unsuccessful and many went out of existence. In July, 1877, violence broke out between striking railroad workers united with crowds sympathetic to their cause and militiamen sent to establish order at the Pennsylvania Railroad's Pittsburgh depot. Before the struggle came to an end, twenty-five persons lost their lives and property damage ran into millions of dollars. Similar violence in other cities led the authorities to take drastic measures against strikers in order to stamp out what appeared to be a labor revolution. The restoration of peace, however, was merely the prelude to further violence. In 1886 another series of strikes swept the nation as workingmen agitated for an eight-hour day. At a mass meeting held on the evening of May 4 near Haymarket Square, Chicago, for the purpose of protesting police violence against strikers, a bomb was hurled at a company of policemen and seven officers were killed. Though the murderer was unknown, a number of anarchists were arrested and four were eventually hanged. The entire labor movement lost prestige among the general public and incurred a series of devastating defeats at the hands of capital. But the strikes continued with full intensity; the great steel strike in Pittsburgh in 1892 resulted in ten deaths, while in 1894, during the Pullman strike in Chicago, President Cleveland sent troops to guard the mails.

The Protestant Witness

Since the membership of Protestant churches during this period was composed chiefly of persons in the middle class, it is not surprising that ordinarily they failed to see social problems through the eyes of labor. Most were at least nominally concerned over the problems of poverty, but fear of socialism, which they associated with labor, prompted them to oppose the unions. In 1879 the Reverend Joseph Cook spoke in Boston on the theme "Are Trade Unions a Nursery for Socialism?" His answer was in the affirmative, emphatically so if the unions were filled with ignorant workers. After the Haymarket disaster of 1886, many Protestant churchmen were inclined to agree with Theodore Roosevelt that labor in general was to blame for the bombing.

Nevertheless, an occasional voice spoke in behalf of labor. Charles Bonney, a well-known Chicago layman, told a congregation shortly after the Haymarket affair that a principal cause of the riot lay "in the greed, the selfishness, the neglect and folly of wealth and power." Frederick Dan Huntington, Episcopal Bishop of Central New York, that same year admonished his fellow clergy for their indifference to social concerns, and William Jewett Tucker of Andover Theological Seminary maintained that the labor question is a legitimate concern of Christianity. A most enlightened approach to labor difficulties was taken by the Church Association for the Advancement of the Interests of Labor, an Episcopal society founded in 1887 in New York City. Working on the principle that labor "should be the standard of social worth," it used every possible means of communication to stimulate interest in the problems of the workingman. Each member was expected to become familiar with at least one labor periodical and with the social and economic issues of the day. Many labor unions soon came to regard the association as a friendly neighbor; the relationship deepened during the 1890's when the association formed sweatshop and tenement committees to work against these evils.

Despite the worthy efforts of a minority of socially minded Protestant leaders, there was no notable influx of laborers into the churches. At least part of the explanation for this situation could be found in a statement by Samuel Gompers of the American Federation of Labor in 1898. He wrote:

My associates have come to look upon the church and the ministry as the apologists and defenders of the wrong committed against the interests of the people, simply because the perpetrators are possessors cf wealth . . . whose real God is the almighty dollar, and who contribute a few of their idols to suborn the intellect and eloquence of the divines, and make even their otherwise generous hearts callous to the suffering of the poor and struggling workers, so that they may use their exalted positions to discourage and discountenance all practical efforts of the toilers to lift themselves out of the slough of despondency and despair.[1]

If the workingman had no desire to be affiliated with the fashionable churches, he was by no means opposed to a Christianity which could speak as progressively about this life as about heaven. Whenever he found a church which spoke to his condition, he was frequently willing to enter into its life and work. In 1894, Herbert N. Casson, formerly a Methodist minister, founded a Labor Church at Lynn, Massachusetts, in the belief that through this means he might win the laboring classes to

[1] Quoted in C. H. Hopkins, *The Rise of the Social Gospel in American Protestantism, 1865–1915* (Yale, 1940), 85.

the church. The membership was composed of those who believed the social problem to be the most vital issue of the day. Casson regularly invited labor leaders to speak from his pulpit. The most that can be said for movements of this kind is that they were sincere attempts to deal positively with the challenge presented by a new frontier. They solved few problems in their own right; their contribution was to suggest a need and to inspire the church at large to seek a solution.

The Roman Catholic Witness

The Roman Catholic Church in America had particular reason to be concerned with the many problems of labor because much of its membership potential lay in the immigrant labor class, a large percentage of which was at least nominally Roman Catholic. At the same time the church was somewhat embarrassed by the situation, for conservatives within its midst held sharply to a policy of non-interference in social issues. Archbishop James Bayley spoke for that group in 1876 when he said that God allows poverty as "the most efficient means of practising some of the most necessary Christian virtues, of charity and alms-giving on the part of the rich, and patience and resignation to His holy will on the part of the poor." Even the more liberally inclined leaders in the church were conservative in their attitude toward the reconstruction of society. The Paulist Fathers, ever sympathetic to the workingman, demanded no marked reforms in economic life, and Cardinal Gibbons observed no glaring faults in the American social structure.

At the same time, liberals of the Gibbons type did what they could to abet the cause of labor unions, while their more conservative coreligionists condemned the unions as destructive to the authority of the state. Particularly suspect were the Knights of Labor because of their pledge of secrecy, their radical economic philosophy, and their large non-Roman Catholic membership. In many dioceses, anti-union preaching was so intense that a number of the faithful felt obliged to withdraw from the Knights of Labor. When Cardinal Taschereau of Quebec obtained from the curia an official disapproval of the Knights of Labor in his province, it seemed to Gibbons that the time had come to submit the case to Rome for a decision. Having received assurances from Terence Powderly, Roman Catholic head of the union, that the union's activities were lawful, Gibbons reported his findings to the eleven archbishops, nine of whom agreed the union should not be censured. In 1887 Gibbons presented a formal opinion to the Prefect of Propaganda, in which he stated that condemnation of the Knights of Labor would have harmful consequences for the church in America. He was also careful to point out that the laboring class in America, unlike that in other countries, held religion in respect. "To lose the heart of the people," he said, "would be a misfortune for which the friendship of the few rich and powerful would be no compensation." A year later the prefect ruled that the Knights might be tolerated; thus Gibbons had won an important victory.

The remarkable cardinal was also able to persuade the Holy Office not to condemn Henry George's *Progress and Poverty* because of its alleged socialistic leanings, an accomplishment which warmed the heart of one of George's ardent supporters, Father Edward McGlynn of New York. McGlynn's persistent enunciation of socialist principles finally led to his excommunication. The liberal element in the church carried the case to Rome and in 1892 Leo XIII restored the much-maligned priest to the church. This action was consistent with the policy set forth by the pope in 1891 in his encyclical *Rerum novarum*, which concerned the relations of labor and capital. While the pope affirmed the right of private property, he condemned selfish interests which reduced the laborer to a position of virtual slavery; the rich had a greater obligation to the poor than the giving of alms. Ironically, each of the opposing sides on the labor issue in America interpreted the encyclical as speaking in its favor.

CHRISTIAN SOCIAL SERVICE

Lyman Abbott spoke for the large element with conservative economic and social leanings in the churches when he maintained that it was the task of organized Christianity "to preach the Gospel to the poor and needy; to provide teachers and places of worship for all, and to make any seeker after God welcome in any Christian church; to show the most concern for those who are in most need." He meant that the obligation of the church to the oppressed was to grant charity and evangelization, that in order to rebuild society one would first have to rebuild men. It was in this spirit that many socially concerned Christians founded programs for the amelioration of social conditions. They were frequently inspired to attempt such work by the reports of need issued by the American Christian Commission, a non-denominational urban social service organization founded at the suggestion of James E. Yeatman in 1865.

City Missions

Among Protestants, the institutional church, pioneered by William A. Muhlenberg as an experiment in charity for the underprivileged, became a standard outlet for the expression of philanthropic concern in the post-Civil War era. St. George's Episcopal Church, located on the East Side of New York, inaugurated an outstanding institutional program in 1882 under the direction of its pastor, W. S. Rainsford. The minister opened a parish house, brought in a trained staff, and offered courses in industrial education. Between 1883 and 1889 the congregation, whose membership climbed from less than 200 to more than 4000, spent over two million dollars for philanthropic purposes. A similar type of work was performed by the congregation of Berkeley Temple (Congregationalist) in Boston. Their program, which stressed classes and entertainment, had a wide appeal for youth. In Philadelphia, Russell Conwell's Baptist Temple began to provide during the 1880's gymnasiums, sewing classes, manual-training courses, reading rooms, day nurseries, and social clubs; the program was staffed by hundreds of voluntary and compensated workers. During the 1890's the Metropolitan Temple (Methodist) of New York, under the leadership of S. Parkes Cadman, began to hold fifty services each week and founded an athletic association, choral societies, a reading room, a sewing school, and an employment bureau. In 1894 a number of these institutional churches decided to organize the Open or Institutional Church League on an interdenominational basis for the purpose of co-ordinating the various programs. The League stood for "open church doors every day and all the day, free seats, a plurality of Christian workers, the personal activity of all church members, a ministry to all the community through educational, reformatory and philanthropic channels. . . ." Its activities undoubtedly had much to do with the multiplication of such churches toward the end of the century.

Much of the success of institutional work was due to cooperative activity in the denominations. The Methodists, for example, organized church extension and missionary societies after 1866, which rendered financial assistance to churches in slum areas and built new churches and chapels. Further help for the institutional church movement came from the Methodist Social Union of New York, founded in 1887 for the promotion of religious work among the poor. Among the Congregationalists, the Chicago City Missionary Society did representative work after 1883, while the American Congregational Union raised funds on a national level for the erection of churches. Baptists, Presbyterians, and Episcopalians carried on similar activities.

Closely related to the institutional church program was the work of the non-denominational city mission. The movement was patterned after the Water Street Mission of New York, founded by Jerry MacAuley, a converted drunkard and burglar, shortly after the Civil War. This rescue mission offered to derelicts not only food and shelter, but fervid preaching which guided them to reclamation and a life of usefulness. Another important mission was the Central Union Mission of Washington, D.C., established in 1884. Not content to provide the transients with board and lodging, it endeavored to secure employment for them. Within a few years many cities in different parts of the country had missions of identical character. Some missions were created to perform a special service. Thus Charles Crittenden, a New York businessman, established a mission for wayward girls in 1883; the Crittenden Home movement soon became a national institution.

Influenced to some extent by the institutional church program, but even more by Toynbee Hall, a pioneer settlement house in East London, was the settlement house movement. It sought to bring together a company of social workers who would live in a slum section of the city and conduct a number of projects for its social betterment. The first American settlement was begun in New York by Dr. Stanton Coit in 1886, but the best known was Hull House in Chicago, founded by Jane Addams and Ellen G. Starr three years later. The latter institution offered day nurseries, classes in arts and crafts, men's clubs, a gymnasium, and an employment bureau, chiefly for the benefit of the foreign born.

Lutheran and Methodist women in particular had a unique opportunity to engage in social service projects through the deaconess movement. Between 1885 and 1900 nearly 150 institutions were founded for the training of deaconesses who would assist ministers in their parish work, particularly that of visitation and the spiritual care of women and children, or serve as nurses or administrators. While the Lutherans were first to enter this field, the greatest use of the institution was made by the Methodist Episcopal Church, which was operating seventy-three deaconess homes by 1900. Methodist deaconesses were soon conducting most of the church's hospitals, homes for the aged, orphanages, and elementary church schools.

Cooperative Projects for Social Service

After the Civil War, the Young Men's Christian Association, for some years concerned with the social needs of the poor, began to devote itself more and more to activities among youth of the middle class. The New York Association set the example in 1869 by adopting a program for "the improvement of the spiritual, mental, social and physical conditions of young men." Due in large measure to the influence of Luther Gulick, physical director of the New York Association, emphasis in Y.M.C.A. work after the 1880's was placed increasingly upon the physical development of youth; in this way bodily exercise became Christianized. For several decades, however, the Y.M.C.A. in certain cities maintained services principally for the poor. The New York Association established a Bowery Branch in 1872 for the purpose of poor relief and the Chicago Association performed the work of a city mission.

The Young Women's Christian Association, organized in England in 1855, was in certain respects the feminine counterpart of the Y.M.C.A. While the first organized body later to be affiliated with the national movement was the Ladies' Christian Union of New York City, established in 1858 "to labor for the temporal, moral, and religious welfare of self-supporting young women," it was not until 1866 that the first Young Women's Christian Association was founded in Boston. This and other associations gradually developed a highly diversified program designed to reach young women of varied backgrounds and experience. While they offered basic services such as providing food and lodging and operating employment bureaus for those in need, their chief emphasis became the cultivation of the "physical, social, intellectual, moral and spiritual interests of young women." Group programs for Christian study and fellowship ranked high among the activities. They also pioneered in such projects as Travelers' Aid and international student centers. In 1906 the local chapters organized themselves into the National Young Women's Christian Association. This body in turn maintained an affiliation with the world association.

The last twenty years of the nineteenth century witnessed an effort by evangelical Protestants to relate religion to social life through the activities of five cooperative organizations. Of these, the Evangelical Alliance and the Convention of Christian Workers were the most important. The Alliance brought prominent religious leaders together to discuss the evils of society and seek a solution to them. Its most salient contribution was to advise the formation of local alliances which would cooperate in finding Christian solutions to social and industrial problems. By 1889 such alliances had been formed in more than forty cities; nevertheless, the movement developed slowly and was not distinguished by exceptional results. The Convention of Christian Workers, established in 1886, was an organization of mission workers. Its purposes were to provide classes and reading rooms, to train theological students and laymen in social work, to help individual churches found missions in run-down areas, and to raise funds for missions. It was a pioneer in the promotion of boys' club work; by 1891 twenty clubs under its auspices were working with nearly 10,000 boys throughout the country. Other organizations which sought to render similar services were the American Congress of Churches, the Brotherhood of Christian Unity, and the League for Catholic Unity, the latter two being as much interested in church union as social reform.

Prior to 1890 the principal activities of the Roman Catholic Church in the area of social betterment were along charitable lines. One of the most important agencies was the time-honored Society of St. Vincent de Paul, a lay missionary movement which endeavored to bring both physical aid and spiritual sustenance to unfortunates. To conservatives in the church, non-sectarian social work was unnecessary; the problems of society could be handled best by the charitable orders. One of the leading benevolent fraternal societies was the Knights of Columbus, founded for Roman Catholic laymen at New Haven, Connecticut, in 1882. Its original goal was to protect the families of its members by means of a system of insurance, but it was soon participating in larger programs for Roman Catholic education and charities. After 1885 the society rapidly developed into a national movement which continued to emphasize beneficence and education. A trend toward better organization of charity began to shape up during the 1890's, the thought being to avoid indiscriminate, haphazard giving. In 1897 the New York archdiocese appointed a General Supervisor of Catholic charities, while a decade later a Diocesan Charitable Bureau was created in Boston. The founding of the National Conference of Catholic Charities, however, had to wait until the opening of the twentieth century.

Social Welfare Agencies

One of the most remarkable religious and philanthropic organizations was the Salvation Army, founded in England in 1878 by William Booth, a former Wesleyan Methodist preacher. The Army was an outgrowth of Booth's East London Revival Society, organized in 1865. Its program emphasized witnessing to Christ by informal preaching and outdoor evangelistic meetings which featured brass bands. After its reorganization along quasi-military lines, the movement became highly centralized and authoritarian, demanding unquestioning obedience from its workers. Its theology was conservative, with stress on sin, redemption, and growth in holiness. The Salvation Army was introduced to the United States in 1880, with the arrival of Commissioner George S. Railton and seven "Hallelujah lasses" or assistants in Philadelphia. Within a few months twelve local units or Army corps and an official newspaper, the *War Cry*, had been established. The informal methods and unorthodox practices of the Army, such as street-preaching, were at first sharply criticized by the churches, but eventually the opposition waned. In 1886 General Ballington Booth, son of the movement's founder, was placed in charge of the Army in America. Indefatigable in zeal, he gradually won his way into favor with religious leaders of the nation, a fact verified by the Reverend Josiah Strong, who was himself "converted to the brass drum and the cymbal." By 1900 the Army, which numbered 700 corps, was conducting more than 11,000 weekly meetings and operating 87 social institutions for the welfare of the destitute. The organization was possibly best known for the work of its Slum Brigades, which went into run-down sections of the cities, held services in saloons and halls, brought relief to the destitute, and preached against vice. As a result of their findings, the Army founded day nurseries for children whose parents could not care for them, rescue homes for prostitutes, food and shelter depots for the unemployed, farm colonies, employment bureaus, and a host of other social service projects.

When Ballington Booth was ordered to return to England in 1896 for another assignment, he refused. Having already become somewhat displeased with the administration of the Army, he withdrew and founded a similar organization known as the Volunteers of America, which was more democratic in government. While its activities were much the same as those of the Salvation Army, the Volunteers worked primarily among a higher class of laborers rather than in the slums and specialized in the reform of inebriates and the social redemption of discharged prisoners.

An outgrowth of the institutional church program was Goodwill Industries, founded in Boston in 1902 by Edgar J. Helms, a Methodist minister. Its purpose was to find employment for handicapped and retired workers. Old clothes, furniture, and other articles no longer desired by their owners were collected by the Goodwill Industries and, having been mended and repaired by the workers, were sold at reduced prices to persons of very limited financial resources. By 1952 the Industries, which were not officially connected with any denomination, were operating 101 factories in the United States and providing employment for 17,545 persons.

THE SOCIAL GOSPEL

While Protestant conservatives were fighting poverty by means of charitable enterprises, a radical group of thinkers was raising a series of embarrassing questions which would force the church to rethink its entire social program. Two men in particular challenged the status quo. The first was a California journalist named Henry George, who analyzed the problems of society in his famous work, *Progress and Poverty,* published in 1879. In it he presented the thesis that persons who improve the land through labor are entitled to the benefits to be derived from such labor and that through a common ownership of land by society their rights must be protected. George's solution to the problem of ownership was certainly naive, but it did constitute a strong indictment of natural resource monopolies. The second thinker was Edward Bellamy, idealistic New England author of *Looking Backward, 2000–1887,* published in 1888. It was a fascinating tale of a utopian society, strangely reminiscent of some of the mid-century perfectionist communities. With all their impracticalities, these two men were able to inspire a zeal for reform which would bear fruit in a number of social movements. One movement which was at least partially influenced by the philosophy of these men was the Protestant Social Gospel.

The Nascence of the Social Gospel

While the main stream of Protestant Christianity in the United States followed a pietistic and doctrinally conservative position which found no culpability in laissez faire capitalism and conceived social progress in terms of organized charities, there was a group of clerical leaders, small at first, that was beginning to ask searching questions about the ethics of the social and economic structure of American life. They made themselves known through a tremendous volume of literature widely circu-

lated, but only gradually did their fellow clergy or the laity respond to
their message. Since they were pioneers, they were not always certain of
the direction they should take and frequently they were in disagreement
as they sought a theology which could speak to the condition of their
times. In their enthusiasm for all that concerned the welfare of men,
however, they were one. It has often been asserted that they were not so
much seeking as attempting to escape from a theology. Clearly they belonged to a generation that was being bombarded by evolution and Biblical criticism and idealistic philosophies and in the process was becoming
metaphysically confused. Yet there was no doubt as to their position
concerning man. They saw him as a child of God with infinite capacities
for moral improvement, who, through earthly progress, could build a
Kingdom of God with life to the full. If they thought of Jesus more as a
prophet of social righteousness than as a divine Saviour, it was because
their metaphysics were subordinate to their ethics. Their Gospel began
with man and moved out to God. It was a typically nineteenth-century
faith, born of the same spirit that motivated men like George and Bellamy
but baptized in the life and thought of the Old and New Testaments.

One of the leading voices at the beginning of the Social Gospel movement was that of Washington Gladden (1836–1918), Congregationalist
pastor of churches in Springfield, Massachusetts, and Columbus, Ohio.
He had been brought up in an orthodox environment and had been nurtured in a theology which stressed individual redemption. It was Horace
Bushnell who imparted to him the concept of the church as a social
institution and of Christianity as a religion of love. Four years on the
editorial staff of the *Independent* in New York inured him to the harsh
realities of urban social relationships yet confirmed his latent desire to
apply to them Christian principles. This he attempted to do through
preaching and through a series of books on such topics as *Working
People and Their Employers* (1876), *Applied Christianity* (1887), and
Social Salvation (1902). He gained valuable insights into the economic
situation, especially the political power of capital, while serving on the
Columbus city council. In his opinion, the competitive basis of laissez
faire capitalism was unchristian. A proper goal was cooperation between
capital and labor, which could be realized if the worker owned a share
in the business. But what was needed most of all in industry was the
"power of Christian love"; it could "smooth and sweeten all the relations
of capitalists and labor." Gladden believed that a more ideal order was
bound to be achieved through the power of love and moral persuasion.
Other contemporary clerics whose thought followed a similar strain were
Theodore Munger and Newman Smyth, Congregationalists, and Elisha
Mulford, Episcopalian.

Three other aggressive advocates of the Social Gospel during the 1880's
deserve mention. Richard T. Ely, a brilliant young economist on the

faculty of Johns Hopkins University, gave a much-needed boost to the movement through his book, *The Labor Movement in America,* published in 1886. In it he maintained that labor should be governed by the principles of Christian ethics. This thesis was made relevant to the work of the ministry by Francis Peabody, who inaugurated the teaching of social ethics at Harvard. Better known to the general public than either of these men was Josiah Strong, Congregational pastor, who stunned the nation by his penetrating analysis of its problems in his book, *Our Country,* published in 1885. It was Strong's contention that greed for money and power was corrupting the country and that so few should own so much and so many own so little was a national calamity. By sounding this note of crisis, he awakened many ministers and congregations to a vital concern over the social situation and gave a powerful impetus to the cause of the Social Gospel.

The Flowering of the Social Gospel

Several events during the 1890's signalized the growth in influence of the Social Gospel. One was the founding of the Brotherhood of the Kingdom, a fellowship of persons committed to the work of Christian social reform which met annually from 1893 to 1915 in New York. The members, of whom Walter Rauschenbusch came to be the most prominent, pledged themselves "to lay stress on the social aims of Christianity." Through their individual writings and group resolutions they exercised a powerful influence on the contemporary Protestant mind. More influential in spreading the Social Gospel was the widely read novel by Charles M. Sheldon, a minister of Topeka, Kansas, entitled *In His Steps: What Would Jesus Do?* Within a few months after its publication in 1897, 100,000 copies had been sold. The story concerned the membership of an average American church and its efforts for an entire year to ascertain and do the will of Jesus in every situation which arose. It was a highly sentimental romantic account, but it touched the hearts of the public and well nigh brought on a national movement for social reform.

Meanwhile, a movement of more radical character was developing under the leadership of an Episcopal clergyman, William D. P. Bliss. Having been won to the cause of labor and impressed by the teachings of Henry George for some time, he organized a Society of Christian Socialists in Boston in 1889. Insisting that the teachings of Jesus lead inevitably to some type of socialism, the society called for the gradual abolition of competition in business and the introduction of profit-sharing, trade-unionism, and municipal ownership. Though the society remained decidedly a minority group, it gained a substantial following and was able to organize local societies in a number of cities.

A most vigorous proponent of Christian Socialism was George D.

Herron, Congregational minister and Professor of Applied Christianity at Iowa (later Grinnell) College after 1893. A speaker of uncommon ability, he was invited to lecture at many universities and seminaries; on such occasions he proclaimed a gospel of "the political appearing of Christ" or the reconstruction of society along socialist lines. The redemptive mission of the church he found to be the erection of a just social order, where the public would own the sources and means of production. This could be accomplished only by the willing sacrifice of self-interests for the interests of others. The views of Herron and other like-minded persons were circulated most widely through a weekly journal, *The Kingdom,* which began publication in 1894.

The chief prophet of the Social Gospel was Walter Rauschenbusch (1861–1918), German-American Baptist who, after 1903, adorned the chair of church history at Colgate-Rochester Theological Seminary. Unlike Social Gospel leaders such as Gladden, whose heritage lay in New England Congregationalism, Rauschenbusch was a product of German piety, doctrinal orthodoxy, and social concern in the tradition of Ritschl. In 1886 he had arrived in New York to pastor a congregation of German immigrants which was conspicuous for its lack of affluence. While there his eyes were opened to the pressing social problems of his day and the solutions proposed by such thinkers as Richard Ely and Henry George. After 1892, when he came out in favor of the Homestead strikers, his political thought moved steadily to the left until it arrived at socialism.

As a religious thinker, Rauschenbusch was essentially conservative; he was never as optimistic about man as the majority of Christian social reformers, for he was not prepared to dispense with the doctrine of original sin. It was typical of the man that he should have offered at the seminary a popular course succinctly entitled The Devil. His central concept, however, was the Kingdom of God, which he saw as a gradually evolving social order based on justice and righteousness. In his first book, *Christianity and the Social Crisis,* published in 1907, he gave an historical analysis of social religion as it developed from the time of the prophets to apostolic Christianity. He emphasized Biblical concern for the poor and oppressed, a concern which he found to be sorely lacking in the modern capitalistic system. In his opinion there was no greater enemy to the divine kingdom than capitalism; it prevented men and women from gaining life's temporal necessities and brought corruption to the social and political order. "Competitive commerce," he said, "exalts selfishness to the dignity of a moral principle. It pits men against one another in a gladiatorial game in which there is no mercy and in which ninety per cent of the combatants finally strew the arena." If the church was to live up to its historic task it must attempt to achieve a thoroughgoing reformation in society, abolishing the hate of economic competition in favor of cooperation grounded in Christian love.

Rauschenbusch is best known for *A Theology for the Social Gospel,* which he published in 1917. It was a frank attempt to find a theological basis for social reform. The author began with a serious consideration of the reality of evil, both individual and corporate, and its peculiar danger in society. It was precisely social sin that was most devastating to morality, whether in the form of war, oppression, or intemperance. Men could not hope to build the Kingdom of God until they made a frontal attack on the Kingdom of Evil. This could come through moral, economic, and social reform, involving the overthrow of capitalism and the establishment of a system not based on a competitive struggle for property and power. As for the progress of the Kingdom, Rauschenbusch was restrained in his optimism; he believed in God's immanence and in progressive perfection but never separated these ideas from his concept of human sinfulness. In this respect he reflected not so much the thought of his own time as of a later time, which was hospitable to Neo-Orthodoxy.

The principal educational center for the propounding of Social Gospel doctrines was the University of Chicago, which featured such celebrated representatives as Albion W. Small, founder of the Sociology Department; his colleague, Charles R. Henderson; and Shailer Mathews, Dean of the Divinity School. Graham Taylor, Professor of Christian Sociology at Chicago Theological Seminary, was also well known for his courses on the social teaching of Jesus and his work at the Chicago Commons settlement. By the opening of the twentieth century a number of seminaries were following the example of Chicago and were establishing chairs in Christian sociology and ethics.

The Reaction of the Churches

From its inception, the Social Gospel movement met opposition from at least two sources. Naturally big business opposed it as a mortal foe and tried unsuccessfully to drive it from the churches. It was also rejected by groups with a strong revivalistic emphasis which held that the principal function of the church was to save men from sin and damnation and prepare them for eternal life in a heavenly kingdom. Nevertheless, the movement gradually gained momentum in the great evangelical churches such as the Methodist, Baptist, Congregational, Presbyterian, and Disciples, all of which adopted social creeds and established agencies to put them into practice. In 1901 the National Council of Congregational Churches appointed a labor committee and the General Convention of the Protestant Episcopal Church approved the appointment of a standing commission on the relations of capital and labor. The Presbyterian Church, U.S.A., created a Department of Church and Labor in 1903 and called to its superintendency the Reverend Charles Stelzle, a man thoroughly conversant with the problems of labor. Seven years later he founded Labor Temple on the East Side of New York as an attempt to bring Christian principles to bear upon the economic and social order. The Methodist Episcopal Church organized a Methodist Federation for Social Service in 1907 and the following year adopted a Social Creed. The Northern Baptist Convention endorsed the Social Gospel in 1908, and the Disciples of Christ organized a Commission on Social Service in 1911.

The capstone of the process was the issuance by the newly founded interdenominational body, the Federal Council of Churches, of a Social Creed of the Churches in 1908, taken largely from the Methodist pronouncement. This Creed was modified by the Federal Council four years later. It called for equal rights for all men, uniform divorce laws, child labor laws, laws against the liquor traffic, protection for workers in their places of employment, old age benefits, labor arbitration, one day of rest weekly, reduction of working hours, safeguards for the rights of workers, guaranteed living wages, and "the application of Christian principles to the acquisition and use of property." Thus official ecclesiastical approval was given to a movement which for more than a generation had been in the process of development. Even so, it seems unlikely that a majority of the laity were won to its cause. With the advent of "normalcy" in the 1920's the movement declined and more than ten years passed before it enjoyed another revival.

The churches were much slower in recognizing the peculiar difficulties which faced the farmer as opposed to the industrial worker, though they devoted some attention to the rural church problem. Many home missionary boards dealt with the plight of rural churches and by 1922 even the Roman Catholic Church, essentially an urban enterprise, was working in this area through the National Catholic Rural Life Conference. As the twentieth century advanced several theological schools inaugurated courses especially designed to train leaders for a rural ministry. The Federal Council of Churches initiated a program of rural church study between 1910 and 1912, but it was not until 1932 that the Council revised the Social Creed of the Churches to include a statement of concern for the economic plight of the farmer. It was symbolic of a new consciousness in American life.

The Churches and

Crusading Internationalism

THAT DEEP-SEATED CONVICTION LONG CHERISHED BY AMERICANS THAT THEIR
nation had been divinely chosen for world mission was nurtured and sustained through the fires of civil conflict and given a new baptism of power
during the subsequent era of geographical expansion and industrial
progress. Many forces combined to magnify the role of Manifest Destiny
in the American consciousness and to encourage popular demand for
expansion. In the realm of science and philosophy, Darwinism seemed to
support expansion through the survival of the fittest doctrine, which was
readily translated by Americans into the thought that by natural selection
the United States had become a superior nation destined to rule the
weaker peoples of the world. At the same time, idealistic philosophies
were emphasizing man's natural ability and interpreting history in terms
of progress, a circumstance which had profound implications for American expansionists. Geographical expansion also seemed justified on the
basis that Americans, having made optimum use of the land and resources in the territorial United States, should make similarly good use of
other dominions for the benefit of mankind. In a period when the nations

of western Europe were progressively furthering their imperialistic interests in Africa, Asia, Latin America, and the Pacific, Americans too heard the call of benevolent empire and believed their mission to be the extension of the blessings of Christian civilization and democratic government through expansion. And so Americans entered with assurance and forthrightness into the effort to gain influence abroad by investing in foreign production, giving governmental assistance to weaker powers, building a large navy to protect national interests, and sending missionaries to Christianize and Americanize the peoples of distant lands. It was an inspired task and it was executed with a zeal born of conviction.

THE EXTENSION OF WORLD MISSIONS

The gradually mounting enthusiasm of the churches for missions in the last thirty-five years of the nineteenth century was a product of national expansionist sentiment combined with deeply imbedded theological motives. The desire to save the "heathen" from eternal damnation belonged to the revivalistic spirit then powerful in American Protestantism which stressed instantaneous conversion and a life directed toward the attainment of perfection. Hudson Taylor, founder of the China Inland Mission, expressed the philosophy of numerous evangelicals when he addressed the convention of the Student Volunteer Movement at Detroit in 1894.

The gospel must be preached to these people in a very short time, for they are passing away. . . . There is a great Niagara of souls passing into the dark in China. Every day, every week, every month they are passing away! A million a month in China they are dying without God![1]

Among many evangelicals the pre-millennial view that the Gospel would have to be preached throughout the whole world before the second coming of Christ was a motivating factor. In some instances, missionaries felt compelled by an irresistible urge to advance American political and economic interests and advocated the use of armed might to compel cooperation with the United States, believing that in the end all would benefit by American occupation. The result was that through their missionary boards the American churches poured a steady stream of volunteers into old and new fields of foreign endeavor. Millions of inspired workers at home and abroad were dedicated to the fulfillment of the prediction in Warren's *Common School Geography* that "there is little doubt that in the course of a few generations the Christian religion will be spread over the greater part of the earth."

[1] *The Student Missionary Enterprise. Addresses and Discussions of the Second International Convention of the Student Volunteer Movement for Foreign Missions* (Revell, 1894), 48.

Denominational Enterprises

While most of the denominations were conducting organized mission work in foreign lands long before the Civil War, it was not until after 1860 that political and economic developments abroad enabled them to conduct their activities to greatest advantage. In Latin America there were more political stability and freedom of conscience after 1850, and Protestant missions made significant gains, especially in Mexico where representatives of the Baptist, Presbyterian, Methodist, and Episcopal denominations came after 1870. Presbyterians were the first to inaugurate a continuing program among the Roman Catholic populations of Central America, having opened a station at Guatemala City in 1882. In Venezuela, the American Bible Society initiated mission work in 1887; the following year the society founded a mission in Peru. Meanwhile, the Methodist Episcopal Church was developing missions in Peru, Bolivia, and Brazil. In the latter country, to which numbers of Southerners emigrated after the Civil War, Southern Baptists, Methodists, and Presbyterians carried on a flourishing program. Presbyterian and Methodist missions were to be found in Chile before the end of the century, as well as in Argentina.

North Africa presented a peculiar challenge since according to strict Moslem codes Christians might not evangelize in their territories; all that was possible was work of a philanthropic, educational, or medical character. The most important Protestant mission in Egypt was that of the United Presbyterian Church of North America, which opened its first station in 1854. The situation was much more encouraging in equatorial and southern Africa, particularly after the middle of the century when the western powers began to invade the interior. In 1890 the American Board of Commissioners for Foreign Missions established stations in Southern Rhodesia. Farther to the north, in the Congo, a most effective mission was begun in 1884 by the American Baptist Missionary Union. During the 1890's the southern Presbyterians and the Disciples of Christ also founded stations in this area, while northern Presbyterians were expanding their mission in the Cameroon. In Yorubaland, on the West Coast, the Southern Baptists renewed a mission founded some twenty years earlier, which had become virtually extinct.

Missionary work in the Near East, strongly Moslem in religious persuasion, was always difficult and many gains were made from among older Christian groups. In Syria the mission begun in 1823 by the American Board of Commissioners was turned over to the Presbyterians in 1870. Possibly their finest contribution in this part of the world was made through the Syrian Protestant College, renamed the American University of Beirut in 1920. In Turkey, the chief Protestant work after 1870 was conducted by the Congregationalists. They too performed a splendid educational service through Robert College and the American College for Girls at Istanbul. In 1870 the Presbyterians assumed responsibility for Persia or Iran and developed a number of centers in that country. During the 1890's the Reformed Church in America inaugurated an Arabian Mission, its most famous missionary being Samuel M. Zwemer. Though some converts were made, none of the missions in Moslem countries can be said to have flourished; Moslems were always difficult to convert and many a missionary counted his work blessed if he could claim a handful of converts after years of service on the mission field.

In India, the missionary situation was greatly affected by political developments. The Sepoy Mutiny of 1857, inspired largely by a reaction to westernization, was finally checked by British arms; the crown took over the government of India from the East India Company and gave direct support to missionary programs, most of which prospered during the remainder of the century. Among these were the Congregational, Presbyterian, U.S.A., United Presbyterian, Northern Baptist, (Dutch) Reformed, General Synod Lutheran, and Methodist Episcopal. Outstanding missionary leaders during this period were James C. R. Ewing, Presbyterian principal of Forman Christian College at Lahore after 1888, and Methodists James Thoburn and William Taylor, who organized missions in numerous centers. The greater majority of converts were won not from the castes, who feared westernization, but from outcastes or primitive animists.

American missionaries conducted a flourishing missionary program in Southeast Asia. In Burma, the Baptists continued an important work begun earlier in the century by Adoniram Judson and succeeded in training a native ministry. They founded several schools and a college in Rangoon. In 1879 the Baptists were joined by a group of American Methodists. The leading Protestant missions in Thailand were maintained by the Presbyterians, who had begun their work in 1840. Their principal evangelistic success was in the North, where they had won 1841 persons to church membership by 1894. Bangkok Christian College was founded in the South. Although there was little persecution in Southeast Asia where Hinayana Buddhism was strong, the efforts of missionaries were impeded by the fact that Buddhists would often continue to adhere to older ideas and practices even after they had accepted Christianity.

Chinese missions also depended to a considerable extent on political developments. As early as 1830 the American Board of Commissioners had begun a mission in Canton, but it was not until the British officer Charles "Chinese" Gordon put down the T'ai P'ing Rebellion of 1848–1864 and the Anglo-Chinese Wars were brought to a successful conclusion that the interior was open to missionary expansion. British operations were highly praised by the American missionaries Samuel Wells Williams and Peter Parker, the latter a medical missionary who eventually became American Minister to China and advocated the annexation of Formosa by the United States. Less aggressive and decidedly devoted to the Chinese was William A. P. Martin, a Presbyterian who translated scholarly works into Chinese and late in the century was made president of the Imperial University in Peking. After 1870, the American Board of Commissioners for Foreign Missions virtually abandoned its work in the South in order to pour its resources into new missions which were opening in North China.

In 1890 the Northern Baptists pioneered in the western province of Szechwan, while Southern Baptists were opening new stations in the cities of Kiangsu after confining their activities for some time to the area around Canton. Before 1868 the chief center of Protestant Episcopal missions was Shanghai; after that time stations were maintained in the cities of Wuchang and Hankow, in the interior. The outstanding Episcopal missionary in China was a Jewish Lithuanian convert, Samuel Schereschewsky, who translated the Bible and the Book of Common Prayer into the Mandarin dialect and in 1875 was elected bishop of his church for China. Between 1860 and 1895 Presbyterians developed a strong missionary program in South China and established stations in various parts of the empire, while Southern Methodists concentrated their activities in the eastern provinces of Kiangsu and Chekiang. One of the more famous converts to the latter body was Charles Soong who, after receiving his education in the United States, was assigned a Methodist circuit in China; two of his daughters later became the wives of Sun Yat-sen and Chiang Kai-shek. The ethical bent of the Chinese mind, nurtured by both Confucianism and Buddhism, may account for much of the enthusiasm shown by the Chinese for the emphasis on health and education in the American program, while adherents of the Buddhist Amitabha or Pure Land School found much sympathy for the other-world teaching of bliss beyond death in Christianity.

American missions in Korea were made possible after the United States concluded a treaty with the Korean government in 1883. The following year the first Presbyterian missionary arrived from America; in 1885 the Methodist Episcopal Church sent two missionary families. These two denominations maintained the principal mission work in Korea, though Southern Presbyterians and Southern Methodists founded stations toward the end of the century.

As in the case of Korea, diplomatic arrangements preceded organized Protestant missions in Japan. In 1854 Commodore Matthew Perry concluded the first American treaty with the Japanese, thus establishing diplomatic relations between the two countries; according to a treaty of 1858, Americans in Japan were to have the right to worship according to the dictates of their consciences. The following year missionaries representing the Protestant Episcopal Church, the Presbyterian Church,

U.S.A., and the Reformed Church in America arrived in Japan and founded stations at Osaka, Tokyo, Kanagawa, Yokohama, and Nagasaki. In the face of opposition and suspicion, the missionaries gained few converts during the first decade and it was not until they were able to win the Japanese confidence that significant progress was made. After the fall of the Tokugawa Shogunate in 1867 and the restoration of government by the Emperor Meiji, Protestant missions flourished and many converts were won to Christianity. The American Board of Commissioners for Foreign Missions opened a mission in 1869; the next decade saw the arrival of representatives from the American Baptist Missionary Union, the Methodist Episcopal Church, and the Cumberland Presbyterian Church. During the 1880's, Protestant missions enjoyed phenomenal growth so that by 1888 their 249 churches numbered 25,514 communicants. The results were due in part to the fact that in 1877 the congregations founded by Presbyterians, U.S.A., Dutch Reformed, and United Presbyterians of Scotland, merged to form the United Church of Christ in Japan and as a united body were consequently more effective in their witness. By the 1890's, however, the churches began to suffer serious losses due to a rising tide of nationalism which branded Christianity as a foreign religion. Not until the opening of the twentieth century did Christianity enjoy a new period of substantial growth.

In Hawaii, the American Board of Commissioners for Foreign Missions, after forty-three years of service, turned its activities over to the self-governing Board of the Hawaiian Evangelical Association in 1863, which supplied the churches with a native ministry. The Mormons developed a program during the 1860's and the Methodists began work in 1890. But little of a significant nature was accomplished until the annexation of the islands by the United States in July, 1898.

The Work of Cooperative Agencies

Late in the nineteenth century many American Protestant leaders awoke to the possibility of cooperation in the work of world missions, while others sensed the value of a strong movement under the auspices of laymen. This latter ideal was made concrete in the formation of the Student Volunteer Movement for Foreign Missions in 1888. At Mt. Hermon, Massachusetts, Dwight L. Moody's conference center, 100 students were inspired during the summer meeting of 1886 to become missionaries. The following year one of this group, Robert Wilder, visited many colleges and seminaries in the United States and Canada and won 2106 persons to the cause of missions. In 1888 this enthusiasm was channeled into a continuing organization, the Student Volunteer Movement, under the chairmanship of John R. Mott, a Methodist layman. Three years later its first Quadrennial Convention, soon to become a highly influential institution, was held. In nations all over the world Student Volunteers were organized to enlist Protestants in the work of missions; through their efforts a high percentage of men destined to become missionary leaders in the twentieth century were recruited. Possibly the most outstanding product of the student missionary movement was the Presbyterian layman, Robert E. Speer.

Other lay organizations which had initiated world mission activities prior to the end of the century were the Y.M.C.A., the Y.W.C.A., and the Christian Endeavor Society. By 1890 several Young Men's Christian Associations had been founded in Christian colleges in Asia. The first secretary to be sent from the United States to India arrived in 1890; a year later there were thirty-five associations in that country. The first secretary was sent to China in 1895. To a lesser extent the Y.W.C.A. carried on work in these same countries. During the 1880's the Christian Endeavor movement was brought to India and was so well received that by 1897 it numbered about 200 local societies. The movement was introduced to China in 1895, a society being founded in Foochow.

The last half of the nineteenth century witnessed a growing effort on the part of world missionary leaders to achieve cooperation in their common tasks through a series of interdenominational conferences. As early as 1858 missionaries from the United States, the British Isles, and continental Europe held a conference in South India; a second conference which included Ceylon was convened in 1879. In 1877 and 1890 Protestant missionaries in China met in conference. Missionaries from North America sought to improve interdenominational cooperation through the Foreign Missions Conference of North America founded in 1893, which eventually included the vast majority of Protestant missionary societies in the United States and Canada. It met annually for the discussion of mutual problems and opportunities; its executive agency was the Committee on Reference and Counsel. As a result of its activities many educational institutions in foreign countries came under interdenominational auspices and in a number of mission fields cooperative agencies began to function.

NATIONALISM AND WORLD MISSIONS

The last two decades of the nineteenth century saw an increasing wave of expansionist sentiment which would sweep the United States into war and introduce an era of unequalled enthusiasm for world missions. To the average American Christian the extension of national influence and power and the propagation of the faith were but different sides of the same coin. The synthesis to some extent had been achieved by the writings of missionaries, who called for the advance of American political influence in order that backward countries might be saved from native despotism or European imperialism. It was also furthered by Josiah Strong's *Our Country* (1885), which promulgated Anglo-Saxon racial superiority and called upon the race to realize its historic commission from God to civilize and evangelize the inferior races of the earth. "This race of unequalled energy," he wrote, "with all the majesty of numbers and wealth behind it—the representative, let us hope, of the largest liberty, the purest Christianity, the highest civilization—having developed peculiarly aggressive traits calculated to impress its institutions upon mankind, will spread itself over the earth."[2] Thousands of readers felt the impact of that argument and accepted its thesis. In much the same spirit Theodore Roosevelt, in his *Naval War of 1812* (1882), and Captain Alfred T. Mahan, in his *The Influence of Sea Power on History* (1890), called for a more powerful navy to promote the imperialistic mercantilism of the nation and to spread superior culture. Roosevelt and Mahan also presented the doctrine, new to Americans, that war was not the worst of evils and might at times be the best means of insuring the triumph of God's righteousness. At first a shocked electorate greeted the thesis with disapproval; particularly opposed were peace societies, farmers, and labor groups. In less than a decade, however, it had received the public's general approbation and even the religious leaders of the country were finding ways to reconcile it in the light of God's will. By 1898 the nation was ideologically prepared for a crusade; its citizenry found it in the Spanish-American War.

The Churches and the Spanish-American War

For some years certain influential leaders in government, among them William H. Seward and James G. Blaine, advocated economic domination of the Caribbean, an area valuable to the United States for its raw materials. During the 1890's American interest in Cuba was especially strong, not only for economic reasons but because of its control by the Spanish who were regarded in the United States as cruel obnoxious tyrants. When Spain's harsh colonial policy prompted the Cuban people to rise up against their oppressors in a long and unsuccessful revolution which lasted from 1868 to 1878, American sympathies were overwhelmingly on the side of the rebels. A second revolution, lasting from 1895 to 1898, brought American tempers to the boiling point. Businessmen, statesmen, expansionists in every walk of life, and humanitarians believed that Cuba should be freed from Spain and brought more closely into the American sphere of influence. Few wanted war, until sensationalistic journalists such as William Randolph Hearst stirred the public by lurid and largely fictional accounts of Spanish atrocities. By 1897 thousands of chivalrous Americans were clamoring for war in the name of humanity;

[2] J. Strong, *Our Country* (Baker and Taylor, 1885), 222.

THE CHURCHES AND CRUSADING INTERNATIONALISM 503

the tension mounted throughout the year, reaching its height with the sinking of the *Maine* in February, 1898. Two months later the United States was at war with Spain, with the full blessing of the churches.

The war turned out to be more than a crusade to save the Cubans from corrupt Spain; to most Protestants it also became a divine means of extending their faith to the Philippines and Puerto Rico and ending Spanish misrule and Roman Catholic authoritarianism in those areas. Throughout the summer and fall of 1898 the pulpit and the religious press expounded to the American public their duty and opportunity in the Caribbean and the Asian archipelago. President McKinley expressed the sentiment of the average churchman when he confided to a group of his Methodist friends:

. . . I am not ashamed to tell you, gentlemen, that I went down on my knees and prayed Almighty God for light and guidance more than one night. And one night late it came to me this way . . . there was nothing left for us to do but to take them all and to educate the Filipinos and uplift and civilize and Christianize them and by God's grace do the very best we could by them, as our fellow men for whom Christ also died.[3]

To another audience, however, and on a different occasion, he spoke of the "commercial opportunity to which American statesmanship cannot be indifferent."

The swift and smashing victory over Spain, achieved by such gallant leaders as Commodore George Dewey and General William R. Shafter, made it necessary for the government to come to a decision as to the disposition of the conquered lands. To the objection of anti-imperialists in the Congress that the retention of the one-time Spanish colonies by the United States would be contrary to American democratic principles, Senator Albert Beveridge of Indiana countered with a religious argument. He maintained that God "has made us adept in government that we may administer government among savage and senile peoples" and that "He has marked the American people as His chosen nation to finally lead in the regeneration of the world." It was as Beveridge wished. By the terms of the treaty signed with Spain at the end of 1898, the United States gained the Philippines, Puerto Rico, and Guam; Cuba was permitted to set up a republic. With the restoration of peace, the United States was well along the way to becoming a great world power.

Crusading Missions

Expansionist policy provided a strong impetus to foreign mission work, enthusiasm for which reached its height in America between 1898 and 1917. The mission enterprise was now popularly conceived to be a

[3] C. Olcott, *The Life of William McKinley* (Houghton Mifflin, 1916), II, 110–111.

patriotic venture. Throughout the country church benevolences for
foreign missions increased by staggering proportions, a development
which was reflected in the statistical reports of the missionaries; there
were more workers, more converts, more churches, schools, and hospitals
than ever before. Bigness had invaded the mission field. At the same time
there was an unusual change in the motivation behind the mission program. Gone was the stress on rescuing the heathen from eternal damnation. In the light of the new theology, which emphasized the dignity of
man and his supreme worth in the sight of God, it seemed somewhat
inconsistent to talk of a merciful loving Father sending persons to perdition for not accepting a Gospel they had never heard. Conservative
theologians still held to the older view, but they found it poor strategy to
hold it too often before the general public. Democratic and humanitarian
philosophies, if not as yet successful in creating official modifications of
theology, were undoubtedly contributing to the recession of certain concepts such as the idea of eternal damnation, and ecclesiastical leaders
were powerless to halt the change in ideology.

Another potent fact was that the missionaries of this period were far
less likely to combine religious with imperialistic interests than were their
supporters at home. In many instances there was open antagonism
between missionaries and western merchants who sought to exploit the
natives. It was the consensus that businessmen frequently were a hin-
drance to the missionary program since they created an unfavorable
impression of Christianity. It was ironic that these same missionaries
should have received so much support from businessmen at home who
conceived of missions in a very different light. For example, the Laymen's
Missionary Movement, founded in 1906 in order to finance the enterprise
which was attracting so many devoted workers, was made up almost
entirely of businessmen. The organization had been effected as a result
of the enthusiasm engendered by that year's quadrennial convention of
the Student Volunteer Movement and developed as an interdenominational fellowship.

American humanitarianism and radiant optimism over the success of
the missionary enterprise were sharply revealed in the Student Volunteer
Movement after 1898. In 1900, Robert E. Speer, advocate extraordinary of
missions and a secretary of the Presbyterian Board of Foreign Missions,
declared that "the world needs to be saved from want and disease and
injustice and inequality and impurity and lust and hopelessness and
fear. . . ." John R. Mott, beloved chairman of the Student Volunteers,
was certain that these needs could be met, and in 1900 he assured
Protestant Christians in his book entitled *The Evangelization of the
World in This Generation* that if they would combine their forces in a
wholly committed effort his suggested goal was not impossible of attainment. By 1915 more than 5000 men and women had been enlisted as mis-

sionary workers, chiefly through the appeal of the Student Volunteers. Additional incentive for the foreign mission enterprise was created by the Missionary Education Movement, initiated in 1902 to further missionary education in all Protestant communions. Forty-seven denominations came to be affiliated with this body, the chief activity of which was the publication of missionary literature.

Missionary fields which excited the greatest popular interest in America immediately after the Spanish-American War were, of course, those in countries recently annexed by the United States. Before entering Puerto Rico in 1899, which had previously been untouched by Protestant missions, the Baptists, Congregationalists, Disciples of Christ, Methodists, Presbyterians, and United Brethren met in conference and agreed to divide their fields of mission. In Cuba, the denominations also divided their spheres of responsibility; they had gained almost 17,000 communicants by 1915. As the years passed there proved to be a greater need for interdenominational cooperation in the Latin American countries. To that end the Committee on Co-operation in Latin America was formed among Protestants in 1914, with headquarters in New York City. Through holding conferences at Panama in 1916 and Montevideo in 1925, it made an important contribution to Protestant missions in Latin America.

In the Pacific, the Protestant denominations at the termination of the war began to evangelize Guam and the Philippines. The American Board of Commissioners for Foreign Missions sent missionaries to Guam in 1900. Ten years later they were recalled; the next missionary program was inaugurated by American Baptists in 1911. Before instituting activities in the Philippines, representatives of denominational mission boards met in New York City in the summer of 1898 to allocate areas of responsibility. Though impeded by the Filipino insurrection of 1899–1902, led by the guerrilla Aguinaldo, Northern Methodists and Presbyterians, U.S.A., were at work in 1899. A year later the northern Baptists arrived, while in 1901 and 1902 the first representatives of the United Brethren, the Disciples of Christ, and the Congregationalists were sent out to found stations. In 1901 Charles H. Brent of the Protestant Episcopal Church was elected missionary bishop of the Philippines. The first important interdenominational work was begun in 1901, when the Baptists, Congregationalists, Disciples, Methodists, Presbyterians, and United Brethren formed the Evangelical Union of the Philippine Islands. A union theological seminary was founded in Manila for the education of a native ministry.

Throughout the mission fields the period after 1900 witnessed the growth of interdenominational agencies and increasing recognition of the importance of native leadership. Especially was this true in Japan, the most progressive of the Oriental countries. In 1907 three Methodist missions merged to form the Japanese Methodist Church, which was placed under Japanese control. Four years later 80 per cent of the native Christians were organized into a Japanese federation of churches. A similar federation was born in India as the result of conferences held in 1909.

While the Roman Catholic Church in America had been generous in its monetary contributions to the world-wide missions of the church, many of which had been established for centuries, as late as 1906 only a dozen or more American Roman Catholics were serving in foreign fields; these represented the Franciscans and the Sisters of Charity. The first school for training foreign missionaries was St. Mary's Mission House in Techny, Illinois, founded in 1909. Maryknoll, the first American society dedicated to foreign missions, was organized at Hawthorne, New York, in 1912; six years later it commissioned its first priests for China.

After 1900, possibly the most remarkable Protestant missionary program was conducted by the Seventh-day Adventists. A relatively small denomination, they were fired by the conviction that the second coming of Christ was imminent and that Christians were expected to labor with dispatch to the end that the Gospel might be made available to all men. Before the opening of the twentieth century they had established footholds in such countries as Natal, Rhodesia, South Africa, India, Japan, Australia, New Zealand, Tahiti, Fiji, Hawaii, Java, Chile, Argentina, Brazil, and areas of Central America. These missions, which developed slowly at first, became flourishing during the twentieth century and additional stations were opened in such lands as Burma, China, Korea, the Philippines, Jamaica, British Guiana, Venezuela, Ecuador, Peru, and Bolivia.

THE PEACE MOVEMENT

Long before Theodore Roosevelt presented his famous justification of war, a movement for the preservation of peace had gradually been gaining momentum. Once strong in America, it had suffered a serious setback during the period leading up to the Civil War era, and did not begin to enjoy a revival until the 1860's. The activities of the American Peace Society, for many decades the leading champion of peace on the American scene, were supplemented after 1866 by the Universal Peace Union and after 1889 by the Department of Peace and Arbitration of the W.C.T.U. Denominational organizations such as the Peace Association of the Friends, founded in 1869, also did much to bring the cause of peace to the attention of the American public. The rising tide of popular interest in the achievement of world peace was reflected in the Universal Peace Congress held in Chicago in 1893, and the Lake Mohonk (New York) Arbitration Conferences which were initiated in 1895 by the Quaker businessman Albert K. Smiley. These conferences helped to spark the Conference of Friends which was convened in Philadelphia in 1901 solely for the purpose of discussing peace. Another direct outgrowth of these annual conferences was the movement for international arbitration, which was highly endorsed by American statesmen. In 1899 the representatives of twenty-six nations met at The Hague to discuss plans for the promotion of universal peace. This conference formulated principles for the conduct of warfare and founded a Permanent Court of Arbitration with headquarters at The Hague. An equally successful second Hague conference with delegates from forty-four countries was held in 1907.

After the Spanish-American War, proponents of peace throughout the nation multiplied rapidly. Among many groups the crusade for peace was identified with the campaign against imperialism. In view of a mounting enthusiasm for colonialism, it seemed judicious to anti-imperialists and peace advocates to join forces for the advancement of their mutual interests. Prominent intellectuals such as William Graham Sumner, William James, Jane Addams, Mark Twain, and William Jennings Bryan argued passionately that in the long run imperialism would prove ruinous to the nation and would lead to horrible conflict and the destruction of basic human rights. But it was obvious after the election of 1900 that a majority of the electorate had not yet subscribed to these views.

Nevertheless, in the years immediately following 1901 the peace movement made notable strides in the churches. In 1902 a group of clergymen met in New York City and organized the American Association of Ministers for the advancement of peace. Thereafter the peace movement in the United States was definitely on the offensive. Through its Department of Peace and Arbitration, the W.C.T.U. published a study course entitled "World Peace" for Sunday Schools, youth groups, and women's organizations. It reported in 1905 that more peace sermons had been delivered that year than at any time previously. The American Peace Society more than doubled its membership and took on new vigor as it reestablished its headquarters at Washington, D.C., in 1912. Many denominations regarded it fitting to attack war as uncivilized and unchristian and issued pronouncements to that effect. This sentiment was movingly expressed in the Episcopal Address before the General Conference of the Methodist Episcopal Church in 1912:

Even while the churches are calling upon rulers to submit all international disputes to arbitration, our own republic answers with more doves of peace made of steel, breathing fire and winged with death. . . . The people can and must assert their nobler love of country by demanding that no American battleship shall disgrace its colors in a war for trade, or in any war, until every peaceful resort has been thoroughly tried. . . . Let every Methodist pulpit ring out clearly and insistently for Peace by Arbitration.[4]

[4] Quoted in Sweet, *Methodism in American History*, 371.

On the interdenominational and interfaith levels, various agencies betokened the rising influence of the movement for world peace. Leaders of the Federal Council of Churches, newly founded in 1908 as a voice of cooperative Protestantism, became interested in holding a world conference of churches to consider the peace question and the organization of a world peace association. In 1911, Dr. Charles S. Macfarland of the Federal Council conferred with European leaders on these matters. Three years later Andrew Carnegie contributed two million dollars for the work of the churches toward peace; the funds were administered by the Church Peace Union, a foundation with representatives from Protestant, Roman Catholic, and Jewish bodies. Through a grant from the Union, a conference of delegates from European and American Protestant communions at Constance, Switzerland, in August, 1914, was made financially possible. The conference, however, was little more than a futile gesture since by this time Europe was being drawn irresistibly into the vortex of war. At a conference held at Berne in 1915 the association, temporarily obstructed but undaunted by the horrible conflict, named itself the World Alliance for Promoting International Friendship through the Churches.

Meanwhile, peace enthusiasts in the American churches had for a decade been assuring themselves of the certain triumph of their cause, seemingly oblivious to the ominous rattling of sabers in Central Europe. The tenor of the times was irenic, the national world view exultantly optimistic. What was so remarkable about the era was that the impulse toward internationalism was being welded to the campaign for peace, so that America's role as a leader in world affairs was increasingly being seen as that of peacemaker. The power of the nation must be directed to the achievement of lasting international peace. The clergy had no monopoly on this idea; it had been enunciated with great clarity and persuasiveness by such distinguished laymen as Charles W. Eliot and Nicholas Murray Butler, in education; James J. Hill, in finance; and William Howard Taft and Woodrow Wilson, in government.

When trouble broke out on the Mexican border after the Mexican Revolution of 1911, it was principally the Hearst papers that urged governmental intervention; the public was much less enthusiastic, and many expressed horror at the thought of sending American boys to fight on foreign soil. This attitude was most evident in the official policy of neutralism with which the United States greeted the outbreak of hostilities in Europe. A steady barrage of allied propaganda, especially the highly exaggerated reports of German atrocities in Belgium, evoked from the shocked American public a general reaction of contempt for the "German Hun," which was intensified by German submarine attacks resulting in the loss of American lives and by the German refusal to accept President Wilson as a mediator of the peace. While the religious press and the pulpit continued, on the whole, to favor the administration's efforts to keep the United States out of war, there was a gradual shift of sentiment, notably in the East, toward intervention. By April, 1917, Americans had been persuaded that, in the words of their President, "the world must be made safe for democracy," and that the war was not an imperialistic conflict but a crusade for the triumph of good over evil. And so the United States entered the maelstrom of war, with self-justification born of a sense of divine calling. Through America's intervention, succeeding generations might raise their children in a better, safer world.

THE CHURCHES AND WORLD WAR I

In no previous conflict had the American people supported their government with such exuberance as in World War I. Whatever elements of pro-German or neutralist sentiment were still existent by April, 1917, were drowned by a vociferous demonstration of patriotism. Every talent and every strength was mobilized for the country's service. The tremendous overseas operation demanded far more than a well-trained fighting force; there was need of skilled workers for munition factories, experienced farmers to produce an adequate food supply, doctors and dentists to care for the sick and wounded, and persons of artistic and literary ability to minister to the psychological needs of combatants and civilians. The rapidity with which the normally independent American citizenry adjusted to the demands of a society at war was little short of phenomenal. It was possible because of their deep sense of purpose and destiny which propelled them to volunteer for whatever service they might be qualified to render. There were those who found no sympathy for the war, but they were anathema.

The Religious Reaction to War

No American group rose more enthusiastically to the occasion afforded by the government's declaration of hostilities than the churches. Denomination after denomination greeted the news of America's entry into the Great War with official pronouncements which reflected their approbation of this course of action and affirmed their complete loyalty to the national cause. The Protestant Episcopal Church, for example, through its House of Bishops, assured President Wilson and his cabinet in October, 1917, of "our patriotic support of the Government, pledging ourselves to cooperate in every possible way to aid, sustain, and protect the brave soldiers and sailors of this great Christian nation in the heroic efforts to destroy the oppression, tyranny, and brutality now threatening the world, and to establish justice, righteousness, and liberty among all nations." While the bishops abhorred war, they recognized that every citizen should consecrate himself to the service of his country. "To express this, we must not only work for the Red Cross and give generously in money and comforts; we must also be ready to pay heavy taxes cheerfully and to buy Liberty Bonds."[5]

Possibly no religious body was more eloquent in its support of the crusade than the Troy Conference of the Methodist Episcopal Church, which resolved in 1918: "We see the trembling lines above which float the Tricolor and the Union Jack, as the hellish Hunnish hordes beat against them to seize the panting throat of the world. We hear the cry 'Hurry up, America,' and we go with fierce passion for world freedom to twine with Union Jack and Tri-color the Stars and Stripes and say to the sinister black eagle flag of Germany, 'You shall not pass.'"[6] The General Assembly of the Presbyterian Church, U.S.A., declared in 1918 that the war was "most just and holy." Just ten days after America's entry into the war the Roman Catholic archbishops meeting at the Catholic University, adopted this pledge of loyalty:

Our people, as ever, will rise as one man to serve the nation. Our priests and consecrated women will once again, as in every former trial of their country, win by their bravery, their heroism and their service new admiration and approval. We are all true Americans, ready as our age, our ability and our condition permits, to do whatever is in us to do for the preservation, the progress and the triumph of our beloved country.[7]

All over the country patriotic clergymen preached the righteousness of America's cause and exhorted their congregations to do their utmost that a full and quick victory might be assured. To many ministers, the Sermon on the Mount was something of an embarrassment, as was the gentle Christ who turned the other cheek. More palatable were the stern prophets of the Old Testament and the indignant Christ who cast out the moneychangers from the Jerusalem temple with a whip of small cords. John Henry Jowett, eminent preacher at the Fifth Avenue Presbyterian Church, New York, counseled his people to regard themselves as Christian soldiers, in a sermon preached on January 6, 1918. He said: "Fight to make God's love known! Fight to get God's will done! Then the new year in Christ will be a glorious year, the best of all the years, full of life, full of purpose, full of joy, and full of victory." Across the river in Brooklyn, the colorful Newell Dwight Hillis of Plymouth Congregational Church eloquently extolled the glories of military service. "That battlefield yonder in France to-day is sending earth's richest souls upward to heaven as the seas exhale their whitest mists, their purest clouds. In this

---

[5] Quoted in J. Addison, *op. cit.*, 308.
[6] Quoted in Sweet, *Methodism in American History*, 374.
[7] Quoted in T. Maynard, *The Story of American Catholicism* (Macmillan, 1943), 534.

great hour, therefore, look toward your son and say, 'My son he is; God's soldier let him be. I could not wish him to a fairer death.'" Cardinal Gibbons spoke for his coreligionists in April, 1917, when he told a group of newsmen: "The primary duty of a citizen is loyalty to country. This loyalty is manifested more by acts than by words; by solemn service rather than by empty declaration. It is exhibited by an absolute and unreserved obedience to his country's call."[8]

Harry Emerson Fosdick, the ascending star of the Protestant pulpit, gave wholehearted support to the war effort, taking leave from his professorship at Union Theological Seminary to work abroad with the Y.M.C.A. At the same time he felt that war was unchristian and under no consideration could be regarded as a safeguard against further conflict. He could not agree with the venerable Lyman Abbott, who wrote: "The armies of the Allies are in the strictest sense of the term officers of peace. They are fighting for peace. They might as well bear upon their banners the inscription, 'Blessed are the peacemakers, for they shall be called the children of God.'"[9] Equally restrained was Robert E. Speer, Secretary of the Presbyterian Board of Foreign Missions, who appealed to his Christian brethren to "be rid of our prejudice and passion, to chant no hymns of hate, to keep our aims and our principles free from selfishness and from any national interest which is not also the interest of all nations. . . ."

In the public utterances of certain Christian leaders there was evidence of a bitter and vindictive spirit. Thus the man who hated everything German, Newell Dwight Hillis, was moved to remark that "lovers of their fellowmen have finally become hopeless with reference to the German people. They have no more relation to the civilization of 1918 than an orangoutang, a gorilla, a Judas, a hyena, a thumbscrew, or a scalpingknife in the hands of a savage. These brutes must be cast out of society." Billy Sunday, that peripatetic foe of sin, followed the same line of thought when he prayed in the United States House of Representatives in January, 1918: "Thou knowest, O Lord, that no nation so infamous, vile, greedy, sensuous, blood-thirsty, ever disgraced the pages of history. Make bare thy mighty arm, O Lord, and smite the hungry, wolfish Hun, whose fangs drip with blood, and we will forever raise our voice to thy praise."[10] Applause followed the prayer. Popular prejudice against Germans, fanned by a flood of propaganda, extended even to the language; several states passed legislation against the use of German in public services, a fact which had much to do with the rapid shift to the use of English among German-speaking Lutherans.

Both the government and the public meted out harsh treatment to

[8] Quoted in J. Ellis, *American Catholicism* (Chicago, 1956), 136.
[9] Quoted in W. Garrison, *The March of Faith* (Harper, 1933), 240.
[10] *Ibid.*, 243.

opponents of the war. Labor organizations such as the Industrial Workers of the World, which promoted great strikes in the copper mines and lumber camps, felt the full impact of an irate public. There was also much contempt shown for members of pacifist denominations and individual conscientious objectors. By law, adherents of such recognized pacifist bodies as the Friends and Mennonites were exempted from military service, but there was considerable confusion in dealing with conscientious objectors, many of whom were thrown into prison camps. The less than 100 clergymen known to have held pacifist positions were persecuted for their views. John Haynes Holmes, prominent Unitarian minister in New York, was vilified for his stand against the war and was repudiated by his own congregation. Paul Jones, Protestant Episcopal Missionary Bishop of Utah, was investigated by the House of Bishops on suspicion of political disloyalty and in the face of pressure resigned from his episcopal post. Due to the distemper of the times, there were even instances in which pacifist ministers were mobbed, beaten, tarred and feathered, or otherwise mistreated by overzealous patriots.

The Churches and Wartime Service

Merely a cursory study of denominational histories will reveal how vigorously the churches supported the war effort. In a thousand ways they boosted the morale of the nation through activities which ranged from the sale of Liberty Bonds and the dedication of service flags to the entertainment of military personnel and the knitting of socks, caps, and sweaters for them by ladies' groups. The Federal Council of Churches, representing the evangelical denominations, founded a General Wartime Commission to act as a clearinghouse for information and to coordinate the work of the churches.

In August, 1917, Presiding Bishop Daniel Tuttle of the Protestant Episcopal Church appointed a War Commission to minister to combatants and assist the work of the denomination's 212 chaplains in the army and navy. It enlisted nearly 100 civilian chaplains to complement the work of military chaplains in camps and cantonments. The churches' Joint Commission on Army and Navy Chaplains screened applicants for the chaplaincy and was instrumental in persuading the Congress to increase the quota of chaplains to one for every 1200 men. Seven of the Lutheran bodies cooperated through the National Lutheran Commission for Soldiers' and Sailors' Welfare, organized in October, 1917. The Commission helped to recruit 100 military chaplains, supported 150 camp pastors, and operated four service houses in eastern cities. It raised more than a million dollars for the benefit of the boys in uniform. Similarly the Methodist Episcopal Church created a National War Council which was concerned with Methodist chaplains (of whom there were about 325), visiting clergymen in the camps, activities for service men, and war industry work. Methodists both North and South, like many other denominations, furnished the men in uniform with books, tracts, pamphlets, and multigraphed news sheets.

Roman Catholic contributions to the war enterprise were channeled through the National Catholic War Council under the chairmanship of Father John J. Burke, editor of the *Catholic World*. It carried on such varied projects as assisting Roman Catholic chaplains and promoting the Liberty Loan drives. The church set a precedent in the appointment of a Chaplain-General, under whose ecclesiastical jurisdiction were placed the more than 1000 Roman Catholic priests in the armed forces.

Various church-sponsored and non-denominational service organizations ministered in countless ways to military personnel at home and abroad. Next to the Red Cross, the most valuable welfare agency among the troops was the Y.M.C.A. By appointment of the War Department in 1917 the Y.M.C.A. was commissioned to operate the official canteens and to "provide for the amusement and recreation of the troops by means of its usual program of social, educational, physical and religious activities." Its agents were authorized to wear the regulation army uniform with appropriate insignia. More than 11,000 workers served abroad with the American Expeditionary Forces. In addition to canteen services, the Y.M.C.A. distributed a large quantity of religious literature and sent leading clergymen to preach to the troops in camp.

The activities of the Knights of Columbus, principally among Roman Catholic soldiers, were similar to those of the Y.M.C.A., and for a time the Knights were under the aegis of the latter. Special programs for Jewish men in arms were provided by the Jewish Welfare Board and the Young Men's Hebrew Association. Canteen services were also rendered by the Salvation Army, while the American Bible Society gave away more than a million testaments in fulfillment of its slogan, "A Khaki Testament in Every Kit."

Despite the fact that the war withdrew from the churches many of their most responsible workers, organized religion suffered no lack of attention or support. Most congregations were beehives of activity and their programs, necessarily modified by the war, featured services by ladies' groups and men who had not been drawn into military service. If their religion was unruffled by winds of doctrine, it did not matter; the Kingdom which they sought would come through the work of their hands, and never were hands busier in laboring for a righteous cause.

As the war progressed the denominations became more engrossed in plans for the evangelization of the world as soon as the return of peace made that possible. Baptists, Disciples, Methodists, Presbyterians, and other denominational bodies launched great drives to raise funds for world missions. In 1918–1919 the Methodist Episcopal Church inaugurated a five-year program in commemoration of the beginning of Methodist missions in 1819; its projected goal was to raise forty million dollars. Financially, the drive was a notable success, for by 1923 more than fifty-five million dollars had been collected. Equally successful were the Disciples of Christ in their Men and Millions Movement, which endeavored to enlist 1000 persons for Christian service and raise six million dollars for colleges and missions. The Presbyterians, U.S.A., through their New Era Movement, raised their Home Missions receipts from $558,253 in 1918 to $1,020,716 in 1922. Much less satisfying were the results of the Northern Baptist New World Movement; between 1919 and 1924 only half of the desired sum of one hundred million dollars was raised. This was the first time that the churches used professional techniques on a large scale for raising funds; the campaigns, however, were costly and much money was wasted through careless and lavish spending, a source of displeasure to many thoughtful church members.

The most grandiose scheme to come out of the period was the Inter-Church World Movement, founded at the close of the war in the hope of achieving a federation of the evangelical churches and raising a large sum for religious and charitable purposes. It had been born of a mounting desire for cooperation and union among American Protestants. Essentially it was a five-year plan to consolidate the programs and budgets of the participating denominations. An immense campaign of promotion was undertaken in the assurance that staggering sums would be pledged, but the public wholly failed to respond according to expectation. The heavy campaign debts finally had to be turned over to the cooperating churches for payment. It was apparent by 1920 that the age of idealism, of crusading internationalism, was rapidly drawing to a close. Just ahead lay the erratic years of national introversion, financial boom, and reckless abandon, ending without glory in the silent, lean years of depression.

26

Religious Cults Since the Civil War

THE CULT PHENOMENON, A DISTINCTIVE FEATURE OF RELIGION IN THE UNITED States, reached its full flowering in the rise of modern, urban, industrial America. Multitudinous forces contributed to this interesting circumstance in which religious minority groups, most of them on the fringe of Christianity, were nurtured and developed. Most basic was the voluntary principle, which admitted no state church and encouraged the fullest freedom of religious expression. Equally important factors were the heterogeneity of American society, the competitive impulse in religion as well as business, and the spirit of individualism which fostered the development of splinter groups and unique religious emphases. Undoubtedly, the relative lack of traditions and conventions in American life gave incentive for experimentation and made for instability.

Social, economic, and cultural factors played a significant role in the evolution of the cults. For the poor, crowded into vermin-possessed tenements and forced to lead what seemed an inconsequential existence, some of the cults offered refuge and release. They provided an escape whereby the disconsolate might retreat from the sordid world of reality and find identity and peace in a fellowship of the concerned. They likewise provided a refuge for those with acute emotional needs and gave them a sense of belonging and a resuscitated hope for the future. Many of the cults thrived because they appealed to the American obsession with both inward and outward success. Especially did they appeal to the desire for status and well being, promising financial prosperity, good health, peace of mind, and a successful marriage. Some took obvious advantage of the American predilection for the sensational and treated a public thrilled by Barnum and Bailey to fantastic exhibitions of the bizarre and occult. To the initiated they offered revelations of esoteric knowledge, often transmitted from ancient times by mystic seers who had attained remarkable insights into the mysteries of life. The mental science cults in particular seem to have had an unusual attraction for women, possibly because of their intuitive appeal and their emphasis upon peace and health, and it is probably not accidental that women should have figured prominently in the founding of such cults as Spiritualism, Christian Science, I Am, Unity, and Theosophy.

DEVELOPMENTS IN MORMONISM AND SPIRITUALISM

The decades immediately following the Civil War witnessed a long and involved struggle between the Church of Jesus Christ of Latter-day Saints and the federal government over the question of polygamy. Joseph Smith had reported plural marriage to have been divinely revealed and it had since been indulged in by a small percentage of the Mormon community, Brigham Young setting an example with twenty-seven wives. Most non-Mormons regarded the institution as an effrontery to Christian morals; aroused by public opinion, as early as 1862 the national government passed the Morrill Act which made polygamy illegal. The Mormons fought this law all the way to the United States Supreme Court, but the decision in 1878 was against them. According to the provisions of the Edmunds Act of 1882, actual polygamists might be punished by disfranchisement and imprisonment. In 1887 the government dissolved the corporation of the church, confiscated much of its property, and fined and imprisoned hundreds of polygamists. Three years later the head of the church, President Wilford Woodruff, directed that plural marriage cease, a decision which was approved by a general conference of Mormons. When Utah was admitted as a state in 1896, the third article of its constitution expressly prohibited polygamy.

A perennial danger in the opinion of non-Mormons in the late nineteenth century was what they deemed a highly autocratic ecclesiastical system which aimed to dominate the state. Unquestionably the church was structured along hierarchical lines. At its head was a President and two Counselors, constituting a First Presidency. Below them were the

Council of the Twelve Apostles which supervised the work of the church and ordained ministers, the First Council of the Seventy, and a series of lesser offices. The church was divided geographically into stakes, composed of wards or parishes, and missions. Mormon ecclesiastical polity, however, seems not to have unduly influenced the church to seek domination of the state. That the church's voice, because of its numerical strength, is heard in the legislative halls of Utah in no wise proves that the church stands opposed to the traditional separation of church and state.

As opposition to Mormons gradually waned with the progression of the twentieth century, the church enjoyed unusual vitality. Believing as it did in continued revelations from the Lord, in the establishment of Zion on the American continent, and in the personal reign of Christ upon the earth, it felt the necessity of spreading these beliefs as widely as possible; consequently it developed a flourishing mission program in the United States, Europe, and other foreign lands, which it maintained through the devoted giving of time and substance of its membership. By 1957 the church enjoyed a membership of 1,339,638.

Spiritualism had suffered no significant losses as a result of the exposé of the famous Fox sisters. Professional mediums continued to attract a following, especially in the cities, and by 1863 the movement, now under the leadership of the well-known clairvoyant Andrew Jackson Davis, was large enough to justify a national organization which lasted nine years. The first permanent organization on a national level was the National Spiritualist Association founded in Chicago in 1893. Thereafter the movement took on the definite character of a church. Its teaching emphasized the love of God, the Golden Rule, the continuation of personal identity after death, and the possibility of communication with the deceased. While Spiritualists continued to stress the importance of seances or communications with the departed, most of their churches held services much like those of evangelical Protestants.

The fact that from 1916 to 1926 Spiritualism enjoyed the phenomenal gain of 74 per cent in membership may be explained at least partially by the awakened concern over the meaning of death evoked by World War I and the popular hope that contact might be established with loved ones killed in action. This awakened interest was stimulated by the work of the Society for Psychical Research and by the writings of Sir Oliver Lodge and Sir Arthur Conan Doyle. Many persons who retained their affiliation with the major denominations were so deeply influenced by the investigations of these famous men that they frequented Spiritualist centers in the hope of receiving messages from the departed. Especially popular were the summer assemblies held at Lily Dale, New York, and Chesterfield, Indiana. The two larger bodies of Spiritualists by the mid-twentieth century were the International General Assembly of Spiritualists, organized in 1936, and the National Spiritualist Association of Churches; their combined reported membership for 1957 was about 173,000.

CHRISTIAN SCIENCE AND THE NEW THOUGHT CULTS

Various forces contributed to the rise of several cults in the late nineteenth century based upon philosophical idealism and emphasizing the attainment of right states of mind and healing by faith. These cults were encouraged indirectly by New England Transcendentalism, particularly as expressed by Ralph Waldo Emerson and Bronson Alcott in their attacks on materialism and their proclamation of divine immanence and the essential goodness of human nature. A more direct influence may be traced to Franz Anton Mesmer, a German physician who conducted studies in psychotherapy from 1774 to 1814 and concluded that a mysterious magnetic fluid was the explanation for the mental power one might exercise over another. Mesmerism or hypnotism was introduced to America in 1838 by the Frenchman Charles Poyen; in the audience at Belfast, Maine, was a man destined to become the pioneer American mental healer, Phineas Parkhurst Quimby (1802–1866), of Portland. The son of a blacksmith, he received little formal education but read rather widely in the fields of philosophy and science. Becoming interested in hypnotism in 1838, he associated himself with another hypnotist and offered his services to patients, diagnosing their ills and prescribing remedies through the aid of hypnosis. Becoming increasingly convinced that the healing process was mental, Quimby began to experiment with healing through suggestion without use of hypnotism. He believed that this was the method Jesus and his disciples employed in their acts of healing and that such seemingly miraculous cures were really quite natural and could be performed in every generation. Since disease was merely the result of wrong belief, his remedy for suffering patients was to disabuse them of their errors and plant truth and healing in their place.

Christian Science

One of Quimby's patients was a frail, sickly woman with neurasthenic tendencies, Mrs. Mary Baker Glover Patterson Eddy (1821–1910), a native of New Hampshire. Formerly a weak and impressionable child, she had been for some years a partial invalid. Indeed, it was not until she was past forty that she began to travel the road which would lead her to Christian Science. During one of her frequent attacks from a spinal infection, she heard of the healing work of Phineas P. Quimby; in 1862 she became his patient and was healed. There can be no doubt that she was deeply impressed by Quimby's ideas, despite the fact that she later denied

Quimby's influence in the development of her teachings. In an article in the *Portland Courier* for November 7, 1862, she wrote: "But now I can see, dimly at first, and only as trees walking the great principle which underlines Dr. Quimby's faith and works, and just in proportion to my right perception of truth is my recovery. . . . The truth which he establishes in the patient cures him. . . ."

According to a later statement by Mrs. Eddy, it was in 1866 that she discovered Christian Science. That year she was injured by a fall on the ice and her doctor informed her that she would never walk again. In two days, however, she did walk, a joyous experience which she later referred to as "the falling apple that led me to the discovery how to be well myself and how to make others so." During the years following 1866, Mrs. Eddy devoted much of her time to reducing her thoughts to writing and giving organization to her textbook of Christian Science appropriately entitled *Science and Health,* which was issued in 1875. This same period found her training students as practitioners in Lynn, Massachusetts. By 1875 she had effected the first organization of a society, composed largely of factory workers and other artisans. In 1879 she and her followers were granted a charter for the Church of Christ (Scientist), with headquarters in Boston. Mrs. Eddy remained in Lynn, where she founded the Massachusetts Metaphysical College in her home in 1881; its purpose was to train healers. Dissatisfied with her small number of converts, she decided to move to Boston. This decision proved to be one of the wisest she ever made. To no group in American society was her therapeutic ministry more appealing than to hysteria-ridden city dwellers who longed for the promise of health and long life. The result was that her lagging movement took on a sudden spurt of vitality.

By 1890 the movement had won nearly 9000 members meeting in more than 200 local groups, a majority of which were in the larger cities of the Middle West. It was apparent during this decade that Christian Science was beginning to appeal more to persons in the higher income brackets and that it was becoming increasingly well-to-do. In 1892, Mrs. Eddy organized the "Mother Church" in Boston as the national church and invited Christian Scientists all over the country to unite with it. Twelve charter members were appointed to pass upon all candidates for membership. The church was governed by rules approved by the Board of Directors and a collection of by-laws written by Mrs. Eddy, which together constituted the *Church Manual.* An additional by-law issued by the foundress in 1895 declared the Bible and *Science and Health* to be "pastor on this planet of all the Churches of the Christian Science denomination," thus replacing individuals who had served in that capacity.

Mrs. Eddy's teachings were grounded in acosmic pantheism, which found spirit alone to be real and eternal and matter to be nothing more than "an image in mortal mind." She defined God, the only reality, as "the great I am; the all-knowing, all-seeing, all-acting, all-wise, all-loving, and eternal; Principle; Mind; Soul; Spirit; Life; Truth; Love; all substance; intelligence." She also spoke of God as the Trinity of Life, Truth, and Love and as God the Father-Mother, Christ the spiritual idea of sonship, and divine science the Holy Comforter. To her the significance of Jesus Christ was not that he rendered an objective atonement but that he showed men the way to union with God.

Salvation, for Mrs. Eddy, was "Life, Truth, and Love, understood and demonstrated as supreme over all; sin, sickness and death destroyed." Sickness and death were illusions and sin consisted in regarding them as realities. Such error could be overcome in this existence; indeed, the realization of Christian perfection was an ideal possibility to be accomplished by the reception of "truth through flood-tides of love." Mrs. Eddy refused to limit salvation to this life, for man was spiritual and therefore immortal. Life went on upon another plane or state of existence. As for morality in this life, Mrs. Eddy's teachings followed the pattern of late nineteenth century evangelical Protestantism by repudiating tobacco, intoxicating drinks, and sensuous pleasures. Social work did not become one of her interests, probably because poverty, like sickness, was an error of mortal mind.

The authoritarian manner in which Mrs. Eddy governed the affairs of Christian Science led to conflicts in the church and in some cases schism. The most notable withdrawal came in 1909 as the result of friction between Mrs. Eddy and Mrs. Augusta E. Stetson, wealthy and highly successful leader of the Christian Science organization in New York. Mrs. Stetson's followers remained loyal to her and joined her in founding a new group called the Church Triumphant. The main body continued to flourish, especially in the idealistic, optimistic period which lasted through World War I. Since the church has officially prohibited any membership reports, it is impossible to estimate its numerical strength. The last Census of Religious Bodies taken in 1936 reported a membership of 268,915.

New Thought, Unity, and Psychiana

After the death of Phineas P. Quimby in 1866, his movement, which later came to be known as New Thought, was carried on by Warren Felt Evans, a Swedenborgian minister, and by Julius Dresser, both of whom had been healed by Quimby. The movement continued to grow in strength and in 1894 the first national convention was held in San Francisco. The International New Thought Alliance was organized in 1914. According to a statement made by its leaders in 1916, its purpose was "to teach the infinitude of the Supreme one, the Divinity of Man and his infinite possibilities through the creative power of constructive thinking and obedience to the voice of the Indwelling Presence which is our Source of Inspiration, Power, Health and Prosperity." Philosophically, New Thought was monistic, but it was frequently difficult to ascertain whether its followers held to pantheism or simply to a pronounced doctrine of immanence. Clearly the teaching was not that of acosmic pantheism, for it accepted the reality of the material world, referring to it as mind in form. As for man, he was a spiritual being made in the image of God, who was the Good. Evil had no independent existence but was, in Platonic fashion, merely the absence of the good or pleasing. Heaven, which was a state of harmony, health, and happiness, might be attained by anyone who sought it through constructive thinking. Since New Thought neither organized as a church nor sought exclusive membership in its groups, no meaningful statistical data can be given. What is certain, however, is that through the writings and lectures of such leaders as O. S. Marden, Ralph Waldo Trine, Elizabeth Towne, Emmet Fox, and Ernest Holmes, the movement has exercised considerable influence on the American public.

Another organization of the New Thought variety was the Unity School of Christianity initiated at Kansas City, Missouri, by Charles and Myrtle Fillmore in 1889. Once attracted to Christian Science, the Fillmores had broken with Mrs. Eddy because of her alleged authoritarianism; until 1906, and from 1919 to 1922 they were affiliated with the New Thought Alliance, but being more orthodox in their doctrine of Jesus Christ, they found it unsatisfactory to remain in the New Thought fellowship. Starting with the publication of a magazine entitled *Thought,* the founders built up a publishing center which circulated thousands of books, periodicals, and pamphlets annually. Despite Mr. Fillmore's dislike of organization the movement gradually developed a churchly character with Unity Centers or congregations and, after 1933, a denominational assembly known as the Unity Annual Conference. The headquarters of the movement were subsequently moved to a 1300-acre farm near Lee's Summit, Missouri. Such theology as Unity professed was essentially practical, a guide to good living. Its view of God was like that of Christian Science, but it differed from the latter in affirming the reality of the material world and sickness and death. While it taught reincarnation until the individual, through attaining the Christ consciousness, could merit habitation in a spiritual body, its emphasis fell on finding life abundant on earth. This could be achieved by "living the Christ within." In order that persons in sickness or trouble might find wholeness, the department of Silent Unity was established as a prayer-offering service for any person who might request meditation and prayer on his behalf.

A more recent branch of the New Thought movement to come into existence was Psychiana, founded by Frank B. Robinson at Moscow, Idaho, in 1929. Scion of New Thought, Robinson established what might be fairly described as a mail-order religion and brought it to the attention of the public through his advertisement, "I Talked With God." His published lessons emphasized health, happiness, and prosperity which were available to every person who learned how to release the power of God; the technique was explained in the lessons which, within fifteen years, went out to a million people.

MISCELLANEOUS CULTS

While space will permit only a cursory examination of the many additional cults in the United States, certain representative groups may be discussed briefly. Some are wholly indigenous; others bear the distinct mark of oriental philosophies. Some are otherworldly; others are frankly materialistic. Each has had a unique appeal for certain segments of American society.

Jehovah's Witnesses

The Watch Tower Bible and Tract Society, commonly known as Jehovah's Witnesses, was founded by Charles Taze Russell in Pittsburgh in 1872. Tortured as a youth by his fear of hell, he had been driven to infidelism, a study of oriental religions, and finally a fresh scrutiny of the Bible. As a result of the Biblical studies, he became convinced that the Bible did not teach hell and that the second coming of Christ, in invisible form, would take place in the autumn of 1874. On subsequent tours about the country he had tremendous success with the poorer classes who found it comforting to believe that a new order was about to be established in which there would be peace and prosperity. In 1879 Russell began publication of a magazine entitled *Zion's Watch Tower and Herald of Christ's Presence*. The first formal organization was effected five years later under the name Zion's Watch Tower Society. In 1909 Russell set up headquarters in Brooklyn, from whence he issued immense quantities of printed material and furnished Bible lessons which were syndicated to newspapers. After his death in 1916, leadership of the movement passed to Judge J. F. Rutherford, during whose administration the name of the organization was changed to the Watch Tower Bible and Tract Society in 1939. Rutherford was succeeded in 1942 by Nathan H. Knorr. All members of the organization, which met locally in Kingdom Halls, were required to give a certain portion of their time to witnessing and distributing literature.

The theology of the movement, set forth principally by Judge Rutherford, emphasized the coming theocratic rule of Jehovah over the earth. Jesus Christ, the perfect man and the beginning of God's creation, was God's representative on earth, sent to save men and establish the Theocracy. After Christ's resurrection he ascended to heaven, but returned in 1914 to reign as king in the midst of his enemies. This reign of course could be understood only in a spiritual sense. Antecedent to the establishment of the Theocracy was the battle of Armageddon and the destruction of evil, imminent events according to Judge Rutherford. The righteous would survive the battle and remain forever on the earth. Then would follow the resurrection of the dead and a thousand-year reign of peace. After that time Satan and the wicked would be destroyed. The Witnesses have been openly critical of the churches, claiming them to be enemies of the truth. They have also come into conflict with the government over their refusal to salute the flag and their efforts to persuade the government to recognize their male members as ministers and therefore exempt from conscription.

Theosophy and the Esoteric Cults

Theosophy is one of those groups which proved attractive to a number of nineteenth-century Americans who desired to delve into the mysteries of Eastern religions. It appealed to liberally minded persons of idealistic sympathies, especially those who found interest in things esoteric. The movement was founded by a Russian noblewoman, Madame Helena Blavatsky, who came from Paris to New York in 1873 and there established a club which later became the Theosophical Society. She was assisted in her work by Henry S. Olcott and William Q. Judge. Madame Blavatsky claimed that during a visit to Tibet she had made contact with the "Trans-Himalayan Masters of Wisdom," from whom she derived her distinctive teachings. Whatever their real origin, they definitely bear the imprint of Buddhism. After Madame Blavatsky's death in London in 1891, William Q. Judge carried on the work in America. Due to his influence the American group seceded from the world organization in 1895 and formed the Theosophical Society in America. In 1906, Mrs. Annie Besant, former atheist and Spiritualist, became president of the society. It was she who provided Theosophy with a systematic presentation of its thought, blending Hindu and Buddhist pantheism with a Christian moral outlook. Jesus, like Krishna, Lao-tze, and Confucius, was an incarnation of a lesser cosmic being which acted as an agent of God. The goal of man was to evolve through successive incarnations and finally to become a cosmic being. In 1926 the movement established its headquarters at Wheaton, Illinois.

Though decidedly more than an esoteric cult, the Liberal Catholic Church is intimately connected with Theosophy as well as with sacramentarianism. An offshoot from the Old Catholic Church, it was founded in England in 1916 by Bishop James I. Wedgebody and the Theosophist Charles W. Leadbeater, who was consecrated a bishop. In 1917 the movement was brought to the United States; Irving S. Cooper was chosen bishop and his episcopal seat established at Los Angeles. While the movement had a definite Christian orientation and doctrinal standards as well as Catholic forms of worship, it permitted a thoroughgoing syncretism in religious thought, teaching that all religions are divinely inspired.

The Vedanta Society, a cult which looks for authority to the Vedas, Upanishads, and Bhagavad-Gita of Hinduism, found its American origins in the teaching of Swami Vivekananda at the World Parliament of Religions at Chicago in 1893. The society was formally organized in 1898 by Swami Abhedananda and soon developed centers in a number of American cities. Its purpose was to show men how to attain wisdom by the method of the ancient philosophy of India, but it was not dogmatic. Indeed, it stressed the essential unity of all religions. A similar movement was the Yogoda Sat-Sanga or Self-Realization Fellowship, which taught the Hindu practice of yoga.

Bahaism, which was not introduced to the United States until the late nineteenth century, originated in Persia in 1844 as an offshoot from Islam. Its founder, the Bab, claimed to be the Door to divine truth and the herald of righteousness. He was executed in 1850 and the leadership passed to Baha'ullah, who taught a religion of universal peace and love and sought to unite all men in a common brotherhood of faith. The movement made its American debut in Chicago at the World Parliament of Religions. In 1912 Baha'ullah's successor, Abdul Baha, journeyed to America and dedicated ground for a temple at Wilmette, Illinois; a truly remarkable edifice, its nine sides symbolized perfection and the unity of all religions.

An interesting cult, the I Am Movement, was founded at Chicago by Guy and Edna Ballard in 1934. Guy Ballard claimed to be the recipient of special revelations from St. Germain, the chief of certain "ascended masters," and published them in his work entitled *Unveiled Mysteries*. Through circulation of his book and the organization of classes in many cities, Ballard was able to convince a multitude of persons fascinated by the occult that he had the truth. He taught that I Am or God was the only supreme reality, but there were hosts of cosmic beings to whom one might look for all manner of help, the emphasis being placed on healing. The movement declined after Ballard's death in 1939 and Mrs. Ballard's indictment the following year by a Federal Grand Jury for fraudulent use of the mails. Her conviction was subsequently reversed by the Supreme Court.

Communitarian Cults

The planting of religious communistic communities was by no means confined to early nineteenth century groups such as the Amana Society or the Oneida Perfectionists; it was much in evidence around the turn of the twentieth century. One of the most representative groups was the

Christian Catholic Apostolic Church in Zion, founded by John Alexander Dowie at Zion City, Illinois, forty-two miles north of Chicago. Dowie, a former Congregational minister in Australia, had abandoned the ministry in 1878 and had founded a sect devoted to faith healing. The year 1893 found him teaching at the Chicago World's Fair and winning converts to his message of divine healing, personal repentance, and strict moral purity. He soon announced himself to be Elijah III (John the Baptist was Elijah II) or Elijah the Restorer, who had come to establish a theocracy. He established his church in 1896 and five years later founded Zion City, which he governed as "first apostle." Industries were started in which hundreds of converts invested, and the community was regulated by a series of strict "blue laws," which included the prohibition to eat pork or to use tobacco, liquor, drugs, or medicines. Beyond the confines of Zion City, however, Dowie's work was distinguished by lack of success. A tremendous campaign in Madison Square Garden, New York, in 1903, fell flat; within two years the Zion enterprises were hopelessly insolvent. Dowie was repudiated by his followers and the leadership of the movement passed to Wilbur Glenn Voliva, a former Disciples of Christ minister and able administrator. The fiscal fortunes of Zion City were noticeably improved as a result of his leadership. The community retained its extreme Biblical literalism, its repudiation of science and medicine, and its insistence that the earth is flat. It also held to its expectation of the immediate second coming of Jesus Christ. After Voliva's death in 1942, the exclusive character of the community gradually broke down and persons of other religious persuasions were welcomed to the city.

A decidedly more erratic community was the House of David, founded by "King Benjamin" Purnell in 1903 at Benton Harbor, Michigan. Purnell claimed to have received a revelation in 1895 to the effect that he was the "seventh messenger" of Revelation 8:6 and that his mission was the "ingathering of Israel" and the preparation of his colony for the imminent end of the world. His followers were required to turn over all their possessions to him; their subsequent support was derived from a "commonwealth fund." A suit brought against Purnell by several members of the community in 1923 resulted in a judgment against the leader for unfair apportionment of the colony's goods and irregular sexual practices. The case went to the Supreme Court of Michigan, but before that court rendered a verdict in his favor, Purnell died. The community continued to prosper, seemingly unaffected by his demise.

Father Divine's Peace Mission

Among the many cults which have appealed chiefly to Negroes, Father Divine's Peace Mission has been one of the most colorful. Born of former slave parents in Georgia, George Baker (probably his real name) under the assumed name of Major Morgan J. Devine, set up a communal religious house in Brooklyn in 1915. Four years later he moved his community to Sayville, Long Island. His followers came to accept him as a divine being, conferring upon him the title "Father." With the continued growth of his movement, Father Divine was obliged to seek larger quarters in Harlem; later he moved his headquarters to Philadelphia. In his various "heavens" he regularly put on sumptuous banquets at nominal cost; on such occasions there would be testimonies, prayers, and singing. Some persons claimed to have been healed of disease. The celibate life was a chief characteristic of the movement, with husbands and wives dwelling in separate quarters. Father Divine has spoken in a positive way to the social and economic needs of his people, endorsing democracy, condemning segregation, and offering temporal security to the downtrodden. Like all the cults which have made an impact on American life, the Peace Mission has fulfilled the needs of a certain element in society and has catered to the American obsession with success. It has been reflective of the basic materialism which has gripped religious life in the United States.

Movements Toward

Christian Unity

A SALIENT FEATURE OF THE AMERICAN RELIGIOUS ENTERPRISE IN THE EIGHTY years antecedent to 1960 was a trend toward greater cooperation and unity. Estranged families of faith, once given to inter-communal polemics, found it increasingly possible to join forces in a common effort to further the Kingdom of God. Contributory to this development was the growing liberal spirit, which placed more emphasis on a maturing Christian life than on an acceptance of right doctrine. Revivalism, long a champion of the sudden conversion experience and the transformed life, was progressively becoming expressive of the ethos of smaller denominations and sects, while major denominations tended to view the Christian life in terms of gradual growth sustained by Christian nurture. The gigantic educational undertaking made necessary by this latter concept called for the utmost cooperation on the part of the churches.

Production of the International Sunday School Lessons was only one answer to this need. Another was the formation of interdenominational, even interfaith, associations to provide inspiration and knowledge of educational techniques for the religious institutions of the country. One of the most valued of these organizations was the Religious Education Association, founded in 1903 as the result of a conference of religious leaders called by President William Rainey Harper of the University of Chicago. The membership of the Association was largely Protestant, but persons of all faiths might be admitted if they so desired. Contributions of the organization to religious education included fostering the teaching of Bible on a college level, encouraging theological schools to establish departments of religious education, and working for the improvement of curricula and teacher training in the church schools. It was the first body to achieve religious cooperation on a national level among orthodox Christians, liberal Christians, Jews, and unchurched idealists. The International Council of Religious Education, formed in 1922, became an accredited educational agency of more than forty Protestant evangelical denominations. While the chief function of the Council was to promote better educational programs in the churches, it offered assistance in a number of related fields and fostered cooperativeness among the several denominations. A further impetus for Christian unity came from the increasingly influential non-denominational seminaries and divinity schools of the larger universities. Graduates of such leading schools of theology as Union in New York, Yale, and Harvard unquestionably tended to develop a broad point of view and a proclivity for the widest possible ecclesiastical fellowship.

Other factors also played their part in the impulse toward unity. Complex social problems in the great urban areas seemed to call for the combined efforts of the denominations for a solution; the work of such socially concerned organizations as the Y.M.C.A. and the Y.W.C.A. represented the cooperative efforts of Christians of many communions. The rapidly expanding world missionary program likewise necessitated a pooling of denominational resources in order to achieve optimum results. A trend toward greater cooperation in this area was evident in the founding of the Foreign Missions Conference of North America in 1893. Also to be considered was the steady breaking down of geographical separation, which served to make American Christians more internationally minded and more conscious of the need for unity in order to withstand the onslaughts of anti-Christian systems. The Spanish-American War and the great world wars of the twentieth century were potent forces in demonstrating the need for community and the desirability of a united Christian voice to speak peace to a disordered world. To a lesser extent Christian unity was fostered by the community church movement quite prominent after the Civil War, which featured the gathering of local congregations composed of communicants from various denominations but not organically bound to any communion. Such interdenominational unions on a local level contributed in a minor way to broader movements in the direction of Christian unity.

NATIONAL FEDERATIONS OF CHURCHES

As early as 1838 the eminent Lutheran divine Samuel Schmucker developed a plan for the union of the Protestant denominations on a federated basis; the new body was to be named the Apostolic Protestant Church. Schmucker's proposed institution never was realized, but the general idea which he set forth was taken up again and carried forward by the distinguished Swiss-American Reformed church historian Philip Schaff. It was eventually achieved in the establishment of national federa-tions of churches.

Nineteenth-Century Alliances

The Evangelical Alliance, which had been founded in England in 1846 as a reaction to the Oxford Movement and other high-church trends, was introduced to America in 1866 by Dr. James McCosh; the following year the American Evangelical Alliance was formally organized. It hoped through the promotion of evangelical union to further the cause of re-ligious freedom and to check the swelling tide of rationalism and skepti-cism. The Alliance was a voluntary organization of individual Christians rather than an official agency of the churches. Until the end of the cen-tury the Alliance was a flourishing organization; in many cities ministerial associations were formed in connection with it. After 1900, however, it entered a period of decline, becoming practically defunct long before its formal dissolution in 1944.

In May, 1885, an American Congress of Churches was organized at New Haven. Its stated purpose was "to promote Christian union and advance the Kingdom of God by the free discussion of the great religious, moral and social questions of the time." Most of the major denominations were represented at the meeting. It was decided that the Congress should regularly convene at intervals of two years, but interest soon died out and the organization crumbled. In 1895 a Federation of Churches and Chris-tian Workers of New York City was organized, having been proposed by a group of Union Seminary alumni. Its goal was to relate "the gospel to every human need," and to so readjust and direct "its agencies that every family in the destitute parts of our city shall be reached." It was not long before federations with similar purposes were being founded in various other cities.

Five years after its founding the New York federation called a joint meeting with the Open and Institutional Church League, an organization which had opposed pew rentals and had furthered the work of institu-tional churches. The result was the formation of a National Federation of Churches and Christian Workers. Local churches and city federations comprised the bulk of its membership, though there were also repre-sentatives from several state associations. The inordinate size of the organization rendered efficient functioning impossible and suggested the need for a more practical system. Thus at a meeting in 1902, the General Secretary Elias B. Sanford called for the establishment of a federation officially endorsed by the denominations and with a membership appointed by them. As a result the Interchurch Conference on Federation, with official representation from the various denominations, convened in New York in 1905. Out of its deliberations came a plan for the formation of the Federal Council of Churches.

The Federal Council of Churches

The organizational meeting of the Federal Council of the Churches of Christ in America was held in Philadelphia in December, 1908, the constitution of the new body having already been approved by twenty-eight denominations. Thereafter the Council was to meet quadrennially. Its five objectives according to its constitution were to express the catholic unity of the Christian Church, to foster cooperative endeavor on the part of the churches, to promote mutual counsel in spiritual matters, to broaden the moral and spiritual influence of the churches, and to encourage the organization of local federations. An executive committee which met annually administered the affairs of the Council, while various permanent committees gave their attention to evangelism, missions, and other prominent interests of the member churches. That the Council appealed to denominations of both liberal and conservative theological orientation was due to the fact that it focused attention on practical problems and refrained from making theological pronouncements. The activities of the Council covered a broad area. It was concerned with such interests as world missions, religious education, evangelism, care of the Negro churches, support of needy Protestant churches in other lands, social service projects on the national scene, and encouragement of local and state federations.

At the first meeting in 1908 the well-known Social Creed of the Churches was adopted, a forthright expression of growing interest on the part of the churches in programs for social betterment. The Council further represented the concerns of socially minded Protestants in opposing the Open-Shop Movement organized by a number of employers at the close of World War I for the purpose of breaking the labor unions. Though certain employers tried to counterattack by accusing the Council of socialist or communist leanings, their campaign was on the whole unsuccessful. From that time until 1950 the Council spoke frequently on behalf of its member churches concerning social problems, particularly that of race relations, and thus bore witness to the increasing harmony among denominations in dealing with matters of social importance. Some opposition to the Federal Council came from a smaller organization, the American Council of Christian Churches, founded in 1944 by a group of fundamentalist churches which were ultra-conservative in theology and opposed to the Social Gospel movement.

State and City Federations

While the Federal Council was building unity on a national level, various state and city federations unrelated to the Council arranged for interdenominational cooperation within a more limited geographical area. On a city level the federations were usually staffed with an executive secretary and directors of specialized ministries such as Christian Education, the Institutional Ministry, Research and Church Planning, Social Welfare, and Youth and Young Adults. Some fifty city federations could boast paid executives on their staffs by 1936; by mid-century the number was much larger. The federations contributed significantly to the work of church planning by arranging for comity agreements among denominations in the establishment of new churches. Their high degree of success in this area testifies to the willingness of the denominations to cooperate. In the realm of religious education and related fields, both state and local federations often encountered greater difficulty inasmuch as local churches were ordinarily committed to denominational programs which for one reason or another frequently did not allow for programs of a local interdenominational type. As the twentieth century progressed, however, many federations found solutions to this vexing problem and were able to conduct successful educational programs.

The National Council of Churches

Simultaneously with the nascence of the Federal Council there were developing certain interdenominational federations of mission boards or other administrative agencies of the churches. These federations were the Foreign Missions Conference of North America, the Home Missions Council of North America, The International Council of Religious Education, the National Protestant Council of Higher Education, the Missionary Education Movement of the United States and Canada, the United Stewardship Council, and the United Council of Church Women. As the result of a formal proposal by the Federal Council, these federations merged with the Council in December, 1950, to form the National Council of the Churches of Christ in the United States of America. This was a remarkable step forward in interchurch cooperation, for it placed under the care of a single agency all phases of interdenominational activity. Support of that agency was guaranteed by the twenty-nine member denominations, which were represented by nearly 600 official delegates. Provision was made for the Council to be governed by a General Assembly which convened biennially. When the Assembly was not in session, the business of the Council was to be conducted by a General Board chosen by the participating communions. The four major divisions through which the Council functioned were Christian Education, Christian Life and Work, Home Missions, and Foreign Missions. In addition, Joint Departments were concerned with such areas as evangelism, family life, stewardship, and religious freedom. Unquestionably the National Council became the outstanding expression of American Protestantism united.

DENOMINATIONAL UNIONS AND ALLIANCES

Concomitantly with the movement toward federal union in Protestantism there developed a trend toward the realization of organic mergers among the denominations. One of the first communions to take a positive stand in favor of union was the Protestant Episcopal Church which, in 1886, issued its "quadrilateral basis" for unity, the four requirements for union with that communion being acceptance of the Nicene Creed as a sufficient statement of the Christian faith, the Bible as the Word of God, the sacraments of Baptism and the Lord's Supper, and the Historic Episcopate, "locally adapted," as the basis of organization. The invitation resulted in no mergers, the chief stumblingblock being the requirement of the Historic Episcopate which many Protestants could not bring them-selves to accept. Around the middle of the twentieth century the Protestant Episcopal Church carried on negotiations with the Presbyterian Church in the U.S.A. and later with the Methodist Church, but as of 1959 no mergers had taken place. Other leading advocates of union were the Disciples of Christ; indeed, union had been one of their major interests since the inception of their communion. Like the Episcopalians, however, their prerequisites for union were such as to discourage other denominations from possible mergers.

Intra-Family Unions

The twentieth century witnessed a number of important mergers between denominations which sprang from common roots and enjoyed similar beliefs and organization. First to unite were the Presbyterian Church in the U.S.A. and the Cumberland Presbyterian Church. The merger, which came about in 1906, became possible when the former body revised the Confession of Faith to remove any stigma of "fatalistic" teaching, always a sore point with the Cumberland Church. The reunited body retained the name Presbyterian Church in the U.S.A. A small minority in the Cumberland Church refused to take part in the merger and so continued the separate identity of that denomination. In 1920 the Presbyterian Church in the U.S.A. united with the Welsh Calvinistic Methodist Church, a body with Calvinistic theology and Presbyterian polity which grew out of the Evangelical Revival of the eighteenth century. From time to time the Presbyterian Church in the U.S.A. proposed union with the Presbyterian Church in the U.S. and the United Presbyterian Church of North America. After long negotiations the Presbyterian Church in the U.S. failed to give its approval; the United Presbyterian Church, however, eventually endorsed the plan, and the union forming the United Presbyterian Church in the U.S.A. was consummated at Pittsburgh in May, 1958. The new body had more than three million communicant members.

In the Baptist family, the year 1911 witnessed the merger of the Northern Baptist Convention with the Free Baptist Churches, the latter group being Arminian in its theology. The union had been made possible by a trend among many Baptists away from traditional Calvinist theology. The united body retained the name the Northern Baptist Convention until 1950 when it was renamed the American Baptist Convention. Those Free Baptists who did not favor the union of 1911 retained their identity as Free Will Baptists.

During and after the World War I period many Lutheran churches in the United States exhibited decided propensities for cooperation, the result in some cases being organic union. The earliest mergers were among the Norwegian and German bodies. In the case of the Norwegians one of the strong pro-union forces was the sense of Norwegian nationalism which tended somewhat to obscure conflicts over pietism, ecclesiastical formalism, and theological orthodoxy. By 1917 harmony among the Norwegian Lutheran bodies had developed to such an extent that Hauge's Norwegian Evangelical Lutheran Synod, the Synod of the Norwegian Evangelical Church of America, and the United Norwegian Lutheran Church in America could unite to form the Norwegian Lutheran Church of America. As the members of this body gradually became thoroughly assimilated into the American environment, the church lost much of its Norwegian nationalistic spirit; and in 1946 the name of the communion was charged to the Evangelical Lutheran Church. Common language, doctrine, and practices contributed to the merger in 1919 of the Wisconsin, Minnesota, Michigan, and Nebraska Synods to form the Evangelical Lutheran Joint Synod of Wisconsin and Other States.

Most important was the merger of 1918 which resulted in the organization of the United Lutheran Church in America. For some years there had been steadily increasing cooperation among the General Synod, the General Council, and the United Synod of the South, all of which had stemmed from the tradition of Muhlenberg Lutheranism. In 1917 these bodies, motivated by the spirit of the Quadri-Centennial celebration of the Reformation, voted to merge. The following year they constituted the largest Lutheran denomination in the United States with nearly 800,000 confirmed members. A further Lutheran union took place in 1930 when the Joint Synod of Ohio, the Iowa Synod, and the Buffalo Synod, all products of German immigration, merged to form the American Lutheran Church.

The process of Lutheran unification received new impetus around the middle of the twentieth century. With the exception of the Missouri Synod, which was extreme in its theological conservatism, most of the major Lutheran bodies made definite progress toward the achievement of organic union. After negotiations between the Missouri Synod and the American Lutheran Church collapsed in 1947 because of failure to reach doctrinal agreement, the latter body opened discussions with the Evangelical Lutheran Church, the United Evangelical Lutheran Church, and the Lutheran Free Church. By 1958 all but the Lutheran Free Church had agreed to merge in 1960. Another contemplated merger, not to take place prior to 1962, includes the United Lutheran Church in America, the Augustana Lutheran Church, the American Evangelical Lutheran Church, and the Finnish Evangelical Lutheran Church (Suomi Synod). When combined, these denominations will realize a membership in the neighborhood of three million.

During the 1920's three mergers took place among smaller denominations of like faith and practice. In 1922 a union was consummated between the Evangelical Association and the United Evangelical Church, thus healing a schism which had taken place in the 1890's. Both of these denominations, united under the name the Evangelical Church, had a doctrine and polity similar to that of the Methodist. In 1924 the Reformed Church in the United States, formerly the German Reformed Church, united with the Hungarian Reformed Church in America; the merged body held the name Reformed Church in the United States. The following year there occurred a union between the Congregational Churches and the Evangelical Protestant Churches of North America, the latter denomination, of German background, having been governed by congregational principles. This composite body continued to be known as the Congregational Churches.

One of the more impressive unions of the present century took place in 1939, when the Methodist Episcopal Church, the Methodist Episcopal Church, South, and the Methodist Protestant Church united to form the Methodist Church. Since 1911, when the first definite proposal looking toward unification was made, conferences had been held to accomplish that purpose. Certain obstacles, however, had to be overcome. The southern church still experienced many of the grievances which had grown out of the Civil War; in theology it was more conservative than the northern body, while in polity its bishops were permitted to exercise more power. The Methodist Protestant Church had no bishops. These difficulties were ultimately resolved, it being decided to retain the episcopal form of government; and in 1939 a Uniting Conference composed of some

900 delegates met in Kansas City, Missouri, and consummated the union. The new Methodist Church, with more than eight million members, became the largest Protestant denomination in the United States.

Among the Friends, a merger of the Religious Society of Friends of Philadelphia and Vicinity (Arch Street Meeting) and the Philadelphia Yearly Meeting of the Religious Society of Friends (Race Street Meeting) was achieved in 1955. The united body, which continued to be known as the Philadelphia Yearly Meeting of the Religious Society of Friends, was associated with the Religious Society of Friends (General Conference), an agency for the advancement of Quakerism.

Inter-Family Unions

An even more striking evidence of the growing desire for union was the consummation of several mergers between denominations of different heritage and tradition. In 1931 the Congregational Churches united with the Christian Church, a product of the New Light movement of the early nineteenth century, to form the Congregational Christian Churches. Though their backgrounds were dissimilar, their union was not unnatural inasmuch as they embraced nearly identical ideals and principles.

Lutheran and Reformed traditions were mingled in the union of the Evangelical Synod of North America and the Reformed Church in the United States in 1934 to form the Evangelical and Reformed Church. The Evangelical Synod was the American counterpart of the Evangelical United Church of Prussia, a body composed of both Lutheran and Reformed congregations. In 1957 the Evangelical and Reformed Church consummated a union with the General Council of the Congregational Christian Churches in Cleveland, Ohio, thus constituting the United Church of Christ. The most noteworthy feature of the merger was that it brought together denominations which had been governed by modified Presbyterian and Congregational polities. However, no constitution and statement of faith were adopted at that time, the matter requiring further study. The second General Synod in 1959 approved a Statement of Faith.

The merger of the Evangelical Church and the Church of the United Brethren in Christ in 1946 to form the Evangelical United Brethren Church was less unusual. Both denominations had a doctrine and polity similar to that of Methodism.

World-Wide Denominational Federations

A trend toward greater cooperation among world denominational fellowships was begun in 1867 with the calling of the Lambeth Conference of Anglican Bishops. The Conference, which met roughly every ten years, gave much of its attention to attaining closer fellowship or union with other communions. Among the most active participants in the work of Lambeth were the bishops of the Protestant Episcopal Church. Just ten years later the Alliance of the Reformed Churches Throughout the World Holding the Presbyterian System convened for the first time at Edinburgh. It provided incentive for the American churches to found the Council of Reformed Churches in the United States Holding the Presbyterian System in 1907. The Ecumenical Methodist Council, known since 1951 as the World Methodist Council, was organized in 1881 to integrate Methodist activities throughout the world. Ten years later the International Congregational Council was constituted in London. The Baptist World Alliance was founded in 1905 in the English capital. In 1919 the National Lutheran Council, a federation organized the previous year by ten Lutheran bodies in the United States for the purpose of achieving greater Lutheran unity, proposed the establishment of a world federation of Lutheran churches. The result was the formation of the Lutheran World Convention in 1923, which body changed its name in 1947 to the Lutheran World Federation. The Disciples of Christ organized a World Convention of Churches of Christ in 1930.

THE ECUMENICAL MOVEMENT

The Ecumenical (from the Greek *oikoumene,* meaning the inhabited world) Movement may be defined as that process whereby Christian communions in every part of the world strive to discover and express a common faith and life centered in commitment to Jesus Christ, their redeeming Lord. The word ecumenical has enjoyed a long and honorable history, but only since 1937, when it was used at a conference held at Oxford, has it become popular in Protestant circles.

The World Missionary Movement

During the nineteenth century, the "great century" of missionary expansion, Protestant leaders in Europe and America began to realize that if the world missionary movement were to be effective there would have to be interdenominational teamwork. To that end an interdenominational meeting was convened in 1854 in New York City and followed by another that same year in London. Further meetings of a similar nature were held in 1860 in Liverpool, in 1878 and 1888 in London, and in 1900 in New York City. Much more significant was the World Missionary Conference convened in Edinburgh in 1910. Since its membership consisted of delegates formally appointed by the several missionary societies, the Conference enjoyed a more official character than did previous assemblies. Among the delegates were representatives of the "younger churches," whose origin was the direct result of missionary endeavor. While these delegates constituted only one per cent of the total representation, their presence was significant and presaged a mounting influence on the part of the "younger churches." Before the Conference adjourned it appointed a Continuation Committee to carry on its work. The chairman, American Methodist leader John R. Mott, founded what became National Christian Councils in a number of nations prior to the outbreak of World War I. His goal was to further cooperation in the planning and implementation of missionary programs. These efforts were merged in 1921 with the creation at Lake Mohonk, New York, of an International Missionary Council. This Council was composed of national and regional missionary councils but was not a legislative body. Under its auspices a number of eventful international missionary conferences were held, notably those at Jerusalem in 1928 and Madras in 1938.

The Progress of Ecumenicity

One of the outstanding members of the World Missionary Conference was Charles H. Brent, Missionary Bishop of the Philippine Islands of the Protestant Episcopal Church. Inspired by the thought of a reunited Christendom, he and two other leaders persuaded the General Convention of their denomination to call a World Conference on Faith and Order. All churches which "accept our Lord Jesus Christ as God and Saviour" might send representatives. World War I interrupted the enterprise and it was not until 1927 that the conference convened at Lausanne, Switzerland. All the major Protestant denominational families in America sent delegates. Eastern Orthodox representatives were also in attendance. As might be expected there were wide differences of theological opinion, but they were dealt with in a spirit of Christian charity. The principal agreements to come out of the conference were that the faith of the church universal was that expressed by the Apostles' and Nicene Creeds, and that episcopal, presbyterian, and congregational forms of government all had an appropriate place in a reunited church. A second Conference on Faith and Order was held at Edinburgh in August, 1937. Four main subjects were on the agenda: the doctrine of Grace, the Word of God, the Ministry and Sacraments, and the Church's Unity in Life and Worship. Most of the dissension was over the Church and the Ministry, there being no agreement as to the meaning of a valid ministry and apostolic succession. In regard to the matter of Grace and the Word of God there was much more unanimity.

A second movement which endeavored to further ecumenicity through practical activity, especially by applying Christian principles to the economic, social, and political orders, was the Life and Work Movement. At the close of World War I, Archbishop Nathan Söderblom of Uppsala, primate of Sweden, called for an ecumenical council to "consider urgent practical tasks before the Church." The conference met at Stockholm in August, 1925. It was not distinguished by success. German Lutheran theologians, who found the principal duty of the church to be the preaching of salvation and the performance of charitable works, came into conflict with the American "Social Gospel" proponents, who felt it necessary to relate Christianity to economic, social, and political problems. A second Life and Work conference held at Oxford in July, 1937, was more auspicious. Among its most important contributions were the approval of a plan for the establishment of a World Council of Churches and the issuance of a *Message* which appraised the church's responsibility in a world over which the gray shadows of war were already beginning to fall.

The World Council of Churches

At a meeting in London in 1937 of representatives from the various branches of the ecumenical movement, plans were made for the creation of a single body which would unite the work of the various movements without infringing on their independence. Having been approved by the Faith and Order and Life and Work movements, a Constituent Committee was appointed to draw up a constitution for the proposed World Council of Churches. This document, sent to the churches in 1938, provided for admission to membership of all communions which accepted Jesus Christ as God and Saviour. It was proposed that the functions of the Council be as follows: "(1) To carry on the work of the two world movements for Faith and Order and for Life and Work. (2) To facilitate common action by the Churches. (3) To promote cooperation in study. (4) To promote the growth of ecumenical consciousness in the members of all Churches. (5) To establish relations with denominational federations of world wide scope and with other ecumenical movements. (6) To call world conferences on specific subjects as occasion may require, such conferences being empowered to publish their own findings." August, 1941, was set as the date for the convening of the Assembly of the World Council, but by that time World War II had broken out and the Assembly had to be postponed indefinitely.

After a long delay the World Council of Churches convened at Amsterdam in August, 1948, continuing in session for two weeks. Its official delegates, who numbered 351, represented 147 churches in 44 countries. There were no representatives from the Roman Catholic or Russian Orthodox Churches, and two large American groups, the Southern Baptist Convention and the Lutheran Missouri Synod, refrained from sending delegates. Fundamentalist churches refused to take part in the World Council and proceeded to found a rival organization known as the International Council of Christian Churches. Still the World Council was the most comprehensive Christian body yet to assemble, with representation from all five continents.

According to the provisions of the constitution adopted at Amsterdam six active presidents and one honorary president were to be elected. It seemed fitting that the honorary presidency went to that revered patriarch of ecumenicity, John R. Mott, by acclamation. G. Bromley Oxnam, Methodist Bishop of New York, was chosen as one of the active presidents, while W. A. Visser 't Hooft of the Dutch Reformed Church functioned as general secretary. A ninety-member Central Committee was also nominated.

The main theme for discussion by the assembly was "Man's Disorder and God's Design," the subject being divided into four sub-topics which dealt with the Universal Church in God's Design, the Church's Witness to God's Design, the Church and the Disorder of Society, and the Church and the International Disorder. Though there was general agreement among the delegates concerning basic Christian principles, certain conflicts also appeared. The principal controversy took place in the discussion of "The Church and the International Disorder," a debate between John Foster Dulles, American Presbyterian layman, and Josef L. Hromadka, Czech theological professor, over the merits of capitalism and communism. On the whole, however, the assembly was an overwhelming success and did much to further the cause of Christian unity.

The Second Assembly of the World Council of Churches was held at Evanston, Illinois, from August 15 to 31, 1954. Since Amsterdam, the World Council's membership had expanded to include 163 communions in 48 nations, some of which were under Communist domination. A record number of 502 delegates officially represented the member churches throughout the world. Thirty denominations in the United States were affiliated with the World Council by 1954, the Southern Baptist Convention and the Lutheran Missouri Synod still being conspicuous by their absence. The Russian Orthodox Church did not participate and the Roman Catholic Church continued to hold itself aloof, but it was encouraging to note the arrival of new member groups such as the Coptic churchmen from Egypt.

The major portion of the time at Evanston was spent in historical review and planning for the future, worship, theological discussion, and the adoption of a budget. A principal concern of the Assembly, which was reflected in the official report, was "Inter-church Aid and Service to Refugees." The central theme for deliberation was "Christ—the Hope of the World," a subject which called forth sharp differences in theological viewpoint. European theologians found their hope in the Saviour Christ, the risen Lord whose work was to call men out of the world and prepare for them a new creation; they saw Christ in the two-fold capacity of judge and redeemer. American theologians, on the other hand, placed more emphasis on ethics than eschatology as popularly interpreted to mean the "doctrine of the last things." Professor Robert L. Calhoun of Yale Divinity School suggested that "eschatology is the doctrine concerned with the limits or boundaries of our living, in time and existence, toward which at every moment our whole lives tend." Thus, in his thinking, the Christian hope belonged as much to the present as to the future. The Assembly found it impossible to reach any real unanimity as to the meaning of "Christian Hope" or eschatology. The result was a final report which found room for both points of view.

Many delegates went away from the meetings with the conviction that the choice of theme had not been judicious, that first things had not been placed first, and that the resultant disagreements had hindered the progress toward unity. Others thought that theological issues of this type would have to be faced but that they could not be dealt with in seventeen days and then put to a vote. Time was needed for careful study and prayer, and in the discussions the points of view of laymen and parish ministers as well as ecumenical leaders were essential to the achievement of lasting unity. Probably the most important contribution of the Assembly was the effect which it had upon the world. Few gatherings in modern times have received such attention; unquestionably, thousands were heartened by the spirit of unity which existed in the face of diversity and fortified by these words which appeared in the *Message* adopted on August 31: "We do not know what is coming to us. But we know who is coming. It is he who meets us every day and who will meet us at the end—Jesus Christ our Lord."

It will be some time before it will be possible to evaluate the Ecumenical Movement as a whole. Clearly it has already achieved highly significant results. But there are definite problems which are also observable. As yet the Council is by no means as inclusive as it would like to be. The second largest Protestant denomination in the United States, the Southern Baptist Convention, is still not represented; neither is the Russian Orthodox Church. More serious, the Council is conceived by the rank-and-file churchgoer to be a top-level movement, sponsored by ecclesiastical dignitaries. Indeed, even the term "ecumenical" is still a strange word to the average Christian layman. If the Ecumenical Movement is to play its full role in the life of contemporary Christianity it will have to capture the attention and the support of parish churches all over the world. Should this possibility become fact, the Ecumenical Movement might become one of the most important Christian developments since Pentecost.

28

The Retreat to Normalcy

WORLD WAR I, THE WAR TO END ALL WARS WAS OVER. A HEAVY SILENCE lay over the battlefields where men had poured out their life's blood in the service of their country. Yet few in America paused to take careful measure of the sacrifice. There were glory and fanfare, tickertape and shouting, but only the bereaved and the survivors of battle knew the awful cost of the Great War. That same ebullient noisy enthusiasm with which Americans greeted the brief but bitter conflict was still conspicuous in the proud flush of victory. After all, the world was better for what they had done, a step closer to that inevitable utopia which lay just around the corner. To the victors at Versailles, terrible in their righteousness, it did not seem inconsistent to mete out a stern revengeful punishment to the vanquished in the name of divine justice and then in idealistic fashion turn to building a lasting world peace. It was one of the last naively optimistic acts of an age already in its dotage, a superannuated age about to be replaced by an era of reckless uncertainties and swaggering doubts.

During the brief period of elation and high resolve which followed the war, President Wilson was in France, prepared to commit the United States to the cause of international justice and peace through participation in a League of Nations. But even as he poured his energies into this new dream, the forces of reaction in his own country were undermining his work. A vast, unpredictable American public was suddenly growing tired of being dedicated to an international ministry and was turning abruptly to isolationism. In Congress, which had been lost to the Democratic party as early as 1918, the Wilsonian dream was subjected to abuse and acrimonious repudiation. His health broken, Wilson retired from the national scene and left the stage to Warren Gamaliel Harding and Normalcy. The high tariff walls erected by Republicans upon their return to power were fitting symbols of the dominating insular nationalism. While the United States did enter into an international conference on naval power in 1921 and affirmed its pacific intentions in the Kellogg-Briand Pact of 1928, such events called forth relatively little interest from the citizenry when compared to domestic affairs. Nevertheless, there was a strong popular sentiment during the 1920's in favor of outlawing war, and by the end of the decade many denominations had officially adopted anti-war resolutions. To a certain extent the churches were experiencing pangs of conscience over their wartime militancy which had aided the forces of secularism and thus contributed to their loss of influence.

RELIGIOUS LIFE IN THE PROSPEROUS TWENTIES

The Challenge of Secularism

The 1920's witnessed a drastic change in the relation between society and organized religion. Though ecclesiastical institutions flourished, intellectuals increasingly came to think of the churches as socially and intellectually inept and smiled with approval at the raging secularism of Clarence Darrow and H. L. Mencken. Far more serious was the fact that religion was gradually losing its power in the lives of men, being patronized but not obeyed, while the churches were being relegated to the role of spectators stationed on the sidelines. Obvious signs of religion's divorce from the vital issues of life were the decline in family devotions, except perhaps among the Jews for whom family worship was central, the casualness with which growing numbers of Americans regarded regular church attendance, and even the trend toward conducting services for the dead in funeral parlors rather than in the church. It was not an irreligious age, but vast multitudes managed to live without cultivating more than a nodding acquaintance with religion and went to their graves without the sustaining power of a dynamic faith.

Certain sociological factors also played a part in the decreasing influence of religion. The increasing transience of the population, made more practicable by the automobile, was an important factor in the growing reluctance of Americans to become deeply involved in the life and work of communal organizations such as the church. At the same time the automobile encouraged population movements to suburbs and towns on the fringes of the great cities, leaving downtown areas to business and apartment-hotel dwellers. Most churches in downtown centers were forced to give up all thought of a true parish ministry and become preaching stations manned by outstanding sermonizers who attracted a heterogeneous mass of people from every part of the metropolis. Well-to-do suburbanites, among the more settled elements of society, were somewhat more likely to participate in parish programs, especially if they had families; they were, however, also highly susceptible to the philosophy that the Sabbath was made for relaxation and it was not seldom that the lure of the open road proved more enticing than the peal of the church bell. Still another type of migration, involving poverty-stricken classes such as Negroes moving to the cities of the North, farmers fleeing from the "dust bowl," and Mexican laborers pouring into the Southwest, created unusual problems for organized religion inasmuch as these transients did not adjust easily to their new environment and often abandoned their formal religious connections.

Organized religion reacted to the challenge of secularism in numerous ways. Recognizing the need for mass media to reach the public with the claims of religion, Christian and Jewish bodies began to copy the methods of successful corporations. Experts in public relations were employed by many denominations to give adequate publicity to their programs and create popular interest in their work. Some of the larger communions established religious lobbies for the purpose of seeking legislation favorable to their interests. Religious presses intensified efforts to hold the public's attention by including literature of a secular nature in their journals and by raising the general quality of their publications. Brilliant sermonizers such as S. Parkes Cadman of Central Congregational Church, Brooklyn, brought scintillating messages to millions via radio, a ministry which reached its apex with the eloquent radio sermons of Harry Emerson Fosdick and Ralph W. Sockman of New York.

A singularly successful organization, designed to coordinate the affairs of the Roman Catholic Church and act as a channel of communication between the hierarchy and the American public, was the National Catholic Welfare Council, established in 1919 and renamed the National Catholic Welfare Conference in 1923. Its Administrative Board was composed of ten leading members of the American hierarchy, thus giving immediate stature to the enterprise. Departments of the Conference were Executive, Education, Press, Social Action, Legal, Catholic Action Study, Youth, and Lay Organizations. In each case the leaders proved to be able interpreters of the mind of the church.

A somewhat unusual effort to combat secularism was made by the Oxford Group Movement, founded by Frank Buchman (1878–   ), a Lutheran minister. As a young clergyman in charge of a small congregation and a successful settlement house in Philadelphia, he came into conflict with his board of trustees; finally he resigned and went to England. While worshipping in a small chapel in Cumberland he had a strange mystical experience in which all bitterness and resentment were purged from his life. It was this event which prompted him to organize a fellowship in which he could share the joy which had come to him. On the whole, his greatest appeal was for the intellectuals and persons in the upper income brackets, and on the campuses of Oxford and Cambridge he created quite a stir. His most characteristic way of reaching people was through house parties, the first of which was held in China in 1918. By this method, which Buchman and his followers soon introduced to the United States, prospective converts were invited to a "party" which lasted four to ten days. Each was assigned a spiritual guide to whom he was to confess all his sins and from whom he was to learn techniques of private prayer. Through prayer, confession, and personal surrender he was expected to become a changed person. Such gatherings were not designed as a substitute for the church; indeed, participants were urged to affiliate with a congregation. In the United States the movement was headed for a time by Samuel M. Shoemaker, rector of Calvary Episcopal Church, New York. He later withdrew from the organization. The principal criticism of the movement was that it was too preoccupied with problems of money and sex and overly sentimental in its approach to them. Doctrinally it presented no teaching of an unorthodox nature; however, it seldom dealt with doctrinal matters, preferring to emphasize experience.

In 1938, when ominous war clouds were hovering over Europe, Buchman made a speech in London in which he called for a new international program of Moral Re-Armament to save the world from destruction. "The nations must re-arm morally," he said. "We need a power strong enough to change human nature and build bridges between man and man, faction and faction. . . . God alone can change human nature." After that time the movement was known as Moral Re-Armament. Its philosophy was much the same as before, except that it now related personal change to social betterment. From its American headquarters, first in Washington, D.C., and later in Los Angeles, it released a flood of literature and directed programs in all parts of the nation. By the opening of World War II, however, the movement entered a period of decline from which it has not yet been able to recover.

The Social Status of the Churches

If religion was not in the most robust health during the twenties, this fact was not revealed in the statistics of church membership. From 1920 to 1930 the percentage of the total population officially numbered as church affiliates rose from 43 to 47 per cent. Religious illiteracy and secularism could increase with regularity without affecting growth in church membership, for formal religious affiliation was becoming an accepted feature of American society. Convention was replacing commitment as motivation for membership in the church.

Financially, American religious institutions had never been so prosperous. After the brief slump of 1921, American economy enjoyed a steady climb until reaching its zenith in 1929—and then it fell with a resounding crash. The churches reaped the full benefits of the era of prosperity. Clerical salaries, long the bane of the ministerial calling, were beginning to reveal signs of improvement, while current expense and benevolence budgets soared higher with each passing year. Americans might allow the idealistic Interchurch World Movement to fail, but they were not at all hesitant to pour large sums into building magnificent church edifices. From 1920 to 1927 the estimated annual value of new construction of religious buildings rose from $55,000,000 to $179,000,000. Between 1916 and 1926 the value of church property more than doubled. Similarly, denominational enterprises for special purposes, such as the Methodist Book Concern in New York, and church-related colleges entered tremendous building programs, increasing the value of their real property by millions of dollars. All too often, however, they contracted debts of unusual magnitude, being confident that their financial receipts would grow indefinitely; the result was that when the depression came many congregations had to face foreclosure, while denominational colleges had to suspend faculty members or drastically cut their salaries. In Protestantism particularly there was much inefficiency in church planning. Due to overchurching, thousands of smaller churches continued with memberships of three hundred or less and an overhead so great that the major part of their budgets had to be devoted to current expenses. Many of them were staffed by inadequately trained ministers who were woefully unprepared for their responsibilities, but who remained at their stations pouring out sectarian convictions to congregations which found them strangely irrelevant to life.

No denomination made more efficient use of its material resources than the Roman Catholic Church. A strong undivided church built along clear-cut organizational lines was of inestimable advantage in the promotion of a church program. Significant gains were made in the area of parochial school education during the twenties as a result of the general financial prosperity. By the late 1920's, 98 per cent of the nation's private elementary schools and two-thirds of its private secondary schools were operated by the Roman Catholic Church. The position of parochial schools was greatly strengthened by rulings of the Supreme Court of the United States in 1923 and 1925 which affirmed the right of parents to educate their children in other than state schools.

The Recovery of Worship

Concerning worship in the sanctuary, many larger denominations found themselves in that never-never land which separated the simple, unadorned, didactic rites of Puritanism and pietism from the rich, ceremonial, mystical services of the liturgical churches. Despite a certain distrust of ritualism on the part of low-church conservatives, increasing prosperity and aesthetic sensitivity prompted experimentation in the fine art of public worship. The Methodist Episcopal Church offers an excellent case in point. Throughout the 1920's there was a general drift toward ritualism discernible in orders of worship, wearing of vestments, and use of liturgical music. Choirs took the place of quartets and semisecular, sentimental music was gradually being abandoned in favor of sacred music. The Lord's Supper became the Communion, and this sacrament was administered with increasing dignity and propriety and in keeping with the set forms of the church.

Liturgical churches such as the Protestant Episcopal also experienced a demand for constructive liturgical development. Work on a second revision of the Book of Common Prayer had already begun in 1913 with broad churchmen cooperating with high churchmen; the revision was given final approval by the General Convention of 1928. While many Protestant features of the work were preserved in the face of objections by high churchmen, there were certain Catholic innovations, among them a larger use of the Apocrypha in the lectionary and the adoption of the Catholic Breviary form of absolution after the Confession. Simultaneously there was a liturgical movement under way in the Roman Catholic Church, its American headquarters being the Benedictine Abbey of St. John, Collegeville, Minnesota, its chief agency for promotion being the Liturgical Arts Society, founded in 1930. This movement did much to encourage congregational participation in Gregorian chants.

Considerable interest in the recovery of worship was stimulated by a number of well-written volumes which came from the press in the 1920's and early 1930's. A few of the more important were *Reality in Worship* (1925) by Willard L. Sperry, *Modern Worship* (1927) by Von Ogden Vogt, *The Technique of Public Worship* (1928) by J. H. Odgers and E. G. Schutz, and *The Recovery of Worship* (1931) by George W. Fiske. In many instances they inspired liberal ministers whose principal attraction was the Social Gospel to introduce into their services the ancient hymns and creeds of the church, not because they endorsed their theological teachings but because their use helped to establish a sense of continuity with the universal communion of the faithful in all ages.

The trend toward dignity in worship was reflected in religious architecture. In place of the auditorium-like structures which had been popular early in the century, edifices with a more decidedly religious character were coming into favor. On the whole, the movement did not follow denominational lines, for one might find on one corner a Baptist church which looked like a Gothic cathedral and on the opposite corner a Roman Catholic church which looked the part of a colonial meetinghouse. The Gothic revival reached its height under the leadership of that eminent architect Ralph Adams Cram and found permanent expression in majestic cathedral-like edifices such as Riverside Church in New York and the university chapels at Chicago, Duke, and Princeton. Romanesque and Byzantine architecture also gained a certain favor, as did Spanish and Italian Renaissance in the Southwest. As the twenties advanced there was increasing use of modernist design in church architecture inspired in large measure by the inimitable Frank Lloyd Wright.

TRENDS IN RELIGIOUS THOUGHT AND EDUCATION

In no area was the impact of secularism felt more acutely than in the realm of intellectual life. For more than a generation theologians of the liberal school had been serving up a curious mixture of absolute idealism rooted in New England Transcendentalism and Hegelianism, evolutionary philosophy, and Biblical ethics. Their enthusiasm for the ethical teaching of Jesus, however exemplary, did not hide the fact that their theological foundation was more secular than Christian. Whether it was conscious or not, they were accommodating themselves to the intellectual currents of the new age, an age which venerated science and found in the philosophy of science its way of life. The representative man was no longer the clergyman in his pulpit but the scientist in his laboratory. The ethos of the time was geocentric, even anthropocentric, and the religion which could best meet its recognized needs was one which offered a therapeutic ministry to persons of neurotic tendency. Christian theology as the exposition of final truth was being progressively neglected by intellectuals in favor of the psychology of religion. The public in general continued, though with growing reluctance, to practice a complacent pietism grounded in a Bible which they respected but did not know.

The Impact of Liberal Philosophies

Philosophy, once the handmaiden of theology, now found itself in the role of judge, armed with a mandate to test the claims of religious authority and determine whether they were deficient. At the same time it attempted to find its own answers to the problems of religion. After World War I, absolute idealism, which had long been America's dominant philosophical position and whose most recent outstanding champions were Josiah Royce (1855–1916) and William E. Hocking (1873–), was unseated from its throne by the empiricism of William James

(1842–1910) and others. James' pragmatic philosophy grew out of his dissatisfaction with materialism, absolute idealism, and theological orthodoxy. Fittingly described as empirical theism, it affirmed the existence of God on the basis that such belief was more satisfactory to the volitional and emotional aspects of man's nature. This God could not be known through dogmatic theology, but only through the human consciousness that the nobler part of man was "continuous with a wider self" which magnified his personality and gave him incentive for creative living. Religion was true because it worked. Perhaps the outstanding attempt to deal with theology as an empirical science was made by Professor D. C. Macintosh of Yale Divinity School in his *Theology as an Empirical Science* (1919). His method was to verify hypotheses about God experimentally through the attainment of a personal awareness of the divine presence and activity.

A further challenge to complacent religious thinking came from the humanist philosophy of John Dewey (1859–1952). While Dewey rejected the metaphysical God of dogmatic theology, he found a place for a deity which represented the sum of natural forces dedicated to the realization of ideal ends. The purpose of religion was to realize lofty social goals, inspired by experienced values. In order to be workable, however, these goals had to be derived from experience which could be shared with others. Private religious experience was unreliable and could not claim universal validity. Only a small percentage of the clergy accepted this humanistic teaching; nevertheless, by tearing down the distinction between the sacred and the secular and identifying religion with the social aspirations of man, it contributed to the undermining of orthodoxy. A far more militant but less effectual foe of organized religion was the American Association for the Advancement of Atheism, founded in 1925 for the purpose of attacking the God concept through the circulation of atheistic literature.

The most profitable mission field for thinkers of liberal bent was the college campus; in hundreds of institutions students studied and discussed humanistic philosophies and were sufficiently impressed by them to abandon their allegiance to organized religion. Even among students for the ministry there was some shifting of theological emphases and persuasions as a result of the new intellectual currents. There was a growing tendency to stress the natural as opposed to the supernatural, to refrain from the quotation of scriptural texts as final authority, and to deal with revelation as though it were something that man discovered about God through experience. A penetrating study of the beliefs of 500 ministers in Chicago and 200 students in various theological seminaries by G. H. Betts in 1929 indicated a liberal trend, particularly among the students. Only 33 per cent of the students, as opposed to 77 per cent of the clergy, believed the New Testament to be an infallible standard of religious truth. Less than half of the ministers and only five per cent of the students accepted the Genesis account of creation. Belief in miracles was rejected by 32 per cent of the clergy and 76 per cent of the students.

The Conservative Reaction

During the opening decade of the twentieth century Protestant Fundamentalism, with its famous five points of theological orthodoxy, had sprung up in answer to theological liberalism. By 1919 it had gained sufficient strength to warrant the organization in Philadelphia of the World's Christian Fundamentals Association, a body pledged to the annihilation of modernist teaching. It was not until the 1920's, however, when a large-scale reaction to secularism and all forms of theological accommodation to it was setting in among Protestants of conservative inclination that the movement came into its own. The issues on which fundamentalists and liberals divided were hardly minor; they covered the entire scope of Christian religion. Fundamentalists worshipped a transcendent Deity who had revealed Himself through a verbally infallible Bible and in Jesus Christ, whom to accept as God Incarnate and personal Saviour was prerequisite to life eternal. They saw the work of the church to be the preaching of a Gospel of redemption and the preparation of the faithful for the second coming of Jesus Christ in power and glory. Consequently they could not endorse the world view of those who saw Christianity as essentially a religion of good works performed by inherently good men dedicated to the building of a Christian social order. Fundamentalists were interested in personal salvation, not society.

The fundamentalist determination to stamp out wherever possible teachings which appeared to contradict Scripture manifested itself in several ways. One of the most notable was the effort to keep the teaching of evolution out of the public schools. In Tennessee fundamentalist influence was powerful enough to pressure the state legislature in 1925 to adopt legislation making it unlawful to "teach any theory that denies the story of the divine creation of man as taught in the Bible." At Dayton, Tennessee, a high-school teacher of biology, John T. Scopes, continued to teach evolutionary views; when this fact was brought to the attention of the authorities, he was arrested. The ensuing trial was farcical, becoming not so much a test of law as a theological debate. On one side was William Jennings Bryan (1860–1925), three-time candidate for the presidency on the Democratic ticket and ardent champion of fundamentalist Christianity, who made an impassioned defense of the Bible as an infallible work, as inerrant in matters of science as in faith. Opposing him was the eminent lawyer and agnostic, Clarence Darrow (1857–1938), who presented a sharp ridicule of Biblical literalism and attacked the anti-evolution law as unconstitutional. An entire nation followed the proceedings much as they would have viewed a prizefight; both Bryan and Darrow were colorful figures. In the end Scopes was convicted, not because Bryan had disproved evolution, which he had not, but because the defendant had violated an outrageous law. A week later Bryan lay dead, a victim of the heat and excitement which had enveloped the stormy courtroom. As for Scopes, his case was carried to the Supreme Court of Tennessee which expediently reversed the decision on the ground that the trial judge had improperly imposed the fine. The anti-evolution campaign, nevertheless, did not then draw to a close. Two other states, Arkansas and Mississippi, adopted legislation similar to that of Tennessee, and there was considerable agitation for the passage of such laws in other parts of the country. But as time passed fewer thoughtful people took seriously the fundamentalist claims and the issue virtually passed from the American scene.

Unable to halt the alarming trend toward secularism, fundamentalism turned away from a "sinful" society and proceeded to create its own world. In that world the center of life was the church, which preached the "whole Bible," and the Bible institute where the faithful could study doctrine untainted by the inroads of modernism. Though rigidly authoritarian, it was a comfortable world blessed by the assurance that it knew the full truth and that its salvation was secure. There was no consistent pattern in fundamentalist organization. In many cases persons of that persuasion remained in the larger denominations while at the same time grouping themselves into congregations with a fundamentalist character. In some instances conflict within a communion led to the withdrawal of the conservative wing to found a new denomination or to the loss of individuals who were drawn to some dynamic evangelist and his revivalistic methods. One such evangelist was "Sister" Aimee Semple McPherson, who founded the International Church of the Foursquare Gospel in Los Angeles and became famous during the twenties for dramatic and sensational services.

In several of the major denominations the fundamentalist-modernist controversy grew to gigantic proportions. None was more shaken by the conflict than the Presbyterian, U.S.A. During the painful theological controversies of the late nineteenth century, the church had held to its official position of Biblical inerrancy. In 1910 when a complaint was made to General Assembly that the New York Presbytery had licensed three ministerial candidates whose theological views were somewhat suspect, the Assembly ruled the following articles of faith were necessary for ordination: the inerrancy of Scripture, the Virgin Birth of Christ, the miracles of Christ, the substitutionary atonement, the Resurrection of Christ. No mention was made of premillennialism, a necessary article for fundamentalists. Though the Assembly of 1910 and the Assemblies of 1916 and 1923, which reiterated the five-point requirement, had no intention of reducing the church's theology to these five articles, the conservative element in the church tended to treat the articles in precisely that manner. The general effect was to increase tension and encourage heresy-hunting.

A widely publicized aspect of the conflict concerned the position of Harry Emerson Fosdick (1878–   ), a Baptist minister and professor of practical theology at Union Theological Seminary, at the First Presbyterian Church, New York. Dr. Fosdick had become stated preacher at the church in 1919 and, much to the displeasure of fundamentalists, had preached liberal theological views. When, in 1922, Dr. Fosdick delivered a ringing sermon entitled "Shall the Fundamentalists Win?" the tension became explosive. Complaints were brought before the General Assembly and in 1924 that body invited the controversial minister to enter the Presbyterian Church and subject himself to its discipline or terminate his relationship with First Church. Dr. Fosdick took the latter course and assumed the pastoral leadership of the liberal Park Avenue Baptist Church and later that of the famous Riverside Church, both in New York.

Meanwhile the Presbyterian conflict continued unabated. In 1924 a document signed by 1274 ministers and known as the "Auburn Affirmation" was issued in protest to the five-point doctrinal requirement which had been imposed by the General Assembly on the ground that it was unconstitutional. About the same time a controversy was shaping up in Princeton Theological Seminary, where Professor J. Gresham Machen was calling for the downfall of liberalism. In his book *Christianity and Liberalism* (1923) he insisted that liberalism was a wholly distinct religion from Christianity and that its adherents should not be permitted to remain within the church. Though most of his theology was rigidly orthodox, he embraced a doctrine of the church which was unorthodox to Presbyterianism. He held the church to be a voluntary society composed of persons who accepted a common theological position, an idea closer to Congregationalism. Growing tension among the faculty led to the decision of the General Assembly to investigate the situation at Princeton; the result was a reorganization of the Seminary and the withdrawal in 1929 of Machen and some of his followers to Philadelphia where they organized the independent Westminster Seminary. Later he and other conservatives organized the Independent Board for Presbyterian Foreign Missions. The General Assembly directed that all Presbyterians withdraw from this enterprise; Machen refused to abide by the directive and was suspended from the ministry. In 1936 he and his associates organized the Presbyterian Church of America, a body which suffered schism one year later when a faction withdrew to form the Bible Presbyterian Synod. The former body changed its name in 1939 to the Orthodox Presbyterian Church. With the exit of Machen and his following the Presbyterian Church in the U.S.A. settled down to enjoy theological peace.

The Baptists too were torn by theological dissension. Baptist fundamentalists in the North had organized the Fundamental Fellowship of the Northern Baptist Convention in 1920 and had attempted to persuade the Northern Baptist Convention to adopt a uniform confession of faith as a safeguard against liberalism. The New Hampshire Confession of Faith of 1830 was proposed to the Convention of 1922 for adoption as a fitting conservative symbol; instead, the Convention affirmed the New Testament to be "the all-sufficient ground of our faith and practice." The Southern Convention, however, though decidedly less troubled by theological liberalism, pronounced the New Hampshire Confession in 1925 to be expressive of the faith of most Southern Baptists. Meanwhile, in the North tension between liberals and conservatives continued to mount until, in 1925, the latter wing founded the Eastern Baptist Theological Seminary in Philadelphia in order to ensure the continuation of orthodox leadership. Extreme fundamentalists withdrew from the Convention in 1933 and organized the General Association of Regular Baptist Churches (North). Further dissatisfaction among conservatives who remained in the Northern Convention led to the founding of the Conservative Baptist Foreign Mission Society in 1943 and the Conservative Baptist Association of America in 1947.

Among the Disciples of Christ the hottest subject of debate was the admission of unimmersed adults, who were satisfied with their earlier baptism, into church membership. The conservative *Christian Standard* abhorred the practice which was fairly common, while the liberal *Christian Century* praised it. Even the Methodist Episcopal Church felt the force of militant conservatism. Repeated efforts were made at the General Conferences of 1916, 1920, and 1924 to force the Commission on Courses of Study for ministerial candidates to select only those works which the conservatives regarded as orthodox and to persuade the Conference to insist on strict conformity to the church's doctrinal standards; they met with failure. In the Protestant Episcopal Church there was a brief unpleasantness between orthodox and liberal factions; it was accentuated by a Pastoral Letter issued by the House of Bishops in 1923, which insisted on the historicity of the Virgin Birth and the Bodily Resurrection of Christ. But liberalism was by that time too widespread among the clergy, even among bishops such as William Lawrence of Massachusetts, to permit effective disciplining, and so the issue was quietly dropped.

With the advent of the 1930's and new manifestations of theological conservatism the fundamentalist movement began to lose something of its force. It gradually took on a more negative character and polemic spirit, directing its chief criticism toward scholars who denied the plenary inspiration of Scripture. To an era which was feeling the challenge of a dynamic Christo-centric faith, fundamentalism's Biblio-centrism seemed woefully passé. The result was that fundamentalists withdrew into their own spiritual cloister or made their home among the minor sects which offered a mixture of doctrinal conservatism and emotional extravagance.

Movements in Religious Education

In no area of the church's total program was the trend toward scientific attitudes more discernible than in the field of education. For some years there had been an emphasis on the improvement of lesson materials and teaching methods in keeping with the newer philosophy of child-centered instruction. Scientific methodology in religious education received an additional impetus through the studies of G. Stanley Hall at Clark University concerning the psychological characteristics of various age groups. A more important influence came from the Columbia University philosopher and educator, John Dewey. According to Dewey: "The aim of education is the reconstruction and reorganization of experience which adds to the meaning of experience and which increases ability to direct the course of subsequent experiences." Purposeful self-expression on the part of the student was prerequisite to effective learning; the fruits of sound education were social activities of a positive and creative nature. Professor George A. Coe of Union Theological Seminary, New York, spelled out the implications of this philosophy for Christian education in his important volume entitled *A Social Theory of Religious Education* (1917). The aim of Christian education, in Coe's view, was the "growth of the young toward and into mature and efficient devotion to the democracy of God, and happy self-realization therein." Optimistic in his view of human nature, he rejected the classical view which distinguished between sinful and redeemed man and developed an educational method designed to treat religious experience as a process beginning at birth rather than as a once-and-for-all decision made at the moment of conversion. Theologically it rested upon the liberal affirmation of divine immanence and the evolutionary view of history seen in terms of moral progress.

The 1920's witnessed a shift by many of the larger Protestant denominations from content-centered to experience-centered curricula. Hand work, construction work, story telling, and purposeful play replaced the older method of simply imparting knowledge of the Bible. Once again religious drama, long repugnant to orthodox Protestanism, came into its own. The guiding spirit behind this development was Professor Fred Eastman, teacher of biography and drama at Chicago Theological Seminary after 1926. Religious drama was found to be an excellent means of arousing the religious interest of young people and adults as well as children, particularly through the awakening of the imagination and the translation of ideas into action. Many churches discovered that the presentation of dramatized Bible stories, pageants, and tableaux enriched the worship experience of the entire congregation.

As the larger churches became increasingly concerned with the problems of education, more attention was given to leadership. Many congregations employed full-time Directors of Religious Education who became responsible not only for the program of the Church School but for all youth activities, leadership education, staff retreats, Vacation Bible Schools, and countless other educational enterprises of the church. The training of adult laymen in child and youth psychology, in Biblical content, and in administration was numbered among their more important functions.

Fundamentalist congregations remained generally aloof from the newer educational philosophy, although they frequently used modern equipment. For a time many returned to the old Uniform Lessons with all their weaknesses. Then, in 1933, the Moody Bible Institute issued the All Bible Graded Series, a marked improvement over the older lessons. This curriculum, while Bible-centered, conformed to the best pedagogical methods of reaching the child and the adolescent.

CHANGING EMPHASES IN WORLD MISSIONS

While Americans were enjoying a brief respite from involvement in world affairs and spending money freely in projects for their own benefit, a crisis was developing on the world mission scene. In eastern countries, which had long been under the domination of Western powers and had been made to feel inferior in the presence of Western culture, a reaction was fast setting in. Eastern peoples had come to see the benefit of the scientific and technological skills to which they had been exposed, and these they accepted. But they were demonstrating a growing reluctance to conform their religion and culture to European and American patterns. In many countries such as India and the Moslem nations there was an upsurge of nationalist sentiment and a subsequent disinclination to see in Christianity anything more than a vehicle of Western imperialism; in some countries, among them China and Turkey, there was a wave of antireligious zeal which threatened to ostracize not only Christianity but such well-entrenched religions as Taoism, Buddhism, and Islam. In Japan considerable resentment was engendered toward American missionaries as a result of the ban on Japanese immigration imposed by the United States in 1924. Part of the solution to these harassing problems was the creation of national churches such as the Church of Christ in China in 1927 and the training of outstanding indigenous clergymen such as the Japanese Protestant leader Toyohiko Kagawa.

Nevertheless, on some mission fields there were evidences of notable gains. In Latin America, Roman Catholicism and Protestantism in particular enjoyed a marked growth; this became increasingly true after 1929 with the development by the United States of its "good neighbor" policy.

On the whole, the greatest progress was made among those peoples which had most recently encountered Western civilization and were being brought into conformity with it before they had the opportunity of understanding what they were being led to accept. This was the situation in Africa south of the Sahara and in the islands of the Pacific. Among the primitive peoples of Burma and the despised classes of India there were also numerous accessions to Christianity.

Such gains by no means concealed the fact that the world missionary enterprise was in grave condition. The general decline in missionary interest and benevolence giving for world missions by the middle 1920's, a circumstance which was amplified during the great depression, was prophetic of increasing deficiencies in the missionary program. Even more discouraging was the mounting indifference among young people of college age toward missions. Prior to the First World War dedication of one's life to missionary service was popularly conceived to be the highest act of Christian commitment; on the college campus no force was more potent than the Student Volunteer Movement. After the war a certain apathy toward missions began to set in and the Student Volunteer Bands gradually disappeared from the colleges. There was still ample humanitarian zeal among college students, but their interests were directed more toward social and economic reform and the achievement of world peace.

Some Christian leaders believed that the reason for much indifference toward the world missionary enterprise was due to its outmoded philosophy and methods which resulted in a program in many respects irrelevant to the problems and needs of the modern world. They were convinced that the time had come for a full reevaluation of the motives for missions and consideration of a thoroughgoing reformation of the entire world missionary movement. Such a reformation would have to be accomplished with relative dispatch. In 1930 a group of American businessmen who had become disturbed over the decline in missionary zeal organized the Laymen's Foreign Missions Inquiry. Its purpose was to make a study of the current missionary programs, an evaluation of their effectiveness, and suggested changes for improvement. Research analysts were sent to India, Burma, China, and Japan to gather and assemble data on denominational missions in those countries; the result was a highly detailed and comprehensive report. The next step was to send a smaller group of distinguished Protestant leaders to these countries in 1931–1932 to make observations and appraise the material previously gathered. The report of the commission, which was chaired by Professor William E. Hocking of Harvard University, was published in 1932 under the title *Re-thinking Missions*. While the report was complimentary of numerous aspects of world missions, it was also moderately critical of Western missionary motives and methods and offered recommendations for appropriate changes. In a section entitled *General Principles* it exhibited a tolerance toward the non-Christian faiths which to many evangelicals seemed to constitute an abdication from responsibility to confront unbelievers with the claims of Jesus Christ. According to the report the hour had arrived "to set the educational and other philanthropic aspects of mission work free from organized responsibility to the work of conscious and direct evangelization." Mission boards should accept their Christian duty to "give largely without any preaching; to cooperate with non-Christian agencies for social improvement; and to foster the initiative of the Orient in defining the ways in which we shall be invited to help."

Though the report was well received by most liberal churchmen and by a number of denominational mission executives, it was sharply attacked by conservatives of all types, especially by fundamentalists and ardent missionary bodies such as the Seventh-day Adventists and the Christian and Missionary Alliance. The best exposition of a theology which held to the complete discontinuity between Christianity and the non-Christian faiths was given in *The Christian Message in a Non-Christian World*, a widely circulated work published in 1938 by the well-known Dutch professor of religion Hendrik Kraemer. Of the two views the latter was probably the most representative of the attitude shared by the rank and file of church members.

SOCIAL RELIGION IN TIME OF NORMALCY

That social life in the 1920's revealed a shocking inconsistency between the religious affirmations of the American public and popular conduct and morals was not as surprising as it might at first seem. At no time in American history had formal religious connections been more socially admired and dynamic religious living more casually ignored than in that morbidly gay and effervescent period known as the Jazz Age. Theodore Dreiser mirrored the times in his *An American Tragedy*, the story of a youth whose Salvation Army background did not dissuade him from drinking, visiting houses of ill fame, and finally committing murder. Not even the clergy could escape the agile pen-thrusts of that acrid critic of American society, Sinclair Lewis, as witness his *Elmer Gantry*.

If Dreiser and Lewis were intemperate in their criticism of contemporary society, it was not because criticism was undeserved. Whether in public or private life there was all too much evidence of scandalous conduct. In government the weak and ineffectual Harding regime, plagued by such disgraceful episodes as the Teapot Dome scandal, became symbolic of corruption in high places. It was a time of sensational murders, flourishing bootleggers and gangsters, and uncontrolled theft. Yet it was not the flagrantly wicked age that moralists frequently insisted it to be. It was an age in transition, recoiling from the drab moralism of the Victorian era and reacting in adolescent fashion to its new-found freedom.

To persons of an older generation such spectacles as college men in raccoon coats, women in knee-length dresses with bobbed hair who smoked cigarettes, and youth who rocked and swayed to the beat of syncopated rhythms were undoubtedly unnerving experiences. But these merely bore witness to radical changes in manners. Divorce was on the incline and sex information was no longer a matter of embarrassment, yet there seems to have been no significant increase in sexual irregularities and the number of illegitimate births remained low. Professional vice decreased markedly and the practice of lynching was moving toward extinction.

Prohibition and Repeal

The zeal for social reform which brought about the achievement of national prohibition at the close of World War I did not at once expire after the return to normalcy. The churches which had worked so diligently for prohibition together with the Anti-Saloon League continued to issue pronouncements from time to time in favor of the legislation. By the 1920's, however, the idealistic spirit which had attacked liquor for the purpose of redeeming the drunkard and reforming society was fading into the background. In its place stood a righteous and stern spirit which contemptuously regarded every drinker as an outlaw and an enemy of society. This changed attitude which revealed less concern for the humanitarian aspects of prohibition may have been natural under the circumstances, but it did not win respect for the churches.

Reactions to prohibition varied greatly with locality. Rural areas were principally dry; the urban Atlantic Seaboard was the wettest in the country. With the exception of cities such as Miami, New Orleans, Chicago, St. Louis, Reno, and San Francisco, the South, Midwest, and Far West were relatively dry. Social groups which opposed the ban on alcoholic beverages were the inveterate drinkers, the wealthy patricians, the rebel "Bohemians," and the Continentals for whom beer and wine were normal parts of their daily fare.

If prohibition was unpopular with certain elements of the population, it made little difference to moralists. What was important was that there was some reduction in drunkenness, a factor which contributed to a decrease in poverty and an improvement of family relationships. It has been estimated that 50 per cent less liquor per capita was consumed in 1926 than in 1918. But even the most ardent foes of liquor recognized that prohibition was not a glorious success. Bootlegging became a prosperous industry in spite of its risks, which in some areas were not great due to bribery of state and federal agents. At the same time the metropolitan press, essentially anti-prohibitionist, was using its vast resources for moulding public opinion to support repeal.

Of all the denominations the Methodists, through their Temperance Boards of the Methodist Episcopal Church and the Methodist Episcopal Church, South, were the most active in fighting repeal. The Baptists and Presbyterians ran a close second and third. Never were these bodies, especially their southern branches, more eloquent than after Governor Alfred E. Smith, Democratic candidate for the presidency in 1928, repudiated the Prohibition enforcement plank of his party's platform. These churches joined forces with the Anti-Saloon League and exerted such an influence on the public as to have contributed significantly to Smith's defeat. The Federal Council of Churches favored the continuation of Prohibition but refrained from denouncing wet candidates for public office. National opinion, however, was moving in the opposite direction and many Americans who recognized the evils of liquor were coming to the conclusion that the Eighteenth Amendment was not the ideal way to curb them. With that change came a sharp decline in the prestige of the churches as framers of public morals. Before the advent of the Roosevelt administration, which promised repeal, the Congress initiated the proper constitutional steps and, with the approval of the states, the Twenty-first Amendment became law in December, 1933, thus bringing Prohibition to an end. In subsequent years most of the denominations which had favored Prohibition continued to issue resolutions in its favor, but these seem to have made little impression on the public consciousness. Thoughtful Americans nevertheless realized that repeal had not solved the problem and that the liquor traffic was a serious menace to society. A partial answer was presented by the Federal Council of Churches in 1946; its report called for revision of the alcoholic beverage tax structure, careful regulation of the sale of liquor, and the placing of controls on advertising by the liquor industry.

Social Tensions in American Life

An unfortunate concomitant of the return to national insularity was a false "Americanism" inspired by a revival of bigotry and the intense fear of every form of radicalism. The year 1919 witnessed a "red" panic brought on by excited reports of communist plots to overthrow the government and destroy the property rights of American citizens. The decision of left-wing Socialists to affiliate with Moscow contributed to a wave of hysteria, despite the fact that relatively few persons followed the communist persuasion and most of the organizations which they formed were short-lived. The finger of suspicion was pointed indiscriminately at persons of liberal political views, and many persons with alleged communist leanings were prosecuted in the courts. Even the Federal Council of Churches was accused of radicalism, chiefly because of the sympathy it had showed to the cause of labor. In the excitement of the times it was not possible to keep the scales of justice in strict balance, as in the case of Sacco and Vanzetti, Italian anarchists who were charged with murder in 1920 and finally executed after being convicted on circumstantial evidence.

Simultaneously there was a resurgence of that nativist spirit which identified Americanism with Anglo-Saxon Protestantism and found Roman Catholics, Jews, and sundry aliens from southern and eastern Europe to be a menace to that way of life inaugurated by the founding fathers of the nation. One of the most uninhibited exhibitions of racial and religious bigotry could be seen in the revived Ku Klux Klan, an organization composed largely of lower-middle-class southern whites opposed to Negroes, Jews, Roman Catholics, and aliens in general. This secret oath-bound society, once the terror of the South, was reorganized in 1915 at Stone Mountain, Georgia, by Colonel William J. Simmons, who became its first Imperial Wizard. It was not until 1920, however, when Edward Clarke assumed the financial management and began a publicity campaign in which memberships were offered for a fee of ten dollars that the Klan reached truly national proportions. By 1925 it numbered perhaps four or five million adherents. Its method was to appeal to latent prejudices in American life and arouse the hatred of malcontents toward certain social and racial groups by planting fear in their minds. Religiously, it reflected the ideologies of Protestant fundamentalism and its concern over possible Roman Catholic domination and growing influence on the part of Jews. In areas where the Klan was most militant, there was often violence, which in some cases resulted in death or mutilation.

In both North and South the Klan was active in the political arena. It worked for legislation to prohibit parochial schools, endeavored to gain control of state governments, and fought in 1924 the nomination and in 1928 the election of Alfred E. Smith, Roman Catholic candidate for the presidency on the Democratic ticket. Numerous ministers actively supported the Klan, particularly in its opposition to Smith; and some rose to high positions in the order. They were rabid in their antagonism toward Roman Catholicism, being convinced that it was determined to gain control over the United States government. Smith publicly affirmed his belief in the separation of church and state and the equality of all religious groups before the law, but his statement fell on unbelieving ears. With the defeat of Smith, however, came the decline of the Klan, the criminal activities of which were now being exposed to public scrutiny. Unfortunately there was not a similar decline of race hatred and religious bigotry. The next decade would witness the rise of fascist anti-Semitism.

Though many individual church adherents succumbed to the "hate psychology," official Christianity raised its voice in opposition to intolerance and bigotry. In 1920 the Federal Council of Churches issued its pronouncement against racial discrimination, the first of a series on the subject; but seldom did it present anything more than the separate but equal doctrine. Segregation remained as firmly entrenched in the churches as in other American institutions, organized Christianity for the most part having resigned its responsibility to seek a solution to this vexing problem which had been heightened by heavy Negro migration to northern cities and terrible race riots during World War I. Future progress in this sphere would come largely through social and political action, initiated and carried forward by such groups as the National Association for the Advancement of Colored People. At least one positive step, however, was taken in the warfare against prejudice by the formation in 1928 of the National Conference of Jews, Protestants, and Catholics, later known as the National Conference of Christians and Jews. Its principal functions were to allay prejudice among religious groups and encourage cooperation in the achievement of common goals by means of an effective adult educational program.

Religion and the Economic Order

During the 1920's the cutting edge of the older Social Gospel was progressively dulled by the tendency of the churches to emphasize issues such as Prohibition, the questionable morality of motion pictures, and the decline of Sabbath observance, and also by the failure of socially concerned organizations such as the Federal Council of Churches to do more than reiterate the basic ideals which they had been promulgating for years. Of social concern there was ample manifestation, but it was based on a naively idealistic theology inadequate to meet the needs of the changing time and consequently had no more driving ambition than to maintain the *status quo*.

Immediately after World War I, a group of business executives endeavored to break the power of labor unions through the organization of an "Open-Shop Movement." Though this unsuccessful strategy was widely condemned by Christian leaders, the widespread fear that labor unions were in league with Russian Communists gave rise to a popular antagonism toward labor. It was believed by many that the great strikes of 1919, which involved some four million workers, had been inspired by Communists; actually only a small minority, such as those led by William Z. Foster, followed the Communist persuasion. Nevertheless the secular press led the public to believe that the unions were controlled by radicals.

The churches preferred to study the evidence more carefully before reaching a decision. In the case of the U. S. Steel strike (1919), the Inter-Church World Movement and the Federal Council of Churches conducted a thorough investigation, the former body issuing a report sympathetic to labor's demand for an eight-hour day to replace the then current twelve-hour working day. As a result the two organizations were bitterly assailed by management and accused of radicalism, a circumstance which un-doubtedly contributed to the downfall of the Inter-Church World Move-ment. The strike was crushed, but wide support for labor soon began to build up among Protestants who read the report, and labor's demands were endorsed by a number of denominational journals. The National Catholic Welfare Council and the National Council of Rabbis joined Protestant groups in calling for reform in the steel industry. Their voices were heard, and by 1923 the twelve-hour day for steel workers was a thing of the past.

At the same time powerful ideological forces were preparing a rebuttal to the pro-labor argument. One came from the well-known writer, Bruce Barton, who tried to convince the public in his best-selling biography of Jesus entitled *The Man Nobody Knows* that Jesus was the founding father of advertising and business, a veritable executive concerned with the problems of management. The suggestion of the book was that busi-ness was already Christian and therefore beyond the pale of justifiable criticism by labor. A far more influential argument was that Christian ethics had no relevance to social problems and the churches should con-fine their pronouncements to theological matters. This latter view gained little acceptance among the clergy, but it was generally adopted by the laity. While there was little that laymen could do to curb the social pronouncements of ecclesiastical dignitaries, they could and did bring a halt to the preaching of the Social Gospel in their parishes. A minister might feel called to preach a social message, but it was difficult for him to resist the will of those on whom he was financially dependent. There were, of course, clergymen who fought for their rights; as a result, many of these were without pulpits. Big Business was enthroned in the churches and professing Christians worshipped before the altars of material pros-perity. Then, in a moment, the Jazz Age, the age of normalcy, was over and a sorely chastened America struggled through stormy years of poverty and war at whose end there was no rainbow.

29

$\mathcal{R}$eligion in an $\mathcal{E}$ra of Crisis

LIKE A THIEF IN THE NIGHT, STEALTHILY AND VIRTUALLY WITHOUT WARNING, came the Great Depression, leaving behind it a nation in the throes of panic and poverty. Few persons then living could remember a time of such paramount crisis. From the vantage point of the early 1930's, World War I seemed most regrettable; but only a minority could recall the full intensity of its fury. The Depression was different. It worked its wrath on all classes and conditions of men—rich and poor, young and old, male and female—and drew them irresistibly into the fellowship of suffering and despair. The sad effects of this American tragedy were not immediately discernible; only gradually did it become evident that a profound ideological change was working itself out in national life. And yet where once there was almost complete trust in the perfectibility of man and belief in a utopian society just around the corner, there were anxious doubt and spiritual gloom. There was no indication that the malaise was prompting a return to sixteenth century ideas of the sovereignty of God and the depravity of man; the American reaction to crisis might be mercurial but it was not volcanic. The most that could be said was that the nation was suffering from tribulation so patently meaningless that a careful reappraisal of life seemed justified, even necessary. The result was an idealism stringently modified by realism, in which man's goodness was seen against a backdrop of evil and his accomplishments challenged by

562

the persistent fact of sin. It was a less buoyant, less assured philosophy than before, but it was not without hope.

RELIGION AND THE DEPRESSION

Though the Depression may be said to have begun with the fateful crash of October, 1929, it was not until 1932 that the public fully grasped the seriousness of the situation; not until a concerned electorate swept Franklin D. Roosevelt into the presidential chair and confronted the awesome spectacle of an official bank holiday followed by breath-taking action on the part of Congress did they realize how far they had sunk and how high they could climb.

Religious institutions throughout the country felt the full impact of the Depression. Many a congregation which had contracted unusually heavy debts for building programs during prosperous times had to face the bitter fact of foreclosure. Collections dropped almost 50 per cent from 1930 to 1934; in urban areas this invariably meant a sharp cut in ministerial salaries, while in the rural parishes it frequently necessitated dispensing with full-time pastoral services for the remainder of the crisis. The Methodist Episcopal Bishops spoke the mind of millions of churchmen when they declared in November, 1933: "Our resources are reduced below anything we have hitherto experienced. The means of aid at our command are tragically depleted." Religious attitudes toward the financial debacle were varied. Protestants in general regarded it as a punishment for sins, the Episcopal *Churchman* going so far as to pronounce it a judgment upon an economic system which was "rotten to the core." Roger Babson, careful student of finance, attributed the collapse to men's willingness to forsake Christ and follow selfish purposes. Roman Catholic interpreters usually emphasized the remedial function of current suffering and pointed to the eschatological hope of a better life in the world to come. Fundamentalists found the Depression to be a certain portent that the end of the present dispensation and the second coming of Christ were imminent.

It was widely supposed by religious leaders that hard times would cause Americans to make a fresh scrutiny of their religious needs and motivate them to seek out the ordinances of religion. Their hopes did not see fulfillment. The record shows that between 1930 and 1940 the churches gained at only one-half the percentage rate of the previous ten-year period. In 1940 membership in all religious bodies was reported at 64,-501,594 or 49 per cent of the nation's population. While these figures may be correct they denote at best a nominal membership and reveal nothing concerning the spiritual pulse of a people. The spirit of secularism had in no wise diminished and the decline in regular church attendance proved it. Women's organizations suffered considerably during the early thirties, possibly in large measure because of new vocational and avocational interests. The participation of youth in organized church activities continued to drop at an alarming rate.

Only among the extreme evangelistic Protestant churches and sects were there evidences of phenomenal membership increases during this period. The secret of their attractiveness was unquestionably in offering the financially distressed a better life in that glorious world which would soon be established after the return of Christ. Particularly successful were the Pentecostal and Holiness sects, which presented a strongly evangelistic and revivalistic message in a decade which was experiencing a dearth of revivals. The religion of a Saviour who cares for each sinner who comes to Him in the arms of faith met a definite emotional need of the disinherited, while the promise to lead the convert to the perfect life gave him a sense of status and well-being. Negroes especially found these sects appealing, as witness the large number of Negro accessions to Holiness bodies. The membership of the Church of the Nazarene, for example, climbed from 63,558 to 136,227 in the decade of 1926–1936, an increase of 114 per cent. During this same period the Assemblies of God, founded in 1914 in Arkansas, raised their membership from 47,950 to 148,043, a gain of 208 per cent.

During the early years of the Depression, the churches did what they could to minister to the needs of the suffering through the time-honored method of charity, but without notable success. The task was far too enormous to make possible effective results, to say nothing of the independent spirit which prompted many proud citizens to refuse charity. To find a solution for the problem was clearly the responsibility of the government; thus when the Roosevelt Administration began to take positive action, the churches hailed the step forward and promptly curtailed their efforts to provide relief. The New Deal manifested something of the spirit of the Social Gospel, remarkably so in the provisions of its National Industrial Recovery Act of 1933 which sought to insure higher wages, create additional jobs, and establish better working conditions. Church leaders were, on the whole, sympathetic and, though skeptical of the results, did what they could to promote the plan. The N.R.A. turned out to be a disappointment, having created as many industrial problems as it had solved, and many liberals greeted its downfall in 1935 with a sigh of relief. By this time two trends of utmost importance were distinguishable: America was gradually recovering from the Depression and once again the Social Gospel was coming into its own. As the economic picture began to brighten, however, the international picture darkened. As the decade advanced the attention of the government would be drawn increasingly toward maintaining national security, while the churches would direct their major efforts toward moral reform, improved industrial relations, and the preservation of peace.

RELIGION IN A DECADE OF GLOBAL CONFLICT

The rise of Hitler to power in 1933 and the subsequent extension of the brown shadow of the German Wehrmacht over the Rhineland, Austria, and Czechoslovakia, together with Japan's aggressions in China, brought deep concern to many thoughtful Americans who could see war clouds relentlessly blotting out the sunshine of peace. Despite governmental efforts to maintain neutrality, it was clear from the many international incidents in which there was loss of American lives and property that it was just a matter of time before the United States would be drawn into the vortex of war. Reluctantly the nation began to arm for its defense.

Pre-War Movements for Peace

As America drifted toward war many Christian leaders were still suffering pangs of conscience for the part they had played in World War I. Throughout the 1920's there was an increasing resolve on the part of large numbers of the clergy never again to bless another war. Among them were such prominent preachers of the Social Gospel as Harry Emerson Fosdick, Ralph W. Sockman, and Ernest Fremont Tittle. Strong pacifist sentiment among the clergy was manifested in 1931 when *The World Tomorrow* polled 19,000 Protestant ministers on their attitude toward war and learned that 12,000 would disapprove of any future war and more than 10,000 would decline to take an active part in one. A second and somewhat larger poll taken in 1934 revealed the same overwhelming repudiation of all armed conflicts. Denominations, other than the Society of Friends, the Brethren, and the Mennonites which included pacifism as part of their creed, issued official pronouncements in condemnation of war. The General Conference of the Methodist Episcopal Church, for example, declared in 1936 that the church "does not endorse, support, or purpose to participate in war." Youth conventions throughout the country adopted anti-war resolutions. Current pacifism, however, was significantly unlike the idealistic type of 1914. Its model was to be found in Mohandas Gandhi's program of resistance through non-violence, which resistance was rather removed from the teaching of Jesus. A common conception among pacifists was that each side in any conflict was equally to blame, a notion which made them incapable of appreciating the difference between aggression and defense.

Meanwhile, a reaction was beginning to set in among certain liberals to what they believed to be misguided pacifism. It was born of the conviction expressed eloquently by the Union Theological Seminary theologian Reinhold Niebuhr (1892–   ) in his provocative *Moral Man and Immoral Society* (1932) that the fundamental error of the time was the attempt to sanctify the social order and conceive it as an absolute good pitted against an absolute evil. Niebuhr found no absolutes, only relatives, in the social order; thus to wage or not to wage war became a choice between relative evils. It was conceivable that under certain conditions it might be more immoral to maintain neutrality than to fight. In any case, the non-pacifist could hardly go to war in the spirit manifested in 1917, for he knew that his action, though unavoidable, constituted sin. From that time Social Gospel liberals tended to divide into pacifist and non-pacifist camps.

It was perhaps ironic that as the national government moved away from isolationism and put into effect a policy of rearmament, Christian liberals of pacifist persuasion found more occasion for fellowship with political conservatives and minority groups which for one reason or another wanted to keep America out of war. Thus for a time the socially liberal *Christian Century* and the politically conservative *Chicago Tribune* traveled the same road though in most respects they had little in common. Unfortunately the pacifist groups were frequently used by anti-British and pro-Nazi forces to give respectability to their cause.

While church organizations generally approved the Lend-Lease program for aid to friendly nations adopted by Congress in 1941, the decision in 1940 to draft men into military service was greeted with loud cries of protest. Pacifist Christians could support a program of material assistance to beleaguered nations, but they were inalterably opposed to any action which appeared to be a step toward actual participation in conflict. Individual clergymen such as Harry Emerson Fosdick used their pulpits for the preaching of neutrality, while groups of ministers such as the 100 who signed "An Affirmation of Christian Pacifist Faith" in 1939 pledged themselves not to participate in war. At their Uniting Conference in 1939 the Methodists declared that they would support all members who claimed exemption from military service as conscientious objectors; the Federal Council of Churches successfully agitated for a change in the draft bill which would grant recognition to all conscientious objectors, whether church members or otherwise. Some pacifists, however, among them ministers and theological students, refused even to register and were sent to prison.

As America moved toward intervention, the cleavage in the churches and among the clergy over this issue widened. The International Convention of the Disciples of Christ in May, 1941, petitioned President Roosevelt "to keep this nation out of the war now raging in Europe." Other denominational bodies presented similar resolutions. On the other hand, a group of distinguished churchmen headed by Reinhold Niebuhr founded in 1941 the periodical *Christianity and Crisis* to counteract the pacifist influence. Its principal thesis was that despite all considerations of sinfulness in English and American life the Axis nations were promoting wicked ends and "the halting of totalitarian aggression is prerequisite to world peace and order." Although many Roman Catholics of Irish origin were unenthusiastic over the prospect of giving aid to England, they recognized the menace of Nazism and on that basis were drawn toward interventionism.

It was Pearl Harbor that decided the issue. After that fateful event, the majority of pacifists reluctantly admitted the necessity of America's entrance into the war and the churches, many of which had fought intervention, issued resolutions in support of the war effort. Throughout the nation religious people greeted the conflict with an attitude of resignation; this was no crusade, no holy war, but simply a job which had to be done if the world was to know any semblance of peace and justice. Of enthusiasm there was none, only a quiet and determined resolve to get on with the work.

The Churches and World War II

If the institutions of religion could not bless the war as holy, they could and did throw the weight of their support behind the national effort to gain a victory as quickly as possible and with the least loss of life. The Sunday after the Japanese attack on Pearl Harbor Protestant clergymen preached on such themes as "Love of Enemies"; "The Task of Christians and of the Church in the Present Crisis"; and "Post-War Reconstruction." Nearly two weeks later the Roman Catholic hierarchy in the United States resolved to "do our full part in the national effort to transmute the impressive material and spiritual resources of our country into effective strength not for vengeance but for the common good, not for national aggrandizement but for common security in a world in which individual human rights shall be safeguarded. . . ." At the next meeting of the Northern Baptist Convention in June, 1942, the assembled delegates resolved to "do anything for the welfare of our country within the full sanction of our individual consciences to achieve a Christian victory and secure for the world a just and lasting peace, regardless of personal cost or sacrifice." The resolution of the General Council of Congregational Christian Churches passed that same year was more moderate and included the viewpoint of the pacifist element within the denomination.

Though many church bodies gave their official blessing to conscientious objectors, only about one per cent of all registrants elected to seek that classification. These persons were ordinarily assigned to non-combatant service in work camps, performing duties in the area of land reclamation, public health, and forest and park service. By the end of 1944 about 8000 men were working in forty-seven Civilian Public Service Camps which were under the general direction of the Selective Service System. Camp necessities were provided by the government but the men received no wages and had to depend in large measure upon the churches for support. The outstanding work in this area was conducted by the American Friends Service Committee. All together the several participating denominations contributed about $4,500,000 to the program for conscientious objectors. It was largely a Protestant enterprise since the number of Roman Catholics and Jews taking a pacifist position was minimal.

One of the most important ways by which religious bodies ministered to the men and women in uniform was through the provision of chaplains. In the autumn of 1940 the government announced the policy of providing one chaplain for every 1200 men in army service, there being three Protestant chaplains for each Roman Catholic chaplain. Ordinarily the average large camp would be assigned only one Jewish chaplain. The principal work of the chaplains was to conduct services of worship and patriotic exercises, provide classes for religious instruction, and act as counselors to service personnel. Additional duties included visiting the sick and officiating at baptisms, marriages, and funerals. Since chaplains were given full responsibility for religious activities in the camps, the government adopted the policy of barring special organizations such as the Y.M.C.A. and the Knights of Columbus from having their own buildings in military areas. There was frequently close cooperation between the chaplains of the various faiths, a circumstance which fostered tolerance and understanding. The non-sectarian character of Protestant chapel services was responsible not only for a declining interest among servicemen in denominational distinctions but for an increasing non-denominational spirit.

The procurement of ministers, priests, and rabbis to be sent to training schools for chaplains required close cooperation between the institutions of religion and the government. The Federal Council of Churches developed an agency known as the General Committee of the Churches for the Army and Navy to act as a clearing house through which ministers from the several Protestant denominations might apply for commissions as chaplains. The Roman Catholic Church maintained a similarly functioning office which was responsible for the church's work among Roman Catholic servicemen. Endorsement of Jewish chaplains was made by the Jewish Welfare Board, an agency which represented all three branches of Judaism. Through the efforts of these and like commissions more than 8000 chaplains had entered the service before the end of the war. The high quality of their ministry brought prestige to the chaplaincy and conclusively established its importance to the spiritual life of men in uniform.

Wishing to support the cause of religion in the camps, Congress in 1941 appropriated $12,816,880 for the erection of 604 chapels in army posts and camps throughout the nation, each designed to seat several hundred persons. The buildings were so designed that altars, pulpits, and lecterns could be moved in order that each faith might employ its own accouterments of worship. The greater majority of American citizens approved the government expenditure for chapels, although some protested that it constituted a further violation of strict separation of church and state.

Social and recreational activities were also provided for servicemen by the government, with the cooperative assistance of Christian and Jewish benevolent agencies. Recreation buildings erected by the government were staffed by the United Service Organizations which coordinated the work of the Y.M.C.A., the Y.W.C.A., the National Catholic Community Service, the Salvation Army, the Jewish Welfare Board, and the National Travelers' Aid Association. U.S.O. clubhouses, established throughout the nation, provided free entertainment for men off duty, their staffs doing everything possible to supply the guests with all the comforts of home and assist them with personal problems. Part of the duties of these organizations was to make available religious guidance for those who desired it and to work with local churches and synagogues in ministering to servicemen. The 1027 U.S.O. clubs in the continental United States, together with 88 in other areas of the world, were financed through individual and group donations; they were open to all members of the armed forces irrespective of race or creed.

A special service for the spiritual edification of men in uniform was rendered by the government through the provision of Testaments, hymnbooks, and devotional literature. One of the most popular publications was *The Song and Service Book, Army and Navy, for Field and Ship,* a work divided into three sections for the use of Protestants, Roman Catholics, and Jews. It included selections from the Bible, responsive readings, prayers, and hymns. The American Bible Society distributed millions of Bibles and Testaments among the armed forces, the pocket Testaments containing a foreword by President Franklin Roosevelt. The Roman Catholic Church furnished its members in uniform with Testaments and prayer books, while Jewish groups distributed prayer books and Psalms among their adherents. Christian Scientists received copies of *Science and Health.* Many local churches or denominations endeavored to keep in touch with their members in service by sending monthly letters or news sheets telling of the work at home and giving practical spiritual guidance. The Lutheran Church, Missouri Synod, rendered a highly appreciated service by sending a monthly devotional leaflet to more than 110,000 members in the armed forces.

From the earliest days of the war the churches had been interested in helping refugees come to this country and assisting them after their arrival. This program was conducted by the American Committee for Christian Refugees, the National Refugee Service, the National Catholic Refugee Service, and the American Friends Service Committee. The latter body performed a host of humanitarian services such as feeding needy children in the European theater, operating ten ambulances in Western

China, furthering rehabilitation projects, and helping persons of Japanese ancestry who had been evacuated by the army from the Pacific Coast to resettle.

The Churches and International Responsibility

The war had not long been under way before the churches turned to the all-important task of laying the groundwork for a lasting peace. As early as 1942 the Federal Council of Churches' Commission to Study the Bases of a Just and Durable Peace, chaired by John Foster Dulles, issued a report which was adopted by a national study conference convened at Delaware, Ohio, in March of that year. The report, which was widely circulated, influenced in considerable measure the thinking of American churchmen. It presented the following Six Pillars of Peace:

I. The peace must provide the political framework for a continuing collaboration of the United Nations and, in due course, of neutral and enemy nations.
II. The peace must make provision for bringing within the scope of international agreement those economic and financial acts of national governments which have widespread international repercussions.
III. The peace must make provision for an organization to adapt the treaty structure of the world to changing underlying conditions.
IV. The peace must proclaim the goal of autonomy for subject peoples, and it must establish international organization to assure and to supervise the realization of that end.
V. The peace must establish procedures for controlling military establishments everywhere.
VI. The peace must establish in principle, and seek to achieve in practice, the right of individuals everywhere to religious and intellectual liberty.

In November, 1942, the National Catholic Welfare Conference, speaking for the hierarchy, called for the "establishment of an international order in which the spirit of Christ shall rule the hearts of men and of nations." Its report charged that totalitarian governments could not support a lasting peace. "The State that usurps total powers by that fact becomes a despot to its own people and a menace to the family of nations." The following month the American Institute of Judaism, meeting in Cleveland, proposed the foundation of a World Council of Christianity and Judaism to work for the establishment of righteousness and brotherhood in the post-war age.

When the war finally drew to a close in 1945, the religious institutions of the United States became even more actively engaged in the furtherance of their international responsibilities. The use of the atomic bomb in order to shorten the war with Japan, they recognized, placed upon the United States the duty to give moral leadership in the area of atomic power and show how such a potent force could be used for the accomplishment of peaceful ends. Another responsibility the churches recognized was that of caring for and rehabilitating suffering peoples in war-torn lands. Thus Northern Baptists, for example, raised more than $16,000,000 in their World Mission Crusade for this purpose, while Presbyterians, U.S.A., through their Restoration Fund, contributed over $23,000,000 for reconstruction work in Europe and Asia. Church World Service in 1946 came under the auspices of the Federal Council of Churches, the American Committee for the World Council of Churches, and the Foreign Missions Conference of North America; its major work was to send food and clothes to stricken countries.

It was perhaps inevitable that the churches should have devoted more emphasis in their international programs to practical relief, health, and education. The evangelistic motive was less in evidence, in large measure because indigenous churches in former mission territory had assumed the function of caring for the spiritual needs of their countrymen. Besides, as Americans came into contact with peoples whom they had known for so long as simply the "heathen," they came to think of them primarily as persons with whom they could share a rich fellowship rather than as objects to be manipulated according to the dictates of church dogma. What was distressing to missionary leaders in the United States was the decline in prestige of Christianity in many countries at a time in which nationalism and Communism were making rapid strides. That Christianity seemed to scores of people in Asia and Africa to be static rather than dynamic and the symbol of a decadent culture was a source of deep concern to mission executives in Europe and America. During the occupation of Japan and afterward the churches regained some of the ground which they had lost during the war, but this was small comfort to churchmen who comprehended the significance of those nationalist forces which were promoting a resurgence of Islam in Indonesia, Buddhism in Burma, and Hinduism in India. Nor could missionary leaders smile at the collapse of Nationalist China and the victory of the Communists in China; they knew it to be a portent of the church's martyrdom at the hands of revolutionists.

Sensing that the achievement of world peace depended in large measure upon an effective international organization, the religious bodies of the United States gave their overwhelming endorsement to the formation of the United Nations. In March, 1946, the Federal Council of Churches declared that the "United Nations offers a hopeful procedure whereby governments can peacefully adjust their disputes and advance their common interests." Nevertheless, it warned that the mere establishment of the United Nations was no guarantee of peace; governments would first have to "subordinate their national interests to a higher moral law and to the welfare of the whole family of God." The Roman Catholic hierarchy of the United States, in a statement issued in November, 1945, took issue with the Security Council provisions but pronounced the United Nations a step in the right direction. Similarly the Central Conference of American Rabbis in 1947 affirmed its commitment "to the world-wide purposes for which the United Nations stand: the moral influence of united mankind; the pursuit of peace and security; the advancement of humanity."

Despite the efforts of peace-loving countries to promote good feeling, the United Nations was swept from one international crisis to another during the first unpropitious decade of its existence. Most serious were the cold war between the Communist and free worlds and the hot war in Korea, instigated by North Korean aggressors in June, 1950. Though the authority of the United Nations was vindicated by the intervention of the United States and other member powers, the war was unpopular among Americans. Most citizens admitted that intervention was unavoidable but were appalled by the magnitude of the sacrifice and the indecisive nature of the conflict, which dragged to its formal close in 1953. As for the forces of organized religion, the war prompted them to intensify efforts in behalf of world peace, particularly through the development of a sense of community.

RECONSTRUCTION IN RELIGIOUS THOUGHT AND EDUCATION

If theological liberalism had emerged triumphantly from the conflict with fundamentalism during the 1920's, it did not have long to glory in its victory. Already forces were being released in American society which would prove destructive of the radiant idealism and evolutionary meliorism, long the dominant philosophies in national life. The American might naturally tend to be an optimist, but he found it difficult to maintain that condition in a generation which witnessed such a series of calamities as the failure of the League of Nations, the collapse of church "world movements," the Depression, World War II, the Korean War, and the mounting threat of Communist aggression. Self-confidence did not explode at once, Americans preferring to regard their misfortunes as undeserved tragedies brought on them by demonic powers from without. But gradually they began to give consideration to the disastrous consequences of personal sin and to some extent develop an experiential awareness of their own guilt. Out of this situation was born a revival of interest in theology.

Symptomatic of the new ideological trends was the transition in American religious philosophy. By 1925 absolute idealism, which had nurtured liberal theology, had fallen into retirement; vying for its former place in the sun were various conflicting systems, the more important of which stood for some form of realism. Supernaturalism was being sorely tested by the religious humanism of John Dewey, but humanism, on the other hand, was being weakened by the theistic naturalism or empirical theism of Henry N. Wieman of the University of Chicago, who defined God as "that character of events to which man must adjust himself in order to attain the highest goods and avoid the greatest evils." At Yale Divinity School, Douglas C. Macintosh was promulgating theological realism via the empirical method, while at Boston University, Edgar S. Brightman was using the same method to arrive at his concept of a personal but finite God; at the same time Brightman was placing a fresh emphasis on the seriousness of evil in the cosmic process. At Haverford College, Rufus Jones was seeking out the World-Mind by mystical intuition, rationally verified. Alfred North Whitehead of Harvard rejected all pantheistic identifications of God with the world because they could not account for positive evil and postulated a God that deals with evil and transforms it into good.

Most significant for religious philosophy was the importation of existentialism from Europe. This system, which came to be known in America primarily through the work of the nineteenth-century Danish philosopher, Sören Kierkegaard, and the twentieth-century Spanish Catholic, Miguel de Unamuno, struck at the roots of idealism with its tragic picture of human life estranged from God and rooted in sin, frustration, and despair. Out of it grew theologies which stressed the sinful nature of man's action, his utter need of divine grace, his personal encounter with the living God, and God's gift of salvation.

The first significant manifestation of theological existentialism in America came through the crisis theology of the Swiss Protestant theologian, Karl Barth (1886–   ). Writing in 1919 for the edification of a disillusioned German citizenry, Barth, in his commentary on Romans, startled his readers by introducing them to a God who confronts man in a demand for his decision to accept or reject the divine will. This God, who is the "wholly other," the transcendent, speaks to man through Jesus Christ alone; He speaks to him in a moment of crisis, an existential moment, in which man's sin stands uncovered and he responds to the divine will humbly in an act of total commitment. This dynamic encounter is possible not through natural theology or reason but only through faith which is a gift of God; it involves not the perception of an ultimate principle of truth but the reaction to a personal will. Much of Barth's thinking permeated the teachings of another leading crisis theologian, Emil Brunner (1889–   ) of Zurich. They parted company, however, over Brunner's insistence that there is some revelation outside the Bible and that original sin does not completely obliterate the image of God in man. Still Brunner believed that God could not be known truly through philosophy but only through a dynamic personal "I-thou" relation. One of his most important contributions was to relate this principle to Christian ethics.

Main Currents in Contemporary Theology

It was not until 1928, when Barth's *The Word of God and the Word of Man* was published in English, that Barthian theology began to make a vital impression on American thinkers. Even so, it had no wide impact until the critical days of the Depression, and then it appeared in a considerably revised American form which was known principally in academic circles. A considerable number of the American revisionists had been nurtured in liberalism but reacted to its theological naïveté. Thus Walter Lowrie, in his *Our Concern with the Theology of Crisis* (1932), wrote critically of liberalism and sympathetically of the new European theology which was coming to be known as neo-orthodoxy. Equally critical of liberalism were Edwin Lewis in his *Christian Manifesto* (1934), George W. Richards in his *Beyond Fundamentalism and Modernism* (1934), and Walter Marshall Horton in his *Realistic Theology* (1934). Not all theologians in America, to be sure, followed in the steps of Continental existentialism. There were some who preferred the more moderate theology of Englishmen William Temple and John Oman, the *agape* motif of the Lundensian (Swedish) theologians Anders Nygren and Gustaf Aulen, with its emphasis on God's free self-giving grace, the scholastic neo-Thomism of Jacques Maritain which was being promoted in the Roman Catholic Church; or the religious interpretation of history and the mystical theology of the Eastern Orthodox thinkers Nicholas Berdyaev and Sergius Bulgakov.

During the late 1930's Princeton Theological Seminary, under the presidency of the eminent ecumenical churchman John A. Mackay, became the chief center of theological existentialism in the United States. To its faculty were brought such able exponents of "crisis" thinking as Otto Piper, exile from Hitler's Germany, and Elmer G. Homrighausen. Guest professorships in 1938 and 1939 went to Emil Brunner and the Czech theologian Josef Hromadka. Probably the outstanding influence of Continental existentialism in America came through the work of Paul Tillich (1886–   ), German emigré who served as professor of philosophical theology at Union Theological Seminary from 1933 to 1954, thereafter becoming university professor at Harvard University.

The John the Baptist of the new theological movement, the primary revisionist and interpreter of existentialism in the United States, was Reinhold Niebuhr (1892–   ) of Union Theological Seminary. Reared in the tradition of conservative Lutheran and Reformed theology and attracted to the ethical implications of the Social Gospel, he had become vitally interested in the social witness of Christianity while serving as pastor of a congregation of factory workers at Bethel Evangelical Church in Detroit. Later, at Union Seminary, his keen analysis of social problems and his criticism of the liberal effort to achieve the Kingdom of God through human efforts in *Moral Man and Immoral Society* (1932) constituted a clarion call for theological and social reconstruction.

At the heart of Niebuhr's theology stood the doctrine of original sin, not in the classic sense of an inheritance from Adam but in the sense of a natural leaning toward pride and magnified self-interest. Man's only salvation from sin is through the grace of God; in his encounter with the divine he comes to the realization that it is through God's power alone that his pride and sinful trust in his own sufficiency can be overcome. But this salvation does not free man entirely from the effects of sin nor from the complex problems of human society. Frequently even the Christian must face the necessity of choosing between the lesser of two evils rather than an absolute good and then doing the best he can in an undesirable situation. Since social groups always represent a strange mixture of good and evil, it is possible for individual acts to be performed on a higher moral plane than social acts. This is because a society can more naturally express the original sin of self-interest and pride than can an individual. It can make claims for itself which would appear ridiculous if asserted by a private citizen.

From his studies of the New Testament and observation of the savage struggles for power in the social order, Niebuhr reached the conclusion that Jesus' ethic was one which demanded perfection and was therefore impossible of attainment. Indeed, it stood in judgment over every ethical situation and summoned the Christian to recognize his moral inadequacy and seek forgiveness. Niebuhr's concept stood between the pessimism of Barthianism which saw the Kingdom of God only as a future hope and the unqualified optimism of American liberalism which confused the Kingdom with human progress. For Niebuhr the Christian way was to work for every possible reform, recognizing the difficulty of moral progress but trusting that each task performed in faith would have significance in the unfolding of the divine purpose.

By the mid-1930's it was obvious that the old order of liberalism had passed and a new theological era was in the making. Harry Emerson Fosdick, the dean of American liberal preachers, dramatized the change in 1935 in his startling but provocative sermon, "The Church Must Go Beyond Modernism," delivered at Riverside Church. Fosdick's indictment of modernism was that it had placed too much emphasis on intellectualism, that it had been overly sentimental, that it had humanized the concept of God, and that it had conformed too much to the standards of the modern world. The time had come for Christians to stand apart from the "prevailing culture" and challenge it. These views were endorsed by such liberals as John C. Bennett, Walter Marshall Horton, and Henry P. Van Dusen.

But if there were changes they were not all in the direction of Barthianism. In addition to the theistic naturalism of Henry Wieman and the neo-orthodoxy of Reinhold Niebuhr there was developing a school which might be termed neo-liberal. Its position was most clearly delineated in a chapter contributed by John C. Bennett to a symposium entitled *Liberal Theology: An Appraisal* (1942). Bennett maintained that the best in liberalism should be preserved and integrated with the best in orthodoxy. Thus the liberal views that man as a creation of God is essentially good, that he is a rational creature, and that he is free and responsible for his thoughts and deeds were indispensable. On the other hand, it was important to realize that sin is real and ever present in society, corrupt-ing men and persuading them that their evil acts are righteous, that a utopian order could not be achieved on earth even though some progress might be expected, and that repentance is constantly necessary in order to save men from the sin of pride and self-righteousness.

Among the distinguished American theologians who have been in-debted to both liberalism and neo-orthodoxy, mention may be made of H. Richard Niebuhr, Robert L. Calhoun, and Walter M. Horton. Pri-marily a historical theologian, H. Richard Niebuhr of Yale Divinity School has dealt critically with the church's role in a profane order, emphasizing the tension between Christian consecration and secular involvement. Yet if his *The Social Sources of Denominationalism* (1929) presented a de-spairing picture of the American religious situation, his *The Kingdom of God in America* (1937) offered a positive and hopeful reading of Ameri-can Christianity. In his theology Niebuhr has stressed the sovereignty of God and the grace of Jesus Christ as necessary in the redemption of society and the need for the Christian movement to be revolutionary and dynamic, committed both to worship and work for the salvation of the world. Niebuhr's colleague, Robert Calhoun, has held similarly to a religious realism gripped by neither radical pessimism nor uncritical optimism. Calhoun's God is ever at work in the world, communicating with men and laboring with them to bring them from sin to repentance and life in love. Walter Marshall Horton of Oberlin Graduate School of Theology has repudiated liberalism as a system of theology and has adopted a liberal evangelicalism. His theology has stressed God as per-sonal and transcendent and religion as redemptive; while it admits the possibility, even the probability, of tragedy in human history, it finds that history is necessarily moving toward the fulfillment of God's purpose.

By the 1950's there were signs of a resurgence of strength among funda-mentalists or Biblical literalists. While their position remained essentially unaltered, under the leadership of such thinkers as Edward J. Carnell, Carl F. H. Henry, and Cornelius Van Til they presented a more rational and philosophical defense of their faith and demonstrated a willingness to enter the wider arenas of theological discussion. They also manifested an interest in social ethics quite unknown to fundamentalists of an older generation.

With the publication of Reinhold Niebuhr's two-volume work on *The Nature and Destiny of Man* in 1941 and 1943 there was inaugurated a new era of system-building in American theology. It developed slowly and cautiously and at first only specific aspects of Christian thought were treated by the constructive theologians. Thus Niebuhr's masterpiece attempted to deal with no more than human nature and human destiny. About the same time Nels F. S. Ferré of Andover Newton Theological School (more recently at Vanderbilt University), a Congregational minister of Swedish birth who had been influenced by the Lundensian theology, began to publish a series of volumes which presented a system half-way between the Swedish school and neo-liberalism. Ferré has found the Agape Love of God to be the distinctive motif of Christianity. Such love, which is made known supremely in Jesus Christ, is resisted in history by moral evil but in the end it will triumph. So far has Ferré carried this idea that he arrives at an ultimate monism and a universal salvation.

More than any other man, Paul Tillich offers promise of becoming the Thomas Aquinas of contemporary American Protestant theology. So versatile a thinker can scarcely be summarized in a few descriptive sentences, especially since what promises to be his *magnum opus,* the *Systematic Theology,* has been completed only through the first two volumes (1951 and 1957). Nevertheless, through the study of these and other important works such as *The Shaking of the Foundations* (1948), *The Protestant Era* (1948), *Love, Power, and Justice* (1954), and *Theology of Culture* (1959) it is possible to reach certain tentative conclusions concerning his major contributions. Tillich fits into no ready-made category, though it might be said that he combines in his thinking elements of both liberalism and neo-orthodoxy. His theology is developed in the five dimensions of epistemology, God, Christ, the Holy Spirit, and the Kingdom of God.

For Tillich, theology begins with the problem of fallen man, with man's ultimate concern which determined his being or non-being in relation to God who is Being itself. The central problem of life is to find the courage to be, to participate in the ultimate power of being. Christian theology deals with this problem in its presentation of Christ as the center and meaning of history, as the means whereby man finds the answer to his existential self-estrangement and meets God in a dynamic encounter. Religious knowledge, therefore, involves the unity of the knower and the known rather than cognitive knowledge of an external reality. This does not rule out historical revelation unless one thinks of it in terms of revealed doctrines; nevertheless, as event and experience, revelation can be described in theological terms.

The heart of religion for Tillich is the Biblical message of justification by faith, the paradox that sinful man is accepted by God as if he were righteous. With the realization that God has accepted him as he is, man can overcome his feelings of guilt and anxiety and his pretentiousness and can confront the ambiguities of life without rationalizing them away. Through faith he is freed from himself and grasped by a power greater than his own. Protestantism must bear witness to this free grace of God which points men beyond themselves and must protest against any heteronomous inclination to place either dogma or the church in the place of God. Any giving of one's ultimate concern to that which is not ultimate, such as the state or the church, is idolatrous. One's ultimate concern must be the living God.

Trends in Religious Education and Culture

Although the contemporary architects of theological reconstruction have not yet permeated the grass roots with their thinking, there has been at least on the popular level a renewed interest in the Bible. This interest has been evidenced in the number, quality, and popularity of the more recent translations, among them a revised edition of the Moffatt translation (1935), Goodspeed's *The Bible, An American Translation* (1931), John Bertram Phillips' *The New Testament in Modern English* (1958), and the highly important Revised Standard Version, the New Testament being published in 1946 and the Old Testament in 1952. The Confraternity edition of the New Testament, a translation by Roman Catholic scholars, was issued in 1941. Since that time a number of Old Testament books have been translated by scholars of the Catholic Biblical Association of America and have been published. No important Jewish edition has appeared since 1917, when the Jewish Publication Society of America published *The Holy Scriptures According to the Masoretic Text, A New Translation*. In the area of Biblical study, a commission of leading Protestant scholars issued a twelve-volume commentary known as *The Interpreter's Bible* from 1951 to 1957. It has proved to be the most popular work of its type to appear in the twentieth century.

The awakening of interest in Christian doctrine and Biblical theology since the 1930's has had a profound effect not only on the curricula of theological seminaries but of church schools as well. Indeed, it has contributed to a changed emphasis in the entire program of Christian education. As late as 1940, Harrison Elliott of Union Theological Seminary was defending the liberal philosophy of education in his *Can Religious Education Be Christian?* But it was a lost cause. The trend was to produce lesson materials which placed more emphasis on theology and on the relevance of the Bible for contemporary living. This is not to suggest that religious education was reverting to the older type of content-centered curriculum. Quite to the contrary, the learner was still central and through the study of psychology the program was being geared more effectively to his needs. These new developments in educational philosophy were indicated in *Christian Education Today,* a report published in 1940 by the International Council of Religious Education. According to Paul H. Vieth's *The Church and Christian Education,* brought out in 1947, "the foundations of Christian Education are to be found in the nature and condition of man who is to be educated, in the faith which the church professes, and in the principles of education which define how learning takes place."

With the reemphasis on theology came a recovery of the communal aspects of the Christian life, notably upon the church as a divine fellowship, upon the significance of the Christian home, and upon the importance of a close correlation between religious guidance in the home and in the church school. New denominational curricula issued during the late 1940's and 1950's included material specifically for parents and helps for family worship and education as well as lessons for Sunday classes. Among these were the Presbyterian, U.S.A., *Christian Faith and Life Series,* the Congregational-Christian *Pilgrim Series,* and the Protestant Episcopal *Seabury Series.* Many churches have geared the entire parish program around the family, encouraging their communicants to worship as families; some have inaugurated special family services, featuring music by junior choirs, while others have arranged for children to be present for a time at the traditional morning service of worship and then to be dismissed to the care of the church school. Along with the trend toward family-centered programs has come a growing stress on the recruitment and training of lay staffs to carry on the many and varied duties of religious education. In many cities local federations of churches have joined with neighborhood congregations in offering content and methods courses for training teachers and prospective teachers.

RELIGIOUS DEVELOPMENTS ON THE DOMESTIC SCENE

The Resurgence of the Social Gospel

While the 1930's witnessed a revolt from the older "Social Gospel" liberalism, there was no concomitant departure from a sense of social responsibility. What was lost was the buoyant optimism born of the conviction that through man all things were possible. What was gained was a fresh awareness of the depths of human pride and passion and the wide disparity between the ethical accomplishments of men and the Kingdom of God. In America, however, this did not result in an eschatological faith which looked for social justice almost wholly in the Second Coming of Christ as a future event; rather, out of it came a renewed zeal to relate God's will to the social order so far as this was possible in a society embroiled in the struggle for power and addicted to the absolutizing and deifying of its own relative interests.

Despite the transformed and revitalized character of the Social Gospel, the churches were unable to recapture the standing in secular society which they had held prior to the 1920's. It was an age of increasing secularism, outwardly respectful to religion but patently indifferent or unconcerned. The principal strength of the new Social Gospel was among the clergy, particularly those of liberal political persuasion. This group, suspected of "socialism" by influential conservatives in the laity, was opposed by the Church League of America, founded in 1937 to make known to the clergy "the viewpoint of laymen, the members who really support the churches and who have a great stake in the private enterprise system in this country." The result was that the chief agitation for social reform came from denominational and interdenominational leaders whose pronouncements frequently did not reflect the will of a majority of the laity.

In this setting the Federal Council of Churches undertook in 1932 to issue a revised version of its Social Creed. On the whole it was a decidedly less ambiguous document, forcefully pointing out the dangers of "speculation and the profit motive" and the need for "collective bargaining and social action." New clauses were added on "Social planning and control of the credit and monetary systems and economic processes for the common good," and "Economic justice for the farmer in legislation, financing of agriculture, transportation, and the price of farm products. . . ." Similarly, the Roman Catholic Church developed its program of social reconstruction through the organization of the Catholic Worker Movement in 1933 and the Association of Catholic Trade Unionists in 1937.

After the late 1930's most of the battles between management and labor were fought without recourse to ecclesiastical opinion. For instance, when Republic Steel fought with John L. Lewis' Steel Workers' Organizing Committee in 1937 over union recognition, 100 prominent clerical leaders appealed to the company to negotiate with the union; only the slightest attention was given this appeal by the press. By this time organized labor had little need of support by the churches, so great had become its power. With power, unfortunately, came potential and in some cases realized corruption, causing many religious leaders during the 1950's to reflect on the need for reform in other areas of the economic order.

The single besetting problem of American society in the era of crisis was race. An awakened Negro minority, increasingly aware of its rights and opportunities, was insisting that the "separate but equal facilities" principle was unjust and was making demands for legislation on behalf of public integration. Though the fullest application of segregation was in the South, throughout the country there were evidences of discrimination through "restrictive covenants" in residential areas, refusal to admit Negroes in certain hotels and restaurants, and numerous other restrictions. While the churches had been championing the rights of minority groups for some years, they had been slow to take a position for integration. The Federal Council of Churches took this step for the first time in 1946 and admonished its member churches to work for a "non-segregated society." Several denominations took similar action. The following year the Archbishop of St. Louis ordered Roman Catholic parochial schools in his archdiocese opened to Negro students; a similarly firm stand was taken in the Archdiocese of San Antonio and New Orleans. In many cases Roman Catholic and Protestant clergy met defiance from their membership when they called for integration. Certainly there were relatively few congregations which functioned on an integrated basis. The decision of the United States Supreme Court in 1954 that racial segregation in public schools was unconstitutional created tension in some quarters. Most Americans, however, acquiesced in changes which they knew to be inevitable and prayed for wisdom and charity to see them through a difficult period of adjustment.

During the late 1930's, a revival of anti-Semitism nurtured by such clerics as Father Charles Coughlin and the Reverend Gerald L. K. Smith called forth the opposition of Roman Catholic and Protestant churches alike. On the positive side, the National Conference of Christians and Jews promoted the study of interracial and interreligious problems and thus did much to destroy bigotry and prejudice.

By the 1920's the right of women to vote and to participate in public life had been assured. Since that time a number of churches have permitted women to serve on local or national boards. In regard to ordination the denominations have been more conservative, though by 1959 women might be ordained in such bodies as the African Methodist Episcopal Zion, the American Baptist, the Disciples of Christ, the United Church of Christ, and the United Presbyterian in the U.S.A. The Methodist Church granted women the status of "local elders" without permitting them membership in conferences. The Roman Catholic Church continued to welcome women into the orders but did not consider their ordination to the priesthood.

New Emphases in American Judaism

The assimilation of Jewish immigrants into the American environment brought with it profound changes in Jewish life and thought. Socially, there had been a steady rise in status on the part of the East-European group, which during the second and third decades of the twentieth century had largely removed themselves from downtown tenement sections and had moved uptown where they had formed mixed communities with

Jews who represented an older settlement. With material advancement, however, came an alarming indifference toward the traditional faith, especially on the part of the younger generation. In many cities the Jewish Center became the chief expression of "Jewishness," providing a specifically Jewish orientation for cultural, political, and philanthropic activities. Religion figured in the community movement, but only as one among many expressions of Jewishness.

The most receptive of the three Jewish bodies to this new trend was Conservatism, which stressed the study of Hebrew and Jewish culture. At the Jewish Theological Seminary considerable interest was shown toward secular Jewish learning and in particular the contemporary Jewish culture emerging from Zionism. One professor at the seminary, Mordecai Kaplan (1881–   ), was singularly motivated to deal creatively with this trend. His approach to the Jewish religion was sociological. As a young man he had developed a deep-seated Jewish consciousness and a passion for Jewish culture without at the same time troubling himself about the concept of God. During his years as a seminary student he began to doubt the Mosaic authorship of the Torah and the historicity of miracles; for him the metaphysical basis of religion gradually dissolved and he came to think of it as the "heightened consciousness of group interests." Central to Judaism were the people of Israel; the Bible was the expression of their striving for self-fulfillment. In 1934 Kaplan incorporated these ideas in a work entitled *Judaism as a Civilization*.

The year 1935 saw the foundation of Kaplan's Reconstructionist movement, the principal goal of which was to promote the establishment of organic Jewish communities which would embrace all Jewish activities and stimulate a sense of Jewish peoplehood. In such communities there would be a place for both religious and non-religious Jews. It was Conservative Judaism, a rapidly growing movement which by 1940 had come under the domination of East-European Jews, that felt the fullest impact of Kaplan's teaching. In general, Conservatism rejected his philosophy but in considerable measure followed his practice of fostering a broad, all-inclusive Jewishness.

Meanwhile, Reform Judaism, also feeling the effects of an influx of East-European elements, by 1930 began to move toward greater use of ritualism and ceremonial. This trend was officially endorsed in 1937 by the Union of American Hebrew Congregations. Three years later a revised version of the Union Prayer Book was published, with slight changes in a ritualistic direction.

One of the most important issues facing the American Jewish community was Zionism. For centuries the belief that Jewish nationality would one day be restored in Palestine was a cardinal feature of Jewish religion. Though repudiated by Reform Jews in the nineteenth century, the greater majority of Jews continued to hope for the restoration of

Israel. This hope was sparked during the terrible persecution of Jews in Eastern Europe late in the nineteenth century; with the publication of *The Jewish State* by Theodor Herzl, a Viennese journalist, in 1896, excitement flared up all over the world and Zionism spread rapidly. Despite the opposition of Reform leaders such as Isaac M. Wise, Zionism gained a foothold in America but it was not until World War I that it assumed the character of a mass movement. Its official agency was the Zionist Organization of America. By 1930 nine national Zionist groups had been organized in the United States with a total membership of about 100,000.

As a result of the terrible mass persecution of the Jews by Hitler, in which six million persons went to their deaths, and as a result of anti-Jewish violence in Arab countries during the 1930's and 1940's, thousands of American Jews who had remained aloof from Jewish activities began to contribute to or work for the United Jewish Appeal or the Zionist organizations. In 1948 alone, the year of the establishment of the State of Israel, $201,000,000 was raised for Jewish relief. It is interesting to note that since 1937, when the Reform rabbis adopted a new platform at Columbus, Ohio, Reform Judaism has officially endorsed the upbuilding of the Jewish state not only as a "refuge for the oppressed" but as a "center of Jewish culture and spiritual life." Among the most influential leaders in this trend toward Zionism were Rabbi Stephen S. Wise and Rabbi Abba Hillel Silver.

Since World War II there has been a revival of Judaism as a religion and a concomitant decline in zeal for the principle of "Jewishness." From 1937 to 1956 the membership of Conservatism increased from 75,000 to 200,000 member families; during the same period Reform climbed from 50,000 to 255,000 families. Orthodoxy suffered a decline in membership but was characterized by a new and remarkable vigor. Jewish schools have similarly flourished. During the 1950's there were evidences of increased attendance at services and a greater inclination to observe the customs and ceremonies of the religion. These changes in American Judaism reflect to some extent the Jewish transition to middle-class respectability; they are also linked to contemporary patterns of religiousness in American culture.

Trends in Religious Communication

Though the period since the Depression has been marked by a singular rise in church attendance, changing patterns of American life have dicated certain alterations in the method of communicating religious truth. Sunday-morning services have been patronized to such an extent that many churches have been obliged to offer a duplicate "early" service. Yet Sunday-evening and mid-week services have generally suffered a decline, largely perhaps because of other interests vying for the churchgoer's time. To the average American church attendant the Sunday-morning service has become the principal hour, possibly the only hour, of weekly inspiration. He has come to expect from it not primarily a learned homily on some theological theme but fellowship with the divine and some "practical" word of guidance to help him meet the day-to-day problems of life.

As a consequence there has been developing on the American scene a revival of worship as a primary means of religious communication. The free church service with its gospel songs and extemporaneous prayers set in a mood of friendly informality is still the dominant national expression of worship. On the other hand, an increasing number of churches have responded favorably to the current liturgical movement. It has resulted not in the abolition of free church forms but has enriched them by fostering a deeper understanding of worship as a corporate act of devotion. In denominations with a long and rich liturgical tradition, notably the Episcopal and Lutheran, there has been renewed emphasis on the rites of the church as symbols of its faith and tokens of its unity in love. Roman Catholicism also has experienced a growing liturgical revival. In many parishes the dialogue Mass, during the celebration of which the congregation recites the prayers with the priest, has been introduced.

American preaching too has been forced to adjust to the demands of the new situation. In the face of a growing religious illiteracy, many ministers have tended to depart from textual and expository preaching which interprets a Biblical passage and relates it to contemporary living; they have preferred to preach topical sermons, life-situation sermons, and book-review sermons which begin with a subject of common interest and proceed to apply the Biblical witness to the religious problem under discussion. Whatever the type of homily, the use of illustrations has figured prominently, for American audiences have proved themselves more responsive to story-telling than to dissertations on the abstract. Successful homiletical craftsmen such as Halford Luccock and William Stidger have demonstrated how the skillful use of illustrations can become a powerful means for the communication of religious truth. In recent years numerous preachers of wide popularity have addressed themselves to national audiences through the publication of books of sermons or magazine articles.

Since the 1920's there has been increasing concern among religious leaders for the spiritual development of youth, particularly on the college campus. The rapid development of state universities in which religion, if taught at all, is dealt with as part of the humanities program has posed a problem for the denominations, which are committed to guide youth to a spiritual orientation and to decision. Many denominations have designated clerical or lay representatives to act as college chaplains to students of their faith. Interdenominational organizations such as the student

Y.M.C.A., the student Y.W.C.A., and the Inter-Varsity Fellowship have also performed a significant work. The general denominational pattern has been to establish a "house" on campus, which becomes the center of student activities. Of late there has been a tendency toward greater co-operation in this work among the several Protestant communions.

Since 1923, when the first religious broadcast in the history of radio was made, there has been a marked growth in the utilization of wider avenues of communication by the churches. They have come to recognize the extreme importance of radio, television, and motion pictures as media for the presentation of inspirational and educational programs. For some years leading radio networks such as the National Broadcasting Company and the Columbia Broadcasting System have granted free time to re-ligious organizations for the production of non-polemical programs of inspiration. For example, N.B.C. has allotted time to the Federal Council of Churches for the "National Radio Pulpit," to the National Council of Catholic Men for "The Catholic Hour," and to the Jewish Theological Seminary of America for "The Eternal Light." C.B.S. has featured the "Church of the Air" and "Wings over Jordan," a program of Negro spir-ituals and inspirational talks. One of the best-known radio ministers was Walter A. Maier of St. Louis who, from 1930 to 1950, conducted the "Lutheran Hour." In addition to national religious broadcasts there have been many local broadcasts over denominationally connected stations. Usually these have been of a more sectarian nature.

During the 1950's television developed into a very useful medium of religious communication. In addition to telecasts of religious programs on Sunday mornings there have been numerous special network presenta-tions of outstanding importance. Among the more notable have been Bishop Fulton J. Sheen's weekly series, the Billy Graham revival meeting in Madison Square Garden, New York, and the several "interview" pro-grams, mostly on Sunday afternoons, which have brought prominent religious leaders before a nationwide audience.

Religious films, the serious production of which dates back to the 1920's, have also become an important means of communicating religious knowledge. Denominational bodies, notably the Missouri Synod Lutheran and the Presbyterian, U.S.A., have pioneered in filming religious pictures. This enterprise has been greatly helped by the Protestant Film Com-mission, organized in 1946 through the cooperative efforts of eighteen Protestant communions which have participated in the manufacture of religious films. Among the finest series of films on Biblical subjects have been the Cathedral Films, produced by James K. Friedrich. Recently commercial firms have shown considerable interest in Biblical themes as in Cecil B. DeMille's extravaganza "The Ten Commandments." In the area of church history the full-length feature of "Martin Luther" has doubtless stimulated considerable popular interest in the Reformation.

Problems of Church and State

Since the founding of the national government, there has been almost constant need for legal definition of the proper relation between religion and the state. The provision that Congress shall make no laws respecting a religious establishment has been broadly interpreted to imply the separation of church and state; actually no separation has existed in an absolute sense inasmuch as churches have received benefits from tax exemption and various chaplaincies have existed in the Congress and the military services. In recent years, however, there has been considerable agitation especially on the part of the Roman Catholic Church to have the traditional view of "separation" modified so that the church may receive additional benefits from the government.

The Roman Catholic policy was indicated in a manifesto issued on November 20, 1948, by the American bishops, who called for "free co-operation between government and religious bodies—cooperation involving no special privilege to any group and no restriction on the religious liberty of any citizen." The exact nature of this cooperation was not stated. An exposition of the Roman Catholic position by the noted theologian Father John Courtney Murray the following year disavowed any inclination on the part of his church to seek a union with the state. On the other hand, the tenor of John A. Ryan and F. J. Boland's work, *Catholic Principles of Politics* (1943), led many Americans to question the church's permanent support of the separation principle.

In recent years non-Roman Catholic writers have given increasing attention to the problem of church-state relationships. One of the most distinguished men to deal with the question was the Protestant Charles C. Marshall in *The Roman Catholic Church in the Modern State* (1928), a most temperate and scholarly discussion. Similarly thoughtful and constructive was the work of the Jewish author Will Herberg entitled *Protestant—Catholic—Jew: An Essay in American Religious Sociology* (1955). Perhaps the most critical treatment of the Roman Catholic position has been that by Paul Blanshard in *American Freedom and Catholic Power* (1950).

Concern over the church-state question and the possible intentions of the Roman Catholic Church in politics has contributed to mounting tension between Protestants who are determined to maintain a strict construction of "separation" and Roman Catholics who favor certain assistance from the government. Among the Protestant bodies, the Baptists have been most active in opposing modifications of the traditional position. Since 1947 the "separation" doctrine has been vigorously defended by a non-denominational organization known as Protestants and Other Americans United for Separation of Church and State. Among its officers have been such eminent churchmen as John A. Mackay, G. Bromley

Oxnam, Charles Clayton Morrison, and Edwin McNeill Poteat. Whether through the mobilization of public opinion or by legal process, it has attempted to curb efforts to break down church-state separation.

One issue of primary concern was the establishment of diplomatic relations with the Vatican. From 1848 to 1867, when the pope ruled an extensive area in central Italy, the United States government maintained a mission in the Papal States. The idea of refounding a mission was not revived until 1939 when President Franklin D. Roosevelt decided to send Myron C. Taylor as his personal representative to the pope. At this time the pope exercised political authority only in the State of Vatican City. Though Mr. Taylor, an Episcopalian, was not considered as a member of the regular diplomatic service, many non-Catholics feared that his appointment constituted a step toward the opening of formal diplomatic relations. A number of Protestant communions passed official protests to the appointment; similar action was taken by various secular groups which favored a strict separation of church and state. In any case, the appointment was continued throughout the administration of Mr. Roosevelt and until 1950 under President Harry Truman; it came to an end only when Mr. Taylor voluntarily resigned.

In 1951, however, Mr. Truman proposed the name of General Mark W. Clark to the Senate for confirmation as first United States ambassador to the Vatican. Immediately widespread opposition was engendered among Protestants, Jews, and other Americans who stood for church-state separation. After several months of bitter controversy, General Clark removed his name from consideration; since that time no further nominations for such a post have been made.

Another problem has concerned religious instruction in conjunction with the public-school system. As early as 1913 a program of week-day religious instruction was inaugurated at Gary, Indiana, whence it spread to other states. Known as the "released-time" plan, it permitted a certain amount of time to be taken from the regular public-school day in order that pupils might attend classes taught by teachers provided by churches and synagogues. In some instances classes were taught in public school buildings by clergymen or trained lay teachers. By 1948 about 1800 communities had adopted the system. Of the small number of students enrolled in the program, two-thirds were drawn from the Roman Catholic, Adventist, and Lutheran groups. Most of the larger Protestant denominations demonstrated relatively little interest in the "released-time" plan.

In 1945 the legality of "released time" was questioned by Mrs. Vashti McCollum, self-styled "rationalist," in a suit before the Sixth Illinois Circuit Court. The plaintiff sought a decision which would forbid the Champaign, Illinois, public schools to allow voluntary religious instruction to take place during public-school time in public-school buildings. According to the then-existing system, arranged by the school board in cooperation with local representatives of the Roman Catholic, Protestant, and Jewish faiths, a thirty-minute period was assigned for the religious education of children whose parents requested it. Other pupils spent the time in study. Mrs. McCollum maintained that the system led to discrimination against her son, who was mocked by the children who took classes in religion. When she lost the decision, she carried the case to the U.S. Supreme Court. In this appeal she was supported by such religious groups as the General Conference of Seventh-day Adventists, the Joint Baptist Conference on Public Relations, and the Synagogue Council of America. After careful deliberation, the court ruled in 1948 in favor of Mrs. McCollum. The decision held that any use by religious groups of "the state's compulsory public school machinery . . . is not separation of church and state" and thus violates the Constitution. Since the ruling had nothing to say about classes in religion held outside school buildings on school time, this latter arrangement, which was pronounced constitutional by the Supreme Court in 1952, was either adopted or continued in a number of states.

Still another important issue concerned the allocation of any tax revenues for the direct or indirect benefit of parochial schools. The Roman Catholic hierarchy has strenuously maintained that the government should grant support to sectarian educational institutions. Its position was clearly set forth by Father Wilfrid Parsons in *The First Freedom* (1948), in which he maintained that there was no basis in the Constitution for a high wall of separation between church and state. Since the end of World War II, the hierarchy has intensified its efforts to obtain state benefits for parochial schools. Some of the concessions made in certain localities have included free textbooks of a non-religious nature, free hot lunches, and free school-bus transportation. This latter benefit became the subject of an interesting case which was fought to the U. S. Supreme Court. The plaintiff, Arch R. Everson, contended that a New Jersey law which extended free transportation privileges to parochial school students was unconstitutional. In 1947 the Supreme Court in a five-to-four decision ruled in favor of the New Jersey law. Of a somewhat different nature has been the willingness of certain states to employ as teachers in the public schools nuns who wear the distinctive garb of their order.

One of the bitterest controversies over federal aid to parochial schools concerned a bill introduced by Congressman Graham A. Barden of North Carolina in 1949. It provided that federal funds should be granted only to public schools. When Mrs. Franklin D. Roosevelt came out in her syndicated column in favor of federal aid to public schools only, Francis Cardinal Spellman of New York bitterly assailed her as "anti-Catholic" and referred to her articles as "documents of discrimination unworthy of an American mother." His highly unjust attack brought down such a flood of public criticism as to cause the red-faced cardinal to issue a more temperate statement and to pay a somewhat conciliatory visit to the lady whom he had vilified. Mrs. Roosevelt reacted to the entire affair with dignity and grace, politely reaffirming her advocacy of church-state separation and demonstrating her complete lack of anti-Roman Catholic bias. Unfortunately, the encounter was but symbolic of a burning issue in American society which promised to become more intensified with the passage of time. It was important that the problem be argued dispassionately and without recourse to bigotry, so that the democratic process might be served honorably and a reasonable solution to a complex and weighty matter be reached.

Religion at the Dawn of the Atomic Age

The dozen years which followed Hiroshima and Nagasaki were troubled by international tensions and anxieties which harassed the spirits of the American people. Confronted by a Russian leviathan which blew alternately hot and cold, Americans could never be quite free from concern that some overzealous leader in the Kremlin might in a rash moment ignite the flame which would destroy mankind in world conflagration. Never before had the relativities of life seemed so complete, certitude so uncertain, disaster so imminent. Everywhere the cry went out for security and came back like a hollow echo from the abyss. Nevertheless Americans refused to abandon their essential inclination toward optimism, believing implicitly that they could find a panacea in the ordinances of religion.

By almost any materialistic standard American religious institutions were becoming increasingly robust. For a full decade church attendance continued to swell as a mass of frustrated, confused, and depressed but still hopeful people looked to religion for reassurance and happiness. The *Yearbook of American Churches* (edition for 1959) reported that by the close of 1957 61 per cent of the estimated national population or 104,-189,678 persons were formally identified with religious groups. Among Protestant bodies in particular there was a renewed emphasis on evangelism and a number of denominations inaugurated special programs for the enrichment of spiritual life in the parishes. A prime example was the New Life Movement of the Presbyterian Church in the U.S.A., which extended from 1947 to 1950. Through a vast program of personal evangelism, conducted in large measure by laymen, 648,583 new members were won to the church. All over the country there was a rising tide of lay religion, and under the salient influence of the well-known Quaker philosopher, Elton Trueblood, and others, greater importance was being attached to the ministry of the laity.

Mass revivalism, ineffectual since the days of Billy Sunday, came once again into popular favor. Traditional in its zeal for the salvation of souls, it was at the same time contemporary in its opposition to secularism, communism, and moral relativism. Its ability to relate the Gospel to the search for peace of mind or to the problem of juvenile delinquency was prerequisite to an effective and beneficial witness. The movement had its beginnings in the Youth for Christ revivals at the outset of World War II. Local rallies designed to minister to the spiritual needs of teenagers and servicemen were conducted by such popular evangelists as Jack Wyrtzen, Torrey Johnson, Billy Graham, and Charles Templeton, the latter eventually becoming an evangelist for the National Council of Churches. Other important exponents of evangelism during the early years of the revival were M. R. DeHaan, Charles E. Fuller, Walter Maier, and the Anglican mission-preacher Bryan Green.

Most popular and ostensibly successful of all the contemporary revivalists was William (Billy) Franklin Graham (1918–   ), Baptist minister and founder in 1950 of the Billy Graham Evangelistic Association. In 1947 he launched a series of evangelistic campaigns which took him to the major cities of the nation. At Houston, Texas; Washington, D.C.; and Boston, Massachusetts, it was not unusual for him to draw 40,000–60,000 at a single meeting. At the New York crusade in 1957, in which Graham reached the apex of his evangelistic career in America, 56,767 persons made decisions for Christ. Using all the usual techniques of a professional revivalist, including the Gospel music rendered by his associate George Beverly Shea, Graham presented his listeners with a compelling but simplified pietistic Gospel which emphasized individual salvation through decision and public profession of one's faith in Christ. The Christian life was conceived largely in terms of daily Bible reading and prayer, winning other souls to Christ, and adherence to the well-established pietistic virtues. There was little if any evidence of social discernment and certainly no effort was made to relate the Gospel to the highly complex problems of contemporary society. On the whole the Graham revivals appealed to the great middle class rather than to the very rich or the extremely poor and constituted a pep rally for that segment of the population which tended most to be identified with formal religion. To what extent the revivals stimulated a continuing Christian experience is difficult to say. Without a doubt the scores of ministers and laymen who served as counselors in the inquiry rooms performed a valuable ministry for those who took the step of publicly professing their faith. The permanent effects of their combined activities have nevertheless been nebulous. No perceivable revival has yet broken out in the local churches; neither have there been indications of an upward trend in the moral life of the great cities.

Simultaneously with the revival of revivalism came the national quest for peace of mind. The trend began as early as 1946 with the publication of Rabbi Joshua Liebman's best seller, *Peace of Mind,* a primer of religious psychology which pointed the way to newness of life through mental discipline. Roman Catholic and Protestant versions of how to attain peace soon followed with Fulton J. Sheen's *Peace of Soul* (1949) and Billy Graham's *Peace with God* (1953). The *pontifex maximus* of the "cult of reassurance," however, was Norman Vincent Peale (1898–   ), popular minister of the Marble Collegiate (Reformed) Church in New York City. Thoroughly dedicated to the spiritual service of mankind, he sought through his preaching and writing to help people find a simple technique to the fine art of living. His solution, which appealed to thousands of anxious but would-be optimistic Americans who viewed religion as a source of "practical" help, was to blot out negative thoughts and turn for guidance to the Bible, to Christ, to prayer. By means of the pulpit, television, magazine articles, and a battery of books which included such popular titles as *The Art of Living, A Guide to Confident Living, The Power of Positive Thinking,* and *Stay Alive All Your Life,* he poured out his religio-psychological counsel to seekers of the easy way. Critics attacked him for the superficiality of his theology; but after all, he was addressing himself to a non-theologically oriented public which conceived religion primarily as a stepping-stone to mental and physical health, happiness, and prosperity. Some credulous segments of this public were even attracted by the claims of prominent faith-healing evangelists such as Oral Roberts, who professed the ability to heal disease in the name and power of Christ.

Ironically, when the "peace-of-mind" cult was at the crest of its influence in the early 1950's, America was gripped by a wave of hysteria brought on by fear of communism unequalled in its history. McCarthyism was abroad in the land and Congressional investigating committees were busily engaged in ferreting out information which might link some of America's most distinguished citizens to the communist conspiracy. Even members of the clergy whose loyalty was unquestionable were exposed to "smear" tactics, as in the case of Methodist Bishop G. Bromley Oxnam who, after his patriotism had been impugned in an address made in the House of Representatives, not only successfully defended himself but went on to criticize abuses in the investigations.

Meanwhile, the trend to religion had continued unabated so that by the early 1950's the new piety had permeated every quarter of American life. At no time in the nation's history had religion been treated with such approbation, skepticism with such scorn. The secular press heralded the return to piety, while motion pictures and popular songs with a quasi-religious theme enjoyed unprecedented popularity. In government, President Dwight D. Eisenhower symbolized the spirit of the times with his simple and unaffected piety; millions of Americans were moved beyond words by the sincerity of the brief prayer which he offered on the occasion of his first inaugural. It was a time which found veteran politicians in Washington traditionally not unaccustomed to a nodding acquaintance with deity in their public utterances, frequenting morning "prayer breakfasts" at which they received spiritual strength for the prosecution of their arduous duties.

Everywhere there was talk of a religious revival sweeping the nation. Uncritical products of the culture accepted it just as they accepted practically everything else in an increasingly standardized society. Religion belonged to decent American living; any other thesis was unpatriotic. The precise nature and form of religion seemed relatively unimportant except to an unconventional minority which required definition for its faith. What was essential was "belief," whatever its character. Thus thousands adhered to little more than a simple, nondescript faith of sentimentalities, with an anthropomorphic theology which pictured God as little more than a kindly Santa Claus or "the man upstairs."

Whence came this mid-twentieth century ethos? At best an answer can be little more than impressionistic. Clearly it is not a direct product of the American Protestant tradition, although undoubtedly Protestant accommodations to rationalism have encouraged the process. It is most definitely not the child of Roman Catholicism, which has continually opposed lack of precision in religious definition. It has assuredly not been authored by Judaism, with its love of regulation in matters of religious practice. Nor has it come by way of the Eastern faiths, although the forces of Buddhism in the United States have been raised by 60,000 through the admission of Hawaii to statehood in 1959, and Moslems have erected a great mosque and Islamic Center at Washington, D.C.

Various analyses of the current religious situation have been forthcoming. Some have interpreted it as the victory of secularism through identity with religion, a process of damnation by faint praise. Others have linked it to the rapid rise of a national cult which has developed coextensively with a trend toward conformity and standardization, the result being all too often the absolutizing of relatives and the relativizing of absolutes. The emerging religion has been characterized by some as humanistic nationalism. Its theology reveals a deity who in the words of Eugene Carson Blake, sometime president of the National Council of Churches, serves as "a combination of whipping boy, servant and even a useful ally in dealing with religious people, who otherwise might get in his way." Such a deity ministers to a people who have no sins, only anxieties.

It seems unlikely that any single contemporary analysis of American religion, however discerning, can hope to accomplish greater results than to stimulate thinking and encourage discussion. The present is too fluid to justify more than the most tentative observations concerning possible trends. Granted, therefore, that there have been evidences of secularism and humanistic nationalism as powerful ideological factors in American religious life, it is equally true that there have been intelligent and dedicated efforts to bring life in a disordered world into conformity to the dynamic will of that Supreme Being who is the Lord of history.

Among many persons of spiritual depth and creativity there has been a mounting conviction that the central religious problem which faces Americans at the dawn of the Atomic Age is as old as man himself. In Tillichian manner they have recognized that problem, whether potential or actual, to be inexorable bondage to a sanctified world of heteronomous, man-made absolutes. In such a world their only freedom is to accede to the static definitions and forms which rule society; their only sin is the longing for a vital and personal transcendental relationship with Being. These concerned individuals stand convinced that Americans must not fashion that kind of world. Rather, against all human vagaries which would make the temporal absolute and the demonic divine, they stress the truth that above the relativities of history abides the living God, whom to know is life and whom to love is perfect freedom. They cannot identify America with the Kingdom of God, but they trust that in spite of human fallibility they can work for its coming. Thus they look for a world which is not yet but which can be, and in loyal devotion to its appearing they make ready for the next brave step into the unknown.

Suggestions for Additional Reading

General Works

Among the more important cultural and social treatments are N. M. Blake, *A Short History of American Life* (McGraw-Hill, 1952); R. H. Gabriel, *The Course of American Democratic Thought* (Ronald, 1940); A. M. Schlesinger and D. R. Fox, eds., *A History of American Life*, 13 vols. (Macmillan, 1927–1948); and H. S. Commager, *The American Mind* (Yale, 1950). Among the more useful reference works are the *Dictionary of American History*, 6 vols. (1940) and the *Dictionary of American Biography*, 22 vols. (1928–1936).

RELIGIOUS HISTORIES AND INTERPRETATIVE STUDIES: Old but standard in the field are H. K. Carroll, *The Religious Forces of the United States*, and L. W. Bacon, *A History of American Christianity* (The Christian Literature Company, 1893 and 1897). More recent works of value are R. H. Abrams, ed., *Organized Religion in the United States* (Annals of the American Academy of Political and Social Science, March, 1948); D. Jenkins, *Europe and America: Their Contributions to the World Church* (Westminster, 1951); H. R. Niebuhr, *The Kingdom of God in America* (Harper, 1937); W. L. Sperry, *Religion in America* (Cambridge, 1945); W. W. Sweet, *The American Churches: An Interpretation* (Abingdon, 1947); and W. W. Sweet, *American Culture and Religion* (Southern Methodist, 1951). For incisive treatments of American Protestantism see J. C. Brauer, *Protestantism in America* (Westminster, 1953); W. S. Hudson, *The Great Tradition of the American Churches* (Harper, 1953); F. E. Mayer, *The Religious Bodies of America* (Concordia, 1954); R. E. Osborn, *The Spirit of American Christianity* (Harper, 1958); and G. M.

Stephenson, *The Puritan Heritage* (The Macmillan Company, 1952). An European appraisal may be found in A. L. Drummond, *Story of American Protestantism* (Beacon, 1951); also S. E. Mead, "The Rise of the Evangelical Conception of the Ministry in America: 1607–1850," and R. S. Michaelson, "The Protestant Ministry in America: 1850 to the Present" in H. R. Niebuhr and D. H. Williams, eds., *The Ministry in Historical Perspectives* (Harper, 1956). For valuable statistical data see the annual editions of *Year Book of the Churches* (National Council of Churches).

SPECIFIC ASPECTS OF RELIGIOUS HISTORY: Excellent discussions of denominationalism may be found in S. E. Mead, "Denominationalism: The Shape of Protestantism in America," *Church History*, XXIII (1954), 291–320, and H. R. Niebuhr, *The Social Sources of Denominationalism* (Holt, 1929). For able treatments of the thesis that the frontier was a leading factor in shaping American life see F. J. Turner, *The Frontier in American Life* (Holt, 1920) and P. G. Mode, *The Frontier Spirit in American Christianity* (Macmillan, 1923). For a historical discussion of the revival phenomenon see W. W. Sweet, *Revivalism in America* (Scribner, 1944).

DENOMINATIONAL HISTORIES: The standard collection prior to 1900 is The American Church History Series, 13 vols. (Christian Literature Co., 1893–1898), which treats the principal denominations. Satisfactory contemporary accounts are R. G. Torbet, *A History of the Baptists* (Judson, 1950); G. Atkins and F. L. Fagley, *History of American Congregationalism* (Pilgrim, 1942); W. E. Garrison and A. T. DeGroot, *The Disciples of Christ* (Christian Board of Publication, 1948); J. T. Addison, *The Episcopal Church in the United States, 1789–1931* (Scribner, 1951); W. W. Manross, *A History of the American Episcopal Church* (Morehouse-Gorham, 1950); E. Russell, *The History of Quakerism* (Macmillan, 1942); N. Glazer, *American Judaism* (Chicago, 1957); A. R. Wentz, *A Basic History of Lutheranism in America* (Muhlenberg, 1955); C. H. Smith, *Story of the Mennonites* (Mennonite Book Concern, 1941); H. E. Luccock, P. Hutchinson, and R. W. Goodloe, *The Story of Methodism* (Abingdon, 1949); W. W. Sweet, *Methodism in American History* (Abingdon, 1954); E. Langton, *History of the Moravian Church* (Allen & Unwin, 1956); G. J. Slosser, ed., *They Seek A Country: The American Presbyterians* (Macmillan, 1955); J. T. Ellis, *American Catholicism* (Chicago, 1956); T. Maynard, *The Story of American Catholicism* (Macmillan, 1943); and E. M. Wilbur, *A History of Unitarianism*, 2 vols. (Harvard, 1945–1952).

Chapter 1: The European Heritage

GENERAL: A number of fine comprehensive works are available in English, among them J. Dillenberger and C. Welch, *Protestant Christianity* (Scribner, 1954); J. H. Nichols, *Primer for Protestants* (Association, 1947); and J. S. Whale, *The Protestant Tradition* (Cambridge, 1955). Particularly helpful for the student of American religion is T. C. Hall, *The Religious Background of American Culture* (Little, Brown, 1930). Able treatments of the Reformation period may be found in R. Bainton, *The Reformation of the Sixteenth Century* (Beacon, 1952); H. J. Grimm, *The Reformation Era, 1500–1650* (Macmillan, 1954); T. M. Lindsay, *A History of the Reformation*, 2 vols. (Scribner, 1916); G. L. Mosse, *The Reformation* (Holt, 1952). For a comprehensive treatment of Protestant theology see A. C. McGiffert, *Protestant Thought Before Kant* (Scribner, 1936). Some of the more important documents of the Reformation may be found in H. E. Fosdick, *Great Voices of the Reformation* (Random, 1952). Able discussions of the Reformation in England are given in T. M. Parker, *The English Reformation to 1558* (Oxford, 1950); F. M. Powicke, *The Reformation in England* (Oxford, 1949); and P. Hughes, *The Reformation in England*, 3 vols. (Hollis & Carter, 1954), the last-cited work being the product of Roman Catholic authorship.

THE RIGHT WING OF THE REFORMATION: Excellent studies of Luther and the German Reformation are available, among them R. Bainton, *Here I Stand* (Abingdon-Cokesbury, 1950); J. Mackinnon, *Luther and the Reformation*, 4 vols. (Longmans, Green, 1925–1930); and E. G. Schwiebert, *Luther and His Times* (Concordia, 1950). A critical treatment of Luther may be found in H. Grisar, *Luther*, 6 vols. (Herder, 1913–1917). The best general treatment of Calvinism is J. T. McNeill, *The History and Character of Calvinism* (Oxford, 1954). For satisfactory discussions of Calvin and his thought see J. Mackinnon, *Calvin and the Reformation* (Longmans, Green, 1936); W. Niesel, *The Theology of Calvin* (Westminster, 1956); T. H. L. Parker, *Portrait of Calvin* (Westminster, 1955). For controversial treatments of the relation of Calvinism to economics see M. Weber, *The Protestant Ethic and the Spirit of Capitalism* (Scribner, 1930) and R. H. Tawney, *Religion and the Rise of Capitalism* (Mentor). Helpful discussions of English Puritanism are W. Haller, *The Rise of Puritanism* (Columbia, 1938) and M. M. Knappen, *Tudor Puritan-*ism (Chicago, 1939). For a special study of Anglicanism see P. E. More and F. L. Cross, *Anglicanism* (Morehouse, 1935).

THE LEFT WING OF THE REFORMATION: Useful accounts of Continental movements are J. Horsch, *Mennonites in Europe* (Mennonite Publishing House, 1942); F. H. Littell, *The Anabaptist View of the Church* (American Society of Church History, 1952); and R. J. Smithson, *The Anabaptists* (Clarke, 1935). For the Friends movement see W. V. Noble, *The Man in Leather Breeches; the Life of George Fox* (Philosophical Library, 1953) and E. Russell, *The History of Quakerism* (Macmillan, 1942).

THE ROMAN CATHOLIC COUNTER-REFORMATION: A good general work by a Roman Catholic is P. Janelle, *The Catholic Reformation* (Bruce, 1949). Able histories of Ignatius of Loyola and the Jesuits are H. Boehmer, *The Jesuits* (Castle, 1928); P. Dudon, *St. Ignatius of Loyola* (Bruce, 1949); P. Van Dyke, *Ignatius Loyola* (Scribner, 1927); and T. J. Campbell, *The Jesuits* (Encyclopaedia, 1921).

JUDAISM: Among the many fine histories are S. Grayzel, *Through the Ages; the Story of the Jewish People* (Jewish Publication Society, 1947); M. Margolis and A. Marx, *A History of the Jewish People* (Meridian, 1927); and A. L. Sachar, *A History of the Jews* (Knopf, 1943).

EXPLORATION AND SETTLEMENT: See J. H. Parry, *Europe and a Wider World, 1415–1715* (Hutchinson's University Library, 1949) and P. Sykes, *A History of Exploration from the Earliest Times to the Present* (Routledge, 1934).

Chapter 2: The Spanish and French Missions

THE MISSIONS OF NEW SPAIN: Good general accounts are H. E. Bolton, *The Spanish Borderlands: A Chronicle of Old Florida and the Southwest* (Yale, 1921); W. Lowery, *The Spanish Set-tlements Within the Present Limits of the United States, 1513–1561* (Putnam, 1911), and H. I. Priestley, *The Coming of the White Man* (Macmillan, 1929). For a more specific handling of religious developments see H. E. Bolton, *The Rim of Christendom* (Macmillan, 1936); C. E. Castaneda, *The Catholic Heritage of Texas*, 6 vols. (Von Boeckman-Jones, 1936–1950); Z. Engelhardt, *The Missions and Missionaries of California*, 5 vols. (Barnes, 1908–1915); and J. M. Espinosa, *Crusaders of the Rio Grande* (Institute of Jesuit History, 1942).

THE MISSIONS OF NEW FRANCE: Standard comprehensive works are H.

I. Priestley, *The Coming of the White Man* and G. M. Wrong, *The Rise and Fall of New France*, 2 vols. (Macmillan, 1928). For able treatments of the Jesuit missions see J. H. Kennedy, *Jesuit and Savage in New France* (Yale, 1950); F. Parkman, *The Jesuits in North America in the Seventeenth Century* (Little, Brown, 1903); and R. G. Thwaites, ed., *The Jesuit Relations and Allied Documents*, 73 vols. (Clark, 1896–1901).

Chapter 3: The Rise and Progress of Colonial Anglicanism

GENERAL WORKS: For able discussions of the political, social, and intellectual background see C. M. Andrews, *The Colonial Period of American History: The Settlements*, Vol. I (Yale, 1934); W. F. Craven, *The Southern Colonies in the Seventeenth Century, 1607–1689*, Vol. I, *A History of the South* (Louisiana State, 1949); T. J. Wertenbaker, *The First Americans, 1607–1690*, Vol. II, *A History of American Life* (Macmillan, 1927); and H. Wish, *Society and Thought in Early America* (Longmans, Green, 1950). The standard Episcopal histories are J. T. Addison, *The Episcopal Church in the United States;* W. W. Manross, *A History of the American Episcopal Church;* and the older C. C. Tiffany, *A History of the Protestant Episcopal Church in the United States*

of America (Christian Literature Co., 1895).

SPECIAL STUDIES: In Chapter II of W. W. Sweet, *Religion in Colonial America* (Scribner, 1949), there is a good summary of church and state relations. Area studies include G. M. Brydon, *Virginia's Mother Church*, Vol. I (Virginia Historical Society, 1947); E. L. Goodwin, *The Colonial Church in Virginia* (Morehouse, 1927); and N. R. Burr, *The Anglican Church in New Jersey* (Church Historical Society, 1954). For a study of problems in church administration see A. L. Cross, *The Anglican Episcopate and the American Colonies* (Longmans, Green, 1902); and D. E. Motley, *Life of Commissary James Blair* (Johns Hopkins, 1901).

Chapter 4: The Puritan Adventure in New England

GENERAL WORKS: Among the basic secular studies are J. T. Adams, *The Founding of New England* (Little, Brown, 1930); C. M. Andrews, *Our Earliest Colonial Settlements* (New York University, 1933); and T. J. Wertenbaker, *The First Americans* and *The Puritan Oligarchy* (Scribner, 1947). The outstanding works are the following by Perry Miller: *Orthodoxy in Massachusetts, 1630–1650* (Harvard, 1933), which presents a recon-

struction of the origin of Congregational polity; *The New England Mind, The Seventeenth Century* (Harvard, 1954); and *The New England Mind, From Colony to Province* (Harvard, 1953). Also valuable are R. B. Perry, *Puritanism and Democracy* (Vanguard, 1944); H. W. Schneider, *The Puritan Mind* (Holt, 1930); A. Simpson, *Puritanism in Old and New England* (Chicago, 1956); and O. Winslow, *Meetinghouse Hill, 1630–1783*

(Macmillan, 1952). For a critical treatment see Vol. I of V. L. Parrington, *Main Currents in American Thought* (Harcourt, Brace, 1954). A fine collection of primary materials may be found in P. Miller and T. Johnson, *The Puritans* (American, 1938).

SPECIAL STUDIES: Among the better intellectual histories are S. Morison, *The Puritan Pronaos* (Oxford, 1936), and K. Murdock, *Literature and Theology in Colonial New England* (Harvard, 1949). Important biographies are K. Murdock, *Increase Mather* (Harvard, 1925); R. and L. Boas, *Cotton Mather* (Harper, 1928); L. C. M. Hare, *Thomas Mayhew, Patriarch to the Indians* (Appleton, 1932); and G. A. Cook, *John Wise, Early American Democrat* (Columbia, 1952). Also worthy of note are G. L. Kittredge, *Witchcraft in Old and New England* (Harvard, 1929), and E. Oberholzer, Jr., *Delinquent Saints: Disciplinary Action in the Early Congregational Churches of Massachusetts* (Columbia, 1956).

Chapter 5: *Religious Minorities in the Middle Colonies*

For a good cursory treatment see Chaps. IV and V of W. W. Sweet, *Religion in Colonial America*. For the development of Roman Catholicism in Maryland see T. Maynard, *The Story of American Catholicism,* and M. P. Andrews, *The Founding of Maryland* (Williams & Wilkins, 1933). Excellent biographies of Roger Williams are S. H. Brockunier, *The Irrepressible Democrat: Roger Williams* (Ronald, 1940); P. Miller, *Roger Williams* (Bobbs-Merrill, 1953); and O. E. Winslow, *Master Roger Williams: A Biography* (Macmillan, 1957). Also see Chap. 8 of R. H. Bainton, *The Travail of Religious Liberty* (Westminster, 1951).

The life of Anne Hutchinson is treated by H. Augur in *An American Jezebel* (Brentano's, 1930). For a fine presentation of the early history of Pennsylvania see Chap. VII in C. M. Andrews, *The Colonial Period of American History,* Vol. III, *The Settlements* (Yale, 1937). Able interpretations of the work of William Penn are E. Beatty, *William Penn as Social Philosopher* (Columbia, 1939); W. W. Comfort, *William Penn* (Pennsylvania, 1944); C. O. Peare, *William Penn* (Lippincott, 1957); and F. B. Tolles and E. G. Alderfer, *The Witness of William Penn* (Macmillan, 1957).

Chapter 6: *The Transplanting of Continental Protestantism*

Satisfactory treatments of the history and religion of New Netherland may be found in C. M. Andrews, *The Colonial Period of American History,* Vol. III; E. T. Corwin, *A History of the Reformed Church, Dutch* (Christian Literature Co., 1895); M. W. Goodwin, *Dutch and English on the Hudson* (Yale, 1919); H. I. Priestley, *The Coming of the White Man;* E. L. Raesly, *Portrait of New Netherland* (Columbia, 1945); S. Van Rensselaer, *History of the City of New York in the Seventeenth Century,* Vol. I (Macmillan, 1909); and F. J. Zwierlein, *Religion in New Netherland* (J. P. Smith, 1910). For the rise of Judaism in New Netherland and elsewhere see A. V. Goodman, *American Overture: Jewish Rights in Colonial Times* (Jewish Publication Society, 1947); and J. R. Marcus, *Early American Jewry,* 2 vols. (Jewish Publication Society, 1951–1953). For Swedish colonial religious history see A. Johnson, *The Swedish Settlements on the Delaware,* 2 vols. (Pennsylvania, 1911). The transplanting of the Huguenots is described in

C. W. Baird, *The Huguenot Emigration to America*, 2 vols. (Dodd Mead, 1895); and A. E. Hirsch, *The Huguenots in Colonial South Carolina* (Duke, 1928). The coming of the Germans is treated in A. B. Faust, *The German Element in the United States,* Vol. I (Houghton Mifflin, 1909); and R. Wood, ed., *The Pennsylvania Germans* (Princeton, 1942). For Lutheran history see A. R. Wentz, *A Basic History of Lutheranism in America;* L. P. Qualben, *The Lutheran Church in Colonial America* (Nelson, 1940); P. A. Wallace, *The Muhlenbergs of Pennsylvania* (Pennsylvania, 1950); and T. G. Tappert and J. W. Doberstein, trans., *The Journals of Henry Melchior Muhlenberg,* 3 vols. (Muhlenberg, 1942). For the history and leadership of other denominational bodies see C. H. Smith, *The Story of the Mennonites;* J. T. Hamilton, *A History of the Church Known as the Moravian Church of the Unitas Fratrum During the Eighteenth and Nineteenth Centuries* (Tinner, 1900); E. E. Gray and L. Robb, *Wilderness Christians: The Moravian Mission to the Delaware Indians* (Cornell, 1956); J. R. Weinlick, *Count Zinzendorf* (Abingdon, 1956); and J. H. Dubbs, *A History of the Reformed Church, German* (Christian Literature Co., 1895).

Chapter 7: *The Scotch-Irish Presbyterians*

General studies of merit include M. W. Armstrong, L. A. Loetscher, and C. A. Anderson, *The Presbyterian Enterprise* (Westminster, 1956); L. A. Loetscher, *A Brief History of the Presbyterians* (Westminster, 1958); G. J. Slosser, ed., *They Seek a Country;* W. W. Sweet, *Religion in Colonial America,* Chap. VIII; and R. E. Thompson, *A History of the Presbyterian Churches in the United States* (Christian Literature Co., 1895). Also of interest are H. Ford, *The Scotch-Irish in America* (Princeton, 1915); and C. A. Hanna, *The Scotch-Irish,* 2 vols. (Putnam, 1902). More detailed studies include W. F. Dunaway, *The Scotch-Irish of Colonial Pennsylvania* (North Carolina, 1944); G. S. Klett, *Presbyterians in Colonial Pennsylvania* (Pennsylvania, 1937); and L. J. Trinterud, *The Forming of an American Tradition* (Westminster, 1949).

Chapter 8: *The Great Awakening*

For the Middle Colony revival see C. Maxson, *The Great Awakening in the Middle Colonies* (Chicago, 1920); G. J. Slosser, *They Seek a Country;* and L. J. Trinterud, *The Forming of an American Tradition.* The work of George Whitefield is carefully analyzed in A. D. Belden, *George Whitefield, The Awakener* (Macmillan, 1953); and S. C. Henry, *George Whitefield, Wayfaring Witness* (Abingdon, 1957). A fine interpretative analysis of the New England revival is E. S. Gaustad, *The Great Awakening in New England* (Harper, 1957). The leading works on Jonathan Edwards are P. Miller, *Jonathan Edwards* (William Sloane Associates, 1949); H. B. Parkes, *Jonathan Edwards, The Fiery Puritan* (Minton, Balch, 1930); and O. E. Winslow, *Jonathan Edwards, 1703–1758* (Macmillan, 1940). For the revival in Virginia see G. M. Brydon, *Virginia's Mother Church,* Vol. II; and W. M. Gewehr, *The Great Awakening in Virginia* (Duke, 1930). The revival among the Baptists is described in R. G. Torbet, *A History of the Baptists.* The nascence of Methodism in England and America is treated in M. R. Brailsford, *A Tale of Two Brothers; John and Charles Wesley*

(Oxford, 1954); R. M. Cameron, *The Rise of Methodism* (Philosophical Library, 1954); F. J. McConnell, *John Wesley* (Abingdon, 1939); and W. W. Sweet, *Methodism in American History.*

Chapter 9: The Aftermath of the Revival

For a discussion of Christian attitudes and work in relation to Indians and Negroes see E. S. Gaustad, *The Great Awakening in New England;* A. M. Gummere, *Journals and Essays of John Woolman* (Macmillan, 1922); R. Reynolds, *The Wisdom of John Woolman* (Allen & Unwin, 1948); and L. L. Haynes, Jr., *The Negro Community Within American Protestantism, 1619–1844* (Christopher, 1953). In S. Henry's *George Whitefield* there is an interesting account of Whitefield's orphanage. The Anglican philanthropic enterprise is discussed in F. J. Klingberg, *Anglican Humanitarianism in Colonial New York* (Church Historical Society, 1940). In L. J. Trinterud, *The Forming of an American Tradition,* attention is given to the founding of Presbyterian colleges. Theological trends in New England are ably treated in C. E. Cunningham, *Timothy Dwight* (Macmillan, 1942); F. H. Foster, *A Genetic History of the New England Theology* (Chicago, 1909); and H. S. Smith, *Changing Conceptions of Original Sin* (Scribner, 1955).

Chapter 10: Religion in the Revolutionary Era

The secular background is skillfully unfolded in M. Curti, *The Roots of American Loyalty* (Columbia, 1946); E. B. Greene, *The Revolutionary Generation, 1763–1790* (Macmillan, 1943); E. F. Humphrey, *Nationalism and Religion in America, 1774–1789* (Chipman Law Publishing Co., 1924); J. C. Miller, *Origins of the American Revolution* (Little, Brown, 1943); and C. H. Van Tyne, *The Causes of the War for Independence* (Houghton Mifflin, 1922). Of special interest is A. M. Baldwin, *The New England Clergy and the American Revolution* (Duke, 1928). For denominational contributions see the histories cited on page 596, and W. W. Sweet, *Religion in the Development of American Culture* (Scribner, 1952).

Chapter 11: The Churches in a Period of Reorganization

The post-revolutionary process of separation of church and state is given general attention in S. H. Cobb, *Rise of Religious Liberty in America* (Macmillan, 1902); E. F. Humphrey, *Nationalism and Religion in America;* A. P. Stokes, *Church and State in the United States,* Vol. I (Harper, 1950); W. W. Sweet, *Religion in the Development of American Culture;* specialized treatments may be found in G. M. Brydon, *Virginia's Mother Church,* Vol. II; and J. C. Meyer, *Church and State in Massachusetts from 1740 to 1833* (Western Reserve, 1930). Satisfactory studies of Deism are to be found in G. A. Koch, *Republican Religion* (Holt, 1933); H. Morais, *Deism in Eighteenth-century America;* and H. H. Clark, *Thomas Paine* (American, 1944). In addition to the above-cited denominational histories, the following works are of importance: for the Episcopal Church, C. O. Loveland, *The Critical Years: The Reconstruction of the Anglican Church in the United States of America, 1780–1789* (Seabury, 1956); and W. A. Beardsley, *Samuel Seabury, The Man and the Bishop* (Church Missions Publishing Co., 1935); for the Lutheran Church, R. Fortenbaugh, *The Development of the Synodical Polity of the Lutheran Church in America to 1829* (1926); for the Methodist Church, F. Asbury, *Journal and Letters*, 3 vols. (Abingdon, 1958); and W. L. Duren, *Francis Asbury, Founder of American Methodism* (Macmillan, 1928); for the Roman Catholic Church, M. A. Ray, *American Opinion of Roman Catholicism in the Eighteenth Century* (Columbia, 1936); C. J. Nuesse, *The So-* *cial Thought of American Catholics, 1634–1829* (Newman, 1945); P. Guilday, *The Life and Times of John Carroll, Archbishop of Baltimore, 1735–1815*, 2 vols. (Encyclopaedia Press, 1922); and A. M. Melville, *John Carroll of Baltimore* (Scribner, 1955). Also see R. W. Albright, *A History of the Evangelical Church* (Evangelical Press, 1942); and A. W. Drury, *History of the Church of the United Brethren in Christ* (Otterbein, 1924).

Chapter 12: Western Expansion and the Second Awakening

Good accounts of America's geographical expansion may be found in R. A. Billington, *Westward Expansion* (Macmillan, 1949); and F. L. Paxson, *History of the American Frontier, 1763–1893* (Houghton Mifflin, 1924). For a general view of religious developments see W. W. Sweet, *Religion in the Development of American Culture*. A fine collection of essays and source materials is contained in W. W. Sweet, *Religion on the American Frontier, The Baptists, 1783–1830* (Chicago, 1931); *The Congregationalists* (Chicago, 1939); *The Methodists* (Chicago, 1946); and *The Presbyterians, 1783–1840* (Chicago, 1936). Also useful are W. B. Posey, *The Baptist Church in the Lower Mississippi Valley, 1776–1845* (Kentucky, 1957); *The Development of Methodism in the Old Southwest, 1783–1824* (Weatherford, 1933); and *The Presbyterian Church in the Old Southwest, 1778–1838* (John Knox, 1952). Peter Cartwright's *Autobiography* (Abingdon, 1956) provides a graphic picture of Methodism on the frontier. Important Roman Catholic studies are M. R. Mattingly, *The Catholic Church on the Kentucky Frontier 1785–1812* (Catholic Univ., 1936); and J. H. Schauinger, *Cathedrals in the Wilderness* (Bruce, 1952), which treats the life of Bishop Flaget. For a general discussion of the Second Awakening see B. A. Weisberger, *They Gathered at the River* (Little, Brown, 1958). The revival in the East is treated in C. R. Kellor, *The Second Great Awakening in Connecticut* (Yale, 1942); C. E. Cunningham, *Timothy Dwight;* and J. K. Morse, *Jedidiah Morse, a Champion of New England Orthodoxy* (Columbia, 1939). For the western revival see C. C. Cleveland, *The Great Revival in the West, 1797–1805* (Chicago, 1916); W. R. Cross, *The Burned-over District* (Cornell, 1950); and C. A. Johnson, *The Frontier Camp Meeting* (Southern Methodist, 1955).

Chapter 13: The Great Missionary Enterprise

General discussions may be found in J. R. Bodo, *The Protestant Clergy and Public Issues* (Princeton, 1954); K. S. Latourette, *The Great Century*, Vol. IV, *A History of the Expansion of Christianity* (Harper, 1941); and W. W. Sweet, *Religion in the Development of American Culture*. Able treatments of home missions may be found in C. B. Goodykoontz, *Home Missions on the American Frontier* (Caxton, 1939); J. B. Clark, *Leaven-*

ing the Nation. The Story of American Home Missions (Baker & Taylor, 1903); W. C. Barclay, Early American Methodism, 1769–1844, 2 vols. (The Board of Missions and Church Extension of the Methodist Church, 1949 and 1950); and C. M. Drury, Presbyterian Panorama (Board of Christian Education, 1952). The nascence of the mission enterprise is described in O. W. Elsbree, The Rise of the Missionary Spirit in America, 1790–1815 (Williamsport Printing Co., 1928). For the development of Negro Churches see L. L. Haynes, Jr., The Negro Community within American Protestantism (Christopher, 1953);

and R. R. Wright, ed., The Encyclopaedia of the African Methodist Episcopal Church (1947). For antimissionism see W. W. Sweet, The Baptists, Chap. IV. The birth of foreign missions is described in W. E. Strong, The Story of the American Board (Pilgrim, 1910). Among the many excellent mission biographies are E. B. Pollard, Luther Rice (Judson, 1928); T. C. Richards, Samuel J. Mills (Pilgrim, 1906); S. Warburton, Eastward! The Story of Adoniram Judson (Round Table, 1937); and C. M. Drury, Henry H. Spaulding (Caxton, 1936), and Marcus Whitman, M.D. (Caxton, 1937).

Chapter 14: Christian Contributions to Education

For a general treatment see W. W. Sweet, Religion in the Development of American Culture, Chap. VI. Tract and Bible societies are discussed in H. O. Dwight, Centennial History of the American Bible Society, 2 vols. (Macmillan, 1916); and G. M. Stephenson, The Puritan Heritage. For a discussion of denominational colleges and parochial schools see W. C. Barclay, Early American Methodism, Vol. II; A. Godbold, The Church College of the Old South (Duke, 1944); P. G. Mode, The Frontier Spirit in American Christianity, Chap. IV; D. G. Tewksbury, The Founding of Amer-

ican Colleges and Universities Before the Civil War (Columbia, 1932); and L. J. Sherrill, Presbyterian Parochial Schools, 1846–70 (Yale, 1932). The Sunday School movement is satisfactorily described in F. G. Lankard, A History of the American Sunday School Curriculum (Abingdon, 1927); and E. W. Rice, A History of the American Sunday School Union (American S. S. Union, 1899) and The Sunday School Movement, 1780–1917, and the American Sunday School Union, 1817–1917 (American S. S. Union, 1917).

Chapter 15: Conflicts in Religious Thought and Practice

LIBERAL TRENDS IN NEW ENGLAND: Excellent general works are H. W. Schneider, A History of American Philosophy (Columbia, 1946); F. H. Foster, A Genetic History of the New England Theology; and J. Haroutunian, Piety Versus Moralism: The Passing of New England Theology (Holt, 1932). Transcendentalism and the rise of Unitarianism and Universalism receive scholarly treatment in W. R. Hutchison, The Transcendentalist Min-

isters (Yale, 1959); P. Miller, The Transcendentalists (Harvard, 1950); E. M. Wilbur, A History of Unitarianism, 2 vols.; C. P. Wright, The Beginnings of Unitarianism in America (Starr King, 1955); A. W. Brown, Always Young for Liberty: A Biography of William Ellery Channing (Syracuse, 1956); D. P. Edgell, William Ellery Channing (Beacon, 1955); R. L. Rusk, The Life of Ralph Waldo Emerson (Scribner, 1949); H. S. Commager,

Theodore Parker (Little, Brown, 1936); and J. E. Dirks, *The Critical Theology of Theodore Parker* (Columbia, 1948). For theological developments in Congregationalism consult S. E. Mead, *Nathaniel William Taylor, 1786–1858* (Chicago, 1942); and B. M. Cross, *Horace Bushnell* (Chicago, 1958).

THE RISE OF NEW DENOMINATIONS: For the East see N. A. Baxter, *History of the Freewill Baptists* (American Baptist Historical Society, 1957); B. Forbush, *Elias Hicks, Quaker Liberal* (Columbia, 1956); W. W. Sweet, *Methodism in American History,* Chap. IX for the Methodist Protestants; and J. H. Kromminga, *The Christian Reformed Church* (Baker, 1949). For the frontier consult W. P. Posey, *The Presbyterian Church in the Old Southwest,* Chap. III on the Cumberland Presbyterians; W. G. West, *Barton Warren Stone* (Disciples of Christ Historical Society, 1954); W. E. Garrison and A. T. DeGroot, *The Disciples of Christ;* W. E. Garrison, *Religion Follows the Frontier, A History of the Disciples of Christ* (Harper, 1931); L. G. McAllister, *Thomas Campbell* (Bethany, 1954); D. R. Lindley, *Apostle of Freedom* (Bethany, 1957), a biography of Alexander Campbell; and R. R. West, *Alexander Campbell and Natural Religion* (Yale, 1948).

PRESBYTERIAN, REFORMED, AND EPISCOPAL CONFLICTS: For Old and New School Presbyterianism see R. E. Thompson, *A History of the Presbyterian Churches in the United States;* and H. S. Smith, *Changing Conceptions of Original Sin,* Chap. 6. German Reformed theology is discussed in L. J. Binkley, *The Mercersburg Theology* (Franklin & Marshall, 1953). Episcopal parties are treated in the general histories by Addison and Manross.

Chapter 16: Immigration and the Changing Religious Scene

The following histories of immigration are of importance: M. L. Hansen, *The Atlantic Migration, 1607–1860* (Harvard, 1940); W. F. Adams, *Ireland and Irish Emigration to the New World from 1815 to the Famine* (Yale, 1932); T. C. Blegen, *Norwegian Migration to America* (Norwegian-American Historical Association, 1931); and C. Wittke, *We Who Built America* (Prentice-Hall, 1939). For special studies of Roman Catholicism consult C. Barry, *The Catholic Church and German Americans* (Bruce, 1953); G. Shaughnessy, *Has the Immigrant Kept the Faith?* (Macmillan, 1925); P. Guilday, *The Life and Times of John England, First Bishop of Charleston, 1786–1842,* 2 vols. (America Press, 1927); H. J. Nolan, *The Most Reverend Francis Patrick Kenrick, Third Bishop of Philadelphia, 1830–1851* (Catholic Univ., 1948); A. M. Melville, *Elizabeth Bayley Seton, 1774–1821* (Scribner, 1951); A. M. Schlesinger, Jr., *Orestes A. Brownson* (Little, Brown, 1939); B. J. Blied, *Austrian Aid to American Catholics, 1830–1860* (Bruce, 1944); and R. A. Billington, *The Protestant Crusade, 1800–1860* (Macmillan, 1938), for an able treatment of anti-Catholic bias. The German and Swedish Protestants are discussed in W. Baepler, *A Century of Grace. A History of the Missouri Synod, 1847–1947* (Concordia, 1947); V. Ferm, *The Crisis in American Lutheran Theology* (Century, 1927); W. O. Foster, *Zion on the Mississippi: The Settlement of the Saxon Lutherans in Missouri, 1839–1841* (Concordia, 1953); C. E. Schneider, *The German Church on the American Frontier* (Eden, 1939); and G. M. Stephenson, *The Religious Aspects of Swedish Immigration* (Minnesota, 1932). For satisfactory discussions of Judaism see N. Glazer, *American Judaism,* Chaps. II & III; and M. Margolis and A. Marx, *History of the Jewish People,* Chaps. 86 and 91.

Chapter 17: The Emergence of Religious Cults and Movements

Useful general accounts may be found in W. R. Cross, *The Burned-over District;* W. W. Sweet, *Religion in the Development of American Culture;* and A. F. Tyler, *Freedom's Ferment* (Minnesota, 1944). Mormonism is discussed in T. F. O'Dea, *The Mormons* (Chicago, 1957); B. H. Roberts, *A Comprehensive History of the Church of Jesus Christ of Latter Day Saints* (Deseret New Press, 1930), a six volume official history; F. Brodie, *No Man Knows My History: The Life of Joseph Smith, The Mormon Prophet* (Knopf, 1945); N. Anderson, *Desert Saints: The Mormon Frontier in Utah* (Chicago, 1942); and R. B. West, *Kingdom of the Saints: The Story of Brigham Young and the Mormons* (Viking, 1957). For satisfactory treatments of religious communal sects see E. D. Andrews, *The People Called Shakers* (Oxford, 1953); M. F. Melcher, *The Shaker Adventure* (Princeton, 1941); A. E. Bestor, Jr., *Backwoods Utopias: The Sectarian and Owenite Phases of Communitarian Socialism in America: 1663–1829* (Pennsylvania, 1950); W. A. Hinds, *American Communities and Co-operative Colonies* (C. H. Kerr & Co., 1908); R. A. Parker, *A Yankee Saint: John Humphrey Noyes and the Oneida Community* (Putnam, 1935); and B. Shambaugh, *Amana, The Community of True Inspiration* (State Historical Society of Iowa, 1908). Adventism is discussed sympathetically in A. W. Spaulding, *A History of Seventh-Day Adventists,* 2 vols. (Review & Herald, 1949); and F. D. Nichol, *The Midnight Cry* (Review & Herald, 1944), a defense of William Miller.

Chapter 18: Evangelism and Social Reform

Ante-bellum evangelism is treated in B. A. Weisberger, *They Gathered at the River;* V. R. Edman, *Finney Lives On* (Revell, 1951); and in T. L. Smith's scholarly *Revivalism and Social Reform* (Abingdon, 1957). For a discussion of perfectionism see J. L. Peters, *Christian Perfection and American Methodism* (Abingdon, 1956); and the above cited work by T. L. Smith. Social reform movements are also treated by T. L. Smith and by A. F. Tyler, *Freedom's Ferment* (Minnesota, 1944); C. C. Cole, Jr., *The Social Ideas of the Northern Evangelists, 1826–1860* (Columbia, 1954); and J. R. Bodo, *The Protestant Clergy and Public Issues.* More specialized works include C. S. Ellsworth, "The American Churches and the Mexican War," *American Historical Review,* Vol. XLV, No. 2 (January, 1940); J. A. Krout, *The Origins of Prohibition* (Knopf, 1925); M. Curti, *The American Peace Crusade, 1815–1861* (Duke, 1929); W. F. Galpin, *Pioneering for Peace* (Bardeen Press, 1933); C. H. Hopkins, *History of the Y. M. C. A. in North America* (Association Press, 1951); and E. M. Robinson, *The Early Years: The Beginnings of Work With Boys in the Young Men's Christian Association* (Association Press, 1950).

Chapter 19: The Churches and the Slavery Controversy

Useful general studies are C. C. Cole, Jr., *The Social Ideas of the Northern Evangelists;* W. R. Cross, *The Burned-over District;* T. L. Smith, *Revivalism and Social Reform;* G. M. Stephenson, *The Puritan Heritage;* A. F. Tyler, *Freedom's Ferment;* and J. R. Bodo, *The Protestant Clergy and Public Issues.* The best work on colonization is E. L. Fox, *The American*

Colonization Society, 1817–1840 (Johns Hopkins, 1919). For studies of abolitionism see G. H. Barnes, *The Anti-Slavery Impulse, 1830–1844* (Appleton-Century-Crofts, 1933); D. L. Dumond, *Antislavery Origins of the Civil War in the United States* (Michigan, 1939); W. P. and F. J. Garrison, *William Lloyd Garrison, 1805–1879*, 4 vols. (Houghton, Mifflin, 1894); and B. P. Thomas, *Theodore Weld, Crusader for Freedom* (Rutgers, 1950). For pro-slavery views consult the above cited work by J. R. Bodo

and W. S. Jenkins, *Pro-Slavery Thought in the Old South* (North Carolina, 1935). Denominational schisms over slavery are treated in the histories by G. J. Slosser, ed., W. W. Sweet, and R. G. Torbet cited on page 596 and in the following specialized studies: W. W. Barnes, *History of the Southern Baptist Convention, 1845–1953* (Broadman, 1954); and J. H. Norwood, *The Schism in the Methodist Episcopal Church, 1844: A Study of Slavery and Ecclesiastical Politics* (Alfred, 1923).

Chapter 20: The House Divided

Important general works related to the Civil War which touch on the history of religion are A. C. Cole, *The Irrepressible Conflict, 1850–1865* (Macmillan, 1934); E. M. Coulter, *The Confederate States of America, 1861–1865, A History of the South*, Vol. VII (Louisiana State, 1950); A. O. Craven, *The Coming of the Civil War* (Scribner, 1942); M. Curti, *The Growth of American Thought* (Harper, 1951); A. P. Stokes, *Church and State in the United States*, Vol. II, which emphasizes the relation of the churches to the state; and H. Wish, *Society and Thought in Early America* (Longmans, Green, 1950). In addition to the general denominational histories

the following works are of significance: C. F. Dunham, *The Attitude of the Northern Clergy toward the South, 1860–1865* (Gray, 1942), which is critical of the Protestant clergy; E. N. Wright, *Conscientious Objectors in the Civil War* (Pennsylvania, 1931); B. J. Blied, *Catholics and the Civil War* (1945); W. W. Sweet, *The Methodist Episcopal Church and the Civil War* (Methodist Book Concern, 1912); L. Vander Velde, *The Presbyterian Churches and the Federal Union, 1861–1869* (Harvard, 1932); and J. B. Cheshire, *The Church in the Confederate States: A History of the Protestant Episcopal Church in the Confederate States* (Longmans, Green, 1912).

Chapter 21: Denominational Consolidation and Expansion

For the churches and reconstruction consult W. E. Garrison, *The March of Faith* (Harper, 1933); E. M. Coulter, *The South during Reconstruction, 1865–1877* (Louisiana State, 1947); and W. A. Dunning, *Reconstruction, Political and Economic* (Harper, 1907). Able discussions of the churches and the Negro may be found in W. E. B. Du Bois, *Black Reconstruction* (Harcourt, Brace, 1935); and W. D. Weatherford, *American*

Churches and the Negro (Christopher, 1957). General works on the frontier are R. H. Billington, *Westward Expansion;* L. Hafen and C. C. Rister, *Western America: The Exploration, Settlement, and Development of the Region Beyond the Mississippi* (Prentice-Hall, 1950); and F. L. Paxson, *History of the American Frontier, 1763–1893.* The standard denominational histories should be consulted for church development on the frontier. Also valuable are K. S. Latourette, *The Great Century;* and W. Hulbert, *The Bishop of All Beyond, Sheldon Jackson* (Friendship Press, 1948). For Indian missions consult the denominational histories, the above cited work by Latourette, and specialized works such as the following studies of Roman Catholic missions: E. Laveille, *The Life of Father De Smet,* trans. by M. Lindsay (P. J. Kenedy, 1915); and P. J. Rahill, *The Catholic Indian Missions and Grant's Peace Policy, 1870–1884* (Catholic Univ., 1954).

Chapter 22: *Americanism and the Immigrant Faiths*

General works of value are K. S. Latourette, *The Great Century;* F. S. Mead, *Handbook of Denominations* (Abingdon, 1951); and C. Wittke, *We Who Built America.* For useful statistical studies see *Religious Bodies: 1936,* 2 vols. (United States Government Printing Office, 1941); and the annual editions of *Yearbook of American Churches* (National Council of Churches), edited by B. Y. Landis. For the Lutheran bodies see G. M. Stephenson, *The Religious Aspects of Swedish Immigration;* and A. R. Wentz, *A Basic History of Lutheranism in America.* Developments in the Roman Catholic Church are satisfactorily discussed in A. Abel, *Protestant Home Missions to Catholic Immigrants* (Institute of Social and Religious Research, 1933); G. Shaughnessy, *Has the Immigrant Kept the Faith?;* A. P. Stokes, *Church and State in the United States,* Vol. II, Chap. XVI; R. D. Cross, *The Emergence of Liberal Catholicism in America* (Harvard, 1958); and J. Higham, *Strangers in the Land: Patterns of American Nativism, 1860–1925* (Rutgers, 1955). The following biographies of Roman Catholic leaders are noteworthy: J. T. Ellis, *The Life of James Cardinal Gibbons, Archbishop of Baltimore, 1834–1921,* 2 vols. (Bruce, 1952); J. H. Moynihan, *The Life of Archbishop John Ireland* (Harper, 1953); P. H. Ahern, *The Life of John J. Keane, Educator and Archbishop, 1839–1918* (Bruce, 1955); K. Burton, *Celestial Homespun* (Longmans, Green, 1943), a life of Isaac Hecker; and J. McSorley, *Father Hecker and His Friends* (Herder, 1952). For Judaism and Eastern Orthodoxy see N. Glazer, *American Judaism;* and C. W. Emhardt, *The Eastern Church in the Western World* (Morehouse, 1928).

Chapter 23: *Christian Idealism in National Life*

In W. E. Garrison, *The March of Faith,* Chaps. IV–VI, there is a good general treatment of religious life in the Victorian era. For biographies of outstanding contemporary preachers see P. Hibben, *Henry Ward Beecher* (The Press of the Readers Club, 1942); A. V. G. Allen, *Phillips Brooks* (Dutton, 1907); and I. V. Brown, *Lyman Abbott, Christian Evolutionist* (Harvard, 1953). The revival of perfectionism is ably treated in J. L. Peters, *Christian Perfection and American Methodism.* The resurgence of revivalism is discussed in B. A. Weisberger, *They Gathered at the River;* G. Bradford, *Dwight L. Moody: A Worker in Souls* (Doubleday Doran, 1927); P. D. Moody, *My Father; an Intimate Portrait of Dwight Moody* (Little, Brown, 1938); W. R. Moody, *D. L. Moody* (Macmillan, 1930); and W. G. McLoughlin, Jr., *Billy Sunday Was His Real Name* (Chicago, 1955). For developments in education and culture consult F. G. Lankard, *A His-*

tory of the American Sunday School Curriculum; R. Richmond, *Chautauqua: An American Place* (Duell, Sloan and Pearce, 1943); L. H. Vincent, *John Heyl Vincent* (Macmillan, 1925); and A. R. Burr, *Russell H. Conwell and His Work* (Winston, 1926). Temperance and Prohibition are given full treatment in E. H. Cherrington, *The Evolution of Prohibition in the United States of America* (American Issue Press, 1920). The new trends in the-

ology and Biblical studies are discussed in the standard denominational histories and in the following specialized works: F. H. Foster, *The Modern Movement in American Theology* (Revell, 1939); L. A. Loetscher, *The Broadening Church* (Pennsylvania, 1954), a scholarly treatment of Presbyterian theology; H. S. Smith, *Changing Conceptions of Original Sin;* and R. D. Cross, *The Emergence of Liberal Catholicism in America.*

Chapter 24: Social Religion in Modern America

Comprehensive discussions may be found in W. E. Garrison, *The March of Faith,* Chaps. IX and X; and A. M. Schlesinger, *The Rise of the City, 1878–1898* (Macmillan, 1933). C. O. Gill and G. Pinchot discuss *The Country Church: The Decline of its Influence and the Remedy* (Macmillan, 1913). For the churches and labor see H. F. May, *Protestant Churches and Industrial America* (Harper, 1949); and H. J. Browne, *The Catholic Church and the Knights of Labor* (Catholic Univ., 1949). Christian social service work is discussed in A. I. Abell, *The Urban Impact on American Protestantism, 1865–1900* (Harvard, 1943); H. A. Wisbey, *Soldiers Without Swords: A History of the Salvation*

Army in the United States (Macmillan, 1956); C. H. Hopkins, *History of the Y.M.C.A. in North America;* and M. S. Sims, *The Y.W.C.A.: An Unfolding Purpose* (Woman's Press, 1950). Good discussions of the Social Gospel and its theology may be found in J. Dombrowski, *The Early Days of Christian Socialism in America* (Columbia, 1936); C. H. Hopkins, *The Rise of the Social Gospel in American Protestantism, 1865–1915* (Yale, 1940); H. S. Smith, *Changing Conceptions of Original Sin,* Chap. IX; D. R. Sharp, *Walter Rauschenbusch* (Macmillan, 1942); and B. Y. Landis, compiler, *A Rauschenbusch Reader* (Harper, 1957).

Chapter 25: The Churches and Crusading Internationalism

Good general studies are W. E. Garrison, *The March of Faith,* Chaps. XI and XVI; and M. Curti, *The Growth of American Thought,* Chap. XXVI. For the history of missionary expansion see the standard denominational histories and K. S. Latourette, *The Great Century in the Americas, Australasia, and Africa,* Vol. V, *A History of the Expansion of Christianity* (Harper, 1943), and *The Great Century in Northern Africa and Asia,* Vol. VI in the same series (Harper, 1944);

P. A. Varg, *Missionaries, Chinese, and Diplomats: The American Protestant Missionary Movement in China, 1890–1952* (Princeton, 1958); and B. Mathews, *John R. Mott, World Citizen* (Harper, 1934). For the peace movement and World War I consult the denominational histories; also see A. P. Stokes, *Church and State in the United States,* Vol. III, Chap. XXI; and R. H. Abrams, *Preachers Present Arms* (Round Table Press, 1933).

Chapter 26: Religious Cults Since the Civil War

Among the more important general accounts are G. G. Atkins, *Modern Religious Cults and Movements* (Revell, 1923); M. Bach, *They Have Found a Faith* (Bobbs-Merrill, 1946); C. S. Braden, *These Also Believe* (Macmillan, 1950), a very readable book; E. T. Clark, *The Small Sects in America* (Abingdon-Cokesbury, 1949), an encyclopaedic work; C. W. Ferguson, *The New Books of Revelations* (Doubleday, Doran, 1929); and J. K. Van Baalen, *The Chaos of Cults* (Eerdmans, 1947), in most cases highly critical. For New Thought see H. W. Dresser, *A History of the New Thought Movement* (Crowell, 1919). Christian Science and its founder are treated in E. S. Bates and J. V. Dittemore, *Mary Baker G. Eddy* (Knopf, 1933), critical; E. F. Dakin, *Mrs. Eddy: The Biography of a Virginal Mind* (Scribner, 1929), critical; L. Powell, *Mary Baker Eddy* (Macmillan, 1930), sympathetic; S. Wilbur, *The Life of Mary Baker Eddy* (Christian Science Publishing Co., 1923), an official biography; and C. S. Braden, *Christian Science Today: Power, Policy, Practice* (Southern Methodist, 1958). Other cults of some interest are discussed in E. R. Pike, *Jehovah's Witnesses* (Watts, 1954); H. H. Stroup, *The Jehovah's Witnesses* (Columbia, 1945); C. E. B. Roberts, *Mysterious Madame, Helena Petrovna Blavatsky* (Harcourt, Brace, 1931); A. H. Fauset, *Black Gods of the Metropolis* (Pennsylvania, 1944), Negro cults in the North; J. Hoshor, *God in a Rolls Royce* (Hillman-Carl, 1936), a biography of Father Divine; and W. M. Miller, *Baha'ism; Its Origin, History and Teachings* (Revell, 1931).

Chapter 27: Movements Toward Christian Unity

The definitive history is R. Rouse and S. C. Neill, *A History of the Ecumenical Movement, 1517–1948* (Westminster, 1954). A briefer work is N. V. Hope, *One Christ, One World, One Church* (Church Historical Society, 1953). Useful interpretative and historical studies are R. S. Bilheimer, *The Quest for Christian Unity* (Association, 1952); W. A. Brown, *Toward a United Church* (Scribner, 1946); W. E. Garrison, *The Quest and Character of a United Church* (Abingdon, 1957); L. Hodgson, *The Ecumenical Movement* (Sewanee, Tenn.: University Press, 1951); C. C. Morrison, *The Unfinished Reformation* (Harper, 1953); and H. P. Van Dusen, *World Christianity* (Abingdon - Cokesbury, 1947). For works confined to American ecumenicity see H. P. Douglass, *Church Unity Movements in the United States* (Institute of Social and Religious Research, 1934); J. A. Hutchison, *We Are Not Divided: A Critical and Historical Study of the Federal Council of the Churches of Christ in America* (Round Table Press, 1941); and C. S. Macfarland, *Christian Unity in the Making: The First Twenty-Five Years of the Federal Council of the Churches of Christ in America, 1905–1930* (Federal Council of Churches, 1948). For the World Council of Churches see W. A. Visser 't Hooft, ed., *The First Assembly of the World Council of Churches* (Harper, 1949); *Man's Disorder and God's Design* (Harper, 1949); World Council of Churches, *The Evanston Report. . . . 1954* (Harper, 1955); and J. H. Nichols, *Evanston, An Interpretation* (Harper, 1954).

Chapter 28: The Retreat to Normalcy

A comprehensive treatment of the period may be found in G. G. Atkins, *Religion in Our Times* (Round Table Press, 1932); and W. E. Garrison, *The March of Faith,* Chaps. XVII and XVIII. The Oxford Group Movement is discussed in C. H. Braden, *These Also Believe;* and A. J. Russell, *For Sinners Only* (Harper, 1932). Trends in religious thought are analyzed in H. E. Fosdick, *The Living of These Days* (Harper, 1956); L. A. Loetscher, *The Broadening Church,* Chaps. 11–15; N. B. Stonehouse, *J. Gresham Machen* (Eerdmans, 1954); S. C. Cole, *The History of Fundamentalism* (R. R. Smith, 1931); and N. F. Furniss, *The Fundamentalist Controversy, 1918–1931* (Yale, 1954). For changing emphases in world missions see K. S. Latourette, *Advance Through Storm* (Harper, 1945). The important social issues of the decade are discussed in P. A. Carter, *The Decline and Revival of the Social Gospel* (Cornell, 1954); R. M. Miller, *American Protestantism and Social Issues, 1919–1939* (North Carolina, 1958); and P. W. Slosson, *The Great Crusade and After, 1914–1928* (Macmillan, 1930). Studies of prohibition include H. Asbury, *The Great Illusion: An Informal History of Prohibition* (Doubleday, 1950); C. Merz, *The Dry Decade* (Doubleday, Doran, 1931); and V. Dabney, *Dry Messiah: The Life of Bishop Cannon* (Knopf, 1949). For the Ku Klux Klan see J. M. Mecklin, *The Ku Klux Klan: A Study of the American Mind* (Harcourt, Brace, 1924).

Chapter 29: Religion in an Era of Crisis

General works of considerable value are S. M. Cavert and H. P. Van Dusen, eds., *The Church Through Half a Century* (Scribner, 1936); H. E. Fosdick, *The Living of These Days;* J. Knox, ed., *Religion and the Present Crisis* (Chicago, 1942); and H. W. Schneider, *Religion in 20th Century America* (Harvard, 1952). For studies of the Depression see S. C. Kincheloe, *Research Memorandum on Religion in the Depression* (Social Science Research Council, 1937); and D. Wecter, *The Age of the Great Depression* (Macmillan, 1948). Religion in a period of global conflict is treated in R. H. Abrams, "The Churches and the Clergy in World War II," *Annals of the American Academy of Political and Social Science* (March, 1948), 110–119; and A. P. Stokes, *Church and State in the United States,* Vol. III, Chap. XXI. A number of important works deal with reconstruction in religious thought, among them S. E. Ahlstrom, "Continental Influence on American Christian Thought Since World War I," *Church History* (September, 1958), 256–272; G. Hammar, *Christian Realism in American Theology* (Uppsala: Appelberg, 1940); C. F. H. Henry, *Fifty Years of Protestant Theology* (Wilde, 1950), and *The Drift of Western Thought* (Eerdmans, 1951); W. Hordern, *A Layman's Guide to Protestant Theology* (Macmillan, 1955); A. S. Nash, ed., *Protestant Thought in the Twentieth Century* (Macmillan, 1951); H. S. Smith, *Changing Conceptions of Original Sin,* Chap. 9; D. W. Soper, *Major Voices in American Theology* (Westminster, 1953), and *Men Who Shape Belief* (Westminster, 1955), the latter two works being brief discussions of the religious thought of America's most eminent Protestant theologians. For works devoted to the contributions of individual thinkers see D. R. Davies, *Reinhold Niebuhr: Prophet from*

America (Macmillan, 1945); and C. W. Kegley and R. W. Bretall, eds., *Reinhold Niebuhr, His Religious, Social, and Political Thought* (Macmillan, 1956), and *The Theology of Paul Tillich* (Macmillan, 1952). For trends in social religion the following works are of value; P. A. Carter, *The Decline and Revival of the Social Gospel;* R. M. Miller, *American Protestantism and Social Issues, 1919–1939;* and R. Root, *Progress Against Prejudice: The Church Confronts the Race Problem* (Friendship Press, 1957). Contemporary trends in Judaism are discussed in N. Glazer, *American Judaism,* Chaps. VI and VII; and I. Eis-

enstein and E. Kohn, eds., *Mordecai M. Kaplan, An Evaluation* (Jewish Reconstructionist Foundation, 1952). Issues of church and state are treated in A. P. Stokes, *Church and State in the United States,* Vol. II, Chaps. XIV, XVIII, and XIX; J. T. Ellis, *American Catholicism,* Chap. IV; and L. Pfeffer, *Church, State, and Freedom* (Beacon, 1953). For a penetrating analysis of the contemporary religious situation consult A. R. Eckardt, *The Surge of Piety in America* (Association Press, 1958); R. E. Osborn, *The Spirit of American Christianity* (Harper, 1958); and M. E. Marty, *The New Shape of American Religion* (Harper, 1959).

Index

A

Abbott, Lyman, 450, 466, 484, 511
Abhedananda, Swami, 524
Abolitionism, 363, 365, 369–73
Acadians, 98
Act Against Heresy (1646), 72
Activism, 446, 477
Adams, Abigail, 200
Adams, John, 200, 215, 288
Adams, John Quincy, 292
Adams, Samuel, 196
Addams, Jane, 486, 507
Adler, Cyrus, 439
Adler, Felix, 436
Adopting Act (1729), 153
Adventism, 343–45
African Methodist Episcopal Church in America, 280
Ainsworth, Henry, 79
Aitken, Robert, 216
Albright, Jacob, 237
Alcott, Bronson, 342
Alemany, Joseph, 33
Alexander, Bishop, 442
Alexander, Archibald, 336
Allen, Ethan, 219
Allen, Richard, 279
Allouez, Claude, 36
Altham, John, 94
Amana Society, 340–41
American Bible Society, 292–93, 391, 497, 513, 569
American Education Society, 287
American Federation of Labor, 481
American Home Missionary Society, 265, 267–69, 270
American Missionary Association, 394, 405
American Protective Association, 434–35
American Sunday School Union, 291–92
American Tract Society, 293
Americanism, 558–59. See also Roman Catholic Church
Ames, Edward R., 396, 401
Ames, William, 63, 145
Alva, Fernando, Duke of, 11
Amherst College, and the second revival, 257
Amish (Ammenites), 131
Anabaptists, 17–18
Anderson, James, 152
Anderson, William C., 279, 327
Andren, O. C. T., 422
Andrew, James O., 377
Andrewes, Lancelot, 92
Andrews, Jedediah, 147
Andros, Edmund, 59, 87–88, 124
Anglican Church: and the American Revolution, 197–99; in the colonial Carolinas, 54–55; in colonial Delaware, 57; in colonial Georgia, 55–56; in colonial Maryland, 44–45, 97–98 (see also Commissaries); in colonial New England, 58–61, 87; in colonial New Jersey, 57–58; in colonial New York, 56–57, 127, 128; in colonial Pennsylvania, 57; and colonial Swedish Lu-

therans, 126; in colonial Virginia, 43–44 (see also Commissaries, Parishes); decline of, in colonial America, 192, 193; disestablishment of, 211–214; in Jamestown, 41–42; origins and doctrines of, 13–15; religious practice of, in the English colonies, 48–50. See also Episcopal Church
Anglican Society for the Propagation of the Gospel, 182, 183
Anglo-Chinese War (1858–1860), 498
Anne, Queen of England, 58
Antes, Henry, 142
Anthony, Susan B., 360, 464
Anti-imperialism, 507
Antimissionism, 271–74
Apostolic Christianity, and the Reformation, 1
Architecture, church, 546–47
Armenians, in the United States, 444
Arminianism, 153, 265; in Methodist theology, 176; among New England Baptists, 171; in the Puritan system, 156; in the second revival. See also Church of God; Cumberland Presbyterians; Free Will Baptists
Arndt, Johann, 137
Articles of Confederation, 210, 216
Asbury, Francis, 177, 178, 205–206, 225, 226, 236, 252, 253, 260, 261, 279, 291, 364
Associate Reformed Church, 244
Atheism, 548
Athenagoras, Archbishop, 442
Atkinson, George H., 268
Atomic bomb, 570–71
Auburn Declaration, 314
Augsburg, Peace of (1555), 6
Augsburg Confession, 328, 330–31, 422, 465
Augustine, influence of, on Puritanism, 76, 77
Aulen, Gustaf, 574
Austin, Ann, 110
Avalon. See Newfoundland
Avery, David, 196
Avilés, Pedro Menéndez de, 27
Ayllón, Lucas Vasquez de, 26, 27

B

Bab, 524
Backus, Isaac, 172, 204
Bacone, Almon C., 416
Badger, Joseph, 267
Baer, G. F., 477–78
Baha, Abdul, 524
Bahaism, 524
Baha'ullah, 524
Bailey, Jacob, 60
Baird, Robert, 327
Baird, Charles W., 449
Baker, George. See Devine, Major Morgan J. (Father Divine)
Baker, Osmon C., 396

Foster, George B., 472
Fourier, Francois, 342
Fourteenth Amendment, 400
Fox, Emmet, 521
Fox, George, 19, 110, 112–13
Fox, Katie, 345–46
Fox, Margaretta, 345–46
France: in the age of exploration, 24;
  capitalism in, 10. *See also* Missions;
  Reformation
Franck, Sebastian, 19
Francke, August Herman, 136, 139
Frankfort Company, 131
Franklin, Benjamin, 185, 187, 191, 363
Fraser, Thomas, 414
Frederick I, of Denmark, 6
Free Quakers, 206
Free Will Baptists, 301–302, 533
Frelinghuysen, Theodorus Jacobus, 156–57
Fremont, General John C., 393
French and Indian War, 38, 136
Friedrich, James K., 585
Friends: and the American Revolution,
  206–207; and the Anglican Church in
  Pennsylvania, 57; in the colonial
  Carolinas, 55; in colonial Maryland,
  45; in colonial Massachusetts, 110–
  11; in colonial New Jersey, 57–58,
  113–14; in colonial Pennsylvania,
  114–17; in colonial Rhode Island,
  111–12; in colonial Virginia, 43–44;
  inception of the Society of, 19; and
  Mennonites, 131; mergers among,
  535; in New Amsterdam, 112; in New
  Netherland, 124; in the post-Revolutionary era, 233; principles and practices of, in colonial Pennsylvania,
  115–16; in the Southern colonies, 112–
  13; the weakening of, 117; and westward expansion, 254; in World War
  II, 568
Froebel, Friedrich, 458
Frontier: anti-Calvinist bias of, 304–305;
  churches on, 242–56; influence of, on
  American development, 238–39, 264;
  post-Civil War, 410–11, and church
  extension, 411–15; revival on, 257–
  63. *See also* Western expansion
Froude, Richard Hurrell, 318
Fugitive Slave Act (1850), 372
Fuller, Charles E., 590
Fuller, Margaret, 341–42, 360
Fuller, Richard, 379
Fuller, Samuel, 70
Fundamental Constitutions (1669), 54
Fundamental Orders of Connecticut
  (1639), 74
Fundamentalism, 474, 530, 549–553, 576
Funk, Christian, 207
Furman, Richard, 273

G

Gadsden Purchase, 31, 266
Gallaudet, Thomas H., 360
Gallican Confession, 10
Gallitzin, Dmitri, 255
Galloway, Joseph, 199
Galusha, Elon, 379
Gano, John, 172, 205
Gano, Stephen, 250
Garcia-diego, Francisco, 33
Garrettson, Freeborn, 226
Garrison, William Lloyd, 353, 367, 368–69, 371, 374

Gatch, Philip, 206
Gelston, Samuel, 152
George II, of England, 139
George III, of England, 194
George, Henry, 484, 489, 490, 491, 492
Gerard, Conrad, 208
German Reformed Church: and the Amer-
  ican Revolution, 203; in colonial
  Pennsylvania, 141–43; liturgy in,
  449; nationalization of, in the post-
  Revolutionary era, 231–32; in the
  nineteenth century, 331. *See also*
  Mercersburg Theology
Germany. *See* Reformation
Ghent, Treaty of (1815), 264–65
Gibault, Pierre, 38–39
Gibbons, James, 431–32, 483–84, 511
Gilbert, Humphrey, 41
Gilbert's Creek Church, 249
Gillespie, George, 148–49, 152
Gladden, Washington, 451, 468, 490
Gloria Dei Church, South Philadelphia, 126
Godwyn, Morgan, 50
Goetschius, John Henry, 142
Going, Jonathan, 270
Gompers, Samuel, 482
Gooch, William, 151, 161
Goodwill Industries, 489
Gordon, A. J., 474
Gordon, Charles "Chinese," 498
Gordon, George A., 451, 469
Gordon, Patrick, 59
Gorges, Ferdinando, 75
Gorton, Samuel, 73, 104
Gough, John B., 355
Gould, Jay, 461
Gould, Thomas, 108
Graeco-Roman world. *See* Hellenistic mind
Graham, Bill, 591
Graham, William (Billy) Franklin, 585, 590
Grant, General Ulysses S., 387
Gratz, Rebecca, 333
Gray, James, 474
Greece, philosophy of, in the medieval synthesis, 2
Greek Orthodoxy, in the United States, 442
Greeley, Horace, 346
Green, Ashbel, 311, 312
Green, Beriah, 370
Green, Bryan, 590
Greene, Nathanael, 206
Greenwood, John, 64
Griffith, Benjamin, 109
Griffith, David, 223–24
Grimke, Angelina, 360, 370
Grimke, Sarah, 360
Griswold, Alexander Viets, 317
Gronau, Israel Christian, 138
Guilds, decline of, 3
Guldin, Samuel, 141
Gurley, Ralph, 367
Gustavus Vasa, King of Sweden, 6
Gustavus Adolphus, King of Sweden, 125

H

Hagan, John, 396
Hague, The, conference (1899), 507, (1907), 507
Haldane, J. A., 308
Half-Way Covenant, 86, 156
Hall, G. Stanley, 553
Hall, Gordon, 282

Olympia

WASH.

Salem

OREGON

IDAHO

Boise

MONTANA

Helena

NORTH DAKOTA

Bismarck

SOUTH DAKOTA

Pierre

CALIFORNIA

Sacramento

San Francisco

Carson
City

NEVADA

WYOMING

Salt Lake
City

Cheyenne

NEBRASKA

Lincoln

Denver

UTAH

COLORADO

KANSAS

Los Angeles

San Diego

ARIZONA

NEW MEXICO

OKLAHOMA

Santa Fe

Oklahoma City

Albuquerque

Phoenix

TEXAS

Tucson

El Paso

Austin

San Antonio

THE UNITED STATES